AGE OF
THE FRENCH REVOLUTION
by Claude Manceron

AGE OF
THE FRENCH REVOLUTION
III

"LES FOLIES"—SYMBOL OF THE YEARS 1783–84

Their Gracious

Pleasure *1782–1785*

CLAUDE MANCERON

Translated from the French by Nancy Amphoux

A TOUCHSTONE BOOK
Published by Simon & Schuster Inc.
NEW YORK · LONDON · TORONTO · SYDNEY · TOKYO

Touchstone
Simon & Schuster Building
Rockefeller Center
1230 Avenue of the Americas
New York, New York 10020

Published by arrangement with Alfred A. Knopf, Inc.
Originally published in France as *Les Hommes de la Liberté III, Le Bon Plaisir* by
Editions Robert Laffont
TOUCHSTONE and colophon are registered trademarks of Simon & Schuster Inc.
Manufactured in the United States of America

10   9   8   7   6   5   4   3   2   1   Pbk.

Library of Congress Cataloging in Publication Data
Manceron, Claude.
  [Bon plaisir. English]
  Their gracious pleasure, 1782–1785/Claude Manceron; translated from the
French by Nancy Amphoux.—1st Touchstone ed.
     p.   cm.—(Age of the French Revolution; v. 3) (A Touchstone book)
  Translation of: Le bon plaisir.
  "Published by arrangement with Alfred A. Knopf, Inc."—T.p. verso.
  Bibliography: p.
  Includes index.
    1. France—History—Louis XVI, 1774–1793—Biography.   2. France—
History—Revolution, 1789–1799—Causes.   3. France—History—
Revolution, 1789–1799—Biography.   4. France—Biography.
I. Title.   II. Series: Manceron, Claude. Hommes de la liberté.
English (Simon and Schuster, inc.); v. 3.
DC145.M3513   1989 vol. 3
[DC137.5.A1]
944.04'0922 s—dc20   89-11295
[944'.035'092]   CIP
ISBN 0-671-68020-X Pbk.

ILLUSTRATION CREDITS

*All of the illustrations are courtesy of the Bibliothèque nationale, Paris, except for the
following:* page 10: *New York Public Library;* pages 70, 210 (Pitt), 241 (Experiment): *Photographie Bulloz, Paris;* page 95: *Collection Viollet, Paris;* pages 100, 368
(Vauban): *Photo Giraudon, Paris;* page 360: *Carnot Family Archive.*

*Most of the illustrations were provided through the courtesy of the Service iconographique of
Editions Robert Laffont.*

To Regis Debray

You are quite right, my dear Philippe, to call this mania of ours for universal freedom a kind of leprosy. But oh, it is a holy and a blessed leprosy, in this age of overwhelming apathy, that can keep alive the sacred fire of avenging indignation against the iniquity called order and legitimate authority. I should rather call it a madness, or better still a passion, like love.

—LUIGI ANGELONI,
letter to Philippe Buonarroti,
July 13, 1834

The French Revolution will remain totally impenetrable to those who try to look at it alone. The only rays of light that can illuminate it must be sought in what went before.

      —ALEXIS DE TOCQUEVILLE, *L'Ancien Régime et la Revolution*

The Bastille is still standing, though we have razed it to the ground in prose; but fall it must, one day.

      —LOUIS-SÉBASTIEN MERCIER, *Le Tableau de Paris* (˙782)

Whenever I think how we are consuming the very marrow of the country, I cannot contrive to calm my mind. Our political and moral world stands upon ruins, hollow caverns, subterranean cloaca. No one considers that they all support each other, no one wants to contemplate that fact, any more than the living conditions of the people who inhabit them. Only those who are a little better informed will understand more readily what is happening when the world topples and strange voices are heard rising from the sewers.

      —GOETHE, note written in 1782

Oh, my beautiful, my beloved France, where everything was so glorious in those days, despite the *lettres de cachet,* the *corvées,* the destitution of the poor, and the gracious pleasure of their kings and ministers!

—CASANOVA, *Mémoires sur la société*
du XVIIIe siècle

Politics is the great word of the discontented poor.

—DUC D'AYEN, *Nouvelles à la main sur*
Madame du Barry

Sire, the State is in grave danger . . . A revolution in the principles of government is approaching, brought about by the fermentation in men's minds. Institutions held sacred, which have enabled this monarchy to advance through so many centuries, are being transformed into problematical issues, cried down as injustices . . .

Every author sets up to be a lawmaker. Anyone putting forward an outrageous proposal, anyone wanting to change the laws, is sure to find readers and followers.

Such is the unfortunate progress of this effervescence, that opinions which had seemed totally reprehensible but a short time ago today appear reasonable and just. And that which is an offense to good people today may soon pass as respectable and legitimate. Who can tell where this incontinence of opinion will end?

—COMTE D'ARTOIS, PRINCE DE CONDÉ,
DUC DE BOURBON, DUC D'ENGHIEN
and PRINCE DE CONTI,
address to the King, December 12, 1788

Contents

Acknowledgments

The large numbers and extreme kindness of those who are continuing to assist me have forced me to be brief in the expression of my gratitude; I would hate to seem to be forgetting someone, especially where press and bookshop sales promotion are concerned, when there has been such unforeseeably favorable response to the first two volumes.

I am no longer alone in my canoe. For this volume, an enormous effort has also been made by the Laffont iconographic section, led by my friend Jean-Marc Gutton. Mme Colette Laly, in particular, procured kilogram after kilogram of facsimiles of unpublished or out-of-print material for me, which she photocopied herself at the Archives or Bibliothèque Nationale.

Once again, the entire Laffont staff has been my nursemaid. Robert Laffont even thought up a new present he could give me—his patience, wrapped in the warm smile that has illuminated my writing career from the very beginning.

By doing me the honor of attaching me to his private staff during the 1974 presidential election campaign, François Mitterand, whom I always knew to be a totally fearless man, showed further proof of his courage when he dared to plant my immovable self in the very eye of the storm. He gave me an unforgettable experience and enabled me to live a chapter of history at firsthand and in the present tense.

I'd like to say once more that my dedication at the beginning of *The Twilight of the Old Order,* "To Anne, through Anne," applies to the whole series. She has literally worn herself out helping me at every level in a labor that becomes a little more hers—ours—with every passing week.

The biggest "thank you" hasn't yet been said; it is for those who read me through to the end.

—C.M.

Preface

The main idea of the *Age of the French Revolution* is to explore the roots of the Revolution by the method of intersecting biographies. In each volume, we make or renew our acquaintance with the characters who will become the leading actors of 1789–1797.

They don't know each other. Unawares, they will approach one another during the fifteen-year reign which rejected the Revolution, thereby endowing it with its messianic character: a cleavage in time to serve all time. Once under way, the Revolution will set the stage for their meeting: they will love, unite, defy, tear to shreds, destroy each other—or survive now and then owing to luck, betrayal, or patience. From 1789–1797 they will enact a *chanson de geste,* each episode of which is part of our existence, destined to become the very tissue of it: the Peters, Johns, and Magdalens, the Pontius Pilates and Judases bearing the glad tidings of liberty. Whenever possible I shall try to bring them out of obscurity, to personify them, to capture the reality of their daily lives.

Over a thousand people, then, a hundred of whom we shall stalk. Their biographies are woven into the main thread of chronological events.

Running heads at the top of each page show the reader where he is at all times. On the left is the date of the incident, on the right its contents in a nutshell. The names used in the titles are those of History: "Louis Phillipe and His Cousins," for example, shows the future King of the French—then only Duc de Valois—in the care of his new "governor," Félicité de Genlis. In running heads the spelling of names is that of the revolutionary period; in the narrative, however, it is that of the period to which the episode belongs. Thus the title "Dumouriez, a Privileged Prisoner" refers to the adventures in 1774 of Colonel du Mouriez, and "Biron Courts the Queen" deals with the person known as the Duc de Lauzun in 1775.

The alphabetical index at the end of the book will help those who prefer to follow the thread of a single biography straight through the series.

The numbered notes toward the end of the book contain bibliographic references and details of use to students and researchers. Asterisks and daggers refer to the footnotes on the page—of which I am as sparing as possible—required for an immediate understanding of the text, especially where approximate equivalents of sums and measurements are concerned.

The estimated amounts allow for the very substantial differences in prices and consumption of goods under Louis XVI and today—what one might call the shift in lifestyles. In *Their Gracious Pleasure* the franc compared with that of Louis XVI is the franc of the 5th Republic (1959), still (in 1976) commonly called the new franc.

Instead of chapters, sequences. A guiding rule: objective truth as to dates, facts, acts, spoken and written words. A bias: the desire to enter into the psychology of each person, whatever his role in the Revolution—hence respect for Charette as well as Marceau—in an attempt to reconstitute his inner movement. A technique: combining anecdotal material with events to provide the background for a portrait and to make a figure live again in his own times through simultaneous sensations and impressions. The Revolution was also David, Talma, Gossec, Ledoux, balloons, visual telegraphy, and Fulton's experiments, just as the liberation of France was also Aragon, Eluard, Camus, Giacometti, Gérard Philipe, and Le Corbusier. An ambition: to steer a course midway between the analysis of economic and social spheres that shape mankind and the study of a particular person's unpredictable influence on those spheres, thereby exploding the framework of determinism. Napoleon and revolutionary Europe; Lenin and the Russia of 1917; De Gaulle and the French Resistance.

Finally, an explanation: my sifting through thousands of episodes resulted in retaining (trifling as they may seem—an operatic aria, an epigram, an academic reception, a love letter) only those things which enhance the understanding of a quarter-century containing all centuries. A conceivable, if insufferable, subtitle comes to mind: "Poetic and historic manual for bringing about instant total change in myself and others."

—Claude Manceron
from *Twilight of the Old Order*

Translator's Note

Politicians did not exist in France, of course, until there was a forum for political debate; when it was created, many of the most important figures to emerge came, as is traditional in Anglo-Saxon democracies, from the law. The débuts of several of these men are recounted in this volume, in a number of chapters referring to lawyers, law courts, and legal procedure. Sometimes the terms are translated, sometimes left in French. There is no consistency, and neither method is satisfactory: translations are not really equivalent and thus misleading, while the French terms are totally meaningless to nonspecialized modern readers (in French as well as in English). The eighteenth-century judicial system in France was amazingly complex, with a multiplicity of branches—ecclesiastical, seneschal, fiscal, provincial, royal, ducal, municipal, and so forth—and overlapping jurisdictions within a single branch. I have not wished to interrupt the narrative with too many necessarily superficial explanations; any reader whose curiosity is irritated into action may consult a history of French law for assistance. A point worth bearing in mind, perhaps, is that the system was entirely hierarchical and therefore vulnerable to corruption-generating pressures; but it was also collegial. Most courts had a *président* and a number of assistants (assessors, councilors) who might themselves be *présidents* in another court or for another case. A *président,* thus, is a judge; juries were unknown.

—N.A.

Their Gracious Pleasure

COLLOT D'HERBOIS

I THE BIRTH OF
THE DAUPHIN

NOVEMBER 1781

The . . . People Have an Older Brother

In Rouen, on November 5, 1781, Jean-Marie Collot d'Herbois rings up the
curtain on the real reign of Louis XVI by performing a play of his own creation
to celebrate the birth of the dauphin. A tiny tinkling ring it is, lost in the
murmur sweeping across France: Hallelujah, something's finally going to happen! People had been in such a hurry to believe that everything would be all
right the moment Louis XV died; but his grandson has needed time to adjust
to the throne, and as he's no sprinter it has taken him six years—just as it took
him eleven years of wedlock to produce, via the Queen, this beautiful baby
boy who is the despair of Monsieur, the Comte d'Artois, the Orléanses, and
the Condés because he edges them all a little further from the throne but who,
for that very reason, is equally the delight of all right-minded people. Louis
XVI, already being nicknamed Louis-the-Just, will see his son, a new Beloved,
ready to take his place sometime around 1820. Long live the future Louis
XVII!* Because the Grand Dauphin, remember—Louis XIV's son—was born
the same year Mazarin died, and that was when the young Sun King first took
a firm grip on his reign. And right now, under the eaves at Versailles, another
wizened old Mazarin lies dying—Maurepas, the Eminence Rose of Louis
XVI's first reign. Exit Maurepas, enter the dauphin!

Here we are in Rouen, under the heavy rains that have been lashing northern
Normandy for days. "The Seine is pissing in her bed," as folks say in these
parts. It's the right weather for the time of year, and it packs 'em into the
Théâtre des Arts, the only theater in Corneille's home town, so rich in other
monuments, in churches, abbeys, and fancy townhouses.[1] But Rouen is a city
of stiff-necked bourgeois whose rigid *mores* can tolerate actors only in small

*In fact, the dauphin born on October 22, 1781, will not be the Louis XVII of History: he
dies of an illness in June 1789, and it is his brother, born in 1785, who becomes Louis XVII.

doses. For instance, the curtain goes up, by order, "at exactly two o'clock, whether or not there is anyone in the audience, so that the play will be over by half-past four."[2] The people in the pit break happily into a repeat of M. d'Herbois's refrain, as sung by a cast of eight:

Vive Louis! Vive Antoinette!	[A cheer for the Bourbons and lily
Chantons Bourbon, fêtons les	so fair:
lis!	Long life to Louis and his Queen
Pour tout Français, c'est le cri	Antoinette!
de la gloire:	Vive Louis! Vive Louis!
Vive Louis! Vive Louis![3]	For every Frenchman that's the best
	cry yet!]

This verse is sung before the intermission of *Les Français à la Grenade, ou L'Impromptu de la Guerre et de l'Amour* [The French at Grenada, or The Impromptu of War and Love], "a comedy-divertissement in two acts composed on the occasion of the victories won by the armies of His Most Christian Majesty in America during the 1779 campaign."* The closing verses are even more irresistible:

Vivent notre Reine et notre	[Long live our gracious Queen and
Roi!	King!
Vivent les princes du sang de	And all the princes of the blood of
France!	France!
Vivent notre Reine et notre	Long live our gracious Queen and
Roi!	King!
Chacun d'nous les aime plus que	Whom we love more than any other
soi!	thing!]

Grenada and d'Estaing are old hat by now, though. There's been plenty of action in the last two years. Everybody knows we're winning a war somewhere on the other side of the world,† although nobody's too sure exactly where. The wind from America is blowing the right way, and has just swept in to merge with the news of the heir to the lily throne back home. One wave from America, another from France, and the two flow together in the head of Collot d'Herbois. What are actors for, if not to invent a tune for the new contredanse of the Two Worlds?

The curtain rises again, on the set of *La Fête dauphine, ou Le Monument français* [The Dolphin Fête, or The French Monument], "a comedy in one act combining song, spectacle, and divertissements," which Collot and his fellow

---

*Capture of the island of Grenada by the Comte d'Estaing.

†The English capitulated at Yorktown on October 19, but France didn't hear about it until the end of November; the general rumor, however, was that Cornwallis had his back to the wall.

actors have just thrown together and staged in a week. A true-blue backdrop, framed in yellow and green and smelling pleasantly of fresh paint: "The scene represents a Normandy village on the sea coast"—but what's that in the middle, that fat, cardboard pyramid topped by a sort of white animal that looks like it fell off a fairground stand? The argument: "A simultaneous celebration of the inauguration of a fountain built by the munificence of our King, the capture of an English ship by a son of the village, and the birth of the dauphin." This is explained to the characters in the play and the audience by the architect of the monument—Collot himself. He's cast himself in a part that suits his playboy style. "Still very young,* he has a handsome figure, a sonorous voice, a slender waist, and an expressive face" set off by black hair that often hangs loose in his neck. Tonight it is bound up in a neat pigtail, as befits the character of the "engineer of the fountain" who declaims to the public as he points to it:

"This monument, small as it is, is proof of the King's fatherly affection for his people. To bring this healthful spring hither required sums that could not be produced by the inhabitants and so, at the behest of our intendant,† the good monarch, in his ardent desire to grasp every opportunity to relieve his subjects, has borne the entire expense."

The whole play drips with the same syrup. Why did the architect crown his fountain with that colossal dolphin? He had a presentiment. Who comes to announce the blessed event to the villagers? Their lord, a marquis with a heart of gold whose knees they run to kiss. Whereupon the inevitable young shepherd lad breaks into a cavatina in which he swears he wouldn't mind if his fair young maid were unfaithful to him, "for the sake of our dauphin, for the sake of our dauphin." At this point on comes an old bell ringer, Daddy Simon, gasping his last. He's walked six leagues** to take part in the festivities but gives his son a terrible tongue lashing for not having come to meet him, bearing tidings of the royal birth:

---

*Collot d'Herbois was born in Paris in 1750 or the year before; his birth record has disappeared and he had a tendency to cut a few years off his age. He becomes a member of the Convention and a delegate to the provinces, chiefly Lyons, in 1793, where he applies a policy of violent terrorist repression: he also becomes a member of the *Comité de Salut public* [Committee of Public Safety], where his name and that of Billaud-Varenne become linked like Castor and Pollux. They are deported together in An III (1795) and both die in Guiana. [The Comité de Salut Public, the most notorious body to emerge during the Revolution, was the executive organ of the government of the *Terreur*. It was set up in April 1793 and led by Danton until July, when Robespierre took over. It was dissolved with the Convention in 1795. Collot d'Herbois and Billaud-Varenne were the members responsible for domestic policy.—*Trans.*]

†Civilian administrator of a province. A few years later he would have written "our prefect."

**[A league is a somewhat indefinite linear distance, say 2.5 to 3 miles; it was the ordinary unit of measurement in those days.—*Trans.*]

You've stolen twelve hours of good cheer from me! . . . I don't love you anymore, and I'll never forgive you! Why didn't you come running, quick as ever you could, to tell me, "Father, our Queen is in good health and the French people have an older brother?" Then you could have run off, if you wanted to, but it would have been such a comfort to me. You can laugh, the rest of you, you're out on the high road, and you're the first to hear the good news. But is a laborer any less the subject of the King because he's buried in the countryside? Who's the first to feel the influence of a good king, a good queen, good ministers? It's the man in the country.

Vigorous applause from the house, which does not of course contain a single peasant—what the devil would a peasant be doing in a theater? In the first place, his curé wouldn't let him go, and besides, the peasants around Rouen are in no mood for jollifications: the region was a center of agitation in 1775 during the Grain War, and in 1777 two women and three scallywags were hanged for insubordination in Old Market square.[4] No: this ripple of satisfaction emanates from the few hundred big import-export dealers who rule the roost in Rouen and call the tune for the sixty thousand inhabitants of the "largest, most populous, most active, and wealthiest town of the kingdom, capital of the province of Normandy, with a rich archbishopric whose incumbent bears the title of Primate of Normandy, with a parlement, a court of aid,* a chamber of accounts, a généralité, a présidial, a bailliage, an intendancy, a mint, a handsome collège, a literary Academy, etc."[5]

No danger of any peasant blouses or bonnets in the Théâtre des Arts: the ladies and misses there come to show off their Indian taffeta caracos and their "coëffures straight from the root with curls." They wish their actors (who do not sit down at their dinner tables) to play docile, proper peasants imbued with devotion to every possible authority. The Rouen merchants deal in peace, even when there's a war on: "textiles and ship outfitting, to a lesser extent grain and flour, wines and spirits, above all sugar and coffee, cotton made up locally or in the Caux region, wool for the Elbeuf looms"[6]—where a proletariat earning day-wages is beginning to crowd together, and it's a good idea to keep them on our side. The Rouen merchants also have interests in shipbuilding and the slave trade with the Islands; and if naval battles make a temporary dent in profits there, they boost them up again by joining forces with the privateers, sharing risks and booty. . . . These form the audience of Collot d'Herbois.

"Oh, forgive my error, father!"

"And a serious error it is, too, because I brought you up according to all the right principles. Do you recall when the good King got married, how we sang praises to the beautiful Antoinette, how we blessed her? . . . We did it under our humble thatched roof, but the words went to heaven as straight as

---

*A sort of court for deliberation and arbitration of tax disputes.

if they came from a palace . . . Ah, but now we have a dauphin, kiss me, I forgive you."

It's all so fresh and gay and dancing. Even the theater is new, built less than ten years ago. On the ceiling, well-padded muses lavish upon Corneille the type of caress that would drive a Polyeucte to damnation, in a blue and gold apotheosis painted by one Lemoine. And the curtain falls on the jaunty final couplet that unites:

Ce que tout bon Français adore,   [What every good Frenchman adores,
Le Roi, la Reine et le Dauphin.   The King, the Queen, and the
                                    dauphin.]

Yeah. . . . But then who wrote these other verses, newly confiscated in a Rouen bookseller's shop?

D'un Dauphin la naissance   [The birth, at last, of a royal son,
Enchante tout Paris;   Has set all Paris at sixes and sevens;
Sa subite existence   But the sudden existence of this
Trouble le Paradis.   little one
"Qui diable l'a produit?"   Raises an eyebrow up in the Heavens.
Dit le Verbe en colère;   "Who the devil begot him?" asks
"C'est quelque coup du   the Word in a yell.
    Saint-Esprit   "The Holy Spirit, it must be, in one
Car jamais personne n'a dit   of his moods;
Que le Roi fut son père."[7]   'Cause the King, so far as I've ever
                                       heard tell,
                                    Was never the one to deliver the
                                       goods."

. . . "Au diable soit l'affaire"   . . . The Comte d'Artois now
Dit le comte d'Artois.   chooses to comment:
"Si j'en eus voulu faire   "Devil take the whole sordid affair!
Il n'eut tenu qu'à moi.   If I had wanted, at any moment,
J'aurais pu procurer [*sic*]   'Twas easy as pie to have laid her there.
Cette race bâtarde.   But I kept my eye on my child's
Mais, pour le bien de mon   welfare
    enfant,   (Though I could have founded the
J'allais tranquillement   bastard house),
Baiser ma Savoyarde."*   And went off like a good boy to
                                       comb my hair
                                    And fuck my legitimate Savoyard
                                       spouse.]

*Reminder: the Comte d'Artois, like his brother Provence, married a daughter of the Savoy dynasty, which was ruling in Turin.

Six verses crescendo, with an especially sharp dig in the last one aimed at one of Marie Antoinette's closest girlfriends:

C'était la princesse d'Hénin.
Comme elle est tribade et catin
On la prit pour la Reine.
	[The Princesse d'Hénin it must have
	  been.
	And as she's both trollop and
	  lesbi-een
	They all mistook her for the
	  Queen.*]

Did Collot know about it? Nothing indicates that he did. The badly printed broadsides, pulled from an amateur press, were making the rounds of a few chosen drawing rooms in concentric circles around Versailles. This particular one came drifting down the Seine in the wake of the messengers announcing the dauphin's birth. No peasant has heard about them either, of course. It takes more refined spirits to appreciate this kind of filth. But there's undoubtedly a false note somewhere in the chorus.

Another false note can be detected in the "gloomy and anxious air," the joylessness of Jean-Marie Collot d'Herbois as he walks home sunk in those blues so familiar to any habitué of lectern or stage, arm in arm with his pretty, insignificant little wife, the sort of woman about whom nobody, not even her husband, can ever think of anything to say. She plays minor parts, she looks after his costumes, she replaces the prompter. She is not sufficient compensation for the renown he wants, that of a Beaumarchais or Molière; and the triumphs on which his resentment can feed are so puny. "I have no fondness for these towns in which quality is not appreciated and there is no respect for talent . . . Actors are degraded in them. If a decent man finds something to admire in you he doesn't dare say so aloud; he only dares to call himself your friend when there is no one about to hear him."[8]

Jean-Marie Collot has no more d'Herbois in his blood than Monsieur Caron has de Beaumarchais. Where did he pick up that name, in the early days of his roamings? Nobody knows. Like his more famous contemporary, probably, by rubbing up against some conquered ground. The only two things he's ever really had in his blood are Paris and the theater.

He was born on the Rue St. Jacques in the home of his father, a Parisian goldsmith. He spent his boyhood wandering among the quacks and charlatans on the Pont Neuf; at fifteen, he was playing buffoon for a puppeteer. We find him at twenty in Saint-Brieuc, in the company of somebody named Pillemont. The wheel turns: Avignon, Bordeaux, back to Paris to fail the entrance examination at the Comédie Française, then Angers, Amiens, Bordeaux again,

*To my knowledge, this is the earliest text to speak so openly of the Queen's alleged irregularities of behavior.

where he's already being called d'Herbois more often than Collot and where he fulminates against the provinces and yearns for Paris, and is already married and already disenchanted. A nervous breakdown at Nantes at the age of twenty-three, serious enough to bring him up for questioning before the criminal court on September 9, 1773. And no wonder: he beat the ticket-taker and smashed the floorboards "with the cannonball that served as a thunder machine".[9] To Angers again, and Douai, where he met his great friend and faithful confidant, the actor Desroziers. Collot writes plays, copies Beaumarchais, and plagiarizes, pretty heavily, his *Eugénie* (a morose drama of love and business) in his first work, *Lucie, ou Les Parents imprudents* [Lucy, or The Imprudent Parents]. Grimm deigned to take note of him:* "I have not met M. Collot d'Herbois, but if he is, perchance, a young man, then he is not lacking in resources. His play is worthless, but there is one new feature in it, highly piquant and quite original, that is the part of an old soldier who, as a favor to his former captain, to whom he is devoted body and soul, pretends to be his valet."[10]

Collot gets his scripts published in Bordeaux, Nantes, Marseilles, Avignon, and even The Hague, playing the part of himself as the occasion arises, setting off in pursuit of fame too soon and too fast—compelled to repeat himself, dishing up his one character, his valet-soldier Francoeur, over and over again. Five acts in Saumur: *Clémence et Monjar,* a flop. *Le Bon Angevin,* "in honour of Monsieur, brother of the King, Duc d'Anjou" and also Comte de Provence, written just after the accession of Louis XVI: "an explosion of sensibility," according to Collot himself.[11] "I saw tears of joy and pleasure flowing from the eyes of the magistrates and assembled citizens whenever the prince's praises issued from the actor's mouth and were echoed in every heart." Provence, his head turned by this first whiff of incense, doled out 1,200 livres.† Collot becomes his certified hymnster: "O, Henri! It is indeed thy blood that flows in thy grandsons' veins! How proud we must be of our masters! . . . O, truly perfect prince, brother of my King, you were born for the joy of mankind!" And off we go, for *Le Seigneur d'Anjou, ou le vrai généreux* in 1776, *Le Vrai généreux ou les bons mariages* in 1777, *Le Nouveau Nostradamus, L'Amant loup-garou* . . . which was an unblushing copy of *The Merry Wives of Windsor,* cribbed from the translations of Shakespeare that were just beginning to come out in France. His Falstaff was called Rodomont, presto change-o. And he also perpetrated a *Paysan magistrat* that was a tracing from Calderón.

But time was passing, the critics were unconvinced, and La Harpe hit him dead center: "A poor imitation of a bad Spanish play."[12] Then he wrote *Le*

---

*Although Collot didn't know it, because Grimm's copy, like every other issue of his *Correspondance littéraire,* was sent in sealed envelopes exclusively to a small number of monarchs and princes of Enlightened Europe.

†6,000 modern francs [$1,200].

Bénéfice, in 1778, with the same results. The best part in the play was a dog called Thisbe. So he did the only thing left for him to do, which was to keep pace with the times like a cabaret M.C.: to write *Les Français à Grenade* followed by today's *Fête dauphine.* Ten plays written and performed by the age of thirty—a fine trash-heap. At least he's got no illusions about himself. Today in Rouen he's already planning ahead to Lyons,* but always with Paris as the ultimate carrot. It's as though his boot licking goes sour on him every time he finds himself alone—or rather facing the cheap four-penny ream on which he pours out his soul in lengthy epistles, written in a jerky hand but with comparatively respectable spelling, to his beloved Desroziers:

> I have never felt so strongly as now the dreadful emptiness of our condition. To be attached to no one, forever in danger of falling prey to one's own soft heart or the foul play of others; to be pitied without true concern, never praised sincerely; to be often forced to seem harsh and compelled to appear wicked or unreasonable: those are our affections, that is what occupies our time. The best among us is the one who best hides his secret hatred and envy of his fellows. We help one another without loving one another, and the greatest trick is to do a public favor to those whom we privately tear to shreds. What a lot of reasons, my dear friend, for not being pleased with myself or anyone else![13]

He doesn't sound too happy, does the actor Collot d'Herbois. Vive Louis! Vive Antoinette!

FATHER JUNIPERO SERRA

2

MARCH 1782

Giving Away What We Did Not Possess

Far, far from France and its festivities and dauphin, a few human ants are clinging grimly to their obscure paths in corners of the earth so different from Europe that they might be on other planets, in other centuries. One of them is Fray Junipero Serra, a son of Our Seraphic Father St. Francis, as he is called in his Order, whose task on this March 18, 1782, is to bless the founding of a new city, Los Angeles, in New Spain.†

---

*Where he settles in March 1782 and baptizes himself the "first actor of spectacles" at the Théâtre des Terreaux.

†The canonization of the Franciscan Junipero Serra (1713–1784) has now been hanging fire in the Vatican for two centuries; he is regarded as the founder of the state of California, and in

Lined along the four sides of the few furlongs of sandy ground forming the "main square" of Los Angeles stands the sparse and heteroclite population that has just been transplanted here to the banks of the "rio de la Porciuncula" (in remembrance of Assisi). Wearing the starched and congested air characteristic of such compulsory attendance, they move docilely through the ritual they have learned from their masters in white magic—benediction, exorcism, then unction, and a tap, "in the name of Our Lord Jesus," on the small coppery heads of the eighteen children. Junipero, although not a bishop, has been empowered by the Pope to perform the sacrament of confirmation in his capacity as padre of all the missions of Upper California—a province large as the Lowlands—which a handful of Franciscans and soldiers have just brought forth from the void.

One could hardly call it a scintillating gathering. Los Angeles isn't very sure it exists yet, and today's confirmation ceremony is more like a symbol, a mortgage on a hope. In this uncertain land between ocean, mountain, and desert, a village needs a few years to "take," and the "founding colony" arrived only last December, in this place four leagues north of San Gabriel—another and equally shaky mission. What could anybody do with such a motley crew, the "first-class parishioners" unearthed by the governor of Lower California a hundred leagues farther south and virtually deported up here with an escort of a dozen soldiers? Eleven men, eleven women, and twenty-one toddlers. "Among the eleven men, there are only two Spaniards and even they are married to Indians; then there is one half-breed married to a mulatto; four redskins,* one married to a mulatto and the other three to Indian women; and two Negroes and two mulattoes married to mulatto women."[1] And with that we're supposed to found a city for His Most Catholic Majesty, king of all the Spains? It's no sinecure, being a missionary in the Western Indies.

> Ave, maris stella
> Dei mater alma . . .

Even so, they all bleat out the chants in their funny way, in that Latin language of which they understand not a word, but that only makes it an even better medium for transmitting the tremor of the sacred. It's God's talk. They kneel, and would prostrate themselves on the ground, too, if required, in front of the blue and gold banner that Junipero Serra unfurls wherever he goes to preach. It bears the figure of a braid-bedizened lady crowned and costumed like a queen—and she is a queen, *Nuestra Señora, la reina de los angeles;*—who

---

1927 Calvin Coolidge placed his effigy among the hundred-odd Founding Fathers on Capitol Hill in Washington.

*The Spaniards had taken over the French habit of calling the American Indians "redskins," whatever their latitude or actual skin color—perhaps because they sometimes dyed their skins with red earth.

appeared so conveniently in December 1533 to Juan Diego, an Indian newly converted by the Franciscans, and asked him to build a sanctuary in her honor in Guadalupe, just as the battle over the nature of the redskins was raging most fiercely between Dominicans and Franciscans, with the former insisting that these cannibals were obviously animals, several steps below the gorilla,* so what was the point of evangelizing them? Spain's entire colonial policy depended upon the outcome, for if the Indians weren't human, then it was legitimate for the *gente de razon,* or rational whites, to massacre them or in a pinch train them as slaves. Priority, hence, to the soldier. But if they've got souls like ours, then they have to be baptized, respected . . . The Virgin ruled in favor of the missionaries, who now take first place wherever, as here, seeds are being sown on unknown ground.[2]

What a victory for a lame old man! Junipero Serra is about as big as a button,[†] he wheezes so hard you expect him to keel over at every *Oremus;* and how, with his rotten leg, does he manage to stand up again after his genuflexions? A scorpion stung him thirty years ago when he was just beginning his wanderings in Mexico, and to try his servant God willed that the infection should rise from heel to knee, so that he now drags behind him a swollen, pustulant limb that "contains, as a token of my sins, more foul matter than there is blood in the rest of my body,"[3] and that he refuses to treat by any means other than the concoction administered to ailing mules—a mixture of tallow and herbs fricasseed in a frying pan.[4]

A two-peso conquistador with no idea that he is becoming the father of a nation or that his asthmatic lungs are breathing life into California. This scattering of human spectators is witnessing a genesis; a Spanish infantry corporal has drawn out the main square of Los Angeles as Romulus and Remus drew the walls of Rome, a rectangle three hundred feet long by two hundred wide. *Fiat urbis!* Let there be a city! This vacant lot has been extended in the form of a cross by four streets** lined by reed huts, a first step toward the sandy terraces full of prickly thorn and the gallop of hills rising into mountains on the horizon. In the middle of it all flows the "Porciuncula",[‡] a stream one of whose loops outlines the site of the settle-

*The human sacrifices and sacred cannibalistic festivities of the last Aztecs had given rise to a fierce debate in Spain and a large number of more or less mythological books; Torquemada got into the act and the pope had to intervene, to confirm the Indians' membership in the human species.

†His bones were measured in 1909; he was 1.57 m. tall [just under 5 feet]. In March 1782 he was sixty-eight years old and suffering badly from chronic asthma; he choked to death in 1784.

**Running northeast-southwest; the rectilinear old Spanish town has been preserved in the heart of the megalopolis, lost like a relic encrusted within the rectilinear American "old town" that grew up around it in the days of the gold and oil rushes, but running north-south.

‡Our Lady of the Angels of the Porziuncola is the name of the little chapel near Assisi that St. Francis restored with his own hands at the beginning of his mystic's career. The stream is now called the Los Angeles River.

ment, awaiting strangulation "in this landscape of steppes."⁵ It will irrigate our sweet potatoes and corn, and our stock will drink from it. "Every head of family received four horses, two yoke of oxen, two cows and a calf, two sheep, two pigs, a mule, a plow, a spade, an axe, a sickle, a gun, and a large shield" along with "a large tract of arable land and a lot to build on, one hundred twenty by sixty feet."⁶

Tonight they'll eat a whole young bull roasted over tree trunks, but now it's only noon and they're singing the *Te Deum* and the *Domine salvum fac regem* in honor of Charles III. Each person steps forward in turn to kiss the hand of the wizened little old man who smiles through his tears in the vast dry light of this rainless land, refreshed and salted by the nearby Pacific Ocean. This really is the end of the earth, a vague place where nobody really knows whether the Indies are East or West. Northwest of the explored regions, where America pushes out a sort of enormous shoulder beyond "the seraphic bay of our father Francis,"* it's all question marks, mainland or islands. Wounded sailing ships, half-unmasted passing Cape Horn or on the long trip northward, wander there for months on end: the English, such as Admiral Vancouver, the French and Portuguese, and who knows who else? Adventurers or soldiers sent out on some desperate mission by a monarch who may already be dead. Russians, too—in fact, they're the commonest, and also the most dangerous, they're the people who actually covet this part of the world and act as though the whole Pacific belonged to them. People say you can even get to their land on foot if you go far enough into the cold. But that's not our problem. The problem in the missions of Upper California is how not to boil in the sun†—and yet the reason why the Grand Council of the Indies let the Franciscans loose here back in 1770 was to beat the Russians to the draw and occupy the coast before they did. Every Indian baptized by them makes one less for the Lutherans and schismatics [Orthodox].

Junipero's victory, thus, is multiple: over the Russians; over the English with whom Spain has been fighting a war, so they say, for the last three years; over the 178 Jesuits booted into Corsica in 1767; over the Dominicans who were frantically tugging at the Holy Father's hem in their eagerness to supplant the Franciscans in New Spain (as though the disciples of Thomas Aquinas had anything to teach a follower of Duns Scotus on the questions of sufficient grace, sanctifying grace, and predestination!);** and above all, and much more, over his fellow countrymen!

*Where San Francisco has just been founded.

†Los Angeles is at the latitude of Teheran, Rabat, and Athens.

**The son of a farm laborer, Junipero Serra was born at Palma, Majorca, where he was for nine years a professor of philosophy and a historian of the great Franciscan philosopher Duns Scotus. The quarrel between Thomists and Scotists was one of the great theological disputes of the Middle Ages; it was settled by a pope in favor of the Thomists, but not until the nineteenth century.

For over ten years now Junipero Serra has been waging a furtive war, using every weapon of humility and passive obedience at his command, against the rapacious Spanish military leaders and, most dangerous of them all, the noble Fleming with the unpronounceable name, for a Spaniard, of Theodore de Croix, whom the king has appointed "Commander General of the Provinces of America," ruling over Serra and the rest as a favor to his protector in Madrid, the high and all-powerful Lord José de Galvez, "universal minister of the Indies"—the king's shadow over half the earth . . . Galvez is the Colbert of the Spanish colonies, which he is sculpting out of the thickness of distance and time with great gouges of his goose quill. The apple of his eye, the object of his most maniacal ministrations, is his latest paper infant, this Upper California on which he will never set foot. In the field, the result of his torrent of orders and instructions—every one containing twenty pages of meticulously ruminated paragraphs, all that office work for an abstract America —is open warfare between two men who address each other with expressions of infinite courtesy but are so infuriated at each other that neither addresses the other at all except in writing: Junipero Serra and Felipe de Neve. The battle of rosary against saber.

Neve is not here in Los Angeles; his kinglet's throne is farther south in San Diego, from which he emits alternating threats and prosecutions in the direction of the Franciscans whom he has been empowered, by the *Reglamento para el gobierno de la Provincia de Californias,* to treat like parish priests confined to things spiritual and not like missionaries possessing full powers in Indian lands. "I thought I was dreaming," Junipero wrote to his superiors, "when he first spoke to me of it. Once I was certain of being well and truly awake, I replied that for thirty years I had supposed I knew the difference between a mission in heathen country and a parish in Christendom"—that is, between a priest who must confine himself to his pulpit or altar and a missionary who metes out spiritual and temporal sustenance in equal portions to the initially mistrustful Indians. Holy water, hosts, and religious images, but also smoke-cured meat, beans, and flour. By this method he had succeeded in evangelizing six hundred Indians of the Pames tribe. "Before," they told him, "we did not understand and we were hungry, which is why we did not like saying prayers, but now everything is different." And how! Junipero adds, "Faith went into their heads by way of their stomachs."

And this *Reglamento,* which that wicked suborning thief of a Neve wrote himself and got the king to sign by using his friends at home, this diabolical document would transfer all temporal power to the military, who would have sole authority over the organization of villages, distribution of supplies, and, most important of all, management of the funds delivered in hard ducats chinking and slithering in the flanks of the king's ships, the "fund of piety" with which so many tangible goods can be purchased.*

Junipero knows perfectly well why the soldiers want to have a free—or full, depending on how you look at it—hand: so they can keep the best meat for themselves, the richest lands, and the biggest incomes. Otherwise, how is it that Neve himself, who arrived in Mexico a poor man ten years ago, has already managed to plan for his retirement by buying up acres and acres of land in Old Castille? Another and nastier reason why the soldiers want to get away from the missionaries' control is because they are even wickeder than the Indians. These so-called protectors our king has sent over to us: what scum! "Every morning"—at San Gabriel—"they ride off into the distance in groups of six. Having learned how to catch cattle and mules with lassos, they go hunting for native women, catch them with slipknots, and shoot down the husbands if they try to defend their property . . . They have even defiled the few children taken in by the mission monks."[7]

The quarrel between Neve and Junipero involved more than protocol or hurt pride: the entire philosophy of Spanish colonization was at stake. What is the point of our being here?

The night after he read the *Reglamento* that Neve triumphantly dispatched to him in August 1778, the little priest was almost strangled by his asthma. He and his brothers under the thumb of those brutes, having to obey them as though they were the Holy Father? His universe tottered on its foundations. For the first and last time he thought of handing in his resignation, asking to be sent home to a chalk-white cell at the foot of the orange groves in Majorca. And then, just at dawn, he received a gentle call from Jesus, not exactly an apparition, more like a sort of friendly and affectionate *psst!* of the sort Junipero sometimes heard at the moment of the consecration.

"Come, come, little brother, don't you remember what I've told you all a hundred times? Come on, repeat it: 'I send you forth as . . .' "

"As . . . ?"

" 'As sheep—' "

"Oh, yes, I've got it, Lord. 'As sheep in the midst of wolves.' "

"That's right. And what did I say next? 'Be ye . . .' "

" 'Be ye therefore wise as serpents and harmless as doves.' "

"Until now, Junipero, you've been a little too much the dove. Be a real serpent for once, and go in peace."

His mind made up, Junipero-the-serpent hurried joyfully off to say mass and conferred a cordial kiss of peace upon the military commander whom he

*The "fund of piety" was a sort of "mission budget" allocated by the King of Spain and partly financed from the missions' own income. In 1780 it could muster 1,257,000 piasters, or approximately 80 million modern francs [$16 million].

had determined to disobey in every particular, nodding agreement all the while.

By now, government-by-mental-reservation has gained the whole of California; the military have the honor, the Franciscans have kept the upper hand, and everything is at sixes and sevens. Neve is no fool and is spluttering with rage, but what can he do to prevent Junipero and the rest from handing out pigs the moment his back is turned, and teaching the natives how to sow barley and wheat? Not that the brothers actually distribute the goods themselves; they simply bless the civilians who do, and as luck would have it the civilians insist on asking and following the padre's advice. What can he do against that? How can he make sure that conversation during the long lectures given to the Indian catechumens never strays from the Son of God and His Most Holy Mother around to the best way of cooking vegetables, the dangers of eating raw meat, recipes for biscuits and tortillas and cornpone? Is he supposed to detail a corporal to spy on the catechism classes? And if the soldiers scowl because the missionaries are showing the Indian women how to spin and weave and make mats and trays, they are told that the women are to begin by preparing religious ornaments for the greater glory of the Almighty.

To begin, that is. Who's going to check and see what they're weaving later on?

Once the missionaries adopted this approach, the Indians began to respond in kind. There are already a few specimens of Apaches from the great Mohave Desert, cousins of the ones who were so eagerly massacring Spaniards a short time ago, mingling with the Los Angeles colonists. They're the ugliest Indians in the whole of New Spain, "all are short and bulge like pitchers, and the skin of the men is crusted a finger deep in dirt. Apart from that, this is an earthly paradise, everything grows to perfection, and the animals wallow in fat. I have also observed* that the Indians positively adore their children, and permit them to do exactly as they please. They show little respect for their womenfolk, however, and seem to have scant affection for them, for they are always scolding them and kicking them in the stomach, even when they are pregnant."[8] A few of those womenfolk have sidled up to the little temporary chapel—the first solid structure built in Los Angeles—to make repeated gestures of pitying compassion in front of the image of a Virgin holding a slightly emaciated Child, the result, they assume, of its mother's inability to produce enough milk. "In response to this, some have been seen thrusting their swollen breasts between the grate and lingering bare-breasted there, beckoning us to bring the Infant Jesus for them to suckle."

*Extract from the journal of Fray Pedro Font, a companion of Junipero Serra in the founding of San Francisco and Los Angeles.

And these are the people Junipero is supposed to treat like swine or abandon to the amusement of the soldiers? He loves them better than himself. "They have filled my heart with delight." Just the other day, they saved his life on the San Buenaventura Road* that runs along the ocean shore for twenty-five leagues. "The storm, the raging ocean, and the wind made it impossible for us to travel along the beach and forced us to climb steep slopes to the inland. When shall I be able to repay these dear Indians the debt of gratitude I then contracted toward them? Unfeeling as I am [*sic*] the tears sprang to my eyes when they picked me up in their arms, pulled me out of the swampy ruts, and helped me to clamber up slippery gradients I should never have been able to negotiate either on foot or on horseback. Some accompanied us, in groups, for days. They would sing with me whenever I was moved to sing. Upon seeing this, others came up and asked me to make the sign of the cross upon their foreheads as well. I have long loved them, and they have long been awaiting the Gospel, these dear Indians."

But now, forward march . . . We have to be at San Gabriel tomorrow, for another confirmation like the ones yesterday and before at San Antonio and San Luis Obispo. Two hundred and seventy-one souls in six days, "which thereby dealt 271 blows to commanding officer Neve."[9] "The mothers give me their babies to hold . . . And indeed they are quite elegant, stark naked with their long hair plastered with white clay. They pulled at my sleeve, wanting to take off my robe. They tried to take my porters' trousers from them. If I had given away my homespun to everyone who wanted it we should have enough Indian Franciscans to fill a large convent. It cannot be denied, however, that some have a slight tendency not to return what they borrow, and I had a terrible time recovering my spectacles . . ." The only thing he can really find to complain of in them, and even that isn't exactly their fault, is the laxity of their morals. "It is the custom for a married man to regard his sisters and mother-in-law like so many wives, and no jealousy arises as the result of this among the ladies, each of whom loves the others' children as she does her own and all live on good terms under the same roof. Polygamy is on the wane, moreover, as our faith begins to gain ground. May God cause another infamous vice to vanish as well: in the region of Santa Clara couples of men are, alas, very numerous, two or three to a village."[10]

"Amar a Dios!" (Let us love God!) These are the parting words among the brethren of this communitarian republic of California ruled by a king far across the seas, whose true viceroy, full of sweetness and cunning beneath his

---

*Another mission that gave birth to a large California town, named after the most famous Franciscan theologian, the "seraphic doctor" St. Bonaventure. The towns of this region—San Diego, Carmel, San Luis Obispo, San Francisco, Santa Clara, San Juan Capistrano—all bear names that are Spanish-Franciscan in origin, and now form a tourist circuit, the "Mission Trail."

brown frock and hood, is Fray Junipero Serra, struggling to extricate himself from the embraces of Los Angeles and remount his mule. The Indians who are to be grouped on the outskirts of the little Spanish burg will "live according to the rule of the primitive Church: everyone works for the fathers and receives food and shelter in return. To those natives who are willing, a gift of land and cattle of their own is also offered, but the Indians in these parts do not aspire to responsibility. They prefer to obey and let the missionaries take care of and think for them."[11]

The column moves off, undoubtedly looking very much like the one that escorted three wise men to Bethlehem: in addition to twenty or so cows, seventy pack mules and asses, there are also a few armed horsemen and thirty Indians, the former bearing swords and guns and the latter bows and arrows; plus cooks, muledrivers, sappers to clear the road, and a few interpreters. Once out of sight of the sea, they set their course by astrolabe. They cover five or six leagues a day.*

Before his departure Junipero has to go through a formality one feels is frankly distasteful to him, in connection with that war—totally abstract to him —being fought between Christians somewhere on the high seas: he collects a tax of "two piasters for every rational being and one piaster for every adult Indian" levied by King Charles III throughout the territory of New Spain to fill Spain's war coffers. "Our Indians, who have never seen a peso, are surprised that the king should ask them to give any, or should need them to wage a war, for they themselves contrive so often and so successfully to kill one another without pesos."

Well, he wriggles out of it in Los Angeles the way he has everywhere else, "by using the collection plate from mass and the supplies we sold to the royal stores." No fool, Junipero Serra: he gets the king's intendants to fill the king's coffers. "The missions have accordingly fought"—against the English—"with all the resources at their disposal. Not only have we prayed from the outset"—of the war—"adding the missal prayer *Contra haereticos* to the orisons at all daily masses; but we have also solved, with our penniless Indians, the seemingly insoluble problem of giving away what we did not possess, namely approximately two thousand pesos to further the victory."

*Junipero Serra dies two years later, after baptizing a total of 6,410 Indians in Upper California. The province is taken from Mexico by the United States after the war of 1848.

3

APRIL 1782

A Dead Loss for the Outfitters

Meanwhile off the other coast of America, a drama involving five hundred more human ants was being enacted for an audience of one—God. Scene: the Atlantic Ocean. Duration: four or five months, in the winter and spring of 1781–82. Setting: the coast of Africa, the Ocean, the Islands. Cast: a handful of English sailors under the command of Captain Collingwood, and a large number of nameless extras—blacks, deported, then exterminated on board the *Zong.* Nameless, yet they are the real actors in the drama.

Nameless in any Christian language, that is, because they were not to be baptized until they had been bought by the planters in Jamaica, after which they would be given names that were simple and easy to shout from a distance: Peter, Paul, Thomas, James, Mary, Marian. Who knows, maybe they're also nameless in whichever of the thousand dialects of the "Bight of Benin" they speak, in their homes in the hollow of Africa's huge armpit where "a narrow band of coast extending for thousands of miles had been wholly delivered into the hands of Europe for the slave trade. Between Cape Verde and Cuanza, over one hundred and fifty fortified emporia were ransoming millions of Africans. Intertribal wars were interminable and invariably motivated by the desire to capture the largest possible number of prisoners to be resold as slaves. People were sold to the traders for the most trivial offenses. Husbands sold their wives, parents sold their children."[1]

It's a smothering climate, they're naked under a scrap of cloth, the Equator is not far away. They're young, or in the prime of life: old people wouldn't fetch a high enough price. Men and women of every size and hue of bronze: the sieve of unending warfare has sifted them into ethnic groups. All their family ties have already been destroyed: saleability is the sole criterion governing the composition of consignments of "ebony,"* and tall, fat, short, with children to match, are grouped according to the presumed desiderata of the customer awaiting delivery on the other side of the ocean.

For the moment, they're being loaded. We're in Tacorary [Takoradi] on

*"Ebony" was the slavers' nickname for their trade.

the Gold Coast, where human gold—flesh and muscle—is more profitable than the yellow sort. "Between Cape Three Points and the Volta River is the main center of the slave trade . . . Within a distance of seventy-five leagues there are no fewer than twenty-three forts (English and Dutch), or one every three leagues."[2] This is the puncture through which Africa's lifeblood is leaking; the sails of slaveships on the horizon flap like vampire wings. Today's cargo is going on the *Zong,* a small three-master 100 feet long, inelegant but robust and firmly seated in the billows for the job she has to perform at trawler pace.

She tacks back and forth outside the reefs, waiting for the launches to finish bringing up her cargo from the pens in which the sellers display their wares, like so many calves in the market, anointed with palm oil and shaven smooth to make their age harder to guess. "Those who fetch the highest prices in the herd have lighter skins than the coastal Negroes: buyers reckon they have come from farther away, sometimes a hundred leagues or more in the interior, and will be more resistant." The most time-consuming part of the business is bartering for them, which involves a bazaar-ful of cloth, guns, knives, kegs of spirits, hides, hats, pewter platters, gunpowder, and iron bars. You have to be part grocer when you set out to trade in men—if you can call them that. "Every captive is branded by the ship's surgeon with a hot iron bar, as a distinguishing mark so that he can be recognized in case of escape."[3] The mark for the *Zong,* on this run, is "a pipe under the left nipple."

At last they're stowed on board, packed like sardines into the specially outfitted steerage, and chained, because a suicide epidemic erupts at every departure. When the coastline dips out of sight they often try to leap overboard. Many—those from cannibal tribes—think they're going to be eaten at sea, although the ones who collide with the cudgels of cruel "commanders" will suffer a worse fate. As for the rest—come, come now, you know perfectly well they'll be better off as slaves than they were where they came from: the slave traders' theme song, ballad of the great philanthropists. "The instant they have been brought on board, the ship must get under way. The reason is that these slaves have so intense a love for their homeland that many die of sorrow; more die before leaving port than during the voyage. Some leap into the sea, others beat their heads against the sides of the ship, others hold their breath until they choke to death, and yet others refuse to eat so they will starve."[4] It's no sinecure, making these savages happy in spite of themselves.

The *Zong* weighs anchor on September 3, 1781, heading for Jamaica via the island of Sao Tomé, with a crew of seventeen and a cargo of 442 deportees. It belongs to the old and noble Royal African Company, a reliable concern with good market connections, an offspring of the London "Company of Adventurers trading to Africa and the Indies" founded in the days of Queen

Anne and Marlborough. They were amateurs back then, often forced to kid-
nap the Negroes themselves, sword in hand. Considerable progress has been
made since, however, and now, under George III, this type of import-export
enterprise runs like a well-oiled machine on its triangular track. The slaveships
set out from Southampton or Bristol, Amsterdam, Nantes or Bordeaux, depending on their nationality, touch land somewhere off the coast of Guinea
to fill their holds with human beings, and bounce away to dump their load of
ebony in the English or French Islands (or on the coast of America itself, when
there isn't a war in the way), whence they set sail again for their home port
laden with sugar or tobacco.

Between decks, every seam has been strained to bursting-point to accommodate its human cargo. "The problem is to enclose the largest possible
number of beings in the smallest possible space and at the same time to
guarantee maximum security for the crew."⁵ If it ever occurred to the Negroes
that they outnumbered their escort twenty to one . . . "The captives are stowed
between the hold and the upper deck, on two levels with a total height of four
feet four inches."* But there's a daily exercise period at the end of the crews'
whips and guns, "to empty the slop pails" and keep the slaves fit enough to
make a good showing to prospective buyers. Captain Collingwood isn't really
a bad guy—only a shrewd one. "Every evening when the weather was fine,
he had his cargo of slaves brought up on deck and the men of the crew played
music for them, to make them dance." A reassuring ritual for those who were
worried about being eaten, because you don't ordinarily ask your main course
to dance for you first. "On average, the food distribution was one measure of
corn porridge for every ten slaves, then they walked past the barrels of drinking water in Indian file, received a pint of water apiece, and went back down
to the hold." Captain Collingwood, sole master on board after God, entirely
responsible for the ship's performance and the ebony negotiations, doesn't
concern himself with minor details; he leaves all that to his first mate and
surgeon (who actually functions as a veterinarian, specializing in the conserva-
tion of human flesh), and remains snugly back in the poop, shut into his
handsome cabin with its Utrecht tapestries, where he can revel in "an armchair
in reversed cowhide, four leather chairs and three folding stools *idem,* one
large mirror and one small one for shaving, and seven complete sets of cut-
lery." He sits there among his books and charts like a little sea-king, in a jacket
with gold buttons and embroidery, his sword at his side, his hair in a wig, and
a lace jabot at his throat. A cleverly contrived system of heavy doors and huge
locks and bolts enables the crew to isolate the bridgehouse where the helm
is and barricade themselves inside it in the event of a mutiny among the
"passengers." We have to think of everything. What about the crew? Nothing

---

*In other words, they had to remain lying down or crawl on all fours.

to brag of: drifters picked up here and there in port bars, men turned down by the king's "impress." They do as they're told, though, and profit by it, because they're better paid than sailors on warships and in less danger, except for disease.

The sails are good, the hull both thin and heavy. They can cross the Atlantic in two or two and one half months, skillfully negotiating the usual series of squalls and doldrums. The trick is to catch the trades right, after the Cape Verde Islands, and make tracks at the sight of any Frenchman. The log entries record nothing but the monotonous litany of the predictable deaths of a percentage of the Negroes who were doomed in advance, the least robust. Well, that'll make more food for the rest. Speculators reckon an average loss of one-sixth of the total, which is the risk ordinarily underwritten by insurance companies. A few notes from the logbook, around mid-October:

"One Negro departed this life of fever.—One Negro, suffering from dropsy, departed this life, of that disease.—One Negress dead of a miscarriage, the child also dead and putrid.—One Negro man child taken off by consumption.—One Negro dead of an extreme swelling of the face and head.—One Negro girl child would not eat or drink, dead of stomach flux.—One male Negro dead of a cramp." The usual stuff. The chronicler can hardly rouse himself to a little more sentiment for "the death of a Negress, with exceedingly fine breasts, swollen, possibly of smallpox."

The situation begins to deteriorate toward the end of the journey. There's too much sickness among the Negroes, and the crew members are going down too, with some kind of intestinal flu, presumably caused by the bad quality of the water, or rather the conditions in which it is stored; water is the Achilles' heel of long-range sailing ships. When land is finally sighted—the palms and sharp white quays of Kingston, capital of Jamaica, the big island held by the English—it looks as though our worries may be over.

On the contrary: that's where the real trouble starts, trouble that will light a fire in English public opinion, although it takes a mighty pile of kindling to produce a flame hot enough to scorch the merchants' interests. But it does, and the whole slave trade machine will begin to creak and, gear by gear, grind to a halt in half a century—in England, that is—and all because of the *Zong,* a tiny grain of sand, one of a hundred such ships setting out that year.

It's hard to find out what really happened, or rather how and why.* Following the company's usual practice, Collingwood had been left free to choose his

*The insurance company's investigation, followed by one made by the naval courts before which the case was brought by Pitt months and years later, amassed tons of testimony without shedding an iota of light on the matter, owing to Collingwood's death from natural causes in 1783, and the crew's combined ignorance and total refusal to speak out.

destination in the Islands, but he seems to have suffered some kind of mental paralysis in the Kingston roads. He looks around for the regulation field with a few huts and some guards, where he can park and "season" his Negroes before auctioning them off. He's worried. He's already lost sixty of his cargo, and seven of his crew. He tries to sell off the "worn-out" ones at discount prices—that is, the ones who are shaky on their feet and likely to snuff out in their buyers' hands: three hundred Island pounds a head, why, that's dirt cheap, gentlemen, only half the average price of a healthy Negro.* Even if you lose a third of them, you're still ahead. Few takers. Lines were apparently not forming outside the port authority's doors to begin negotiating for the remaining three hundred Negroes. It's this blasted war that has put a hex on the market. People have been buying fewer and fewer slaves ever since Messieurs d'Estaing and de Grasse started barging around in these parts. Only fifteen or sixteen thousand Negroes a year since 1775: what a comedown! It's natural enough, though. Why should we burden ourselves with slaves if the French are going to hit Kingston one of these days and take Jamaica and Barbados away from us like they did Grenada? And the traders—among whom Collingwood is no exception—demand payment for half their cargo in gold. They won't look at paper money anymore, and they won't take more than half the amount in colonial produce. Collingwood probably wasn't expecting such a cool reception from his prospective buyers. The bottom has dropped out of the market. No fun for a slave trader stuck with a ship full of perishable goods.

Perishable is the word.

Collingwood turns back to sea, his crew and cargo unaltered, on November 9. He hasn't even taken on a load of fresh vegetables or renewed his water supply. Where's he headed? Barbados? He could be there in three days. But instead, he sails round in circles, possibly discouraged by reports from that island. He turns south. Toward Guiana? Or the American ports still held by Tories—Charlestown, Georgetown? And scurvy is eating into his ship, and the water's going foul, and the crew is beginning to grumble.

"On November 29, 1781, the captain of the *Zong* took stock of his water supplies, too late.† There were only two hundred gallons left, for 392 persons. The captain called his officers and crew together and informed them that if the slaves died of natural causes, it would mean a dead loss for the outfitters—and

*Six hundred Jamaica pounds, the going price for a slave on delivery, amounted to about 400 French livres or 2,000 modern francs [$400].

†This running account is a summary of the case written by a court clerk two years later, when the second trial of the Company *v.* Lloyds Insurance was being brought before the Court of the Exchequer in London.

for themselves, as they received a commission on every cargo—whereas if they were thrown overboard alive, the loss would be for the insurers.

In two days, 133 ailing slaves were thrown into the sea. On December 1 torrential rains fell and filled the water barrels, which had been, anyway, far from empty. There was now enough drinking water for eleven days, but twenty-six more slaves were nonetheless deemed to be mortally ill, laden with irons, and cast overboard. Other slaves who had been brought out on deck for a medical examination witnessed this organized massacre. Ten of them jumped into the sea of their own accord. All drowned. The ship returned to Jamaica on December 22, with the survivors."[6]

This captain, like all the rest, didn't think a job was something to take too seriously, and many another heart like his was beating beneath its fancywork and muslin in the eighteenth century.

Who's going to have a nervous breakdown over an unmarketable cargo chucked into the sea? Just another commercial mishap; and indeed nobody would have bothered about it, for the very good reason that nobody in London would ever have heard of it, if those thickheaded insurance people had been capable of following Captain Collingwood's reasoning. But there's the rub: they weren't. The chaps at Lloyds have no reason to do any favors for the chaps at the Royal African Company, who are asking thirty pounds for every slave still alive at the moment he was thrown overboard.

Lloyds refuses, on "purely legal grounds." No, no, and no again; Captain Collingwood was acting upon a hypothesis which is covered by no clause in the contract. We pay for Negroes slain in a mutiny and for Negroes dying of illness while on shipboard—but not in excess of one-sixth of the total, as stipulated heretofore—and provided that the surgeon's certificate declares them to be "sound and unspoilt" upon receipt. We even pay for Negroes sentenced to death for insubordination, "by a lawful ruling of the captain." But in this case, Captain Collingwood, you have transgressed your prerogatives . . . and the trial, which opens in London in March 1782 and is heard by the King's Bench (where the ship's outfitters win) before being appealed to the Court of the Exchequer (where they lose), employs a legal-commercial jargon worthy of a dispute over a con-signment of wormy kidney beans. "What is the matter?" It is to determine whether the sacrificed portion of the consignment was irremediably doomed before it was thrown overboard. If so, we pay. If not, the "dead loss" is for the Royal African Company. It's not.

Even so, the situation wouldn't have been too bad, Captain Colling-wood's faux-pas could have been written off on the books, if the Gazette of His Majesty's civil courts had not happened to fall into the hands of two young troublemakers farther up the Thames, whose habits were totally incomprehensible to men of both business and law—two members of the House of Commons, politicians, romantics, that's all we need. William Wilberforce and William Pitt, both born in 1759, both Cambridge graduates, both elected in 1780, the year they reached their majority—one Member for Hull and the other for the little town of Appleby, setting out on a debater's career in the House with the appetite of an ogre. Wilberforce has been trying to arouse public feeling against the slave trade for years. He claims spiritual descent from John Wesley, the somber prophet of these English years who is campaigning for moral purity and equality among men. Wilberforce later writes in his diary that "Almighty God has given a great object to my life: the suppression of the slave trade." With Pitt's help he battens on to the *Zong* case and hurls it at the press like a stick of dynamite, engaging in a public battle against the ship outfitters' counsel, who, in turn, try to stir up a counterwave of indignation against these whippersnapper politicians who think they can teach a lesson to established people with holdings in the City. They should mind their own business. "And, so far from the charge of murder lying against these people, there is not the least imputation—of cruelty I will not say, but—of impropriety: not in the least!!!"[7] And the merchants' guild of Liverpool, foreseeing its ruination if anything happens to impede the slave trade, votes a present of one hundred pounds to a pious clergyman, Raymond Harris, who has just published a pamphlet (commissioned by the outfitters) entitled "Research into the Scriptures," in which he sets out to prove, on the strength of three hundred quotations from the Bible, that God approves of and actually ordains the enslavement of the Negroes, "for the purpose of procuring baptism for them in this world and eternal salvation in the other."[8]

Too late. Some people in England can read and have hearts that beat in a certain way. In April 1782 Wilberforce founds his "Standing Committee for the Abolition of the Slave Trade," which is immediately joined by John Wesley, the Bishop of London, twenty Members of Parliament, a dozen lords, and that stripling with the sharp fangs, the famous Chatham's son—William Pitt, heir to one of the greatest political fortunes in the kingdom, whose sights are set high and who has sworn to settle the hash of the slave trade.

Worth watching.

4

JANUARY 1782

An Extraordinary and a Glorious Thing

"It was such a mild winter"—in France, and especially in Paris—"that people feared they would be unable to fill the ice-houses",[1] those big stone cavities in cellars or huge triple-walled wooden coffers in which blocks of ice stayed frozen even in mid-August, for the greater savor of oyster luncheons served with chilled Aÿ wine.

But the champagne began flowing before there was any need for ice, with the festivities starting right after Christmas to celebrate the dauphin's birth. Damp, mild festivities they were, to match the rotten winter and the spring that couldn't make up its mind. Fountains of wine in the town squares, mountains of sausages and rolls provided at the expense of the city elders, a great clanging of bells and squeaking of fiddles from their perch on makeshift platforms: January 21, 1782, Paris's party for the King and Queen,* who dine in public in the courtyard of the Hôtel de Ville, where a sort of palace has been built overnight according to the latest fad, which is to paste canvas and cardboard over all the "old stones" as though they need make-up. "No effort was spared and money had been spent almost extravagantly. In spite of the war, this prince's birth made people wild with joy . . . The back of the Grève being frightful to see,† it was hidden by an immense and very handsome gallery built of solid timbers and magnificently decorated" . . . But "the pyrotechnists had no space"—for the fireworks—"and dared neither light nor feed a fire, of which there was none at all. The Queen seemed displeased with her retenue and with the acclamations, and was rather quiet."[2] Maybe because there was a sort of first-night-flop or rained-out-baseball-game feeling in the air: since the great massacre caused by crowding at the fireworks display for Marie Antoinette's marriage, the Paris chief of police had invented something absolutely new—a crowd-control squad. "This unfortunate example [the massacre]

*Louis XVI will be guillotined a few feet away eleven years later to the day. This passage jumps back some months from the first two chapters, which form a prologue to this volume.

†That is, the side of the square opposite the bank of the Seine, which was an irregular row of unmatching houses.

had at least the merit of producing, on subsequent public occasions, the most severely regulated order, but it was too sudden a shift to the opposite extreme. After that time, the people were invited to public festivities on the condition that they should not attend. The area set aside for them was a desert, they received more cudgel blows than buns, with the result that at the celebration of the birth of the dauphin,* when the King and Queen came to the windows of the Hôtel de Ville to be greeted by the cheers and blessings of the people, there were no people in sight."[3]

There was a lot of noise in other parts of the kingdom, nevertheless, enough to singe the ears of a little gentleman of eight whom the dauphin's birth had edged another step further from the throne: his distant cousin Louis-Philippe, Duc de Valois.† He was uncomfortable enough without this new thorn in his side, for he had just lived through a sort of earthquake when, on January 12, his whole routine, previously dedicated to idleness and play, was abruptly upset. He had been unpotted and repotted like a plant, from the Palais Royal to Saint-Cloud and from there to the Convent of Belle-Chasse. And even more, the little man had been given into the care of a woman—and what a woman: the headline maker Félicité de Genlis. A front-page-event, which has set more salon tongues wagging than the dauphin himself. Did you ever hear of such a thing, a prince of the blood entrusted to a female at training time! And the spicy bit is—this is whispered, but not too quietly because it's virtually public knowledge—that the woman into whose care the poor child is being consigned is his father's mistress. Really, those Orléanses, what a family!

Hardy the bookseller, a solemn and stiff-necked old Parisian who records absolutely everything in his diary, wrote on January 8: "M. le Duc de Chartres** has just dismissed the tutors and instructors assigned for some ten years [*sic*] to the Duc de Valois and the Duc de Montpensier, his two male children, and will in future entrust every aspect of their education to the gentle Comtesse de Genlis, who is already teaching the two princesses, his daughters."[4]

Hardy's wrong on one point: there's a third male child, the Comte de Beaujolais, a babe of three. We won't quibble over numbers; he too is packed off to Félicité de Genlis, who cannot withhold a cry of triumph as she writes to her friend Bernis, the pretty, mincing cardinal who represents Louis XVI in Rome: "For three years I have been governess to Mesdemoi-

---

*This is according to Louis-Sébastien Mercier.

†Who will be in turn Duc de Chartres, Duc d'Orléans, and King of the French, with the title Louis-Philippe I, from 1830 to 1849. He was born on October 6, 1773, and he is the person who will sit on the throne in the years that were supposed to be the reign of the newborn dauphin.

**That is, Louis-Philippe-Joseph, son of "Louis the Stout," the then Duc d'Orléans who becomes the Philippe Egalité of 1793.

selles d'Orléans, and this very moment [January 6] M. le Duc de Chartres has entrusted me with the education of the three princes, his sons, the eldest of whom is eight years old. So these princes will never have a governor, as I am to act in that capacity instead. Each year I shall spend eight months with them in the country; the four winter months they will remain in Paris and will be brought to me at Belle-Chasse every day, where I shall keep them three hours for instruction, which I shall impart to them myself. For the rest, I shall direct all their other studies, I shall also have charge of their households . . . In accepting this hitherto unprecedented mark of confidence I made only two requests: that I should be absolute mistress, and that in payment for my devotion I should receive nothing but the highly distinguished honor attaching to the task."[5] A pure and simple takeover, in fact.

On January 12, therefore, Louis-Philippe plunges headfirst into the new situation officially announced on the 8th and first envisaged in a casual conversation between the Duc de Chartres and his former mistress on the 6th. It seemed so spontaneous, just an idea that suddenly struck me—yes, indeed, why not? It's the answer to all our problems!—but the ground had been prepared like a tapestry by Félicité's deft fingers. It had taken her years of patience.

Philippe (de Chartres) had dropped in for a chat at the house built expressly for her in the gardens at Belle-Chasse; he often did that in the evening after supper, at the hour permitted to persons favored by the nuns (those enjoying the "princes' right" to enter the gates). Handsome in spite of himself, that's his style, with his pleasantly weary air, his well-washed casual appearance, his English tone and bright-hued vest, he always looks as if he just got off his horse, what an attractive man in spite of those pimples all over his face. She was waiting for him, straight as a ramrod whatever she did but a friendly sort of ramrod—I suffer for you and it's a pleasure—she can't stay thirty seconds without some sort of activity. "She was almost always at her desk,* painting flowers or making things out of hair or wax, for it is true that she was never idle."[6] The perpetual mobilization of the entire being to combat the insecurity of a poor girl landed in a nest of nabobs.

Her Chartres is a shade restless this evening; he complains, in his languid nobleman's manner, of his worries about his sons. That poor Marquis de Bonnard, Buffon's friend, the man who was assigned to serve them as a sort of extended nursemaid and guide their early steps—he really isn't up to the mark, he's positively irresponsible. Why, Valois told his father that very morning how he had "thundered at his door." And "in the same conversation he added, on the subject of his walks in the garden at Saint-Cloud, that they had

*According to her pupil Louis-Philippe. It would appear that Mme de Genlis was the first woman to use this article of furniture for the same purpose as did men. Other "literary" ladies had "secrétaires."

been bedeviled by 'relatives,' by which he meant the insects called *cousins"*
[gnats or midges—*Trans.*].[7] What's this, what's this, his cousins the little Duc
d'Angoulême and now the dauphin being equated with mosquitoes: can you
imagine what would happen if the King should ever get wind of it? The boy
must have someone right away, someone who can take him in hand, re-educate
him in fact.

Félicité listened, wearing her inscrutable cat's face. With a delicate paw
she edged forth one name, then another; what about Schomberg, Durfort, de
Thiars—none of whom could possibly fill the bill. Philippe brushes them aside
with a wave of his hand: all pedants, incompetents. She crept slowly toward
the fleeting instant for which you spend half a lifetime preparing. She relates
the incident later, not without relish:

> Then I began to laugh and said to him, "Why, then, what about me!"
> "Why not?" he replied, quite in earnest.
> I protest that I had only meant it as a pleasantry and that, in our previous
> conversations, nothing had ever prepared me for so singular a thought. But I was
> much struck by the expression and tone of M. le Duc de Chartres. I glimpsed the
> possibility of an extraordinary and a glorious thing, and I desired that it should
> take place. I spoke my thought to him quite openly. M. le Duc de Chartres seemed
> delighted, and said to me, "Then that's that. You shall be their tutor."[8]

Louis XVI had to be informed: he had the last word about the education
of every prince of the blood. The next day Philippe tackles him, rather gin-
gerly. But the birth of his son has put the King in a good mood; he replies,
with customary tact:

"Governor or governess, what do I care. I've got a dauphin. Madame is
thought to be pregnant.* The Comtesse d'Artois has children; you can do as
you please with yours."

"On January 12, 1782," Louis-Philippe relates, "I was taken to Saint-Cloud
with the Duc de Montpensier, my younger brother, from whom I had never
been separated since his birth, and there we were handed over to Mme de
Genlis. She had one of my two sisters with her; the elder had stayed in Paris,
with the measles." That means a brief respite before the daunting hours at
Belle-Chasse, but even this is no mean shock: "Immediately upon our arrival
at Saint-Cloud I encountered changes that, despite my youth, made a powerful
impression upon me . . . We dined and took supper alone with my sister
. . . and the only service was common pottery, brown underneath, which made
a sharp contrast with the silver dishes on which we had always been served
before. The food was abominable. That part was run entirely by the Baronne
d'Andlau, the mother of Mme de Genlis,"[9] a stout matron with voracious

*That is, the wife of Monsieur, Comte de Provence. She wasn't, and they remain childless.

appetites who had remarried, after the death of Félicité's father, a man who had once taken a fancy to her daughter but settled for the mother instead. Both of them were expert at capitalizing on anything that came their way.

Poor Louis-Philippe! What's the point of changing châteaus, from the gilded suites of the Palais Royal with their ceilings covered in beautiful and entirely naked ladies to the terraces and cascades of the gardens of Saint-Cloud, as magnificent as those of Versailles; and what's the use of being heir to the biggest fortune in France, the combined assets of the Orléans and Penthièvre families, if all you get to eat is stew out of a china bowl? The little prince has been ensnared into a setting more appropriate for a novice in a monastery; with glittering caskets of jewels all round him, here he is dumped in a brown paper bag.

Face to face, Félicité de Genlis and Louis-Philippe. They're both pretty sharp. They take a long look at each other. Which will it be, war or peace?

He, seen by her: a characterless little boy. Regular features, pale eyes, pretty curling fair hair but left to grow too long on his shoulders, making him look like a girl. Too many shirt-dresses in lawn, too much perfume. "He walks with his head down, both body and knees bent, and he sways from side to side. No old man could climb stairs as heavily and gracelessly as he . . . When I came [to Saint-Cloud] five or six underlings stood round him, whose sole occupation was to spare him the trouble of going to fetch the toy he wanted next."[10] A child in danger of non-existing. He needs shaking up and fast.

She, seen by a little boy: an old woman, as she is for her society and age, in which women are worn out at twenty; and she's thirty-six—but what a youthful old woman! Unimaginable without the huge winged hat she dons every morning as though it were a war helmet. Just six years ago it was, on her thirtieth birthday, when she scandalized the habitués of the Palais Royal by turning up at Mme de Chartres's soirée without a trace of make-up and wearing an afternoon gown. She took to her middle age like a nun's habit; she had said, not without that tinge of theatricality which comes so naturally to her, that she would dance no more, was giving up clothes, cosmetics, and gambling — and, she implied, love—everything, in fact, except writing books. People thought it wouldn't last three months. It has lasted and will go on lasting. Not one grain of powder. The most uncompromising of gowns. And she's writing all right, quires and quires, enough to give her cramps in her fingers. She reeks of will power. She reeks of nothing else.

Under the hat may be observed a mass of chestnut-colored hair, elegantly upswept albeit unpowdered, an ocean enchained, slightly overpowering the little rodentlike face with the upturned nose and arched brows—a sign of humor—and the pointed chin. She's not a beauty; she is pretty. Lively eyes, a mouth that is spiritual rather than sensual. All in all, a face one wouldn't forget and a body to serve it: dedicated to the mind, well cinched at the waist. Every part of her has been mapped and plotted and stands, well-ordered, held in reserve—except for the gleam in the eye, of course, and the high-perched voice that speaks as though it were singing. Champagne that fizzes all the more for being so tightly bottled up.

Mme de Genlis is a child of worry and courage. The father? Respectable lesser nobility fallen upon evil days. The hint of an untamed childhood spent in the "ancient and dilapidated" manor of Saint-Aubin near Orléans, leaning against the Loire but turning its back to it. She used to escape from it sometimes, when she was ten or so, and preach to the gaping loiterers from the terrace looking out over the side of the pond. She would promise them cakes and recite lines or passages from the Bible to them. She's the same today, when she captivates whole salons. A sort of poor man's Germaine Necker* with a father up to his ears in debt and no choice but to raise herself as best she can in the course of an unrewarding adolescence—by the strength of her pretty wrists, which could run so agilely up and down the harp in the farmer-generals' homes where she would entertain the assembly. There was Le Normand (La Pompadour's husband), La Popelinière, the first man who wouldn't have minded confiscating her, but she was only thirteen at the time, and he was sixty-seven. "I was very cross not to be three or four years older, for I admired him so much that I should have been delighted to marry him."[11] Somebody gave a few louis to her or her mother, and some dresses. "She was petted and praised beyond reason, and she would blush to tears."[12] Her full name was Etiennette-Félicité du Crest de Saint-Aubin. More or less by accident she married an extremely easygoing man, Charles-Alexis Brûlart de Sillery, Comte de Genlis, a naval officer who had fallen in love with her portrait when Félicité's father showed it to him during a period of co-captivity in England. So she let him marry her picture, or precious little else at any rate. Where's her husband now, in her days of grandeur? Not far geographically, but light-years from her heart. He is captain of the guard of the Duc d'Orléans and lives apart. He is a close friend of Philippe de Chartres and was standing with him on the poop of the *Saint-Esprit* during the battle of Ouessant. A man of some wit and few asperities, who never interfered with what was going on between his princely friend and his wife. Do the right thing, y'know. He gambles. He chases skirts, up to a point, for the honor of his breed, which is a good one: the Brûlarts were around before Louis XIV. A small man with fine, tired features.

Charles and Félicité were married enough, however, to help each other up the ladder of the Orléans family when they dropped anchor in the Palais Royal thanks to the Marquise de Montesson, Philippe's fat father-duke's Mme

*The future Mme de Staël.

de Maintenon, who was also Félicité's aunt by marriage. It was double love at first sight, first the Duchesse de Chartres and then her husband, when this pretty woman turned up ten years back piquant and poor, and they both discovered that in her company one was never bored. The duchesse loves her with greater constancy and passion than the duke, apart from sleeping-with, which he did more or less in passing during a trip to Forges-les-Eaux, where his wife had gone to take the waters that are supposed to make you pregnant. There was a ravishing little *ménage à trois* that summer of 1772, when the young duchesse was just goose enough to believe that everybody was friends all round. In her embroidery bag she carried the *Office du Saint-Esprit,* which she recited every day on the sly, respecting, by interposed orison, the theoretical commitment that her husband had made upon receiving the Order of the Holy Spirit. The other two, meanwhile, were in bed together. Philippe and Félicité wrote each other a few impassioned love letters in the pastoral vein, calling each other "my child." But she had her eye on the future: "I shall employ my reason, if I have any left, to temper the violence of a sentiment that could do nothing in its present state but drive me to desperation. I do not rightly know what I am doing, since I have loved you."[13] The waters of Forges, moreover, were to live up to their reputation: a year later, the duchesse was delivered of little Louis-Philippe, the child of the *ménage à trois* that has endured platonically for ten years, since the gust of sensuality blew past. All three are really exceedingly fond of one another. Félicité would have been the Pompadour of the Orléanses, if Pompadour had had Marie Leczinska as her intimate friend and ended up as the dauphin's tutor.

LOUIS-PHILIPPE, DUC DE VALOIS

5

APRIL 1782

They Fancy They Must Write

"Do you want to become a man, Monseigneur?"

That very evening, January 12, the laws are promulgated, the boundaries are marked out, the little prince's universe is transformed. He was on his way outdoors, to console himself for his nasty supper by playing in the woods at Saint-Cloud, accompanied by two footmen whose job was to keep all animals away from him, for Louis-Philippe was afraid of dogs.

"The footmen will stay here at the château, Monseigneur, where they will be better employed. Here are your new walking companions . . ."

Two German shepherds! He shuddered but shed no tears. He was intrigued by this woman who was daring to oppose him. His eyes fixed on the ground, he stoically endured a long speech on self-mastery, in which she found the right words to give him a taste for the headiest intoxication of all, for a spoiled child: emancipation from boredom.

"Will you take a turn round the grounds with them? At your age, every child of an English prince has his own pack of hounds."

Oh, well, if the English . . . "Gladly, Madame." The first victory is for her, but it's also one over himself. He reckons that they're even when he returns shivering and proud, but she's waiting on the doorstep: time for his history lesson.[1] And the very next morning come spelling and mythology, and more history with some peculiar new methods all her own; now he's really impressed: 115 little gouache paintings by a Polish artist, "representing the great moments of Greek and Roman history, selected by her, framed and bearing explanations on the back written by Mme de Genlis in a very fine hand and arranged in chronological order."[2] Comic-strip teaching.

Louis-Philippe is caught up in the whirlwind of this ultra-modern pedagogical method being invented day by day as his governess goes along, with him as its guinea-pig—what an adventure! His little sister, the twin with the measles, dies on February 8. The round of lessons continues in mourning, and the surviving sister, Adélaïde, is conscripted into the class along with a pretty little English doll of the same age, Pamela, a child selected by a correspondent in London "among the foundlings maintained by the King of England." She had been sent for three years before, as though from a mail-order house; item, one "pretty, dark-haired little girl, aged not more than six, and it is most important that her nose be not too long and that she speak not a single word of French,"[3] of course, because her role is to be a living textbook for the children of the House of Orléans. "We will take her, but she must have a good accent." A sort of white pickaninny, being brought up in the company of her betters.*

Louis-Philippe soon begins to see some good points in his new turn-of-the-screw lifestyle. He sleeps in the Palais Royal, the grandiose residence of the Orléans family that towers like a cliff above a rubble heap which is raising great cries of complaint among the Parisians: the trees in the gardens have been chopped down, the paths are all ruts and potholes, the earth itself is nothing but pits and hummocks, new shops are springing up, the old familiar fabric of the right bank is turning into a patchwork—what are they doing to

---

*The wildest rumors were circulating, and would continue to circulate, on the subject of Pamela's origins; at one point Philippe de Chartres was alleged to be her father and Mme de Genlis her mother; upon inspection, these suppositions would seem to be unfounded.

our beloved Paris? And all so that M. le Duc de Chartres, the richest man in France, can escape bankruptcy, or at least that's what people are saying, because he lives so lavishly. This maneuver is pure speculation; he's building the shops for rent, and borrowing on every side . . . Louis-Philippe understands nothing of his father's worries and wheeling and dealing. He doesn't like the ugly building-site outside his windows, he'd rather be at Saint-Cloud, but these days it's to Belle-Chasse that he is driven every afternoon in a carriage, crossing the Seine by the Pont Royal. He rolls down the Quai d'Orsay, turns up the "Rue de Belle-Chasse," a narrow street between white houses with larger and larger gaps between them until they give way to open countryside west of Paris, the fields and gardens before the Champ de Mars, and here are the high walls of the Convent of the Ladies of Saint Sépulcre among its bird-thronged lilacs. He enters the private convent that the Duc de Chartres had built inside the main walls, as other men build their "follies," so that Mme de Genlis could bring up the young Orléans ladies along with her own four children.* A big, rather stupid-looking house, pure white, only two stories tall, with a plain façade. The nuns keep the key to the gate and open it only to ladies and noblemen. It is here that Paris now comes to call on Félicité every evening, since Félicité no longer goes calling on it. When Louis-Philippe d'Orléans, Duc de Valois, walks in the door with all the solemnity of a child at play, the building and everybody inside it seem to exist for the express purpose of fashioning him into a man. Here again, his appraising eyes were on the job:

"The entrance to the house was a clue to the oddness of all the rest of it . . . The kitchen was the first thing that struck one's eyes; servants' rooms, extremely dark and damp"—Mme de Genlis's modernity did not extend belowstairs; all very well to lead the way, but only within one's own class—"opened off right and left along a long, equally dark hall decorated with blue signs bearing quotations in English. It was so gloomy there that I was never able to read them . . . On the left was a tower, on the right a parlor, similarly bristling with writing designed to inform society as a whole of the overriding intentions of its occupant, which were to allow as few men as possible inside the house and to live there in the deepest seclusion." His sister's room "was hung with painted medallions depicting Roman emperors and great moments of history; in the middle a thick rope reached down from the ceiling, and we were made to climb it like a tree; between the two windows there was a sort of well containing sandbags, which we would draw up to the ceiling by means of a rope and pulley, as though they were pails of water,"[4] the reason for this complicated chamber-gymnasium being that the nuns were prepared to allow men in the building but not so much as a man-child in their gardens, where

*The nuns' buildings and grounds stood approximately in the space now occupied by St. Clotilde's church and the square adjoining the Rue Saint-Dominique.

the apparatus could more conveniently have been installed. "We would spend the whole after-dinner in Mme de Genlis's room, where we had lessons of all sorts, geography, history, chemistry, and various languages . . . She seldom followed any scheme with consistency or perseverance, although she often claimed she did. Her ideas came from her reading, rarely from her reasoning. Thus they varied with the books that fell into her hands."[5] Which of the two was the better judge of the other, the tutor or the tutored? She had plenty of good sense and he was equally well endowed, spicing sense with his own special variety of humor—the introverted kind. "She read enormously, but usually so quickly that she could only recall what she had read by consulting her notes and summaries: her instruction was artificial and superficial as a result, but I believe she did not mind, for her one aim was to shine . . . She had made numerous chronological summaries for us, assembling all the different periods of different histories, but she could remember none of them . . . She had a marked predilection for the centuries of chivalry and the Romanesque period, which she saw as ruled by women and consequently by passion; these chivalrous sentiments, this *Esclavage pour la Dame des pensées**[Enslavement to the Lady of the Mind], was, according to her, the driving force behind all great deeds. She employed every possible means to stimulate our enthusiasm in this direction; but the love she wanted us to grasp was purely platonic." The heir of the Orléanses had scant inclination to become a knight errant; his mind ran at ground level, but not unintelligently. Even as she was, however, and even as he was, he grew fond of his romantic tormentor. "We were brought up with a vengeance"† . . . and indeed, many witnesses are and will continue to be flabbergasted to see the little prince's character formation carried to the point of placing a hopper on his back filled with 300 pounds of iron and making him climb the spiral staircase in the house beneath it on all fours.[6] But he never complained in later days. Rather the opposite. Perhaps he was grateful to receive an education so unlike that of "those insects called *cousins*" who were being fattened off in their gold and feathers. What Félicité is giving him is far more precious: a childhood of his own.

On Wednesday, April 10, for example, we find them braving the stares of socialite Paris together for the first time, at the new Théâtre Français near the Luxembourg. The play is *Les Femmes savantes:* but at this type of performance, of course, the action takes place as much in the audience as on stage. Five hundred pairs of eyes are fastened upon the boxes of the great. On the left, facing the stage, is that of the Duc de Chartres; across from it on the right, that of the fat Duc d'Orléans: the princes must play their parts first, before the

*Underlined by Louis-Philippe in his extremely interesting *Mémoires,* which the Comte de Paris has recently published.

†He was to tell Victor Hugo fifty years later, when he was king.

actors begin. Philippe de Chartres starts to enter his box, then stands aside to allow Mme de Genlis to precede him, accompanied by her princely pupils. She's wearing her same old hat, broad as a parasol but almost grossly simple in comparison with the scaffoldings bearing down the other women's heads and making the three tiers of boxes look like a display of flowerpots or model crafts. Here and there one can even make out something resembling a ship rolling on the waves of naked shoulders: the *coëffures à la liberté* in honor of the American Rebels, assemblages of colored cloth, wire, and hair depicting three-masted warships in full sail. The immense gowns fall in layers of ruffles over the paniers, which have doubled in width in the last ten years. The dominant hue is dauphin-shit-yellow, all the rage this winter.

The moment she steps inside the theater, Félicité receives the entire house like a vial of acid in the face.

That particular society has had little enough love for her ever since she began publishing book after book in her prolific and effusive style.* A woman of letters is something to be sneered at *a priori,* whatever her letters may be, and especially if they are Christian moralities and blunt arrows aimed at *Encyclopédistes.* † And then, if she's poor, dependent upon the great and above all upon those Orléanses, those counter-kings about whom everybody has so much to tell you . . . And even more, she's taken it upon herself to set *us* an example, by turning her back on society and playing at convent sisters. And now here she is metamorphosed into a "governor" for a prince, that really is the limit!

"The arrival of Mme de Genlis was the signal for a storm of whistles and catcalls lasting an uninterrupted ten minutes. The hurricane had hardly begun to die down when the Duc d'Orléans and Mme de Montesson appeared in their box facing that of Mgr de Chartres and, in a movement of violent opposition, the whole house burst into applause."[7] For Paris and for Versailles, this uproar is the event of the spring, the main topic of conversation, along with the battle of Yorktown. And it didn't end when the curtain rose, either; but she was rather asking for it, after all, by choosing to exhibit herself at *Les Femmes savantes,* of all plays: *"C'est à vous que je parle ma soeur . . ."* [Sister, I am speaking to you . . .] Throughout the performance, every allusion that could conceivably be applied to Mme de Genlis was raucously underlined, to

---

*Inter alia, a *Théâtre à l'usage des jeunes personnes* [Theater for Young People] and a *Théâtre de société* [Society Theater] in two volumes; a large treatise on education called *Adèle et Théodore,* intended to be a riposte to *Emile;* and she was then preparing three octavo volumes entitled *Les Veillées du château ou Cours de morale à l'usage des enfants* [Fireside Evenings at the Château, or a Course in Morality for Children]. In her old age she produces some pleasant, garrulous, and disorganized *Mémoires.*

†I.e., the contributors to the *Encyclopédie* and, by extension, the enlightened or liberal, and the anticlerical or deistic.

the point of indecency. Two lines in particular provoked shouts and stampings of feet, exclamations and sarcastic bravos:

> Elles veulent écrire et devenir auteurs
> Et céans beaucoup plus qu'en aucun lieu du monde.

> [They fancy they must write, it's authors they would be,
> And not just anywhere, but here for all to see.]

She outfaces them. Uncringing, smiling, a shade pale perhaps, she pretends to hear nothing and performs her duty, commenting on the play for her pupils. Maybe she's actually enjoying this plunge into the lions' den: beneath her eyes, washing over her, is the same spray that stung Philippe de Chartres when his moment of glory at the Battle of Ouessant was turned into cowardice —the foam of libelous, epigram-making, song-singing Paris that kills you with pin-pricks. She knows what they resent in her and she's proud of it: she is somebody else. She is not like them. She has a destiny of her own, and what if it is to be their black sheep. A woman who writes books. A woman who lives by her own rules. A woman who thinks. At this moment Félicité de Crest, Comtesse de Genlis, experiences the kind of inverted triumph, the righteous thrill she was looking for as a little girl when she went scampering about in her sabots haranguing the riffraff of Saint-Aubin: she is forcing herself down the throats of people whom she doesn't like and who don't like her. Every eyewitness says she was radiant that evening, although the Duc de Chartres, lurking in the shadows of his box, was white with rage.

Louis-Philippe expresses no delight at the affront, shows no solidarity with those who are insulting his daily torturer. He might have taken this opportunity for revenge, for he is one of those children who immediately grasp what goes on between adults. But he has already chosen sides, and his is not theirs. He places his small hand in Félicité's hardly larger one and sits quietly, pretending to be interested in nothing but the play. He has already understood that he needs her more than the rest of them for the destiny awaiting him, which is to be a living incarnation of opposition to His Majesty, to the reign of gracious pleasure. In this system, where everyone falls prostrate before the King's decrees and disobedience is a sin, the Orléans family has polarized the regrets and nostalgia of a whole society. "Ah, if only it was *them* . . ." For the moment, the flighty Parisians are cheering the father and snickering at the son. But the grandson sees his path clear before him. He knows that he too will be Duc de Chartres one day, and then Duc d'Orléans, and that he will become the leader of the anti-court, the Palais Royal court. Then he will be able to choose: he can grow fat and mind his own business like his grandfather, or he can try to exist in his own right and live up to his image, as his father has been doing, with indifferent success, for the last few years. Either way,

Louis-Philippe will have to risk living, so he's already allied himself with his father, however unhappy that father may be, and to this weird lady his father has inflicted upon him to give him some personality and teach him how to stand up straight.

"I derived much benefit from becoming inured to fatigue, and had I not been so I should never have borne up under what fortune held in store for me . . . One of Mme de Genlis's manias [still according to Louis-Philippe] was never to do what others had done, or at least not to do it the same way. The consequence of this was that she prepared young spirits like ours [his own and his brothers'] which were already enthusiastic by nature, to rush headlong into every innovation of the age . . . She strove mightily to inculcate in us the strictest sort of piety, so that we would be different from the mass of our contemporaries. She turned us, in short, into puritan Catholics."[8] Later, he qualifies the atmosphere of his childhood as one of "puritan republicanism," as though it had been Rousseau lecturing him in percale and velvet furbelows.

He perceives the distinction between the venal, frivolous theater audience and himself; but will this little prince's intensive training course produce a great person?

POPE PIUS VI

6

APRIL 1782

A Young Man's Escapade

In Vienna, on February 7, 1782, Emperor Joseph II of Austria writes to his brother and confidant Leopold: "They still say that the pope will come. I shall be ready for him."[1] Leopold, Grand Duke of Tuscany (which he governs for the Hapsburgs in a benevolent-reformer style), replies on February 25: "At last the pope's journey to Vienna is decided and he will leave on the 27th of this month, the day after tomorrow. He will go by way of Loreto and the Venetian State . . . Everyone in Italy is opposed to this journey of the pope, and to the choice of persons accompanying him." On March 4 Joseph phlegmatically concludes, "So we are now to witness this phenomenon, the pope in Germany. I am sending Cobenzl* to welcome him at the border [of the

*Johann Philip, Count Cobenzl, vice-chancellor of the empire and right hand of Kaunitz, the all-powerful minister. He later becomes chancellor himself and negotiates the peace of Campo-Formio with Napoleon.

Empire] and my kitchens . . . to give him a decent meal." Joseph goes on: "His departure in mid-Lent is a real escapade which can be neither justified nor understood save in relation to that mystical [*sic*: these letters are all written in French and thus contain numerous eccentricities—*Trans.*] longing of his to appear as the savior of the rights of the Church.

"However extraordinary his arrival here, and although it is not possible to prepare oneself for the thought of all that he may propose, perform, or negotiate, he will, I trust, find me a respectful son of the Church, a courteous housekeeper in his dealings with his guest, a good Catholic in the full sense of the word, but also a man who stands above all the fine phrases and tragic acts* with which he might accompany his visit; firm, sure, and unshakeable in his principles, and adhering to the good of the state without regard for any other consideration whatsoever" (March 7).

In other words, the pope may be coming, but he can expect to pay his own expenses. Really, what kind of bee has this priest got in his bonnet? If he means to start giving public lessons to the emperor, he'd better look out: "A disquisition in the Church of the Holy Father would cause an unthinkable scene, for I could not refrain from interrupting him and ordering him to be silent" (March 18).

Joseph II needn't worry. The distinguished sixty-five-year-old who mounts majestically into one of the six carriages waiting outside the Lateran Palace to carry him across the Alps is a pasteboard pope, all sugar and honey, an old ham actor with fine white hair freshly curled every morning and a complexion enlivened by a layer of bright cosmetics. Just a *grande coquette,* Pius VI. The shade of Gregory VII must turn in his grave whenever people mention the trip to Canossa in the same breath as this one, which might in theory be another epoch-making event—the pope outside the Papal States! The pope visiting the emperor! The summit confrontation of lords spiritual and temporal! There's been nothing like it for centuries. But at Canossa, Emperor Henry came to kneel outside the gate, humbled by the threat of excommunication. The medieval Church was the equal of the empire, but now it's raveling away, and it's the pope's turn to do the beseeching. " 'We've got Canossa the other way round now,' malicious observers are saying."[2]

For his journey Pius VI wraps himself in the protective cocoon of his leechlike family—all those Braschis, or rather Onestis, the children of his sister Giulia—whose massive new wealth has incensed even the Romans, old hands though they are at the game of nepotism. Pius VI's nephews are taking them back to the days of the Renaissance: the eldest is a cardinal, and a sumptuous palace† is being built in Rome for the second one, who's been made Duke

---

*Should be taken to mean "spectacular gestures."
†The Palazzo Braschi, which now houses the Italian Ministry of the Interior.

of Nemi. Inside its stables, Luigi Onesti de Nemi will soon align twenty carriages. In the pope's retinue you can see a pretty, painted blond girl decked out in her best finery, climbing into one of the Vienna-bound vehicles: Luigi's child-bride, Dona Costanza, alias Queen of Rome. At sixteen she holds court as though she were a dauphine. "She would entertain the members of the Sacred College, the aristocracy, and prelates with unheard-of luxury . . . And on consistory days she would appear at the Lateran covered in the most precious jewels and receive the homages rendered unto sovereigns. The pope was extremely fond of her and gave her everything she asked for."[3] In the wake of Dona Costanza toils a little Benedictine draped in humility and black, her confessor Father Chiaramonti, chosen because he hails from the Braschis' hometown, Cesena.*

The procession leaves a whispering somnolent Lenten Rome and drives past the Pontine Marshes, now being drained. Pius VI likes to think of himself as a master builder, and St. Peter's has newly been flanked by a bulging hernia of scaffolding under which a sacristy, large as a ministry, is being added to the basilica. They detour by way of Cesena, the birthplace (where the pope's uncle is bishop), and the natives go wild with joy. At Loreto, on the other hand, they sulk: the Home of the Holy Family, transported from Nazareth by angels a thousand or more years ago, has been ransomed. To retrieve the pontifical treasury from bankruptcy, the Roman tax collectors have recently sponged off some of the gold and silver that was dripping from the walls of this peculiar construction (Joseph and Mary seem to have had extraordinary taste), half Roman villa and half baronial folly. They got three million livres† for it. They didn't take it all; but the lowliest vagabond of Loreto regards himself as the proprietor of the ceilings of the Home, now scraped bare as an Incan temple.

The Venetian States, by easy stages: a triumph. Then the Alpine passes. Then the reception of the Austrian authorities, intimidated by this suzerain unlike any other. And another detour to Maria-Zell, the most famous Marian pilgrimage in the empire. Joseph II abhors the idols venerated there: a Virgin in star-studded mantle, a little doll crowned with gold and diamonds. "That is the best place for him"—for the pope (to Joseph, on March 7).

After a month on the road, the encounter. Joseph can hardly make the effort, especially as he has a bad case of conjunctivitis. But finally, "despite the inflammation of my eyes, I decided to go out to meet the pope; I looked upon it as a day of battle in which a few risks must be run, whatever the outcome. I went beyond Neustadt to join him and, to avoid any ceremonies and compliments, it was on the main road and in the presence of the postilions alone that I met him, took him out of his carriage and into my two-seated coach, and

*With Dona Costanza's backing, he becomes a cardinal and succeeds Pius VI as pope (Pius VII).

†Eighteen million modern francs [$3.5 million].

brought him straight to Vienna," to the Hofburg Palace, where Pius VI will sleep "next to me, on the same floor . . . I could only seem to be exaggerating if I told you the number of carriages, people on foot and on horseback lining the road to see us come . . . If I say there were one hundred thousand souls, in sooth I say not one too many."*

"A day of battle" . . . In a way, it is.

If you twisted his arm, Pius VI might find it in himself to tell you that this Joseph II toward whom he marches wreathed in smiles and with blessing hand outstretched is the devil incarnate, the Antichrist who was to come at the end of time. A demiurge planted in the heart of Europe, who has dared to touch the intangible, to overturn the natural order of things: he has attacked the primacy of the clergy! Ah, when the Church of Rome lost his mother it lost everything. "In Vienna a young emperor, consumed by ambition, famished for fame, was awaiting the first opportunity to disrupt the repose of Europe," observes the heretical Frederick II, not without a quiet smile, from his balcony in Berlin.[4] And as "my brother the sacristan"—this is still according to Frederick—"does not possess enough military power to set the frontiers waltzing, he has settled for the priests instead: war upon statues, accounts to be rendered for tapers, censorship of sermons."

Joseph-the-Leveler thumbs his nose at the "special arrangements" of Prague or Budapest. "It has to work, and the monarchy must become a single, equal province once and for all."[5] A single empire, a single language—his, of course, German: to his ears Hungarian, Czech, and Croat are hick dialects. A year ago he was even beginning to find fault with the privileges of the nobles, whom Maria Theresa had permitted to increase their wealth and estates as long as they supported her. But there he was going too far; the indispensable Kaunitz tightened the reins and headed him off toward the monks and priests, whom he also loathed: Kaunitz doesn't believe in God. Josephism was born in 1781, in a haze of edicts: a doctrine of reasoned religion, a sort of pâté of faith and logic in alternating strips. A year ago Joseph brought crashing down the shakiest wing of the structure: the regular clergy. What were all these idlers?† "The monarchy is too poor to permit itself to maintain inactive persons."[6] From November on, no more Carthusians, Cistercians, or Carmelites. Anybody who doesn't want to become a parish priest can leave the

---

*A schoolboy studying with the Brienne priests, Napoleon Buonaparte, eagerly devours the account of this meeting, reported in the French gazettes, as relayed to him by his teachers. Twenty-two years later, when he is host to Pius VII at Fontainebleau, he scrupulously re-enacts every detail of the procedure followed at the pope's reception by Joseph II. The very idea of his coronation ceremony seems less preposterous to contemporaries because this second visit was like an imitation of that of Pius VI to Vienna.

†Parts of his reasoning will crop up again in 1790, in the words of the partisans of a civil constitution for the clergy.

country. With their confiscated goods and chattels, Joseph has endowed a "religious fund" for schools and welfare work. At the same time all parish priests, even bishops, have been turned into civil servants—better paid, but under orders. The emperor himself has assumed responsibility for censorship, which was so tense during his mother's reign. He shifts its center of gravity, giving—a little—more rein to philosophical or libertine writing and casting a more critical eye on theology. Model sermons are prepared for modern-day priests: make way for the Supreme Being, farewell little Jesus, Virgin, and saints. Lots of practical morality, not so many genuflexions. The religious brotherhoods are dissolved. No more ex-votos, no more group recitals of rosaries, no more stations of the cross. The bells will keep silent except on major occasions. "The worship of relics and of the Holy Sacrament during Holy Week have been forbidden as pagan rituals."[7] And as for your embroidery-laden idols, I, Joseph, hereby strip them naked until the day I can get rid of them entirely and have mass said in the vernacular: pure Jansenism, with a wink in Luther's direction. Like all kings of character, he dreams of manufacturing a religion to fit his own ideas. There was fever and shuddering up and down the empire when its great baroque many-colored cloak was torn from its back, north to south and east to west—the cloak that had made religion into a street festival and kept the humble amused, God's state fair. Here and there, a few peasants had even shouldered their pitchforks to defend their sacred statues.

In November 1781, Joseph rang up the curtain on his act of liberation from his mother, his sweet revenge: "There were two measures that Maria Theresa had been determined never to allow:* a declaration of tolerance that would place all religions on an equal footing, and the secularization of the monasteries. One year after her death, both had been made law."[8] The tolerance his text instituted was a little warped, though, like everything else about Joseph II: it favored the Protestants, whose rights were restored and who were placed almost on a level with the Catholics, and it unstitched the yellow bands from the Jews' clothes; but it muzzled the thousand and one little nonconforming sects. "Any who proclaim themselves Deists or anything of the sort shall receive twenty-four lashes" . . . "Tolerance and philosophy on one side," says one lampoon, "and twenty-four lashes on the other. How is it supposed to work?"[9]

There's nothing to work. This is Joseph II. Creaking and groaning, the empire begins to adjust to its new emperor. Kaunitz notwithstanding, he now starts to attack serfdom, in his German states at least, and shake the foundations of the feudal system,[10] but only by fits and starts, and very much more to annoy the gentry than to relieve the peasantry. All the same, if anything at all is

*According to Victor Tapié.

moving in the congealed Europe of 1781, it is in Austria and thanks to him.

The pope wouldn't have batted an eyelash to stop him from changing the status of the serfs; but the administration of the clergy? And not only in Vienna but in Northern Italy too (under Austrian dominion), in Milan, on the confines of the most clerical state of all, that of the Church? What is the world coming to? Joseph is tearing huge holes in a spider web that took centuries to spin out from its hub in Rome until it embraced every Catholic country. And his theological pretensions are putting new breath in the lungs of that ghastly Jansenism, which is such a threat to the opulence of the high clergy that its extermination has been the obsession of every pope for the last hundred years. Joseph encourages Nicholas von Hontheim, the Bishop-Coadjutator of Trier, who, under the alias of Febronius, is trying to reduce the pope's status to that of Bishop of Rome. *Qu'est-ce que le Pape?* [What Is the Pope?] is the title of a pamphlet, subsidized by the emperor, which you can buy in the Vienna book shops these days. And that's why His Holiness has come in person to see what's going on in the mind of this sovereign known as "His Apostolic Majesty." The pope's main demand is the restoration, in the preparation dispensed to students at the imperial seminary, of the Bull *Unigenitus,* abolished by order of Joseph: the bull that destroyed Jansenism. But one wonders if he'll even dare to mention it when he actually comes face to face with the emperor.

If anybody is upset by the visit, in the fullest sense of the word, it is Joseph II. His life as a fussy widower was purring uneventfully along. "I try to get out of doors every day and my life is regular; I work"—often with Kaunitz—"from seven in the morning until two; then I go out; I dine at four and go back to work until around nine, then I go into company until eleven and so to bed," as often as he can a short distance away from his overpowering palace, in "the little house I had built near the Augarten, where my garden enables me to work and also spend some time walking. I have even had a few people to dinner there already . . . The good weather has come, but the frosts did considerable damage to both vines and fruit trees, and I who adore gardening am much pained to see it in my own garden."[11] He's becoming increasingly misogynous: "I found it impossible to continue living at Court with all those women. I accordingly gave out that except for the old women and those who lived apart, all others should make efforts to quit the Court in the course of the summer . . . This is necessary for the present and destroys for all possible future eventualities the bad principles and false manner of thinking of this female republic." At forty he's given up trying to look like a young man, and isn't far from taking himself for an old one: "What little hair I have left is abandoning me and I fear I shall be obliged to have recourse to a wig." The neuroses of the obsessive loner inhabit his tall carcass and long mournful face, adorned as though at the top of a tower with globulous eyes emitting an unforgettable expression, like some mysterious summons. He is foredoomed to illness: stomach, eyes, boils, catarrh, insomnia. An Argan* enthroned. And now all of a sudden that worse-than-woman in a white cassock, the pope, has come to drag him out of his shell, accompanied by those human crowds that sicken and terrify him and, worst of all, will be wasted crowds for him, because every kiss bestowed on the pope's hand will mean one less for the emperor.

Joseph has accordingly opted for a wooden mien and an impeccably amicable frigidity. "For Holy Week the pope has not yet quite decided what he will do, and whether I can take any part must depend upon the state of my eyes." Sometimes, illness is a heaven-sent gift.

In the carriage, "our conversation turned upon insignificant matters." The following day, March 23: "His Holiness came to call on His Majesty and remained alone with him in his chamber for two hours. The talk was mainly of the Edict of Tolerance and, after His Holiness had heard all the arguments He concluded with these remarkable words, that if He had been in the emperor's place He would have done the same."† So that's how you muzzle a pope; was it worth traveling two hundred leagues? The next day Joseph steps across the hall to return the visit and consolidate his advantage: "The chief subject of conversation was the Bull *Unigenitus,* and His Holiness found it quite proper that no more mention should be made of it in any disputation." Another point scored. At their third encounter, on the 25th, the pope, presumably in a state of shock, took refuge in ceremony: "Nothing was decided except that on Holy Thursday His Holiness would administer communion to H.M. the Emperor in the private chapel and wash the feet of twelve poor persons . . ."

Has that finished him off? No. On the 26th, Pius VI takes his courage in both hands and engages in "a conversation lasting three hours with H.M. the Emperor, during which almost all ecclesiastical questions were reviewed more or less heatedly." He's not going to turn stubborn, is he? Joseph breaks the clinch, swallows some medicine and takes to his bed, abandoning Vienna to the intruder over the Easter weekend. Pius VI can bless and officiate to his heart's content. On April 4 the emperor writes to Leopold: "Herewith, my dear brother, is the continuation of the journal of the pope, in which you will see that it is now nine days since I have been able to speak to His Holiness." The Holiness, meanwhile, is doing what he can to pass the time, visiting churches and convents, "holding out his foot to be kissed," hemmed in by throngs of loiterers, those Viennese loiterers who are apparently born to stroll about all day long between two cups of chocolate and who wouldn't miss this unique spectacle for the world. "On April 4 His Holiness neither went out

*[The protagonist in Molière's *Malade Imaginaire.—Trans.*]

†According to the "journal" of the pope's visit to Vienna, which Joseph had written for Leopold and revised himself.

nor said mass but gave a long series of audiences; he received everybody, that is, merchants, clerks, and burghers down to the valets and cooks." The fact of the matter is that the pope is digging in and hoping to weary Joseph into submission. "The *seccatura* [*sic*; that is, the break between us] is beginning to widen enormously and I believe that His Holiness thinks of trying importunity, reason having availed him nothing" (on April 18). Relations become so strained that by the end they aren't even speaking to each other. They write. But Joseph won't give an inch: "Our conversations having concluded by deciding nothing, the Holy Father set out to write down the different items of ecclesiastical policy for me. I replied at once and, in order that you may be informed, I enclose the whole exchange. You will see that the highest courtesy prevails but that we are not entirely in agreement as to the principles, although we both wish to further the welfare of religion."

Pius VI stalls and flees ceremoniously on April 22, provoking a *whew!* of relief from Joseph: "At last, I have just now packaged up [*sic*] the pope! He is traveling by way of Munich and will sleep tonight at Mölk . . . I do not hide from you how glad I am to see him go, for especially in these last few days the thing had become almost unendurable, with all the artifices and humbug he put into his negotiations and his speeches and the truly ridiculous enthusiasm by which the women particularly were affected. Every corridor and staircase in the Court was packed full of people; even with redoubled sentries there was no way to avoid all the things people brought him to be blessed: scapulars, rosaries, images, and so on. And for the benediction he gave from the balcony seven times a day there was a crowd so huge that one could not imagine it if one had not seen it with one's own eyes, for it is no exaggeration to say that there were as many as sixty thousand people at a time . . . For twenty leagues around and more, the peasants came with their womenfolk and children; yesterday one woman was trampled in the crowd beneath my windows."

And those are the very people Joseph wants to knead into a reform, and to start by curing them of what he calls their Christian paganism, meaning all that rattle of telling beads. It was high time the Visitor left: two visions of the world and life have confronted each other at the summit of the century, and neither got anything from the other. Will Europe be big enough to hold them? Here it comes again, the old quarrel of emperor and pope—but this time it looks as if God may have changed sides. For the moment, the pope is the loser since, however many airs he may try to put on, he's coming home empty-handed. "I am only curious to see how he will manage with Pasquin," grumbles Joseph.* Leopold couldn't agree more: "I frankly admit to you that I was not at all edified by the conduct of the pope; his entire journey was a young

---

*Meaning, "with Roman public opinion," which, in that newspaperless city, was expressed through the innumerable graffiti scribbled near an unidentifiable stone bust that the Romans used to call "Master Paschino."

man's escapade and he made no progress from start to finish . . . Since his return to his own States, he has been saying and writing to everyone how enchanted he is with his trip to Vienna and how he has returned with your confidence and friendship, how he has made you change all your resolutions on tolerance . . . , but most of all on the Bull *Unigenitus,* which is dearer to his heart than any other thing, as though he were some zealous Jesuit.* This affectation in the pope to boast aloud of a thing that nobody knows better than himself to be untrue is really an unforgivable and shocking way for the head of the Church to behave, and in matters of such weight." But Pius VI had to throw a little dust in Pasquin's eyes, after all.

Frederick II has the last word on this episode, in a letter to his old friend d'Alembert: "Braschi has just proved that the pope is not infallible, by taking an initiative as futile as it was out of place. For the rest, I am well, send you all good wishes for your own health, and leave to the evil destinies awaiting them the pope, Abbé Raynal, the fanatics, the *philosophes,* the Carthusians, and, above all, the English."[12] In other words, his position is one that, two centuries later, would be called centrist.†

DE GRASSE   SUFFREN

7

APRIL 1782

That National Sentiment . . . Becomes Most Pernicious

On April 12, 1782, France's top naval chiefs gamble their destinies at opposite ends of the earth. One's going to lose his shirt: de Grasse; the other forces luck to play his way—but only just: Suffren. Two of the most important naval battles of the war, Les Saintes and Provédien, are fought between French and English with the sun at the same angle overhead but half a world apart. The stake is the same in both cases: each side wants to put as many trumps as possible in his hand before sitting down to negotiate the peace treaty that everybody knows is inevitable since the English capitulation at Yorktown. The thunder from these cannons will take weeks and weeks to reach the shores of America and Europe, however, and in Geneva, it may not be heard at all. The ten or

*Braschi, a secular priest, was anything but a Jesuit, but it is true that he was accused of sympathizing with the Order banished by his predecessor and having some desire to restore it.

†[In French politics, middle of the road. —*Trans.*]

twelve thousand sailors who face each other today in the Caribbean Sea and Bay of Bengal are naked and alone in their theaters, playing both actors and audience. The tale people tell of their deeds will depend upon their memories, but they won't have much time to store them up. Every minute counts between two gusts of the wind.

In the Antilles, around eight in the morning, two processions of giants bear down on each other for the big match in the 16-mile-wide "canal" between Dominica and the group of islets called Les Saintes [South of Guadeloupe— *Trans.*]: Admiral de Grasse's thirty-one ships of the line against Vice-Admiral Rodney's thirty-six. The English are not only more numerous but faster, because most of their ships have those newfangled copper-sheathed hulls and cut the water more cleanly. But for the moment the French have the wind at their backs and can maneuver better.

This decisive eleventh-hour duel has been postponed again and again by the prudence of both commanders: in a seaman's life, anything is better than losing a fleet, which is why thus far in the war even Ouessant and the battles off New York, and the Chesapeake and the Antilles, have been mere feints and skirmishes. And since Yorktown they've been playing hide-and-seek harder than ever between the waves. Grasse was sick as a dog, haggard with fever; he dragged his ships back to Martinique and began bombarding his minister, the Marquis de Castries, with pleas to be recalled to France. "You would take pity upon me if you could see the state I am in. I can neither speak nor write. My illness grows worse every day and I have no idea when it will end. The longer I live the more I am convinced that a man of sixty has no business being in command of a fleet such as this."[1] At Yorktown, all the glory had gone to Washington and Rochambeau, and that pipsqueak La Fayette picked up the crumbs; all de Grasse got, after making the victory possible by blocking the entrance to the bay, was a polite thank-you note. But Castries didn't have anyone to put in his place, so he played deaf and left him there.

The admiral accordingly resumed his spying on the English between Windwards and Leewards, uncertain whether to attack or defend himself, each side clutching its pawns like the land generals farther north on the continent: the Rebels are now certain of Philadelphia, but the English are still entrenched in both North (New York) and South (Charleston). Facing de Grasse, cat one day and mouse the next, was his adversary Rollicking Rodney, in approximately the same state of mind and body, so twisted up with gout that he had vainly crossed an ocean in search of a more comfortable position, but the ocean, like his cabin-bunk, was still too narrow for him. Whoever saw a case of gout cured by London fog? At least going over there for treatment had spared him the afflicting scene in America last October and given him plenty of leeway to heap scorn and contempt upon the heads of those imbeciles Hood and Graves, who knew nothing about war and had spoiled everything. Now he's back to show de Grasse what the Royal Navy is made of—if the high lords in the Admiralty will only let him. Quaking from the only fear they could ever experience—the fear of blame—each of the two "generals" of the great naval armies has been waiting like a schoolboy for permission to have one real fight, granted via the couriers who took six weeks to reach them from their respective courts and usually arrived at the worst possible moment.

They've finally gotten their go-aheads. Castries's order to de Grasse: capture Jamaica, the last of the major English possessions in the "sugar islands" to leeward, west of the French bases. A paradise of blue mountains and black slaves in a tangle of sugar canes, and the Kingston roads, one of the three safest ports for large ships in those waters. The minister even sent Admiral de Guichen out from Brest during the winter with reinforcements loaded with soldiers, equipment, and ammunition, to help de Grasse do the job. But it's turn and turn about: he now has to send four or five times as many merchantmen back to Nantes and Bordeaux, which were on the verge of commercial asphyxiation.

Rodney's orders are to round up all the available warships on the British coasts, take them over to Barbados* to join Hood, and from there strike, anywhere they liked, to restore at least a moral balance before the peace talks begin. The honor of His Majesty George III could not treat for peace after a defeat: rather let the war go on forever. So the lion of the seas can just improvise something. He can recapture Grenada. He can attack Martinique, Guadeloupe, or Santo Domingo.

He has had the pleasant surprise of advance warning of the big French convoy's preparations for departure and has guessed the enemy's intentions. All he needs to do is sneak up behind de Grasse while his armada is migrating to Jamaica, grab a good wind and charge him, break his back . . . Circling like big falcons flung up from the last little English nests in the south—Barbados, Santa Lucia, and Antigua—his frigates have followed the tracks of the overweight French. In these parts the frigate is queen, except during those confrontations of moving fortresses, the battles between ships of the line; and the English have three times as many frigates as the French.

De Grasse is about to fall into Rodney's trap. He has just decided to do everything he shouldn't.

He sets sail from Fort Royal, Martinique, on the morning of April 8. He orders his thirty-five giants to come out one by one, a cable's length apart. In the

---

*Barbados stands slightly ahead of the chain of little Windwards, an "eastern outpost," the first to greet ships driven from Europe by the trade winds.

center, with the majesty of a seaborne metropolis, the *Ville de Paris* and her 104 guns. After being herded together outside the roads for several days, those damnfool sacred cows of merchantmen now have to be driven along before the warships, there must be 150 of them, of every conceivable tonnage and shape, a forest of masts barely able to drag along at two or three miles an hour, heading for Santo Domingo, where they will join up with Admiral don Solano's Spaniards, take on water, breathe a bit, and separate: the warships to attack Jamaica, the merchantmen to sail back to Europe while the English are occupied defending Kingston. It would be "the richest convoy ever to leave the Antilles for Europe. It held within its hulls the fortune or ruination of thousands of persons, the prosperity or collapse of several French towns . . ."[2]

Yes, but sailing from Martinique to Santo Domingo when Rodney's at anchor at Santa Lucia twenty sea miles away and staring at the French out of every frigate's spyglass is a shade idealistic, to say the least. De Grasse has not lost his mind, however. By April 8 he knows he's going to have the English at his heels. Is he dreaming? Does he suppose he'll have time to turn around and scare Rodney, corner him in one of the island channels while his convoy sails out of danger farther north? That line of reasoning would be all right if he were the strongest, fastest, and most cunning. On the bridge of the *Sceptre,* the ship commanding his rear guard, one clear-sighted officer, the Comte de Vaudreuil, gives his diary a lecture while awaiting the catastrophe: "M. le Comte de Grasse considers that he will not be able to avoid combat. I am rather inclined to think that the general's contempt for his enemies will decide him on this occasion to attack them with inferior forces. That national sentiment which gives confidence to inferiors and may have a good effect upon them becomes most pernicious sometimes in the head of a leader."[3]

They have now been playing "Winds and Islands," the favorite game of the men who toil in Caribbean waters, for four days. In the shelter of an island you're suddenly becalmed, the sails sag, and you beg the dear Lord to send you just one tiny puff. The instant you get round the land's end, it's the opposite, you're lashed on all sides by unpredictable gusts winging in from north or south, and even more by the east wind, which has slipped through the holes in the island net to throw you back on the eternal trail of Christopher Columbus in search of the Indies. The topmen go limp in the rigging, from reefing and letting out sail almost in the same breath. You keep a fleet in line in weather like this! And as for maneuvering for combat, you might as well try to do it in a cocktail shaker . . .

Captain de La Pérouse is the first to see Rodney's sails rising up in the south. He brings his frigate, the *Astrée,* within speaking-trumpet range of the *Ville de Paris:*

"Unidentified fleet in view astern!"

"Unidentified"—a figure of speech. They hug the coast of Dominica, taking advantage of the currents. At dawn on April 9 they try to charge the English vanguard commanded by Hood, who was always sticking his neck out: twelve ships would have been cut off, a hell of a catch if Hood hadn't called it quits first, for once, after two hours of combat, violent in some spots and desultory in others. On board the *Northumberland,* a French ship that had kept its English name after being captured, a colonel of dragoons is finding the time heavy on his hands and calls out to his ship's captain, de Saint-Cézaire:

"You call this a fight? We might as well be taking tea on deck!"

Thereupon an 18-pounder explodes between-decks, a result of the poor quality of the French powder. Eleven dead and twenty-five wounded.

"Hot tea," adds the colonel.[4]

Not to the English taste, anyway, for they break away. De Grasse on his bridge is being implored by his officers:

"Follow them! They're injured, they're still out of range of the bulk of their fleet, this is the moment!"

The big man shakes his head:

"We'll let them run away, after this check. Instruct the convoy to make for Santo Domingo with all speed. My mission is to protect it above all else."

That gains one day. On April 10 they resume their game of cat-and-mouse. "I am still tacking in the Saintes channel to observe from close range whether the English army does not intend some movement," de Grasse writes in his journal. They do their observing four or five leagues apart, hugging the islets, Terre de Bas and Terre de Haut, two volcanic peaks that have broken water here, pure white against the brilliant blue ocean, on which the Whites have managed to plant a little cotton and five hundred wretched Negroes to cultivate it somehow or other: Les Saintes, they're called. Their role is to act as huge fixed buoys in the stupidest French naval maneuver of the century. "The convoy not being far enough ahead of the"—naval—"army for me to follow it, I would protect it more surely by remaining within sight of the enemies."[5] But in that case, Admiral, why didn't you try harder to close your pincers on their vanguard yesterday? De Grasse treats his fleet as though it were some sort of retrenched camp designed to intimidate nomads; but the sea's whims and Rodney's bad temper will knock his fine theories to bits. They tack up and down all day without ever really getting into the "wind of Les Saintes." In the night of April 10–11, loud crunching noises and oaths are heard: two mastodons, the *Zélé* and the *Jason,* have collided while coming about. It's only their twenty-fifth smash in twenty-one months: they're more like marine clowns, whose sailors are developing perforce the reflexes they need to offset their captains' incompetence. De Gras Préville, captain of the *Zélé,* is one of the "red officers" who have gained promotion by birthright and the nobiliary freemasonry, notwithstanding a marginal note in his file: "Knows little navigation and has never commanded."[6] This time he's done for the *Jason,* which de Grasse has to send back to Basse Terre with a wobbly mast to join the *Caton,* severely trounced by the English two days before. That makes two less. Four, if you count the *Sagittaire* and *Experiment* (another *ci-devant* English ship), detached to guard the merchant fleet. De Grasse's remaining thirty-one ships have 1,770 guns.

Rodney's got 2,700.

Will they fight? "On the evening of the 11th it seemed that the French would decide to move off and catch the Guadeloupe wind by the north side of the Saintes channel. They had gained considerably on the enemy, who was then out of sight. Thus, the way to Santo Domingo was free . . ."[7] when crash, crunch, at two in the morning the *Zélé,* deprived of her usual scapegoat, can find nothing better to ram than the admiral ship, and from behind. The *Ville de Paris* is only shaken, as by a seaquake; the other numbskull breaks her bowsprit smack in the middle of her poop and also loses her mizzenmast in the collision. What de Grasse has to say to Gras Préville could almost be heard by the English:

"*Carogno de dréfounté!* [Provençal obscenity—*Trans.*] I know your ship won't sail! I know she steers badly and is top-heavy! But maybe if you learned how to operate her . . ."

Not too much damage on the vast *Ville de Paris,* which can function normally. But the dawn of April 12 finds the *Zélé* out of control. La Pérouse is ordered to take her in tow. With some difficulty, the *Astrée* throws the clumsy oaf a line. The towing operation slows them both; they drop behind. Rodney sends a pack out after them. De Grasse has time to choose: do I sacrifice them or do I risk my whole fleet for them? His decision accords with forty years of honor, but not of brains.

"The honor of the King's arms, my own honor, could not permit me to allow a ship unfit to defend itself to be taken before my eyes. I was not going to increase my inferiority by combining it with cowardice . . . What a blot upon the French flag! What general could have done it?"[8]

Maybe he's reached that end of a sea officer's life at which the temptation to fight or die becomes irresistible. Otherwise, what is the point of having lived?

So that's why they're arming for battle now near Les Saintes, at the worst possible moment and in defiance of all common sense, let alone reason. The bright flames flickering up the signal halyards of the *Ville de Paris* instruct them to form into battle order after coming about all together downwind. At 7:30 in the morning, the first division commanded by Bougainville makes contact with the first English ships. Proud and stately under a blazing sun, the French fleet advances into the lion's maw.

8

APRIL 1782

Fame, That Wisp of Smoke

At that same moment, night had long since fallen off Ceylon, four thousand miles and nine hour-zones away on the other side of the earth. There, Suffren has just finished a tie game with Admiral Hughes's English, but it's worth a victory. It was close, though. What would have happened if the brutal tropical darkness, intensified by heavy monsoon cloud, hadn't blindfolded all the fighters just as they were raising their arms for the fatal thrust? We're almost at the same latitude as de Grasse and Rodney, between Tropic of Cancer and Equator, but here, in place of the infinite clarity of the Antilles we have the climate of Ceylon and southern India, the Malabar and Coromandel Coast, muddied from April to September by the southwest monsoon gliding between the huge island and the continent with its crop of squalls. Never a day without rain. This time it came early, "on an ill-settled, quarrelsome, peevish wind."[1] Everything felt sticky. The men were fighting in a sort of tepid, salty aquarium.

Yet this was the far side of Ceylon and the island gave protection from the spring monsoon, whose fringes reached no farther than the east coast after which there was nothing but the Indian Ocean to the ends of sight, sail, and time. The Dutch, who have been allied with the French since December 1780 but whose aggressiveness toward the English is purely platonic, are the lawful possessors of Ceylon, and do in fact hold its ports, but with such tiny handfuls of men that George III's fleet can help itself in passing as though they belonged to it instead. Trincomalee, the only decent harbor, really out of the wind and a little less than halfway down the right flank of the fat pear that is Ceylon's outline on a map, is the port from which Hughes's fleet set out to thwart the efforts of Suffren and his soldiers to reconquer French India. A little to the southeast of Trincomalee, a peak rears out of the sea—the rock of Provédien. Upon reaching it Smash-All Suffren decides to thwart the thwarters and make it clear to all concerned that the King of France is back in these parts in force. Twelve ships against Hughes's eleven. On the mainland, the Hindus of Haidar

Ali, Nabob of Mysore, were awaiting us with outstretched arms. On the island, the Dutch had doubts about the determination of the French. Everything was unsettled. Given the circumstances, Suffren was right to take chances, unlike de Grasse who ought prudently to have remained the custodian of a favorable situation off America.

Suffren is here to kick. He would never have wanted it any other way; and the people at home knew his character so well that when they detached him from Rochambeau's fateful convoy to America in March 1781 they gave him the barest minimum, a scant dozen ships and captains with bad report cards. Up to him to convey this puny sprout to the Indies and make it perform miracles. He didn't mind: "The smallest favorable circumstance can put me at the head of a fine squadron and enable me to gain fame, that wisp of smoke for which one ventures so much."[2] He'd already given one English fleet a good drubbing at the Cape Verde Islands—and, by the same stroke, saved the Dutch colony at the Cape. Having reached the tip of India after months and months of navigating and sitting in port at Ile de France, he made contact with Haidar Ali, prepared for the recapture of Pondicherry,* and won a sort of pre-tournament and practically bloodless victory (thirty dead and no damage) over Hughes's fleet off Sadras on February 18. Now, at Provédien, Hercules is about to flex his biceps. "I must find the English and beat them. I am in a superb position, commanding twelve ships of the line and have over one thousand five hundred leagues of seaboard. But there are many buts . . . Nowhere could I be so brilliantly employed. In spite of this I have some major discomforts, and one of the gravest of them is not to be able to fuck you, my dear,"[3] he writes on April 1 to his beloved and much-deceived mistress Laure de Seillans. In the absence of a woman, and in accordance with his nature, he embraces fighting with all his boundless appetite for thrills. Provédien . . .

A rough day. This time it's a real naval battle, with the ships grappling to the death like pit-bulls. Suffren gave them the order of no return: "Draw to within half a gun's range," or a whole pistol's range, it comes to the same thing. The English are clinging to the Ceylon coast as though it was their mother on the first day of school. You can see they're squinting at Trincomalee as a possible haven in case of emergency. Fine—we'll just corner them and flatten them between our guns and the shore. First, Suffren commands the classic maneuver: all the French ships side by side in a row perpendicular to the English, who are in single file. Each French ship lines up an Englishman in its bowsprit

*The English had taken the town, two-thirds destroyed, after four months of siege in 1778. They had also taken most of the French emporia in the Indies, which the government had virtually abandoned. Sadras, south of Madras, is one of the northernmost ports on the Coromandel Coast.

and heads for it, then swings a quarter-turn away when it gets in close, and they fight in Indian file along two parallel lines—if all goes well. But it's a devil of a maneuver with these tricky winds. "Holding the line required a precision of movement and uniformity of speed that were lacking among the captains and ships of the French squadron."[4] Suffren himself sets a bad example: in his haste to stick his sword into somebody he detaches his *Héros* from the center of the line and rushes up to rub flanks with the *Superb,* the English admiral-ship. His personal bit of bravura jeopardizes two thousand men's lives. Side by side, the two craft fire almost point-blank from the thirty-seven guns they harbor in each of their flanks. From the top of their poops the duellists can see and insult each other with gestures, almost with speech. Suffren is more disgusting than ever, half-dressed, sweating and stinking under his lumpy hat. Hughes, impeccable and powdered in his blue, gold, and white uniform but just as stout as the bailli—"little mother Hughes" as his tars affectionately dub him—is one of the best English leaders, "swollen, high-colored, garrulous,"[5] screwed into place on his huge gouty legs; but his little eyes go trotting into every nook and cranny.

At noon the rest of the fleets are engaged in the same game as their leaders: stomach-butting. Five of the heaviest in the middle of the line against five of the other team. On either side of the *Superb* are its two "con-sorts," the ships that must accompany the admiral-ship everywhere like a blind man's guide dogs: the *Monmouth* and the *Monarch,* against the two "consorts" of the *Héros,* the *Sphinx* and *Orient.* Also in the center, the *Petit Annibal* and *Brillant* (French) are in a clinch with the *Eagle* and *Burford.* The rest of the French are floundering around: the *Vengeur* and *Artésien* at the head of the line and the *Sévère, Ajax,* and *Annibal* at the tail have all hung back as though they're just lounging outside the firing range, at the risk of giving Suffren a fit of apoplexy; you can be sure their captains will feel the rough edge of his tongue tomorrow. "Cowardice" is a word that springs easily to admirals' lips when they're in the hot-seat themselves—that's how Philippe de Chartres got branded after Ouessant. In 1782, French ships' captains are often fatuous and sometimes imcompetent—shortcomings of the nobility—but the only thing wrong with their courage is that they have too much of it. The fault is not in their valor, it's in the shifting winds, the clouds of smoke that hide the "general's" signals, and the loss of time and energy between the moment when orders have finally been understood and trans-mitted by commanders and the moment when they are carried out in the rigging and at the helm. As always, the Brittany and Provençal crews have been decimated by sickness during the crossing, and the gaps in them filled by recruiting, or rather shanghaiing lascars [a Hindi word for East Indian sailors—*Trans.*] on the Indian coast: tall, gentle fellows benumbed by their deportation, who've never been in anything bigger than a rowboat. Just you try to teach them how to handle canvas rectangles the size of their village squares. And as for getting them to load the guns in the ports and touch them off with a burning wick. . . .

In short, Provédien is a core of fire among ten or twelve ships welded together at the heart of an eddy of other ships. Devilish hot. Suffren scores the first point: the *Superb* begins to burn, and three masts have been torn off the *Monmouth,* crippling her and putting her out of commission. Suffren deserts his darling Hughes to take his *Héros* and finish her off. Mistake: by doing that he opens up a gap between himself and the rest of his squadron, and Hughes, having gotten the fire under control, dives into it with his *Superb.* Now it's the *Héros*'s turn to be surrounded, battered, her masts splintered, her guns exploding. Round two to Hughes. Round three is a tie: the *Orient* and *Brillant* sail up to relieve Suffren, the sun's dipping, they've been fighting for four hours already, over a hundred dead on either side, the *Orient*'s mainsail catches fire and she becomes a gigantic torch; the *Superb,* penned in on all sides, slides behind the drifting, drunken *Monmouth* while Suffren orders his captains after her with oaths that would make God tear his hair out. "Take her, seize her, she's ours!" But it's an Englishman who wins the prize for sang-froid and manages to throw the cripple a line, while both teams' navigators on the poops tug respectfully at their captains' sleeves, do please observe, milord, monsieur, that the wind is driving us ashore and the battle is going to end with twenty ships breaking up on the rocks.

Almost simultaneously, the admirals give the order to reduce sail and wear,* but nobody can stay in line then, it's every man for himself, first to pull off the coastal reefs like bloodsuckers, and then to go on fighting with whichever enemy ship happens to be nearest, catch as catch can. But who's who and what? The French even lose their general for half an hour. The little foretop-mast of the *Héros* has broken; the ship isn't doomed, but she has to slip out of the fight. Splash! The bailli du Suffren's thick, agile bulk has already dropped into a longboat to be transferred to another ship. Rowed between the lightning of parting shots and the lightning of the coming storm, he toils along the surface of the sea toward another hesitant giant, the *Ajax,* and gives its Captain Bouvet the scare of his life when he emerges from the deeps like some Bacchic Neptune, determined to start all over again, herd together three or four ships and hunt down the *Monmouth* . . . But nobody's heart is in it anymore, and a pre-stampede panic is the result. In ten short minutes, around six o'clock, the Good Lord stops the game by slapping two lids on the playing field: an ink-black storm and the tropical night. Suffren has to use signal

---

*[That is, to go about by turning stern to the wind.—*Trans.*]

lanterns to order his ships to break, from the deck of an *Ajax* that grates three times against the coral bottom and has to wrench herself free in the shallows with the flip-flops of a sand-bound walrus. The French squadron has lost five officers, and two hundred and twenty men are either dead or seriously injured. The English have one hundred and thirty-seven dead and four hundred and thirty *hors de combat.* In the end, everybody anchors where he is, rather than sail round in circles or drift in to shore. The ailing *Héros* and *Orient* spend the night in the middle of the English squadron, so close they can hear the enemy voices on deck. But nobody pays much attention to the other side; the whole night long, dancing on the huge swells and scoured by pelting rain, men and ships lick their wounds.

Next morning, calm and quiet fall like a woman's gentle hands on a face in pain, it's a monsoon morning: the sun-filled off-shore breeze with its odors that make you dizzy in the head can change even the sight of death. It's time to believe in life again. The two immobilized fleets are all tangled up together, and *"pagaille à la Provédien"* ["Provédien hodge-podge" would be a rough equivalent—*Trans.*] enters the vocabulary of the French navy. They disengage, taking infinite precautions, like wrestlers floored together with their limbs tied in knots. Nobody wants to rush back into battle. And everybody needs wood, sails, and ammunition . . . Suffren's still in a hurry, though: "We are anchored on a very bad bottom, two-thirds of a league from land and within one and one-half gun's length of the English fleet. There can be but few examples of a mêlée such as this."[6] But "if, in our squadron, five or six captains—half, that is to say— are not changed, we shall never achieve anything and may well lose in any circumstance."[7] As always, fulminating against his own men, twice as mad at them as at the English. Singlehanded, or seconded by men of his caliber, he would have impaled Hughes upon the Ceylon rocks, or so he swears. Hughes is in bad enough shape already, however, with his *Monmouth* in tow and five or six other ships crippled. This being the case, the fleets continue to glare defiance at each other for eight more days—a record in naval fighting—and finally drift dignifiedly apart, pretending they haven't been introduced. The English return to Trincomalee and Suffren goes to heal his fleet farther south, in a funny little Dutch port in Ceylon called Batticaloa.

He's the winner, when everything is said and done. In spite of all the uncertainties and mishaps of battle, he was right to attack: he has broken the English *hauteur* in the Indies and, as soon as his ships are fixed up again he's going back up north to the continent to get in a few more licks.

9

APRIL 1782

The Slaughter . . . Was Immense

Back at Les Saintes, beginning around eight o'clock, the ends of two redoubtable moving ramparts, the fleets about to sail past each other, catch fire. The *Brave* and *Marlborough* begin a cannonade that runs along the line of the fleets like a flame along a fuse. Each of the "naval armies" is articulated into three segments, although their maneuvers have now welded them into two Siamese sea serpents: Bougainville commands the French vanguard; de Grasse, supreme commander, the middle; and Vaudreuil the rear guard. On the English side, Rodney is also personally in command of his central wing, Drake leads the head squadron and Hood the tail. Since the two lines cross in the opening movement of the ballet, it's Bougainville and Drake who lead the way. The French have the advantage of an east wind, and the center sections are soon face to face, de Grasse against Rodney, the one hundred guns of the *Ville de Paris* against the *Formidable*'s eighty.

Another duel of admirals. The carcasses of the two giant ships shudder from the impact of blows received or fired, you can't tell which any more. François-Joseph, Comte de Grasse du Bar and Marquis de Tilly, erect on the poop in the blue and scarlet uniform of a lieutenant general of the naval armies of the King of France, studded with decorations and slashed diagonally by the grand cordon of the Order of Saint-Louis, his powerful torso made even larger by monumental epaulets, is living the moment of apotheosis of the great commander. There he stands, the anchor of his fleet, and all his troubles are blown away by the first shot. Another fat man, like Suffren, but less swollen in front because he's taller. How could he feel anything but contempt for the sickly little creature he can see perfectly clearly across from him: Rodney, also in full dress uniform, but riveted to his chair and crippled with rheumatism?

"He's sucking lemons, gentlemen!" exclaims de Grasse. "May he soon be sucking sea water!"

For it is at that very moment, when the double-or-nothing throw of these men's lives has just left their hands, that Rodney is suddenly visited by a very

British reflex. A sixteen-year-old middy was bringing him a glass of lemon juice, and stirred the sugar in with his sword.

"Boy, come now, boy! You can do that among middies, but not to your admiral! For shame! Drink that slop yourself and send me the steward and some decent utensils!"

Case shot was sweeping the decks. It's too hot, there's too much smoke to wait for the steward. Am I going to have to die with a parched throat? Admiral Rodney snaps his fingers. A lemon is brought, he cuts it himself and squeezes it into his open mouth. De Grasse shouldn't laugh: lemon juice sharpens an old lion's teeth. Things will soon be turning fast, both the wind and the position of the French.[1]

It isn't even nine o'clock, and the fighting has already become pretty deadly when de Grasse understands, too late, that once the two fleets have finished filing past each other and firing haphazardly, the English are going to end up northwest of him, where he was when they started, and will lie between him and that infernal French convoy laboriously plowing along a few hours' north toward Santo Domingo. Whatever happens, he can't get cut off from them; so he orders one of the worst possible maneuvers to perform against the wind and in the thick of a battle: a complete about-face, which would bring all his ships around to face the same direction as the English and run parallel with them, in the hope of overtaking the line they were now descending. He loses the battle of Les Saintes by giving the order too late and giving it wrong, in two parts, first telling each ship to spin on its axis like a top and then, when that doesn't work, ordering the whole fleet to turn like a snake, following the first ship of the vanguard. He also loses the battle because his orders are either not understood or not carried out by the front and rear squadrons, which leaves the center, meaning de Grasse himself, dangerously alone. And in any case, the wind wouldn't have allowed him to do anything else.

Bougainville and the vanguard keep sailing straight ahead, out of the battle zone. The next day de Grasse can find no words harsh enough for this officer from the land army who has never been accepted at sea, an author-traveler "hated and scorned by all the French officers."[2] And de Grasse hurls the sempiternal insult of the top man passing the buck to his subalterns, the old refrain of "cowardice," at Bougainville and the ten or fifteen other French captains who continue maneuvering this way and that, paying little or no heed to their ballet-master's imprecations. Bougainville and Vaudreuil subsequently point out that the only ships to escape destruction were those in their squadrons. Just so! retorts de Grasse, since my center fought on alone, forsaken by them.

But it was also thanks to Rodney's lightning intuition, when he sees the breach opened up by Bougainville's departure between the French vanguard and its center. He has the sudden flash of battle, the comet-streak that makes the big winners: hook it by the hair as it comes past. Fate is decided in a few seconds, in a mind tipping twenty years of caution into two hours of folly.*

"Look sharp, lad!" Rodney bellows at his helmsman straight into the loudhailer. "Hard aweather, and God preserve us!"

More complicated orders run up the *Formidable*'s signal halyards, heeling the English three-masters one after the other into the waves like racing yachts. They have to "alter course on the quarter starboard tack" so that their constantly adjusted sails will engage in a sort of alchemy with the wind. The center squadron ships nearest him get the idea and move quickest. Like drunken bulls, the *Formidable*, followed by the *Namur, St. Alban, Canada, Repulse,* and *Ajax* turn 90 degrees to the left and head straight for the French line, cutting through it a third of the way down. The *Formidable* sails between the *Glorieux* and the *Sceptre,* so close that the French gunners, believing collision imminent, lose their heads and run, flinging their sponges and lintstocks on the decks. What about the rest of them, behind us? Will they get the message? Rodney hasn't had time to confirm his orders to his rear guard. He's in very great danger of finding himself trapped in a counter-trap with six other ships. But the rear guard is Hood, who works by telepathy. His sixth sense sends him and his squadron, led by the *Bedford,* cutting between the *César* and *Dauphin royal.* The French center squadron is "wrapped up in a banana peel." Some of the officers on its poops must have turned a shade paler when they saw their deaths so close ahead. De Grasse is about as far up a creek as he can get.

All they could do was fight it out, flags high. They fought, like Frenchmen. Fire on all sides, anyhow, anywhere, at the pachyderms encircling them. They're so close together that they can hear the enemy's orders. The burning cannon-plugs land in the sails, the men have to put out fires in the rigging twenty feet aloft, hanging from each other's hips and knees. Rows of cannon-balls pockmark the hulls without gouging through them, but when a shell flies through a port it makes mincemeat out of the flesh and wood and iron inside. Perched high in the shrouds and tops, the navy soldiers hurl grenades and shoot on sight at the adversaries' decks, picking out the officers. Down in the lower batteries, on the second and third decks, a passion of naked men with turbaned heads: the gunners, who don't know anything about anything and are leaving the skin of their hands on the incandescent tubes. Automatic gestures, an exact reproduction of hell as they used to see it painted on the walls of their parish church; but they are enduring this hell for their masters' sins, not theirs; the only thing they ever did wrong was get born.

At the end of five hours of intense firing, there are no cartridges left in the hold of the *Ville de Paris.* Powder is rammed loose down the muzzles from

*Many English historians claim that the credit should go to a few officers who were imploring Rodney to act when he himself was hesitant; but in the last analysis the honor of the decision goes to him.

the front, "by the spoon," and a dozen overheated cannons explode, devouring their servers raw. Blood flows along the floor in streams, like in a slaughterhouse.

"We're running short of balls for the muskets, Admiral!"

"Melt down my plate!" replies de Grasse, desperate, a tall statue planted like a menhir at the crossroads of peril. He is beginning to long for death with all his heart.

The ship's forge starts turning out silver shells and balls from the molten knives and forks and platters, which had been engraved with the arms of the de Grasses: a lion beneath three towers. They're about as much help as spitting in the sea: the English are sweeping the French decks with their blasted carronades, those bronze toads squatting on their upper decks which emit floods of case shot that slice through the rigging and mow down the topmen —they are the decisive weapon in the English victory at Les Saintes. One by one, the unsupported French masts topple, carrying their sails with them because there wasn't time to take them in. And the *Ville de Paris* isn't the only cripple: all that remains of the *Sceptre* is a hulk, the *Glorieux* is leaking, and the *César,* its rudder jammed, is going round in circles. A rout.

But de Grasse keeps fighting, trying to answer back, clutching at every straw hope of recovery that snaps between his fingers. At eleven o'clock he sends out an order for a general attack to the entire fleet, including Bougainville who's over the horizon, and Vaudreuil . . . If Bougainville had turned back the vanguard he'd have had the wind with him, he could have been there in no time and caught the English in a crossfire. But at noon the wind dropped. Sixty ships sat, stalled in the smoke blanketing everything at sea level. Five thousand gunners stood with lighted matches, unable to fire on the masses whose outlines they could dimly make out a few cables away, but were they friend or foe? Death's intermission.

At one o'clock, when a Domingo breeze wiped the atmosphere a little cleaner, the scene it revealed was the French central squadron on the scaffold, six bleeding ships in the middle of the English pack. Signal flags were still scudding up and down the admiral's halyards: "General rally": Bougainville's only two miles upwind, Vaudreuil four miles downwind, but Drake's rear guard is closing in. If Vaudreuil can get his ass here fast enough, we can fight another round, so please you guys out there, take advantage of this little offshore breeze! "I then gave the entire army the signal to keep to at the same time," de Grasse writes later. In vain. The Marquis de Saint-Simon,* officer in the engineer corps on board the *Ville de Paris,* records that "notwithstanding all the signals that were constantly repeated and therefore received, one part of the army deemed it more expedient to turn before the wind, crowd on sail, and flee, than to concern itself with the glory of saving the admiral flag."[3]

*Cousin of the future founder of the Saint-Simonist utopists' sect.

Bougainville has the excuse that his squadron is exhausted: his ships fought for two hours that morning, he's almost out of powder, and two of his best captains have been killed, Saint-Cézaire and La Clochetterie, the man who started the war four years before on board the *Belle-Poule*. But Vaudreuil does finally come dragging up, like a man walking out to face the firing squad next to his already fallen comrade. The *Ville de Paris* is shroudless, her masts are tilting, her decks carpeted with dead bodies. France's most beautiful ship, built by subscription by the merchants in the capital, is in her death agony. The *Pluton* offers to take her in tow. De Grasse shrugs. In the thick of the English fleet? Yet even after five o'clock he signals to "re-form the line of battle" in a last dying spasm, just as some of his best ships are surrendering, one after the other: the *César, Hector, Glorieux, Ardent*. Bougainville's squadron, scurrying southwards, is a dance of sails on the horizon. But Vaudreuil and seven more or less whole ships are still close to the center of the combat and in danger of being caught in the gears, if the "general in chief" insists on their hanging around to be the futile witnesses of his death throes.

It is the moment for de Grasse to make the only honorable choice a military leader can make when everything is falling apart around him—that is, consent to lose alone, shoulder the defeat himself, rather than condemn what live forces he has left to go down with him. "I was surrounded on all sides. My misfortune seemed inescapable. I continued to fight on alone, in order to satisfy my honor and that of the ship to which fate had attached me, and to occupy the enemy ships that might otherwise have interfered with the retreat of the squadron of M. de Vaudreuil, who had so meritoriously assisted me."[4] The main thing was to hold out until night, so that all the French ships that were still in working order could get away without being pursued.

Had he been alone then, he would undoubtedly have preferred to die. The failure of an entire life was grinding away at his heart. Admiral de Grasse, the conqueror of the Chesapeake, would go down in History as a portrait in the losers' gallery. "There remained no way to avoid surrendering the *Ville de Paris*, save to blow her up. But the naval regulations did not require me to do so, and I had no right to kill the rest of my brave crew." So the *Ville de Paris* strikes her colors at 6:30 p.m. on April 12, 1782. Vaudreuil, thereby promoted to commander-in-chief, instantly orders the remnants of the French fleet to institute a general stampede and the tropical night quickly lowers a compassionate curtain over the survivors' flight. There are enough left to defend our islands against an enemy that has also been sorely tried.

The English ship nearest the smitten giant is the *Barfleur*, flying the colors of Admiral Hood, who has grappled with de Grasse in many another match over the oceans of the earth. Hood is too tactful to clap his hands and hulloo with glee. One gust of wind in a different direction could have brought him to the same pass at any time these last decades. He sends Captain Lord Granston in a longboat to take possession of his prey.

"Between the fore and main masts," Granston relates, "we bloodied our boots at every step. The slaughter was . . . immense. The blood and limbs of swine and sheep penned on deck mingled with human gore. The top deck was still covered with dead and wounded. Grasse was standing, flanked by three officers. He had received a bruise in the kidneys but was otherwise unhurt, a most remarkable fact, for he had been exposed for many hours to very destructive fire that had decimated his officers and swept the poop clean on several occasions. Tall, robust, with a proud mien, he was at that moment an object of respect, for whom one felt solicitude and sympathy. He could not get over his amazement at seeing his ships taken, his fleet defeated and himself a prisoner in so short a time."[5]

De Grasse was right not to kill himself. Everything is relative in defeat. The immediate consequence of this one is that it shakes the English badly enough to compel them to spend five days making repairs, during which the French merchant convoy can shelter in Santo Domingo and, a few weeks later, set off back to France, taking advantage of the departure of the English ships for New York, which was then in danger. And the big emotional shock of the news, when it reaches Europe, is ultimately beneficial. The French, who were beginning to put on airs, will have to climb down a few pegs, while the English, who were falling back with jaws clenched, can relax. They'll be able to start talking. Which is all both worlds have been waiting for: a few thousand men slain, for the diplomats' dinner.

GRAND DUKE PAUL
OF RUSSIA

THE PRINCE AND PRINCES
DE CONDÉ

10

JUNE 1782

And Three Times As Many Servants

What about Paris meanwhile, and Versailles, and the cities of France? What have they been doing all this time? The writer Louis-Sébastien Mercier* takes

*An author of "philosophical" essays and treaties, remarkable for his nonconformism and immense curiosity. We soon meet him in Switzerland putting the finishing touches to his *Tableau de Paris*.

a dimmish view: "The historian will be hard-pressed, when he comes to depict the mood of the city dwellers in the midst of these great movements that were squeezing out the blood of nations, and the degree of interest shown by townspeople in these tremendous upheavals! How did the whole of Paris rise up in revolt, without really knowing why?—or at least, without having succeeded in drawing the slightest conclusion from its gratuitous opinion?

"The names of American generals and places of war which an ignorant people were forever deforming; the great phrase 'freedom of the seas' in all our ladies' mouths; our elegant blades confusing a ship's masts and rigging as though they had been aboard it; Europe suddenly transplanted to America . . . , all these delirious concoctions delivered at a libertines' supper by men who would have blanched at the sudden entrance of an exempt [a police agent] what a grotesque chapter that would be to write!

"The Parisian, upon hearing of the disaster that had befallen our squadron under the command of the Comte de Grasse, uttered a shriek of pain and indignation. He could not bear the thought of the splendid *Ville de Paris* sailing up the Thames.* One might have imagined that this commotion would imprint a totally new character upon people's minds; but after the most clamorous wailing and lamentations the Parisian abruptly subsided into the silence that is decreed to be his habitual state."[1]

The news from Les Saintes arrived over a month after the event, when the spring weather was creating preoccupations of a very different order for the "average Parisian," who, "at Whitsuntide, takes the *galiote* to Sèves† and runs from thence to Versailles to stare at the princes and the procession of the Order of the Holy Ghost, then the grounds, then the menagerie. On the return trip people tell the story of the Swiss guard at the menagerie, a doorman in royal livery whose job was to feed a dromedary six bottles of Burgundy every day. The animal having died, the Swiss guard submitted a petition requesting the *survival of the dromedary.*

"The largest suites of rooms are opened to the public. The smaller ones, which are the most richly decorated and interesting to see, are closed. At noon everyone crowds into the gallery to contemplate the King on his way to mass, and the Queen, and Monsieur and Madame and Monseigneur Comte d'Artois and Madame Comtesse d'Artois, and then people say to each other:

" 'Did you see the King?'

" 'Yes; he laughed.'

" 'That's true, he did laugh.'

" 'He looked quite pleased.'

---

*She never does; mortally wounded in the battle, taken in tow by the English, the *Ville de Paris* sinks a few days after her capture.

†*Sic;* today, Sèvres. The *galiote* was a stage-barge, hauled down the Seine by horses; its regular circuit was Paris–Meudon.

" 'Upon my word, he has reason to be.

"When the host is raised, every eye is riveted upon the King and nobody kneels on the altar side. At the *grand couvert* [meal] the Parisian observes that the King ate with a hearty appetite whereas the Queen took nothing but one glass of water. This will be the substance of conversation for a fortnight; and all the serving-girls will crane their necks to hear the great news."[2]

For the great news is what's happening in Paris or at Court. The rest of the world can whirl; the only real events are those that take place in this navel of the universe in which the subject of this summer's big stir is the reception of the Comte and Comtesse du Nord, or in other words the Empress Catherine's son Grand Duke Paul, heir to the throne of all the Russias, who's taking a tour around Europe with his wife. The man who will one day rule over "Muscovy" is worth a little fuss: people are beginning to realize, from the writings of Voltaire, Diderot, and Grimm, that a giant is stirring somewhere out there and starting to shake off his crust of snow. Will the man who is to personify it tomorrow be our enemy or our friend? Since Peter the Great's memorable tour sixty years before, in the course of which the founder of modern Russia was converted to European techniques if not European ideas, no comparable event had occurred. It was also an opportunity for high society to obtain a brief respite from boredom—life has been so inexpressibly dull since the top party-boys left for America.

Paul and Marie were accordingly feted at Versailles, Trianon, and the Palais Royal; but the high point, the week that will long live in the memories of all, is their reception by the Condés at Chantilly, a palace overlooked by History but now making up for lost time: you'd think we were back in the days of the first great parties for Louis XIV, except that Molière and Lully aren't there. But otherwise, the occasion is a perfect explosion of extravagance, a smear of luxury and gadgetry far beyond anything anyone could remember. All eyewitnesses are dazzled—things are looking up for the century of Louis XVI!

Vatel had impaled himself on his own sword a hundred years earlier* because the fish didn't come on time. That was at a Condé shindig too, but in those days the head of the family was the prince, of course, the real, true, great man himself, who needed to be forgiven for making war on France and therefore got out his best china when he wanted to throw a party for Louis XIV. It only cost him two hundred thousand écus† and his chief cook's death, which went unnoticed because "Gourville [the head steward] undertook to remedy the

---

*111 years to be exact, in April 1671. The Marquise de Sévigné wrote one of her liveliest letters on the event.

†Two million modern francs [$400,000].

loss of Vatel," as Mme de Sévigné informs us, "and it was remedied. The party dined very well, then there was a light repast, then supper, and a promenade, games, hunting; everything was daffodil-scented and as though enchanted."

Again, on this tenth of June 1782, "Chantilly is the most beautiful place on earth—no longer, as in the days of Mme de Sévigné, carpeted with a thousand écus worth of daffodils, but enchanting, superb," writes the poor man's Sévigné, a nice lady called the Baronne d'Oberkirch who was a childhood friend of the Grand Duchess Marie (Paul's wife) back in the days when Marie was a (German) Princesse de Montbéliard (France). Oberkirch is right on the spot, all wide eyes and little shrieks of delight, utterly absorbed in her coiffure and migraines, to supply us with an account of these festivities which would be absolutely faithful were it not for the fact that she has suffered a total ablation of the critical faculty—whatever is noble is good and right—but that only makes her a better mirror of the people she observes, since they all think so too. "The water, woods, gardens are exquisite; the naiads of the fountains have a courtly air, leaning upon their urns . . ."[3]

The scene is ten leagues north of Paris, between Saint-Denis and Senlis, on the edge of a forest as vast as the capital. "The Paris road crosses it for ten miles," and it is even more than ordinarily teeming with game because every inch of it belongs to the Condés and all churls are forbidden to hunt or trap in it. This game devastates their peasants' lands too, for "they say the *capitainerie,* or paramountship, is above 100 miles in circumference,"[4] with the result that their vassals grow fewer vegetables and fruit than anyone else in the Paris region. But the Condés deserve their hunting rights: for four generations they've done nothing but fight, trade, speculate, and build a dream home that can out-Versailles Versailles in *dolce vita,* and inside which they're better off than kings, less cluttered up with parasites and officials. They're also the direct descendants of St. Louis, a minor branch tucked away in a corner of the family tree, you never know, what if the senior branch were wiped out by smallpox, and then the Orléanses . . . They're about fifteenth, more or less, in line for the throne, and almost able to lay a better spread for the future tsar than is Louis XVI. "We were one hundred and fifty people and at least three times as many servants, not counting those of the prince's household.* Upon leaving table, we found barouches harnessed and waiting. M. le Duc de Bourbon and M. le Prince de Condé drove the ladies themselves, through a thousand surprises, beneath vaults of greenery decorated with streamers, ribbons, and the initials of Their Imperial Highnesses. The weather was everything that could be desired: it was a pure delight"—the smiling coolness of the forest

---

*In other words every guest from Paris or Versailles had brought at least three servants, not counting the eighty-nine persons in the grand-ducal retinue; the Condés' staff at Chantilly numbered approximately two thousand.

north of Paris, which makes Compiègne, Montmorency, Senlis, or Bondy preferable to the damp swelter of Versailles when the hot weather comes in June. You need a horse to show your visitors around the grounds here, the Chantilly estate is city-scaled. Moving out from the old château of the Grand Condé, which wasn't exactly a doll's house, buildings have multiplied on all sides: there's the big house itself surrounded by its moat full of giant carp; the "little château" with its sixty rooms, each gilded differently; an adjoining "masters' lodging" in case they run out of room elsewhere, and the famous stables, "the most magnificent construction of the estate; they could house two hundred and fifty horses in fifty apartments"[5] and were built with the prodigious profits that the Duc de Bourbon, the one who came after the Regent during Louis XV's minority, had adroitly reaped by extricating himself from the Law bankruptcy in time. "It has been said of the Duc de Bourbon, who built these splendid stables and transformed them into an edifice more imposing than the château he lived in, that this prince must certainly have believed in metempsychosis" (Mercier). The Condés' colossal fortune, first planted in those days, has thrived on a compost of shipwrecks and suicides. Since then, they haven't needed to bother learning how to count. All they do is spend. By building, for example, a little farther on, "the château called 'd'Enghien,' a pretty building in the Italian manner, as a sort of hunting lodge."[6]

"Upon our return, we went to the extremely handsome and ornate entertainment hall. The particular feature of this was that the back of the stage could be opened to show a natural waterfall adorned with the figure of a nymph. By means of a tube that communicated with the theater, eight tiers of water rose up, making a most magical effect." Authors had to write their plays for the machinery, cram their poetry into the pipes. Nevertheless, Chantilly is undoubtedly the most successful combination of grass, stones, and water in France. An Olympus whose gods, as on the other one, sit yawning between two cloudbursts. In the last few days, however, it has shaken off its lethargy. "We then found the gardens completely illuminated, and a dazzling display of fireworks. The façade of the château represented the arms of the Comte and Comtesse du Nord with their symbolic initials entwined in love-knots. It was the last word in elegance. Supper was served on the Ile d'Amour" in the center of an artificial lake created by damming up the waters of the Nonette; "there were all sorts of games, tilting, and swings, and then came the ball. It had a gaiety and verve that are never to be found at Court under ordinary circumstances. I have since learned"—Oberkirch speaking—"how keenly the Queen regretted not being present for this fete, but the King would not have permitted it. The throne of France is surrounded by a rampart of etiquette that is exceedingly difficult to cross." Nor are Monsieur, Artois, or the Orléanses present for they, who are also "above" the Condés, would be breaking the rules by appearing as their cousins' "official guests"; so the Condés can play at being kings without fear of censure.

Two generations of failures, ne'er-do-well Bourbons, "princes of the blood" whose only function was to parade around and impress the "lower orders" while sucking up their substance. True, they're more presentable than the branches closer to the throne: better set-up, less obviously degenerate, with muscles and good carriage, capable of sitting a horse. The Prince de Condé (Louis-Joseph), his son the Duc de Bourbon (Louis-Henri) . . . and now the third generation, Louis-Antoine, the grandson—"M. le Duc d'Enghien,* a pretty ten-year-old child who already shows great promise and brings Mme la Comtesse du Nord a huge bouquet of the rarest and most beautifully scented flowers." What else can he do? Condé, the head of the family, is only forty-six and behaves like an old-age pensioner. To offset his minister-duke father, a notorious debauchee, he has affected a gloomy devoutness combined with a fierce hatred of all "libertines." He married a Rohan-Soubise, thereby doubling his fortune. She soon left him a widower, however, and he was content to remain one: the hunt was sufficient for him. In his youth, during the Seven Years' War, he fought against the Prussians well enough to do credit to his name; but all that is left for him now is to relive the pride of his twenties. The war of his middle years is being waged upon the Encyclopédistes and the "new spirit"—that is, anything that might cast doubt upon the justification of his privileges. "He did not share any part of the enthusiasm of the young French nobility for the cause of American independence. This new form of crusade was a matter of indifference or anxiety to him. The institution of a republic was far removed from his subjects of concern and not congenial to his sympathies."[7] "M. le Prince de Condé," Mme d'Oberkirch tells us, "does not like the *philosophes* and has never joined in the infatuation for these men who have done and will continue to do us so much harm.

"'I far prefer,' he likes to say, 'a virtuous mind to a fine mind.'" How he loves the virtuous minds of his right-thinking peasants, for instance, who greet him cap in hand; of his laborers whose lord he is, the fictitious proprietor of their land, on which he levies feudal taxes for a domain as big as a province; and of his day-laborers, too, those who possess nothing, nothing at all, and who sometimes don't have a day's bread in front of them.† Between 25,000 and 27,000 of those virtuous minds are dependent upon him for their living. Not that he's stingy; now and then he flings a few coins at them from the doors of his carriage. He has one daughter, who turned devout and stupid after her projected marriage with the Comte d'Artois fell through because Louis XV, who didn't like the Condés, exercised his veto—"Mademoiselle," they call

*Napoleon has him kidnapped at Etterheim and legally assassinated in the pits of Vincennes on March 21, 1804.

†It would seem, however, that even the Condés had difficulty making ends meet: in the *Livre rouge* on the Court's secret expenditure published at the beginning of the Revolution, it is recorded that Louis XVI paid 25,000 livres a year to the Prince de Condé between 1781 and 1788, making a total of 150,000 modern francs [$30,000].

her;* and a twenty-six-year-old son, Louis-Henri, Duc de Bourbon, who has achieved the signal distinction of becoming a champion at debauchery in the major league of princes, outstripping even the Comte d'Artois and Duc de Chartres, who are no mean contenders. He's a case, however. The only reason why he married (at fifteen) Mathilde d'Orléans (Chartres's sister), who was six years his senior, was to manufacture the infant Enghien and provide a framework for his philandering. They live apart, she plaintively rehearsing to her friends the names of her husband's mistresses—a new one every month in the ranks of high society, not counting the girls of lower estate†—and seeking consolation among the valets. His sexual activities speedily assume the dimensions of an obsession.** A good-looking man, however, robust and spirited, with a basically scarlet complexion veering to eggplant in the evening. His beaters have flushed him some pretty women, Tallyho!

Everybody sleeps for one night and the next morning, except the ladies who have to get up at seven and be tortured by the hairdressers, a regiment of whom have been imported. And off we go again on June 12. "After dinner, as excellent as that of the previous day, we drove through the grounds in barouches" to admire the Bois Vert, the Allée de Sylvie, the temple of Venus, and the Roman pavilion. "Then there was hunting at the ponds; after which, when night had fallen, lanterns were brought out, I believe, from under every leaf. Various balls were improvised in halls of greenery and in the pavilions. Supper was served in the hamlet," which Condé has just built to compete with the one the Queen is putting up at Trianon, a tiny bit bigger and better planned, to mortify without really angering her. "It is a picturesque assemblage of rustic fabrications in the midst of an English garden. The walls of the largest cabin are hung with greenery inside and surrounded outside with everything needful to a good laborer. It is in this thatched cottage, which contains a single room of oval shape, that supper was served at a dozen small tables, each seating ten or twelve"—this supper consisting of a "small service": six kinds of soup, twelve entrees, twelve fish dishes, three roasts, six kinds of fowl, twelve desserts, and "Oriental preserves." Not exactly the menu of the "good laborers" of the Beauvais

*Louise de Condé later takes the veil and, during the Restoration, founds the Benedictines of St. Louis du Temple, a bastion of integrism: "Our ancestors were Huguenots," the noble abbess would say, "and God only knows what sad fate has befallen them in the other world. I shall devote myself body and soul to the Lord to atone for and efface their errors."[8]

†It was she whom the drunken Comte d'Artois slapped in the face at an Opéra ball in 1778, leading to a duel between Bourbon and him.

**The nineteenth-century biographer, or rather hagiographer, of the princes de Condé, with the uninventable name of Crétineau-Joly [roughly, Little-Cretin-the-Fair—*Trans.*], who wrote his entire book in what must have been an uncomfortable position (prostrate), found a piquant expression for the Duc de Bourbon: "His ears were oversensitive to that *whinny of lascivious hearts* mentioned by Bossuet in one of his sermons."[9]

region, whose regular fare consists of "biscuits, bread, salt pork on occasion, meat seldom, vegetables more often; the priests recommend that they do not consume alcoholic or inflammable beverages, which are incendiary. Agricultural workers put three spoonfuls of vinegar in their water so that it will resist putrefaction."[10]

"After dinner, we went to take fruit in a pavilion situated in the middle of the wood, which we had not seen before. This pavilion is a single isolated rotunda, at the top of which invisible places had been prepared for musicians, so that one might, lounging on a sofa, hear music above one without seeing it [*sic*] at all . . . The youngest and prettiest women in Paris and the most agreeable gallants were all at this fete, which could never have been so beautiful in another place. The menagerie is larger and better cared for than that of the King, and as for the stables, everybody knows one can easily drive a four-horse carriage straight through them." Is that all? By no means. Next morning, the hunt. "This most royal of pleasures is especially appreciated by the princesses of the house of Condé. I can understand, when once one has seen their forests, their hounds, and all the paraphernalia of venery . . ." The fanfares swirl through the woods like gusts of wild wind; but can anyone at the Condé end of a gun imagine what real terror the dying fall of a far-off horn may herald? In 1782 the gracious pleasure of princes has enabled a tiny handful of men to reach the absolute summit of the science of hedonism. "The hunt resumed at dawn in the grounds. Several of those attending it had not been to bed at all, including M. le Duc de Bourbon. The stag was chased three hours and brought to bay at the head of the canal, which he crossed, followed by the entire pack." An ecstasy of blood and shouting. The noblest animal of them all falls, his throat cut by "M. le Prince de Condé. His aim was superb and all the huntsmen were thrilled. The honors were, quite rightly, for Mme la Comtesse du Nord. M. le Prince de Condé gave her the stag's four teeth and antlers. She had the teeth mounted in a girandole surrounded by diamonds."

"Someone related a witticism that was already going the rounds in Paris:

" 'In their entertainment of M. le Comte du Nord, the King conducted himself as a friend, the Duc d'Orléans as a bourgeois, and the Prince de Condé as a monarch.'

" 'That is profoundly true,' replied the Comte du Nord. 'It is impossible to speak too highly of the house of Condé; no sovereign in Europe could have done more, if only because of that beautiful place at Chantilly, which has no peer.' " And yet he's just been entertained in Warsaw, Vienna, and five or six German courts, by the pope, by Leopold in Tuscany . . . But between this marginal Bourbon and Catherine's son there was a real rapport. A sort of Russian excess they had in common. In Paul's heart, the true princes of France are the Condés.

" 'We shall welcome you to St. Petersburg with enthusiasm, Monsieur . . .'

" 'Alas, that is only a dream,' replied the Prince de Condé with a sigh."*

And on his way back to Russia, Grand Duke Paul offers the eternal consolation of the rich to another curious person, who was suffering from remorse at the thought of his conspicuous consumption:

"It is not as mad to build palaces as you are pleased to think. The grandeur of princes is that of peoples, and all the money you have spent here has made work and consequently prosperity for your subjects."[11]

In this respect, anyway, Grand Duke Paul Petrovich has nothing on his conscience. But that's the only peaceful side of his character. This enormous stir and fuss of parties, the golden cornucopia of France gushing forth, festivities costing the equivalent of a minor war: it all washes up at the feet of an intriguingly disharmonious couple, a broad, swelling German woman, pink and giddy, bending down when she speaks to a husband who stands a head shorter than she and whose ugliness makes the uninitiated recoil. Can she actually mate with that simian? The future Emperor of Russia is a sort of monster, attained by a degree of degeneracy far exceeding that of the whole tribe of effete sovereigns now reigning or soon to reign by divine right over the nations of the end of the century. Minor detail: he is thought to be insane.

CATHERINE THE GREAT

I I

JUNE 1782

My Bitch of a Nation

Mind you, a man could be crazy for less. Paul Petrovich means Paul son of Peter, but he will never know whether he's really the son of the tsar who was first deposed and then murdered by his wife Catherine;† or of, for instance, Saltykov, one of her early lovers. He had been almost officially assigned to sire a child on the young princess, her husband's semi-impotence having left her

---

*A dream that comes true, but not in the way he was imagining, when, at the end of all his warring against the French Republic, the exiled Prince de Condé seeks asylum fifteen years later, in November 1797, at the court of Tsar Paul I in St. Petersburg.

†In 1762. Peter III was strangled shortly after being deposed, if not by Catherine's order then at least with her tacit consent, for she subsequently heaped favors upon his murderers.

more or less a virgin after eight years of marriage. This question was brought
to his attention in his youth by the anti-Catherine mutterings of an opposition
clique that was backing him to further its members' careers, with the result that
Paul suffers from the same essential doubt about himself as Charles VII at
Chinon: his credentials are defective. Has he or hasn't he any of the blood of
Peter the Great in his veins, that blood which was already sick in the big man
himself but which nevertheless, carried down on the female side, constitutes
the only dynastic reference evoked in Russia by all the male and female
adventurers who have since confiscated its throne on the crest of one or
another wave of guard regiments blown their way? Catherine herself, German
to the fingertips, could not consolidate her usurpation and receive the blessings
of the gilded patriarchs until she proclaimed him, Paul *Petrovich,* then a child
of eight, "heir to the throne and associate in her act of salvation of Holy
Russia, our beloved son." A stunning lesson in how to manipulate hereditary
rights, if he was a bastard after all.

He undoubtedly hated her even then. In 1764, "he asked why his father
had been made to die and why the throne that belonged by rights to him had
been given to his mother. He added that when he grew up he would certainly
redress the situation."[1] That was at the age of ten. People say he already had
that trick of blinking so often to hide the profound gaze which is his only
redeeming feature, the appeal of a soul in chains. But to be catapulted on stage
at the age of twenty-eight with the whole of enlightened Europe in the audience is enough to make anybody blink, coming from the Shakespearean chaos
of the history of the Romanovs.

Peter the Great had had his son and heir assassinated—Tsarevich Alexis
the "opposer." His widow Catherine I mounted the throne at his death and
gave Russia to her favorite, Menshikov, to govern. She died, whereupon the
throne was restored to Peter II, a son of the assassinated Alexis, who was then
ten and who died at fourteen. A "Council of the Nobility" next called to the
throne a sister-in-law of Peter the Great, Anne.* She presented the empire to
her lover-in-chief Biron, the son of a German groom, to rule over as absolute
master for ten years. At her death it was the turn of another child emperor,
one of her nephews, two months old: Ivan VI. Would Biron be able to stay
on top? No. A "pro-Russian" palace revolution wiped out the Germans and
consecrated a Russian in their place, a real one, our little mother Elisabeth,
Peter the Great's second daughter. For the record: this gentle lady, and her
successors, kept young Ivan VI imprisoned for life in the Schlüsselberg fortress, the famous Russian Bastille in St. Petersburg. His jailers stabbed him to
death in 1764, in the course of a mysterious liberation attempt.

---

*She had married Peter's brother, a loony who had to be interned but was nonetheless
proclaimed "co-tsar," His Majesty Ivan V.

Elisabeth was the only woman Paul loved in his childhood, she was his *baba*—the tsarina with no husband and a multitude of lovers, a very gay girl indeed. "If my great-aunt had lived another two years I should be master of everything today,"[2] he said, and his hypothesis was not so far-fetched. Toward the end of her twenty-year reign Elisabeth was indeed toying with the idea of short-circuiting her nephew Peter, the "legitimate" heir she had been compelled to dig up in Schleswig-Holstein owing to her own inability to produce anything other than the progeny of guardsmen or lackeys. Another German? *Ja, ja,* and the "old Russians" were mightily incensed; nevertheless, this Peter was the sole grandson (on the distaff side) of Peter the Great: the magic blood. But alas, he stubbornly stuck to his German ways and also proved at twenty to be not only completely unhinged but completely pickled as well. He was literally never sober. Well, why not demote him, then, and appropriate the son produced by his wife Catherine—another German? But, at least he was undoubtedly sired by a real Russian, and with Elisabeth's blessing too. We can bring him up "in the Russian manner." The tsarina was thinking about it when death overtook her, and it was Catherine herself who, within a few months, undertook to wipe the slate of Russia clean of her drunken tsar of a husband —but not for little Paul's sake: for her own, and for a long time.

Paul had been led in, wearing his toy officer's costume, to pay his respects to the remains of his great-aunt lying in state in the cathedral of Kazan. How could you compare them: that poor lump of dead flesh in a cloth-of-silver gown, covered with lace and paint beneath the golden crown, a rotting cosmetics exhibit bloated with unhealthy fat (Elisabeth had also begun to souse)— and the vital young woman with the long hair and provocative bosom, "Elisabeth the horsewoman who tamed the Russian mare" and whose portraits used to set little lights flashing in the eyes of Louis XV? Nevertheless, it was beside this piece of human jetsam that Paul staged a fit of hysterics long remembered by the older courtiers, for with his darling auntie went his last shred of security, his one staff and support, his haven, and a life began in which nobody would ever again admire him without a price tag in their eyes and death would be ever standing at his bedside—sometimes in the guise of his own mother. No child of seven brought up by a dozen superstitious matrons who had stuffed his head full of witchcraft could turn into a man just like that; it was asking too much of him. From that moment on he never knew a quiet night. He was terrified of new faces, of beggars, and traveling showmen. A slammed door, a trumpet fanfare, a thunderclap sent him running. He couldn't bear the smallest spot on his clothing: everything was blood to him, he would cut the stain out with scissors, even on embroidered brocades.* Then too the

*Paul Petrovich becomes tsar in November 1796 at the death of Catherine II, and reigns, as Paul I, until his own assassination in October 1801 by a group of courtiers alarmed by his

genetic terrain may have been none too sound. "He suffers," the French ambassador informs Choiseul, "from a nervous weakness attributed to the stigmata of a venereal disease inherited from Saltykov."[3]

The lover-and-possible-father wasn't so bad, though, with his long indefinite head at the top of one of those fine hard-muscled bodies of which Catherine was so fond. But when the Europe of the princes first meets the "Comte du Nord" it opts in favor of the hypothetical legitimate father, because Paul looks so much like Peter III, "with his flattened cheekbones, large downward-slanting eyes, and that sort of Pekinese muzzle he has in place of a nose."[4] "A premature baldness contrives to give his face the appearance of a death's-head. The denuded skull, heavy and round, stands atop a short and awkward body upon which its owner vainly endeavors to confer a semblance of elegance by walking with a sway. One might take him for a dish-faced Laplander with the movements of an automaton."[5] If this was his true lineage it might remove the stain of bastardy but could only confirm his predisposition to madness. Catherine, who was never able to abide her son, exploits the situation, sometimes raising doubts as to his heredity (in which case it would be for her, on the strength of her "reforms" and popularity, to found a new dynasty, like a second Peter the Great) and sometimes letting him believe that he must inevitably lose his mind and be removed in turn.

But Paul fights back, writhing away from the precipice with the aid of certain not-negligible resources: an uncramped intelligence, curiosity of mind, and a great faculty for assimilation. Panin, his tutor with the "European and cosmopolitan" leanings, has him reading *Don Quixote, Pantagruel, Gil Blas,* and Voltaire's *Charles XII* at the age of ten, and he knows some scenes from *Phèdre* by heart. Another advantage he has over his "father": he plumps for normal sexuality. He willingly allows himself to be initiated by the ladies designated for the purpose in the proximity of any young heir to a throne; he is madly in love with his first wife, a princess of Hesse with a narrow pelvis who dies in childbirth and in agony; but three months later, when the subject of a new fiancée is broached, he is all eagerness:

"Fair? Dark? Short or tall?"[6]

She was fair and tall and cantankerous, and so shortsighted that she had to bend over like a hen to see where she was going. She was Sophie, of the branch of Württembergs who had found themselves, as a consequence of the endemic irrationality of peace treaties, reigning over Montbéliard: a German family governing a French population with a patriarchal and easygoing hand. There must have been a dozen or so of these Teutonic princelings of micro-

increasing insanity, but also by his tentative plans to conclude an agreement with Bonaparte, who is then First Consul.

scopic realms whose chief activity in life was bringing up their daughters to be offered to greater sovereigns. Stud farms for blue-blood fillies. Sophie won the triple stakes in return for an overnight transformation, as was the rule in her world, from a stern Protestantism to an Orthodox mysticism filled with genuflexions and signs of the cross; she had herself rechristened Marie. Oh, wonder: for the moment, they are a happy couple; their need for each other is intensified by the fact that Catherine stole their two sons almost at hatching, to bring up in her own nest and coddle in the cradle of her wild dream; its objective is revealed in their names—Alexander will reign in the West and Constantine, as soon as she recaptures Constantinople from the Turks, in the East. This maternal abduction does nothing to pacify Paul, who sees it as a repetition, at his expense, of the projected dynastic short-circuit Elisabeth had intended for him. Russian history certainly seems to abound in unwanted fathers.

From afar, however, and pending the day of his possible liquidation, Catherine has also spoiled him. She needed him to exist and maintain a lifestyle that would impress the rabble, but not to set foot in her Council and not to make friends with her ministers. He reigns over a sort of mini-kingdom in his internment camp ten leagues from St. Petersburg, which consists of two palaces close enough together for him to keep moving incessantly from one to the other through the swamps and humid forests of these flatlands: Pavlosk (Paul's place) and Gachina, which he and his wife have turned into a sort of Germanic Versailles and where his very own grenadiers can goosestep among the rosebeds before his eyes. From a distance the statues look like marble, but when you come closer you see that they're only iron, painted white. It is all very inflated and fake. Fake Prussian: Paul's hero, his god, is Frederick, the sovereign his mother can't stomach. And for every Russian gimmick she affects, he counters by Teutonizing himself a little more, in the image of his official father. The princely pair are surrounded by a clique of parasites who stick with them on the off chance, one never knows, of progressing from the tedium of a spare-clothes closet to the government of one of the biggest empires in the world. And a few intrepid souls, instantly denounced by informers, have dared to become regular visitors at Gachina.

But if that's the situation, what is the point of this trip to Europe, where everyone will see him as official pretender and feed his yearning for grandeur? Partly, it's a court maneuver: Catherine wants to get rid of old Panin, who is now minister of foreign affairs and is more attached to her son, and more of a "Frederickist," than she feels is good for him. In addition, she wants to put a stop to Paul's little trick of posing publicly as a reformer in the Senate and giving out that if he were holding the broomstick all those rotten Potemkins would soon be swept away. During their absence she also intends to run a security check on any of his supporters who have stayed at home in Russia, carry out a small purification and purge. Her task was simplified by Sophie-Marie's desire to see her parents again, and by Paul's vanity, his notion that he would be re-creating the journey of Peter the Great. But it took months to talk him out of going to Berlin, and his mother was absolutely determined that there must be no contact between him and Frederick. His itinerary was drawn up for him as though he were a schoolboy, Poland, Austria, Italy, France, and back again. The pre-departure negotiations were rich in tragicomical anguish, with Paul suddenly terrified that he wouldn't be allowed to come home again, and what if Alexander were proclaimed heir in his absence? He shouted and swore that he would not go at all unless he could visit Berlin first, but in vain. The day they left everybody wept, some in rage and some in fear: Catherine wept, and they wept, and the crowd strewn along the way wept too. Like all crown princes, Paul was becoming popular in Russia: the eternal hope. Panin had fallen ill, he was on his way out and knew it.

At this point they've been jolting along the roads for eight or nine months, bumbling down their star-studded path and affording Leopold, Grand Duke of Tuscany and Joseph II's brother, an opportunity to dash off a most perceptive portrait of Paul:*

"In addition to a good deal of wit, talent and reflection, the Comte du Nord has the ability to grasp ideas and things aright and to see all their facets and circumstances at once . . . I believe he will be very active, but there is great vigor in his manner of thinking in particular. To me he seems very firm, resolute, and determined once he has made up his mind, and he is assuredly not a man to let himself be guided by anyone else. It appears that he does not care for foreigners in general, and will be rather severe, will aim for order, subordination without qualification, obedience to the rules, and exactitude. In his speeches he never alluded to his position or to the Empress in any way; but he did not hide from me the fact that he does not approve of all the great schemes and innovations undertaken in Russia, which do indeed prove to have more show and name than substance when carried out. It was only on the point of the Empress's scheme of self-aggrandizement at the expense of the Turks, by refounding the Empire of Constantinople, that he made no attempt to conceal his strong disapproval of the idea, or of any other plan for increasing a monarchy which is already too large and which needs to have attention paid to what is going on within it, to banish all fruitless thought of conquest that would achieve nothing but glory and have no solid advantages but, on the contrary, only weaken the country further. On this point I am convinced that he spoke sincerely."[7] To which Joseph, well informed by a number of Catherine's courtiers (including, possibly, Potemkin, or at least Paul believes so)

---

*In one of his no-punch-pulling letters to his brother.

whom Cobenzl, his ambassador in Petersburg, has bought with no regard for cost, replies, "Domestic intrigues continue in Petersburg, and it is probable that upon his return the grand duke will find more grounds for irritation than he had before setting out upon his travels."[8]

Half of Europe to be waded through, like a labyrinth of old, by this heir to whom everybody kowtows. But at the end of the maze, all he can expect is a noose. Maybe even sooner? In Florence, of all apposite places, at the height of a banquet, it suddenly seemed to Paul that the wine had a peculiar taste. Without further ado he thrust a finger down his throat and vomited before the assembled company. In Bruges, after drinking a glass of beer that was not sufficiently chilled, the same scene. "He turned pale instantly, his features contracted so as to render him unrecognizable, he choked, stiffened, threw back his head, and breathed stertorously."[9] We also learn that he loves his country about as tenderly as he loves his mother. During one of his tantrums, the Prince de Ligne tries to find excuses for her:

"Monseigneur, a woman cannot run everywhere and concern herself with every little detail . . ."

"Damnation, that is why my bitch of a nation wants only women to rule it!"[10]

In Naples someone tries to please him by praising his country's legislation. He explodes, in front of the king, queen, and a hundred guests: "Laws, in Russia! Laws, in a country ruled by a woman who can only keep the throne by trampling every law underfoot!"[11]

And at Versailles he has just nonplussed poor Louis XVI and Marie Antoinette —first and foremost a dutiful daughter—with an outburst in the same vein on the subject of his retinue, all those faces and not one he can trust: "I should have been sorry to see so much as a poodle that was truly attached to me in my retinue, for my mother would have had it thrown into the Seine before we left Paris."[12]

Almost every day meanwhile, that same mother writes the young couple affectionate and benevolent letters, thickly spread with honey, from her palace at Tsarskoye Selo.[13] How Russian these Germans are! Their hearts positively melt in mutual hatred: "M. Alexander, frightfully full of himself after writing four lines to his papa and maman, has recently begun to spell . . . Your letter from Mohilev gave me gooseflesh, when I read that you both had fevers upon reaching Plotsk . . . The profundity of Alexander's questions is astonishing* . . . I sent for the blue and gray misses from the community to entertain your

---

*This is the future Alexander I, Napoleon's "friend-foe," who implicitly condones his father's assassination and reigns over Russia from 1801 until his mysterious death in 1825.

children. Afterwards, I dispatched the whole jolly troop to the hall where they
danced, and our urchins joined in the fun, Alexander very bashful and Constantine never dancing with fewer than two young ladies at once . . . The
appreciation shown you by the Viennese public confirms the opinion I have
always held, which is that the Austrians are good Russians [*sic*] . . . Reading
the outpourings of your hearts in your letters, my dear children, is as sweet
to me as a mother as it is novel to me as Empress, since most of the letters she
receives are ordinarily filled with circumstances, conjunctures, and conjec-
tures, rather than with natural human feelings. Your precious letters are balm
to my blood. I find them far more to my taste than pea soup . . ."

Catherine's soup is turning sour on her these days, however, just as the
"Norths" are wallowing in receptions at Versailles and Chantilly. Thunderbolt: her police pried open the shoeheels of the couriers sent by Bibikov—a
young aide-de-camp who stayed behind in Petersburg but was writing to
Prince Kurakin, one of the people in Paul's retinue—and in those heels they
found the heartrending laments of a few young noblemen with withering
hopes. Pillow-secrets, peculations of the "one-eyed one" (Potemkin), political
intrigues, and general ferment in the place temporarily vacated by Paul. Bibikov: one of the first links in the chain of Russian men of liberty. He longed
to have his cry heard all over Europe: "All I can tell you is that we are in a
pretty pickle and it is impossible to remain so unfeeling while the country
suffers. To contemplate it in cold blood would verge upon the comical, but
unfortunately the heart breaks, and one sees in all its blackness the awful
position of those who, like us, think of the good and have still some energy
in our souls . . . I am sustained only by hope for the future . . . In the name
of God, come back to us soon, we are all too aware of your absence."[14]

So Catherine adds a postscript, informing Paul that she has read this
missive and imprisoned Bibikov, without a hearing, in the Peter and Paul
Fortress but that, because she was such a kindly soul, she did not intend to hang
him. It comes like a thunderbolt at the end of a letter devoted primarily to "the
extremely cold, calm weather prevailing at Tsarskoye Selo this spring, but with
a very cutting breeze from the north":

"Having regard to the Bibikov affair, I must tell you that that man, to
whom, as to his family, I have shown every mark of favor, is an ingrate, his
mind a sea of resentment against your mother. This vice, a destructive force
in any society, is not a feeling to be encouraged. But that such a man should
find friends is proof of many things . . . Bibikov, whose ideas have filled his
chimaerical head with ill-will and steeped him in ingratitude and falsehood,
did the only thing he could do; he repented, implored forgiveness, and
adopted the attitude and behavior of a child who deserved to be whipped and
knew it. This whole affair might serve as a lesson in morality for youth. But
however penitent he may appear, what can be expected of a brain nourished

on gossip? . . . Because of my principles, I have dragged this young man by
his hair from the abyss into which he must otherwise have plunged, because
my style is less tragic than that of my predecessors.* I tell you this, my dear
children, because in my affection for you I desire that you should learn from
it [Catherine's French, literally, is "fatten your cabbages on it"—*Trans.*] now
and in the future."15 She had a weakness for vegetable imagery, pea soup, and
fattened cabbages . . . But Paul knew how his soup was likely to taste when
he got home. Maybe it wasn't such a bad idea for him to practice vomiting.

Under the circumstances, what some people term "madness" may be the
only port in the storm for him. One evening at supper, the fare as exquisite
as usual, Grand Duke Paul leans over to Mme d'Oberkirch and tells her, in
the most casual voice in the world, a story he then makes her swear not to
repeat: "I was in the streets of St. Petersburg one evening, or rather one night,
with Kurakin and a couple of footmen. We had been up late chatting and
smoking, and took it into our heads to go out of the palace incognito and look
at the city by moonlight. It was not cold, the days were growing longer, in fact
it was one of the mildest moments of our springtime, so sickly in comparison
with that of the south . . . At the corner of the street, standing hidden in a
doorway, I saw a tall thin man wrapped in a cloak like a Spaniard, with a
military hat pulled far down over his eyes. He seemed to be waiting for
something, and as soon as we passed in front of him he stepped out of his
hiding place and began walking on our left, without word or gesture. It was
impossible to discern his features; but his footsteps on the pavement rang
strangely, like two stones striking together."

Kurakin, who is also at the table, bends discreetly over the "delicious,
plump, and flavorful little oysters that are said to be found only in the region
of Ostend." However devoted to the Grand Duke he may be, neither he nor
the footmen saw anything that night.

"What? Don't you see that man on my left, in a cloak, walking between
the wall and me?"

"Your Highness is touching the wall yourself and there is no room for
anyone between you and it."

Never mind. Paul went on walking alongside the invisible stranger,
beneath the embarrassed gaze of his three flesh-and-blood companions. A
deadly chill possessed his whole body. And suddenly there came a call,
"Paul!" and "Paul!" again, three or four times, and then, "Paul, poor
Paul, poor prince!" . . . The other three heard no more than they saw.
"With an enormous effort, I asked this mysterious being who he was and
what he wanted of me:

*She means, "because I don't employ the same means of punishment."

" 'I want you not to become too attached to the things of this world, for you will not remain long in it.' "

They walked on over an hour, in silence.

"Look at Kurakin smiling, he still thinks I dreamed it all . . . At last we drew near the great square between the Neva bridge and the Senators' palace.

"Paul, farewell; you will see me again, here and elsewhere.'

"Then, as though he had touched it, his hat lifted slightly by itself, and I could see his features clearly. I drew back in spite of myself, for there were the eagle eye, the tanned brow, and stern smile of my ancestor Peter the Great. Before I had recovered my senses, he disappeared.

"And it is on that very spot that the empress is erecting the famous monument that is soon to be admired by all Europe, representing Tsar Peter on horseback.*A huge granite boulder is the foundation for it. It was not I who told my mother of the spot chosen, or rather foreordained, by the ghost, and I confess that when I return to see that statue I am afraid that I shall be afraid."

The Prince de Ligne, an amiable playboy who lives only for the moment, is also at this supper; he makes bold to shrug:

"But what does your story prove, Monseigneur?"

"That I shall die young."[16]

It was enough to give poor Mme d'Oberkirch one of her migraines, she didn't sleep a wink all night. But it's a proper heart attack she's like to have later when, at another supper, the grand duke, who "was in dizzying high spirits," suddenly called out to her:

"Well, Madame, you were well and truly taken in by my ghost story, weren't you?"

"What, Monseigneur, do you mean it is not true?"

"Of course it isn't true, it never was true. It is just a piece of nonsense I made up to frighten you a little."[17]

Chantilly was the high point of their stay in Ile de France. The illustrious guests, still following in Joseph II's footsteps, soon move on to the provinces —Touraine, Normandy, and that "Lower Brittany, which is a ghastly country, where the people gabble some incomprehensible tongue . . . The men, dressed in skins, reminded the Comte du Nord of his Tatars."[18]

Before leaving Paris the monarchs-to-be visited the manufactury of Sèvres, where they ordered three hundred thousand livres' worth of porcelain.

---

*It still exists, and is undoubtedly the most successful equestrian statue ever made, a miracle of balance and technique. A Frenchman, Falconet, had designed, cast and erected it but, exasperated by administrative red tape, he left Petersburg before its inauguration, which takes place at the very time of this chapter, in the summer of 1782.

"The same day, the royal couple also visited the prisons, wishing to see how the prisoners were treated, and to give them their alms in person. In the different prisons they visited, they distributed over eighteen thousand francs.* As a result, their names were blessed by all."

LA FAYETTE

12

JUNE 1782

What a Contrast!

During his stay in Versailles and Paris the apprentice tsar met three men of liberty. Four if you count Necker, who has been living in pseudo-exile at Saint-Ouen since his dismissal, and whom Paul went to contemplate as a sort of financial trouble-shooter, a wizard kept in reserve for a rainy day here or somewhere else, an expert in royal economics—because every sovereign on earth these days is beginning to need specialists to help him understand his own budget. And also because Necker controls one of the least shaky banks in Europe. But the financier had withdrawn into disenchantment, and the "Comte du Nord" didn't dare commit himself too far with a man in disgrace, so their conversation never got beyond the weather.

The three other liberty-freaks, three of the men who were most dangerous to the system prevailing at the French court in 1782 but who were tolerated because for the moment they were only showing the tips of their tails, were La Fayette, back from America in triumph; Beaumarchais, about to fight the battle of *The Marriage of Figaro;* and Condorcet, who has just been elected to the Académie Française.

La Fayette, as usual, shot back from Yorktown like a popped cork: his homecomings are like the colic, you just have to get used to it. The formalities of the English capitulation were hardly over and the American and French troops settling into their winter quarters when he applied to Congress in Philadelphia for a leave of absence that nobody had any reason to refuse him: after all, he wasn't being paid a single American penny and had just made a fair-sized hole in his own pocket for the rebel cause. And he didn't have to ask the French

*Modern-day equivalents: two million francs for porcelain [$400,000], one hundred and twenty thousand for the prisoners [$24,000].

ministers for permission, because his official status was that of an American officer. He had just experienced the supreme joy of his life. "I count among my finest moments the time when M. de Saint-Simon's division"—he was commanding a French regiment—"was united with my own army, and when I commanded the three camp marshals in turn, with the troops under their orders."[1] And, by holding out in Virginia for a whole year against the enemy and a good many "friends," he had also turned the tide of war southward and been the detonator of the victory. He is now twenty-four, and has chalked up a respectable score in the last five of his years for a child-bridegroom, the runt of the litter of rakes from the Epée de Bois, the provincial orphan who used to dance so badly at Versailles that the Queen snickered. His confused runaway attempt in the summer of 1777 has turned the redheaded stripling into the "Hero of Two Worlds," as certain flatterers are starting to call him. But in America the war's turning gray again. Now they'll just sit down and stare at each other across the snowdrifts. Washington and Rochambeau, the two "official" victors at Yorktown, will be getting better star billing than ever, at the head of their buried armies, pending negotiations or the resumption of hostilities. At the moment of surrender in Yorktown, La Fayette was already mortified to see himself relegated to the status of a mere staff officer. There, he was just one of the winning team, but in Paris he'll be *the* winner—provided he gets there fast enough and can prevent the hysteria of public opinion from veering in some other direction.

He wanted to see his wife again, too, and his mistress and his children, and he wanted to dazzle his in-laws, those Noailleses who had been so snooty to him. From now on, he always needs a political motivation too, so he imagines himself acting as a hyphen between the young republic and the old monarchy, as the man of the Alliance. The Americans were encouraging him; he had official standing with Franklin and the other diplomats. On November 23, 1781, therefore, Congress passed a resolution saying that "Major General Marquis de La Fayette shall be authorized to go to France and to return only at the period that he shall judge most suitable . . . The Secretary for Foreign Affairs shall inform the plenipotentiary ministers of the United States that Congress desires them to confer with the Marquis de La Fayette and take advantage of his knowledge of the position of public affairs in the United States . . . The [American] superintendent of finance, the Secretary for Foreign Affairs, and the War Office, shall give the Marquis de La Fayette, as touching the affairs of their respective departments, all communications that may enable him to accelerate the sending of help that might be granted to the United States by His Most Christian Majesty."[2]

He'll be the Frenchman who knows most about American affairs—considerably more than he knows about those of his own kingdom, which he left a colonel and is re-entering a "camp marshal" or full general of the army empowered, if war should break out on the continent, to take command of vast numbers of men. His appointment, signed by Louis XVI and dating from the surrender at Yorktown, crossed with him on the seas as he winged back aboard the *Alliance*, the ship for which he seems to have a commuter ticket; but on this occasion the winter blasts drive her straight to the port of Orient at top speed and without incident.* And what a change from his first return, in 1778, when he'd been rapped on the knuckles and seated on the sidelines. In 1782, he reaches Paris on that very 21st of January when the crowds are pouring along the sanded streets to the Hôtel de Ville to celebrate the birth of the dauphin and churching of the Queen. The Hôtel de Noailles was empty: everybody in it, including his wife, had gone to the reception. Upon learning of his arrival, Marie Antoinette graciously sweeps the half-fainting Adrienne into her carriage and conducts her to her husband, surrounded by a cheering throng and drawn by the laboring women from the district around the markets, who are called "fishwives" [with implications of strong smell] by those who have never soiled their hands. They come bearing flowers and wreaths of laurel to their little marquis, a sign that his fame is finally seeping down to "the people." From the Queen to the fishwives: who in Paris can do better this year? On February 11 the actress playing *Iphigénie* comes to his box and crowns him with laurels. True, a few of his playmates aren't so enthusiastic: "All the young bloods present disapproved of Mlle Torlay's gesture; they are furious to see M. de La Fayette named camp marshal at twenty-four without having gone through a period as brigadier. They say he has done nothing particular and that they would have done as much if they had had the same opportunities."[3]

So what. Here he is anyway, on June 8, in the drawing rooms of Versailles, for the most spectacular full-dress ball yet given by Marie Antoinette. Tonight Versailles can vie with Chantilly. Everything is beautiful, bursting with light, music, and possibly a shade too much heat, although the tall bay windows stand open, letting in the scent of newmown grass. The Gallery of Mirrors "is the handsomest hall in Europe." It is lit "with about five thousand candles, which seemed many times that number because of the mirrors," and also with *girandoles,* those star-shaped objects in wax and paper that make the very walls dance. "The whole Court was dressed in its grandest attire; the women who danced had white satin dominoes, with small panniers and *petites queues* [little tails, location unspecified—*Trans.*]."[4] This is the achievement of Marie-Jeanne Bertin, daughter of a constable and ex-"apprentress" to a milliner in Abbeville who had "gone up" to Paris—down, actually—and, in ten years, become a

*The difficulties of his first return and his vexations in Paris are related in volume II; on February 2 he cedes his regiment to his brother-in-law, the Vicomte de Noailles, for the trifling sum of 60,000 livres, or 360,000 modern francs [$72,000].

power in Court through the favor of the queen: they call her the "Minister of Fashion." The thirty girls in her shop "at the sign of the Grand Mogul" on the Rue Saint-Honoré have been working on this ball for a month. "Everywhere one looked [in the shop] one saw nothing but damasks, dauphines,* satins, brocades, and lace. The ladies of the Court asked to be shown them out of curiosity, but until the Comtesse du Nord had worn them it was forbidden to publish the models. Mlle Bertin seemed a singular person, inflated with her own importance, talking to princesses as though she were their equal."⁵ Maybe she was? This summer, as the result of an *entente* between the Queen and her, a new color, brought from Bordeaux, has become all the rage.

> The year 1782 saw the advent of the fashion for white. It had been reigning for several years in Bordeaux, whence it was brought by the Creoles from our colonies. There was abundance of gold in that city, yet all one saw was percale and calico; luxury got its due nevertheless, for the rich merchants claimed that the cloth could only be properly washed in the tropics, and sent their wives' gowns, and their own linens, to be laundered in Santo Domingo. The Queen decided that she wanted to dress *à la bordelaise*. Appearing all in white, she dazzled the court; and soon the boulevards of Paris were covered with white gowns . . . There was sharp censure of this simplicity, at first among the courtiers and then throughout the kingdom; and yet, by one of those contradictions that are more common in France than elsewhere, at the same time as people were criticizing the Queen they were also feverishly copying her. Every woman wanted to have the same *déshabillé*, the same bonnet, and the same plumes she had been seen wearing. They flocked to her milliner, a woman called Bertin; it was a positive revolution in our ladies' attire, and conferred a kind of importance upon this woman.

The days of "dauphin-shit-yellow" are over. "One can no longer distinguish between a duchess and an actress!"⁶

France in white from top to toe . . . One of the novelties confronting La Fayette upon his return, along with those scaffoldings so high that one wonders if there will ever be an end to the heavenward ascension of ladies' headdresses and the raising of carriage roofs to accommodate them. The provincial Mme d'Oberkirch is "still unable to overcome the difficulty of sitting fully dressed and coiffed in a carriage from Paris to Versailles; one could not be more uncomfortable, and the women who must act as postilions [*sic*] several times a week must be mightily weary of it."⁷ La Fayette, however, doesn't have much time to sympathize with them.

Where are the lowly huts of Valley Forge, the swamps in which he was

*Dauphine is a brocaded woolen cloth, of several mottled hues. The patronage of the future tsarina was very important to Mlle Bertin, because all the ladies of the Russian aristocracy followed the grand duchess into her shop. Mlle Bertin was then at the summit of her success and had just bought a handsome house at Epinay-sur-Seine where she lived in stubborn celibacy, ruling her household of nephews and nieces with an iron hand.

floundering six months ago on the banks of the York? Gone. He's home again now, inside this ring of two thousand idlers who govern his real world. Like all the rest of them, he is struck by that instant of supreme majesty when the assembled Court stands motionless for the entrance, to the blare of trumpet fanfares, of the royal family. The well-meaning young King has filled out considerably, as he approaches his thirtieth birthday, but he's also learning to smile through the fog of his myopia; Marie Antoinette still has "the same long, regular face, the nose at once aquiline and yet pointed at the tip, the high forehead, the lively blue eyes, the lily-and-roses complexion, and small pouting mouth," the mark of the Hapsburgs—but she's grown a lot heavier and fuller-breasted since the birth of her second child. She has become a real woman. Nobody could stand straight or walk better. Behind the royal couple, Provence with his spare tires, Artois with his chin, and their wives, the two ugly ducklings from Savoy; and a fat, jerkily moving girl—Elisabeth, the King's younger sister. Followed by a Niagara of chamberlains, torch-bearers, equerries, senior officials in gold, silver, and diamonds . . . a procession a thousand years in the making. With every fiber of his heredity and upbringing, La Fayette belongs to that ritual. He has to cross an ocean before he can feel himself a republican, and even then his conversion extends no further than allegiance to a sort of elected king named Washington. Tonight, at the very apex of another universe, he is the man of the hour, and in this sense too he's the hero of two worlds.

"The Comte and Comtesse du Nord did not dance, nor did the King nor any of his family nor the princes of the blood, apart from the Queen and the Comte d'Artois who opened the ball with a quadrille and danced very well and often, and then all the brilliant young people. Three quadrilles were danced simultaneously . . . For her dress, the Queen had copied the beautiful painting of 'La Belle Gabrielle.'* I [the Duc de Croÿ] was particularly delighted by a dance she performed most flawlessly, as did he, with M. de La Fayette."[8]

The ladies wish she would hurry up and choose a different partner, for La Fayette's new aura is more than gossip: he has grown stronger, more assured, tanned. His sensual lips underline fine features, a teasing expression. His wife is idiotically in love with him; "the force of her sentiment was such that for some months she nearly fainted when he left her room. Such a fierce passion terrified her by the thought that she would not always be able to conceal it from him and that it would be an embarrassment. To that end, and for him alone, she sought to temper her emotion."[9] Immediately upon his return, her warrior had made her pregnant again. For her that is paradise enough, and she carefully hides from him the fact that she knows he has gone back to Aglaé

*In other words, she was dressed à la Henri IV.

d'Hunolstein—or rather that Aglaé has rushed into his arms. And after treating him so disdainfully in the days when he had barely edged out the Duc de Chartres for possession of her favors, and after replacing him so well and frequently during his campaigns. There was a whole melancholy of his American memories named Aglaé, the times when he used to exhale heavy bivouac sighs about her to discreet friends back home. And here she is again, almost overeager now, still good to handle but she's put on weight too, wears more make-up than she should, and has seen so much of the devil at Bagatelle and Mousseaux that she's got him in her flesh. Tonight Gilbert is also ogling a third woman, one of the few who might be capable of resisting him, Diane Adélaïde, Comtesse de Simiane, née de Damas, whose three brothers belong to his gilded youth club. One of them was La Fayette's companion in America. The prettiest woman in France, they say in this milieu where they always say too much. But she has a nice body, of which her husband apparently makes little use—and the face of an angel one would like to bite. "The sense of these advantages has instilled in her, from childhood, a desire to avoid becoming the subject of envy."[10] An *insaisissable.* Poor La Fayette has a very busy homecoming, what with the three women of the traditional panoply: the legitimate spouse, the official mistress, and the infinitely desired. Ah, there's dancing and quadrilles tonight, in the blaze of Versailles's five thousand candles; and a man is only twenty-four once in his life, and will there be a second Yorktown? Will the future tsar make two trips from Petersburg to compliment a conqueror of the English? And will the springtime belles ever again have such extraordinary "waterfall" hairdos, "extremely stylish but rather cumbersome, with little flat curved bottles made to follow the shape of the head, containing water in which the stems of real flowers are dipped to keep them fresh among the curls"?[11] Lip-level gardens. Let's dance. And then let's sup at Mme de Lamballe's, it's only midnight. "The circle was small but very select. After supper there was lotto, a game that is all the fashion, and a great deal of money was lost. After the lotto, there was more dancing, and the Queen performed another quadrille. This little ball was incomparably gayer than the other one. The King only looked in and then retired"—these occasions always put him to sleep. "After his departure, pleasure was not cramped by protocol, and all were delighted with this form of intimacy, which the Queen did nothing to discourage."

But there's an end to everything. Even they have to go to bed sometime, around about the hour when the clods who work for and are governed by them are getting up. "It was a radiant morning and daylight had come, the peasants were going about their daily tasks. What a contrast between their calm faces and our own drawn features," observes Mme d'Oberkirch, who is not often given to philosophizing. "The rouge had gone from our cheeks and the powder from our hair . . ."[12]

The hour at which La Fayette tends to wake up, too, like the peasants, whenever the thought of America and the Insurgents—still at war, still threatened—tickles the side of him that never goes completely to sleep. The English have sent Grenville to Paris as unofficial negotiator, to see which way Franklin is blowing and sound out Vergennes. On June 2 Franklin notes, "The Marquis de La Fayette came to see me and stayed to dinner. He is worried by the delay. He cannot leave for America until he knows with certainty whether or no there will be a treaty."[13] On June 10 Gilbert goes to make a scene to Grenville in person: "I have remained here longer than I should have done in order to see whether we would have peace or war, but as I see that the hope of peace is only a game and you are merely trifling with us, I do not intend to stay longer, and shall leave in a few days."[14] And then there's the eternal opacity of Vergennes, who has become, since Maurepas's death, the weightiest if not the principal minister. Impossible to figure out what, or indeed whether, he's thinking. On June 20 La Fayette, at the end of his patience, calls on Franklin again: "The marquis has seen M. de Vergennes, who received M. Grenville, but he can tell me nothing of what passed between them."[15] At least as long as Maurepas was lingering, there was some recourse, somebody to turn to when one could obtain nothing from the ministers of foreign affairs and war. But there is no way to say so much as a syllable to the King directly about what goes on in his kingdom, and when his chief clerk Vergennes starts making like a stone wall, where is one to turn to try a cushion-shot approach? And here's another novelty, the most singular of all at the time of La Fayette's homecoming, which also marks the watershed of this reign: Louis XVI has not replaced Maurepas. *L'Etat, c'est lui.* For the time being there is no "principal minister" or supercounselor, although God knows there'd been enough speculation on the subject. Some people were betting on Vergennes, but the King presumably finds him too boring: others were speculating on the recall of Necker or even Choiseul, the eternal hope of the Queen's camp. One can't imagine Miromesnil, Ségur, or Castries outside their fields of justice, war, and navy; they haven't got the stature. Joly de Fleury, who took over Necker's job at the treasury, is an insignificant place-keeper. So who?

The spirit of contradiction that forms the substratum of Louis XVI's character is undoubtedly what has induced him to fox them all. Keeping one's court on tenterhooks really is a pleasure for a king; and it also suits his pathological inability to make a choice. "We observed that the King was truly delighted to see all the intrigues foiled, that he did not find it so difficult as he had imagined to govern alone, and we never saw him looking better pleased, or more decided, or indeed more cheerful . . .

"To understand the state of utter prostration of Versailles at that time, one must remember that courtiers have a sort of absolute, official need to know where to go toadying, whether it is to the prime minister, his confessor, his valet, friends or mistress, or to the mistresses of the King, if he has any, and down to their lowliest attendants: one must always be toadying somewhere. Judge, then, of their consternation: they no longer knew where to turn!"[16]

Thus we might now witness the hatching-out of a true head of state—if Louis XVI had it in him. But that's the big question. Maurepas himself was almost nothing, precious little in any event: a rhyming punster. But in his youth at least he had had a sense of the state, and the experience of half a century of pessimism had made him intimately acquainted with every inch of these people swarming over Versailles. With him died government by skepticism; will Louis XVI now replace it with government by vacuum? "The King did not make the slightest change in his life and style. He went hunting and worked at the customary times, seeing each minister alone, taking care to speak to none about anything but his particular business, stopping them if they seem inclined to stray from it, appearing, moreover, quite firm and determined, so that in this respect nothing stood out, and everyone reserved his position."[17] Perhaps France is heading back to the 1740s, when Louis XV also took it into his head, after the death of the old Cardinal de Fleury, to govern alone or pretend to. Twenty million souls in the hands of a man nobody knows. As far as hastening the end of the war in America is concerned, it's enough to make La Fayette foam with irritation. But with him that's also a habit.

On June 24 this year, he officially joins the ranks of that scattering of people throughout Europe who are trying to see a little further than the ends of their noses, the Freemasons. In the absence of a more substantial King, a subterranean republic is being formed, in a sort of public clandestinity employing rituals parallel to those of the religions it aspires to transcend. Back in 1775, when Gilbert was hardly more than a boy, he had been allowed to attend a meeting of "La Candeur" lodge in Paris, but only as an observer. In America he had also visited two or three lodges with Washington, who was a Freemason himself. But now he becomes a full member of "the Reverend Lodge of St. John of Scotland of the Social Contract, Mother Lodge of the Scottish Rite in France," which, along with the "Nine Sisters," has the most influence on "enlightened" opinion in Paris. A fair share of his companions-at-arms or at-leisure are fellow members. He's no longer alone, even in his political dreams. A new springboard:

> In the year of the Venerable Lodge 5782, on the 24th day of the 4th month, the R.L. of St. John of Scotland of the Social Contract, Mother Lodge of the Scottish Rite in France, duly convened and regularly assembled under the geometric points known only to the children of the Light . . . the proceedings were opened in the accustomed manner; the record of the preceding assembly was read out, after which the R.L. masonically applauded . . .
>
> A brother Master of Ceremonies having announced that brother La Fayette was outside the door and seeking entry to the temple, the Venerable having dispatched several Scottish knights to receive this brother, preceded by two

Masters of Ceremonies, the Venerable Lodge wished, by admitting brother La
Fayette with the honors ordinarily accorded only to Masons of the highest degrees, to give him a tangible mark of the esteem in which it holds his military
talents, whose example is certain to form heroes.[18]

THE MARRIAGE OF FIGARO,
ACT 4, SCENE 9

13

MAY 1782

My Sober Self and My Frivolous Creation

The soirée arranged for the Comte and Comtesse du Nord on May 26 is also
part of a cunning and highly subversive plot against the state, although our
wide-eyed Comtesse d'Oberkirch completely misses the point—she thinks it's
just another Parisian lark. "On our way back from the Opéra we went to the
home of Mme la Comtesse du Nord where a special pleasure was in store for
us . . . : M. de Beaumarchais was to read his *Marriage of Figaro* to Their Imperial
Highnesses; at that time it was not yet known to the stage, as the authorities
had refused permission to perform it."[1] The trouble, dear baroness, is that in
this case "the authorities" is Louis XVI himself. Beaumarchais has been working on his play for six years. Six months ago it was approved "by acclamation,
by the French Acting Company." Two months ago, the royal censor appointed
for the occasion—a man named Coqueley (whose name was instantly decom-
posed by the Parisians into Coqü-et-ley) [cocu: cuckold; "et-ley" may be *ailé*
(winged), or *et laid* (and ugly, as in "poor but undeserving")—*Trans.*]—gave
his authorization with a grudging jab of his pen. But six weeks ago, Louis XVI
tossed the first veto of his reign into the balance. This is one of those instances
in which old boneheap Maurepas was so useful as a screen between the King's
prudery and the prevailing tone of the age. If the Mentor had been alive, he'd
have let Figaro go hang himself wherever he pleased, with a shrug.

But a new play by Beaumarchais, whose *Barber of Seville* set Paris on its
ears seven years ago and whose *Mémoires* against Parlement in the Goëzman
case almost caused riots a little earlier, is an event requiring the King's personal attention. His obsession, the prime password of his reign and the moral
legacy left him by his father, is "to protect religion from the wicked." Louis
XVI accordingly determined to see for himself what this authorization was
permitting.

"When I entered the Queen's inner closet," relates Mme Campan, her lady of honor,[2] "I found her alone with the King; a chair and a small table were already placed before them, and on the table lay an enormous manuscript in several notebooks. The King said to me:

" 'This is Beaumarchais's play. You must read it to us. Some places will be very hard to follow because of the corrections and additions . . . You will speak to no one of what you are going to read.'

"I began. The King kept interrupting me with exclamations, always well founded* whether of praise or censure. His most frequent comment would be:

" 'Very poor taste! The man is forever indulging in that vice of the Italian *concetti.*'†

"At Figaro's monologue, where he attacks various elements of the administration, and even more when I came to the tirade on the state prisons, the King rose quickly to his feet and said,

" 'This is abominable. The play will never be acted. It would be necessary to destroy the Bastille before the performance of this play could be anything other than a dangerous indiscretion. The man is making light of all that should be respected in government.' "

With these words Louis XVI is born. Neither fool nor churl, this man who has so little talent for enjoying himself is primarily a politician, of the most conservative species. People were expecting him to react to Count Almaviva's *jus primae noctis* or the flutterings of the Countess and Suzanne around a half-naked pageboy, but he couldn't care less about them. Louis XVI is not deaf. "The tirade on the state prisons" in which Mirabeau has lost his youth and into which poor Desgranges has just been thrown untried (he was a young life-guardsman who was bragging—anything's possible, after all—that he had slept with the more than commonly unprepossessing Comtesse d'Artois): the Bastille, from which Linguet has only just emerged fuming with rage;** and the Château d'If and Pierre-en-Scize north of Lyons; and Doullens; and the Fort de Joux; and thirty more in the King of France's game of hide-and-seek. No; he stuck it out for five acts, until he came to those few lines that transform the *Marriage* into a political weapon, when Figaro's voice changes tone in the midst of his soliloquy *(O femme! femme! femme! créature faible et décevante*—O, woman, woman, woman! weak and deceitful creature) while waiting for Suzanne. The wrapping on his discourse is pretty transparent, and Louis XVI,

---

Sic. When Mme Campan publishes her *Mémoires,* under the Restoration, she is running a pension for aristocratic young ladies and aspires to be a character-former of the "right-minded."

†A term that was beginning to be used to mean an impertinent and rather anti-establishment witticism.

**After being disbarred in Paris he had founded a periodical, his famous *Annales,* in London, but was ambushed by the French police during a quick trip to the continent.

who is not a ladies' man, has no difficulty grasping the true subject of the speech: "Just because you are a great lord, you think you are also a great genius! . . . Birth, fortune, a rank, positions, they all create so much pride! What have you done to deserve so much? You gave yourself the trouble of being born, and that was all." The life of the poor blighter with his conjuring tricks flicks past like the pages of a picture-book against a background of the Gallery of Mirrors, and here come the words that bring Louis XVI bounding out of his armchair: "Having not a sou to my name, I write about the value of money and interest; and instantly I see, from the depths of a coach, the drawbridge of a fortress dropping down before me, and all my hope and freedom died inside its walls. *(Rises.)* How I should love to get my hands on one of those four-day potencies who are so nonchalant about the evil done by their order, once his pride had been tamed by a resounding disgrace! I should say to him that absurdities in print have no power except where their course is dammed; that without the freedom to criticize there can be no flattering hymns of praise; and that only little men fear little writings."[3]

More than enough to give one little king a big scare.

But for Beaumarchais no battle is ever over. He goes on flailing about in the fog: "Read well or ill, or commented with evil intent, *they* pronounced the play to be abominable, and without knowing in what I had offended, because of course no explanation was given, I submitted myself to the inquisition, compelled to guess what my crimes were, and I judged myself to be tacitly proscribed; but as this proscription by the Court merely inflamed the curiosity of the town, I was also condemned to give innumerable readings."[4] Well, if ever a condemned man connived at his torture it was he; private readings were the only weapon he had left with which to assault the royal fortress. He had to lay siege to Louis XVI by creeping from drawing room to drawing room as though they were so many trenches. But what a delectable war, to be fighting them with themselves! His whole life for the past thirty years. Just as he learned how to take watches apart working for his father, he's also learned a few tricks about manipulating this society he abhors although every millimeter of his skin adheres to it.

He read the play to the Fronsacs (son of the old Maréchal de Richelieu) and to the Vaudreuils, to Mme de Lamballe and the Polignacs, to farmers-general and financiers, and even to a few of those high-court judges he scourges in the character of Brid'Oison. First take Paris, then move on to Versailles. Trianon would be the toughest nut to crack. Once the Queen made up her mind, the King wouldn't have much say. But Beaumarchais is a long way from that now. He snatches at the opportunity for a little blackmail made possible by the visit of the "Norths": Catherine II, informed by her gossip-spy Grimm, had given out that nothing would please her better than to have the play performed in Petersburg (most of the sovereigns of the day liked to seem more French than the King of France). Beaumarchais wasn't too eager. His battlefield was here at home: a watchmaker's son is naked anywhere else. Also, he had already burnt his fingers once, in his dealings with Maria Theresa. But it does no harm to let the Court of France know that one might conceivably do without it. Grimm plays go-between to the illustrious travelers and the muzzled author, in the hysterical style befitting a man who has spent thirty years pleading not-guilty. "You are to know, Sir," he writes Beaumarchais on May 24, "that there was much talk of the *Marriage of Figaro* today at dinner in the home of M. le Comte du Nord, that M. le Comte and Mme la Comtesse showed a keen desire to know the play, and that it was agreed that the author would be invited to come Sunday around seven in the evening, and to have the goodness to bring his play and read it . . . I believe that this reading must not be refused and that, far from damaging the plan to have it performed, it might considerably assist the project, because if, as I make no doubt, the play produces the impression it habitually does, the listeners will be all the more encouraged to undertake some action on behalf of its performance. I thought it my duty to inform you of the state of affairs but I do most earnestly entreat you, Sir, not to compromise me, for in giving my opinion I have been no more than an onlooker."[5]

Beaumarchais has an auxiliary advantage: he's the only decent author Paris has got to show the grand duke. Abbé Raynal and Mercier are in exile; Diderot is aging fast inside his shell; this season's craze is Abbé Delille, a clergyman so hot in pursuit of women that his cassock's on fire, notwithstanding a face "all in zigzags, with a large mouth that speaks pretty verse and a pair of eyes, rather grayish and sunken, with which he can do whatever he likes."[6] The only thing wrong with him is that his "pretty verse" is flat as a flounder and capable of sending insomniacs straight into the arms of Morpheus. He has recently perpetrated a gigantic poem in four cantos on *Les Jardins,* which almost attains the absolute in delicate affectation. "In the first canto the author undertakes to orchestrate the water, flowers, lawns, and shade; in the second, flowers, water, shade, and lawns; in the third and fourth, he is still orchestrating the shade, flowers, lawns, and water . . ."[7] And this is the author of the day. So perhaps, instead of Abbé Delille, we might pull Beaumarchais out of his box.

Once the formalities are out of the way he is asked to be seated opposite the future masters of the world, in the apartment filled with Oriental vases and exquisite furniture reserved for them in the Russian ambassador's town house on the corner of the Rue de Gramont and the old boulevard, a slightly eccentric part of Paris that tends to be noisy in the evening. The heavy drapes have been drawn. The spectators are about to watch a scene, played for themselves alone, which very few people have witnessed and very few more ever will: Beaumarchais reading the forbidden *Marriage*. He was fifty on January 17.

Still a fine figure of a man, a shade stout, a trifle ponderous, the kind whose erudition in all matters pertaining to pleasure sends frustrated ladies into ecstasies the moment he walks in the door. The chaste d'Oberkirch feels herself going all limp at the mere sight of him sinking into his chair with the poise he acquired at Versailles in the days when he was teaching music to the daughters of Louis XV: this rogue is one of us. "What a difference, between M. de Beaumarchais and M. de La Harpe:* Just as I was repelled by the weasel-face of M. de La Harpe, so I was charmed by the fine open features of M. de Beaumarchais, full of wit, perhaps a little bold. I was found at fault in this, for he is said to be a worthless fellow. I do not deny it, it is possible, but he does have prodigious wit, is brave as any lion, and unshakeable in his determination . . . A watchmaker's son, he has, by his own merits, achieved familiarity with the most illustrious persons; everyone who has sought to make sport of him has come to grief; he has overcome many obstacles and amassed an immense fortune . . . I am assured that he is passionately fond of his daughter, and a good father can never be a bad-hearted man."[8] And the fact that the said daughter is motherless, at least officially, only adds spice to the story. Eugénie de Beaumarchais was born five years ago, the product of her father's altar- and contract-less marriage with Marie-Thérèse de Willermawlaz, a young bourgeoise of Swiss origin, with heavy features but an unobtrusive appeal, who used to come and ask him, in the days of the Goëzman trial, to play the harp at what may have been a rather compromising hour. She brings him the tranquil side of love, "the vague melancholy of the sun half-hidden by cloud, French superficiality on a pedestal of Swiss dignity,"[9] and she knows how to keep his clerks in hand while he goes gadding. Why hasn't he married her? Because he forgot to, more or less. And maybe because, after two scandal-ridden widowerhoods, he is suspicious of marriage. And certainly because he is still fired by other fuels: a no-holds-barred eroticism with Mme de Godeville, an ambivalent platonicism with "Ninon," the seventeen-year-old provincial girl who writes to him from Aix-en-Provence because he's famous and asks his advice about her troubled lovelife, "in which she has been engaged since the age of twelve." He files these items from a lovelorn column, like all his other papers—for he is a methodical man—in a folder inscribed "Case of My Young Client Whom I Have Not Met."[10] Marie Thérèse has nothing to lose by waiting around. She has one great advantage over all the others, that of being there all the time, in the apartment in the mansion on the Rue Vieille-du-Temple

---

*La Harpe, a verbose and pedantic author who edits a *Correspondance littéraire,* a competitor of Grimm's, is also one of the most influential members of the Academy and has just bored the "Norths" to distraction with a stodgy address delivered at their official reception. "If M. de La Harpe were injured," Beaumarchais said, "he would bleed bile."

above his offices, where, when he's around, he leads the most irreproach-ably respectable existence imaginable between his mistress-wife, his sister Julie, the nephews and nieces he looks after, his friends, and faithful servants.

But just now Beaumarchais is living at least a triple life: there are his rainbow-hued love affairs, ranging from scarlet to forget-me-not blue; his public activities, which are tangled beyond belief (he is becoming less and less of a secret agent and more and more of a dealer in anything with the United States, up to his neck in his own mare's nest and likely to be smothered by it; and the truth of his "immense fortune" is that he's on the verge of bankruptcy because he's been about as crafty as a goldfish and the Congress in Philadelphia is refusing to acknowledge his bills); and finally, his life as a man of letters. He has just founded the Société des Auteurs, he's editing a complete Voltaire in seventy-two volumes, which is giving him no end of headaches; and with a craftsman's loving care he is manufacturing his own little bomb to blow up the century, his *Marriage of Figaro,* which he has been perfecting and polishing with icy passion for the last six or seven years. You don't need to look too hard for him at home or among his friends or his imbroglios: that play is where he is.

No bomb was ever more prettily packaged. The leaves are painstakingly strung together with pink ribbons, and Beaumarchais's marvelous handwrit-ing, so clean and sharply modeled, is even more legible in this copy than in the manuscript submitted to the French Acting Company.* The whole is enclosed in a strong pasteboard envelope upon which Pierre Augustin has calligraphed *Opuscule comique,* like a soldier camouflaging his fortin with branches. Does he plunge right in with Figaro's and Suzanne's opening lines, in the room that Count Almaviva wants to give them "in the Château d'Aguas-Frescas" but that she doesn't want to accept on account of a certain com-municating door?

> *Figaro.* Nineteen feet by twenty-six.
> *Suzanne.* Look, Figaro, how I've fixed my bonnet; do you like it better this way?

By no means: with elaborate care he extracts, instead, an introductory page, which he uses only for this type of reading, and in which he puts his listeners off their guard by comparing himself to a "clever coquette:"†

> Before beginning this reading, I must recount to you an incident that took place before my very eyes.
> A young author, at supper in someone's house, was requested to read one of his works, which was being much talked about in the world. They tried everything, even cajolery, but he would not yield. At last some person took offense and said to him,

---

*Both still exist. The first is in the Archives of the Théâtre Français, and this one, discovered by M. de Loménie, belongs to the Beaumarchais family.

†Unpublished until 1879. Found by M. de Loménie among Beaumarchais's papers.

"Sir, you are like a clever coquette who refuses to give anyone what she is dying to bestow upon all . . ."

"Leaving aside the coquette," the author replied, "your analogy is more apt than you suppose; those fair damsels and we authors suffer a common fate, that of being forgotten once the sacrifice is made . . . Be more just, or ask nothing of us. The hard work is our share; all you have is the delight . . . But, to complete your parallel . . . , I shall yield to your pleadings, inconsistent and weak as one of those fair ladies, and read you my creation."[11]

That gets them nicely softened up. How could an author who plays the ingenue like that be a real threat? Just another troubadour, one of those people we've been tossing coins to for centuries. The great can indulge without fear in the pleasure procured by equivocal situations and mirth-provoking repartee: "To drink when we are not thirsty and make love in every season, Madame; these are the only things that distinguish us from the animals . . ." An author who can actually make us smile. And he knows so well how to reassure us, too, poking fun at himself in front of everybody! "Oh, weird sequence of events!"—his life, that is, that famous comedy which Pierre Augustin Caron has been performing before the Two Worlds for so many years, now described by Figaro for our greater self-content. He's his own fall guy. Side-splitting, the way he says it—and drawing room laughter ripples over his tale, even after the tone of the speech turns distinctly sober.

Oh, weird sequence of events! How did this happen to me? Why these things and not other ones? Who fastened them to my head? Forced to pursue the path I took without meaning to, just as I shall leave it without desiring to, I have strewn its banks with as many flowers as my gaiety would allow. My gaiety, too; I call it mine without knowing if it belongs to me any more than the rest, or even what this *me* is with which I am so preoccupied: a shapeless assemblage of unknown particles, then a runty imbecile of a being, a gamboling little animal, a young man ardent for pleasure, possessing every faculty for delighting in it, working at every trade to earn my bread, here a master, there a valet, depending on fortune's whim, ambitious by vanity, hardworking by necessity, but rapturously lazy . . . An orator when danger threatens, a poet for relaxation, a musician on occasion, a lover by wild fits and starts, I have seen everything, done everything, exhausted everything . . .[12]

And there he stands, an old monkey turned solemn for the duration of a thunderbolt, packing his monologue away with the rest in its ribboned box. They applaud. They understood nothing. He has won tonight's round. For those who need a guide to conduct their conversation he has undertaken to summarize his play himself, removing all the explosive from it: it's "the most trifling of tales. A Spanish grandee* is in love with a girl whom he wants to seduce, and the efforts deployed by a fiancé (the one she is to marry) and by

*With its Inquisition and feudal paraphernalia, Spain was so outrageously backward that the injustice and absurdity one wanted to castigate in one's own country could safely be situated there.

the grandee's wife combine to thwart the designs of an absolute master whose rank, fortune, and prodigality render him easily capable of achieving them. That is all, nothing more. The play is before your eyes."[13]

And *this* is what Louis XVI is not allowing to be staged in his realm? The next day Paul Petrovich comes close to letting it be understood that Russia, even his mother's Russia, is a model of liberalism in comparison to France. His wife and he shower compliments upon Beaumarchais, who passes them along to Grimm on May 27: "Monsieur le Baron, it is the very least I can do to send you my first thanks, since it is to you that I owe the most benevolent reception which their Imperial Highnesses deigned to accord to my sober self and my frivolous creation."[14] A reception he's going to use, in the coming days, in his dealings with the Garde des Sceaux, the chief of police, and *tutti quanti,* returning to the charge again and again, not above converting it into black-mail: "M. le Prince Youssoupof, the Grand Duke's first chamberlain, has left this very minute. He renewed his request for my manuscript so that M. le Comte du Nord might take it to the empress. It is impossible for me to send it away until the play has been performed, for a comedy is not really finished until its first performance" (this to Lenoir, the chief of police) . . . What a sanctimonious scalawag:[15] St. Pierre-Augustin, evangelist of Figaro . . . it looks as if he's going to have a long preach ahead. The Garde des Sceaux doesn't even answer. Lenoir is vague. The opinion of the Grand Duke is a matter of supreme indifference to Louis XVI; Russia and France aren't going to fight a war over a second-rate ham. Who cares? All his life Beaumarchais has been remembering where he buried his bones so he can dig them up again when he needs them, even if it's years later.

LES LIAISONS DANGEREUSES,
O U
LETTRES
Recueillies dans une Société, & publiées pour l'instruction de quelques autres.

Par M. C..... DE L...

J'ai vu les mœurs de mon temps, & j'ai publié ces Lettres.
J. J. ROUSSEAU , *Préf. de la Nouvelle Héloïse.*

PREMIERE PARTIE.

A AMSTERDAM;
Et se trouve à PARIS,
Chez DURAND Neveu , Libraire , à la Sagesse, rue Galande.

M. DCC. LXXXII.

14

MAY 1782

One of Those Disastrous Meteors

If anybody had wanted to look further afield than the eternal provocateur Beaumarchais or Abbé Delille, the official sleeping pill, he could have introduced the future tsar to the season's one true author—the revelation of the year, around whom so much noise is being made that you can hardly hear yourself think—and that is the man who wrote *Les Liaisons dangereuses.* Not that anyone would have been likely to arrange the meeting: confront their Imperial

Highnesses with the perpetrator of that unspeakable ignominy? You might as well present them to a streetwalker from the Palais Royal.

Besides, how can you introduce a person who is faceless and homeless (to contemporary columnists, at any rate) and almost nameless? Can you introduce a set of initials? Because that's all you can learn from the book that has created such a stir. It was advertised in the *Mercure de France* on March 23, 1782, as one of the week's new issues: *"Les Liaisons dangereuses, ou Lettres recueillies dans une société particulière et publiées pour l'instruction de quelques autres,* par M. C . . . de L . . ."* [The book is usually known in English by its French title but has been translated as *Dangerous Acquaintances;* the remainder would read, "or letters compiled in one particular society and published for the edification of certain others."*—Trans.*] The opening page of the first edition mentions only "Amsterdam," the (alleged) city of publication, and the name of the (real) publisher; and goes on to say that the book "may be obtained in Paris at the sign of 'La Sagesse,' nephew of Durand, Bookseller, Rue Galande."[1] And a sentence from Rousseau's *Nouvelle Héloïse* rounds it off: "I have observed the customs of my time and I have published these letters."

The customs of my time? A bunch of creatures floundering around in a mudbath, most of them suffocating but a few uttering little shrieks of delight —is that *us?*

It is. Or at least it is in the mind of the author, that mysterious adjunct of Beaumarchais. What Pierre-Augustin is trying to get onto the stage with his *Marriage,* Monsieur C . . . de L . . . has just published in his *Liaisons.* A major revelation, one no society likes to contemplate: the image, far worse than that of its death, of its putrefaction. *Iam foetet.* *

Speaking of rot, that hoary sepulcher La Harpe has just yelped a warning to Grand Duke Paul and "enlightened" Russia, over which he thinks he has mentor's rights, in his *Correspondance littéraire* (aimed chiefly at St. Petersburg): "The author was apparently seeking to outdo Versac in the *Egarements* of Crébillon *fils* and Richardson's Lovelace.† His hero, M. de Valmont, is far more refined than the former and a great deal more horrible than the latter . . . One of the greatest shortcomings of this type of novel is that it gives out as the manners of the century (and the author expresses himself thus in his epigraph) what is at bottom nothing but a tale of some twenty smug wretches and sluts who think themselves possessed of great superiority of intelligence because they have elevated libertinage into a principle and made a science of depravity . . . Gross artifice, wantonly revolting atrocities and ridiculous hor-

---

*Martha's words to Jesus in the story of the resurrection of her brother Lazarus, as told by St. John (11:39): "By this time he stinketh."

†Lovelace (in *Clarissa Harlowe*) and Versac were two models of the perverted seducer in novels that had been in vogue for the past few years. Richardson had popularized the "epistolary-novel" form, which Laclos adopted for his book.

rors: such is the substance of the book, and yet its author is a man of wit,"[2] confesses a slightly crestfallen M. de La Harpe who, in his subconscious mind, would undoubtedly have cut off his right hand to be able to have written one page of the *Liaisons* as compared to his thirty cemetery-tomes.

. . . And this abomination is selling like hotcakes. The two thousand copies of the original edition went in two weeks, even at the stiff price of thirty livres,* and on April 21 the author signed a new contract with "Durand's nephew" for a second edition "on the same terms as the first."[3] Within the year, a dozen book pirates come chasing up for booty and, as is the usual practice with a book that sells, publish a dozen copies, supposedly from Geneva or Neuchâtel, for their own exclusive benefit. Marie Antoinette orders a copy in May, in spite—or because—of the clamors of the right-minded, and reads it without telling her husband, taking the precaution of having neither the author's initials nor the title stamped on the binding.† It becomes the year's breviary for many of her friends, mainly those lucky enough to set sail for the last little round in the American campaign to gain some glory fallout. On board the ship carrying them to Boston, Lauzun, the Vicomte de Broglie, the Ségur boy, and Alexandre de Lameth positively whinny with laughter when the little Baron de Montesquieu admits to being the only person present who hasn't read it. Shortly thereafter, their ship has a run-in with an English frigate, which fires a curious projectile at them, composed of two cannonballs joined by an iron bar.

"Look, friend," somebody shouts to Montesquieu. "There are the *liaisons dangereuses!*"[4]

Alexandre de Tilly, one of the Queen's young pages who had just emerged from the provinces, bears witness—much later, during the Restoration—to the furor that has made the palace of Versailles into a sort of suburban branch of the Durand bookshop. Tilly, who in riper years abandons himself to repentance after abandoning his youth to bedhopping, and becomes something like a character out of the *Liaisons* after a very cold shower, proclaims that he has "to reproach himself with having been an impassioned admirer of the book, and above all, with lending it, when it was new, to two or three women who took greater pains to hide from each other the fact that they had read it than they did to hide the fact that they did everything it taught . . . If anyone should chance to be surprised [by Tilly's remorse] it is because he looks upon *Les Liaisons dangereuses* as a mere novel to be closed after reading it in one's youth, whereas I see it as one of those disastrous meteors that appeared in a fiery sky at the end of the eighteenth century."[5]

The newsmongers are still trying to discover the name of the planet that

---

*Over 150 new francs [$30], which is a lot, even for four duodecimo volumes.
†The Queen's copy is preserved in the Bibliothèque Nationale.

has emitted this meteor. Another Paris "correspondent" (writing to London, this time) named Moufle d'Angerville is getting warm: "The book in fashion . . . is attributed to one M. de la Clo [*sic*] an officer of the artillery who has also written several smaller pieces in prose and verse" (April 29). On May 14 he fills in: "The novel *Les Liaisons dangereuses* has produced so many sensations, because of the allusions which people pretend to see in it and the maliciousness with which each reader applies the portraits in it to well-known persons . . . that the police have forbidden further sales of the book together with its mention in the catalogues of any public places where it was being read. The author is the son of a M. Chauderlot [*sic*] senior clerk of an intendant of finance; he is already much distressed by the publicity given to his book. He has portrayed monsters, and for that reason people insist that he must be one . . . He has now returned to his regiment, where he will strive to clear his name."[6]

As often, Grimm is the best informed and puts his initiates in the know way back in April: "M. C. . . de L. . . is M. Choderlos de la Clos [*sic*], an artillery officer; in the past he was known only for a few fugitive pieces in the *Almanach des Muses* . . . It has been said of M. Restif de la Bretonne that he was the 'Rousseau du ruisseau' [Rousseau of the gutter; Restif de la Bretonne was the only author of the age to write about "the people."—*Trans.*]. One might be tempted to call M. de La Clos the Restif of good society."[7] This is followed by four pages in which he utterly demolishes the book, notwithstanding the fact that it is the first great novel of modern times, the best constructed and best written, and the only one that can be read from start to finish two hundred years later without a jot or tittle of boredom. But in battles between literati there is no such thing as giving quarter. Grimm, jealous as the rest, tramples all over the filthy rag and puts parents on their guard against this danger to minors. "However bad an opinion one may have of society in general and that of Paris in particular, I believe one would encounter few liaisons in that city more dangerous to a young person than the reading of the *Liaisons dangereuses,* by M. de la Clos."[8] War has been declared on all mirrors by the people who can't stand to look at themselves anymore. Louis XVI settles Beaumarchais's hash by himself; with Laclos, everybody gets into the act.

And yet if you look a little closer, the book is nothing more than a parable of cruelty. One man and one woman, the Vicomte de Valmont and the Marquise de Merteuil, have elected permanent domicile in the camp of antimorality. What Sade in his prison writings is beginning to express in terms of physical suffering, Laclos describes in the more confined realm of cerebral orgasm: the delectable pleasure of hurting others, that conquest of the human race. There are two revolutionary innovations in his plot: firstly, the partners in perversion have so few illusions about themselves and their intentions that they become positively transparent to each other's gaze, like diamonds of the first water; and secondly, it's a woman, Mme de Merteuil, who takes the initiative. This must be the first book in the history of the world in which equality between the sexes has reached so high a level. Lovers they have been and promise to become again, at the end of the human manhunt they plan to organize, for their private pleasure and vanity, on the human acreage within their domain, lasting just long enough to suck the blood from a few more lives and add a few more to their score of broken hearts—those absurd hearts that will keep beating for love. The tightly knit action of the *Liaisons* proceeds almost with the classical rigor of the traditional theater, respecting unity of time if not of place: the first letter is dated August 3rd, the last January 14th of the following year. A five-month hecatomb. The dénouement comes when Mme de Merteuil discovers that Valmont is teetering on the brink of the trap in which he has ensnared poor Mme Tourvel and is within an ace of falling "in love" with her, as the vulgar herd understands the term. She pulls out and compels him to slaughter the doe at bay. But he, meanwhile, has moved beyond their alliance and, his mission accomplished, feels nothing but fury against his accomplice and inspiration. Their pact becomes war. They destroy each other, and the process lasts long enough for them to immolate not only the wretched Mme Tourvel but little Cécile Vollanges as well, who immures herself in a convent, and the young chevalier Danceny who joins the Order of Malta after killing Valmont in a duel. Mme de Merteuil is herself ruined, disfigured by smallpox. At least the wicked are punished, even if the good gain little by way of reward. In his preface the author swears by all that's holy that he wanted to write a moral novel, and this contention is supported by many a passage in the book, which is only lightly stippled with erotic allusions of a far milder kind than those to be found in so many other books on the shelves of so many bookshops of the time.

But what the censors of 1782 find intolerable, as do the people who deny the reality of the world Laclos has portrayed, is the tone of his "epistolary novel"—its irrefutable veracity. "If this book burns, it can only burn like ice. It is a book of History* . . . At the time of the French Revolution the French aristocracy was a physically debilitated race . . . Libertine books, therefore, can explain and account for the Revolution . . . This is a moralist's book, as lofty as the most elevated and as deep as the most profound." Elsewhere: "Quintessentially French book. A book of sociability, terrifying, but only underneath the chatter and propriety. Yes: a book of sociability."[9] In

*These sentences were jotted down by Baudelaire when he was conceiving the (unrealized) project of writing a book about *Les Liaisons dangereuses.* Of all the book's critics he understood it by far the best, and summed up its political importance in these few brief notes, followed by another highly significant phrase: "All books are immoral."

his last hours a cry breaks from Valmont's lips: "Is this how people love?"

This is how; this is how Choiseul "loved" his sister, then his wife; how Louis XV loved la Pompadour, how Philippe de Chartres loves the great ladies of his orgies at Mousseaux and how La Fayette, now that he's dying for Mme de Simiane, is beginning to "love" Aglaé d'Hunolstein; not to mention their elders, covered with mistresses and lovers like doughboys covered with lice —the Contis, Richelieus, the Maréchale de Luxembourg and Princesse de Rohan-Guéménée—"for such is this country," writes Besenval who knows what he's writing about,* "that, so long as one is opulent and bears a fine name, not only is one forgiven everything but one can spend one's old age basking, after a youth of utter ignominy, in the esteem and respect of all."[10]

CHODERLOS DE LACLOS

15

MAY 1782

Leading a Double Life

Where is he in this month of May and what is he doing, this maker of monsters, whom people insist "must be one too"? Is he really as upset as he claims to be by all the fur flying around him? He asked for it, after all, it's his revenge upon that tomblike silence. Pierre-Ambroise-François Choderlos de Laclos is forty years old, the age at which genius must either out or choke to death.†

Perhaps it's the far-off Spanish origins of his family, who settled in Franche-Comté in the days of Charles V, that give him that gauntness and the beanpole height. And his shyness, too, and glowering pride. He's sensitive. Artillery Captain-Major Laclos will tolerate nothing half-hearted in the (usually excellent) reports of his superiors. When he was a "sub-aide-major" one of his comrades, Burtin, was promoted "aide-major" of a neighboring regiment ahead of him, and Laclos's protestations filled a hefty folder in the office of the military governor of the Dauphiné: they should give him the rank of

*The Comte de Besenval, an "accomplished" Swiss gentlemen who, at sixty, is the "old man" in Marie Antoinette's immediate circle.

†He was christened in the Saint-Michel parish of Amiens on October 19, 1741, but the spelling in the church records is "de la Clos"; after 1782 he signs himself "Laclos." As is customary, the name by which he is known is the last in the series, François.

"aide-major" too, even without the pay. They did in the end, but not without a sarcastic comment by the inspector: "This officer will never perform his duty save for ambition."[1] These days, we find him in the La Rochelle stagecoach that shuttles him twice a year between Paris, where he goes to negotiate with his publisher and see for himself how his book is selling, and his garrison on the island of Aix. "A tall, thin, sallow person in black" to those who don't like him;[2] but he loves to don his handsome royal blue uniform, specially designed for the new artillery corps, with the scarlet facings and epaulets that make up for his narrow shoulders, all glittering with gold buttons. That spareness, the fine features, and the pallor "are illuminated by beautiful blue eyes and a willful and probing expression,"[3] the expression shared by great writers and ragpickers, always on the lookout for anything left lying around.

Chartres, Châteaudun, Vendôme, Tours, Poitiers, Niort . . . The high-road to Charente that grows greener and greener, with more and more copses along the roadside, and little fields in which a sprinkling of cherry and apple trees is beginning to blossom. Three nights at the inn, chosen at the whim of the coachmen and according to the condition of the road; heavy rain adds another day to the journey. Inside the big wooden box that shakes the passengers until their teeth rattle, what notary from Saintonge or châtelaine from Poitou could ever guess that their traveling companion is the man who's keeping Versailles awake nights? Laclos has little in common with Beaumarchais—one short hour with the latter and you're breathing a different air. But there is nothing immediately striking about Laclos either, and he was brought up in Picardy, where children are seen and not heard.

True, as Moufle d' Angerville says, Laclos is the son of one of the King's officials, but a by no means insignificant one: his father, Jean-Ambroise Choderlos de Laclos, who is old but still alive and who took considerable pains with his son's education and seems never to have crossed his inclinations,* was "secretary to the office of the intendant of Picardy and Artois," and as such, serving Intendant Chauvelin, he had come to know all the ins and outs of provincial doings and beings. The fate of a Turgot: it enriched the heart and the intelligence but not the pocketbook. "It does not surprise me," wrote a lady-friend of the family, "that M. Choderlos should write well: wit is hereditary in his family."[4] Nineteen uneventful years, during which all the important things were decided. In 1759 François entered the army by the new, and only, door open to the children of "good family" without fortune: the "artillery corps, which tended to be filled with sons of the bourgeoisie and lesser nobility

---

*He dies in 1784; his mother, "Dame Marie Catherine Galois" came from the upper middle class of Amiens, and there is no evidence of conflict between her and her son. Both parents cultivated "the taste for belles-lettres." He has one brother, four years his senior, who is in the India Company.

who had ability in the sciences but few friends at Court."[5] To become an officer there, being born wasn't enough; you also had to work.* At the La Fère school he was "an avid scholar,"[6] and it was all the easier for him because the place was close to home: the school had been opened thirty years before, in Thiérache on the Paris–Valenciennes road. His first big thrills were "the mathematical figures that we used to work over again among ourselves in the refectory at night, after they had been superficially demonstrated in the class-room that morning, and which we wrote out on the doors, the pewter plates, and window-shutters."[7] Thus he never left Picardy until he was twenty, in the days of the Seven Years' War; and his first big trip was from north to west, to La Rochelle where the "colonies Brigade" was being trained before, it was hoped, recapturing India or Canada from the English. Laclos imagined himself a general at twenty-five, as La Fayette was to be . . .

. . . And finds himself, twenty years later, a captain-major, after treading water in one garrison after another. The disastrous peace of 1763 had snapped the thread of his hopes and broken his youth.

His middle years? The barracks merry-go-round. The "Colonies Bri-gade" became the Toul regiment, and in it François de Laclos, drone-by-seniority after dreaming of eaglehood, lumbers one square forward every five years in an endless game of hopscotch across the face of France. From Toul to Strasbourg, Strasbourg to Grenoble, Grenoble to Besançon, and Besançon to Valence. He wasn't even detached for the Corsica campaign, as some of his comrades were. After these eons of military life that look more like a proces-sion, he can count himself lucky to be found worthy, thanks to the new war, of a slight change of service, applying his technical abilities and experience to the fortification of the island of Aix below Rochefort, just in case the English should conceive a desire to attack it. And he's been harnessed to this task, more mechanical than military, since 1779.

All right, but what else? If you're a man of his quality, you can't spend twenty years in a professional vacuum without some sort of pastime, some form of escape; yet it appears that he could. He's a bachelor. He has not been noted as a pursuer of either girls or married women (another point of disparity between him and Beaumarchais), but neither has he fled them. He has seized, without committing himself, whatever came his way, but he never takes any-one into his confidence. Ah, they're a tight-lipped lot in Amiens. "I had in my possession a few rather spicy anecdotes from my youth"[8] is all he ever says, later, to Tilly, and by "youth" he means that twenty-year Sahara between his arrival at La Fère and the *Liaisons.* These days, he must be feeling as though

---

*These were the same considerations that induced Charles de Buonaparte to enroll his second son at Autun in 1778, before placing him at Brienne.

he's finally beginning to live something a little bigger than "my youth." With
and by his book.

Is that all? Like the majority of his comrades, he becomes a Freemason.*
He turns an occasional verse, no worse than anybody else's, an *Epître à
Margot,* which was said to have angered La du Barry, who thought everybody was out to get her in the last days of Louis XV, and some licentious
and/or tender poems: *"Le souvenir de ce qu'on aime / Est au moins l'ombre du
bonheur"* . . . *"De penser, la triste habitude / M'obsède encore malgré moi"* . . .
*"Heureux par elle, entre ses bras / J'oubliais tous les noms de France / Et le plai-
sir n'y perdait pas"* . . . *"Ce temps que j'emploie a t'écrire / Est sans doute un
temps que je perds. / Jamais tu ne liras ces vers, / Margot; car tu ne sais pas lire"*
["The memory of what one loves /Sheds at least a shadow of happiness"
. . . "The grievous habit of thought / Still rooted in my unwilling self"
. . . "Made happy by her, in her embrace / I forgot every name in
France, / But pleasure was none the poorer for that" . . . "These moments I spend writing you / Are wasted beyond all doubt; / Lines you
will never read, / Margot, for you cannot read at all,"] and a pretty little
piece against jealous husbands who do exactly as they please while forbid-
ding their wives to move an inch:

De ces messieurs, Paris abonde.	[In such men does Paris abound.
On ne voit qu'eux dans le grand monde,	At the top there's naught else to be found:
Bien scélerats, bien séduisants,	Villains, yet charmers at work.
Petits despotes de tendresse,	These tyrants of love's innocence
Un peu français par la faiblesse,	May be French by inconsequence
Mais bien turcs par les sentiments.	But their feelings are unmixed Turk.]

In 1777 he concocted a pedestrian libretto out of a pedestrian novel by
one Mme Riccoboni, a society lady. The music was written by the Chevalier
de Saint-Georges, a young mulatto who was the drawing-room craze for two
or three seasons, and the whole thing ended with a single performance of a
deplorable *Ernestine,* who was booed off the stage.

Empty froth . . . he was within an ace of missing the train.

But he had his eyes open all the time. Watching everybody, everything,
everywhere. Laclos, the spy of provincial society. Who could be suspicious of
him? He was well bred, had a nose for the best tables and knew how to

---

*And attended "La Candeur" lodge when in Paris; his signature is often supplemented by
masonic symbols.

appreciate good food, but as though in passing, absent-mindedly, owing to that part of him that was engaged in the automatic observation of things; it had become his life habit. In Grenoble he set down his bags in an inn that a man named Rivière, who had come up from Montelimar, had just opened on the Rue Pertuisière in the snarl of alleyways behind the cathedral.* He passed the word to his comrades in the "Toul regiment"; why don't we set up headquarters there? By way of children, Rivière just happened to have the four prettiest girls in Grenoble. He soon had plenty of customers too, and so did his daughters: when Laclos left at the end of six years, the Rivière fortunes were made, and the good man was always ready to name the man he had to thank. But if François took any interest in one or another of the girls, he did that absent-mindedly too. He came from a good family and was accordingly received by the "best society" of this secretive town squeezed into the ring formed by the faraway mountains and the corset of its ramparts. It was just a step along the "Grand'rue"—you could touch both sides of it if you stretched out your arms—from the Grenette (grain-market square) to the imposing town house on the Rue du Pont Saint-Jaime where the wife of Président de Vaulx, an angel of virtue, received so hospitably. What a dream, to trouble those still waters! *I have only one thought in my head; I think about it all day and dream about it at night. I really must have that woman, to spare myself the humiliation of falling in love with her.*† In the draft of his manuscript, already quite far advanced, she becomes the wife of Président Tourvel. [10] But for one angel of purity, how many discoveries of another sort did he make in the course of his evening promenades in the Jardin de Ville, the only part of town that was lit after nine o'clock; or in the gloom of the Rue Chenoise and the Rue Brocherie, dark as country lanes, along which ladies groped in hooded capes that hid everything. Lord, but Grenoble was dull! Nothing but nothing to do, except dine out and then spend the night gambling, with an occasional authorized noonday visit to the ceremonial *toilette* of this or that local queen . . . those moments when the hunter stands aquiver at the edge of the thicket.

The female monster had been in his head since Toul or Besançon, someone he needed to pay back for one or two nasty tumbles into a briar-patch, and he finds more models in La Rochelle. But it was in Grenoble that he had the most time in which to mix his potpourri, possibly starting with that crippled little old lady full of tales to bring blushes to a regiment's cheeks, whom Laclos would wind up and set talking interminably in her château half way up the

---

*Today, Rue Alphand and Place Sainte Claire. On the strength of his early success Rivière moved into the larger establishment of "Les Trois Dauphins" on the Rue Montorge, made famous by Napoleon's transits. When Laclos, then a general, comes back that way in 1800 Rivière welcomes him gratefully and entertains him lavishly.

†To indicate their source, extracts from *Les Liaisons Dangereuses* like the above will be italicized in this chapter.

Lancey: the Marquise de La Tour-du-Pin-Montauban. She used to tell how she had made the men dance in the old days, with whip and riding-crop . . . He took a nibble here, no doubt; but the essence of La Merteuil he found north of Grenoble, on the right bank of the Isère down a league or so through the broad valley hugged by the Chartreuse and Vercors ranges, riding toward a pretty little hillside village called Voreppe, dead gray on a sunless day but bright blue in summer—Voreppe, *vorego alpium,* the gate to the Alps. There he came upon two châteaus, square and inconvenient like everything else built by the Dauphiné gentry, on the slopes of a hamlet called "Le Chevalon." One was besieged by all the garrison officers and noblemen of the vicinity because of its heiress, a pretty child of seventeen named Marguerite-Françoise de Blacons: Cécile Vollanges. In real life she did not enter a convent but married, in 1780, the lord of Voreppe, a Comte d'Agoult—and Laclos, like the rest, must have thought her an idiot for preferring somebody else to himself. In the *Liaisons* he vents his spleen abundantly upon the stupidity and latent vulgarity of such sweet young things who are transformed in one night from prudery to more than obligingness. *"We are forever being told to have soft hearts. And then we are forbidden to follow where they lead, when it is toward a man! That is unfair!"* Laclos even caught the trick of green-little-girl speech: *"He didn't look at me but he had a look as if he was ill . . . As the moment to write him draws closer, my heart beats so hard you couldn't conceive."* Cécile finds her official fiancé too decrepit for words: *"Can you imagine, he can't be a day under thirty-six!"* Which was within three years of the age of the Comte d'Agoult. She irritated Laclos, but at first he was intrigued by her: *"That contrast of naive candor with forwardness of speech does, I confess, have an effect; and I do not know why it should be, but I am no longer interested by anything except these curious mixtures."*

Higher up, on the other side of the road, stands an old château which must already have been melancholy in those days,* damp, glued to the cliffside on which the sun never shines for more than three hours a day; but it sheltered a unique creature in the form of a noble Arlesian dame who didn't worry about chills or the view as long as she had a few men within reach. She was an aunt of the Comte d'Agoult, what a handy coincidence, only a short walk from one château to the other, from Christine-Marie-Félicité de Loys de Joinville, Marquise de Montmaur—there she is, that's La Merteuil, "whose conversation was slightly *décolletée*"†—to little Marguerite-Françoise de Blacons, who could so easily be plied by her liberated elder with those recommendations and almost lesbian incitations that M. de Laclos, with never a quiver in his fingertips as

---

*And is positively lugubrious today, cornered between the quarry-pitted mountain and the Grenoble–Lyons superhighway.

†According to Stendhal, soon to be born in Grenoble, who was deeply influenced by Laclos's novel. For him (in *La Vie de Henry Brulard*) there can be no doubt: Madame de Montmaur is La Merteuil.

he sat, playing backgammon or reversis during the evening gatherings at Le Chevalon, could see as clearly as if he were in the room: *"I counseled her to lie down, which she did; I served her as chambermaid. She had made no toilette and soon her hair fell loosely over her shoulders and completely uncovered bosom; I kissed her; she lay back in my arms . . ."*

This was all taking place in a world of privileged idlers, the same world in which Beaumarchais sets his *Marriage.* The magistrates who had had Mandrin flogged twenty-seven years before loathed the officers and yet entertained them nightly, and could at least concur with them in their contempt for and vilification of the Court nobility, all those people in Versailles whose places they would so gladly have taken. Laclos, too, imprisoned in his Vauban-fashioned cul-de-sac, was thinking about Versailles. For four years* he's been working on "a highly scandalous manuscript of three hundred pages" listing all the great nobles of 1778 with notes on their morals, as viewed by the provinces.[11] In his head Laclos has been traveling back and forth nonstop between Le Chevalon and Trianon, between what he could see and imagine where he was and what he heard reported from afar, and slowly it was all coming together to form a new society in which love was replaced by cruelty, both here and among the great at Court—the society that had turned him into one of its little tin soldiers. Around the edges of the disenchanted twitchings of lives dessicated at twenty by drawing-room boredom, we also find a backdrop of peasantry, but not idealized as it is in Beaumarchais: here, the peasants are deadened by poverty. Valmont takes a little tour among them, to perform a good deed and impress Président de Tourvel's wife. The stony ground is hard to plow in the Voreppe coomb, and there's scant grazing for livestock; only little stands of walnut that give a cool shade but nothing can grow beneath them, and vineyards that yield a wine so sour it burns holes in your stomach. *"Today, in the morning, they were to seize the goods of an entire family that could not pay the taille†* . . . *I enter the village, I see a great to-do, I approach, I question; I learn what is going forward and, yielding to my generous compassion I nobly pay fifty-six livres ** for the want of which five persons were being cast out into despair and the night* . . . *A young peasant, leading forward a woman and two children, said to them: 'Let us all kneel at the feet of this image of God!'* . . . *It seemed proper to me to repay these poor people for the pleasure they had procured me. I had ten louis with me, and gave it to them."*

Oh, the Pleasure, the gracious pleasure of the little feudal baron—the same as that of the King—the pleasure of giving alms to affirm one's omnipo-

---

*Again according to Stendhal, who read the manuscript in Naples but, alas, let it out of his hands, and it has vanished.

†A form of direct taxation that every family had to pay to its lord, either the local aristocrat or the King.

**About 350 new francs [$70]. The ten louis of alms represent around four times that amount, in the neighborhood of 1,200 francs [$240].

tence and one's right to give orders "in the image of God": it culminates in Valmont (and for Valmont we hardly need to look for models; he's the man Laclos longed to be, to get back at them all), through his author's invention, in the 1780's, of the supreme manifestation of aristocratic gracious pleasure: the voluptuousness of self-destruction by mutual consumption. *"You now have them both in the palm of your hand"*—Le Chevalon at Voreppe is no bigger than a chessboard—*"love and hatred, you need but choose, they both sleep under the same roof; and, leading a double life, you can caress with one hand and strike with the other."* In the provinces, people know how to behave, which means that debauchery is only for two, plus some surreptitious servants (in *Les Liaisons* there is a valet, Azolan, a bastard cousin of Figaro, who writes his master letters of smutty and obsequious insolence). But Laclos has heard enough to recount the rituals of the Great: "The men abandoned themselves, the women submitted. There was hatred in all their hearts, yet their words were affectionate. Gaiety aroused desire, and desire in turn found fresh delight in gaiety. This astonishing orgy lasted till morning."

Patience, patience: give us another one or two idle and ambitious generations and by the end of the reign of Louis XVI the "people of quality" in Grenoble and La Rochelle will be holding their own, in the gracious pleasures sweepstakes, with those who crossed the line ahead of them in Versailles. The kingdom will be united by free competition in an open market between the cruelty of women—(La Merteuil): *"I am certain that if I had wit enough to leave him now it would plunge him into despair; and there is nothing more diverting than the despair of the lovelorn. He would call me perfidious, and that word perfidious has always been pleasing to me; after 'cruel,' it is the sweetest sound a woman's ear may hear"*—and the cruelty of men: *"Never, since early youth, had Valmont taken one step or uttered one word without deliberate intent, and he had never had a deliberate intent that was not either dishonest or criminal . . . He could reckon to a nicety what horrors a man may permit himself without being compromised; and, in order that he might be cruel and wicked without danger to himself, he chose women for his victims."*

The supreme objective: an absolute, the equal of a religion. This form of gracious pleasure is evangelical; it will rally all the joyboys on earth in the society of higher freedom that the wealthy are busily constructing for the wealthy: *"I shall have that woman;* * I shall abduct her from the husband who profanes her. I shall boldly ravish her from the very God she worships. What exquisite pleasure for me, to be now the object, now the vanquisher of her remorse! . . . She may believe in virtue if she likes, but sacrifice it to me she shall . . . Then, I consent, she may tell me, 'I adore you' . . . I shall truly be the God she will have preferred."*

This is what has been haunting François de Laclos throughout his long peregrination, and more specifically those six months of leave he took in La

---

*Valmont is speaking here of President de Tourvel's wife, of course.

Rochelle during the second half of 1781. He had just come from Grenoble, and his sack was full. His book was ready. All that remained was to polish it, in another town rife with ramparts and delicious little scandals but against a backdrop of ocean instead of the mountains and in the shadow of the batteries aimed at England. "After studying a trade that could bring me neither great promotion nor great consideration, I resolved to write a book that would be something out of the ordinary, one that would make some noise, and whose echo would resound on earth after I myself had quit it . . . I did my best to polish my style and, after a few months of final revision, I launched my book upon the public."[12]

It's done. Laclos is not exaggerating when he uses the language of the terrorist, but he was standing too close to his target when he hurled his bomb, and can't avoid the shrapnel. After a scant two months of clandestinity he has made his name in the literary world, all right, but a fat lot of good it's done him: that apology for a military career he has grimly built up stone by stone has now been seriously jeopardized. On May 24, 1782, he steps out of the stagecoach at La Rochelle a finished man. The Maréchal de Ségur, minister of war, has just ordered him to leave his post on the island of Aix and return to his sempiternal "Toul regiment," which had been dispersed along the coast and was now reassembled at Brest. Ségur senior is a bigot of the first water, and all the more outraged in this instance because his son, the viscount, appears to be following in Valmont's footsteps. In the past, nasty books had at least been perpetrated by civilians; if the officers want to start horning in, what will become of us? He'll teach that fancy intellectual in La Rochelle to go getting inkstains on his fingers.

But Laclos likes the place. He's fond of climbing up the Baleine tower in the evening, where "an assemblage of"—oil-fed—"lamps under a dome made all of glass forms a globe of fire that serves as a beacon." This is where he came to dip his pen in the ocean to make it even more saline and corrosive, and where he melted down the details of his past into a mould of the governing class stripped naked in what he saw as its most secret part—its sexuality. From up there, on clear days, he could take in at a single glance the islands of Oléron, Ré, Brouage, Marennes, and Aix, to which a lighter bore him to work on the huge toys of war. All last year he sat there contemplating, from far above and far away, the puppet-show he had been witnessing for the past twenty years, and as he scoured away the paint some strange deformities emerged from beneath the masks. "One sees the remains of the famous dike directed [sic] by the Cardinal de Richelieu. It measured 747 fathoms long. When the tide is out, one can observe it quite plainly. These works, their duration, extent, and strength, seem almost greater than human power. The capture of La Rochelle cost over thirty millions."[13] There, one hundred and fifty years before Laclos, one half of France had succeeded in throttling the other half, in order to teach it to believe in transubstantiation, and Richelieu had become what is commonly called a great man, worthy of his blood-colored robe.* Who knows the primal deeps of piracy and savagery that spawned the merciless elegance with which the men of gown and sword now slip each other down between their fingertips, like oysters?

Laclos is unwell, he's caught some kind of flu, a dizzy fever from the Charente swamps "by which everybody here is affected."[14] Thus far, his book has brought him one thousand and six hundred francs, for the rights to the first edition,† but his move to Brest and payment of his debts in La Rochelle compel him to ask the ministry for a grant of six hundred francs "to meet the remainder of his expenses."** He has a hard time getting it, but does so with the help of his immediate superior, the Marquis de Montalembert, director of works on the island of Aix. This officer has conceived a great respect for the abilities of Laclos, who managed, in three years, to construct a large wooden fort on this square league of sand supporting a scatter of little white cottages lost in the ocean, for less than a million francs.‡ Nobody believed in it, they said the fort would collapse from the blast of its own cannons. On October 6, 1780, Laclos had every gun fired at once, and not one beam creaked. Even in routine, he's an innovator. "He is my second self!" Montalembert pleads with the increasingly ill-tempered Ségur, who drily retorts "that the Sieur de Laclos is to take immediate steps to enable one of his officers to replace him, so that there may be nothing to hinder his return to service with his regiment."[15] Brest, here we come. Just one more stage on the journey, and he knows there's a long road ahead. He sets off armed, by way of consolation, with a letter from good old Mme Riccoboni, co-author of their forlorn flop *Ernestine,* who informs him that "all Paris is rushing to read you, all Paris is talking of you. If it is a happiness to occupy the thoughts of the inhabitants of this immense capital, then you should rejoice in the pleasure: for no one has had so great a chance of it as you."[16] But the truth is that he has never felt more alone and forsaken. He tries to cover it up with pride, but pride is no real balm for bitterness. So that's what you get for denouncing the manners of your day. To Mme Riccoboni, who keeps preaching at him full tilt, he replies "that the moralist's law commences where the written law falls silent . . . I wanted to arouse a salutary indignation in the public against those vices it no longer seems to find offensive. Now Mme de Merteuil and Valmont are raising a general hue and cry. But if you think back on the events of our time, you will see a host of traits similar to those of my creations, whose possessors,

---

*The cost of the siege of La Rochelle can be very approximately estimated at 200 million modern francs [$40 million]. The budget of Louis XIII never recovered.

†A little less than 10,000 modern francs [$2,000].

**3,600 francs [$750] nowadays.

‡Multiply by six to obtain the modern equivalent [$1.2 million].

of both sexes, have been or are being all the more esteemed and honored for them."

And the more people talk about him, the more taciturn he becomes.

CONDORCET

16

JUNE 1782

That Vast Collection of Truths

On June 6, 1782, the heir to a feudal past is officially presented to a spokesman of the future: Paul Petrovich and his wife go to "take place" as guests of honor at the Academy of Sciences in Paris. They are welcomed by its secretary general, the Marquis Nicolas Caritat de Condorcet, already highly regarded as a mathematician in St. Petersburg. The princely retinue, both French and Russian, were dreading this unavoidable chore, an hour of slumber in an uncomfortable armchair. Nevertheless, it has to be gone through with, it's part of the routine: a compulsory tour of the academies, those mini-republics of distilled tedium, is one of the privileges of sovereigns and highnesses visiting Paris.

Was the "Comte du Nord" bored on this occasion? He may have been, although there was plenty of material in the speech to keep him interested— because Condorcet is feeling an ever more imperative need to apply his geometry to politics. He launches a short sharp offensive aimed at Paul alone, and so much the worse, or better, for the rest of his audience. One man's anguished appeal to another, masquerading as an academic harangue—at last, a chance for the man who thinks he's discovered the mathematical laws of History to speak his heart (and mind) to one of the future rulers of the world.

After an opening in which he places Paul on a level with Peter the Great ("Sixty-five years later, the great-grandson of this prince comes to occupy the same place . . . and show us that he is destined to inherit the grand designs of Peter I no less than his empire"), Condorcet displays first the wisdom of the serpent and then the innocence of the dove. He abstains from the ritual references to Catherine II, whom d'Alembert or La Harpe would have enshrined as a model of enlightened despotism; not one word about her in the entire speech, as if she didn't exist.[1] Thanks to this little ploy, her son can feel as though he's being treated as an adult, almost a sovereign; and for that reason alone Paul may have been one of the few to hear him out. It is true that whenever the Grand Duke's demons left him in peace he showed unmistakable signs of intelligence, as in the suddenly soothed waters of a storm-tossed lake.

To clear the air, Condorcet starts off with a statement expressing all the pride of the scholar who no longer has to kowtow to potentates: "The fortunate consequences of this protection"—of the sciences by enlightened princes —"have been so rapid and far-reaching that it has, in a manner of speaking, ceased to be necessary. The love of study, a sense of the usefulness and dignity of the sciences, is become too universal for them to require outside assistance any longer; and it may be said that the greatest service that princes have rendered to the sciences was to make them independent of their power." That turns one page, anyway; so much for the researcher's subjugation to the open or closed hand of a patron. Now we can talk man to man about the considerable but very relative progress that has been made: "Casting one's gaze upon the state of the sciences in Europe, one is struck by the rapid strides they have taken in the last half century, by that vast collection of truths unknown to our forefathers, by the great number of new methods and, one might almost say, new sciences that have been added to the force and wealth of the human mind . . . But one also sees that several aspects of the sciences have escaped this general drive forward,* and one observes that they are precisely those in which genius can find neither resources nor a reward for its efforts unaided; those in which an important discovery can be made only at the cost of several centuries and the efforts of several people"—in other words, nothing less than an embryonic international brain bank—". . . To speak on such an occasion of what further aid the sciences are entitled to expect from the monarchs is to speak of our hopes."

Hope, that's the key word for Condorcet, who's becoming the prophet of happiness conceived as the product of an addition of science to politics. Here it comes; knowing smiles begin to raise the corners of all those habitually disdainful mouths. This year Condorcet has also become the scapegoat of the skeptics, the village idiot of the Palais Mazarin, ever since February 21, when he began his speech of admission to the Académie Française with a sort of hymn to the joy of living in his age. The eternal choirboy; wasn't even Turgot's downfall enough to teach him that there is no Santa Claus?

Condorcet is forty. He lives in a tête-à-tête with the human race and is thought to be incapable of marrying anything else, in the apartment that goes with his job in the handsome Hôtel des Monnaies, brand new and shining white, which

---

*Today Condorcet would have called these the "human sciences," those that require statistics and large numbers of superimposed observations: the "collective" sciences.

overlooks the left bank of the Seine across from the Louvre.* Turgot had gotten him appointed inspector of the Mint, in which position, assisted by regiments of clerks, he kept a rather remote and disinterested eye on the striking of gold and silver marks, big silver écus, louis, and even deniers, liards, and double-liards in copper—the *monnaie de billon* or base (alloy) coinage as it was called—but only for Paris, one-sixteenth of France. Every coin was stamped with an A to distinguish it from those minted in La Rochelle, Perpignan, Metz, or Lille (marked H, Q, AA, and W, respectively), and so on, not to mention the coins struck in Pau, which were stamped with a cow.[2] When Turgot was dismissed, Condorcet tendered his resignation to Maurepas because he hated Necker and didn't want to serve under him. They pacified him by telling him he was not directly attached to the comptroller-general's office and could therefore stay on in this setting that was too big for him but in which he could at least dream the world as he liked it, drawing inflated portraits of men, extending and uplifting them to the heights of universal generosity. He left it now and then to visit his small group of friends, always the same men and women a shade too far ahead of their age, wandering into their salons with his wig askew, his coat unbrushed, and his nails untrimmed: Condorcet, a teeming solitude.

Those same friends had just propelled him into the Académie Française, his election to which was "one of the greatest battles won by M. d'Alembert over M. de Buffon."[3] The big men of the day spent a lot of their time on such trifles. "The latter [Buffon] was absolutely determined to favor M. Bailly, author of the *Histoire de l'astronomie ancienne,* the *Lettres sur l'Atlantide,* and *Sur l'origine des sciences;* at the previous election, M. de Chamfort was only three or four votes ahead of him.† His new rival [Condorcet] had fewer literary works to his credit," and it is true that his baggage is pretty meager outside the realm of geometry: some *Eloges académiques,* a few anti-religious tracts, and almost as many tirades against Necker. Enough to shut the gates of any paradise in his face. "In the eyes of the Académie Française, these works must have been just so many reasons for keeping him out . . . It required all of M. d'Alembert's intellectual adroitness, all his political energy, and even, it is said, all the eloquence of his tears to carry the day on behalf of his client [*sic*]." Sixteen votes to fifteen. But Buffon was at a disadvantage because he was so seldom around: way off in his Burgundian Montbard, he was majestically laying, at two-or-three-yearly intervals, the latest fat tome of his oeuvre for

---

*The Mint (Hôtel des Monnaies) had just been completed. It was designed by Jacques-Denis Antoine and built on the site of the former Hôtel de Conti; standing between the Pont Neuf and the Pont des Arts, it remains today a perfect illustration of the architecture of the period of Louis XVI, which was beginning to refurbish the banks of the Seine.

†Giants playing marbles. The great Chamfort had thus "beaten" Bailly to the Académie in 1781. And Bailly will be the first mayor of Paris in 1789, presiding over the Tennis Court Oath.

eternity like so many dodo's eggs: Man, Nature . . . The shriveled-up asthmatic old d'Alembert, surviving half-petrified like a spider at the heart of his web in some forgotten corner: all he was good for anymore was to creep over to the Académie now and then and dump an atheist into its midst.

On February 21 Condorcet thanked them with a paean worthy of an eighteenth-century mystic. What is the world coming to when the devotees of holy reason begin outchanting the monks? Envy-green Grimm lacerated his "inferior speech, lacking in warmth, harmony, elegance, filled with trite ideas and an artificial and precious metaphysics, and even more remarkable for a host of improper and tasteless expressions such as this exclamation, so absurdly bombastic: 'Witnesses to the final strivings of ignorance and error, we have seen reason emerge victorious from the long and painful struggle, and at last we can cry "Truth has conquered! The human race is saved!"' . . . In what hoary homily did our philosopher disinter this fine spate of eloquence?"[4]

Grimm gives himself away a little further on: "In the speaker's eyes everything becomes larger than life." That's the real bone of contention between the surviving mummies of the society of Louis XV who had spent their whole lives diminishing things, and these opening notes of visceral optimism, the song of the future, the harbinger of a tidal wave whose origin and destination are still unknown. This year, Condorcet is a prophet.

"Lacking in warmth"—really?

> For the first time . . ., the method of ascertaining the truth has been reduced to an art,* to formulae one might even say. Reason has finally recognized the road it must follow and grasped the thread that will keep it from going astray. These primary truths, these methods that have spread among every nation and been carried to both worlds, can no longer be annihilated; the human race will never again know those alternating periods of darkness and light to which it was long believed to be eternally condemned by nature . . .
>
> Every century will add new enlightenment to that of the century preceding it; and this advance, which nothing now can stop or suspend, shall know no limits but those of the duration of the universe.
>
> And yet is there not a time when the natural limitations of our mind will render further progress impossible? No, Gentlemen: as our enlightenment grows, so our methods of instruction become more perfect; the human mind seems to be growing too, its limits retreating. When a young man leaves our schools, he is filled with more true knowledge than could be acquired by the greatest geniuses, I shall not say of Antiquity, but even of the seventeenth century, and at the end of lengthy studies. Ever more refined methods follow one upon the other, and in little space assemble all the truths that the men of genius of an entire

---

*This is from the February speech after his election to the Académie: in fact, it's the first manifesto of scientific romanticism. The speech made at the Academy of Sciences in June (the one attended by the tsarevich with which I begin and end this chapter) is an echo and extension of it.

century were endeavoring to discover. In every age, the distance that the human mind sees before it will always appear infinite; but the distance it leaves behind at each moment, the distance separating it from its infancy, will also widen unendingly . . .

It would be simple for me to confirm this truth. As a professional observer of the progress of the sciences I see every year, every month, almost every day marked impartially by some new discovery and some useful invention. This spectacle, at once sublime and reassuring, has become the habit of my life and a part of my happiness. These sciences, created almost in our own lifetime, whose subject is man himself and whose immediate goal is human happiness, will stride forward no less surely than the physical sciences; and that most alluring thought, namely that our nephews will know more than we do and be wiser than we are, is no longer an illusion.[5]

It must have given that public of withered turkey-cocks a big thrill to hear that the young were about to start knowing more than they did: talk about a world overturned.

Yes, and then on June 6 we come back to the charge; not such a bad idea to put the future Paul I a little more in the picture by treating him as one of those "nephews," especially since he seems to have such a grudge against his mother's century. Willy-nilly, Condorcet is compelled to turn to those prehistoric relics, the sovereigns, for a helping hand in his promotion of the human race. He's an optimist, all right, but not crazy enough to imagine a world without kings. However, there's nothing to hope for from Louis XVI, that premature dotard impermeable to any form of political innovation, who's likely to keep France stagnating for half a century or more; so the heirs of the Encyclopédistes have no choice but to try to run round their own ends, as it were, toward Leopold of Tuscany, Joseph of Austria, or Paul of Russia, who might become agents of change if all else fails.

The sheep gazes up at the monkey, Condorcet raises his myopic eyes to the beautiful gilded silhouettes he dimly discerns in a haze of armchairs facing him, and tosses out his lines like a man fishing for the moon (in a soporifically monotonous voice, it is true, for he's a deskman with no gift for oratory and fumbles with the sheets of his speech):

Everything concurs to establish that the whole of nature is subject to regular laws; any apparent disorder merely hides an order that our eyes cannot discern. It can become known only through the observation of facts, which must be seen in their entirety or chronology before the underlying order can become perceptible to our weak sight . . . In vain have we covered the surface of the earth, dug into its innards, described and analyzed the very substances within it . . . We create systems; and as soon as we take one step more on the surface of the earth, or delve a few feet deeper into its bowels, these phantoms of the imagination begin to dissolve. How shall such ephemeral beings as we surprise the secret heart of operations that nature prepares at a rhythm so immense, in comparison with the span of our lives? How shall a man grasp a whole whose parts are spread as though at random over so huge a surface that it would be impossible for him, though he devoted his entire life to the task, not only to observe its whole extent but even to cover it, not only to examine but merely to see it all? . . .

The links between a man's physical constitution, his moral qualities, the social order and the nature of the climate in which he lives, the soil he treads and the objects around him, can be known only by a long sequence of research simultaneously embracing different climates, different mores, and different political constitutions. From this must come an important science, and that science will not be truly created until a huge sum of constant and precise observation has founded both the results of that observation and the certainty of those results upon calculations . . .

Sovereigns alone possess the means of rendering these achievements independent of time and chance. They alone can command and have carried out, on a single plane, these lengthy and arduous efforts that cannot be performed for glory alone. Who shall shape these great undertakings whose value can become visible only in the distant future; who but a prince, able to conceive his plans not in the terms of one man's life but in those of empires? Only the sovereigns, by joining together, can expand the scientists' research to the dimensions required by one entire branch of the sciences whose component parts nature has scattered throughout the world.[6]

. . . Nothing less than a universal science, based on empire-wide statistics. Over to your good heart, Paul Petrovich! "The despot and the scholar"—a fable for 1782.

BRISSOT

17

JUNE 1782

An Impious War

Condorcet's question is answered almost on the rebound, but not by the Russian autocracy: the agent is the French monarchy, and in particular Vergennes, the man about whom nobody knows anything, including whether he is going to be officially appointed principal minister. In any event, he has certainly acquired more influence over the mind of Louis XVI than anyone else this year. Vergennes does not carry out French foreign policy: he decides it unassisted, under the umbrella of royal inertia. For example, it is he who orders the French army to besiege and then invade Geneva in July 1782 . . . The freedom of the tiny Swiss republic will have lasted eighty-four days, one scant springtime.*

Brissot, with his big revolution-scenting nose, came to take a sniff round a little while ago; but it was already too late by the time he left Paris, where he was living and partly living by his pen, between his setback in London, his rest periods with the Dupont family in Boulogne, and five or six schemes in perpetual transformation. His eye had been bewitched by the mirage of freedom in Geneva. Who knows; maybe he could find some role to play in this latter-day Athens—found a publishing house or a newspaper with Europe-wide resonance. He set out laden like a mule with the "prospectuses" of his friend Marat, to be distributed along the road in the hope of interesting local scientists in the physics and medical experiments Jean-Paul was conducting in Paris. By June 6, however, the news was already so bad that he was writing to Marat from Lyons, "The troops are continuing to close in on Geneva"— six thousand infantry commanded by the Marquis de Jaucourt, those troops so badly needed to accelerate the freedom of America; what a lot of them, soldiers like blue ants tramping down every road in the Forez and Dauphiné. "They say the siege is to begin on the 20th of this month, so that I shall not be able to go there directly. I leave next week for Lausanne; but send your letters to Lyons if you want to give me any news." As for those advertisements about "the apparatus for measuring internal fire," "I have not forgotten you, either at the Oratory or the booksellers', but the professor of physics at that

*[The event to which this and the following chapters refer took place on April 8, 1782, when a group of liberal townsmen in Geneva, led by the men described hereafter, took over the town in a bloodless *prise d'armes*. The situation was as follows: a small number of patrician families ruled the town through the Petty Council, a fifteen-man emanation of the Grand Council or Two Hundred, itself elected from the General Council, which consisted of everyone who had the right to vote. Electorally, the population was divided into Citizens and Burghers, who had that right, and Habitants (immigrants, predominantly but not all working class) and Natifs (their native-born children), who did not. Politically, it was divided into those in control, the Constitutionnaires, who upheld the former constitution and resisted all attempts to incorporate anyone else into the decision-making processes (not surprisingly, they were also known as Négatifs), and the Représentants, who had legally obtained some minor changes in the rules of representation and government in February 1781. The Négatifs were trying to have what they called the "gun-point edicts" invalidated; the Représentants were prepared to fight for them. The Habitants and Natifs were divided: some, led by Isaac Cornuaud, sided with the old guard, others with the reform party. The quarrel had been building up for years. The Geneva "revolution" presents, nonviolently and in very reduced dimensions, all the forces, relationships, and interferences at work in France a few years later, and the same elements of deliberate intention, misunderstanding, backfire, and ricochet. It also served, as will be seen, as a proving ground for many of the major figures of 1789 and after.—Trans.]

college is an old fogey who gives very bad demonstrations and is a thousand leagues away from your ideas. I keep exhorting them all to regard your works as true classics [but] old fellow, you have enemies in the provinces as well as in the capital. I met one doctor in particular, with whom I was obliged to argue at great length . . . People object that one does not bring physics books to the provinces as though they were novels."[1] Come to think of it, it's no great wonder if Marat, helped along by his incipient paranoia, should be starting to believe that the whole world is against him.

But Brissot's itch to see Geneva is too strong to be stopped by a mere siege. He leaves Lyons on June 10, "by the last stagecoach that was to carry passengers there."[2] He arrives on the 12th, to witness the death agony of his first revolution.[3] What does it matter if one minute ant on the world's sidewalk gets squashed? That same day, the old sage Court de Gébelin* has the following exchange with one of his friends who was questioning him in the flippant Parisian mode:

"There must be an amazing number of people in this town of Geneva, for everyone to be talking about it so much?"

"My friend, the kingdom of France has towns five or six times the size of Geneva, and nobody ever mentions them. But freedom, morality, and education triple men and turn them into giants. If Geneva were a fief of France, she would be just another burg; free, her name is everywhere."[4]

From Brissot again: "Before I got here my eyes were afflicted, in the region of Gex, by the sight of vehicles and teams bearing in large print the words "Army of Jaucourt"; it was an impious war my country was waging upon Geneva, for it was fought against the people's party and to support the aristocracy, and my soul was dismayed by the sight. Upon entering the unfortunate city, I saw anxiety and care written on every face; it seemed to me that they could see me only as an enemy, because I was French."[5] The spectacle of the last hours of a calm despair in a city removed from time. There was a hive of men in black on the fortifications wielding the most primitive tools and looking like a Reformation engraving, the Gueux of the Netherlands awaiting assault by the Duque de Alba's killers [Gueux: "beggars," in French, here refers to the Protestant resistance to Spain in sixteenth-century Holland—*Trans.*]. Drill on the ramparts, deliberations in the churches and town hall, but no illusions in either place. The "Powers" didn't even give us time to enact a little exemplary legislation and plant our garden à la Rousseau on the shores of Lake Geneva. Why vote edicts we'll never be allowed to apply?

The Genevans have known what was in store for them for the last two

---

*A Genevan pastor who had been engaged for years on a monumental historical research project in Paris. He has enormous influence over men as dissimilar as Bailly and Rabaut Saint-Étienne.

months. Almost as soon as their *prise d'armes* was over, they began hearing from well-informed travelers that the "Courts of France and Sardinia,* as well as the cantons [Zurich, Bern] were going to send troops against them."6 All the sovereigns and partisans of the established order in Europe were backing the forces of repression. The great Frederick himself, that eminent model of enlightened despotism, has just intimated "to the Praiseworthy Canton of Bern" (on which he can exert considerable pressure) what turn *he* thinks events should take.

> It is to be feared that, the Republic of Geneva being abandoned to itself and its own destiny, attitudes of partisanship and ambition will invade the different parties, and its fate will be decided by the law of the stronger,† engendering anarchy, which will lead in turn to the ruination of this otherwise blessed Republic . . . All that remains to be hoped is that your two Cantons and the High Crown of France . . . will take, in word and deed, sufficiently vigorous and effective action not only to prevent renewed and greater trouble in Geneva but also to restore a form of government in which the old fundamental Constitution will be preserved . . . and to establish a legal force and power that may ensure peace and tranquillity hereafter.7

Virtually every atom of the energy of the new regime in Geneva, hence, has been mobilized to resist aggression from without rather than to construct policy within. And yet so little has changed! Thirty or so families who effectively personify Geneva's economic expansion and vitality have evicted thirty or so stale crusts from their armchairs, with the support of the more disgruntled elements among the Natifs and Habitants—a few thousand politically aware men of the people. The only really "revolutionary" measure adopted was that they elevated five hundred of the latter to the status of full citizenship. Everybody else was sitting on the fence, passive and generally mistrustful, and one section of the Natifs, commanded by the "traitor" Cornuaud, has remained faithful to the *ci-devant* Messieurs. The pre-revolt councilors have even retained their functions as commissioners. What about the evictees? Those who didn't flee have been locked up, two to a room, in the Hôtel des Balances, where they are enjoying—at their own expense, true, but their goods were not confiscated—the finest fare in Geneva. And this is the barbarian explosion that has alarmed old Frederick himself? Ah, but these Huns of the clock-and-watch industry were crying "Freedom" a mite too loud: and the Europe of 1782 is sunk so deep in torpor that a sneeze is enough to jounce its mattress.

To the ramparts, everybody! To the ramparts! Under the leadership of the Baron du Châtel, a former officer in the Austrian artillery, the Genevans are

---

*The curious expression "Court of Sardinia" means, we recall, the monarchy of Savoy, which reigns in Turin and also over the Sards.

†Meaning the people, in this instance.

repairing the ramparts of Saint-Gervais and the bastion of Saint-Jean, after discovering that their beautiful fortifications, admirably restored on the advice of Vauban, have been used so seldom that they've sunk into decrepitude, like a fringe of hoary locks around the town's bald pate. Beginning on April 28, "more than five hundred persons were assigned to the defense works, even during the religious service[!]." "One former pastor, Isaac Salomon Anspach, a member of the Committee of Security [the name of the provisional government] was haranguing the improvised laborers and, to encourage them, told them it would take sixty thousand men to capture Geneva."[8] But now, in June, the rats are deserting the ship through every leaky seam: "Natifs and Négatifs have taken fright and, in various disguises, are seeking refuge at Carouges, in Savoy, and in the country of Gex, despite the stern orders of the Committee of Security, which is employing woman-searchers [*sic*] who operate at the city gates and even look under the women's skirts . . . There is much peroration in the circles in the evenings, especially at the Circle of Equality [a totally new word outside the Masonic lodges] where Clavière and du Roveray complain that only the leaders are out and at work while the rest of the citizens sleep in peace and at ease; at the Circle of Good Stews, an address was adopted, written by a notary named Richard, conveying an expression of general gratitude to Clavière and du Roveray."[9]

Clavière, good old Clavière, the man of accounts and speculations:* Brissot finds him dressed as a dragoon with a comical round helmet on his head, in the midst of the militia mounting guard outside the town hall. "To those who urge him to save his strength for some more useful task he replies: 'In the past I tried to make myself useful with my pen; this is my pen now!' And he points to his gun; if someone expresses surprise to see that he is not even an officer, he answers back: 'What I want is to be the equal of my fellow citizens. Besides, they won't take me alive. I always have my pistol about me.' "[10]

The situation has deteriorated considerably since the first happy rush out to the ramparts when old Anspach was saying that sixty thousand men couldn't capture Geneva. Now, one-tenth that number are enough to sway the hesitant. Since May 5 the Genevans have known that the King of France is sending Jaucourt's six thousand men against them, and the King of Sardinia another four thousand, commanded by the Comte de la Marmora; plus the detachments sent by the "Cantons" (a rabid Bern, dragging a very unwilling Zurich in its wake; proof that the Geneva disease is dangerously contagious: "the tone of Zurich is strongly Représentant").[11]

Hunger is stalking the city, too. The region of Gex will no longer supply anything but trivial foodstuffs, and even those are smuggled in. At the Gre-

---

*We shall be meeting Etienne Clavière many times again, until his tragic death in 1793; in the interim he will be minister of finances under Louis XVI, then under the Convention.

nette (grain market square) wheat is scarce and expensive. Emigration is on the increase. But the main body of the victorious bourgeoisie has stuck together. "They drill in squadrons in the bastions every day, and patrols are guarding the lake. Two companies of grenadiers have firing practice in the curtain running from the Cornavin gate to the Chantepoulet bastion, and from the Cornavin bastion four cannons fire shells and case shot under the eyes of the Représentant leaders and the ladies who have come out to watch. Moreover, there are some girls from Saint-Gervais [the poor part of town] among those learning to fire the weapons, while their less spry mothers prepare cartridge pouches and lint[12]—the women of Geneva leave Brissot gaping: a new species of human being, female citizens!

> Several Genevan women take part in political conversations. I had brought my French prejudices with me; there, politics seemed a weighty and tedious science, not worth the attention of a pretty woman. To give pleasure and entertainment was the great art that women were supposed to spend their lives learning . . . A woman engaging in politics seemed like a monster to me, or at the very least a sort of new breed of *précieuse ridicule.* There can be no doubt that if I had but troubled to reflect upon my opinions, I should soon have discovered their absurdity and turned my mockery against myself rather than expending it upon political women; but in most of the external circumstances of my life, swept along by the current, I have been a slave of public prejudice more often than an apostle of the truth . . . I possessed a goodly share of that scathing and flippant attitude that is so rightly held against my compatriots; and when I think back upon my conduct in Geneva and everywhere in Switzerland, I believe my good Genevan friends must have found me very *French* indeed* . . . All praise to the Genevan women of 1782! No country (for at that time I had not seen the United States) had offered a more attractive sight to my eyes.[13]

But these women and their menfolk were sipping their chocolate in the shadow of the gallows. In June the circle tightened to choking-point. A Bernese general with the resounding name of Robert-Scipion de Lentulus, Baron de Redekin, advanced at the head of two thousand Swiss from the Cantons and set up his headquarters in the Château de Coppet, which belonged to Necker, who had stayed prudently behind with his family at Saint-Ouen: Necker the flittermouse, half Genevan–half French but with his sympathies on the side of the Représentants, insinuates that France would not have intervened if he had still been minister, but keeping an eye to the future, is careful to make no public statements on his friends' behalf. "On June 13 M. de la Marmora moved into the Château-Blanc"—almost at the gates of Geneva—"where he kept great state" among his Piedmontese: the traditional nightwatch, eat, drink, and

*Brissot's italics.

be merry, for tomorrow we die. "M. de Jaucourt is at Ferney, where a prodigious number of people have rushed from all sides to see him."[14] Ferney! The
château that Voltaire left four years ago, to go to his death in Paris. His heirs,
the Marquis de Villette and his wife—the famous "Belle et Bonne"—are a
trifle overenthusiastic, perhaps, in their reception of the soldiers marching up
to wring the necks of Rousseau's disciples. The great confessor had been
prophetic in his defense of the lower orders here; and the men who are trying
to seize power today are fans of his. The *Confessions* have just been published,
too, adding fuel to the fire, and Brissot devoured the book before coming to
look at Geneva through Jean-Jacques-colored spectacles. Voltaire, of course,
had sided with the Négatifs, although not unwaveringly—partly out of hostility to Rousseau but partly because of his congenital loathing of fuss. He adored
the people, no doubt, but only so long as the people kept quiet and worked.
And now the soldiers of the King of France are encamped at Ferney with their
guns aimed at Rousseauist Geneva, and Europe is looking on from the balcony
as, only four short years after the deaths of the two intellectual giants, armed
manifestations of their thoughts prepare to enact the first physical expression
of the dispute between what they stood for. Overheated ideas, ink turned
homicide . . .

On June 23 the regiments of Médoc, Normandy, and the Dauphiné are
encamped on the Prégny heights as far as Morillon and the Grand Saconnex.
M. de Jaucourt's twenty-two pieces of artillery are installed at Meyrin, and he's
expecting twice as many more, coming up in forced marches from Saint-
Claude and the region of Gex. The royal grenadiers are lined along the
frontier of the Vaud. Geneva is almost out of bread.

But not one shot has been fired. The misty early summer heat, only
slightly relieved by the lake-breeze in the evenings, has wrapped the infant war
in a layer of cotton. Are we really going to fight, or is this some sort of
nightmare? It all depends on the scattered centers of decision and instigation:
1) the Représentants, who have taken control of the town; 2) the Constitutionnaires, or in other words the Négatif hostages in the Hôtel des Balances, who
can still pull plenty of strings outside; 3) the chiefs of the invading armies, each
having latitude to interpret his minister's orders more or less loosely; and 4)
the Natifs who have gone over to the French and are grouped around Cornuaud at Tournay . . . another Voltaire property. Negotiate? Make mayhem?
Turn Geneva into "a new Saguntum" buried beneath its ruins?* Surrender?

---

*Saguntum, an Iberian town allied with Rome and sacked by the Carthaginians in 219 B.C.

CLAVIÈRE

18

These Chimaeras Belong to Us

Brissot has no trouble making contact with Geneva's new masters, those on whom the decision about whether or not to shed blood ultimately depends. He moves from one to the other through that sort of anxious euphoria which often marks the beginning of successful but doomed revolutions. "No town exhibited a greater tranquillity than Geneva, despite the military paraphernalia installed on its ramparts and the hostilities threatening it from every side; the safety of the individual was respected at all times, and not one murder or brawl occurred throughout the long interval of this people's dictatorship.

"The moment Divernois* learned of my arrival he hastened to my inn; I could almost have taken him for a Frenchman. He had all the vivacity, loquacity, and superior airs of one, but in other respects his frank and open manner, his pleasant and considerate ways, and his spirited conversation imperceptibly covered over the effects of these shortcomings. He introduced me to the people's leaders: Clavière, Duroveray,† Vieusseux, Grenus, and Dentand."[1] All of which "people's leaders" are, as one might have expected, very upper middle class: Dentand, a lawyer, is working on a massive *Essai de législation criminelle;* Vieusseux, Clavière's son-in-law, assists him in his financial undertakings; Jacques Grenus is a senior official in the administration of the little Genevan army.**

Francis d'Ivernois himself has all the qualifications to emerge as the archangel of the band. One reason why some of the Genevan dames are so enamored of their revolution is because he is there to personify it—so young and handsome, only twenty-five, so fiery and slender, his attire enhanced by all those little nuances that identify a man as "an elegant" in these parts ... He has retained the long Morvan nose of his Protestant ancestors, exiled from Cussy (north of Autun) in the last days of the wars of religion. His

*The more common spelling is Francis (or François) d'Ivernois.

†Who does spell his name like that during the Revolution, when he is part of the "Mirabeau clique," but at this point writes it "du Roveray."

**In 1791 he is elected a substitute member of the French Legislative Assembly and thereafter becomes one of the revolutionary leaders in Geneva.

grandfather Abraham even moved back and tried to settle at Marvejols in Gevaudan, where heretics were tolerated but not enough to prevent his son (Francis's father) from opting for exile again, in Geneva. Hatred and bitter contempt for French intolerance have throbbed in the d'Ivernois breast for two hundred years. The family had a tidy nest egg and managed to invest it profitably in the clock industry. Ten years before Francis was born, his father was promoted from the rank of a mere "Habitant" to that of "Bourgeois" of the town, in exchange for a substantial payment: "1,100 white écus and 10 écus* for the library."[2] "Only five Natifs a year could benefit from this mark of favor, so that to some of their ears the name of fatherland was no more than a synonym for a heap of coins."[3] Be that as it may, young Francis was born a full-fledged citizen of Geneva and finds no reason to complain of it. He mostly thinks of himself as a citizen of the world like Rousseau, whom his father had bailed out innumerable times in the days of his Genevan tribulations.† And since his father died too early (in 1778), leaving six children to fend for themselves, Francis became a printer and bookseller at the age of twenty-two (by special dispensation, as he was still technically a minor) and embarked upon a crazy undertaking: the publication of the *Oeuvres complètes* of that same newly departed Rousseau.

He has been and still is wrestling with this labor of Hercules, but he has also been very much engrossed in politics since the Geneva troubles began to loom. He flung himself into the fray body and soul and even went to Versailles on his own, with instructions from nobody, to plead the Représentants' cause; he was admitted by Maurepas, who pretended to listen to him, and shown the door by Vergennes, who had a horror of Geneva liberals even then. He next proceeded to cook his own goose by sending the minister a torrid *Mémoire:* "Democracies are tumultuous only among idle, ignorant, and superstitious peoples. We assuredly suffer from none of those failings and if we have some reputation as an educated people it is because we have been compelled to work with uncommon dexterity in order not to go hungry." The poor rube gets so heated up that in the end he's writing to Vergennes as though the man had a heart: "We are ready to bury ourselves beneath the ruins of our freedoms. And however much those freedoms may be called chimaeras, Monsieur le Comte, these chimaeras belong to us."[4]

Vergennes almost had him thrown in prison. "The sieur d'Ivernois is an intriguing fanatic . . . After having schemed by every means to make himself the advocate of the Représentants at Court, he has now addressed to myself and the ministers of the King three items that I send herewith.[5] Before showing them to the King and receiving H.M.'s instructions as regards the treat-

---

*Or 20,000 modern francs [$4,000].
†For which his reward was a stream of invective in the *Confessions.*

ment to be administered to a foreign [sic] individual who permits himself such behavior, I am having these three items transmitted to the first councilor of Geneva."[6] D'Ivernois gets back in time to cover his tracks and publish his texts, which make him famous and are qualified by Négatif leaders as "the pleadings of an infernally dangerous viper,"[7] when in reality they contain nothing worth writing home about. Brissot sees at first glance that d'Ivernois is simply an intelligent young conservative, of the same type as William Pitt in London, and that "all his efforts were bent upon maintaining his country's initial constitution while reforming the abuses that had crept into its administration."[8] But imbecilic Négatifs had built so broad a dike across his path that he lost his temper trying to scrabble over it, and is now standing there, naked sword drawn, a youngster whose first idea was simply to promote his own class. . . . Such are the anomalies of revolutions.

Jacques-Antoine du Roveray is ten years older but no less infuriated, and has the same youthful enthusiasm as d'Ivernois although he is sharper and more cutting: a commercial lawyer who has made his way up from next to nothing and prospered in the wake of Clavière, with whom he has a great deal in common. He's the Représentants' wild boar, with his wide low forehead, straight, carefully powdered hair, and bushy eyebrows above eyes that shoot you dead point-blank. He, at least, is not infatuated with the "people," whom he defends more out of duty than conviction. "Although he was proud and haughty with the Négatifs in general," writes Cornuaud, ringleader of the "traitors" and thus in the opposing camp, "I stood up for him against my friends who could not stomach the man. He was a virtuous young man, interesting, a good son, husband, and father, full of enthusiastic love of freedom but carried to excess by his age and the flattery of the former demagogues."[9]

Young, thus more energetic and also better speakers, d'Ivernois and du Roveray are the coming men. But the real leader of the Représentant movement is Etienne Clavière. His surface covers the whole of rebel Geneva, in which money still continues to play so great a part. He's a banker, owns business concerns, is wealthy, and could easily sit back and let his already diversified holdings fructify on the world's markets: Geneva and Neuchâtel, and London too, and Paris, and Philadelphia any day now. But he's been contaminated by Necker's affliction, that itch of virtue, in the Roman sense of the word, which is beginning to trouble some of the money manipulators— a product of their sense of honor and, in some instances, a more intelligent grasp of their own interests as being linked to the evolution of societies. This is the beginning of his friendship with Brissot:

"The man who attracted me most of all, the one I began even then to look upon as my friend, my Mentor, was Clavière. His conversation seemed sounder, wittier, and more agreeable to me than that of all the rest; his ideas, like his manners, were more akin to those of the cosmopolitans, the *philosophes*. There was nothing conceited or presumptuous about him, as there was about most of his compatriots; he was unsure of himself, mistrusted facts and men, and was at the same time continually occupied in increasing their welfare"[10] . . . and possibly in hinting, from their very first meetings, that a polemicist of Brissot's ilk might be eligible for some of that "welfare," which would go down in the books as an investment. The leaders of the invisible hydra otherwise known as the Protestant bank often thought straight and weren't too bad at talking, but everything they wrote was cottage cheese. A pen, a real one with the right kind of ink, that of a Linguet, a Mirabeau, a Beaumarchais, a Brissot, is a weapon worth paying for. Clavière invites Brissot to dinner at the height of the tension, on the eve of the day when the Représentant leaders decide to send their families to Neuchâtel "to spare them the horrors of a siege. The lake greatly facilitated this sort of emigration. Nothing could be more heartrending than these separations of so many families! The hapless people behaved as though they were looking their last upon each other . . . Clavière's wife* possessed by nature that delicacy of feeling and refinement of mind that Marivaux and Crébillon fils had made fashionable in Paris; and his daughter† combined a gentle physiognomy with a soundness of judgement rare in a person of her age. She loved her husband with complete sincerity and dared to say as much, which seemed somewhat provincial; but I fully understood her affection when I saw the worthy young man [Vieusseux] who is goodness personified."[11]

In this little group Etienne Clavière acts the part of elder statesman. He was born in Geneva on January 15, 1735. In appearance he is fragile and indomitable, a sort of hothouse asparagus who leans toward people when they speak to him because he is hard of hearing. "Of delicate health, suffering from frequent inflammations, he became deaf at the end of his childhood. However, compulsory exercise occasioned by frequent trips to Frankfurt-am-Main, where he went to change Empire currency for the money of France, fortified him, and he soon reached the height of five feet five inches."[12] As the son of a dealer in linens and muslin, and a demoiselle Rapillars from a cloth-merchant family in Lausanne, he'd been living in the chink of coin and fog of account books since he first opened his eyes. He had followed his father, Jean-Jacques Clavière, from Amsterdam to London and Paris, where intelligent treatment substantially improved his hearing. The father died in 1776, leaving a fortune

*Née Marthe Louise Garnier; a cousin of her husband. The daughter of a Marseille merchant, she brought a dowry of 30,000 livres (180,000 modern francs [$36,000]) to their marriage in 1758.

†Jeanne-Josephine, born 1761 and married in 1780 to Pierre-François Vieusseux, whom Brissot has just named as one of the "people's leaders."

to be divided equally between Etienne and a brother named Jean-Jacques, who had no head for business and allowed him to assume sole control of the "Maison Clavière et fils" and the further assets that Etienne, a careful manager, grafted onto it. He dealt in grain, wax, hose, and silks and even more in lotteries, loans, real estate, and annuities, becoming more and more of a financier and less and less of a businessman. By the time Brissot meets him, his ball of yarn is winding up by itself, thanks to knots tied with the best bankers in Paris, London, Amsterdam, Leghorn, and Dublin. He has over twenty clerks in his Geneva offices. His fortune amounts to 150,000 livres in capital.*

But the man of money is only one side of Clavière. He also dreams. Something inside him has escaped the world of numbers. He was visited by a very peculiar thought in Paris one day in 1780, when he too was trying to win France over to the cause of the Représentants . . . He caught du Roveray by the sleeve as they were walking past the Hôtel des Finances, in which Necker was then ensconced: "My heart tells me that some day I shall live in that building."[13]

Ambition? No doubt; but perhaps in the higher sense of the word. In any event, he soon forgot his premonition and plunged into the Geneva conflict. "He applied politics and moral philosophy to the details of trade;† he had no physical courage at all and was timid by temperament, yet he put himself in situations demanding much intrepidity of character; it seemed as though his mind and character did not match; he was always attacking authority, although danger frightened him; one might have called him . . . the most enterprising poltroon in the world . . . Despite his republican ideas he was fond of luxury and show; there was a sharp contrast between the elegance of his tastes and the austerity of his principles, but he never sacrificed probity to opulence."[14] On this last point, Clavière was abundantly pleased with himself: "I have been working for twenty-five years; never have I caused anyone loss or hardship through any inexactness on my part. I have always made provision ahead of time to meet my commitments; on every occasion I have done what foresight requires in this respect of a man who does not wish to lose the esteem of himself and others."[15] As far as losing his own is concerned we need have no worries, apparently.

This evening we find him in that strange state of nervous exuberance that sets him apart from the rest. He's happy in it, it's his natural condition. And if he is so involved in politics just now, it is because he is convinced that "although political disputes in a free state may do harm they did even more good, and put everyone in a more pleasant frame of mind than the insipidity of repose."[16]

*About 70 million modern francs [$14 million].

†According to another of his Swiss friends, Etienne Dumont, whom Clavière brings into Mirabeau's circle.

He's got what he wanted: a dispute a hundred thousand voices strong raging across all Europe, with him plumb in the middle. Who cares what happens to him afterwards, even if he shudders to think of it? At least the name of Etienne Clavière will no longer be unknown.

CORNAUD

19

JULY 1782

This Form of Happiness

The others, meanwhile, have not been standing idle. The Négatifs being held as hostages in the Hôtel des Balances are mobilized by Antoine-Saladin de Crans,* a fine-featured fifty-year-old beau with a well-cared-for look and the large staring eyes of those who stick to their ideas come what may. He plays the young tenor in this chorus of dyspeptics, urging them to refuse all negotiation with the new regime,[1] a few of whose members have been trying to initiate a hostages-for-parley exchange with the generals of the foreign armies. No: we'll settle this among Genevans; none of us wants a military occupation, a horde of uniformed ruffians in the streets . . . Saladin de Crans is adamant; they must pin their hopes on the invaders: "I contend that in the present situation we cannot negotiate anything whatsoever; that the Représentants must submit and comply with the demands; that their leaders are insane to think of resisting three united Powers, cowards to hold us hostage in order to ensure their personal safety, and vile, base souls to treat us as they are doing."[2] So there.

Not all the reactionaries are under lock and key, however, far from it. There is the great and noble François Tronchin,† friend of Voltaire, Grimm, and Diderot, the octogenarian whom some would like to call the Franklin of Geneva, trundling off down the back roads in a chaise carried by two stout valets to join M. de Jaucourt at his headquarters "and tell him which roads to take in order to reach Geneva without damaging the property of the Constitutionnaires. Tronchin himself lived at Les Délices, where Voltaire used to visit; the house would be in great danger in the event of a siege."[3] Two or three of his colleagues, equally venerable and equally at liberty—you've got to

---

*Born in 1725. His eighty-year-old mother was killed on the day of the *prise d'armes* by a stray shell that landed on her balcony.

†His cousin, a doctor in Paris, treated Voltaire, and treated him cruelly.

watch out for these granddads—including Councilor Rilliet and the former syndic Jean-Antoine Guainier, go to dine with the Sardinian general, M. de la Marmora, and provide him with the same information. The ramparts of Geneva might better be called a sieve for stoolies. At Nyon, the generals from Bern and Zurich are even better off: it's Cornuaud himself, chief of the passive-Natifs and deadly enemy of Clavière and the Représentants, man of the people and foe of the bourgeois, who does the tattling to and heckling of General de Lentulus, doddering a little at the end of his career "and not knowing the first thing about affairs in Geneva."[4]

Funny bird, Cornuaud. Quite a character; one can become acquainted with it by reading the copious *Mémoires* in which he speaks of very little else from the first to the final page of ten fat manuscript notebooks, each five hundred pages long. He's still under forty,* and there is not a single Natif who has not come under his influence in recent years, since he took to politics like a duck to water: vigorous, cunning, a good speaker, physically courageous, but never free of that fundamental aggressiveness of the self-made man who doesn't intend to be imposed upon by any Messieurs. The Représentants' claim to personify the aspirations of the people makes him as angry as if somebody had stolen his watch. There's only one man who knows what the Natifs really want and how to talk to them and that's me, Isaac Cornuaud, because I am one and, like them, I've forged my life out of whatever materials I could lay my hands on.

Since the siege began, he's been at Tournay or Ferney, the two plots of earth over which Voltaire was lord, in the company of a large contingent of other Natifs who have also opted for the old order and who cluster around him like the kinsmen of Abraham when he went forth from Ur of the Chaldees. He is their prophet and provider. "More than one hundred and fifty individuals, men, women, and children were living [as refugees] at Ferney, and I was mightily occupied with providing for their subsistence and keeping proper order among some of them . . . A great many had no resources of their own and it was only just that they should be maintained. To some I paid a fixed amount weekly; to others, who were staying at the inn, I gave so much per meal and informed the innkeeper that I would pay nothing extra† . . . I had twenty-six people living in my rooms, and even so I was the only person at Ferney to have a whole room to myself. I often invented more business there than I actually had, in order to enjoy my precious freedom and abandon myself to my dominant passion for reading and study . . . The impatience, the

*But only just; he was born in Geneva on August 15, 1743, son of a couple of "Habitants," Protestants hailing from Poitou (his father) and Geneva (his mother).

†Where did he get the money? Cornuaud had no personal fortune. D'Ivernois claims, and Cornuaud never denied it, that he was being heavily subsidized by the Court of France.

unreasonableness, the flood of futile words and exaggerated fears of the crowd surrounding me, to whom the same things must be said over again every day, were just so many ordeals for me."⁵ Nothing resembles the problems of a revolutionary leader so much as the problems of a counterrevolutionary leader. But Cornuaud also has a sense of irony that never forsakes him; he's capable of watching himself in action and making fun of his grand adventure on the scale of the "political atom" with which he equates Geneva. There's something of Restif in him, a Swiss and most of all a Protestant Restif, which obviously excludes the eroticism but not necessarily the romanticism or the plain common sense.

How did this Genevan Natif, the descendant of Poitevin refugees— apprentice at twelve, turned watch-case-maker, turned unlucky master crafts- man with six workers, turned accountant, turned mathematics teacher—be- come the leader of a party on which the King of France and the "Constitution- naires" of rebel Geneva are relying for help? If the city's new masters feel so unsure of their position in the event of an invasion the reason is that Cornuaud, by dint of patience and prestige, has managed to neutralize a large portion of the Natifs, making them believe that equality of political rights would bring them nothing, that they would be better off to drop their demand for it, separate from the Représentants, who were all upper-crust anyway—their exploiters, their economic masters enriched by their labor—and ally them- selves with their natural protectors, the great aristocrats of old . . . The eternal temptation of Bouvines and the Fronde: an alliance of the aristocracy and the people against everybody in between, all those ideological bourgeois who hide the reality of their class ambitions under a spate of fine words.

Isaac even claims to have outmaneuvered them and led the loathed bourgeois into the very jaws of the trap. For years the Représentants had been engaging in legal obstructionism, impeding the work of the munici- pal government. So by putting their backs to the wall for once, obliging them to defy the laws, making part of the people say "We dare you" to them so that they have to unmask, emerge from their holes, and find themselves suddenly abandoned by the mass, reduced to their own num- bers, listening for the dread footfall of the bogeyman—that is, the kings and the other cantons—we've got them where we want them at last! Cor- nuaud's rubbing his hands with glee. For him, these days, everything's just dandy. What a revenge after a lifetime in the mud.

"My mother"—who was pious—"made my life burdensome to me, al- though with the best intentions, by teaching me several cathechisms, each more profound than the last but all beyond the reach of my years or any human understanding. I was so discontented with my lot that an extremely singular idea came into my head and occupied my thoughts intensely and for a long time: the regret that I had not been born a girl." He got over it by reading, which he learned by struggling, one word at a time, through two books pinched from his father: *Robinson Crusoe* and *Gil Blas.* True enough, his early youth was much like that of Restif, even Rousseau. "My desire to learn to write found satisfaction elsewhere. I was responsible for the correspondence and diary of a drunken vinegar-manufacturer who could neither read nor write. A chambermaid also kept me busy writing love letters to her swain in London." Apprenticeship came at twelve, to a watchmaker who used to thrash him like new-mown wheat. He bore it stoically, but his parents found out. He was moved to another master, a good one this time, where he could stretch his wings. "For me my master's home was a true paradise. That was the only time in my life when neither men nor events nor my passions opposed me . . . At seventeen I found myself free, in a position to earn four louis a month.* What a fortune! What a sudden change! It is not possible for those reared in comfort to have any accurate idea of what it means to a young man when he sees the first money he has earned by his own labor." That was the age of his exposure to Voltaire and Rousseau, the wound that left so many scars on young people toward the middle and end of the century, and made them not quite the same as their elders. Love gets off to a good start with "a girl of seventeen, a pretty blue-eyed brunette with a slender waist, who sang well, spoke gracefully, was filled with gaiety and sallies, simple like me" . . . but she dies in two days from one of those sudden fevers lurking at the corner of every fountain. "Forsaken and homeless, I found myself in a dreadful void; one object was missing, and so I had nothing." He tries to get over her by going to work in Paris—but "Paris, seen superficially by a thoughtful young man who has known nothing but his tiny fatherland and whose head is full of republican ideas, is most assuredly a monstrous spectacle." Return after six weeks, as though to the promised land: "I shall never forget what I felt when, after crossing the mountains, I first saw the lake and magnificent valley encircled by the Alps and the Jura, in which Geneva stood out as the capital and mistress. I felt a pure and tender joy that caused me to shed tears of pleasure: it was my country, it was my homeland I was seeing again, and I was happy." But not for long: the emptiness in his heart weighs like a stone. "That time was dangerous for my freedom, and circumstances rendered it fatal" by precipitating him into marriage with an abandoned girl "of modest appearance, not at all pretty . . . And that is how I have always decided the most important matters in my life; that is how I decided the most important one of all, the choice of my companion. I thought less about it, and for less long, than many people do before choosing the color of a new suit of clothes." The marriage was unhappy from the start, the young people did not love each other, and with the birth of their first child poor Marie-Judith Cornuaud sank into a lasting inertia.

*About 500 modern francs [$100].

"More than once I thought of quitting life . . . But although sorrow kills, one does not often kill oneself for sorrow; the chiefest cause of suicide is boredom," and that's one disease from which Isaac does not suffer. With a little capital, he tries to found a watch-case manufacture, and goes bankrupt. He may be able to sway thousands but he can't command six workers. He goes into exile as first hand in a more successful factory in Neuchâtel. "I set to work like a slavey to pay off my debts, which totaled one hundred and forty louis,* a considerable sum for a worker in my profession who had nothing but his two arms. I lived alone like an anchorite, hardly ever going out of my house, wrapped in a brown overcoat, working sixteen hours a day to feed my family while paying off my creditors." To render this penal servitude bearable, he found the girl he ought to have met before, a Neuchâtel woman who looked upon him kindly: "A friendship, the most intense, most affectionate, and purest, made me as happy, for nearly ten years, as anyone can be who is compelled to seek happiness outside his own home . . . For a delicate heart any union other than the legitimate bond is rife with shoals and sorrows; this form of happiness scarce deserves the name: it is a necessary attachment that gives life to tender souls, but gives them misery too."

1779. Back to Geneva. Farewell to Neuchâtel and his consolation there. Plunging, this time a mature and aware man, into the world of the Natifs, the pariahs of Geneva. He gives up clockmaking. He retrains in mathematics. "It seemed quite a novel thing to see a thirty-year-old craftsman and father of a family leaving his workshop every day at two to go and listen, in the company of young students, to the arid lectures of a professor of mathematics. At first the youths made fun of me, but my desire to learn and the indulgence owing to their years made me insensitive to their pranks." Now his head begins to whirl over algebra and geometry. "I could work at that subject from four in the morning to eleven at night without minding. My parents, my friends, and neighbors of both sexes absolutely had to learn, one arithmetic, the second algebra, another geometry. My wife was the only person to resist. She groaned when she saw my plan to change professions, and I suffered a good deal from her ill humor" but not enough to do anything about it and the next thing we know he's a mathematics teacher, earning hardly enough to support his family and begin to publish his writings. "Perhaps if I had been happy in my affairs of the heart, that passion for love which is so active in me would have outweighed the passion to make a name for myself that drove me into a new career . . . But circumstance makes sport of men sometimes, causing them to turn left when they mean to turn right. However that may be, from the year 1779 until 1782 my existence was purely political . . ." Helped along by the fact that,

*Over 15,000 modern francs [$3,000].

beginning in 1780, "a pension was paid to him by one of the members of the Committee of Constitutionnaires."

In other words, Cornuaud sold himself without the slightest scruple since, as one of his "right-minded" biographers puts it,[6] "he was the first to understand, with rare clairvoyance, who the Natifs' only allies could be. Despite all their fine promises, the bourgeois Représentants, jealously attached to their mercantile and professional privileges, are the natural foes to whom the Natifs have foolishly subjected themselves. The aristocratic Constitutionnaires, on the other hand, never cross them on any ground and can be their sincere allies."*

Joy among the conservatives: the good people have finally seen how pure are our intentions and how providential our mission! Rage among the Représentants, intensified by the fact that their consciences are none too unblemished. "It was this wrath that incited them to call all Natifs who were not on their side by the nickname of *Grimauds,* alluding to a scoundrel of that name who was said to have brought the plague upon Geneva in older days,"† Cornuaud relates before going on to say, not without pride (modesty being a relatively recessive character trait in that age), "The Natifs were insulted by the appellation until that of *Cornualistes* was conferred upon them by the people's faction of the Bourgeoisie, also as a term of abuse. After 1780 the Représentants generally applied it to anyone, Citizen, Natif, or Habitant, who did not share their political views. In this I find that they were involuntarily doing me great honor, and I can give myself the credit for seeking to deserve it."

Cornuaud's main idea is to short-circuit the parliamentary bourgeoisie. No more middlemen between Powers and people. " 'You refuse to raise us up a little,' I would sometimes say to Représentant citizens. 'Well, then, we'll see if we cannot bring you down to our level and then, one way or the other, our conditions will be more nearly the same.' " He starts flooding Geneva with so many pamphlets "that upon seeing them appear so frequently my friends would say, 'Cornuaud's sneezed again!' " but in a few short months they won him as wide a hearing as any great orator; his method consisted simply in hammering away at the Natifs, making them blush for being "stupid as the geese that saved the Capitol, by helping the Représentants on more than one occasion. Let us create a life for ourselves that will be our own; let the Natifs become respectable, and let people cease to look upon us as clients, as shadows, as the satellites, perhaps, of half the Bourgeoisie."[8]

*This is the first formulation of the sociological triad, people-bourgeoisie-aristocracy, which serves as a backdrop to all the episodes of the French Revolution seven years later.

†The "Messieurs du Haut" [Gentlemen on the Heights] also had a curious name that they used among themselves when speaking of the "yellow laborers" and unemployed who formed the bulk of Cornuaud's battalions: they called them "Mammelus."[7]

They hear him all the way to Versailles. How could Vergennes not lend an ear to such comforting noises? "I succeeded"—this is still Cornuaud talking —"in bringing Versailles to see the Représentant party as isolated, as a thousand lesser aristocrats agitating in a population of twenty-eight thousand souls whose peace and quiet they were disturbing." He certainly has the primary quality needed to make an impression upon the Great: plenty of cheek.

His personal apotheosis, thus, has been a success. While waiting to reënter Geneva in the vans of the besiegers, he lives through a moment of exquisite weightlessness. "During those critical days, there was never a want of moments of gaiety. We had suppers attended by all the most agreeable members of the Constitutionnaire party: MM. de Saussure, Tronchin, Lullin de Châteauvieux,* de Chapeaurouge, Huber père"—the painter-caricaturist of Voltaire —"etc. Benoît-les-Bigarrures [*sic*; Benedict-the-motley—*Trans.*], a few other Natifs and myself made up the company, and we passed some delightful evenings together."

VERGENNES

20

JULY 1782

Dare to Live!

One day, however, we'll have to quit prattling and partying, and actually *do* something about these *enragés,* as Louis XVI has just termed the Représentants in a letter to his ambassador Castelnau.[1] Vergennes's voice has risen to a positive shriek: Geneva hurts him, physically hurts him; it "has fallen into anarchy. The first step to take to restore order is to reëstablish the legitimate government. His Majesty believes that humanity and sound policy demand that Geneva should cease to be a school for sedition whose destructive dogmas would soon infect everything surrounding the city."[2] But it isn't pain that's making him scream so loudly—it's fear, the born conservative's visceral fear of anything that moves; Vergennes has spent his whole life sounding the alarm. "I hardly need dwell upon the reasons that cause the King to desire that Geneva should have a government in which the largest share should go to educated people and to the old families . . . [Otherwise] it would be not

*Who gave his name to a Swiss regiment levied by himself for the King of France—the very regiment that mutinies against Bouillé at Nancy in July 1790.

unreasonable to predict a circumstance in which the multitude, easily won over by some enemy power, might cause us embarrassment."[3] He's been dreading the explosion for two years: "I should be deeply chagrined to see the demagogues' project gain favor because it would serve as bait for the French in the southern provinces who, certain of entering the bourgeoisie without difficulty, would repair to Geneva and settle their families there. The King could not contemplate this innovation with indifference."[4] Which is one reason why Vergennes gave such energetic support to the ejection of Necker last year: he knew the Genevan would try to save at least the lives and property, if not the power, of his Représentant friends, and without him, since May 18, 1781, Vergennes has had a free hand against free Geneva.

Brissot just manages to squeeze in a "pilgrimage to Ferney," accompanied by "a younger brother of Marat, as original a specimen as the other. He had dropped a few writings into the political torrent swirling through Geneva, but was not well-known there and his family was not prosperous, so he opted for exile to Russia where he joined the 'tutorial party,' in which one could at least earn money, if but little consideration."* Nobody pays any attention to the two young men, in shirtsleeves because of the stifling heat; "we were not able to pass the gates of the château; General Jaucourt was master of the place." Through the wrought-iron grillwork they could glimpse the nearby church that Voltaire had designed and inside which the Villettes had deposited his heart. "Built under his direction, it bore the one word *Deo,* which should take the place of all those inscriptions cluttering up the entrances to every temple in which the Eternal is worshipped."[5] But "the combined armies were encircling Geneva ever more closely. There was a daily threat of gunfire. General Jaucourt issued a proclamation ordering all French within the town to leave it under pain of hanging. Thus I had to depart from the unhappy city, anticipating its dishonor more than its destruction. I made my way toward Bern."[6] Exit Brissot on June 17. He has other trips to take; his rendezvous with the scaffold is not in Geneva.

On Sunday June 23, tallyho! The heavy military machine is set in motion under the leadership of the French. The dragoons take the Petit Saconnex while the Nassau infantry regiment (German mercenaries in the King's service, brought up from Saarlouis [Saarlautern] in forced marches) occupies the Peney district, still outside the walls.

    A quivering pastor gives the peasantry their instructions: make no waves. "The colonel called upon him and entered into relations. Every family is

*This is David Mara, born in 1756, the second brother of Jean-Paul Marat. David follows Gilbert Romme's path to Russia but unlike Romme, he stays—and marries a Frenchwoman; he dies there in 1829.

remaining quietly in or near its home."[7] But no ramparts have yet been stormed, and d'Ivernois is still optimistic: the people on his side are reacting as they should. "Five minutes after hearing the news, the whole town was up in arms, even before the Noble Committee of Security gave the order to sound the alarm. In that critical moment, when everyone believed that the French were about to scale our ramparts, we had the satisfaction of seeing over five thousand men armed in a twinkling, filled with courage and loyalty."[8]

Poor d'Ivernois didn't know how busy the termites had been. Ten or fifteen shrewd councilors had informed the military leaders that an assault would be the worst possible ploy because the Genevans would make it a point of honor to resist, whereas by letting disenchantment slowly ripen, along with internal quarrels and anxiety . . . the fruit would drop off the bough by itself. In the following week, therefore, the besiegers did nothing but tighten their ring around the town and make various intimidating gestures. "At the instigation of the parish priests, Savoyard women who were boarding Genevan children brought them back to the town, fearing that if their parents were killed in the fray they would be left with the children on their hands"—and the soldiers let them through the lines, why of course, the poor little darlings! How is the "Noble Committee of Security" supposed to maintain its Roman stiff upper lip with all these women and babies underfoot? Most of the men's families were still in town; you needed Clavière's bank account to send them across the lake.

The pastors, another force of inertia, now get into the act. By no means a secular state, Geneva is more like an anti-Rome, in which the clergy delegates power to laymen under the unrelenting supervision of the "Company of pastors, which had absolute control over the educational system at every level. It also had a say in the appointment of the hospital director and holders of various public offices. It had the right"—as did the parlements in France, but with more authority—"to make remonstrances to the government."[9] Its president, elected for a term of one week only—which indicates the frequency and importance of its meetings—bore the ineffable title of "Monsieur le Modérateur" and the word perfectly expresses the Company's policy throughout the revolution. Immediately after the uprising of April 8, its mood was funereal. "Having unanimously deplored the present state of affairs and the fatal outcome that may issue from it for our beloved homeland, we decided . . . to delegate four of our oldest members to wait upon M. le Premier Syndic, to impress upon his bosom the affliction we feel at the sorry state of the Fatherland." Do they think the town's been taken over by the devil or the pope or something? Not at all; but they are highly suspicious of these disciples of a Rousseau whom they were so instrumental in driving out of Geneva, these Représentants who read the *Encyclopédie* and only come to church out of courtesy. With one or two exceptions, like Reverend Vernes, they adhere with every fiber to the Constitutionnaire party, to the men who have always sat in the front pews at services and made the largest contributions to charity. And they are in close touch with their colleagues in Bern and Zurich, despite the fact that the two Cantons are half at war with Geneva. So that's one side of the resistance gone flabby, and another open sieve for signals and mediations among reasonable folks. On April 9, "it was resolved that the following passage relating to our unfortunate situation should be added to daily prayers in church:

"'O God . . . we humble ourselves beneath Thy powerful hand, and we freely acknowledge that we have truly deserved the punishment that Thou hast inflicted upon us . . . We have turned away from Thee, prosperity has corrupted us, ungodliness has sprung up among us and, by Thy just judgment, Thou hast permitted us to become the prey of long-lasting and dangerous dissension whose weight is growing greater . . . O God, have mercy upon us in Thy great compassion! May the blows of the rod that is striking us awaken our sleeping consciences! May religion recover her empire over us and her influence over our ways!'"

Not quite what you'd call a Magnificat; more like a premature Miserere.

On April 26 the Company announced, "with respect to the different orders which may now be issued in the villages, that the country pastors have no concern in things military, and are to offer no opposition but to confine themselves to their ministries." That explains why the local clergy has made no trouble for the occupying forces. At the plenary meeting on June 21, moreover, "there was a discussion of the lamentable condition of our fatherland, and mutual exhortations to redouble our efforts and zeal in softening people's attitudes." A fine state of mind for a bunch of besieged pastors. It was only one step more, and that step was taken on Monday the 24th at two o'clock, "to send members of the Company to the ministers of the Powers in our neighboring areas, to depict to them the intensity of fermentation in our city . . . describe to them the dangers that could result from this, and conjure them to employ only the mildest of measures, which would not expose the Fatherland to the ultimate woe . . . The Company empowered these gentlemen to appear as its delegates. They set out in the afternoon."

Jaucourt is jubilant. He takes a quick finger count: for the French, there's been Cornuaud and his "Cornualists" from the start, and now, like the Burghers of Calais, here come the pastors shambling up. "In substance, M. le Marquis de Jaucourt replied that he considered the approach made to him by the clergy very well-considered and that it was one of their duties to instill feelings of mildness and moderation into their flocks. He then stated, and repeated, that he wished no harm to anyone whomsoever; that he had come with the intention of pacifying Geneva,* driving out dissension, and establishing a firm order and peace."

Amen. Forward march.

The Noble Committee of Security is beginning to feel a slip in the conveyor belts issuing out of the town hall, where it adopts increasingly fierce resolutions which turn to jelly in the streets at the bottom of the town, among the pastors and tradesmen and society ladies and all those soft underbellies Cornuaud's been kneading away at. D'Ivernois loses his illusions but stubbornly grits his teeth: "There remained"—this is him writing—"the legitimate hope of obtaining an honorable capitulation from the three Powers"—that is, one leaving some leeway for the new laws—"by announcing resistance to the utter death [*sic*] in a place that it was equally in the interests of all three to preserve. In this hope, the very wise precaution was taken of removing seven thousand of powder,† which had been deposited in the lower town where the attack would begin and storing them, as a further precaution, inside the cathedral." The object of this maneuver, which elicited a loud wail from the Company of pastors "and two houses situated in the heart of the aristocrats' district," was to ensure that the said houses would be blown up with the rest in the event of defeat, or cause Vergennes to draw back at the thought of his allies' annihilation, and "abandon the idea of the personal vengeances that he was believed to be preparing to exact." That last clause shows the extent to which even the die-hards' determination to go down in the ruins had been enfeebled before a single shot was fired.

Also in the high town, meanwhile, searches were being carried out in the homes of suspected Négatifs still at large, followed by confiscation of the caches of weapons they had stored with the intention of firing on the siege defenders from behind. This was the occasion for a tragicomic incident: a few of them refused to open their doors and barricaded themselves in with their family, friends, and servants. The grenadiers were greeted with blunderbusses, a rash of mini-sieges erupted inside the main siege; yet these were no more vigorously prosecuted than the principal one: the recalcitrants were simply isolated.

One of them was the noble scholar, geologist, and naturalist Horace-Bénédict de Saussure,** who had been even crabbier than the rest during the past three months, and had turned his home into a full-fledged fortress com-

---

*With six thousand troops and fifty cannons; this meaning of "pacification," we may observe, is not an invention of neocolonial warfare.

†In one-pound bags.

**One of the first, in 1788, to climb the Mont Blanc; he leaves a pleasant, highly romantic account of his ascent.

plete with a cannon, or so he alleged, to defend it with. And what a home! A brand-new little palace, three stories with eleven windows each,* Greek demi-columns set into its stately façade, and a triangular pediment bearing a mythological scene in bas-relief. Tall trees and high walls stand all around.[10] Not so pretty as the Petit Trianon but more imposing. And the ousted rulers of Geneva possess another twenty or thirty "homes" just like it, symbols of their power and influence. The people who thought they were going to sweep all that away in one kettle-boil must have been dreaming. When the Committee of Security ordered its men to force their way into the home of Horace-Bénédict de Saussure with grenades at the ready, and bring along a team of sappers to blow up the whole shebang in case of resistance, the nearby citizens came rushing in to protest. You can't be meaning to spoil our lovely neighborhood!

Herein lies the cause of the bankruptcy of this revolution: how many Genevans really took it seriously? A bare two or three thousand of the lower classes, those of April 8 now waiting on the ramparts, and the handful of twenty or thirty Représentants who have burned their bridges and are feeling increasingly isolated in the atmosphere of uncontested but passive respect prevailing in the majestic town hall into whose great chamber their impotent officers can ride directly on horseback, thanks to a ramp erected by François I long before. But when they do it's only to deliver alarming news. Are we going to have to fight the whole neighborhood just to get the better of old Saussure? Dentand, who's chairman of the commission that day, shrugs:

"If we want to put a stop to this kind of conflict we should have to destroy the entire generation."[11] And it is clearly not this bunch of agitated pacifists who either would or could do the job. Let Horace-Bénédict play swashbucklers inside his fortified camp. At least, we can cut off his water supply.† And the Noble Committee of Security, true to the end to its humanitarian principles, passes a resolution—one of its last—to the effect that "provision shall be made for dogs and cats abandoned during the evacuation of the Saint-Gervais district."

At dawn on June 29 the bugles blow beneath the ramparts. A summons is officially handed to the guard at every gate by messengers whose brasses are adorned with dazzling standards bearing the arms of France, Sardinia, Bern, and Zurich: the "Powers" allied to stamp out "this volcano in a molehill."[12] They have combined tactics and joined forces under the command of the French general (Jaucourt) who, following the advice of his fifth column, has

---

*Geneva having been spared by two World Wars, it can still be admired, along with the town's other old houses.

†On June 28 he capitulates, but on his own terms, thanks to the mediation of the syndics. None of his household is harmed. This takes place shortly before the French enter the town.

opted for a combination of intimidation and moderation. The ultimatum naturally demands the restoration of the former regime, and its former leaders as well, to their pre–April 8 status, together with the release of the hostages; but it imposes no further retribution than the removal of twenty-one leaders of the revolutionary movement to any place of their choosing outside Geneva, provided it be at a distance of at least twenty leagues. This means the members of the "Committee of Security" plus ten of their most seriously compromised sympathizers. The list is headed, of course, by the names of Clavière, d'Ivernois, Vieusseux, Grenus, du Roveray, and Dentand. A shrewd move: their fellow citizens are not required to hand them over to be hanged, which would have rallied everybody to their side; all that is asked is that they should go away, in return for which "the besieging forces undertake to make no attempt on the freedom or independence of the Republic and to withdraw once peace has been sufficiently restored." Who's talking about occupation? This is just a symbolic dress parade.

Well, it's worth thinking about, and the ultimatum gives them twenty-four hours in which to do so. What a perfect ending to the interminable palaver that has formed the substance of the Geneva revolution, at least in the center and at the top of the town. The people holding the ramparts are the only force that can really be counted upon. *They* believe in it. Jacques Mallet du Pan,* a pastor's son who's been trying his hand at journalism lately and who is on the aristocrats' side by nature, cannot help observing that day:

"One must try to imagine the heartrending picture of this population of artisans, impoverished by idleness, buoyed up by fanaticism, gaily facing the gravest perils, heedless of their own fate and that of their families, spending the whole day admiring the cannons and fortifications or performing never-ending military drill . . . and running heroically to their doom. Every individual [on the ramparts] was a soldier, artilleryman, statesman, or commander."

But what's the use, if the leaders are chickening out? The Geneva revolution is rotting from the top. It's a bad sign when people start discussing an ultimatum; if they really want to fight they send the talkers to the devil. The fissure made in the leaders' minds by this apparently guileless offer is far more effective than any attempt to storm the walls. "The first to speak of capitulation were several pastors. Reverend Waldkirch, in particular, kept stressing the idea that true glory in this instance consisted in yielding rather than standing fast with no hope of success."[13]

As for the "twenty-one" whom the ultimatum put in such an impossible position by making the town's safety depend on them and them alone, the attitude they adopt may be heroic, when they agree as a body "to sacrifice

*Now thirty-three. His father, Reverend Mallet, married a du Pan girl, which meant so much in Geneva that the son adopted his mother's maiden name. Together with Joseph de Maistre, Mallet du Pan becomes one of the chief theorists of the monarchy.

themselves for the public weal," but it is also demoralizing. Those nearest them are tempted to take them at their word and nudge them gently toward the exit. But tempers are rising on the ramparts, meanwhile, where the scene is the same as it was three months ago during the uprising. One section of the people—the non-Cornualist Natifs and Habitants—want to hold out, and they're the ones whose plight really is dangerous and who'll be massacred in the event of a bombardment. It's the rhetoricians, the orators, the men who've been feeding them on fiery words, who're trying to wriggle out.

Jaucourt shrewdly extends the deadline—two days, three days—while his soldiers dig trenches and the defenders barricade the streets. But Geneva is lost when, at the pastors' suggestion, it is decided to hold a general delibera-tion to which, "for the twelve circles of the town,* one hundred citizens who must all be homeowners or have families" are sent as extraordinary delegates. Unlikely to be a gathering of firebrands. It meets at five in the afternoon on July 1.

Cacophony. Everybody shouts at once and, behind a screen of highflown verbiage, the champions of surrender make more noise than the rest. D'Iver-nois argues that they can't quit without a fight. The response to this is a text by Rousseau, published by d'Ivernois himself, a letter Jean-Jacques had written to d'Ivernois senior in 1768:[14]

> You are ready to go down beneath the ruins of the fatherland. Do more. Dare to live for its glory at a time when it will exist no more. Yes, Gentlemen, one course remains open to you and it is, I venture to say, the only one worthy of you. It is not to stain your hands with the blood of your fellow countrymen, but rather to deliver up to them these walls which ought to be a refuge for freedom and shall become a tyrants' den instead. It is to come out, all of you together in broad daylight, with your womenfolk and children in your midst. And if irons must be worn, let them at least be those of some great prince and not the intolerable and odious yoke of your peers.

"Dare to live!" Well, if *Rousseau* says so . . . The partisans of capitulation are yelling even louder than before. But the men on the ramparts have heard what's going on and come running up with loaded guns to create one dickens of a disturbance. If you've got to have all this talk about gunpowder, maybe we should start by shooting a few of the people who want to give in. The first men to be seriously threatened are the cowards, which makes a just reversal of the usual order of things. The initial ballot produces a narrow majority in favor of resistance, whereupon the reassured warriors surge back to the ram-parts through a night of crippling heat, an oven in which the thought of death comes almost like a cooling breeze. But they ought to have forced the meeting

*Spontaneous assemblies that had gradually grown up but had no legal status. They might also be called "clubs."

to end while they were still there: the moment their backs are turned, the pro-surrender party calls for a second and more orderly ballot. Fifty-seven for surrender, forty for resistance. It's one o'clock in the morning. The uproar swells. Lawyer Grenus waves his sword in the faces of those who voted to give up. Someone named Brusse, alias Lamotte, breaks his across his knee. After this, who'll ever believe the Genevans are quiet folk! Lapels are clutched amid loud vociferation, arguing whether to have a third ballot. But Clavière, d'Ivernois, and du Roveray, standing with folded arms in the eye of the storm, have understood, and hang their heads. "We may be permitted to dispose of our own lives," asks Clavière, "but what gives us the right to dispose of those of ten thousand women and children?" Farewell, Republic of Geneva! In which a few members failed to possess the form of will to live that means courage to die. Well; let's at least try to bring down the curtain with dignity.

And since no blood is to be spilled, let's also spare that of our hostages. There then ensues a curious procession of conquered-conquerors: the twenty-one exilees walk through the gloom from town hall to Hôtel des Balances, to release their prisoners and make sure that the people don't cut them to shreds. The atmosphere is ghastly, perspiration-bathed yet glacial. They're not going to start congratulating each other, are they? The men in arms feel cheated and are beginning to growl again; back they flood, for the last time, from the posts at which they have now become useless, to settle their score with the leaders who have abandoned them.

Drums begin rolling in the French and Sardinian camps, the troops rush to arm: what's going on inside the town? What's all this firing, apparently not aimed at the besiegers? It's the people of Geneva, wild with rage, firing into the air or through the windows and then breaking their guns in order not to surrender them. Fireworks for a dead illusion.

And as the mob's wrath must have its scapegoats, a hefty escort party looking more like a posse is formed to accompany the voluntary exiles, our dearly beloved leaders, who are spat out of town that night from the landing stage, where a light craft awaits them on the calm surface of the lake. Charon's bark about to ferry its cargo over the Styx. Into the water with you, Clavière, d'Ivernois, du Roveray, Dentand, Vieusseux, and the rest! One infuriated man wounds du Roveray with a sword thrust. The minute the oarsman pulls away a hail of shells pours down upon them, fired by their friends, as though the physical act of their flight had precipitated the hatred around them. Most of the men in the boat drop down and hug the gunwales, but there always has to be one to play the figurehead, standing erect with folded arms, waiting "for a shell to put an end to my days sooner than remain alive with the memory of this night." On this occasion it's a clockmaker named Ringler; but death won't touch him.

"Thus," ironically comments the Négatif Rochemont, "the only praise-worthy action they performed in the course of these events, which was to have the courage to tell the people that they must not attempt to defend the city and thereby raze it from top to bottom, nearly led to their own destruction."[15]

The little craft bearing the spirit of the Revolution disappears God knows where. At dawn, the French, Sardinian, and Bernese troops march into the city with drums beating and standards unfurled. Vergennes certainly can't complain about the results of his "Geneva coup."

MIRABEAU

21

AUGUST 1782

A Cotton Scarecrow

Like a stone dropped into the still waters of 1782, the news of that same "Geneva coup" spread across Europe and the rest of the world in concentric circles, giving well-informed people a few quickly forgotten, quickly calmed shudders. The "masses" never hear of it at all, of course, as neither their priests nor their almanachs refer to it. But a few of those in the know prick up their ears at the sound of "this first squall before the tempest," the expression Cornuaud used to describe it ten years later.

One of them was Manon Phlipon, now Mme Roland and bourgeoise of the fair town of Amiens since her marriage two and a half years before.* The couple had a friend in Geneva, a physicist of thirty with a limp caused by an injured knee, "the good and learned Henri-Albert Gosse," as Roland calls him after making his acquaintance in Paris where Gosse was studying and preparing his dissertation on the "means of protecting gilders from the diseases of their occupation."[1] Gosse was a supporter of the Représentants and had hurried to Geneva to stand and fall at their side before following them into exile. On August 23, 1782, Manon, in Amiens, writes to another and even younger friend of theirs in Paris, Bosc d'Antic.†

*She is now twenty-eight.

†This is the first of Manon Roland's letters to Bosc that has been preserved; we shall see more of him in future, and with reason. He was born in 1759 into a Protestant Cevenol family. The Rolands met him in 1781 at the "Jardin du Roi," now Jardin des Plantes, where he, like themselves and Gosse, was attending Daubenton's and Jussieu's natural history classes.

I have received a letter from M. Gosse that I believe you will be interested to read, and I send it on to you. You will see how the generals of the combined troops of France, Savoy, and Bern behaved when they took possession of Geneva . . . To my mind those poor Genevans conducted themselves in the worst possible manner: one might think them a troop of blind men, willingly delivering themselves up to a few traitors who had sold them and whose maneuvers were perfectly plain. I lost all patience with them I don't know how many times as I was reading it, and my blood is still boiling in my veins . . .

That hot blood that colored her cheeks like a painting by Greuze in the days when she was a virgin, and is still tormenting her now that she is married to old Roland, the husband desperation allowed her to find acceptable. She is emerging from a long struggle she has been waging against her own body and all givers of good advice, as a result of her determination to breastfeed, for over six months, their pretty little daughter, born on October 4, 1781, and saddled with the romantic name of Eudora. The milk rose as from a bottomless well into those beautiful breasts that had given such palpitations to the gentlemen on the Place Dauphine. "One hour after her birth, Eudora was put to her mother's breast, and she had so much milk that the child could never suck enough."[2] A deluge. They gave her a second baby to nurse, but there was still too much. They called in the professional "sucklers," a corporation related to the midwives and wet-nurses: women who were paid to relieve overendowed mothers or to pump breasts that had gone dry to bring the milk back again. Manon has been living on porridge, roasts, oysters, fresh butter, and stewed apples, as recommended by her breviary for that year, *L'Avis aux mères qui veulent allaiter leurs enfants* [Guide for Mothers Desiring to Breastfeed Their Babies], a best-seller by Mme Le Reboul, published by Panckoucke in 1777 and avidly devoured by every Rousseauist. But neither "small beer" nor quinine nor "the good wine of Spain" nor sorrel soup nor herb teas nor barley-water could quench her insatiable thirst. She could have drunk all the water in the Somme. Suddenly, through some process of mutation or resurgence, a new facet of the urban Parisienne Manon had come to light, as earthy and deep-rooted in the old soil as a Picardy peasant woman. But once the numbness of her first months of maternity had worn off, the intellectual Manon raced back to her one unfailing outlet: letter writing. Not to the Cannet sisters anymore, the confidantes of her adolescence who are now her neighbors and to whom she no longer has much to say, as is always the case with the people who are our consciences from afar but whom we promptly lose all desire to see when they are visible all the time. Now she writes to Gosse, Bosc, or another youth of the same caliber called Lanthenas,* a doctor, exactly her age

*Born at Le Puy on April 18, 1754, Lanthenas knew the Rolands in his student years and lived in the same building as they in Paris. He follows them into politics during the Revolution and is a member of the Convention.

(Bosc is younger and Gosse not much older). In place of the overripe old maids in Amiens, the respectable Amiens housewife is now corresponding with overheated young men in Paris. In August 1782 few of them are likely to have received another letter as profoundly and passionately political as this from a beautiful young woman. Here is our first glimpse of the real Mme Roland, on the subject of a failed revolution:

> . . . I pity from the bottom of my heart those people who were unable to see which was the best side in spite of their excellent intentions, or rather who did not have influence enough to impose it; but it seems clear to me that on the whole Geneva was not worthy of freedom; one cannot find in them even half the energy that would have been necessary to defend so precious a quality or die beneath its ruins; and this only increases my hatred of the oppressors whose proximity had corrupted the republic before they arrived on the scene to destroy it.
>
> Gosse tells me that his friend in Paris is in the aristocrats' party and that he has not wanted to see him since the loss of freedom . . . I would have wagered no less: the person in question is a M. Coladon whom I used to call Celadon, no more than a pretty boy whose honeyed ways smelled of slavery a league off, and I'd have given a hundred like him for one cripple of Gosse's worth.
>
> The only hiding place left to virtue and freedom is in the hearts of a tiny number of honorable people; a fig for the rest, and for every throne in the world! I would say it in the teeth of sovereigns: it would be laughed at, coming from a woman; but I swear that had I been in Geneva I should be dead before I would hear them laughing.

These days, the vanquished Genevans who "dared to live" (and how easy it is to cast the first stone when one is in Amiens, or anywhere else) are trickling into Neuchâtel, under great Frederick's wing. They meet, put their heads together, catch their breath, and await developments on the shore of that long, long lake, the most capricious in Switzerland. Here, the sovereign who helped to defeat them is prepared to leave them alone as long as they pipe down. All they are asked to do is keep quiet and let people forget them.

What a curious rendezvous: Brissot was waiting for them, of course; but they see another man of liberty heaving into view, too, and from a very different quarter. Who would ever have dreamed of finding him here? Why, it's Gabriel-Honoré de Mirabeau himself, popping out of his box and strolling away arm in arm with the Geneva revolutionaries. Chance or intuition? A bit of both. But this brief association, lost in the mists of time, looks almost like a cue.

He's been playing daddy's boy all winter long, a part for which he is badly miscast; but then, he's becoming such a fine actor . . . Having duly liquidated Sophie, Mirabeau also sheds his sensitivity, and his spirit was broken in Vincennes; so that now he's back on his feet again, his appetite is concentrated solely on the only two objects that will count for him hereafter, money and power. "Why should one feel oneself a man, unless it is to succeed always and everywhere?"[3] As far as money is concerned, he chose his butcher-father's camp at the wrong moment, Mirabeau père having just lost an avalanche of lawsuits against his wife and daughter, Louise de Cabris, and become utterly ruined, or as ruined as a nobleman could be in those days—only one château, one pied-à-terre in Paris, half his former household staff, and fewer horses in his stables. Enough to make you believe in immanent justice: where did it get him to persecute his wife and daughter all these years?* But now, after jumping back and forth between his parents so many times, Honoré's choice is made and can't be unmade. (After Sophie, nobody ever calls him Gabriel again.) He emerged from Vincennes only to be placed "under the hand of his father" by the King's *lettre de cachet,* and is as dependent upon him as a newborn babe. One frown from the old man and Honoré will be back in jail. And the neurotic hatred that his sister Louise has nursed toward him—not without some justification—since their incest became public knowledge has cut off any chance he had of attaching himself to the winning side. His one hope of clearing the slate and finally leading a more or less normal life—at thirty-three—is to tame his father and, with his support, try to recover his wife, if only for appearances' sake. Also, the vast fortune of the Marignanes could put them in clover again. First step: regain his legal freedom. So he's had to keep his nose clean . . .

. . . All autumn long and all through the early winter at Bignon, in a dreary tête-à-tête with that failed and embittered genius of a father with whom he had never spent so much time before. Mme de Pailly, "the black cat," the Swiss mistress who's been reigning over the place since Honoré's childhood, has been on a long vacation in her native land because her public "concubinage" with the marquis would have been a mark against him while the lawsuits were pending. A skyful of tedium stretched above the "pretty basket of grasses" drenched by autumn rain and the insistent, penetrating fog of the Loing. The pearls of water grew heavier and heavier, finally dragging the leaves to the ground outside, where the rich Gâtinais mud clings to your boots. Surrounded by the joyless labor of ill-paid gardeners, these two men, father and son, paced their bent way through the sodden gusts, leaning into the winds of their lives. They had every reason to hate each other; for a few months they pretended it was love. A masterful performance. Farther south, at the Château de Mirabeau beneath a mistral-scoured sky, the bailli was still shaking his head and lecturing away at his brother:† "Consider that the best manner to succeed at

---

*"All" Mirabeau senior will have to live on from now until his death is an annuity of 15,000 livres (90,000 modern francs [$18,000]), punctually paid to him by his brother the bailli: the income from an endowment from the days of their opulence.

†Reminder: the bailli is the Marquis de Mirabeau's younger brother, who entered the Order of Malta for the same reason as everybody else—that is, the law of primogeniture—had a respectable career there (observing, like Suffren, the vow of celibacy but not that of chastity) and looked

nothing is to pretend to think for others, and try to lead them according to one's own liking and not according to theirs." Those two have been bickering back and forth across France for the last thirty years, they couldn't live without it now, they're hooked. But lately their quarrel has changed tack: for years the bailli stuck up for his nephew, and now he's trying to moderate the father's singularly overdue infatuation for his son. The Friend of Man was making "a great effort at paternity":

"I began, immediately upon his arrival, to stuff him, in writing, full of principles and of all that I know. [Thus far] all he has done, by long and solitary study, is to increase the tangle inside his head, which is an upside-down library ... He is no more thirty-three years old than I am sixty-six ... That head will always be that of a child; it counts for nothing with him to have a mentor." The infernal Mirabeau fils, meanwhile, was playing his part to perfection, and maybe not wholly tongue in cheek—when he starts to act, he goes all the way. "My only concern is my father, and his concern for me is my joy ... He will always be greatly deserving of renown, whatever the public may think today," he wrote to Jean-François Vitry, his love-at-first-sight friend for 1781. Vitry was an official in the ministry of foreign affairs, who has become the startled witness to this fleeting reconciliation and to the meek-as-a-lamb phase of Gabriel-Honoré de Mirabeau. "I emerged too late from my swaddling clothes and cradle." He was trying to stop believing he was destined to rule the world. "Simply wanting to be a beacon does not make you one" (again to Vitry). But certain evenings by the fireside, in the space left inside him between the old man that his blighted youth had made him and the Marignane's pimp that seemed likely to be his future vocation, he was still dreaming far and high, although of nothing he could put a name to: "I am tormented by my own agitation. When the candle that has been lit at both ends is used up, it will go out; but at least it will have shed a bright light for such a tiny lantern." The marquis, meanwhile, was dreaming of the return of his "black cat." This couldn't last much longer.

E finita la commedia. Word came that Mme de Pailly was on her way to Bignon. The approach of spring hits Mirabeau like a teenager. He goes roaming again, with his father's provisional blessing: after all, he had to "put his head back on his shoulders," the head that had been sliced off in effigy on the main square of Pontarlier five years earlier. If he didn't want to vegetate his life away under the *lettre de cachet* that was protecting him from civil justice, he was going to have to do battle with the lawcourts of Franche-Comté, give himself up and get himself tried in flesh and blood, in order to invalidate the

---

after their estate in Provence. His correspondence with the "Friend of Man" is one of the unpublished treasures of eighteenth-century French.

contempt of court charge. Whew, we're off, we're moving. Bye-bye daddy.

"I want to show what, in this century of inertia and slavery, still remains possible for a man of courage." Mirabeau's back in voice, it would seem, and his father is certainly back in grumpiness: he sends the bailli a funeral oration for six months of illusion. "Notwithstanding the bitter ugliness, the intercadent gait [*sic*], the trenchant precipitousness, breathless, inflated, and the expression, or to put it better the hideous brow of that man* when he is listening or thinking, something told me that he was nothing but a cotton scarecrow . . . But what a head, if head there be! The weakest in all Europe."

Mirabeau fils' little caravan moved off, for better or worse, in February 1782, quitting the Gâtinais for the still snowbound roads of the Jura. *Dramatis personae:* the eternal infant with the oversized head, happy as a schoolboy on holiday; a lawyer, or rather a sort of "legal adviser" called Des Birons, "under whose supervision his father placed him, in pursuance of the full powers granted him by the King, a copy of which was in his possession;"[4] and one terrific manservant worthy of a novel on his own, a Figaro whom Mirabeau had just recruited at Bignon and who sticks with him to the bitter end: Aimé Legrain,[5] a Picard born in 1752 and thus almost the same age as Honoré, with an equally ticklish sense of honor. "Having heard the saying 'prostrate as a base valet' a hundred times over, he had become disgusted, not with serving, but with being servile."[6] He was the lackey-accomplice, a typical *ancien régime* character whose master, having once made his acquaintance, would sooner part with both arms and legs than with his man. Legrain gorged like Gargantua, drank like a fish, and fucked like . . . a Mirabeau. Somewhere around Sens, after Des Birons had retired to his chamber, the two playmates indulged in a few out-of-the-way competitions. At last, one time in his life, Honoré was being allowed to spend his father's money; somebody had to pay for the trip, after all. Sade, too, before embarking upon his prison career, had introduced his beloved Latour into his damsel-torturing alcoves. But in the paternally financed festivities of Mirabeau and Legrain, there was no perversity; it was all joy. At Brinon, "a seventeen year-old cook, with a pretty face and a pretty bosom" accorded her favors to them both with very liberal impartiality. The next day an axle broke, and they had to wait for it to be repaired.

" 'Sir, I'd have been much happier if the coach had broken down at Brinon . . .'

" 'I know what you mean, I know what you mean . . .' M. le Comte said to me, in the same tone of voice."†

In the shivering little town of Pontarlier, on which Mirabeau dropped like

---

*This isn't the first time that the "Friend of Man" has spoken of his son in such terms.
†From Legrain's manuscript diary.

a bomb, the warden of the hovel they called a prison, which had never
harbored an inmate of such distinction, turned over his own lodging to
Honoré and transported himself and his family into the cells, "with the smug-
glers, deserters, thieves, and fevered* whose howls drive sleep from their
neighbors' weary lids."† Somebody could have written a ballad about that
jailer's family: the father and mother were always drunk and the two "young
ladies," seventeen and nineteen, volunteered their services as the docile hand-
maidens of master and valet alike; and when the latter, who was free as the
wind, was dispatched on some errand, both girls devoted themselves to Mirabeau, who thus took his full revenge upon six months of compulsory chastity
at Bignon.

Legrain even contracted Honoré's furious hyperactivity. More useful to
his cause than all the lawyers in the world, he whisked back and forth across
the Swiss border like a weaver's shuttle, digging up witnesses and imploring
and intimidating them—for want of funds to corrupt them with. Mirabeau's
defense was a pellucid crystal of bad faith. He had been convicted of "abducting a married woman," and Sophie and he together stood convicted of "adultery." Abduction? What abduction? Prove that I took the woman away by
force! Adultery? Which adultery? A hundred people had seen them together,
but that was in Switzerland and Holland; for their testimony to have any legal
weight, they would have to come and submit it to the judges in Pontarlier. The
wall Legrain built was high and strong: not one citizen of Verrières-Suisses
dared scale it. He even instigated a sort of mini-terror in Pontarlier, harrying
the magistrates at their very doors and swingeing the King's own counsel, M.
Pion, in broad daylight:

"There were some dogs running after me in the main street, and among
them happened to be M. Pion, sworn enemy of my master and no friend to
his servant. As I had a good coachwhip with me and knew how to use it, but
I didn't want to slash his eyes, I only gave him a cut across the face and both
ears . . ."

The fact that Legrain suffered no punishment for this attack** is a clear
indication of the atmosphere of this topsy-turvy trial, in which the incarcerated
contumax was defying the whole leathery little society that had executed him
in absentia. His response to the hypocrisy of these people who thought heads
had to fall for adultery was a rousing campaign of provocation, like a streetwalker flaunting her buttocks in their faces. They may have been asking for
it, but they certainly got it. The Franche-Comté discovered Mirabeau's titanic
humor. At one of the few public hearings (most of the case took place behind

*That is, lunatics in the straitjacket stage.

†According to Mirabeau, who heavily dramatized the conditions of his detention in Pontarlier.

**Except an interrogation in Besançon.

closed doors, in discreet questioning, exchanges of written statements, and muted interviews), he rose up before his judges:

"Gentlemen, I am accused of seduction. To this my one reply and sole defense is to request that my portrait be deposited with the clerk."

The poor nudnik of a clerk didn't catch on and sat there blankly. One of the judges had to give him a prod:

"Nincompoop! Look at the gentleman's face!"

These tactics were not likely to hasten the day of victory, however, witness the fact that they kept him in the lockup for over five months. Every lawyer's man of them, from Pontarlier to Besançon, was sticking tight to his colleagues and even tighter to Président de Monnier, the venerable half-dead cuckold himself* who was defending what he termed his honor to the death and nursing the hope of a sizable compensation in hard cash. The sentence delivered *in absentia* granted him nothing less than forty thousand livres in damages, of which neither Mirabeau, père or fils, could raise the first penny.† As the weeks went by Honoré sensed that he was being nudged gently toward a lifelong debt and a verdict that would still be defamatory to him, so he fell back upon the tried and true form of self-defense he had adopted in his days in the Château d'If, Fort de Joux, and Amsterdam: incendiary *Mémoires,* which were published in Besançon and even in Paris and appealed to public opinion. They brought the case to the notice of one part of the outside world, namely the gossipmongers at Court, of whom there was no scarcity, heaven knows. And from them Versailles and Paris learned that some weird little owl's-nest out there in the mountains was giving a libertine a hard time. And that's just the word for him, says Mirabeau père, stricken and seething anew. The talk was driving him out of his mind; he became ill every time the family name was uttered in the street. "After all this, turning to print is a swordthrust in my side; . . . that *Mémoire* is visibly dedicated to the libertines . . . You cannot imagine"—this to the bailli— "what he calls his defense. I have never seen him so extravagant: he has humiliated the witnesses, exasperated the judges, insulted everybody. And he believes himself to have acted in innocent good faith, he is downtrodden, moderate, and magnanimous! . . . These *Mémoires* will break his neck for good, and will pillory the preposterous madman." The "Friend of Man" was fiercely regretting those six wasted months, but what hurt him most was his vanity. Can a fellow remodel his son after thirty years? Well, that's over now, they won't catch him trying that one again, and he savors every drop of the incoercible hatred rising in his gorge once more, his hatred of his large-headed child. An old man's joy.

*He dies on March 4, 1783, but that made no change in Sophie's situation; she couldn't forgive her relatives and settled in Gien.

†240,000 modern francs [$48,000].

The child, meanwhile, was having a ball. Smash—there's one for the Marquis de Monnier and his graybearded impotence. Bam—and another for the daughter by his first marriage and his son-in-law, the Valdahons, "their offensive vanity, their satirical humbug, their insatiable and sordid cupidity!" One, two, three *Mémoires;* people were reminded of the ones Beaumarchais was writing against Goëzman a few years ago and sat back to guffaw at this revival of "Punch Thwacking His Judges." The third and final blow is for the assistant prosecuting attorney, a man named Sombarde who was conducting the case despite the fact that he was a relative of Président de Monnier! "Sombarde, perfidious Sombarde, come hither and let me reveal your crime . . . You are related to M. de Monnier, you have extorted citations in foreign countries, you have threatened, seduced, and suborned witnesses; you have been present while they were testifying; you have paid them with your kinsman's coin." Modest as ever, Mirabeau writes to Vitry, after rereading this diatribe; "If this is not a degree of eloquence unknown to our slavish centuries, then I know not where to find that gift of heaven, so alluring and so rare."

At least he's recovered the backbone of his former personality: his boundless self-confidence.

Okay, okay, don't rock the boat; please, stop the slaughter! Backstage negotiation is the only solution; the case is finally settled at the expense of the one person who isn't there, never opens her mouth, and is ready to endure anything, Sophie de Monnier, buried alive at Gien. The "Friend of Man" had sent his prolific and flabby son-in-law, the Comte du Saillant, to Pontarlier; he was always useful for such errands. He offered the Valdahons a deal—they being the only people who could act officially on behalf of Président de Monnier. He also had to calm the indignant outbursts of his brother-in-law, who didn't like people doing business behind his back. But a little money laid out to pay for some Arbois wine and a great many peaceable words to assure Honoré that he could go on playing the star part . . . To the very end Mirabeau tries to persuade himself that he has been Sophie's best possible defender, even after all parties have signed a treaty endorsing the Monniers' separation in flesh and in cash, divesting Sophie of the rights and dowry guaranteed by her marriage contract, and confining her to her residence at Gien, in exchange for which her husband magnanimously agrees to pay her an annuity of 1,200 livres.* He drops his suit against her and against Mirabeau; there was no abduction, no seduction, no adultery. Their little Gabrielle-Sophie is dead, thank the Lord. The Pontarlier magistracy consents to rescind its sentence. If you twisted his arm, Honoré would be tempted to tell you that it was for Sophie's sake he had

*7,500 modern francs [$1,500], which the Valdahons continue to pay after de Monnier's death. This is virtually her only income.

undergone the martyrdom of prison. "When one considers that Mme de Monnier had more than I [to answer for] by a proven flight from her husband's home and the equally proven birth of a child after an absence of nineteen months, you [to Vitry] would find me miraculously accommodating."[7]

If he is to forget Sophie with a clear conscience he has to convince himself that he had, after all, given the woman who was guilty of loving him beyond reason that scrap of tranquillity with which all females should content themselves and not make a fuss. Sophie was silent as the tomb, which must mean that on her side everything was fine, right?

On his, it was only so-so. He was no longer threatened by civil justice, but he was still "under the hand of the King"—and thus of his father—by virtue of that infernal *lettre de cachet.* And the father in question is now out to get him again and won't cough up a sou, being far too infuriated by the thought that his son has used *his* money to print those accursed *Mémoires.* Honoré can just paddle his own canoe down to Aix to undertake the next phase of his grand design—that is, the retrieval of his wife and rank, and never mind if he's broke as yesterday's toothpick and reduced to a state of civil infancy. That's his business. And above all he can refrain from showing his big head at Bignon again, where Mme de Pailly has just resumed sway, the dear creature, accompanied by a nice bit of capital that couldn't have arrived at a better time. If the marquis hears that his son is prowling around Paris, it'll be Vincennes or the Bastille and no mistake.

Honoré has had plenty of time to weigh up the situation during the interminable weeks of his confinement in the jailkeeper's house pending completion of the laborious legal formalities officializing the treaty between Pontarlier, Besançon, Dijon (for Sophie's parents), and Gien. The future is not rosy. His morale sags whenever his pockets are empty. His response to the congratulations of his sister Caroline du Saillant is bitter: "I am very far from able to subscribe to the sanguine omens with which your kind heart has favored me. Mine is torn, and the wound will never heal. My father's contempt and hatred are out in the open at last, he has bared them to the bone. The contempt may be assumed, but that only renders the hatred the fiercer . . . What can I do? What must I do? Except avoid arrest and thwart his prophecies by exiling myself forever from my native land and family."

It's not such a bad idea: he's almost touching the frontier, and he knows every mountain path on the road to Verrières-Suisses as well as any smuggler, from the days when he frequented them so assiduously as lover. And from Les Verrières there's a fine dry road through the pine forests that will bring him tumbling down to Neuchâtel, where his *Essai sur le despotisme* was printed. Fauche the printer can be his banker, Mirabeau's got trunkfuls of manuscripts to unload on him. The summer heat is setting in, but so mildly at this altitude, where the air of freedom seems twice as sweet when he is finally released on

August 13. With Legrain, to whom he owes three months' back wages, at his heels, he shoots away to Neuchâtel, the refrigerator of the banished Genevans, from which Brissot has just departed en route for Paris.

MERCIER

22

AUGUST 1782

A Dream If Ever There Was One

When they get there they're going to disturb the peace of a strange person who's been living so quietly in Neuchâtel that he could almost have gotten himself elected mayor—Louis-Sébastien Mercier, who sank prudently out of sight here after Abbé Raynal was banished from Paris in 1781 following the explosive reprint of his *Histoire des Deux Indes*. When the fur starts to fly, he reasoned, you're better off under cover, especially when you yourself have unleashed two or three wildcats into the literary jungle and are busily sharpening the claws of a few more. "Here all my time is my own, I revel in every instant of its duration, my leisure is perfect and no distraction takes me from my study . . . Here I regret that there are not seventy-two hours in the day, I am neither utterly alone nor assailed by urban noise, I need curry no favor, and at last I am writing in a free country under the protecting hand of a great king who knows how to wield the pen himself."[1] Voltaire's old illusion about Frederick was hard to kill, it misled nearly all the writers of the day. But in this case the King of Prussia had an added virtue, that of being a hundred leagues away from Neuchâtel, where "literary discord has never penetrated, for I am the only man holding a pen,"[2] as Mercier was still purring in June. Poor fellow! Here comes competition, and so much the better for the Neuchâtel printers who have almost the monopoly on the little town's wealth, as the watchmakers do in Geneva. But Mercier doesn't seem to mind too much, sitting in his hillside house on the slopes on the outskirts of Neuchâtel,* where he can look down on the lake and gaze out at the mountains. He was living there with "a friend to whom I am bound by love of literature and chemistry,"[3] but it isn't all milk and honey; they quarrel and spy on each other like lovers—yet Mercier was not totally indifferent to women, and seriously set out

---

*Absorbed by the growing town in the nineteenth century; Mercier's room has been a sort of little museum for almost fifty years.

to court his publisher's daughter. After a few months the friend walks out on him, tearing wails of agony from Mercier's breast; a touch of cold shoulder from a chemist and he's at death's door, writhing in depression, neurasthenia, and what-have-you. Perhaps this Parisian's bliss in his Neuchâtel retreat is less unmitigated than he would have us believe, but in him everything is a mixture, friendship and love, gravity and platitude, revolt and affectation; he's a bouil-labaisse, a culture medium, you can fish anything up out of the stew and there'll always be enough left to go round. *Le Courrier de l'Europe* even announces that he actually expired of grief in the arms of Abbé Raynal, "who was confessing me and giving me absolution," what an illustration for the history of eighteenth-century literature.* He has to write the *Journal de Paris* to let them know he's not quite dead yet,[4] although it's true that he was complaining of a sort of agony:

> How solitary everything around me seems! Has the hour come? Yes; I seem to hear the angel of destruction hailing me to the place to which so many mortals have descended . . . I read pity in every face, but it is cold and transient. Every look tells me: he's going to die. In vain I call for help from the consoling voice of friendship; there is no reply. Friendship, yes, friendship itself is weary of my lamentations, the sight of my afflictions has become importunate to it . . . The storm in my breast is more tumultuous than that which flattens and uproots the trees on the mountainside. The cloud of death advances. I hear a funereal voice cry out to me, 'Thou shalt die!'[5]

You need your ears cleaned, Louis-Sébastien; it was "Thou shalt write." The author of the first modern novel of political anticipation, *L'An 2440*, is now putting the finishing touches to his *Tableau de Paris*, a philosophico-picaresque documentary essay like nothing before it and nothing since, on the capital of the kingdom of Louis XVI.† His squeezed-lemon lamentations are just a smokescreen for his doubts about the quality of his work, and leave his readers utterly unmoved. The man himself, moreover, usually hides his private anxieties behind a round chinless face, well-groomed and close-shaven, with a slug-nose thicker between the eyes than it is at its distant tip glued onto a flat face, a domed intellectual's forehead under rather sparse powdered hair, the whole lit by ferret eyes; the mouth is relatively thin, neither excessively sensual nor excessively kind. A defensive man;[6] he'll never suffer longer than he has to.

To work, Mercier! "I left Paris the better to depict it,"[7] but not before having "done so much running about to produce the portrait of Paris that I can truly

---

*In fact, Raynal is in Berlin with Frederick in 1782, and Mercier lives on until 1814.

†From the beginning, I have taken many sketches and scenes in my characters' Paris from Mercier's *Le Tableau de Paris;* see references.

say I painted it with my legs." He had published two volumes that were already impertinent enough before Louis XVI's turn of the screw, coinciding with Necker's dismissal. Then he started all over again and, in two years, will produce eight more volumes, six hundred and seventy-four chapters, while simultaneously turning out four (insignificant) tomes of *Portraits des Rois de France* and another four of satirical miscellany about everything and nothing, entitled *Mon Bonnet de Nuit* [My Nightcap]. Not bad for a basket case. He's reached the period at which a creator has to start burning his phosphorus and let everything else go hang. Who among us knows how long he can stay aflame?

He's a true son of that Paris he castigates and sings hymns to in almost the same breath; this is an Oedipal passion. He was born there in 1740, on the Quai de l'Ecole where his father Jean-Louis Mercier kept a sword-cutler's shop at the sign of "La Garde d'Or et d'Argent," and Louis-Sébastien is not ashamed of the fact.

"Demosthenes, I believe, was the son of a manufacturer of swords," he scribbled in a draft of a poem, proudly adding "And so am I" in the margin before going on, still in the unassuming vein so fashionable in those days: "My name is very common, but I rhyme in steel."

His mother was the daughter of a well-off mason and died when he was four. Only one of his brothers survived, Charles-André, who is also his friend; he kept the hôtel on the Rue de Tournon which became famous after Joseph II stayed there. A comfortable family, thus, honored in the world of trades and corporations: under Louis XV the sword-cutler was "guard and juryman of the community." Their home had only two rooms, one above the other on top of the shop, with heavy, solid furniture and a quantity of pots, flambeaux, and silver platters. Sébastien grew up in this humble ostentation of the Parisian artisan, in which anything that happened must have happened in silence, for he virtually never refers to his childhood and it's about the only subject he doesn't cover. His father remarried, of course, after a year, like everybody else; but Mercier hasn't left one word about his stepmother and precious few about his father. We know more about the dancing and Latin masters who were imported to give him polish, like some little *bourgeois gentilhomme.* What followed them was a lot less fun—that is, his first lessons in adult ferocity in old Toquet's boarding school. Toquet was one of those bloodthirsty school-masters to whom children were sacrificed in the name of a primary education. "Crowded together in close, dark, airless rooms, we were not permitted to whisper, stir, or raise our eyes from the book; at the sound of doctor A.B.C.'s voice we trembled in every small limb. The cane was perpetually suspended over our heads . . . Whoever has seen one boarding school, has seen them all . . . In each, the children had their hats stolen and their clothing torn, were bored in their captivity, cursed their ignorant and disheartening tutors, passed on to each other all the elements of vice, gnawed on bones miscalled meat at the refectory table to please the niggardly mistress,* who, like the master, held a fistful of rods at the ready."[8] At nine, he found himself a day pupil at the Collège des Quatre Nations.† "Up at six in the morning, my arms too short to reach round my Greek and Latin dictionaries," he had only to cross the Pont Neuf to reach the splendid edifice in which he had such a deadly time that now, thirty years later, in volume V of *Le Tableau de Paris,* he's still scourging "that most beautiful, richest and largest of the colleges of the Université de Paris, which is at the same time poorest in skilled teachers and learned scholars." The first person he encountered there every morning was "the under-principal, whom the scholars called *yard-dog* because, like a shepherd's dog, his occupation was to contain the schoolboy species in a large courtyard until classes began. He was authorized to mete out justice of the lower and middle degrees." In class, the poor kids were faced with "pedants whose heads had been turned and who believed themselves capable of educating a crown prince because they had donned the purple belt. There is no arrogance comparable to that of professorial conceit . . . One's first glance at this purple personage inflated with pedagogy is a glance of derision, the second a look of pity." The pupils were beaten bloody on the slightest pretext in front of the professor's pulpit and forced to count the strokes themselves. Here Mercier learned Roman history, contempt for the human race, and masturbation. "Some masters surreptitiously gave us the most famous forbidden books to read. Mass was the pupils' preferred moment for perusing the *Ode to Priapus;* some sang the obscene lines at vespers, in the faux-bourdon of the *Magnificat*.[9] At seventeen he was hanging around the Théâtre Français and Café Procope, which cured him of all desire to do anything but write: his revenge, the chance to affirm himself, to exist. Which is why he goes on and on now, writing about absolutely everything; all that matters is the sound of his own words in his ears. He himself had a vague skirmish with teaching, when he was twenty-three, as "form-master" to a class of thirteen-year-olds, in the days when the void created in many schools by the expulsion of the Jesuits had to be filled with whatever they could scrape up. But that was only to earn an absent-minded living. For ten years he was primarily a scribbler: tragedies, tales, "philosophical reveries," nothing; blackened paper. In 1770 he became a real writer, one of the strangest and most neglected, along with Restif de la Bretonne, in all of French literature; that year *L'An 2440, ou Rêve s'il en fut jamais* [The Year

*The lower schools were often run by couples.

†Where he may have rubbed elbows with another day pupil who was equally remote from the "Quatre Nations," Antoine-Laurent de Lavoisier. This school, today known as the Palais Mazarin and seat of the Académie Française, was instituted by Louis XIV to indoctrinate "well-born" children from the four "foreign" lands he had conquered: Alsace, Flanders, Roussillon, and the territory of Pignerol.

2440, or A Dream If Ever There Was One] was published anonymously, in Amsterdam, by van Harrevelt, in one octavo volume which went almost unnoticed by Grimm and Bachaumont. The critics of that age could not tolerate anything disconcerting in any area, and where was one to put this unclassifiable object? "It is a species of apocalypse that would require lengthy discussion."[10] We've been waiting a long time for it; in fact, we're still waiting at the end of the twentieth century.

In that book Mercier existed. His *An 2440* remains the pride of his life, and rightly so. He keeps coming back to it, referring to it, brandishing it. What a fox in the chicken-coop. He took optimism and generosity as his guides, borrowing a phrase from Leibnitz* for an epigraph: "The Present is quick with the Future." That's Mercier, all right: his thought is a projection onto the screen of the visible. He wastes very little time on the window dressing that gives his book its fictional hue, showing far less concern for it than Swift for Gulliver in Lilliput or Brobdingnag. Chapter I: a young Parisian converses with an old Englishman—a perfect exponent, naturally, of the British superiority over France and the French—who sets the tone from the start by abusing Paris: "In your kingdom everything is done for this capital. Cities and whole provinces are sacrificed to it. Ha! But what is it, more than a diamond on a dungheap? What an inconceivable mixture of wit and stupidity, genius and folly, grandeur and ignominy!"[11] Chapter II: "I am seven hundred years old"; shamed and stricken by the preceding conversation, the young Frenchman has slept the centuries away and wakes in a totally transformed Paris. "My brow was creased with wrinkles, my hair white, there were bones protruding sharply beneath my eyes; a long nose and a pale, livid complexion had spread over my whole face. The moment I tried to walk, I found myself leaning automatically upon a stick, but at least I had inherited none of that ill-humor which is so common among old men." And off we go, dot and shuffle, for four hundred pages of utopia. "Everyone pressed around me with most particular consideration and respect. The people were all burning to question me, but discretion tied their tongues, and they merely whispered among themselves:

"A man from the century of Louis XV! Oh, how exceedingly curious! . . ."

But it is as a man of his own century that Mercier rebuilds Paris, France, and the World of *L'An 2440.* He lacks true power, true wrath, and gropes his way among clever tricks and valiant impulses. Everything seems different to the narrator because "I observed the movement of the vehicles"—still horse-

*Leibnitz (1646–1716), one of the great German philosophers, scholars, and "universal men" of the preceding century, had a very strong influence on eighteenth-century thinkers and was a living encyclopedia and a model of tolerance. His motto: "There is almost nothing that I hold in contempt."

drawn; no shadow of a motor in sight—"how each one going in one direction drove on the right and each one coming in the other was on the left. This wonderfully simple means of avoiding manslaughter had only just been thought of, so true it is that the most useful discoveries are last to be made." You may smile; but in the Paris of Louis XVI over two thousand pedestrians were killed every year because coachmen drove exactly where they pleased. Starting with an immeasurably larger number of victims—the peoples bled to death by war—Mercier takes the bit between his teeth and returns at full gallop to the monstrous Europe in which he has no choice but to try to live, that rats' nest of sovereigns known as the Age of Enlightenment. His real gift is for polemics, not imagination. His utopia ought to be the exact opposite of what exists; well, at least what exists gives him a solid springboard:

> Oh, singular and deplorable constitution of our political world! Eight or ten crowned heads maintain the human race in chains, writing back and forth, helping each other to hold it tightly in their royal hands so that they may squeeze it at will until it twitches in convulsions. Conspiracy is not hidden in the shadows; it is public, open, conducted by ambassadors. Our complaints can no longer mount to their august ears. Cast your gaze over Europe; you see nothing but a vast arsenal in which thousands of powder-kegs await one tiny spark to burst into flame.* Often it is the hand of a muddle-headed minister that touches off the explosion. The flames catch, North and South, and spread to the ends of the earth. How many cannon, bombs, guns, balls and shells, swords, bayonets etc., of murderous puppets obedient to the lash of discipline, await nothing but the order emanating from some cabinet to play at their bloody games? Mathematics itself has profaned its divine attributes: it fosters the dementia of sovereigns, now ambitious, now insane. With what precision an army can be destroyed, a camp razed, a site besieged, a town burnt! I have seen the members of academies coolly calculate the capacity of a cannon. But stay, Gentlemen; wait until you have so much as a principality of your own. What do you care whose name is to reign in which country? Your patriotism is a false virtue, dangerous to mankind. For let us consider a little the meaning of that word *patriotism.* To be attached to a State one must be a member of that State. Apart from two or three Republics, there is no longer any such thing as a *patria* in the true sense. Why should an Englishman be my enemy? I am bound to him by trade, by art, by every possible tie: between us there is no natural antipathy. Why then do you insist, beyond some arbitrary line, that I separate my cause from those of other men? Patriotism is a fanaticism invented by kings, and augurs ill for the universe. For if my nation were three times smaller I should have to hate three times as many people; my affections would be dependent upon the changing boundaries of States: in a single year I should have to carry the fire to one neighbor and make peace with another whose throat I was cutting but the day before. No: in my eyes the Europe of the future must form a single huge State; and the hope I dare to express is that it may become

*Need we recall that this passage was written thirty years before the Napoleonic wars?

united under one and the same domination. All in all, and upon careful reflection, that would be a great advantage: then I could be a patriot. But what is freedom today? Naught but the heroism of slavery.

One can see why the book was published anonymously, when its author calmly announces, forty pages on, that "prejudice is always seated at the right hand of the throne,* ready to pour its errors into the ear of kings," or that "if divorce were permitted, marriages would be happier. People would be less wary of contracting a bond that would not chain them to their unhappiness." In 2440 people divorce as they please; but we can't ask Mercier to go much further than that: his path was traced in his twenties when he, like so many others, opted for Rousseau in preference to Voltaire, for virtue over libertinage. The women in his utopia are excruciatingly dull. The only change in their lives in 700 years is that they wear no make-up and go about attired all in white, followed by hordes of offspring. As for social structures: they become more flexible but remain essentially what they had been before. In seven hundred years of inspired slumber Mercier has not done away with fathers, elders, authorities, kings, or God.

> Can you believe it? The revolution has been accomplished effortlessly and through the heroism of one great man. A philosopher-king, worthy of the throne because he disdained it, . . . offered to restore the former prerogatives of the Estates . . . Absolute sovereignty was abolished. The leader retained the name of king but did not undertake the insane task of seeking to bear alone the burden that so weighed down his ancestors. The assembled Estates of the kingdom possessed all legislative power. The administration of affairs, both political and civil, was entrusted to the Senate, and the monarch, armed with the sword of justice, ensured that the laws were respected. The Senate is responsible to the king and the king and Senate are responsible to the Estates, which assemble every two years. All decisions there are taken by plurality of votes, including those relating to vacant places and the redressing of wrongs.

"A dream if ever there was one," really? The coffin-lid of our gracious pleasure—"as the King wills, so wills the Law"—must have been crushing indeed for a scheme as timid as this to seem extraordinary in 1770–80! Here and there, Mercier nervously allows the tip of his pen to slip out in a snarl or two, a sort of furtive graffito: "Man! if you are still capable of choice, choose to be happy or wretched; fear tyranny, abhor slavery, shoulder your arms, die or live free!" Or, "Everything on the face of this earth is revolution; the human spirit makes infinite variety in the national character, alters books so as to render them unrecognizable. Is there a single author who can boast of not

*No connection with "right" and "left" as they become defined politically in 1789, except that by "right" Mercier means the favorites, the privileged persons whom the sovereign places on his right by preference.

having been hissed by the next generation? Do we not jest at our predecessors? Have we any idea of the progress our children will make?" And then out of the blue, at the base of his placid pyramid: "Why should not the French support the republican government? . . . French honor, an ever active principle higher than the wisest institutions, could one day become the soul of a republic." He did write "republic," although in passing.

The entire book is an escape from the present, the price that has to be paid some day by anyone lucky enough to be able to write, to wage the battle of the imagination. At the end, everything starts whirling around in a kaleidoscope: Mercier abandons the new Paris and the new France to outline a world regenerated (undoubtedly under the influence of early editions of Raynal's *Histoire des Deux Indes*) by love and shared interest. A series of mini-chapters, passages ten or twenty lines long: from Peking, from Jedo [*sic*], the capital of Japan, from Persia, from Mexico City, "which has just regained its former splendor under the domination of the descendants of the famous Montezuma"; from the city of Asunçion in Paraguay, from Philadelphia, Morocco, Siam, the Malabar Coast; from the Magellanic Land (Patagonia), the Land of the Papous, the Isle of Tahiti in the South Sea, from Petersburg, Warsaw, Constantinople, Rome (whose bishop goes to call on the Emperor of Italy and "withdraws on foot with all the humility of a true servant of God"); from Naples, Madrid, London, Vienna, and The Hague, we see converging an internationale of optimism. Will he finish off back in Paris again, where, of course, "the monarch dwells in the very heart of the capital. There he is, to be seen by the multitude. His ear is ever open to their cries. He is not hidden away in some kind of desert, surrounded by a host of golden slaves"?

No. Surprise postface, a stroke of genius: if the king is living in Paris, what's happened to Versailles? The man who wakes up in the year 2440 ends his travels there.

XLIVth and final chapter: Versailles. I enter the town and gaze around looking for that sumptuous palace in which the destinies of several nations were decided. What was my surprise to behold nothing but debris, gaping walls, mutilated statuary, a few up-ended porticoes hinting confusedly at former magnificence. I was walking among these ruins when I encountered an old man, seated on the capital of a column. "Oh," I asked him, "What has happened to this great palace?" "It fell!" "How was that?" "It collapsed on its own foundations. One man in his overweening pride sought to violate nature here; he precipitated edifice upon edifice; in his desire to satisfy his capricious will, he exhausted his subjects. Here all the coin of the kingdom was entombed. Here flowed a river of tears to fill those fountains of which not a trace remains. Here is all that survives of the colossus that a million hands erected with so much painful effort. This palace was a faithful image of the grandeur of him who built it, for it was weak in its very foundations . . ." "But why do you weep?" I asked him. "Everybody is happy now, and these ruins signify nothing less than a destitute society." He raised his voice and said, "Ah, wretch, know that I am Louis XIV, who built this ill-fated palace. Divine Justice has rekindled the torch of my life so that I should contemplate my deplorable works at first hand . . . How fragile are the monuments of pride! . . . I weep, and shall weep forever. Ah, had I but known!"

23

JULY–SEPTEMBER 1782

The Right to Resist

From Brissot's *Mémoires,** after his disappointing Geneva expedition:
   "At Neuchâtel I found Mercier, then occupied with the printing of the continuation of his *Tableau de Paris,* a work whose simple philosophy, more readily accessible to the people than that of Raynal, did much to hasten the Revolution by opening the eyes of the French to a host of prejudices and abuses. More than one hundred thousand copies of these two works [of Mercier and Raynal] went into every corner of Europe within a few years. Eight editions of the *Histoire philosophique*[1] were being printed at once. Fear of the Bastille and the desire to put as much life as possible into his scenes had led Mercier to choose this retreat. But although he had a pleasant life there, he seemed to me to be missing the entertainments and little suppers of Paris, where he had spent half his time. Solitude was not so congenial to his eyes as it was to mine. He preferred to observe men and *ridicules* in town, rather than revel in himself and nature in a lonely countryside.
   "Let all friends of solitude seek refuge in Switzerland; that is their true homeland!"
   Notwithstanding these exhortations, Brissot himself spends a bare three months there before flying away toward Paris and London, while Mercier endures three long years in Neuchâtel. How the literati love each other! Jealousy drips from every word in that passage by Brissot, although he had some justification: at this point Jacques-Pierre is a mere polemicist paid by the piece whereas since *L'An 2440,* and that was twelve years ago, Mercier has gained the clandestine renown which the authors of that time looked upon as

*Written years later, when he was already playing a leading role in the Revolution.

their Promised Land. Nevertheless, the two men were destined to meet and work in the same direction, if not as friends. They shared the same printer: the encounter was inevitable. From Brissot again: "I lived [in Neuchâtel] with the banneret* Osterwald who had established a huge printshop from which issued almost all the worthwhile political and philosophical works then inundating France. From there they were smuggled across the Jura mountains to Lyons, which offered facilities for their subsequent distribution throughout France. In this branch of commerce Neuchâtel had taken over from Holland, and France paid an immense tribute to this little State in order to receive the light emanating from her own bosom, whose proscription was at once an absurdity and a crime of its government . . . The inquisitors in the cabinet at Versailles imagined they had shuttered every chink through which a ray of light might creep by garnishing the Flemish frontier with their sbirros. But the spirit of freedom simply changed place, transporting its workshops to the heart of the mountains . . . I admired M. Osterwald's establishment in a charming and well-chosen situation on the lake. Osterwald was a learned old man; but his daughter, widow of the minister† Bertrand, surpassed him by her remarkably extensive knowledge. She was truly worthy of the place to which the Elector Palatine has since called her at the head of a house of public instruction in Mannheim"[2] . . . and she was also, therefore, worthy of the assiduous court paid her by Mercier, to which, judging by a few letters that have been found, she apparently responded with her whole large Swiss heart.[3] Will we ever know what prevented Louis-Sébastien Mercier from ending his days as a respected schoolmaster and father of a large family in Baden-Württemberg where the Rhine and Neckar meet, far from the turmoil of Paris? Maybe Brissot was right when he said Mercier was homesick.

Almost all of them cross one another's paths and meet one another's minds at some point during that summer, in the large, airy, new rooms of the "Société typographique de Neuchâtel," the most highly respected, momentarily the largest, and therefore the most threatened firm in the canton; but that's a fate printers have in common with munitions manufacturers.** Mercier, Brissot, d'Ivernois, Clavière. The first three come bearing manuscripts and remain to see them through the printers; the fourth comes bearing funds, for Clavière

*An old title of the lesser nobility dating from the Holy Roman Empire; originally a banneret was a minor aristocrat whom the emperor had authorized to arm banner-bearing companies in his service.

†That is, the reverend.

**Frédéric Samuel Osterwald, Banneret of Neuchâtel and a much-esteemed man in the town, so highly prized as a speaker that he had been nicknamed Golden-mouth, had hardly recovered from the legal censure pronounced against him by the governor of Frederick II "for publication of bad books" and goes bankrupt in 1784.

knows how to choose his authors and suffered little loss (except in real estate) from the Geneva uprising. Big banking is already simulating the starfish: cut off an arm here and it grows back again on the far side of the frontier. He advances a hundred louis to Brissot* for the lightning production of *Le Philadelphien à Genève, ou lettres d'un Américain sur la dernière révolution de Genève, etc.* † [The Philadelphian in Geneva, or Letters from an American on the Late Revolution in Geneva, etc.]. While waiting for the 216 pages of this opus to get written Brissot amuses himself polishing his epigrams in a series of pamphlets, insults flung at the conquerors of Geneva like pebbles rattling on a coffin-lid, which Osterwald brings out by the fistful. "When matters come to such a pass [as occupation by a foreign army] all hope must be abandoned. A tiny republic in the hands of a Persian Sophi** is a mouse between the paws of a cat. He toys with it for a time, then throttles it. Such may be Geneva's fate."4 Or, "What is a crime of state? Authors apply this term to any event in a democracy that tends to tamper with the established constitution, to the detriment of the people's happiness. As a man, and an American [*sic*], I have reason to believe that this definition can be applied to every form of government; for in every government the people's happiness should be the proper goal of the administration; under every government, when a people is oppressed and crushed by tyranny, it is entitled to protest, it has the right to resist. This principle is one of natural law."5 Finally, drawing attention to the inevitable link between the prostration of a down-trodden people and its moral deterioration: "You have no idea . . . of the change that has taken place in customs and principles in Geneva in the last three months. Two prostitutes, their heads shaved, have been put on the wooden horse‡ to provide a new form of entertainment for the poor Genevans, enslaved by three powers that find themselves quite bemused by the ties binding them together. Is this the right way to put a stop to such forms of disorder? . . . More to the point: will the daughters and wives of Messeigneurs du Magnifique Petit Conseil be put on the wooden horse when they are found guilty of licentiousness?"6

D'Ivernois has aged ten years in three months. It's a mature man, a veteran stripped of the young seducer's braggadocio, who comes to badger Osterwald's compositors and printers about a revised and supplemented version of his *Tableau historique et politique des Révolutions de Genève dans le XVIIIe siècle*†† [Historical and Political Tableau of the Revolutions in Geneva in the

*About 12,000 modern francs [$2,400].

†He hardly has time to start the book in Neuchâtel and completes it in England. The edition in my possession is unsigned and dated 1783; Dublin is (falsely) given as the place of publication.

**As the shah was often called in those days.

‡A form of pillory, sometimes mobile, employed in Germanic countries.

††A first edition, killed in the egg, had been run off during the uprising by Quiby and Boisselier in Geneva; the book is almost wholly based on papers left by his father.

Eighteenth Century]—dedicated, oh irony, to Louis XVI! The book will be
hunted down by every police force in Europe, except that of England.

All these dignified gentlemen, dressed in black but exchanging lily-
white handshakes, topped by large heads inside which worlds are whirling,
pace respectfully back and forth in the clatter and clank of the presses,
stops, and presser-feet, between the huge typesetting room where the compositors manufacture each book like a cake, aligning the wooden bases of
the lead letters—the most beautiful fonts ever designed by man—one by
one in their forms, and the printshop where the presses stand like trees,
their geometrical branches growing up to the ceiling to brace themselves
against the shattering blows. With infinite care the printers, in tight knee-
breeches, short rolled hair, and leather aprons, place the forms emerging
from the wetting-room on the ever slippery skating-rink block and slowly
insert, sheet by sheet, the opening trickles of a torrent that will tear old
systems up by the roots, a flood of puny ink, the only weapon that could
be used against entrenched old fogeys. Every writer who comes through
the door automatically begins to feel a bit like a laborer. Mercier's positively churning it out, as though stung to action by the arrival of the Geneva refugees. In August he hands Osterwald a few of his most virulent
passages on his beloved Paris, which he demolishes like an abandoned mistress. "The insults offered her are true lovers' reproaches, the reproaches
of a lover who longs to see her as beautiful and radiant as she could ideally be."[7] He says the bitterest thing a lover can say, coldly remarking that
his ex-beloved is falling to pieces—that the Paris of Louis XVI is being
hurried into her grave by poverty and opulence.

> How can Paris be protected from the hunger that perpetually threatens two-thirds
> of its inhabitants? . . . The great misdeed was done when society consented to,
> and endorsed by its very laws, a prodigious inequality of fortunes, since which
> time everyone has been compelled to devise his own personal means of survival.
> There is an unending struggle in which all forces conspire against the boulder of
> wealth, seeking to chip away some pebble of it. In this there can be no question
> of the laws of Plato; what we have to contemplate today is the overturning of
> natural society, the monstrous consequences of luxury, and the general depravity
> it has engendered. The State is a sick and gangrened body; we have not therefore
> to impose upon it the duties of a sound and vigorous one, but rather to treat it
> as its almost incurable condition requires.
>
> Luxury alone can heal the wounds of luxury. It is a poison that has become
> necessary to the whole. The first law is survival. The most appalling spectacle is
> that of idle misery awaiting death with folded arms and uttering a few inarticulate
> moans; and as the capital is a confused and incoherent conglomeration of men who
> have neither time to cultivate nor manufactures to direct nor duties to perform,
> who are crushed by the daily burden of indigence and who can continue to exist
> only through prompt and private industriousness, then it is needful—the evil

having been committed and every manner of abuse tolerated—it is needful to give means of subsistence to this horde of men who might otherwise do worse.[8]

In Neuchâtel, thus, this is how you get from Geneva to Paris, by moving from one box of type to the next in Banneret Osterwald's printshop. Maybe Vergennes was right to be so apprehensive; maybe, failing any larger solution, he was wise to throw up his little dike in an effort to stave off the tide of the times. At any rate the Marquis de Jaucourt, commander-in-chief of the punitive forces, is certainly the man for the job. He loathes the natives entrusted to his care and hastens to inform Vergennes: "The more I learn of the character of the inhabitants of Geneva, the more confirmed does my opinion become that there cannot be another like it in the world. It has all the disadvantages of pride, self-interest, weakness, mischievousness, and intrigue. And bad faith thrown in for good measure, because one does not know on whom or what one can rely."[9] He wastes no time. Four hundred newly promoted Bourgeois are hurled back into the political void as Natifs. "Showing proof of great clemency . . . Sieurs Dentand, Ringler, Grenus, Vieusseux, Flournoy, Clavière, Lamotte, Bonnet, Chauvet, du Roveray, Guerre, and d'Ivernois, the last-named bearing the seed of several Catilinas* in himself and standing out as the most dangerous subject in a policed society [sic]" are exiled for life. D'Ivernois, however, ties for top honors with his elder, Clavière, "who shall be pronounced infamous and have his name stricken from the citizens' roster. He is forbidden on pain of death ever to appear in the city or territory of the Republic [of Geneva], the Republic undertaking never to pardon him. The tutelary powers further promise never to tolerate him on their territories. On the tower of St. Peter,† at great height, shall be placed an inscription blighting the memories of Clavière and Dentand."[10] Vergennes most heartily concurs: "It has been my constant aim to deprive the bourgeoisie of the means of drawing authority into its hands because, had it retained them, there would never be peace in Geneva. Every time I have thought I saw a tendency, in the drafts of laws, to give the multitude some influence in government, I have asked that they be altered."[11]

On November 21 a General Council is rounded up and railroaded into adopting, "to the sound of ringing bells and prayers of thanksgiving," the pacification edict that restores full powers to the retrograde aristocracy. One hundred and thirteen courageous voters** (including most of the pastors— and about time!) reject the diktat, Article XXV of which actually states that

*Leader of a popular party in Rome in the first century B.C. who often employed violence and was himself assassinated at forty-six. We know him only through the diatribes of his adversaries, especially Cicero, "who made him the very model of youth demoralized and depraved by civil war, going to any lengths to satisfy its ambitions" (Petit Robert des noms propres).

†The cathedral. This project is never carried out.

**Against 524 ayes; the usual attendance at General Council meetings was more like 1,500.

every resident of Geneva must swear an oath of obedience or leave town. One hundred and thirty-six persons refuse to swear and go into exile, after this mini-revocation of the Edict of Nantes.[12] With the people gagged and the bourgeoisie in despair, order may be said to reign anew in Geneva.

So what. If Geneva is no longer in Geneva, we'll move her somewhere else. D'Ivernois is the first to voice the scheme for a "New Geneva." He's young, and still capable of seeing that when the notion of fatherland becomes oppressive it makes no more sense than the notion of family. To free minds it is only smoke, a mist: blow on it and it vanishes from the sight of clear eyes. A fatherland can have no *raison d'être* except when it breeds life and liberty. Anything else is dead wood in an old tree.

Upon what is Geneva founded, apart from a questioning mind and the spirit of Calvinist criticism? What is its other essential component? "Manufacture." That almost collectivist effort of masters, craftsmen, and skilled workers to assemble and export the finest timepieces in the world. The "Geneva manufacture" needs enthusiasm and fraternity, though; in the rarefied atmosphere that Louis XVI has just imposed upon it, it will inevitably wither. "One project alone can soften the bitterness of our lot, avenge us upon our tyrants and give tyranny the greatest lesson it may ever have received. That project is to transplant the Republic to England—or at least the most commendable part of the Republic, by which I mean everything associated with the manufacture of timepieces, in other words half the town."[13] The men already in exile will set the plan in motion and lead the way, and the provisionally subdued Genevans will prick up their ears and follow, in the greatest human hemorrhage of the end of the century. D'Ivernois: "I am sacrificing to this plan the remnants of a tumultuous youth and a dilapidated fortune." By midsummer, a few of the Genevans' English friends have become interested (in every sense of the word). A colony of manufacturers of watches, the universal gadget of the age: it would attract capital, build new towns, create juicy investments, and lend its promoters a nice blush of liberalism. Encouraged by some of the English ministers, Lord Shelburne in particular, and bearing Clavière's endorsement to his London correspondents, d'Ivernois sets out for England on July 29 to be followed by du Roveray within a fortnight. If the attempt to found a New Geneva on the main island proves problematic, owing to the economic crisis in the United Kingdom and competition from English watchmakers, we can always fall back on Ireland, an authentic colony whose Roman Catholicism matters as little to its Protestant occupiers, liberal or otherwise, as does Greek Orthodoxy to the Turks or, later, Islam to the French. The perfect terrain for an experiment in industrial development. "Ireland," writes a contemporary English specialist, "is almost in a state of nature" in autumn 1782. "Her fields and her inhabitants are equally uncultivated. The linen manufacture is the only one fully established . . . By nature, this country is superior" to England; but "Irishmen . . . are meager in their faces, filthy in their dress, and dwell in hovels."[14] The graft of an active and virtuous Protestant scion onto that stock, a sort of industrial *Mayflower* . . . Worth watching.

But the Genevan emigrants are being solicited on all sides. Joseph II would like nothing better than to lure a few over his way. The more Protestants he has (in Constance, he proposes), the happier he'll be. And there's also the Margrave of Baden, the Elector Palatine, the Grand Duke of Hesse, and the Grand Duke of Tuscany . . . They're all trying to entice the outcasts. Frederick II has first option and would like to settle them in Magdeburg, unless he simply decides to tell his governor in Neuchâtel to give them all the help they need there. Clavière prudently installs himself in the town for the time being, at the crossroads of capital and industry. On August 19 he receives permission from the canton authorities to remain as long as he likes: "An appeal was addressed to his good will to make whatever effort he may deem proper on behalf of the Chamber of Charity."[15] By mid-September he has resumed his financial dealings with Delessert in Paris, Rivier in Bordeaux, Crawley in London, and Owermann and Meyer, also in Bordeaux; he sends Vieusseux to represent him in Paris, where his son-in-law, unlike himself, is free to elect domicile. He invests substantial sums with Louis Féline (Nantes) and Girardot, Haller et Cie (Zurich). Wherever his friends end up, they aren't going to run out of bread.[16]

One of them now gets a look in on the first good deal of his life: Brissot. Not that he was obsessed by money, he hardly gave it a thought; but need exasperated him because it deprived him of his means of expression. In Neuchâtel, the Brissot-Clavière alliance is signed and sealed for better or for worse.

"Instead of thanking them for their generosity, people had driven them out with blows of their gunbutts and I saw [Brissot talking] Clavière abused more than once. I could not credit such ingratitude toward a man who had sacrificed his fortune [to a point] . . . his repose, and his life to the people.

"The Genevan outcasts scattered in the vicinity of Neuchâtel; several were living in a village called Pésieux, half a league away; they were the most considerable of the group. I rented a room there for a fortnight, the better to profit from their conversation. Du Roveray and Clavière* passed on a wealth of precious material to me, part of which I later consigned to my *Philadelphien à Genève* . . .

"The Genevans differed as to their next move. They wanted to found a colony; but where? France, which was putting them in irons, was loathsome to their eyes. The emperor was calling them to Constance. But what faith can

---

*And d'Ivernois too, of course; but Brissot was soon to quarrel with him in England, and tends to neglect him in his *Mémoires*.

be placed in the promises of a despot? Switzerland seemed to be proposing brothers; but secret jealousy was gnawing at the hearts of those brothers. All eyes gradually turned to England. Its constitution offered the most certain guarantees of freedom; Ireland might see the rise of a new Geneva. The plan was formed . . .

"To turn my friend Clavière's thoughts from his sorrows, we conceived the idea of touring the countryside around Neuchâtel. These voyages were profitable to me in every sense. Clavière, matured by his years, his experience of civil and political life, and the practice of trade and of men; Clavière, who owed everything to himself and drew only upon his own resources, whose power lay wholly in his own strength, was constantly correcting my reflections and giving weight to my ideas. He had seen in my works a great facility for writing, fertility, clarity, method, and most of all a lively sensitivity; but he rightly considered that I was abusing these qualities, that there was no indication of depth, that the thinking was too superficial, and he wanted to teach me to pursue my ideas further, make me dissatisfied with myself and more exacting in my productions. It was then that I underwent my second education, and I owe all the benefit of it to him alone . . . Clavière had everything I lacked, and in part I could supplement what he did not possess. Another bond between us was a shared sensitivity to things beautiful and good, a common desire to be useful, a need for disinterested expansion beyond ourselves . . . He was for me at that time as I have known him since, that is, a true father and wise mentor. He gave me sound advice in regard to the establishment I wanted to set up in England and, although he knew nothing of my means, was well aware that prosperity was not the common lot of men of letters; he offered me a credit of two hundred louis on a house in London."[17] Brissot has found his father substitute.

After d'Ivernois and du Roveray, it is now his turn to leave the nest, equipped not only with full pockets but also with the indispensable blessing of the bank. These fellows are part gyrfalcon. Brissot climbs into a *carabas** and rumbles over the mountain roads to Besançon, meaning to make only a brief stopover in Paris and set off again for London as soon as possible, now that the signature of the peace treaty is known to be more or less in the offing. At least the United States are free, and nobody can change that. In England he'll start a newspaper, with the help of funds from the New Geneva, at last he'll become a second Linguet, reaching out to influence the whole enlightened world . . . He starts dreaming again.

There's one little detail to be dealt with first, however: sweet Félicité, his mistress since 1780. It wouldn't be so bad if she were alone, but he has become a sort of pasha to four females: her mother Mme Dupont, the kindly hostess

*Possibly a deformation of "charabanc."

in Boulogne, and Félicité's two sisters also dote on him. "I was bidding farewell to France; was I to leave my friend behind? To take her with me before my establishment was built on any firm foundations seemed imprudent. We therefore determined upon a separation, which could not be for long; but before leaving her the best of mothers secretly united us, before the eyes of friendship alone . . .*18

"I returned to Boulogne with my mother-in-law and remained there a few weeks, surrounded by filial and fraternal affection and the counsel of friendship. My marriage had given me three sisters, that is, three friends; but there was only one soul in all that family."19

Exit Brissot from Neuchâtel; a few days later, enter Mirabeau.† Their paths crossed, the one on his way to Besançon and the other on his way from Pontarlier, with nothing in his pockets and everything in his head, now "back on his shoulders" and fixed even more firmly in place by twelve thousand livres of debts to friends, printers, and lawyers, contracted during his last trial, which his father was refusing to pay.

Mirabeau's sole capital is his manuscripts. His first visit is to his ex-printer-accomplice Samuel Fauche, who is an important rival of Osterwald but far less squeamish about licentious or subversive copy. He had already printed Honoré's *Essai sur le despotisme* back in the days of his semi-liberty in the Fort du Joux—the days of Sophie. Friend Fauche, will you buy my fresh *Conversion*, my *Espion dévalisé*, and my *Lettres de cachet et des prisons d'Etat?* A salmagundi that has gone slightly sour since Vincennes, where he wrote the first drafts or one might better say finished products, since he is virtually incapable of revising his work: one piece of trashy porn; one jumble of juicy anecdotes on the Court and government of Louis XV, weighted down with a hymn to Turgot and the text of the *Appel aux Hessois,* which Mirabeau had written in Holland to deter the Hessians from going off to fight against the Rebels;** and lastly, one loud roar, with all its petty vindictiveness and noble thoughts. Fauche's arm needs no twisting, especially as he can always hope to boost sales by

*On September 17, 1782. This doesn't mean that some sort of family ceremony took place with Mme Dupont officiating; Brissot married Félicité Dupont very much according to Hoyle in the parish church of Saint-Sulpice. It was kept a secret from relatives and even friends, however, because of the job as assistant governess that Félicité had recently landed in the household of Mme de Genlis—the name of a controversial polemicist could not be allowed to tarnish the glitter of the House of Orléans.

†Most historians have supposed that they met and became acquainted there, but this is not so, as is proven by Mirabeau's first letter to Brissot in 1783, published in the latter's correspondence. Although they knew each other by reputation, they never came face to face until then.

**The whole lumped together under the title of *L'Espion dévalisé.* Such mixtures were fairly common in those days, and were called "compendia of anas" after the Latin suffix, meaning a collection of information or odds and ends (e.g. Americana).

playing opposing groups of readers off against one another and is anxious to recoup the two thousand or so francs Mirabeau has been owing him since 1776 as the result of distribution problems with *L'Essai sur le despotisme.* The one sure way for an author to get published is to be in debt to his publisher. So here goes for three new books bearing no author's name and fictitious places of origin. No harm in trying.

Meanwhile, Mirabeau will seduce the Genevans. He's counting on it and was already plotting his course back in his prison in Pontarlier, where Legrain brought him the gazettes to read. Step no. 1 ? While he was in Pontarlier a man named Théophile Rilliet, a childhood friend of Clavière and a Représentant, had written to him, apparently to compare notes about their respective legal troubles, and Mirabeau had answered. "Oh, no less virtuous than hapless man!" (From Mirabeau to Rilliet, July 19, 1782) "Eloquent man, who caused me to shed bitter tears, but who also comforted my heart and uplifted my soul by the force of your sensitivity and the noble spectacle of your qualities! Allow me to do you homage once again." He tells Rilliet he will be in Neuchâtel early in August. "I shall hasten, Monsieur, to bring you my tribute of zeal and devotedness, and we shall speak of the affairs and errors of your Republic."[20] He hits town like a one-man traveling sideshow, with his bulldozing ways, his aristocratic poise, his mysterious air of being in on all the secrets. He picks the best inn in town, the "Faucon," "very pleasantly situated, in an area covered with vineyards that produce a good red wine."[21] An ideal place for Clavière and du Roveray (still a few days from his departure) to make his acquaintance and find a common ground that they never again forsake.

Mirabeau doesn't stay long at the "Faucon"; Clavière takes him by the arm and leads him to the best house in the canton, that of a man named du Peyrou who has amassed a huge amount of money in Surinam (Dutch Guiana) by God alone knows what shady dealings and built a little palace fit for a king on the hill above Neuchâtel. All he rules over, though, is conversation. "In this city there are more handsome and elegant buildings and town houses than in any other in Switzerland."[22] Frederick II's hospitality was by no means confined to exiles and nervous penpushers: the place was positively seething with businessmen of every description, also in search of a bit of breathing space. Clavière, too, did not linger long in his fleabag of a hotel at Pésieux; he was already living in du Peyrou's house and it was he who got his host to invite Mirabeau, who takes like a fish to these luxurious waters, which have nearly drowned Brissot: "My only regret" (Brissot writing) "was being surrounded by too much wealth. Although a *philosophe,* M. du Peyrou lived in a magnificent palace that had cost him more than a million to build,* for it had often been necessary to violate nature† and bring either materials or furnish-

*Six million new francs [$1,200,000].

†The "du Peyrou house" is built into a friable hillside.

ings from afar. The gilt drawing room, more appropriate to Paris than to the lonely mountains, made too marked a contrast with the simplicity of its owner, the amiability of his wife, and the bust of Rousseau that was worshipped there."[23] It was, on the other hand, a perfect hothouse for the germination, sprouting, and development of the Clavière-Mirabeau relationship, which ripened from mutual appreciation into friendship. Until this point the former had known nothing but petty bourgeois, Brissot included, whom he made use of for want of anything better. But here at last, at his mercy or at least within his grasp, was a nobleman bursting with energy and ideas. "Clavière loved Mirabeau,* loved him, I believe, better than all his other friends. If I am not mistaken the cause for this attachment lay in the Genevan's invincible penchant for revolutions and those who could carry them out."[24] No doubt; but there's also that shared sense of ease by the side of a snapping fire, when powdered footmen glide past like shadows to fill your glass with the wine of Aÿ at the end of an eight-course meal, and the immaculate napery, and the crystal. Could any atmosphere be more propitious to the shedding of mellow tears over injustice and poverty?

Money doesn't come into those early conversations; Clavière's friendship is enough to renew Mirabeau's confidence in the future. But Mirabeau, driven as always by one of those double-edged impulses that is intended to make the world better but only succeeds in making his own position worse, immediately gives Clavière an earnest of his good faith by firing off a massive epistle to— Vergennes! It begins with the personal question: he begs the minister to destroy that *lettre de cachet* he will have hanging over his head again as soon as he sets foot in France, so that he can begin his legal joust against the Marignanes in Aix. On this point Mirabeau might have had a chance in spite of Vergennes's grim austerity, for the minister was a vague cousin of Sophie's parents, had followed the trial closely, and was fully aware that the prosecution of the two lovers had been a monstrous miscarriage. Next comes the altruistic part: to show proof of his good intentions to Clavière and his friends, Honoré appends to his personal request a staggering sixteen-page *Mémoire*[25] in which he addresses the minister in the authoritarian tones of a special envoy dispatched to set everybody straight about events in Geneva, dishing out warnings and advice and almost making the minister's decisions for him: withdraw the occupying forces, clear the slate, prevent emigration and the dispersal of Genevan industry, restore the rights of the bourgeoisie, and give the people back their freedom. Acting like the thirty-three-year-old boy scout that he is, Mirabeau treats Vergennes as though he were some sort of idiot or liberal or something. Nevertheless, he strikes the right tone: that inimitable matter-of-

*By Brissot, in his *Mémoires,* much later, and not untinged with bitterness. In this connection Brissot recalls that Clavière was an "inexhaustible mine of rough diamonds."

course attitude adopted by people of their class when talking among themselves about anything at all, a woman, a footman, a people, "come now, old
boy, you know perfectly well that . . . " They take each other by the arm. They
sprinkle the whole with a scattering of witticisms. They casually drop a few
items of valuable information just in case the other chappie might feel like
knocking off some work between two yawns. The shoptalk of the aristocracy.
Topshop talk. As he turned over the pages before giving them the axe,
Vergennes may well have had a passing thought that Mirabeau might just
come in handy one day, somewhere between Madrid and Constantinople. He
had passed his entrance examination to the antechamber of diplomacy:

"You may believe a man who respects you too much to flatter or mislead
you. The troubles in Geneva are not the work of the sacrificed party; they are
a masterpiece of machiavellianism by the other party . . . Allow me to say it:
had you once intimated to the aristocrats that the faults of the governed are
most often those of the governing, the mere accents of your beneficent voice
might have calmed the Genevans and put an end to their dissension."

Here and there we catch a glimpse of the statesman. The best of Mirabeau
talks to the best of Vergennes, as from one planet to another:

"Take care you be not deceived. The Genevans who have now been humiliated
are the part of their nation most highly esteemed by the whole of Europe . . . I
repeat, therefore, Monsieur le Comte, that emigrations are in the offing in Geneva, and that to my mind there is not a single one of its neighbors who does not
feel most definitely concerned by the fact. If Geneva became no more than a
storehouse for the commerce of Lyons and the South of France in their dealings
with Switzerland, Italy, and a large part of Germany, it would still be a highly
important city; but Geneva has also been the chief source of the trade and
manufacture from which Switzerland derives her prosperity. Geneva fertilizes the
stony soil of Savoy, waters it with what little money is in circulation there, supports
its day-laborers, and shares its abundance with that region, the most desolate in
all Europe. Geneva has a similar influence upon the French provinces adjoining
it. France, to which the opulent town lent one hundred millions under M.
Necker's ministry, benefits more than any other country from this little State's
activity, commerce, and industry; not to mention the fact that Geneva is the only
military post already equipped for war ready to cover the kingdom from the
Rhone to the Mediterranean, and defend the river crossing. Beyond all doubt, in
my opinion, France can desire nothing more than that Geneva, in this extremity
of her territory, should remain ever industrious and populous."

That's not just talk. What strange genius inhabits this putrescent failure,
that makes him speak of European affairs more wisely than a Choiseul or a
Bernis? In the whole chicken-coop of courtiers at Versailles there aren't twenty
people so well-informed about the economics of Geneva—which won't, of
course, prevent him from being reëvicted from Neuchâtel: *Des Lettres de cachet*

has been selling well, too well in fact. The first edition, nine thousand copies, is sold out, and four thousand of the second have gone when the police, at a frown from Frederick II who has suddenly remembered that there are Bastilles in Prussia too, after all, march into Fauche's printshop one morning. According to the Swiss censor of the book who wakes up to the fact a trifle late in the day, "the author sought to destroy religion by causing it to be seen as a human invention and, what is more, he seemed to be inviting the French to set limits upon the allegedly absolute authority of their sovereign."[26]

So the eternal wayfarer sets out again, but at least in the desired direction —that is, Provence. Vergennes has not rescinded the *lettre de cachet,* but Mirabeau père has authorized his accursed son to stay with the bailli at Mirabeau during the preliminaries to his suit against his wife. Not much richer than before: Fauche, who's just incurred a tidy fine for the *Lettres de cachet,* claims he hasn't even covered his costs. Perhaps Clavière tactfully deposits a purse in the right place at the right moment; no one will ever know. In any event, those two will meet again.

SCHILLER

24

SEPTEMBER 1782

Hand in Glove with the Lord of Hell

Stuttgart doesn't sleep too well on the night of September 22, 1782. The routine of the capital of the dukes of Württemberg, ordinarily so placid, has been shattered by the mammoth reception that its sovereign Charles Eugene is giving for the year's most notorious tourists, the Comte and Comtesse du Nord, on their way back to St. Petersburg. True, Duke Charles Eugene's weekend château is outside the city walls, but all those heavy carriages thundering over the cobbles, the tradesmen's carts, the galloping messengers . . . The local burghers, who do not receive invitations to gentlemen's residences, could hardly be expected not to toss with vexation in their high beds at the thought of the fairy tale taking place on their doorstep, and at their expense.

For Friedrich Schiller, on the other hand, who has chosen this moment to make his escape, the party is a blessing. A new life. A break with his youth. The crack in a destiny that divides everything into before and after. Farewell

Stuttgart. He's off. He's going to start looking like himself at last; in two months, he'll be twenty-three.* First, however, he has to get through the town gates, which were shut at ten as they are every evening. But who's going to notice two hungry-looking youths in nondescript attire? All they have to do is wait until it gets dark enough and the guards grow weary of the unwonted bustle of traffic. The only real danger is that somebody might recognize the young doctor of the Augé regiment stationed in town—because he's deserting it, is this regimental physician, this species of sub-officer who is entitled to neither stripes nor sword and has to apply for permission every time he wants to leave his post. So he now wages his first battle, the only one that counts—against his own army.

He worked today as usual, so that nobody would think anything was amiss, treating his customary squad of feverish, diarrhetic, or syphilitic soldiers in the quarantine station, the regimental infirmary where they stuff them in three to a bed. His cattle. He scorns them. He ignores them. He would frankly have preferred to be a veterinarian: cows would certainly understand him better, him and all the things he's carrying round in his heart and head.

> To rob, to kill, to wench, to fight,
> Our pastime is, and daily sport;
> The gibbet claims us morn and night,
> So let's be jolly, time is short.
>
> . . . . . .
>
> And, when with Rhenish and rare Moselle
> Our throats we have been oiling
> Our courage burns with a fiercer swell,
> And we're hand in glove with the lord of hell
> Who down in his flames is broiling.
>
> For father slain the orphans' cries,
> The widowed mothers' moan and wail,
> Of brides bereaved the whimpering sighs,
> Like music sweet, our ears regale.[1]

A puny little shrimp like him, can you imagine! That's the kind of tune he's been humming in his bath ever since he wrote *The Robbers,* his first play, and saw it performed in Mannheim last January. Germany wants him anaesthetized, the better to hogtie him; and he wants to give Germany a good goose with his writing. Above all—because he's counting on support from another Germany, one of heroes and giants, the Germany of the Rhine toward which

*He was born at Marbach in Swabia on November 10, 1759.

he is now fleeing—above all, he wants to arouse that infernal Swabia of his childhood with Württemberg in its center, that "land of castrati."

At eight in the evening he's back in his room awaiting his companion, his friend, his chosen one, his pal or buddy a later age would say, Andreas Streicher. They're bound together by the strong single vibration with which they respond to everything, the vibration that is the substance of young friendship, and so they're going to run away together too. Streicher is only twenty, and his infatuation with Schiller dates from their last year on the benches of the king's school. He wants to become a musician and will head for Hamburg, where he can kneel at the feet of his idol Karl Philipp Emanuel Bach.* Wrapped in a flowing black cloak as befits a conspiracy, he drives cautiously through the center of the old town in a two-horse cabriolet hired with their last florins. Although the younger of the pair, it is he who has looked after the luggage and packed Schiller's trunk as well as his own, because Friedrich can't even keep track of his gloves and boots. On top of the vehicle, between the two trunks, Streicher has hoisted and lashed down the whole of his earthly fortune: a little piano.[2] For an extra touch of the romantic, he has also stuck a brace of pistols into his belt, "one of which had no hammer and the other no flint, and neither of which was loaded."

He taps at a ground-floor window of a house on the Kleiner Graben (now the Eberhardstrasse), where Schiller sublet a room from the Gnädige Frau† Dorothée Louise Vischer, who occupies the lower part of the building. Another reason for the late hour of their departure is that they have to wait for her to drop off to sleep. Since becoming her tenant, Schiller has also been intermittently her lover and he has no desire to sully the pure joy of escape with floods of tears. He is feeling slightly sullied himself, however, less on account of their embraces than because he is really and truly attached to the tall widow, who is blond and blue-eyed but also flat as a pancake and knobbly as an old vine and ten years his senior, and who has six children. About as far as you could get from the Lorelei; but she played the piano for him and sang lieder to melt his heart. She's the only woman he has ever possessed. Schiller is definitely not a lady's man: in choosing the Palatinate tonight, he's also choosing Streicher and friendship.

Ready, comrade? Streicher tiptoes into Friedrich's lair, a perfect image of his youth: "a hole, reeking of tobacco and every other sort of smell, in which, apart from one large table, two benches, a narrow wardrobe, and a few pairs of threadbare breeches hanging on the wall, there was nothing to look at but bundles of copies of The Robbers in one corner, and in another, a heap of

---

*Second son of Johann Sebastian. He became a sort of pope of music: Mozart (three years older than Schiller) also made the pilgrimage to see him. Streicher later becomes a noted pianist.

†Honorable Lady, literally [a polite term of address—Trans.].

potatoes mingled with bottles and other assorted objects in indescribable confusion."

No, the comrade isn't ready. Elbows on the table, he's deep in contemplation of the *Odes* of Klopstock, one of his favorite poets.* Beside the book, a ream of paper on which he is now scribbling feverishly—inspiration has swooped upon him like a night owl, it's her hour, and he has begun an ode on the same subject as one of the great German master's, just to prove he can do as well.

"Listen, listen to this; you've got to tell me what you think of it right away."

Streicher knows his friend pretty well, but this staggers even him. Waste time *tonight?* But poetry is never a waste of time. So he paces back and forth fuming while Schiller declaims a (unfortunately lost) rough draft. "At last I brought my friend down to earth again, not before having given my opinion, which was that I thought his verse very much superior to that of Klopstock." They climb into the closed coach, and Streicher drives slowly away between the rows of old houses with their bright-colored paint and oriels that stick out like so many gossips' pointed caps, peering after them with dead eyes. Narrow little streets, you can shake hands with a person standing on the other side. Then a little bridge over the Nisselbach, around which, century by century, Stuttgart's twenty thousand inhabitants have ringed themselves to spin silk, wool, and cottons, dry tobacco, work gold and silver, and make ropes. A town of hard earners, a shop for every house or almost. Small danger of colliding with much poetry there; ah, Swabia! The gates with their huge studded leaves, opening out to the three big suburbs that have already sprawled into the distance, are almost symbolic, a sort of corset.

To baffle any potential pursuers, the escapees exit by the east-facing Essling gate, although that's not the way they're really going. Also, there's less light on that side. The sentry orders them to halt, a lanternless noncommissioned officer steps forward, demands their names and the object of their journey, and doesn't give a damn. He is promptly informed, and promptly forgets, that "Doctor Wolff and Doctor Ritter† are traveling to Essling on business," and the way is free. They then make a long detour through Esslingen, the largest and prettiest of the suburbs, full of beautiful, broad, arrow-straight streets: Stuttgart's breathing space; and turn due north, their true direction, toward Mannheim, via Ludwigsburg. But in the distance, on a hilltop half a league from Stuttgart, they see a great blaze of brilliance in the

---

*Yet Klopstock, the aging author of *The Messiah,* was a solemn religious poet, the only quality of whose works—today virtually unreadable—was to open the way to Romanticism for better men. Schiller found in him an echo of his adolescent mysticism.

†In German, of course, "Doktor" does not mean only a physician but also refers to the holder of a university degree.

night: the palace of Duke Charles Eugene of Württemberg, whose name, "La Solitude," is rather inappropriate at the moment, ninety thousand lamps having just been lit in it to honor Paul and Marie of Russia. The setting is one of legendary magnificence: with the statues, the torchères, and the mirrors, you can't tell if you're indoors or out in the garden. "It's the palace of the Sun!" exclaims our old friend Baronne d'Oberkirch, who is, of course, a member of the party. Three thousand bewigged footmen (a thousand of them borrowed from the army) stand fastened to their candelabra, rivaling the statuary. As a little surprise for his guests, the duke has changed all the furnishings in his residence, and everything has been sent out from Paris in the last three months. Earlier in the day there was a hunt; tiers were erected near the Barensee in order that the guests might observe "the arrival of four thousand stags and does marching in a herd for the kill. It was the most singular sight imaginable. The hunters were full of enthusiasm, but the onlookers felt pity for the unfortunate animals, which were doomed in advance, and there was a horrible slaughter. Wagons were filled with them and given as presents by the duke."[3]

Suddenly, as they turn away from the blazing château, Schiller the sword-flourisher, off to rape every nun and burn every bourgeois alive, begins to behave most peculiarly. He clutches his friend by the arm and points to one side of the illuminated scene, the wing of the palace where his parents live— where old Johann-Kaspar Schiller is peacefully ending a colorful career as barber-surgeon-soldier in the position of head nurseryman to Duke Charles Eugene; at his side, as always since 1749, the gentle and tender Elisabeth Dorothée, daughter of a Marbach innkeeper, who has given him three daughters in addition to Friedrich.*

And the man-child, the genius snorting contempt for all mankind, turns to Streicher with his eyes full of tears and lets gently fall one word: *"Mutter."*

His mother and elder sister were the only people he had confided in, and they were also the only women who ever found favor in his eyes. They had been the light of his childhood. Both inhabit all his plays, in one form or another. His father was undoubtedly not a bad man and never let him want for anything; but can you talk to a father? A father is someone you obey. Father, colonel, duke, they're all the same: gags to self-expression. "My sister was the heroine of my first dreams." They went to grade school together, Christine and Friedrich, in the big Swabian village of Lorch hemmed in by pines and rustling with falling water. "Those were the days when everything went so well," writes Christine,[4] the days "of the narrow garden gate, the swallows' nests in the corner of the casements, the hedge behind which I [Friedrich] lay in ambush and played hide-and-seek with the dog . . ."

*In 1782 Schiller's parents are sixty-nine (his father) and fifty-nine (his mother) years old.

He had grown too fast, inheriting his mother's tall, slender figure, weak lungs, redhead's complexion with skin soft as a girl's and peppered with freckles, and the pinkness around the eyes. At Lorch, his birthplace, he discovered the deep marks left by the great emperors of yore, especially Frederick Barbarossa of the auburn beard like the one Friedrich himself hoped to sport when he grew up; and the giant centuries-old linden tree on whose trunk naive statues of the twelve Hohenstaufens had been carved.* Those emperors, knights, pages, brigands had become part of him, like all the things one learns at play. When he was six, Reverend Moser gave him a painless introduction to Latin; the pastor's son and he were thick as thieves, which helped. This was his first encounter with friendship, "the soft, silent hand, early sought and soon met, that bandages wounds and shares all burdens" and that for him always comes before love.

The first break came soon afterward: Mr. Schiller's garrison life transported them all to Ludwigsburg, the Versailles of the dukes of Württemberg. From country to town, and what a town: a golden rats' nest, a cheese inhabited by eleven thousand parasites arrayed in silk and bobbed wigs, moving about between the vast capes, so stiff they looked as though they were made of iron, of Charles Eugene's grenadiers. It was here that Friedrich first saw the man who would take over from his father as master of his fate: "the prince, still young in aspect,† with round red cheeks and proud allure, drawn in his carriage by eight horses behind a fanfare of eighteen mounted coronets, wearing a little hat trimmed with gold braid, his hair in plump frizzled curls, a scarlet coat with yellow frogs, nankeen breeches, and top boots." He's "the god of the earth,"⁵ a man from whom one nod can, and does, make the joy or misery of the wide-eyed child watching him roll past and already asking himself questions.

Funny sort of god. Parisian scandal mongers concentrated on the caprices of the superstars: Louis XV's mistresses, the gigolos of Catherine the Great, Frederick's catamites, and the seventeen children of Maria Theresa. For them that was enough to give a little spice to the age. But the lottery of Westphalian treaties had strewn Europe's belly with a proliferation of mini-tyrants who spent their time aping the real sovereigns in their fifty-square-league territories outlined by the anomalies of inheritance. The people of wonderful old Germany endured them as they had endured everything else, the sword, the axe, the burgomaster, the Communes, and, after the concordats in Luther's day, the alternating pastors or priests, depending upon the faith of their reigning prince. *Cuius regio, huius religio.* The Württembergers, for instance, had been enduring Charles Eugene since 1744 when, upon reaching his majority at

*Dynasty of German emperors with semi-legendary history, originating in Swabia and reigning from 1100 to 1254.

†Charles Eugene of Württemberg, born in 1728, inherited the ducal throne (under a regent) at his father's death in 1737.

sixteen (only possible for princes, of course), he began what he himself called his *Lebensgaloppade,* * his wild career through his reign, marked by a series of orgies and a degree of extravagance that would have left an ogre lost in admiration. "I was," he says himself, "an untrammeled devil, but how should there be anything surprising in that? Everybody was forever bowing and scraping to me."[6] Swabia's pretty maidens abducted by the police for ten leagues around, for the duke's pleasure; Swabia's youths sold as mercenaries by the thousand (six thousand to France during the Seven Years' War), to pay for the duke's new castles. (Major Johann-Kaspar Schiller, like so many others, had acted the part of pimp—that is, had been a recruiting sergeant for the duke's human livestock.) By the time Friedrich became a gifted pupil in the Ludwigsburg school the duke was settling down, at least outwardly, thanks to his own version of La Pompadour, the good-natured and pretty Franziska von Leuktrum. She was a mistress with the unofficial rank of duchess, long before becoming a real one (in 1785), when Charles Eugene's first wife, the Margrave of Bayreuth,† finally consents to die. Good grades at school brought the poor boy no luck, however, for the Duke of Württemberg also creamed off all the clever subjects in his territory to serve in his army or administration. You wanted to be a pastor, did you, Friedrich? (His religious crisis was over by then, though, and Rousseau's deism was undermining the bastion of reformist dogma. But at least being a pastor is one way of being yourself . . .) Well, you'll be a creature of His Most Serene Highness instead. Until you run away in September 1782.

SCHILLER

25

SEPTEMBER 1782

The Trumpet of Rebellion

On January 16, 1773, when he was fourteen, Schiller's high grades, oh irony, earned him a transfer to the Ludwigsburg military academy, where they trained the men who would subsequently train Württemberg in obedience. He went "in a state of mental agony".** This was a second and worse break, the

*Headlong course through life.
†Repudiated in 1756; she left some interesting *Mémoires.*
** *Mit zerrissenem Gemüt.*

object of which was to force a round head into a square hole. The Karlsschule, or "Charles University," had been built next to "La Solitude" and boasted a façade seven hundred feet long.* Within its fastnesses were locked three hundred toy pupils uniformly decked out in pretty blue and white tin soldier's uniforms and bicorne hats; their places, however, were assigned not at all uniformly but rather as for the Day of Judgment: the sons of the nobility on the right, those of the bourgeoisie on the left. "The nobles did not sleep, eat, or wash with the bourgeois. Only the nobles wore silver epaulets and powdered wigs; only they were allowed to kiss the duke's hand; all commoners were allowed to kiss was the hem of his coat." They were made to maneuver all day long like automatons: "When someone cries 'Eat!' everybody eats"[1] . . . "The human heart experiences a singular pang of discomfort when confronted by the spectacle of these youths shut in for their meals. Their every gesture is regulated by a sign from the supervisor. It is a painful sensation to see human creatures treated like marionettes."[2] Never a holiday, never a visit, no woman could come within the confines of the school.† Sole outlets for sexuality: pederasty and masturbation. But you had to be quick about it, because informers received substantial rewards. The slightest infringement of discipline earned you a beating, solitary confinement, or three days on bread and water. At "La Solitude," the pupils were never alone, not even at night.

But along with all this, there was also a constellation of excellent teachers hired from neighboring countries and paid their weight in gold; in particular, there were several Frenchmen, who were meant to give what the duke called "the French tone" . . . One of His Most Serene Highness's greatest thrills was to play inspector. He was forever sticking his nose into everything and distributing resounding whacks to "his dear children" with his august hand. Once, during an inspection, one boy requested permission to attend his father's funeral, to which the curt reply was:

"Silence! Henceforth, I am your father!"

This is where Schiller lived out his youth, from 1773 to 1780—a compulsory graft, but onto what branch? The army? He was too frail. Architecture? Too full of crazy ideas. The "Artists' Conservatory" where pupils were trained as actors, musicians, and dancers for the pleasure of the duke and his guests?** He had a falsetto voice and was about as graceful as a giraffe. For want of anything better they set him to learning medicine, which may have saved him

---

*Before being moved, in 1775, next door to the ducal palace in Stuttgart, where the duke could keep an even closer eye on it.

†Except for great ladies and their attendants, on authorization from the duke.

**And where an English visitor, Burney, observed "the presence of eighteen castrati, the Court having at its service two surgeons from Bologna who are expert at this type of royal manufacture."[3]

from ending his days as an adolescent suicide. He became fascinated by the most concrete and sometimes most repugnant aspects of the human body: humors, mucus, pus, the digestive and genital functions. He clung to medicine as to a rough-barked raft riding the waves of superficial and useless concepts. Medicine was the reality of things. It was an authorized weapon to express his rejection of illusion; and it was perfectly compatible with poetry, which was his more clandestine form of resistance. "Love of poetry was an offense against the laws of the Institute in which I was reared, and in contradiction with the plan of its founder. For eight years the thrust of my life had to strive against military discipline, but the passion of poetry is ardent and strong as first love."[4] What poetry? Not the French style, for sure. He abhorred all things emanating from the land of Louis XV and XVI, on which his instructors had tried to force feed his sensitivity. Except for Rousseau, of course, but to him Rousseau was no more a Frenchman than Homer: he was the bard of the new world. He had a horror of cadenced lines, pastorals, and convention. "In France, accursed propriety has castrated the man of nature. The cothurn has been transformed into a dancing-pump. In England and Germany nature is exposed, if I may use the expression, down to her very sex; her pimples and birthmarks are enlarged under the magnifying glass with ruthless determination."[5] Where would he have met the true greatness of France, alongside which he walked unawares? He had never seen the best of Diderot, never even heard the name of Restif de la Bretonne. The kinds of words and rhymes he needed to express his revolt would have to bellow, and at the age of fifteen he began dreaming of a play in which right would be on the side of the wicked: *"The Robbers,* that monstrous union of insubordination and genius"[6] as he tried to define the work in 1784.* And it is true that the vast paraphernalia of the Karlsschule, its wasted millions, and its regulations, will have achieved that if it achieved nothing else, like a winepress in which one grape-seed turned out to be pure diamond: it achieved Friedrich Schiller, the first great spirit of pure revolt.

At fifteen or sixteen the adolescent-plaything, slave in a world sculpted to endure for centuries, began to boil. The main traits of his personality and behavior were already formed: "My Schiller," writes Scharffenstein, his best friend at that time, "had a truly comic aspect: he was extremely tall for his age; his thighs were almost the same distance around as his calves; he had a very long neck and a pale complexion, with small red-rimmed eyes. Of all the boys he was among the dirtiest. Inspector Nies used to mutter, 'What a pig!'† And no words could describe his frumpish head covered with curlpapers and an enormous plait."[7] . . . "Damnable plait!" as Schiller used to growl every morning when he had to braid his hair before leaving the dormitory, and two

*The word genius being used here in the Romantic sense—that is, "poetic genius" or inspiration.

†*Schweinepelz,* literally pigskin.

or three compassionate comrades would plait it for him in a rush, just as they would lean helpfully against him to prop him up when he staggered into line in the refectory after secretly drinking himself into a stupor. In later days, O Learned Doctor, might we not detect "schizoid or even schizophrenic tendencies" in this desperate youngster? He takes snuff like a grenadier, mainly at night when he gets up to write. And "when he ran out of tobacco he would sniff dust to irritate his olfactory membranes."*

Along with the tobacco and alcohol, however, he was imbibing a mass of other scents emanating from "modern books," all of which were duly banned and kept hidden in desks, under mattresses and sometimes between the roots of trees: Wieland, Lessing, Herder, the untamed Goethe of *Werther* and *Goetz von Berlichingen,* the plays of the already aging Klinger, including his *Sturm und Drang*† written in 1770, which gave its name to all those chaotic strivings of men who wanted to shake up their worlds but were totally unaware of the label to be stuck on them later, like stuffed wild animals. At that point they were still in the opening phase of the great eruption. "Nature! Nature!" was the cry of liberation that Klinger may have been first to utter but that was now rising in all their throats, including that of the stiff young man whose career prospects consisted in transfers from one prison to another, as when, on December 15, 1780, he left the Karlsschule for the subaltern position of *regimen medikus* or military doctor in the lowliest of Württemberg regiments, where he was paid eighteen florins a month** to take care of the Augé grenadiers. Let's have another look at him, through Scharffenstein's eyes (in 1781: this time, the escapee). We need not trouble learned professors to give us a scholarly exigesis—the *Sturm und Drang,* storm and stress, *is* Schiller.

> Long-legged and long in the arms, his chest thrown far forward and arched, his neck inordinately long; there was something boardlike in his appearance, no whit of elegance in his turn-out. The forehead was broad, the nose straight and dead white, with an extremely sharp, angled, and pointed tip bent over like a parrot's beak. His eyebrows were red and set very close to dark gray eyes sunk deep in their sockets, and so close together that they almost touched at the bridge of his nose. This part of his face was expressive and had something intensely moving about it. His mouth was also highly expressive; his lips were thin and the lower one protruded but one had the impression, when Schiller grew excited, that this was simply the result of the enthusiasm and ardor driving him; it showed great energy; his jaw was powerful, his cheeks pale and hollow, strewn with freckles; his eyelids almost always red and inflamed; his hair thick and tangled, auburn in

---

*According to Petersen, another of his friends.

†Half concrete, half abstract, has any movement ever been more ambiguously personified? *Sturm* is the storm, the tempest; *Drang* is impetus, impulse, pressure, violence, but usually "stress" when applied to the literary movement.

**About 800 modern francs [$160].

color. His whole head, bespeaking virility less, perhaps, than the strangeness of an apparition, had great distinction and energy even in repose.[8]

"Shall I let myself be forced into a corset and my will bound by laws? No law ever gave birth to so much as one great man; but my freedom can breed colossi, and madmen . . . I dream of an army of stout fellows like myself: then Germany would be a real republic, and Rome and Sparta would look like nunneries alongside her."[9]

So speaks Karl Moor the rabid, the good-bad-man of *The Robbers,* when he first appears on the stage of the Mannheim theater on January 13, 1782. What Beaumarchais with all his connections, his artful dodging and his talent, can only hint at in his *Marriage* (still banned in France), a stripling of twenty-two lets off in the face of the Holy Roman Germanic Empire and thereby earns instant fame throughout the Rhineland,* although he was no more its prophet, nor any better paid there, than in his own infernal Württemberg thirty leagues away, where he resumed his persona of the failed student every time he came back from Mannheim. There was small danger that Duke Charles Eugene would tolerate even the sale, let alone the performance, of a work whose author had proudly proclaimed to his friends, "We shall make a play that will be burned by the executioner on the Place de Grève."† The municipality of Leipzig forbade performance of the play during the local fair with the piquant comment: "Quite enough robbing goes on here already." The play was pro-hibited in most of the larger states of the empire.** But on the German edge of the Rhine lay that rubble heap of princely or episcopal molecules decorated like operetta settings, where severity was less highly prized than nonchalance and "libertines" could deftly slip dangerous books from hand to hand. There, princes and people left each other alone as long as the latter let the former amuse themselves as they pleased. Thus the first edition of *The Robbers* (no author's name, printed by Metzler in Stuttgart but fictitiously domiciled in Frankfurt) sputtered along the border of Germany like a fuse on a charge of dynamite. "The play‡ is a declaration of war on society. The world is badly made, and that explains the presence in it of the Robbers, a sort of 'sovereign company' or 'republic' developing in opposition to a senile and rotten society. All the social foundations are crumbling; ministers are 'panders' [*Kuppler*]; lawyers are prevaricators; the country squires milk the people; the priests are

*The play shows clear evidence of Shakespearean influence, although at this point Schiller had read only Wieland's mediocre translations of *Richard II* and *III, Henry VIII, Lear, Macbeth* and *Hamlet.* The only French author to have made any impression on him at this point was Mercier (in his dramatized historical essays).

†You slipped up there, Friedrich—a French allusion! The Place de Grève in Paris was famous as an execution ground.

**Its first performance in Vienna, at the Burgtheater, does not take place until 1850.

‡According to Robert d'Harcourt.

'apers of divinity'; all men in 'gold braid' are sordid wretches. Everything in the community that has power or is respected without question must be swept away. The world must be made anew, rejuvenated; and it is the Robbers' mission to perform this task."[10]

A spark, a breath of air, a stir, especially among the young. In 1782, thousands of Germans mutilated by enforced confinement recognized themselves in the prisoner of "La Solitude," just as they had recognized themselves in Werther six years before. But this time the object was not to caress the pangs of disprized love; it was to experience the thrills of social protest. "I was Karl Moor; we all were, all of us young people," writes Kerner, a friend of Goethe. And when the Karlsschule pupils learned that one of their classmates had succeeded in publishing this sacrilegious opus—for nobody can keep a secret, everything makes the rounds in whispers, and besides, Friedrich had read the play to a few friends out in the woods—they began passing round and feverishly recopying the first anarchist tracts: "All for black bread and freedom! Down with slavery! Better to eat dry beans in freedom than frosted cakes in chains!"

"No event in the history of eighteenth-century German literature can be compared with the explosion caused by *The Robbers*. Timme, the critic of the *Gazette érudite d'Erfurt*, called Schiller a German Shakespeare."[11]

In less than a year the book's success forced the play onto the stage of one of the few liberal theaters of the age, the Mannheim theater on the banks of the Neckar. Money was the main consideration: Baron von Dalberg, the theater manager,* was a shrewd operator with a nose for a quick profit. He offered the army surgeon a contract and Schiller floated away on cloud nine, agreeing to everything and putting up with anything just to see his play on the boards. Most of the seditious and ribald tirades were cut and so, regrettably, was the scene of the nuns' rape in the forest; the action was moved back in time to the fifteenth century although the resulting anachronisms were worthy of the worst tabloid serial; and the latent anticlericalism and call to free love were filtered out, act by act. The play Schiller finally saw performed as he sat gnawing his knuckles was almost goody-goody, an abortion of his revolt.

But even "almost" was enough to stagger a society. "People came in droves from leagues around, from Heidelberg, Darmstadt, Frankfurt, Mainz, Worms, Spire, on horseback and by carriage, to witness the riot of the first performance," according to Streicher. And to applaud a most incredible concoction. Shakespeare had indeed left his mark on the august old man torn between Cain and Abel, sequestered by his bad son (Franz) who is after his money while the good son (Karl) enlists the aid of the robbers to release him.

---

*Cousin of the famous Bishop of Mainz who (later) becomes one of the German dignitaries of the Napoleonic empire.

There follow five acts of rip-snorting adventure packed with owls and armor, ghosts and scoundrels, cascading along until the old man's final appearance, livid but alive, and a family massacre that pretty much clears the stage. The audience goes wild: "The theater was as though transformed into an insane asylum; eyes were rolling in their sockets, fists were clenched, feet were stamping and hoarse voices were bellowing, people who had never seen each other before were embracing and sobbing, women were fainting."[12] It hadn't been possible to emasculate everything; even this travesty contained one or two touches of the sort that could uproot the mountains of convention under which people were lying pinned. Here's Karl again, shouting:

"Men! Men! false! treacherous crocodiles! . . . Would I were a bear of the north, and could arm my ravenous kind against those murderers . . . Oh! I could poison the ocean, that they might drink death in every source! . . . Oh! that I could blow the trumpet of rebellion through all nature, and summon heaven, earth, and seas to war against this savage race."[13] And it's Amelie, the rather conventional and flat Juliet/Ophelia of this man's play, who brings down the first-act curtain, turning to face the—empty—box of the Elector Palatine:

"The world is then unhinged—outcasts are kings and kings are outcasts! I would not change the rags of that poor outcast for the imperial purple! What must be the look with which he begs his bread! . . . a look that dazzles into naught the splendor of the proud, the pageant triumphs of the rich and great."[14]

When you come to think of it, maybe Schiller's youth in that children's prison camp wasn't a total loss after all.

So OK, but then what? He was famous for a fortnight, except that nobody knew his real identity outside his own inner circle. The play was only performed four times at Mannheim because the potential audience, the number of people capable of transporting themselves to a theater and buying a ticket, was not large. A few articles filtered into the press but didn't even get as far as Schiller, who received from von Dalberg exactly enough to cover his trips to Mannheim and who now found himself back in the Augé regiment pricking and pomading his grenadiers' hides. He published a first collection of verse,* in which death puts up a good fight but is conquered or at least surmounted by universal love. Something was pushing from behind but couldn't yet force its way through, a new image of joy, hands joined in unending circles and the outpouring of millions of throats. Inside his narrow chest all mankind was seeking expression. "With the same omnipotence as in the eternal and silent mechanisms of astral nature, love reigns in the spider web of our poor carcasses abandoned to desire."[15] In the final songs—hymns

---

*Baudelaire was inspired by it.

to friendship—we hear a new voice speaking from the human heart: "Oh, joy, oh joy, I have met thee. Of all the millions of beings it is thee whom I embrace; of all the millions of beings it is thou alone who art mine . . . Hatred makes us into dead men; love's embrace transforms us into gods. That sacred need for love we find at every step of creation. Linked together and ever higher, we mount the spiral till we throttle space and time in the ocean of unending splendor."[16]

Schiller might have been able to keep up this shuttle between his secret routine and his celebrity—it was rather picturesque, after all—long enough to compose a few more poems and two or three plays he had in mind. But Charles Eugene of Württemberg was not the kind of protector to be easily mystified. He had received protestations and demands from numerous right-minded souls; was he paying his menials to wield firebrands? On September 1, through official channels, he gives his regimental doctor notice that he is "forbidden, under pain of dismissal, to write any more plays for the theater." Has Schiller forbidden him to rule? But it's an unequal contest, so the only way out is "my desperate step,"* the leap into the unknown. Desertion, flight. An attempt to make his life coincide with his work.

It's a beautiful morning, that September 24, when the two escapees reach the gentle town of Mannheim and its romantic promenades, where the authorities welcome them like stray dogs. But that is another story.

PRINCE DE ROHAN-GUÉMÉNÉE

26

OCTOBER 1782

A King . . . Imbecilic and Rabid by Turns

Now, what about this peace; are we making it or not? Everybody seems to have forgotten the fact, but there's still a sort of a war on out there on the other side of the earth. True, the American and French victory in Yorktown has settled the English hash, not only in Virginia but in the overall scheme of things; but King George's men are still sitting in New York, and no battle yet has ever done the work of a treaty.

For a year, it looked as though some of the belligerents were letting things slide on purpose: the English in the hope of tipping back the scales, and their

---

*Der verzweifelte Schritt (as he said to Streicher).

revenge on de Grasse at Les Saintes has done nothing to dissuade them from pursuing that idea; and the French (meaning Vergennes in this instance) on speculation, reckoning that if the war is simply allowed to rot everybody will be thrown a few bones, such as fishing rights off Newfoundland, some territory in the United States, a couple of islands for the English, and why not a tip for the Spaniards, our blessed allies and millstones around our necks? The only people in a hurry to get it over with are the ones who have the war on their land and in their flesh—that is, the Americans. The Gentlemen of Congress, safely reënsconced in Philadelphia at last, are not too pleased with their ambassador to France—the great, the revered, the immortal Franklin. They can hardly criticize him publicly or send him a letter of reprimand, he's the living incarnation of the Alliance, but they sometimes wonder if he isn't so Allied that his French half has gotten the better of the American one. They have accordingly dispatched two new ambassadors extraordinary to Madrid and Paris, to "assist" him: John Adams and John Jay. Two tough guys to prop up the softie. Their arrival takes place against a background of exquisite courtesy by which Franklin is not deceived. He is aging fast, though, cooling down, beginning to look upon any sort of dispute as incomprehensibly absurd; and his real friends, of both sexes, have increasingly become the lights of Versailles, Paris, and Auteuil, the intimates of his beloved Mme Helvétius, the survivors of Turgot's dream.

But in late 1782 these people are far more interested in the skeletons in their own closets than in settling any accounts with Insurgents; why, how can the war not be over, since La Fayette's home again? And with the bankruptcy of the Rohan-Guéménées on our hands, how could we possibly think about anything else?

On September 30, 1782, *Le Journal de Paris* gives public voice, in extremely circumspect and indefinite terms, to what has been the sole topic of Court and salon conversation for several weeks: the Prince de Rohan-Guéménée has been forced to declare himself bankrupt like any vulgar banker. He has referred three thousand creditors to the magnanimity of the royal treasury and the skill of his liquidator-magistrates for payment of their due. His total debts amount to thirty-three million livres. From the uproar, you'd think some minor throne had toppled. It is a throne, and woe betide anyone caught beneath it when it falls.*

Roi ne puis; Duc ne daigne; Rohan suis. [King I may not; duke I deign not; Rohan am—the family motto.] This is one of the twelve or fifteen families who regard

---

*The Rohan-Guéménée debt equaled about 200 million modern francs [$40 million] in all, but the figure was only revealed by degrees as the enormity of the scandal became known, and the final amount was not made public until all the details of the affair came to light, in April 1792. At this point the figure being quoted is sixteen to twenty million.

themselves as the equals of the Bourbons, even of the Capetians. And the title of prince—which their motto does not disdain—has belonged to them automatically for almost a thousand years. Descended from the first rulers of Brittany, the main trunk flourished at Rennes and was holding the land of Rohan near that town in the year 1100. Branches had spread throughout the west and as far as the Pyrenees: the Rohan-Montbazons, Rohan-Chabots, Rohan-Soubises, and, by a Montbazon graft, the Rohan-Guéménées, who emanated from Guéménée-sur-Scorff in the Morbihan, five leagues from Pontivy, where their huge château, thrice demolished and thrice rebuilt in the course of the wars of religion,* towered over a town of one thousand souls. To avoid splitting up the fiefs and if possible to consolidate them, there had been a good deal of intermarriage between cousins over the centuries. In the end, they had grown to be one of those princely states within the state, which the King himself had to treat with respect (except when a king like Louis XIV happened to cut off one of their heads, but those days were long gone now) and which could compel ministers, even reforming ones, to bite their tongues.

Under Louis XV the Rohan-Soubises were in the driver's seat. They converted to Catholicism at the right time, one becoming a cardinal and another—the elder—a maréchal, who made the name of Soubise famous by his long meander through Germany in quest of his enemy, leading to his defeat at Rossbach. Protected first by La Pompadour and later by La du Barry—a feat in itself—he had been one of the King's most loyal friends in his old age. Since 1704, the Rohans of that branch have held the bishopric of Strasbourg from father to son, so to speak, although in this instance it was uncle to nephew. And the pope, almost as a matter of course, allotted them a cardinal's hat into the bargain. At the time of the bankruptcy, Prince Louis-René had just stepped into the dual office at less than fifty years of age, and was resting there after the magnificent pomp in which he had been living as His Majesty's ambassador to Vienna, where he kept so many girls and so much gambling in his immediate proximity that Maria Theresa had taken a strong dislike to him. He often visited Versailles, in his capacity as grand almoner to the King, and he had a hearty appetite. The Queen, duly warned by her mother, also found him objectionable. But among the cousinry there was a Rohan-Soubise girl, who married a Rohan-Guéménée boy, and this couple has occupied stage center for the last ten years. Marie Antoinette was fascinated by the Princesse de Rohan-Guéménée, a past-mistress of the best trick of the courtier's trade, that of keeping her patron amused with her aplomb, her laughter, her risqué stories, and her mordant wit. A high-class hoyden. At Versailles she presided over the table where the highest stakes were played—millions a night. She was ap-

---

*Some of the Rohans became leaders of the western Protestants, opposing Richelieu. With Buckingham's help, the first Rohan-Soubise nearly broke the blockade at La Rochelle.

pointed "governess to the Children of France," like a school prize-day award, before they were even born, but she never had time to teach the dauphin how to play so much as reversi, for like all the great Court *noblesse* she was staggering under her own weight, under the burden of unproductivity and idleness. Every family dragged a train of parasites at its heels and was facing insurrection because it no longer paid them. That's why the Orléanses were "developing" the Palais Royal, and Monsieur himself was speculating in Guiana. The Guéménées, however, carried improvidence beyond even unreasonable bounds, so they are first to fall. Willy-nilly, it's time to 'fess up; there will be no further payments made by them, either to their biggest creditors or to their regiments of footmen, doormen, and fiddle players. The clamor is rising from every floor of the house, from lowly and lofty alike, even from literary people like Abbé Delille or the Marquis de Villette, Voltaire's friend, who had lent them 28,000 livres.* If we have to start doing business with society scribes . . .

Heads must fall. Louis XVI accordingly chops—those of the Rohan-Guéménée's notary and estate manager, who are thrown into prison. The prince is requested to retire to his lands in Navarre, and the princess (they live apart) to return to her father in Brittany . . . whither she repairs, taking the precaution of abducting two or three lovers to keep her company, as you never know what resources the locals can produce. The King, in return, digs into the pocket of his kingdom, the Cardinal de Rohan into that of his bishopric in Strasbourg, and old uncle Soubise gives up a few of his girls at the Opéra. This holy alliance settles a few of the more pressing debts and shuts the mouths of the biggest bawlers during the "three months of suspension" needed to avert a cascade of public lawsuits—long enough for the wind to turn and for any creditor obstinate enough to persist in his claims to be intimidated. By the end of the year, everybody at Court is shedding tears of compassion for—the Rohan-Guéménées; they miss their princess.

Oh yes, she was supposed to be governess to the Children of France, wasn't she? Her "resignation" is requested, in exchange for a tidy annuity. Will she be replaced by someone above reproach? Rumor says so, so loudly that all virtuous souls are lying awake nights in dread. And indeed the King's finger is hovering in the direction of no less a person than his aunt, the inevitable, eternal Adelaïde,† who positively scrambles into the ring. She's been perishing of boredom at Bellevue, heaping scorn and abuse upon this century of libertines. "Mme Adelaïde, for whom the King feels the most absolute veneration and trust, has offered to assume responsibility herself for the education of His Majesty's children."[1] Louis XVI quite likes the idea— one of his father's sisters, at last somebody who would be capable of teaching

*180,000 modern francs [$36,000].

†One of Louis XV's four daughters—the shy Madame Sophie—has just died, leaving Louise in her Carmelite nunnery at Saint-Denis and Adelaïde and Victoire in their home at Bellevue.

his children what they need most—religion. A collective shudder runs through the "Queen's party": think of the forty-year culture gap between that little bigot of an Adelaïde and her cousin Louis-Philippe d'Orléans, who's receiving what could almost be called a progressive education at the hands of Mme de Genlis. Marie Antoinette herself rejects the old lady predicant; but will she look for some acceptable alternate who is actually capable of teaching? Not she. She's got just the thing right here. Really, the Rohan-Guéménée collapse hasn't taught her much: their momentary low-calorie diet will simply put more flesh on another family of favorites. This is the year of the Queen's great affection for Mme de Polignac, and what's the point of power if you can't use it to spoil the people you love?

"As soon as the King, who had intentions regarding Mme Adelaïde, received the resignation of the Princesse de Guéménée, he entered the Queen's chambers.

" 'Well, Madame,' he said to his august spouse, 'to whom shall we entrust these important duties?'

"Mme de Polignac happened to be there.

" 'Here,' replied the Queen, taking her by the hand, 'is the person we need.'

" 'So be it,' said the King; 'I can but respect and applaud your choice.'

"Mme de Polignac threw herself at the monarch's feet, and he raised her to embrace her."[2]

La Guéménée was already overpainted and exhausted by surfeit of pleasures. As her successor, Comtesse Jules de Polignac had one strong card: the head of an angel. This wasn't the first time it had won her a jackpot, and while raking it in she said, without pausing for breath, how very essential it was that another little angel, saucier and sharper than herself, should become Lady of the Queen's palace: her sister-in-law Louise de Polastron, whose appointment was being opposed by all the families of other potential candidates. "They say that to become Lady of the Palace at seventeen would be quite unprecedented."[3] Furthermore, the Noailleses were pushing Mme de La Fayette for the job. But the little angel of seventeen had caught the eye not only of her sister-in-law Yolande but also of Marie Antoinette (who, with Fersen still in America, seems more and more inclined to keep the men at a distance and the women, especially very young ones, at close proximity) and the Comte d'Artois to boot, who had often sought access to Louise's bedside when she had the measles the year before.* Who could hold out against a coalition like that? With Yolande de Polignac installed as the dauphin's governess and Louise de

*She becomes his mistress in 1787 and goes into exile with him in 1789. Her influence upon him is "felicitous," at least as far as his morals are concerned; she becomes a surrogate wife to him but it is not until her death "of consumption," in 1804, that the future Charles X turns to religion.

Polastron as the Queen's new fancy doll, the Polignac clan has edged out the Rohans for top honors. And this is the kind of *real* news in the barnyard that makes us totally incapable of noticing another ten or twenty thousand casualties on the other side of the ocean.

Anything else to report? Well, another big novelty this autumn is that the literati are beginning to stare at each other in the most peculiar way, as though they were looking for warts on the tips of one another's noses. This is the result of the growing popularity of a translation of several tomes full of plates, figures, and portraits, entitled *L'Art de connaître les hommes par la physionomie*, the original German text of which came from Zurich, where its author, Gaspard Lavater, is first pastor of St. Peter's church.* A rather unusual pastor, part mystic, part scholar, and part philosopher, but mostly prolific writer. For the last ten years he's been flooding his own country with a seething stream of verse and prose that is now beginning to overflow into Europe and is attracting a certain amount of attention, although not on account of its elephantine style. Is there a new magus in Zurich? In any event, he's just invented a new science, called Physiognomy, "which consists in seeking the relationship between the facial features and the character and feelings of the soul."[4] What a break it would be if we could judge what we're up against, in love, friendship, and work, at one glance! His followers are tempted to carry little pocket rulers around, to measure their partners in conversation. "The eyebrows, moreover, the protrusion of the eye-bone, tautness of muscle between the brows, breadth of the bridge of the nose, depth of eye, elevation of iris; how expressive all these parts are, taken separately or together!"[5] Up to that point nothing earth-shaking; but now Lavater brings in geometry: "My readers may find this claim wanting in reason. However that may be, the propensity that urges me to seek out the truth compels me to suggest that by forming a right angle from the zenith and extremity of the horizontal and perpendicular lines and their relation with the diagonal, one may generally learn the capacity of the forehead from the relationship between these lines. As I write this, I am engaged in devising a machine† by means of which it will be possible, even without the aid of silhouettes, to take the form of every skull and determine with sufficient accuracy the degree of its capacity." Not everyone has jumped on the bandwagon, in either Zurich or Paris, where physiognomy is chiefly treated as an entertaining subject for debate. Grimm, for example, doesn't hide his skepticism: "The doctrine of M. Lavater is too contagious. Let us refrain from *physiognomizing* in our turn. And, moreover, could it be performed successfully in a country in which every face, in its desire to resemble every other, is disfigured by some mask?"

*He was born there in 1741.
†Which he never perfected—or, thank God, put on the market. Imagine Lavater's contraption in the hands of the vocational guidance counselors!

There never was a mask that didn't slip one day, though. Even those of kings. At the theater of Versailles, and in Paris, the French Acting Company is rehearsing its first production of Shakespeare, to open in January. Until now he was read only in English and sneered at, except by Diderot, as an author of Byzantine gibberish. But this time Ducis, an amiable academician, has performed upon the text of *King Lear* such a labor of smoothing, rubbing, and polishing that the work has become almost digestible to the French stomach and, again according to Grimm, the play is certain to be a hit. "The thing to bear in mind is that the range of combinations to which our dramatic system seems sensitive is infinitely limited. Its resources have been exhausted, and it may be impossible for genius itself to obtain any noteworthy results in this area today without breaking totally new ground* . . . For indeed, what could be a more extraordinary idea than to venture to present, upon the French stage, the portrait of a king despoiled by his own children, whom misfortune and desperation have driven imbecilic and rabid by turns?"[6]

But—what about that peace?

THE SIEGE OF GIBRALTAR

27

OCTOBER 1782

All the Enguiens are Lucky

Since Yorktown, operations have been continuing in four theaters, as the military chroniclers call them, and on this occasion the term is relatively apt because, with one or two exceptions, there has been less action than dress parade.

The land armies on the "New Continent" have stayed where they were; in Gibraltar, the Franco-Spaniards are trying to wrest the rock from the English; on the high seas, after the disaster of Les Saintes, the naval war has degenerated into corsairs' raids in which John Paul Jones is still swashbucklingly prominent; and in the Indies, Suffren—with his fleet, his little expeditionary corps, and his Hindu allies—is ramming everything in sight.

In the United States, thus, General Clinton's English are holed up in New York and vicinity, the Rebel army is in Philadelphia, and Rochambeau's men are at the tip of the Chesapeake, where Washington has asked them to perform

*The bard's plays then being the best part of two hundred years old.

the thankless task of dismantling the English fortifications and divesting the two dead towns (York and Gloucester) "of the corpses of men and horses, scattered books, gutted furniture,"[1] the spume of battles. "Only after this roadwork [sic] had been completed did Rochambeau's army take up quarters some few leagues from there, in Williamsburg" and begin to rot from boredom. Fersen, still one of Rochambeau's aides-de-camp, is determined to come out of it alive. "Until now my health has been very good and, by taking care, I hope to keep it so. The country in which we now are is very unhealthy, and the fevers that we call *frassan* in Sweden are very common. We have many down sick; not even the natives are spared. This must be attributed to the inconstancy of the weather and the sudden shifts from hot to cold, which are very abrupt.* We have already had unbearably hot days followed by snow and freezing cold. This is a dreadful climate.† By taking care not to get chilled and always dressing warmly, I believe one can overcome the inconstancy of the weather and avoid illness."[2] He finally seems to have understood that warfare consists, first if not foremost, of catching cold in your barracks.

The English, cut off in the south, have evacuated Charleston, followed by Savannah, in small boatloads, to the great chagrin of the local Tories who welcomed them so cordially. Then, news of the battle of Les Saintes nailed all troops to their campsites. It took Rochambeau almost six months to ease his men back up to Baltimore, there to meet Washington again and agree that nothing could be agreed. The situation had been reversed: now it was the warriors in the far corners of the earth who were waiting for word from the diplomats back home. Rochambeau himself, ravaged by those famous Virginia fevers, reëmbarks at Annapolis in November 1782, leaving the pretentious carper Viomesnil to make preparations for the French troops' return home, which the ministers Ségur and Castries had commanded in September, once Versailles realized that peace was now only weeks away. The gazettes say that Louis XVI conversed "at great length" with the man who won his reign's war, but Rochambeau's audience actually lasted only half an hour, and Louis didn't give him the Cordon bleu (of the Order of the Holy Spirit) for another ten months.[3]

Apart from New York, then, the thirteen United Provinces have spent 1782 settling the minor scores of a dying civil war behind closed doors: hangings and pillaging, unidentifiable partisan gangs. The losers, that is, those who were friends to the English, learned that their choice would cost them plenty; but when they were on top, consideration for the Rebels hadn't been their long suit either.

*This letter, to his father, was written on March 25, 1782.
†His morale was pretty low that day . . . Williamsburg is at roughly the same latitude as Algiers.

The biggest noise of the year, or at least the one most audible to the ears of the French Court, was made during the summer and autumn at Gibraltar. And it was noise in the literal sense: what a waste of gunpowder! When that many cannon start spewing forth at once in Europe, it's advisable to lend an ear; fires can always spread.

Figurative noise as well, though: Louis XVI's brother and cousin have gone out to fight, the royal family is at last being allowed to commit itself personally to battle. The Comte d'Artois and Duc de Bourbon (the very two who fought a duel in March 1778) have run down to show the Spaniards how to end a siege and what stuff a Frenchman is made of. They start by crossing the peninsula in easy stages, with a retinue so sumptuous one would have supposed them on their way to a wedding. The Spaniards, who were feeling just a mite shame-faced in regard to their recent military fiascos, made up for it in the realm of hospitality, where they consider themselves unbeatable. June and July were one long series of festivities, thirty parties in honor of a massacre, from San Sebastian to Cadiz. In Versailles, everybody was bloated with optimism. From Fabvier-la-perruche* on August 10, 1782:† "The siege of Gibraltar seems to have been quite forgotten; the only news from Spain being discussed in conversations is the reception of M. le Comte d'Artois. The prince had taken some magnificent jewels with him but found them paltry in comparison with those that were offered to him there, so our jewelers are now engaged in manufacturing still more precious articles. As for the allegedly impregnable rock, its conquest is regarded as a *fait accompli*. The officer who brings us the news will teach us nothing we do not already know. Our imagination is soaring far beyond, to the total eviction of the English, which M. d'Estaing will be instructed to undertake in the West Indies with the fleet he is to conduct there after the capture of Gibraltar. The Comte d'Artois, meanwhile, covered in laurels, will travel here with the Infante don Carlos,"[4] heir to the Spanish throne. War really can be such a pretty thing sometimes, seen from afar! Even close up it has a certain charm in the eyes of the great. Our valiant princes' first days of duty were positively euphoric. From the Saint-Roch camp, which the beseigers set up north of the microscopic appendix formed by the Rock of Gibraltar, Bourbon wrote his father on August 24:

> Until now, all has gone well. Wednesday we had an alarm: at five in the afternoon the enemy threw a grenade that ignited our new works. As we went out at once to attempt to extinguish the flames, they began firing very energetically upon the entire trench. M. de Crillon being at Algeciras at the time, M. de Lassi, who commands the artillery, undertook to reply in order to protect our men

---

*Author of another *Correspondance secrete,* presumably intended for the King of Poland and published by Lescure in 1866 [Fabvier-la-perruche: Fabvier-the-parrot—*Trans.*].

†The throne of France has exactly ten years to the day of life left.

at their work; so the firing became general. M. le Comte d'Artois and I went up on horseback and approached the edge of the sea within close reach of the trench, for we could see the balls flying out perfectly clearly on either side. In the absence of our general, he was extremely keen to venture farther, but was persuaded that it would be useless. I have never seen anything so fine, the cannonade went on for a good two hours; the English fired eighteen hundred times and we about twelve hundred; we lost very few people, a dozen men killed or injured, Spanish or French. The Lyonnais regiment, which was working to put out the fire, conducted itself impeccably; they had the fire out within two hours; only twenty-two fathoms were burnt, but they will soon be made good again, and the incident will not delay the great attack. This rock of Gibraltar bristles with batteries; every night they make an infernal racket firing but do no great damage . . . It appears that they are very short of supplies but are firmly preparing to receive our attack and are hoping for relief from the great [English] fleet. The officer told us they had built six hundred forges in order to shoot red-hot balls onto our floating batteries . . . Apart from that, I have not yet been able to open my house here, a kitchen had to be improvised out of nothing. I have dined with M. le Comte d'Artois, M. de Crillon, and M. Bressole, and hope to be able to give a dinner myself by the beginning of next week.

I am very glad to know there are big stags in Chantilly; you will certainly find some at Dammartin and Nanteuil; I believe I shall not have the honor and pleasure of seeing them. In all probability I shall arrive in time for the staggarts* in the high season. The heat here is dreadful and the hounds would go very badly, for there has been not one drop of rain in the last seven months. I am delighted to hear that M. de Choiseul has killed a cream-colored fallow doe to put in the natural history room, for they are exceedingly rare at Chantilly.[5]

The reply comes not from Bourbon's father but from his son, the little Duc d'Enghien who has just had his tenth birthday. Despite the fact that he doesn't yet know how to spell his title, his missive is a fair summary of the conditioning in caste-pride that has been given him in lieu of an education: "My dear papa, my first letter [sent a few days earlier] is more like a letter by a girl than by a Condé. I shall now write one in my own manner. Yes, papa, gain glory; give the English a good beating, take Gibraltar. After taking it, come home, come home to us. Then leave again, go to America, and show that you are a Condé. I hope to be able to show it too one day, and I await that moment with impatience. The Grand Condé was also called Duc d'Enguien [*sic*] when he won the battle of Rocroy. Perhaps the name will bring me luck, for all the Enguiens are lucky; the one of the battle of Cerizoles,† the one who won the battle of Rocroy; I hope I shall be too."[6]

Meanwhile the wind has sent the Versailles weather vanes spinning; in less than a month Fabvier has changed his tune about "the capture of Gilles-le-batard [Gibraltar; his poor pun: Giles-the-bastard] as our vulgarians call it

*Staggart: a four-year old.

†Ceresole d'Alba in the Piedmont; a victory over the Imperials won in 1544.

... The news received by the Court of late is highly unsatisfactory. The floating batteries are mere machines, difficult to operate and of uncertain effect; the assaults that were being planned are now seen as futile and rash; in one night, the sorties of the besieged can destroy the fruit of several weeks of immense labor. Let us wait another week, however [on September 2, 1782] before adopting any final decisions as to the fate of this memorable undertaking."[7] Two weeks later, in a few short hours, the siege of Gibraltar did indeed fail; and true enough, the cause was "the disaster of the prasmes."*

The day is lived through, and most picturesquely recorded, by a young "naval guard" or officer-in-training, on board the *Dictateur*,† one of the big seventy-four-gun French ships taking part in the siege under the orders of the Comte de Guichen. As a product of the lesser nobility of the Nivernais, the Chevalier de Cotignon's only, and very slender, hope of advancement was in the navy. He therefore attended the naval school at Toulon and is delighted to be seeing his first action at Gibraltar. He is especially delighted as he has just been transferred from a frigate to one of these imposing vessels whose decks all sailors longed to tread: "The difference between this ship and a frigate! I found a whole new world; on a frigate one can scarcely budge whereas on a ship one can run about and walk, at least from poop to forecastle, and along a charming gallery, and in the council room, and another large fine room, and in the batteries. I soon grew used to the tumult."[8]

At first, Cotignon and his friends shared the optimism of the rest of the besiegers: how could combined land and naval forces of such size fail to overcome that little bit of a boulder? But they didn't realize how easy to defend Gibraltar is, with its hundreds of invulnerable batteries embedded in stone. For two months, on board the *Dictateur,* Cotignon functioned as a sort of civil servant of death. Every morning work started at eight; that is, they moored broadside onto the English ramparts and shelled them until midnight while the Spanish and French artillery did the same from their camp at Saint-Roch. The rock and its little town gave back tit for tat. "Sometimes the whole of Gibraltar was firing upon us." This daily letting-off of steam didn't do much real damage, however. "During that time we had no more than ten or twelve men killed on the two ships, but many injured by shell fragments."

They could have gone on like that forever. But now everything's about

---

*The word was also written *prames* or *prammes.* These were the famous floating batteries that we will soon see in action. They were designed by the naval engineer d'Arçon, and their inventor was fiercely but unfairly criticized after this incident, for his prasmes were the precursors of armored battleships.

†One of the few French ships to be copper-sheathed, thus slower sailing but less vulnerable to barnacles than wooden-hulled ships. The engaging Jean-Jacques de Cotignon was born at Poussignol near Château-Chinon on December 17, 1761, and retires early, in 1790, to his parents' modest country home where he writes the *Mémoires* that have just been published, fortunately, by Physician-General Carré of the Naval Academy. His home may still be seen in its fine upland setting near Château-Chinon.

to change: these are the days when war, like work, is beginning to learn that machines can help it. There are vague dreams afloat, of submarines or *"scafandres"* in the water and flying machines in the air. As for Gibraltar: "At Algeciras* nine ships were being built, called prasmes or floating batteries"— modeled after those that had been so laboriously towed from Toulon—"to bombard the ramparts of the town from close up, so as to make a breach in the walls in preparation for the assault. Every day, troops were arriving, Spanish and French alike, including the Lyonnais, Royal Swedish, Brittany, Piedmont, etc. regiments." While waiting for the big moment they amused themselves as best they could, when the sea was calm and they had shore leave.

> One day there were four of us naval guards taking a walk. They might fire as they liked, we kept on coming; but when we saw that they were starting to lose their tempers, we mimed pants-down and showed them our behinds. Just then a shell thumped down in our midst and made us cover up our compliment, after which we very prudently withdrew.
>
> The entire camp had witnessed our prank. Some reproved us, and those were the wisest, while others laughed and made fun of us, one of them being a sublieutenant named the Chevalier de Mons-Villeneuve; so we dared him to do as much. He wagered he would do better, and kiss the very gates of the town.
>
> Nobody wanted to wager, but he went all the same; he was allowed to draw near, there being nothing to fear from one lone man. They did fire a few rounds at him, though, which he braved, and carried out his plan; he even chalked his name on the gate and returned safe and sound.

Not the sort of escapade to worry General Elliott, the governor of Gibraltar—one of the toughest-skinned English commanders in this war. "He always stood fast, and outfaced the thousands of shells fired at him. He had been watching the construction of those floating batteries right under his eyes with perfect equanimity, for he knew very well how he would parry the blow . . ."

On September 12 all is ready.

> The floating batteries were finished, we prepared to put them into service, and the fleet was ordered to stand by to support them. We set sail, shipping all the troops in Cadiz assigned to the expedition, and that evening we anchored at Algeciras.
>
> Next morning, there being nobody more to come, the nine batteries were moored within pistol range of the ramparts of Gibraltar, after being loaded with all the troops required for the assault. There were about two thousand men on each. The whole fleet also moored within half-cannon range, to back up the prasmes. Firing began at 8 in the morning.

*A small but strong Andalusian town with a well-protected port on the western side of the gulf of Gibraltar only three leagues away. It was also called Old Gibraltar, and the English could observe it through their spyglasses.

I cannot help shuddering at the very thought of what ensued; I can easily say that it was the most exquisite horror that ever was or will be. Elliott, who had been observing our preparations for a long time, had made his plans accordingly, and as the only thing he could do to save himself was to fire molten balls, he did.* The firing had not been going on above half an hour, and the nine batteries, each aiming forty twenty-four-pounders, would soon have made the breach and were preparing to follow it up, when his balls fell and set them afire.

First, five prasmes blew up into the air and the rest followed suit soon afterward; one can imagine a little of what happened, but one needs to have seen it. Each prasme had enough powder on board for two days' firing. Conceive of the explosion! In the instant, we saw whole men, arms, and heads flying into the air. Both sides immediately ceased firing, so that help could be given to the unfortunate people; we lowered all our longboats and pinnaces; I was sent with ours and fished out eighty men, and very nearly perished with them because the boat was so loaded that we came within an ace of sinking a thousand times before getting back on board. Happily the sea was calm, but how many of those poor wretches I left behind with nothing to help them, in order to save the ones who seemed least damaged!

In the end we saved all we could, but credit must be given to the humanity of the English who, anticipating what would transpire, had boats ready to come to our aid, and they saved over half the men† . . .

After this event we all set sail for Cadiz where we unloaded the troops. The Saint-Roch camp broke soon afterwards.

The noise of the explosion of the prasmes was heard in Cadiz, which is twenty leagues away, but it was heard farther still. The concussion was so great that not one pane of window-glass was left in either the town of Gibraltar or in Algeciras, and the inhabitants thought there had been an earthquake. We ourselves were deaf for several days.**

This made the war look a little less pretty, even at Versailles. On September 30 "the disaster of the prasmes, and especially the loss of the brave people manning them and the very great likelihood that many more will be needlessly sacrificed, made the deepest impression upon our monarch. This latest reverse reopened the wound that those preceding it had made in Our Majesty's paternal heart. 'It must be confessed,' he told the ministers of

---

*The "code of war" had previously regarded incendiary cannonades using red-hot or flaming balls as dishonorable. But the exception sometimes proved the rule.

†The motivation of these "lifeboats" wasn't as charitable as all that: they were gunboats which Elliott had stationed there to finish off the prasmes at close range and, with no more mission to accomplish, why shouldn't they salvage a few survivors?

**We learn from Physician-General Carré that d'Arçon had foreseen the possibility of a cannonade of red-hot balls and invented a water-based cooling system, "which, by soaking the wooden walls of the floating batteries, was to neutralize the effects of the incendiary projectiles." But the badly trained commanders didn't dare turn it on for fear of wetting their powder. And to top it all off, there was an indescribable mix-up between French and Spanish.

the war and navy, 'that this is a fine and glorious campaign for my arms!'

"The courtiers, who always stand to gain from a change of ministries, are convinced that the end of the campaign will see one. The Duc de Choiseul and Mme de Maurepas are said to be making overtures, and the two parties that have divided our court may now unite."[9] Aha—rumors of a cabinet reshuffle, that means matters are grave indeed. Maybe the time has come to sign that peace. But what about our last great hope in the Indies? Isn't Suffren out there avenging Dupleix?

SUFFREN AND THE
HAIDAR ALI

28

DECEMBER 1782

I've Seen You, I've Seen Everything

It takes the news five months to cover the distance. France has only just learned, at the end of October, of the victory of Provédien, which brings some consolation for the catastrophes of Les Saintes and Gibraltar and gives the ministers in London something to fret over, after depopulating their garrisons and fleets in the East to bolster their armies in the Americas and Mediterranean and leaving the English crown to defend its Asian trading centers with only "fifteen or twenty thousand sepoys,* crack troops it is true, and three or four thousand Europeans"—English and Hanoverians. "These were all the forces they could muster against us on the Coromandel coast."[1] And there were about the same number on the Malabar coast and in Bengal. More or less enough to cope with Suffren's raids and a skeletal French expeditionary force shrunk by disease as a result of the voyage and change of climate; but they might be woefully inadequate if the Grand Nabob Haidar Ali, the most impressive chieftain to hold sway in southern India for the last two centuries, continues to arm and prosecute his anti-English rebellion—war would be a better word, for this is his home ground—and it's starting to spread like wildfire. His manpower resources are virtually inexhaustible; he's the suzerain of almost all the rajas, that dust-cloud of local princelings; and he has substantially overestimated the help he can count on from the King of France, on the strength of his envoy Suffren's success in checking the English fleet. To Hindu eyes, a warship, a fire-spitting monster, is something supernatural,

*Natives recruited and trained locally. This estimate was given by the Chevalier de Mautort.

for the Hindus have nothing but dhows for coastal trade and fishing barks.

Suffren is not about to undeceive Haidar Ali: a general uprising in the Indies is France's last hope—the English evicted, an empire to "protect" dropping ready-cooked into our hands, four or five times the size of the "United Provinces" over which this war has been fought. On July 26, 1782, Louis François de Mautort,* captain in the Austrasie regiment† and a newly arrived liaison officer assigned to Haidar Ali, is an eyewitness to the meeting between the native chief and the bailli du Suffren. He might almost believe he was attending a summit conference between a god of Hindu legend and a god of the sea, and the two principals are not likely to argue with him. On that day in 1782, after Suffren had played a second murderous tie game with the English fleet off Nagappattinam,** a tiny group of men briefly experienced the very essence of the picturesque somewhere near Cuddalore.‡ When you come to look at this year, so misprized by all historians, what a lot was going on! Mautort has entered a world as alien to a Frenchman as the moon: India —mammoth, evanescent, awesome.

> This was the first time I had occasion to see that enormous mass†† in motion, and I found, beneath the appearance of disorder, what was in fact a high degree of order. One hour before beginning to march they sound what they call the *langara.* For this, a man climbs onto an elephant carrying two stout cymbals, and strikes them slowly and rhythmically; the claps can be heard at a great distance. He continues this throughout the whole march, especially if it is at night, and the sound indicates the route to follow. Infantry and cavalry march in several columns; guidons, standards, and flags carried with the *langara* mark out the new camp and tell each corps where it is to go. The bazaars have their own flags too, but the merchants usually do not arrive until the second day. Whatever is not military travels in separate columns. One needs to have seen all this panoply to have any idea of it; the descriptions one reads in Quintus Curtius of the armies of Darius are quite faithful reflections of what we saw passing before our eyes. Over one hundred and fifty thousand persons of all ages and sexes were on the move. Here would be the seraglio of some prince, there that of an army chief escorted by soldiers. The unfortunate women—I do not believe their lot is to be envied— robed in white, were hidden from head to foot; they traveled in open wagons

*Born at Abbeville on April 3, 1752, a younger son of the lesser nobility, struggling to make a career in the infantry.

†Product of a division of the Champagne regiment in 1776.

**On July 6, 1782. At the end of it, the English again withdrew to Madras. Suffren was still fulminating against his captains, accusing them of having deprived him of a decisive victory for the second time. He has just committed the atrocity of handing over eight hundred English prisoners, captured during his recent battles, to Haidar Ali—that is, to a high level of refined torture, for the Nabob never gave quarter.

‡A small port on the Coromandel coast, taken by the French on May 6, which gave them a foothold on the continent again.

††Haidar Ali's army.

drawn by oxen or costly horses. They tranquilly followed the line, without permission to speak to anyone. Then elephants paraded past bearing their *giroles,* which is a sort of palanquin, very elegant in form. The mahouts drove them seated on the animals' necks, armed with nothing but a two-foot stick at one end of which was a paddle-shaped iron. After them came herds of camels laden with tents and equipment. Carts pulled by teams of buffalo formed another column. The number of beasts of burden was incalculable. To give an idea, one need only say that the nabob had sixty thousand to supply his army and draw his artillery.

This multitude of men and beasts formed endless columns and, owing to the conformation of the Coromandel coast, which is a flat country without relief, all reached their destinations with little difficulty . . .

I have yet to speak of the style in which Haidar Ali traveled. When the *langara* began to sound, his lancers, the troops who were to escort him, his elephants, his hand-horses, and in short everything that formed his cortege and guard assembled in the square in front of his tents. When he was ready, he climbed into a superb palanquin and, surrounded by his lancers, had himself carried with great expedition to the camp they were to occupy."[2]

For Suffren, in spite of his panic at the thought of having to wear a tight-collared dress uniform, the trip was worth the effort. To talk, man to man, to the possessor of power like that! What were France's other allies by comparison? Mere handfuls of men, uppity Rebels, ragged Spaniards, middle-class Dutch militia! Game as ever, the bailli marches to the *durbar* * as though he were mounting the scaffold; and his officers march away from it in roars of laughter that echo through the mess halls for years:

The palanquins and a detachment of cavalry were sent on ahead and, on the appointed day, M. de Suffren, followed by several of the chief officers of the squadron, came up to the middle of the escort . . . Around seven in the evening he set off again for the camp, with our general and the first officers of our army, and then went on to the *durbar,* which was to open at nine o'clock. The ceremonies were the customary ones. The Nabob† was highly diverted by the Commander's difficulties and the fatigue occasioned by his unfamiliarity with the custom of sitting on a cushion in the Asian manner. The extreme stoutness of his body, combined with his very short stature, his great vivacity, the movements he was continually obliged to make to keep his position, and the heat inside the tent, were all highly discommoding to him. Several more cushions were brought, one after the other, to prop him up on the side that seemed most likely to collapse. These mounds of feathers provoked an ever more abundant perspiration all over his body. There was no discussion of business that evening, which fortunately short-ened the session. Around midnight we withdrew. M. de Suffren proposed that the Nabob should come to see his squadron. He wanted to offer him a shipboard

*A court held by a prince, a formal reception.
†A tall, well-set-up man, very dark-skinned, still youthful in appearance despite the illness that was beginning to undermine him.

reception and simulate a naval battle. But the Indian princes, and especially Haidar Ali, were naturally mistrustful and would not have risked placing themselves in the hands of foreigners at sea. To extricate himself Haidar Ali shrewdly replied, "Suffren, I've seen you; I've seen everything."[3]

Courtesy, humor, both? Who can tell with these expressionless copper-hued people?

In any case, the alliance looks like it's going to stick. Suffren, proud of his supreme sacrifice, hurries back to Cuddalore and prods his fleet into action, though some of its ships are still bruised and bleeding from previous frays; he aims them back toward Ceylon, where, between August 22 and September 2, he pulls off one of the finest coups of this campaign, beseiging and then capturing the splendid naval base of Trincomalee, which the English had taken from the Dutch—the "lawful" owners of the big island. Once again, Suffren is quicker than "little mother Hughes," who's been looking for him farther north but who sails him down the very next day and blocks him inside his new conquest. Shall the bailli be trapped? Never! Suffren orders his fleet out on September 3 for an engagement in the open sea, judged suicidal by his captains. Maybe that's why they again show so little enthusiasm about rushing to the fore; or is Suffren's irascibility beginning to soften his brain? Some of his ships are crippled or have been leaking for weeks . . . This offensive looks like it's being waged by a disabled veterans' association. And it's yet another tie, the third, but this time it really is touch and go: the English don't decide to call it a day and head back to Madras until long past nightfall. Trincomalee remains in Suffren's possession, but all he can do with it is turn it into a hospital for his ailing men and ships. Inevitably, the mill of his belligerence starts grinding away; who can he blame now?

At last the monsoon comes with its downpours and hurricanes, and gives everybody time to breathe. Suffren tries various ploys to make the English believe he means to winter at Trincomalee but actually sails off through apocalyptic storms to fasten himself to the Dutch in Sumatra and intimidate the local Malay sovereign, the King of Achem, who is none too overjoyed by this unexpected visit, which might bring him some additional guests in the guise of the English.

And there they are when the worst thing that could happen to them happens: on December 7, 1782, Haidar Ali dies, "of a carbuncular tumor between the shoulders." He was only sixty-three. He had had time to pass on the bulk of his succession (always risky among Hindu feudalities) to his oldest son Tipu Sahib, an influential young man who is just as hostile to the English as his father. But will Tipu Sahib be able to get them all under his thumb? Does he have the kind of genius required to hold everything together and negotiate this war cautiously, month by month, which was his father's great gift? In Sumatra, the demoralized French prepare to resume their Penelopean labor in the spring, a little wearier than they were the year before, a little less certain of their ally.

While in Versailles, where nobody knows anything of these latest developments, the Marquis de Castries has persuaded Louis XVI, on the strength of Suffren's first dispatches, to send out reinforcements and invest more heavily in the Indian gamble. The tragedy of Gibraltar has released Admiral de Guichen, the "navy man on the way up," just as de Grasse and d'Estaing are on the way out. He is given a convoy and troops—embarked, very badly, on four lots of ships, which stray through the southern seas until after Christmas before anchoring in the vicinity of Ceylon.

In keeping with its general level of efficiency, the Court of France, which may be only five months behind as far as news from India is concerned, is a good thirty in arrears when it comes to imagination. True, the great general sent out to give Suffren a hand, the man who's finally going to even up the 1763 score with the English, does actually know the terrain. They called him "the right hand of Dupleix" in the last war; he's the great and glorious Marquis de Bussy, "Indian Bussy!" Bravo. We're back under Louis XV, we've come full circle. There's just one tiny hitch, which is that Bussy, aged sixty-four, looks ten years older and is racked by gout. Two tiny hitches, rather: gouty is one thing, but he's gaga too.[4]

GEORGE III OF ENGLAND

29

JANUARY 1783

George, Be a King!

Deep down, neither England nor France is eager to fight to the death over the Indian emporia alone, with uncertain odds, vanishing allies, and exhausted armies on both land and sea. After all, this is supposed to be the "American" war, and on that side of the world, it's over; and the Americans couldn't care less about the Indies and Gibraltar. Throughout the whole of 1782, therefore, the fore-stage has been occupied by diplomats executing complicated maneuvers reminiscent of a slow-motion ballet.

The "official" conferences—nine, from May to July—take place in Paris:

between Vergennes, firm as a rock with all eternity before him;* Franklin (pro-French and increasingly disgusted with England), flanked by Adams and Jay, who don't trust either Franklin or Vergennes; Grenville, descendant of an illustrious family of icicles, who is the official envoy of the English Foreign Ministry but similarly supervised or counterbalanced by Richard Oswald, the delegate of the Minister for the Colonies, a cunning old merchant whose instructions are to pacify Franklin; and lastly, Aranda, representing the Spaniards, whose hauteur is no help to anybody and who are clamoring for Gibraltar with every breath. "The Spanish ambassador is a veritable crown of thorns!" sighs Vergennes.[2]

After July 24 the conferences become less official and more efficient as they move, table by table, from Paris to The Hague to London. "By the time the negotiations† ended, the different negotiators were agreed upon one thing at least, and that was their exasperation."[3] The Americans wanted Canada and the land as far west as the Mississippi, the Spaniards were demanding Gibraltar and Florida, the French were trying to snatch as many islands as possible and recover their ports in the Indies, the English wanted not only to keep Canada but to have exclusive fishing rights off Newfoundland, and were insisting that protection be given to the American Tories, whom they called "loyalists." Piecing that quilt together in a year was out of the question at their snail's pace. But the real action was not around the conference table; the eye of the war was in London, where the wind from America had finally swept into the center of that tightly closed circle upon which everything depended, the English Parliament. One might have supposed it would be paralyzed for centuries, but in 1782 it is actually where the molecules are moving fastest, and human history begins to thaw in the heat. We really ought never to swear that nothing can ever change anything.

The battlefield? A few square furlongs under a Gothic vault, in one of the most conformist settings imaginable: the ancient chapel of St. Stephen next to Westminster Palace, deconsecrated to accommodate a parliament from which every religion and political system in the world could learn a thing or two. Inside, opposition and majority sit facing each other and even switch places when the occasion arises.** The nostalgia of men of liberty the globe over has

---

*For Joly de Fleury, on the other hand, the colorless magistrate who has taken over from Necker as comptroller-general of finance, time is of the essence: in March 1782 Vergennes estimated the total cost to France of its assistance to the Rebels, from 1776 to the end of 1782 (extrapolating from sums paid out in advance), at twenty-eight million livres or 170 million modern francs [$34 million]. At that rate the royal treasury, which was already full of leaks, would soon go under.[1]

†According to Bernard Faÿ.

**Destroyed by a German bombardment on May 10, 1941, the Commons Chamber has been restored to its former bleak stateliness, complete with all its former inconvenience.

been eddying round this hall since the first orator rose to speak there, idealizing as they fantasized. No speaker's platform. No government bench. Everybody talks from his seat. The ministers, including the prime minister, sit on the lowest bench on the majority side, facing the opposition leaders on the other side. Between the two, a gigantic solid wooden table on the gleaming surface of which rests a sort of heavy silver club (the mace) signifying power —which no one is allowed to touch. At the end of the table, under a little canopy, sits Mr. Speaker, stuffed into an enormous wig; but he has little more authority than one of the ushers: all he does is call upon or reprimand the orators. Overhead, burning night and day through the light dimmed even in bright sunshine by the thick panes of glass in the high windows, hangs an overpowering chandelier in the Dutch manner, the smoke from its candles blackening the vault above. On the low benches, crowded together in their gold-trimmed coats, their hair curled and powdered, their necks wrapped in three-tiered cravats, many leaning on sticks and canes, their elbows in each other's ribs, and—save in the king's presence—their three-cornered hats firmly clamped to their heads, perch a gang of thieves from a county fair who wouldn't give up their seats for a cannonball, the honorable gentlemen, the squires,* almost all of them sons of Lords (true peers, that is) who will end their days in the House of Lords: the members of the nation's Parliament. Nobody raises his voice. The object of the game is to shut everybody else up by imposing yourself quietly; disapproval or criticism is expressed only by an occasional distinguished grumble. The orators perform in the muted register, making their effects by means of delicate shifts of timbre. The greatest, like the glorious Pitt the Elder (Lord Chatham), end almost in a whisper, and the silence enveloping them at the end of their speeches subtly transmits agreement or opprobrium. One Tory speaker once tried to play the Roman tribune, going to such outrageous lengths of bad taste as to bellow, "If I lie, let the first man to say so stab me with this weapon!"

And, plucking a knife from his bosom, he tossed it onto the great table. A deep and total silence ensued while three or four hundred startled gentlemen contemplated the unwonted object. And into the hush Sheridan, one of the most frivolous members of the opposition, interjected a polite query:

"But what has become of the fork?"[4]

God knows, these people can cut and thrust all right, but it's all mantled in words. They possess, in fact, a formidable aggressiveness, but in the style of debate in which it expresses itself here, murders are committed courteously. The news from Yorktown has put new life into the Whigs, who have been opposing the royal government's brutal treatment of the "Colonies" for nearly

---

*Squires are country gentlemen, farmers who've worked their way up over the centuries.

ten years. But the triumph of a Cassandra is ever bitter. Fox crushes the majority with a few short words of irony:

"I shall not say that I believe the ministers are paid by France. It is not possible for me to prove the fact. But I shall venture to say that they deserve to be so paid."[5] Lord North, the prime minister, whose shoulders have to bear, a little unfairly, the full brunt of George III's short-sighted policy and ill-conceived war, takes the blows unflinchingly as an Englishman should, even when threatened with an impeachment that could lead him to the scaffold. He parries with the eternal language of defeated governments playing for time, by appealing to the name of union:

"A melancholy disaster has occurred in Virginia; but are we, therefore, to lie down and die? No, it ought rather to rouse us into action . . . by bold and united exertions everything may be saved; by dejection and despair everything must be lost!" Their sovereign would never sacrifice the essential rights and enduring interests upon which depend the nation's future strength and security. The American war may be unfortunate, but it was not unjust.

He shouldn't leave himself open like that, it's too easy to answer back and annihilate him, as Burke undertakes to do, bringing up the kind of heavy artillery that only the best orator of the day can manipulate:

The Prime Minister's words froze my blood . . . Good God! . . . Are we yet to be told of the rights for which we went to war? Oh excellent rights! Oh valuable rights! Valuable you should be, for we have paid dear at parting with you. Oh valuable rights, that have cost England thirteen provinces, four islands, a hundred thousand men, and more than seventy millions of money!* Oh wonderful rights, that have lost to Great Britain her empire on the ocean—her boasted grand and substantial superiority, which made the world bend before her! Oh inestimable rights, that have taken from us our rank among nations, our importance abroad, and our happiness at home; that have taken from us our trade, our manufactures, and our commerce; that have reduced us . . . to be one of the most compact, unenviable powers on the face of the globe! Oh wonderful rights that are likely to take from us all that yet remains!

We had the right to tax America, says the Noble Lord, and as we had a right, we must do it . . . Oh miserable and infatuated men! miserable and undone country! not to know that right signified nothing without might; that the right without the power of enforcing it was nugatory and idle . . . Oh, says a silly man, full of his prerogative of dominion over a few beasts of the field, there is excellent wool on the back of a wolf, and, therefore, he must be sheared. What! shear a wolf? Yes. But will he comply? have you considered the trouble? how will you get this wool? Oh, I have considered nothing, and I will consider nothing but my right: a wolf is an animal that has wool; all animals that have wool are to be shorn and, therefore, I will shear the wolf.

*A little more than twice the cost to France, in pounds sterling.

There is no doubt that this is also a war, but one of ideas, or personalities at least. Lord North has been at the helm since February 28, 1770. Twelve years; long enough. But the wrestling match between Whigs and Tories across the top of the big wooden table has been going on even longer; their speeches are the last but also the decisive echo of clamor, street fighting, and riots, with the king's officers hurled into the Thames, Irishmen burned alive in their barns, downtrodden Scots; and they provide a flickering but precious reflection of the infinite wretchedness of eleven million men and women, laborers still working for the most part on farms but already being herded together and sent to the manufactures, often totally forgotten by their elected representatives. What is the English word for *"prolétariat"?*

Round and round goes the merry-go-round, first Whigs then Tories then Whigs then Tories, but careful: the words have changed meaning several times in the last hundred years, like "left-wing" in so many mouths in the twentieth century. In 1688 the Tories were nobles steeped in popery, who remained loyal to the Stuarts and the divine right of kings. The Whigs were the fervent followers of the Anglican church, longing for the days of Elizabeth I, aristocrats themselves but wanting self-government. Nobody mentioned "the people"; they were simply mobilized at the whim of their Lord's religious fanaticism. The Stuart kings showed least intelligence, if only by relying on Louis XIV, whom the English loathed. The Whig aristocracy was cleverer, replacing the Stuarts with the Hanoverian dynasty—stolid, ignorant Germans—and, to govern in their name, George I, who couldn't speak a word of English, followed by George II, who could stammer two or three, but what did that matter? The true names of England were Marlborough, Bolingbroke, Walpole, or William Pitt (the Elder, of course). Until that October 25, 1760, when a twenty-two-year-old George III, charming, by no means a fool, and educated by British tutors, dropped down on the throne before them with the backing of an imperious Mummy who hissed into his ear every morning, "George, be a king!" In his first address to Parliament, he had written with his own hand, "Born and educated in this country, I glory in the name of Briton."[6]

An English king! That's all we need. And off they went again, the do-si-dos, betrayals, realignments, you try to figure out who's really Whig and who's Tory these last twenty years* . . . Whole regiments of the old Tory aristocracy, the Jacobites as they were called on account of James Stuart, promptly abandoned their Pretender by the wayside, drinking himself under the table and chasing skirts from France to Italy, and plumped for what they had always wanted, a monarch with some muscle . . . but who would exert it on their behalf. The Whigs balked. If the king wasn't going to be their puppet any-

---

*Except in America, we recall, where the words had kept their older meanings: Tory *for* the crown, and Whig *against* it.

more, they might as well convert themselves into liberals and move over to the opposition. George III hated them from the very pit of his stomach: his desire was to be an English Louis XIV, but he had turned up a hundred years too late. Just a few days ago, in 1782, one dispute between ghosts had been settled. His Mazarin had been Lord Bute, a man "come up from nothing" said the Whigs—begging your pardon: up from the Queen Mother's bed.* As prime minister, Bute had reaped the laurels of the war that Pitt had wanted and successfully waged: he had concluded the peace of 1763—too soon, according to the erstwhile Whigs; just in time, according to the craven Tories, the "Court party" that formed around George III's favorites. They then transferred their loyalties from Bute to North and would transfer them to the devil if it were His Majesty's gracious pleasure. It was to oppose them that Wilkes got himself elected Lord Mayor of London in 1774† . . . the better to sell himself, once in office, to the king. It was against them** that Pitt the Elder, then Lord Chatham, had risen up at the beginning of the American war, tottering on his crutches, crippled by gout and apoplexy: "I rejoice that America has resisted. Three millions of people so dead to all the feelings of liberty as voluntarily to submit to be slaves would have been fit instruments to make slaves of the rest . . . America, if she fell, would fall like the strong man. She would embrace the pillars of the state, and pull down the constitution along with her. Is this your boasted peace? Not to sheath the sword in its scabbard, but to sheath it in the bowels of your countrymen?"[7] A few days later he was carried away from his bench dying; stricken by a final attack, he was still mumbling imprecations.

But ten years earlier, a timid and ascetic young Irishman nicknamed "the Jesuit" by his friends—Edmund Burke—had made his début in the Commons. Where is his bashfulness today? Maybe it's because of it, because of a constant need to overcome self-doubt, that he has stepped into the shoes of Pitt the Elder and become today the lion of the Whigs.

Not solo. Twenty years ago there was also a man named Fox, who became Lord Holland and moved to the Upper House, and now we have his third son, Charles Fox, who can equal and in fact outdo Burke in pugnacity. Burke and Fox‡ have been hogging half the stage for almost ten years now but have never

---

*He may have been the father of Lord North, who would then be half-brother (born in secret) to George III, and who strongly resembles him.

†In the days when Marat was in London and had a finger in the pie.

**Although not until after he had curried favor with the king in the hope of becoming his tutor, around 1765. George III even restored him to power for a year; but both men were too much of a piece and could never agree for long.

‡The French are most familiar with Charles Fox, because of the peace of Amiens in 1802, when, old and weary, he replaces Pitt the Younger in the English government, too late and for too short a time, and is the only valid British representative in the eyes of First Consul Bonaparte.

been able to steal the leading role from the stalwart ministers installed on the front bench by George III. The king's men don't go in much for purple passages but they're there and they stand fast, like the throne. This being so, what's the use of the golden oratory of the Whigs?

Its use is to challenge, to appeal, to echo across Europe, to fecundate the minds of Brissot and Marat. To give notice that every Englishman is not endorsing England's crimes and thus to found a new concept of Nation and give birth to a sense of solidarity among men of freedom, whatever their camp. All the people in France, from Mirabeau to Condorcet, who are being forcibly silenced by the absence of a national assembly and reduced to issuing anonymous pamphlets—they all envy the lot of the Whig orators. Oh, to be able to speak! To shout in the face of the powers-that-be what they thought and are thinking about the dismissal of Turgot and Necker, and now the downfall of the Rohan-Guéménée family . . . All those words crammed down all those throats: what a load of dynamite!

Since 1780, the gears have been shifting even faster. The Commons were dissolved by the king under pressure of the confused riots that rocked the city and set people shaking their heads and predicting revolution in England. On a certain Black Wednesday that year, the rabble had risen in fury, ostensibly in support of Lord Gordon, a mildly dotty aristocrat who was rabid against the Roman Catholics;* but he was only a pretext for the outpouring of the discontent that was goading them to action. For three days the city was nothing but smashed windows and doors ripped off their hinges, broils between militia and guttersnipes, all the characters of Hogarth pouring out of his drawings and rampaging through the streets. Nobody understood exactly what it was they wanted, but the very walls of Whitehall, where the king was in residence, had been desecrated. The authorities called out the troops, George III panicked and decided to try some new men in Parliament, hoping for sympathy and support at a time when he still thought he could win the war. Poor fellow: the 1780 elections returned the veterans Fox and Burke, followed by a pack of young wolves with razor-sharp teeth, who were beginning to equal their leaders and gathering strength to surpass them: Pitt the Younger, Wilberforce, Fitzpatrick, Townshend, Sheridan. And across from them: nothing. Not one young man, not one popular leader on the king's side. "Operation Wilkes" had failed because it was too blatantly tainted with corruption; all that remained was a compact group of decrepit Tories, most of whom were being automatically transferred (by the death of the older generation) to the House of Lords, and the inextirpable Lord North, who has now discovered the one

---

*At the end of his life Gordon converts to Judaism. [The Gordon riots are dramatically fictionalized in Dickens's *Barnaby Rudge.*—*Trans.*]

sure riposte when the opposition attacks: he simply goes to sleep on his bench every time one of them takes the floor.

Even more preoccupying is the mental and physical deterioration of the king. In less than twenty years he has lost both youth and charm and become, like his forefathers, one of those large-bellied pop-eyed Germans he so wanted not to resemble. No Louis XIV here, that's for sure. He stutters, he sways heavily from side to side as he walks, he's forever regurgitating the same old commonplaces. His private life, surveyed by his eagle-eyed mother, is irreproachable. His mores are heart-breakingly proper. In twenty years he sires fifteen children upon poor Queen Charlotte of Mecklenberg, another German married by arrangement, of course, so ugly and so lucid that she burst into tears at her first sight of her new ladies-in-waiting, all fair and well-endowed. She asked them, "Are all the women in England as beautiful as you?" "The stiff Teutonic corset that she insisted upon wearing even when she slept at night, yet further increased Her Majesty's natural rigidity. Her thin hair, oily and black, was pulled harshly back from her face and one could see her scalp between the pins."[8] George III is faithful to her, but what good does that do? He's losing his mind.

At this stage, the words are a bit strong. Way back in 1765, however, there was a first alarm, serious enough to compel the Tory Grenville, with many circumlocutions, to get Parliament to adopt a "Regency Act" just in case, if, by misfortune . . . What exactly was wrong with the king? Now and then, he simply went off into a fog. He literally strayed. He didn't know where he was or who was with him. He recovered from that first attack so quickly that nobody said anything more about it for fifteen years. But whether as a result of the onset of old age or his American woes or the steady progression of degeneracy, his intimates are now beginning to worry. In 1782 Lord Cavendish takes the bull by the horns when he privately observes, "His Majesty is certainly wrong in the upper storey." And Fox, with gloomy jubilation, comments upon "the king's very strange expression," putting more jubilation than gloom into his irony, perhaps, because in 1782 the Whigs finally have a potential alternate king to back, a Louis XI to pit against their Charles VII: on August 12 that year the Prince of Wales is twenty years old.

WILLIAM PITT

BURKE

SHERIDAN

30

FEBRUARY 1783

This Is Only a Pause

In an absolute monarchy, which this has pretty much become during the reign of George III, the hopes of the men who love their country are ultimately pinned on the king's demise or incapacity; it is one of the few laws of history that works almost automatically. Lacking any better alternative in the last days of the reign of Louis XV, for example, people were longing for the advent of Louis XVI . . .

But George IV, whose coronation day some people would like to hasten, seems a far more promising prospect than the young dauphin of France ten years earlier.* For he's a jolly good fellow . . . "He will be the best-mannered man or the greatest good-for-nothing in Europe. Possibly both,"[1] said the Bishop of Litchfield, one of his better tutors. Others had taken great pains to cultivate whatever differences they could find between him and his father, with some success. The Prince of Wales can conceivably be seen as an anti-George III. The girlfriend of one of his grooms ended his virginity at sixteen, and women have since become a necessity to him. Mary Hamilton, one of his first public mistresses, the one he had in 1779—she was ten years older than he—has left a description of him [actually written by himself in the third person, and sent to her—*Trans.*], which remains valid throughout his youth, and indeed adulthood:

> . . . rather above the common size, his limbs well proportioned, and upon the whole well made, tho' rather too great a penchant to grow fat, the features of his countenance are strong and manly, tho' they carry with them too much of an air of hauteur, his forehead well shaped, his eyes tho' none of the best, and tho' grey are yet passable, tolerable good eyebrows and eyelashes, *un petit nez retroussé cependant assez aimé* [a small turned-up nose yet it has found favor;

*He does become King of England, as George IV, when his father finally deigns to depart this world, which is not until January 30, 1820. But for many many years before that he is "Prince Regent," owing to the eventually total insanity of George III. It is to him that Napoleon addresses his famous letter of surrender from the Ile d'Aix in 1815.

in French in the original—*Trans.*], a good mouth tho' rather large, with fine teeth, a tolerable good chin, but the whole of the countenance is too round. I forgot to add very ugly ears.

His sentiments and thoughts are open and generous, above doing anything that is mean, (too susceptible, even to believing people his friends, and placing too much confidence in them), grateful and friendly to excess where he finds *a real friend* . . . rather too familiar to his inferiors but will not suffer himself to be brow-beaten or treated with haughtiness by his superiors. Now for his vices, or rather let us call them weaknesses—too subject to give loose or vent to his passions of every kind, too subject to be in a passion . . . he's rather too fond of Wine and Women.[2]

He's got excuses: his father won't allow him to be fond of anything else. He wants to move his heir's residence within view, the better to keep an eye on him. He has pared his establishment to the bone. He has refused to let him serve in the army, and even to visit the provincial estates of the great lords of the kingdom. He has separated him from his brothers, cousins, and uncles: monarchy also allows abusive fathers to make another great dream come true, that of destroying their child. But this one "seems ready to burst in his skin."[3] And he has the promising reflexes of the young rooster: one day George III berates him for lying so long in bed. Reply:

"I have observed, Sir, that however late I rise, the day is still long enough to do nothing in."

The Prince of Wales, therefore, surreptitiously before Yorktown and almost publicly since, is leaning toward "His Majesty's opposition" and giving it a second source of vitality, in addition to the bitter pill of being right. Perhaps there will be some possibility of action in the not too far distant future.

For three months at the beginning of this year, they fought the good fight, across the great wooden table, against Lord North's soporosity. At their head the Right Honourable Edmund Burke, son of a lawyer (Protestant?—he claims to be, his enemies deny it, and he couldn't care less) in Dublin, the capital of colonized Ireland. Fifty-four years old in 1782. Poor, skinny, obstinate, always angry. A pen. A voice. Twenty years after his great speech in favor of the Insurgents (made in 1775) Fox instructs the members of Parliament to "peruse it again and again, engrave it upon their minds, imprint it in their hearts. It is there they will learn that democratic representation is the sovereign remedy for all evils."[4] But Burke has been leading the opposition for so many years that he has become the incarnation of it. Nobody can imagine him a minister, and he never will be. What would Jeremiah be doing in a government?

Now he has Fox as running mate, equally gifted at flights of oratory for all his diminutive size, but a bon vivant, a drinker, more of a diplomat, and closer in age to the Prince of Wales, who soon takes a liking to him. Fox is only thirty-five this year. The son of a statesman who brought him up gently and liked to say, "Let's let the young people have their way, they're always right." He gambles away fortunes, drinks like a fish. Almost all these English politicians are professional topers, moreover, including both Younger and Elder Pitts. Positively swimming in gin and port. Fox is one of the worst, though, which accounts for his leaden complexion, his stoutness, and the swarm of creditors dogging his heels, following him to the very doors of the House. "Mr. Fox is the foremost face anywhere," old Walpole said, "the hero of Parliament, gaming-table, and brothel. Last week he spent twenty-four consecutive hours in those three places or in transit from one to the other."[5] But the great historian Gibbon, albeit one of his staunchest opponents,* does concede that "Perhaps no human being was ever more perfectly exempt from the taint of malevolence, vanity or falsehood."[6]

He is the coming generation, or at least the New Wave, the England of tomorrow. Everyone can feel it in the opening weeks of a unique session, made remarkable chiefly by the presence of two very dissimilar debutants. One is Richard Brinsley Sheridan, thirty-two years old and the author of *The School for Scandal* and other plays, a Beaumarchais who has made it in politics, another Irishman but this time from the North, young, handsome, easygoing, a bit of a ham, with romantic allure, a boy who has just succeeded—starting from next to nothing and by virtue of his talent alone—in spanning the "chasm between high rank and good breeding and the common wretches that crawl on the earth," that "tragic feature of the eighteenth century."[7] His "extraordinary voice" and flair for gesture are his finest qualities. "One of the most important social requirements for a man at that time,† and especially for a politician, was to be amusing. Beyond all doubt, Sheridan fulfilled this condition."[8]

Of Pitt the Younger, the other new leading man, it would hardly be possible to say that he is amusing. But the moment his rather frail voice is heard, a shiver runs along the benches, even those of the opposition, where a friend gives Charles Fox a dig in the ribs:

"Look sharp! Remember what your mother used to say! If ever that little shrimp turns against us, he will be a thorn in your side forever . . ."[9]

Amusing or not, he's a Pitt. He is Pitt. He's twenty-two years old and has just gotten himself elected, following the tradition in the great English families, for one of those "rotten boroughs" that made a travesty of three-fourths of the electoral procedure. (The delineation of constituencies having remained

---

*Edward Gibbon (1737–1794), the author of the monumental *Decline and Fall of the Roman Empire.* A little, hunchbacked, extremely sentimental man, he toured all over Europe in his youth and was the spurned swain of the Genevan Suzanne Curchod, who married Necker instead.

†According to Mme Châtel de Brancion, author of an excellent *Sheridan* published in 1974 (see Notes).

unchanged since the days of Charles I,* a member could be put into office by two or three farmers obedient to the wishes of their local lord.) His father lived long enough to put him into orbit but not crush him under his own weight. He emerges from his cradle as the Moses of England, watched by every eye, eagerly awaited. Here he is. A child of the century is born.

Maybe it was because his family doctor brought him up on port that he has acquired such a liking for it. (Four bottles a day on average, after the age of twenty);[10] or maybe the beverage has had some pickling effect upon his nervous system. In any event, he is white, pallid, fragile, and chaste unto frigidity. He never marries. But the Greek vocabulary by heart at fourteen, a Master of Arts from Cambridge at seventeen . . . He has poured his entire life into his hereditary ambition—to become a brilliant orator? Dazzle is not, as it turns out, his strong point. "His speeches are those of a mathematician," according to Wilberforce: "He explains things as he goes along; and then returns to his point of departure with startling ease."[11] Burke, and Fox, and Wilberforce have no trouble understanding his equations. If William Pitt happens to be on their side at the beginning of 1782, it's simply because you can't found a political career on a decomposing government. In the Pitt family you're a minister or you're nothing. Nevertheless, if there is any way to salvage the situation, it's through him.

North's fall, and hence the decision to make peace, which is virtually imposed upon the king, is the outcome of three parliamentary ballots, in December and in January and February 1782. Finally, on March 20, a cold wintry evening with a fall of snow in London, Lord North announces his resignation at the beginning of a sitting that everyone had assumed would be long and so sent their carriages away. With a placid smile he walks out past his conquerors, who stand shivering as they wait for their vehicles. "You see, gentlemen, the advantage of being in the secret. Good night."[12] And climbs into his.

George III is so mortified, after working so hard to become a truly English king, that he threatens to abdicate and retire to his dominions in Hanover. But that would make things too easy for his upstart son; and perhaps already, from afar, he can perceive the discreet signals of young William Pitt . . . He calls a moderate Whig to power, Lord Rockingham, who makes Fox his foreign secretary. Thereupon, the negotiations in France begin to thaw.

Only to freeze up again in July. Pitt was not a clairvoyant, he could hardly have foreseen that Rockingham would die in July after four short months in power. But for the child prodigy this stroke of fate is a big break, coinciding with the great split in the new generation of English politics. George III, this

*In 1782 towns like Manchester and Birmingham, which already had more than twenty thousand inhabitants, do not send a single representative to Parliament; nineteen boroughs in Cornwall, on the other hand, elect thirty-nine members.

time openly advised by Pitt, wisely resigns himself to signing the peace, since there is really nothing else he can do—but with a ministry made to his order, in other words composed of Tories and turncoat Whigs. Prime minister: Lord Shelburne; Pitt becomes chancellor of the exchequer—that is, minister of finance—at the age of twenty-two. Left on the other side are those who never forgive: Fox, Burke, and Sheridan. Not to mention the Prince of Wales. George III had sensed that only a young man of Pitt's stature could outweigh his son's growing popularity. There will be much expatiation on the curious psychology that has led this young politician to hitch his wagon to an aging king. Perhaps an unconscious act of revenge upon his father, who fought George III so long and hard?

The latest move in the game is a coalition among the parliamentarians (including Lord North!) who have been outraged by all this maneuvering, which brings down the fragile royal government at the end of the summer. So it's Fox and North together, now we've seen everything, who sign the peace preliminaries, first with the Americans—in London on September 30, 1782—and then with the French, at Versailles on January 20, 1783 . . . but not under the same prime minister, because Portland has succeeded Shelburne in the interim, during which Pitt spends a few weeks back on his bench, glad enough not to have dipped his pen in the ink of that second treaty, which is hardly a feather in England's cap. And bides his time; it won't be long coming, if he can judge by various winks from the king. Soon there will be an end to this procession of ministries presided over by doddering aristocratic nonentities. And what better way for Pitt to win even more popularity than by spending another little season in opposition, although under the king's wing and giving out hints that (how will they put it later?) with him, the country can have change without loss of continuity. The king's party has found its archangel. Oh, wonderful alchemy of conservatism and youth! The sleight-of-hand is performed in the first three months of 1783, when the Tories, personified by Pitt, become the opposition of a mixed government, "a bastard coalition" in which Fox and North can only cancel each other out and nothing can be done anyway because of the king's loathing for them. "Never shall I place my confidence in such a ministry, and I shall seize the first opportunity to dismiss it."[13] Now that he's got his own man in the wings.

As for the time lapse between the two treaty signatures, two hundred years of French historians will berate the American plenipotentiaries for this incident, calling them ungrateful sneaks for daring to negotiate with the English on their own, without notifying us . . . and passing from generation to generation the tale of a scene fit for a nineteenth-century ballad-vendor's engraving that takes place between Vergennes and Franklin toward the end of September

1782. The latter, looking slightly sheepish, is presenting the French minister with the text of the Anglo-American treaty that had been signed without his knowledge. "Vergennes reeled at the blow." Sez you. Vergennes had never felt anything but contempt for the Americans, and in July he secretly sent one of his best agents, Rayneval, to make a deal in London behind their backs. John Adams, with his sharp puritan nose, smelled a rat the moment he arrived in Europe, and Franklin himself finally agreed that there probably was one. Everybody was cheating everybody and trying to get off as cheaply as possible. France, regarding the Insurgents as mere mercenaries, wanted primarily to negotiate as leader of the coalition and only with the English. The Insurgents, on the other hand, wanted full legal recognition for their nation from the outset. And since the French were being held up by those accursed Spaniards on account of Gibraltar, the American commissioners quietly edged themselves into the imbroglio, like mice between scrapping cats. Well done. Anyway, nobody is really angry, just pretending. And the Americans' precocious peace is ultimately appended to the general treaty whose ratification by all the belligerents, Dutch included, requires the whole of 1783.

America is thereafter independent to the Mississippi; France recovers Pondicherry in India along with the islands of St. Pierre and Miquelon (off the south coast of Newfoundland) and Tobago, and obtains fishing rights off Newfoundland; and she keeps Senegal. England keeps Gibraltar and Canada but leaves Louisiana, Florida, and Minorca to the Spanish. The humiliation of the Paris treaty of 1763 has been mitigated, and France can fortify Dunkerque again. Even the crown of England isn't too badly dented, because she gets off pretty cheaply and pretends to grant enforced concessions "by free and deliberate act."

Opinion among the courtiers gives Vergennes full credit for the successes actually achieved by the fighters in the field. A hymn of praise rises up to the man who, if one can place any trust in the signs, must soon be officially transformed into principal minister. He is sixty-four years old. He is happy and tired. With reason. He has worked hard, day after day, even though his objectives have sometimes changed. His office has been part of the battlefield.

The war that was won by Washington, Rochambeau, and La Fayette is proclaimed to have been won by Louis XVI and Vergennes, who does indeed get a promotion, on February 23, 1783, to the post of "President of the Council of Finance," a relatively honorary position that removes none of the comptroller-general's power but will add another 60,000 livres to Vergennes's annual income.* This is the coming man, I tell you. The big chiefs in Western Europe are very likely to be Vergennes and William Pitt, tomorrow and for a long time to come. Possibly preparing for the third round:

---

*About 370,000 modern francs [$72,000].

there's a touch of chill around the edges of this peace that has sprung so easily to everyone's lips. From his exile in Berlin Abbé Raynal contemplates it unenthusiastically: "It was concluded in haste, and eternal [*sic*] concessions have been made to smooth over momentary difficulties; for that reason one may say that this is only a pause."[14]

ST. BENOÎT-JOSEPH LABRE

31

APRIL 1783

Eighty Thousand Relics

Rome, April 17, 1783, Holy Thursday. Temporary altars are being erected in the city's 364 churches. But there never was a Holy Week like this one. Can you imagine a revolution in the pope's home town on Maundy Thursday? Yet that's what's happening. It starts in the tangle of alleyways around the Coliseum and spreads out to envelop the whole city.

This revolution, however, is one of piety—"superstition," Voltaire would have said. In any event, it's the opposite of sedition. The object of all the pushing and shoving, which seems likely to asphyxiate a few of the mob, is to increase its chances of getting to heaven by touching a little lump of dead body: a saint.

The signal was given at dawn by the children from the houses near that of Signor Zaccarelli, where Benoît-Joseph Labre* died during the night, on the little square of Our Lady of the Mounts—a few cypresses, a fountain, eight or ten ochre-hued façades, and that wonderful Roman paving made of irregular stones cemented by weeds. The children "filled the square and streets with their cries, chanting in chorus: *'E morto il Santo! E morto il Santo!'* Soon Benoît-Joseph's sanctity was being proclaimed by more than the children; the people, the whole of Rome joined in their cries, repeating the same words, over and over: the saint has died.† It was a sort of total commotion; in the streets of Rome almost nothing could be heard but those short phrases: A saint has died in Rome; where is the home of the saint who has died?

"A crowd besieged the house of Signor Zaccarelli; he was forced to open

*Benoît Labre, a manifestation of the current of subterranean mysticism that was sweeping through the Europe of the Enlightenment, is canonized in 1880.

†This is an eyewitness account. There was a reporter in the crowd, Benoît-Joseph's last confessor, whose story, from which these lines have been taken, was published in Italy and France (in translation) the same year.

it, and a guard of Corsican soldiers* was summoned to prevent disorder and contain the multitude."[1]

The excitement continued to grow during the next two days, overflowed on the evening of Easter Sunday—the day of the funeral—and flooded the countryside on Monday, when the movement was reversed by the neighboring towns. People came pouring in from every corner of the Papal States, the rich in carriages, the poor on foot. The shock wave spread as far as Naples in the south and Milan in the north, celebrating a great high mass to beggary.

Because the beggar Benoît-Joseph Labre has finally managed to commit suicide at the age of thirty-four, after a self-imposed agony prolonged for many years. He must have had the constitution of a horse to have held out so long. While his suffering was in the present tense, nobody took him very seriously, except a few priests and nuns and pious souls who were fascinated by his heaven-hued gaze. The vermin infesting him, his pestilential smell, and the fundamental misanthropy hidden behind a mask of meditation, kept the crowds away. His death changes all that, raising him high on a cross-shaped podium at the end of the Roman century. It sends the papal court and the great Roman families into seventh heaven, if one may be forgiven the expression. Their aggressive opulence, their cynical display of idleness and pleasure, are justified by this stampede of one of the poorest peoples in Europe toward the champion of poverty. Can't you see, that's all THEY want, somebody even more wretched than themselves; why, it's their image of bliss, the only one conceivable for them, the bliss of the life beyond. Oh, how fortunate they are, the scum! God has sent them an envoy on purpose to make them ashamed of all the good things in their lives, their little fistful of *maritozzi* (raisin cakes), their yearly Carnival, their jug of thick wine on the *osteria* table on Sunday— even that is too much for them. St. Benoît-Joseph Labre will teach them self-restraint.

One day in June 1782, after the mass he had just celebrated, as he did every day, in the church of St. Ignatius of the Roman college, Abbé Marconi's attention was drawn to "a man whose aspect, at first sight, was unpleasant and repugnant. Half-naked legs, his waist belted by a length of thin cord, his head completely unkempt, poorly covered and wrapped in a worn and ragged coat; all the external attributes, in short, of the most wretched beggar I have ever observed; thus appeared before me, for the first time, Benoît-Joseph." This wreck had come to ask the priest to hear his "general confession."† He was

---

*Since their conquest and exploitation by Genoa and France in turn, the Corsicans had been almost as important a source of mercenaries as the Swiss; they were mainly employed in Latin countries.

†The practice is now falling into disuse in the Roman Catholic church, but was fairly common in olden times and still exists in conjunction with certain pilgrimages or jubilees. However many

already on his sixth. The abbé was quite willing to do so, especially as the man's voice, his expression, and his magnetism were compelling, whenever he deigned (and that was not often) to address a fellow man. "I quickly perceived a remarkable light in the soul of Benoît-Joseph," and Marconi became his weekly confessor, although not without "always taking the precaution of hearing him only in the confessional, so as to make a sort of separation between us" (and protect himself from the vermin that could be seen swarming over the holy man's body; too bad for the penitents next in line, who would have to kneel in Labre's place). Although he couldn't have stayed long enough to leave many crabs and lice behind, for he had virtually nothing to confess. Cudgel his memory as he liked in search of some peccadillo, he had obeyed God's call since childhood; it had sent him away from parents, men—don't even mention women—food, comfort, sleep, and anything else that might bring some sun into a human life. He's been calling his body "my cadaver" for the last ten years. Can a dead man sin?

Over a year ago, he ceased his barefoot peregrinations from Boulogne-sur-Mer to Naples in pursuit of every sanctuary of the Christian world, as though he were making a collection of the houses of the Virgin and Lord. He was so weak that he could only walk a few steps at a time, and it was more like crawling than walking. He had spent half his life on his knees—especially the nights—which had caused two huge, pustulent tumors to grow and spread over his kneecaps, leaking onto the slabs of the church floors. He wouldn't have been bad-looking, in fact, if he hadn't adopted that sort of counter-coquetry—striving to make himself hideous with his gauntness, fiercely prominent cheekbones, dusty reddish mat of tangled beard and hair. The brow was lofty, the eyes crystal-blue, and the body would have been well-proportioned.* But wreck he wanted to be and wreck he became, and he lived his last year among the wreckage of the ages.

"In Rome, in the district of the Amfiteatro Flavio, formerly called the Coliseum, near the Via della Croce, there are some ancient ruins and a considerable extent of half-demolished wall. Having found, in one of these ruins, a space large enough to contain him, Benoît-Joseph thought it would suffice him for a dwelling, and he had no other for several years." A century has to make do with the saints it gets; the scope and the style of their personalities reflect, and indeed caricature, the features of their era. Benoît-Joseph Labre is the saint of Roman decrepitude.

---

confessions, and hence absolutions, one had already made and received, one started all over from scratch and tried to confess every single sin committed since infancy.

*"Six palms and five thumbs" notes the "notary public" in charge of the coffining. Oh, those diabolical systems of weights and measures; that's something in the neighborhood of 1.75 meters [about 5 feet 10 inches].

Lent has just ended; this year he didn't even want to beg for the pittance he used to be given once a day at the monastery gates, "in which he preferred to seek out the peelings and most repellent morsels." He decided to stop eating altogether. "It was only on the eve of his death that, feeling his strength exhausted, he yielded to the urgings of some kind person who brought him hard-boiled eggs"—who knows, maybe he strangled on them?—"and mixed a little vinegar with his water." Note that this excellent confessor, who also acted as Labre's spiritual guide (Benoît-Joseph belonging to no congregation), never once used his authority to incite his penitent to eat decently in the name of holy obedience: "So it is to this, I thought to myself [Abbé Marconi] as I spoke to him, it is to this that his austerities have reduced him: he will shortly die a martyr to penitence. Nevertheless, despite the particular affection I felt for him, it never occurred to me to speak to him of his health, and still less to exhort him to spare himself and temper the rigors of his penitence." Of course it didn't. Saints are few and far between these days, and when you've actually landed one, it's in your interest to promote his exaltation, in every sense of the word. "I would add that I also never thought to invite the Servant of God to show less neglect for his bodily cleanliness and external appearance, or to deliver himself from the bites of his vexatious insects, a torment as humiliating as it must have been intolerable." What more could Benoît-Joseph desire? He had found a confessor who left him alone and let him wallow in the voluptuousness of his sufferings.

On Holy Wednesday, thus, the Poor Man of God dragged himself from his hole to the church of Our Lady of the Mounts, one of the ten or twelve within arm's reach in this populous district. He took his usual route, praying aloud with multitudinous signs of the cross as he went but also cursing and grumbling—the simple ruse he had hit upon long ago to prevent anyone from speaking to him; his bedrock misanthropy could endure no dialogue other than confession. But people weren't too anxious to talk to him anyway, because he was so scary. He vituperated against the age in a confused discourse laced partly with jaculatory orisons but even more with imprecations directed at everything and everybody: Rome would burn, the rich were too rich but the poor would go to hell too because they weren't poor enough. He expectorated the fire of God "against the passions and scandals of the Catholics, the temples profaned" by libertine paintings and frescoes, "the blind heretics." His religion was that of Torquemada. In his eyes nine-tenths of mankind were already damned. A few letters to his parents have been found, in which he says little about Jesus but goes to some lengths to intimidate them: "Meditate upon the fearful sufferings of hell that are endured throughout eternity for a single deadly sin, so easily committed . . . Endeavor to be among the tiny number of the elect."[2] "Above all, take heed for your salvation and the education of my brothers and sisters; watch over their conduct; think of the eternal flames of hell and [again] the tiny number of the elect."[3]

That Wednesday he heard five or six masses, as usual, left the church around one in the afternoon, and swooned on the threshold. He was carried to the nearby house of Zaccarelli, "a merchant noted for his honesty, his religion, and his special affection for Benoît-Joseph." He was laid out fully dressed on a bed and then finished off in a last-minute attempt to stuff him like a goose. By evening it was clear he was going to die. Priests and the superiors of various orders came pouring in, each trying more or less to appropriate him. If, with his dying breath, he would only claim membership of one of them, what a stroke of luck! But he was too far gone; his death was as peaceful as his life had been tormented. At "the first hour of the night, when all the bells of Rome begin to ring announcing that it is time for the faithful to recite the anthem *Salve Regina,* * the servant of the Mother of God, with no convulsions or visible agony, gently yielded up his soul to his creator, on Wednesday April 16, 1783, aged thirty-four years and twenty-one days."

And so ends his long march toward solitude and death, begun at the age of five or six in the "diocese of Boulogne-sur-Mer in the parish of Saint-Sulpice d'Amette," a nearby hamlet where Benoît-Joseph, eldest of the fifteen children born to the flourishing farmer Jean-Baptiste Labre and his wife Anna-Barbe Grandsire (both still living in 1783), was already refusing to join in the games of his brothers and playmates. The influence of his uncle, another Labre—the parish priest of Erin (also in the Boulonnais)—who taught him to read French and Latin from religious books, may have been decisive, and is undoubtedly what gave his nephew that obsession with the never perfect confession: "Benoît-Joseph often repeated this idea, which he said he had found in St. Theresa, that a vast number of Christians were plunged into hell by the crime of making bad confessions." "His submission to his uncle's least desires was already that of a monk to his superior." But the uncle-priest died before Benoît's fifteenth birthday, in the course of a strange epidemic that decimated humans and animals alike. And "in the country, livestock is a poor farmer's whole fortune. Losing his life and losing his animals are almost equal misfortunes. Benoît-Joseph realized this and divided his labors between the ailing humans and the animals belonging to them."[4] However, he had no vocation as a hospitaler, and this is one of the few recorded instances in which he exerted himself on behalf of his fellow man. He was already in pursuit of silence and retreat. Human contacts pained him, beginning with those in his own family. Two years of strife before his parents would let him enter a Trappist monastery,

*A new practice prescribed by Pius IV "to implore the succor of the Mother of God in the present need of the Church."

after the initial rigor of the order had been restored by Rancé's reform. The elders were flabbergasted—our first-born a monk? Who ever heard of such a thing? But by dint of sleeping on the ground and refusing to eat he got his way, and set off for a trial novitiate.

Neither Trappists nor Carthusians could take more than six months of him; unless it was he who couldn't bear a regular association with anyone, not even the great mutes. At the age of twenty, after a last suffocating visit to his parents whom he was never to see again, he set out on his long pilgrimage to escape from the human race. "God is calling me!" But from afar. First France, top to bottom, North Sea to Alps; then the Italy of Loreto, Assisi, and Rome; then the whole kingdom of Naples clear to Bari and back up to Loreto, and the abbey of Our Lady of the Hermits (the word haunted him) at Einsiedeln in Switzerland, and sanctuaries in Burgundy and Germany. He kept going. Glimpsed on the banks of the Rhine in 1776, he was already wearing out, and exhaustion finally overcame him in Rome, where he returned for good, to destroy himself.

Then comes the priests' dogfight to decide which church the Saint is to be buried in, with a nice jump upward in view, in the mass-and-taper market, for the stock of the chosen site. He died near Madonna dei Monti, but his rathole was on the territory of the parish of S. Salvatore. So sorry, objects the priest of San Martino ai Monti, he's under my jurisdiction. The cardinal-vicar of Rome, the next best thing to the pope, arbitrates in favor of Madonna dei Monti, where he had been seen most frequently in the last year.

"Meanwhile the people were losing patience, waiting for the convoy to set out. The crowd increased steadily; the first guard was doubled, and the soldiers accompanying the body to keep order formed a sort of funeral escort." The brief procession from the Zaccarelli house to Madonna dei Monti is pure Roman, with its mixture of tears and breast-beating, the wailing of professional mourners, and general curiosity. A large spot of moving color in the heart of Holy Week stillness. "The solemnity of Maundy Thursday is such that no interment can take place in Rome on that day. The body of the Servant of God was accordingly placed in a part of the church adjoining the sacristy . . . As the devotion of the faithful assumed increasingly extravagant proportions, the cardinal-vicar gave permission to delay inhumation for four days, and at the same time the necessary precautions were taken to prevent tumult and maintain order." A good thing too, for the mob is swelling by the hour, "all ages, all conditions and estates pressing forward and mingling together" to touch the corpse with rosaries and medals or simply "to let flow [*sic*] their lips respectfully over its hands, moisten them with their tears, touch the feet or any other part of the flesh, all of which they found soft, palpable, and flexible and in a perfect state of integrity and incorruption."

The miracles are beginning, in other words, and their numbers grow almost as fast as the crowd. There would be much to say, in this connection, concerning the good taste of miracles . . . Why, on the evening of Holy Thursday, for instance, does Benoît feel moved to produce "the universal sweat which spread over his body so abundantly that the face seemed bathed and entirely covered in it?"

Hey, you guys, are you really sure he's dead?

"Brother Bagnatti, from whom I have this, wiped the face of Benoît-Joseph, by pulling forward and applying to it the hood covering his head. The hood was quickly soaked in this sweat, which I am preciously preserving* . . . The same phenomenon occurred again on Holy Saturday and was certified by several witnesses who had laid their hands upon the flesh of the Servant of God."

Listen, listen, fellows, are you still so sure he's dead? The word "catalepsy" has been in use among the erudite since 1507, although it's true that there are few of their numbers in the crowd inside Madonna dei Monti.

Better yet: on the eve of Easter Sunday, the day set for burial, a notary and some fifty onlookers witness another trick of this capricious stiff. Just before the coffining they decide to clothe the body in the long white tunic of the Brotherhood of Our Lady of the Snows† of which he has posthumously been made a member. Five days after his demise, this should not have been an easy operation; yet the body, far from being stiff as a board, remains in all its parts "flexible, palpable, and without the smallest trace of corruption!" It is placed in an upright position. Everybody cries out: it's leaning over, it's going to fall! Don't you worry: Benoît-Joseph sticks out a hand and braces himself by gripping the back of a nearby prie-dieu. Positively helping them to get him under ground . . . But listen, are you really, truly sure etc., etc.? . . . They nail him down under three thicknesses of wood and seal his coffin with the apostolic seal. Dead or not, he's going to be buried.

At this point the Saint has already effected, on the spot or by remote control, a hundred cures for those beginning to invoke his name, cures for "cancers, fistulas, epilepsies, gangrenes, rickets, scirrhus, varicose veins, impostumes, hydropsies, apoplexies, ulcers, wasting, phthises,**scurvy, blindness, deafness, crushed and fractured bones."‡ Proceedings in his beatifica-

---

*Abbé Marconi speaking.

†Arising out of a miracle that took place in Rome one August 5th sometime in the Middle Ages, when a heavy snowfall marked the future site of the basilica of Santa Maria Maggiore.

** Scirrhus: hard, slow-growing malignant tumor; impostume: abcess; phthises: consumption or tuberculosis.

‡The list of places in Italy and France where these miracles were reported runs to sixty-nine towns, in Abbé Marconi's account (printed in November 1783) and the chain stretches from Arras to Bari.

tion trial are opened at once. From now on he is called "the Blessed Be-noît-Joseph Labre" or, more familiarly, "the Pauper of Jesus Christ."

On September 28, 1783, Abbé Marconi observes[5] that "the portraits of Benoît-Joseph Labre have become so numerous since his death that sixty thousand can now be counted." In Rome, "there is not one painter or en-graver but has worked to limn and present his natural features in paint-ings, medals, wax, plaster, or on silk. Over eighty thousand relics have al-ready been distributed."

32

MAY 1783

The Triumph of That Mountebank

Mirabeau's real life begins at almost the same age and on almost the same day as that of Benoît Labre comes to an end, but that's the only link between the two, and Mirabeau is almost a year younger than the Pauper of God—thirty-three—when he rears his ugly mug "beneath that lion's mane" and his voice rings out for the first time in a big city of France, where he's making news again.

May 23, 1783—the "Aix defense," as this period is later called. In the past he's been known only for his escapades, affairs, pamphlets, and misfor-tunes. The only true Mirabeau was his father the marquis, the "OEconomist," the "Friend of Man," failed minister and protagonist of fifteen lawsuits; but from now on Honoré will no longer be Mirabeau fils. He gouges out his fame with his fingernails, scrabbling up from the pit and not bothering about any worms he happens to crush as he climbs. His first star billing is an improvisa-tion, as counsel for his own defense. Hail Mirabeau and farewell youth! He pleads, with furor, against his wife Emilie:

"Gentlemen: when, in 1772, I blessed heaven for granting unto me the wife my heart had chosen; when, in 1773, I bathed with my tears the fruit of her tenderness whose premature death I was later condemned to bemoan, I little anticipated that in a few short years she whom love had brought to the foot of the altar would be asking the courts to dissolve our union . . ."[1]

His first words, his first ripples of eloquence, his first lies, but it's all grist for his mill. He came here to Aix six months ago to get her back, and failing that, demolish her. He knows he is facing the most decisive battle of his life, and if he had had a cauldron of boiling oil within reach . . .*

"Can you hesitate, gentlemen, to grant me the sight of my wife, to grant me provisionally the right to correspond with her? . . . These things are owed me because the magistrate must not condone an interference with the exercise of my rights; owed me because, my quality being unchallenged, my name of husband must not be a vain name."[2] Not that he had cared so much about his "name of husband" five years before when he was having a high old time with Sophie . . . But now, as in Pontarlier a few months ago, Mirabeau proves himself a champion of bad faith, leaping into the breach that justice in those days left gaping wide between nature and the law: "In our legislation, gentlemen, there can be no doubt that the woman, even separated, remains subject to her husband's authority."[3] Why, of course. And this is me, the author of the *Essai sur le despotisme,* telling you so . . .

. . . In Aix, the "capital city of Provence," which has twenty thousand inhabitants and more than five hundred wig-and-gowners, the cream of whom are on hand to hear, oppose, or judge Mirabeau in "one of the best-constructed towns in the kingdom, situated on level ground at the base of several hills, most of which produce excellent oils, wines, and fruits."[4] Eighteen leagues from Arles, seventy from Lyons, one hundred and eighty from Paris. Spring is tipping into summer, the almond and peach trees have already shed their flowers but a few chestnuts here and there are still covered in pink. To hear Mirabeau, the crowd assembles on "the Place des Prêcheurs or des Jacobins, the handsomest in town, lined with beautiful houses, all very tall and built" under Louis XIV "of cut stone. At one extremity of the square stands the Palace [of Justice] a considerable edifice and one that can lay claim to some beauty, despite its age.† The courtroom is decorated with portraits of all the kings of France, placed high up in square compartments. Those of the last three kings [Louis XIII, Louis XIV, Louis XV] stand out from the rest; they are depicted on horseback, and life-size." A good setting for the maiden performance of one of History's great actors. And he's got a great audience, too, packed in like sardines. All the nobility of Provence is there, so much at home, so closed-in, although possessing less power than that of some other regions

---

*The background to and viccissitudes of the trial at Aix can be understood by reference to earlier volumes, which cover the couple's initial separation at Manosque, Mirabeau's incarceration in the Château d'If and Fort du Joux, the abduction of Sophie de Monnier and their arrest in Holland, Emilie's life at Le Tholonet, his ordeal in the tower of Vincennes, and the death of their son.

†The Palace of Justice in Aix was built under François I, and many of its doors and chair backs bear his emblem, the salamander.

over "a province that is positively emerging from infancy"—according to François de La Rochefoucauld, who has just visited it—"the very structure of its administration and Estates impedes its progress."[5] Here, the high clergymen are still top dogs: Archbishop Boisgelin administers the territory. A large third estate composed chiefly of magistrates has been coming up in the last two generations, however, and today fills half the courtroom. There are even a few representatives of the lower orders, tradespeople and servants, who have managed to force their way in. Mirabeau's been creating such a stir in town that the people are all excited, and have instinctively sided with the poor Monsieur who is trying to get back his wife . . . from the Marignanes, one of the loftiest and snootiest families in the region.

"Despite a triple guard, gates, fences, and windows had all been smashed by the muddled throng."[6] "People climbed onto the roof just to see him, even if they couldn't hear him," writes Mirabeau's father, who knows only by hearsay but is well informed, "and pity 'tis that all were not able to hear, for he spoke, shouted, and roared so that the lion's mane was white with foam and dripping sweat. Only picture the triumph of that mountebank."[7] As at the other public hearings in the trial (there are seven in all), the colors of gowns, rolled wigs, and cassocks mix together like a lark pasty: "The presidents sat at the same bench as the councilors, without heed for protocol, because of the great number of people."[8]

The son of one of those councilors to the parlement of Aix, Eugène d'Arnauld de Vitrolles, is only nine years old,* but his first great memory stays with him for the rest of his life: "On the day Mirabeau pronounced his famous speech my father wanted me to attend the hearing and had me seated on the *huissiers'* bench.† I was just beneath the tempestuous orator, so that I could not turn my head to look at him without being drenched by the shower accompanying his words. Heavens above, what a baptism that was! I can still see his impassioned features, his face so expressively ugly and pitted from the pox, his lion's head, his bull's neck and torso, his extraordinary coiffure, his bold expression."[9]

A born orator? No, manufactured, but instinctively, with the aid of a good pair of lungs and a thorax; he hurls his words in his audience's faces, to seduce them, to "get" them, to make up for his ugliness. "His voice is full, masculine,

---

*The Baron de Vitrolles (1774–1854) plays an important part in history when he rushes to the tsar's headquarters at the beginning of his invasion of France in 1814 and informs him that the road to Paris, unguarded by Napoleon, is open to the Russians. An ultra-Royalist, he also acts as go-between for Fouché and the Bourbons, thus facilitating the second Restoration in 1815, after Waterloo. For these services, his kings reward him with total ingratitude. He leaves some well-written and interesting *Mémoires.*

†[A minor magistrate who serves notices, supervises foreclosures, and so on—not the modern-day *usher. —Trans.*]

resonant; it fills and flatters the ear. Always sustained but flexible, it can be
heard equally well when lowered or raised. He can span every note,* and
articulated his endings so carefully that one never lost the final words."[10] Not
a trace of garlic in his accent, of course—Mirabeau spent only two or three
years in Provence—although expert ears sometimes thought they detected a
hint of "Gâtinais drag" in some of his endings,[11] but one always tends to
attribute to a speaker the accent of his native place. In fact, his language is the
pure French of the middle Loire. He starts out slowly, quietly, without excessive glibness or refinement; he needs to warm up. He is even said to stammer
a bit in the opening minutes. He doesn't waste his effects. In this particular
speech he pauses after each of the charges to be refuted, and there are no fewer
than eight instructions to "Breathe and reply" in his script.

A script that's forty-six pages long and requires almost five hours to read,
with a calculated build-up culminating in the final dénouement. Emilie isn't
there, she attends none of the hearings, but her ears must have been burning
sometime around noon (the hearing began at eight in the morning) when he
came to the accusation which in his eyes was most unjust of all, that of having
slandered his wife:

> For years on end I have been enduring outrages of every description; for years
> on end I have been drinking to the dregs the bottomless cup of misfortune for
> the very reason that I wish to speak no evil of her; and I am said to have slandered
> her? . . . No. I have not slandered her; I should not have been capable of
> slandering her. It is time to show that if I have deigned to abase myself to make
> humiliating apologies, it was not my conduct toward Mme de Mirabeau that drove
> me to do so.
>
> I shall read you, Gentlemen, a letter written by Mme de Mirabeau, which
> I shall hand to the King's representatives in one moment. I had forgiven and
> would continue to forgive, but today forgiveness would be cowardice . . . Here
> is the letter![12]

And with that he slowly extracts a small folded sheet from among his
papers. You could hear a fly buzz.

And yet this isn't their first exhibition; they've been flinging their private
correspondence at each other for three months, with such gay abandon one
wonders if the only reason why the Marignanes and Mirabeaus ever wrote at
all, in their period of love or friendship, was to prepare their evidence for the
day of reckoning. But before that began, there were four months of almost
equally sordid negotiations.

After leaving Switzerland, Honoré turned up at Mirabeau on October 20,

*This probably means "every emotional key"; Mirabeau was a good musician, though, and
had a beautiful singing voice.

1782. He was happy to renew acquaintance with the cradle of his title, although not of his family, where he had never spent more than a few days
before—in 1770, on his way back from the Corsica campaign, presumably at
the time of his incestuous relationship with his sister Louise; and then in 1772
and 1773, long enough for the public abduction of Emilie de Marignane
(Mirabeau is only five leagues from Aix) into a mournful compulsory marriage, a few months of "happy newlyweds" play acting, the conception of their
son, poor little Victor . . . and the contracting of so many debts that he took
flight from a pack of baying creditors in April 1774 and "retired" to Manosque
with the aid of his first *lettre de cachet.* Since that time: nine years of eternity.

He was wondering how he would be received. The lord, or at least
administrator of the place, was the bailli de Mirabeau, his father's younger
brother, who stuck up for Honoré in early days but has been down on him
since the affair with Sophie. So he put on a fairly modest air as his carriage
turned into that bit of Provence, so harsh, more like a mountain landscape than
the Mediterranean, which his marquis-father had always loathed because of
"the burning sky, immoderate climate, and savage aspect; arid walks, rocks,
birds of prey, devouring streams, torrents now empty now overflowing."[13]
Mirabeau fils, on the other hand, felt a kinship between the land's hidden
violence and his own. He liked the far-off view of the big square eagle's-nest
whose six round towers stood guard over a huddle of shanties. Far off, the
purple line of the Luberon mountains—cousin Sade's country. At the foot, a
circle of tawny rocks cut by the hesitant bed of the Durance. The local people
looked just like them. The self-styled Friend of Man found them "unchangea-
ble, strong, hard, and anxious" and had been very cross with his son for
defending them in 1772, when they had offered a show of resistance to him
over the felling of some timber—the only thing that belonged to them. In fact,
that was the date of the first serious dispute between father and son:

"You are earning a reputation as a moderate with your very first appearance in the province," the old grouch had written, "and that is extremely
bizarre."

"The word was rather strong," replied Mirabeau in his great self-defense
penned in prison in Vincennes. "I saw that I should always be found wrong
because I was not loved."[14] But do the locals remember this former complicity
between them and him? He's always had a knack for talking to "the people,"
though he considers himself at least as much their superior as did his forefathers. Cunning? Instinctive impulse? He went out to them with open hands,
as he did to women.

Yes. They remember. There was a little return-of-the-Prodigal air about
his arrival as his carriage climbed up the roadway he had had cut into the rock
face on purpose to accommodate the oversize coach purchased on his wedding
day. "The roadside was sprinkled with fusiliers and speechifiers, and bonfires

were blazing on all sides . . . The pleasure of the country people when they saw me again was quite unfeigned; and indeed I had done them no real harm."[15] The bailli, who wasn't particularly thrilled to have his misanthropic routine upset by the advent of the "count of squalls,"* nonetheless joined in the festivities and loyally reported: "One thing that surprised me was the joy of the people here upon seeing him come, though he is indebted to more than one of them . . . They are indeed very fond of him, and I was touched by their heartfelt expressions." When his nephew first turned up, thus, the stout colossus with the intimidating, icy demeanor, gloomy face, and white hair did not snub him. "I greeted him without too much warmth, nor yet too much standoffishness, to tell the truth . . . He was, I do believe, a little afraid: I reassured him by my welcome, neither cold nor overcordial."[16] And he sticks firmly to his respectable neutrality: "I shall have no hand, near or far, in his repatriation of his wife . . . I shall give him no advice as to how he should recover her" even if, like almost everybody associated with Mirabeau from now on, he confesses to being quickly won over by the sudden emergence of maturity in him. What's happened to the *enfant terrible?* "I begin to think that others have led you to judge him rather worse than he is, and I am very pleased with him,"[17] says bailli to marquis—although he still won't take sides in the battle, which Mirabeau stages pretty much alone, and for an audience of elite, however hard the impotent plebs may be clapping in the top balconies. What he needs is the support of "decent people" to put pressure on the Marignane family, but what happens is that the high society of Aix pretends he doesn't exist.† "Everyone tried to avoid me. I was Anti-Christ."[18]

*Appellation inflicted upon his son by the marquis when Honoré was 20. The bailli was a sort of Alceste [protagonist in Molière's *Misanthrope—Trans.*] who fled women, unlike the other men in his family, and, after trying to become minister of the navy, gave up ambition, too. He had served on the Malta galleys and, when not at Mirabeau, spent his time in a "commandery" in the Rouergue.

†He does find one attorney and a councilor who get the archbishop, Mgr. de Boisgelin, to make a vague attempt to effect a reconciliation, but without conviction. "The archbishop pissed pure water" (from bailli to marquis on February 4, 1783).

33

You Can't Win a Wife with a Constable

What he mostly was was a killjoy for the frivolous, sparkling society of Le Tholonet and Marignane, which had clasped Emilie to its bosom and expelled him from it as an unassimilable graft. What was he really after? Did he actually believe they could ever live together again? Yet he swears that, to him, "legal rape is almost as loathsome as illegal rape." "I must feel, for I have said so so often and loudly, that human freedom is inalienable." Apparently, then, when he first returned to Provence, his idea was less to fight a lawsuit than to reconquer his wife; and maybe in theory the idea wasn't such a bad one. For once, his father agreed with him: "It's only a matter of winning over one chambermaid . . ." If Honoré could just get her alone, he knows how malleable, how suggestible she is at bottom . . . All his charm and virility could have been brought into play, and after all he was her husband before God and man, and she would find him steadier than before. His first move, thus, was to try for that tête-a-tête, which could change everything. Alone, she might not have said no; but she was cloistered, sequestered by her father, her friends, and even more by her lover, the Comte de Galliffet. One by one, the doors were slammed in Mirabeau's face, and Emilie wrote to him, "You yourself must feel that the events which have taken place will always form an insurmountable barrier between us." Then she sent back, unopened, a fifteen-page letter in which he sought, with heavy vibrato, to move her heart and senses by using the familiar form of address as of old.

But plead he must, so plead he will, one man against the whole world, as at Pontarlier. There, in Franche-Comté, it was for the right to live; in Aix it'll be for honor, and even more for cash.

This time, however, the barrage he has to face has been erected not by a little frontier town but by one of the most important municipalities of France, whose nobility is bound by a thousand ties to that of the entire kingdom. "I have come to contend with the most highly accredited family in Aix, that which is held to have the most agreeable society, the most powerful friends, the best cook." For a start, he couldn't even find a lawyer, the Marignanes having mobilized every worthwhile attorney in town: twenty-three of them! They troop into the courtroom like a battalion, led by two nationally known tenors: rough, tough Pascalis and crafty Portalis. Faced with opponents of this caliber, Mirabeau decides, although that wasn't his original intention, to conduct his defense himself, with the assistance of young Jaubert, who was still a student. As a result, his voice first resounds through France almost by accident, but already—perhaps this is less of an accident—in opposition to a coalition of the aristocracy.

On April 1 "the dance has begun," as the bailli informs the marquis, whose hatred and contempt for his son are thereby intensified, if such a thing were possible. Their name dragged through the mud yet again, and what an again! But wasn't it he who had driven Honoré to such desperate straits by evicting him from Le Bignon without a penny, as though he were some sixteen-year-old kid? As for Emilie, *the* Law may not be on her side, but human law certainly is. "You can't win a wife with a constable," sighs the marquis, and he knows whereof he speaks. Emilie had taken too much from Honoré: the tantrums he threw when they were together and his crazy stunts when they weren't, the affair with Sophie that he carried on before the eyes of all Europe, the child he had by her, their own son who was dead. And besides, she's perfectly comfortable with young Galliffet, "in his court of cockcrows and tail-preeners [in French: *dans sa cour de petits-maîtres et de haut-la-queue: cour:* court / barnyard; *petits maîtres:* little masters, roosters; *haut-la-queue:* the lift of tail feathers of a displaying fowl / an erection . . . the French is decidedly crude —*Trans.*]."[1] Therein lies the quid pro quo of the Aix hearings: she's right in being wrong; he's wrong in trying too late to be right.

"Dance?" A cruel six-act ballet, you mean.

Act I: an exchange of paper salvos. Mirabeau demands that the countess come back to live with him, in return for which she demands an official separation.

Act II: March 20. Mirabeau had already made one speech to the lieutenant of the seneschal court and two assessors, pleading with moderation and an affected and rather lachrymose tenderness, which made a great impression upon a courtroom so tightly packed that people were fainting in their seats. In reply to the accusation that he was a bad husband, he read out excerpts from Emilie's passionate letters to him ten years before. Here are his closing lines —a later age would not have swallowed such bathos, but in those days it "went over" fine, and is said to have brought tears to the eyes of the Marquis de Marignane himself: "O you, you who love me still and have never left my heart! . . . Do not fear my victory, it is necessary to your happiness, for otherwise I should not want it." He even dragged in their dead son: "That poor unfortunate Victor, were he alive today, would be pleading for me to his mother." The judges ordered Emilie to accept her husband's visits pending their decision on the substance of the case; but the Marignanes instantly appealed to the parlement, which stayed the judgment, and the couple were not to see each other again.

Act III: May 7, counterattack. Attorney Portalis let loose with a diatribe in which he called Mirabeau a drunkard, debauchee, spendthrift, thief, and even murderer. In support of these insults, he invoked seemingly irrefutable proof, which caused an enormous sensation at the time: a series of letters from the "Friend of Man" to Emilie and her parents, denigrating his son with his own peculiar brand of cruelty, which we know to be inimitable indeed. The father was being used to destroy the son; even the bailli found this a bit much. He wrote to the marquis the next day: "The demon of scribomania must have had a terrible grip on you, to make you write in such a style!" But it's too late now, that hearing deals Honoré a deadly blow. Until then, only "informed circles" were aware of his father's perpetual griping; now it was public knowledge. This move also made it clear that Emilie had burned her bridges; Honoré himself was revolted by it. Even if she had wanted him, he couldn't have stood her. It is at this point that his goal shifts: revenge becomes his sole purpose in continuing the fight. He forgets, of course, that he was the first to introduce their private correspondence into the proceedings.

Which brings us back where we started, to the great speech of May 23 and the crowd hanging on his every word. Act IV.

If it's letters you want . . . He calmly unfolds it and reads it out, it's short but it's enough to destroy Emilie's reputation and quell the Marignanes, at least temporarily. "At last I have recovered my senses, Monsieur, and the first effect of my return to virtue is to notify you that all commerce between us is now at an end, etc." The letter he dictated to her at Manosque in the throes of a towering rage, on May 28, 1774,* to be addressed to "Monsieur le Chevalier de Gassaud" after Honoré, who had already played his wife false several times without the least compunction, learned of the poor young woman's infidelity with her cousin in the Gray Musketeers. She wrote it but he never sent it; he folded it up, put it carefully away, and somehow failed to lose it in the ensuing turmoil. Who says he's nothing but impulse? This looks more like a rare gift for calculation. His vengeance has been cooling nine long years, almost to the day. At the top and bottom of the "confession" he extorted from Emilie he had inscribed in his heavy hand "Mirabeau fils *ne varietur*";[2] and it's true that one part of him—the worst—has not altered.

He was sure of his effect, and he gets it. But it costs him plenty, for now

---

*I was mistaken in volume I when I said that Gassaud received the letter and then returned it; in fact, it never reached him.

he has fallen into the trap set by his adversaries, who've been trying to drive him over the edge for the last three months. In the eyes of the public, no doubt, he has cleared himself to some extent by proving that she "deceived" him too and even that, as far as the evidence is concerned, she did it "first." But in the name of what can he now keep up the fiction of the idyllically happy couple who have been parted by a whim of fate and whom he is longing to reunite? How could a judge find it right or even rational to force two people together who have nothing but resentment in common? Whereupon Mirabeau, in a sort of suicide dive, turns to Portalis—most famous of the Aix lawyers, the one who wrote the brief quoting all his father's insults—and hacks him down with a poleax. There are times when he can't keep his life from pouring out:

"If a lawyer, for his only eloquence, can do no more than vomit injurious declamations, lies, exaggerations, and calumny; if his only ability is to invent or distort the facts, truncate or falsify the evidence he cites . . ., then such a man degrades himself from the freest of conditions into the most servile slavery to passion . . . He is a purveyor of falsehoods, empty words, and insults."[3]

"During this implacable slaughter, Portalis was shedding tears of pain and fury, gnawing at his pencil."[4] But Jean-Etienne-Marie Portalis,* with his thin lips and balding head, his dry gaze beneath prematurely gray hair—the unmoved stare of an applier and even now a maker of laws—is not the kind of man to faint on the witness stand. He's seen plenty and will see plenty more. He was an acquaintance of Necker's and a close friend of the Archbishop of Aix.[5] He already stands out as one of the moderate but enlightened leaders of Provence, light years away from a fulminator like Cazalis, who was the prototype of the cantankerous conservative. Even so, it was no fun for him to sit there and be called a lot of dirty names in front of his home team! He was also squirming because he was known to have been on friendly terms with the Marignanes for years. But he brazens it out on his bench and most certainly does not swoon and have to be carried unconscious from the courtroom, as Mirabeau's partisans later claim, following the bailli's lead and creating a legend that has been perpetuated for two centuries by most of his historians.[6] On the contrary, Portalis demands that "this injurious statement" and the letter "imputed to the party he is defending" be instantly deposited with the registrar. The haste with which the judges comply with his request is clear proof that in their eyes Mirabeau has lost the game, however much he may have won the crowd—especially as, treating his defeat as a foregone con-

*Born at Le Beausset near Toulon in 1746, he occupies a considerable position in the magistrature and administration of Toulon but is far more important in the Consulate when he becomes one of Bonaparte's most influential advisers during the drafting of the "Napoleonic Code"; he dies, a high dignitary of the Empire and laden with honors, in 1807.

clusion, he had dealt the magistrates themselves a few punches in passing.

He was playing "loser wins" again, in a drama that reaches its climax here, although we still have two more acts to suffer through, tying up loose ends.

Act V: Mirabeau's last public statement, on June 17. At this point, when each side could be supposed to have won one game, the crowd is if possible even larger than before. They're hoping for a new sensation, but it doesn't come: the Marignanes, frightened of further scandal, have hinted at a vague possibility of some sort of settlement, if only to keep Honoré from another public eruption. Also, there are two spectators of note in the front row, in whose presence nobody would dare to misbehave: Archduke Ferdinand of Austria (the Governor of Milan) and his wife. He's another of Marie Antoinette's brothers and looks very like her; he has been traveling in France and makes a special detour to catch the star attraction of the year, but all he sees is a magnanimous Mirabeau, claws fully sheathed, reverting to his romantic and sentimental vein. It wasn't worth the price of admission: Mirabeau reaches the heights when he's angry or engaging in political analysis, not when he runs on about "Emilie, my passion for you was too real not to have penetrated your soul. You burn for me and you hate me, you are tearing me asunder . . ." Final, futile stratagem: he has bribed a clerk into letting him see the text of the indictment that, as soon as he finished, the prosecutor, Maurel de Calissanne, was to read out . . . Mirabeau treats himself to a point-by-point refutation of it before the poor magistrate can open his mouth. *This* is the man who actually does faint, more or less—maybe "diplomatically," in order to have the final ruling deferred until July 5,* thus giving Portalis and the Marignanes more freedom to maneuver. Now that they no longer have to fear the prospect of another public drubbing, they drop all pretense of negotiating and lodge a fresh complaint on Emilie's behalf—for defamation this time, for reading out her confession of adultery in public. Mirabeau came on in Act V as long-suffering victim; he exits as thoroughgoing blackguard.

The game's up. Act VI: on July 5 nine judges, all friends of the Marig-nanes, "dismiss and reject" Mirabeau's demands, order him to pay costs, and grant "the chief part of the request of Marguerite Emilie de Covet de Marig-nane de Mirabeau"—that is, separation of body and property, but, unlike the miserable Sophie, with no obligation to live in any specified place. She is free to do as she pleases—except, of course, to remarry.† As for him . . . "This

---

*It was this incident, simulated or not, which served as a basis for the tale of Portalis's fainting on May 23, but which actually involved the prosecuting attorney and occurred on June 17.

†Which she does on June 9, 1792, one year after Honoré's death, in Nice (hence as an émigrée); her second husband is a Comte de La Rocca, by whom she had a child a month earlier. She dies young (at forty-eight), on March 6, 1800, in the Mirabeau residence in Paris, half of which came to her (the other half went to the du Saillants) by inheritance.

ruling parts me [from his wife] only to proclaim my civil death . . . My defenses have been suppressed, my pleading of May 23 overruled. What must my country think of my justification? What must France, nay, the whole of Europe think, when the name I bear, hitherto honored with a renown that will be the ruin of me, shall no longer be heard except in association with a defamatory decree? Had I been guilty, I should have been separated; but my claim was justified and I have been separated even so, and my defenses proscribed. Let my defense be vain, and punished as a crime; but what must be thought of the humble imputations to which I have succumbed! *Bad son, bad husband, bad father, bad citizen, dangerous subject.* It is for these that I have been judged."[7]

He's like an India-rubber-man, forever bouncing off the walls of his epoch. Here he is an outcast from society again, with no money and no position, rejected by his father, politely evicted by his uncle. On the off chance, he goes back up to Paris to see if he can at least prevail upon the Garde des Sceaux to tear up that *lettre de cachet.* He is grimly resolved to do anything—in other words, write for anybody. This case has intensified the obsession by which he was first visited in Vincennes: he must sell himself, sell himself, and sell himself some more. There's nothing else for him to do. He does it.

Although not before reaping the same bitter fruits as Beaumarchais nine years before, after his "censure" in the Goëzman trial. Among the marginals of the eighteenth century a pair condemned is a pair acclaimed. Mirabeau keeps his head high too, none of your slinking away like an Adam banned from the Eden of the magistrates. He picks up his gilded walking stick, dons his finest attire, and takes a stroll down one of the main thoroughfares of Provence where there's little chance that the crowd will fail to notice him, the man anyone could recognize blindfold at two hundred yards on a pitch black night. Mid-June. There he goes, followed by his faithful Legrain and a few friends, along the Cours, which is already famous in Aix,* "the regular promenade of the town, two hundred and twenty canes long. (*The* canne *is a local measure composed of eight* pans, *and the* pan *measures nine* pouces *or thereabouts; the* canne, *therefore, is approximately equivalent to the* toise.†) The Cours is planted with four rows of trees, forming three passages. Two of these are for people on foot. Carriages and other vehicles use the central one . . . In the center of the Cours stand several fountains with basins, one of which pours out a steady stream of warm mineral water. The others are always full of water as well. All the fountains have different shapes and vary in their particular decorations. The Cours is the general meeting place for the town's society: there are good-looking women

*And is known today, of course, as the Cours Mirabeau.
†The *toise* (fathom) equals about two meters (about 6.5 feet). Word of advice to budding historians: choose your subjects in periods subsequent to the creation of the metric system.

to be seen there, but as far as their features are concerned the saying in Provence is, *Men of Aix, Women of Marseilles.*"[8]

Here, Mirabeau wins his first public triumph. What's the racket, what's all the pushing and shoving? People emerge from their shops and come running to look at the Monsieur who has just been condemned by the Messieurs, as though he were the Messiah. They hiss and boo the Comte de Galliffet, they throw stones at prosecuting attorney de Calissanne, "while their applauding hands followed, with redoubled energy, the man known as the *illustrious unfortunate.*"[9] "He created factions in the towns and countryside. Aristocracy, magistracy, and bourgeoisie were split. Without exception, the lower orders were on the side of the Comte de Mirabeau. When he walked out followed by a sedan chair, the urchins and porters ran after him clapping their hands.* 'That is not surprising,' said his uncle the bailli; 'there has always been an attraction between my nephew and the rabble.'"[10]

It doesn't turn his head, though; he knows what their bravos are worth and how long they last, and he regards them as a sort of investment. Who knows, he may be back in these parts one day. He writes to an English friend, Hugh Elliott, "I have become the demagogue of Provence† . . . I have deserved neither the severity nor the indulgence with which I have been treated, and you may be assured that such cheerless success as this will not increase my conceit, especially as no insurrection can ever amount to anything in France."[11]

ROBESPIERRE

34

JUNE 1783

Someone Named Robespierre

In that same year of (prerevolutionary) grace 1783, at opposite ends of France but both times in a courtroom, Mirabeau becomes famous and Robespierre is first heard of. For the former, the Aix hearings were preceded, like the eruption of a volcano, by a long underground rumble of scandal and whispering among the aristocracy, and it was as a nobleman, albeit a persecuted one,

*This is from a letter by Portalis!

†He uses the term in its original meaning, of "one who is beloved of the people, or champions their cause."

that Mirabeau first rose above the crater in a fetid cloud. Robespierre, on the other hand, was totally unknown except to a few burghers of Arras when he made the "lightning rod" speech that brought his name to the attention of the general public—in "advanced" scientific circles, that is. How could anybody have heard of him before: he's only twenty-four. Hardly hatched.*

But the shell's broken now. At the end of June 1783 a doctor named Ansart writes to his friend Langlet, who's studying law in Paris: "Nothing new in our town [Arras] except that someone named Robespierre, newly arrived from your parts, has just made his début here in a famous case in which he spoke at three hearings in such a manner as to discourage anyone aspiring to follow the same career hereafter. They say that by his delivery, his choice of expressions, and the clarity of his speech he leaves all the Liborels, Desmazières [and so on: there follows a list of the most noted lawyers of Arras] far in the rear. You† are reckoned to be the only pretender with any chance of dimming this flood of light."[1]

For the moment, he's living with his sister Charlotte on one floor of the du Ruts' house on the Rue des Teinturiers; in other words, in the home of his Aunt Henriette, one of his father's two sisters who married late, after their brother's death—in her case, to Gabriel-François du Rut, a physician. "For the moment" is certainly the right expression: the only noteworthy feature of Robespierre's early years as a lawyer is his inability to stay put. When he first came back from Paris with a crackling new lawyer's diploma under his arm and all his years of school and youth rolled up inside it (because he'd never had what you could call a real "youth"), he had a vague falling-out with the du Ruts over an inheritance and tried to set up housekeeping with Charlotte on the Rue du Saumon. But that way he was headed for ruin, because his only wealth in the world was rolled up in another parchment, issued by the "office of administration of Louis-le-Grand collège":**

"Having regard to the Principal's account of the high ability of the Sieur de Robespierres [sic] scholar of the Collège of Arras now about to complete his course of study, and to his good conduct during the last twelve years and

*He was baptized Maximilien-Marie-Isidore on May 6, 1758, and was lucky enough to escape the usual custom and to be called by the first of his given names; one somehow doesn't imagine an Isidore de Robespierre blazing such a bright trail through history.

†In 1787 Langlet does in fact become not only a noteworthy member of the Arras Bar but also one of Robespierre's political friends.

**Where he rubbed remote elbows with another boarder three classes below him, the young Camille Desmoulins, from Guise. The two were not friends at school. There were about fifty boarders and four hundred day pupils at Louis-le-Grand, which gave it an essentially Parisian personality.

the excellent results he has obtained both in the University prize awards and in his examinations in philosophy and law, the office has unanimously agreed to grant the said Sieur de Robespierres a gratification of six hundred livres,* which will be paid to him by the head paymaster of the Collège d'Arras and the said sum shall be allocated to the account of the said paymaster upon return of this minute together with the receipt of the said Sieur de Robespierres."[2]

Add to that a few crumbs inherited from his Carraut grandparents (the brewers) and his youngest sister Henriette, who died, poor thing, of *"langueur"* in 1780 . . . In all, not enough to hold out for a year, or until his law practice might begin to produce some income, and everybody knows that a novice lawyer has to possess himself in patience. He therefore made up his quarrel with the du Ruts and probably paid them only a token rent. But he leaves them as soon as he can, accompanied by Charlotte, and moves into a house on the Rue du Collège (at the end of 1783), to end up in 1787 in the pretty building on the Rue des Ratsporteurs. Wherever he lives, however, his young-old bachelor's existence is the same, regular as clockwork.

Charlotte is its witness, almost its servant.† She too might seem like an old maid at twenty-three (in 1783) and has been prepared for a life of sacrifice and submissiveness by her term in the charitable Collège des Manarres, in Tournai; because who would ever marry the dowerless daughter of a runaway lawyer who's been up to God knows what? She "was maintained and fed for nine years; when she left, she was given clothing befitting her state. Two mistresses were attached to the boarding-school: one was responsible mainly for internal economy," or as we might say today, domestic science and the balancing of a modest budget, which is all Maximilien requires. "The other" mistress "taught the pupils the principles of religion and instructed them in writing, sewing, and lacemaking. The product of the incumbents' [*sic*] handiwork formed a substantial share of the income of the establishment."[3]

Charlotte, thus, had had even less of a childhood than her brother in order that he might, upon his return from Louis-le-Grand, find a sort of lay sister trained to bow to him in every circumstance and relieve him of "material cares," just as she would have done (should one write "with a little luck") for a husband. The divining rod dips above buried pools of vinegar.

Come to think of it, wasn't there a younger brother? Augustin-Bon-Joseph, born in 1763, so quiet, docile, and mild that he was nicknamed Bonbon in his infancy. He has now left Arras, doing a switch with his older brother who was able, on the strength of an academic career of unimpeachable steadiness al-

---

*About 4,000 modern francs [$800].

†Her *Mémoires,* written by Laponneraye under the Restoration, cannot of course be taken at face value; but they contain, especially in the early parts, unquestionably accurate particulars of the brother's and sister's everyday lives in Arras.

though lacking in brio, to give his junior this tiny boost. In 1780, shortly
before leaving Louis-le-Grand, Maximilien had written to the Most Reverend
Father Abbot of Saint-Vaast requesting that one of the scholarships held by the
all-powerful Benedictines, the real masters of Arras, in the Paris school which
had absorbed that of their own order (a little lower in the Latin Quarter) be
transferred to his brother. The Father Abbot had graciously deigned to comply: another lad like Maximilien, obedience-conditioned from birth, would be
a welcome ally in his struggle to inject some meeker raw material into the third
estate of Arras, which could be so rambunctious on occasion. Augustin accordingly left the school in Douai for Paris just as Maximilien was coming home
again.

By the way: we are not to imagine this Father Abbot officiating at the back
of the choir with the magnificent carved stalls in the Abbey of Saint-Vaast. He's
hardly ever set foot in the place. This is a "commendatory abbot," a fictitious
superior appointed by the King to one of the ecclesiastical "livings." It is he,
wherever he may be, who receives the annual stipend actually earned by the
monks, their servants, and the abbey's farmers. "The annual income of the
Abbey of Saint-Vaast amounts to about one hundred and forty thousand livres,
fifty thousand of which are for the abbot . . . The monks, fifty in all, are
governed by a prior who has six thousand livres of income for his own use.
Then there is another monk, the provost"—or chief of household police on
the monastery grounds—"and he receives five thousand livres. The collector
has three thousand livres, the annuitant two thousand* and so on for the other
officers"—that is, those occupying a specific office—"of the House."[4]

Perhaps less by the way is the identity of this "commendatory abbot of
Saint-Vaast" who rakes in fifty thousand livres of gracious royal pleasure
gleaned from the sweat of the Artesians' brows: he is the cardinal-prince Louis
de Rohan, Archbishop of Strasbourg, holder of similar positions in six other
and equally lucrative abbeys in France, not to mention the sumptuous income
he derives from his own diocese and his share of the family property. He's a
partisan of the easy life, and even though Marie Antoinette can't stand him and
Louis XVI looks down at him, the Rohan-Guéménées could still get everything they wanted at this point in their history, thanks to that darling princess
in such high favor at Court.

Which is why, through the beneficence of Cardinal de Rohan, Augustin
de Robespierre follows his brother's footsteps into Louis-le-Grand Collège.

On days when he has a case in court Maximilien gets up an hour earlier than
usual—at six instead of seven—and sets straight to work, in his dressing gown,

---

*Translated into modern francs: total income of the abbey: 850,000 F [$170,000]; for the
"commendatory abbot," 300,000 F [$60,000]; the prior, 36,000 [$7,500]; the provost, 30,000
[$6,000]; the collector, 18,000 [$3,600]; the annuitant, 12,000 [$2,400]; the last two were
responsible for collecting the signorial tithes owing to the monks.

on the neatly docketed briefs in his study, where he remains until eight or nine. Then, every morning of the week, the local barber comes in to shave him and arrange and powder the plump curls of his light brown hair. This, along with his rather high-quality clothes, is his only item of "luxury" expenditure. He acquired one habit in his Louis-le-Grand days that his life in the law courts is turning into a conditioned reflex, and it is one he will never lose: that of making an appearance.

Next, he ingests "a meal of dairy products" and goes back to work until ten, when he dresses and repairs to the courtroom on foot. His hearing over, he punctually returns to "dine" with Charlotte upon the meal she has prepared for them. They pool their money and share their table, for Charlotte has invested her pittance of an inheritance in their household. "He ate little and drank nothing but [wine-] reddened water. He expressed no preference for any particular food. Many times I asked him what he wanted to eat for his dinner, and he replied that he had no idea. He was fond of fruit and the only thing he could not forgo was a cup of coffee."⁵ After this one substantial meal of the day—consumed, as was the custom among almost all bourgeois of that time, around four in the afternoon—he leaves the house, whatever the weather, for the hour-long health-walk made fashionable by Rousseau. Sometimes he calls on friends in the course of it. Then he comes home and works at his briefs again until about eight in the evening. Then what? A touch of family gathering with his aunts, who often come to see Charlotte, or some conversation with the small group of friends that these two likeable and modest young people have rapidly made in the proper quarters of the old society. "When we played cards or talked of insignificant things, he would withdraw to a corner of the room, lean back in an armchair and muse, as though there were no other person present. He was naturally cheerful, however, and could sometimes joke and laugh till he wept."

Is he still a virgin? It seems likely; because he's shy, or reserved, or because he wants to show that he has none of the extravagance that led his father so far astray. He's perfectly willing to "flirt,"* however, and chatter away about the birds and flowers to the pretty girls in his society. He neither runs after nor from them. When he wants to shine in their eyes, with the most honorable of intentions, he presents them with copies of his creations—his speeches—as a pastry cook might send the object of his affection a cake. Last year, for instance, he sent a letter to a Mademoiselle Dehay (a friend of Charlotte's)† about the canaries she had given them, in which, after alluding

---

*[A curious case of language borrowing: *conter fleurette* (literally, prattling about the flowers) became *fleureter,* before going to England to become *flirt,* in which form it has recently returned to France, where girls now call "mon flirt" what English-speakers would call "my boyfriend."— *Trans.*]

†On June 22, 1782: this bit of badinage, known as "the canary letter," has given rise to pages of fruitless exigesis on the part of many of Robespierre's biographers. It is, however, the earliest

inter alia to "the doves reared by the Graces to pull Venus's chariot," he announces, in a postscript, the dispatch of three copies of the *Mémoire* [written submissions] in the Beugny case, which he has just had printed (together with six other lawyers). The case concerned a Protestant (converted at the age of sixty-four) who had disinherited his nephews and nieces "out of hatred for the Catholic religion." No joking matter in Arras, and Robespierre and his colleagues had no difficulty in breaking the will of a man guilty of the compounded crimes of being dead and a heretic.[6] When he crosses the center of Arras on his way to court, pacing through the two marketplaces—one big and one small, all askew yet somehow fitted one inside the other, with their Spanish-looking houses whose roofs cut back as they rise like steps marching heavenward—his route takes him past the chapel of the Sainte-Chandelle in the *petite place* (similar to the Samaritaine at the end of the Pont Neuf in Paris). Here, since the year 1105, an enormous taper has stood embedded in its stone shrine; it "is lighted once each year and is said never to grow any shorter."[7] The Holy Virgin had given it to Bishop Lambert and two "instrument-players" that year, the day she landed on the cathedral spire to halt "an epidemic of ardent fire." That's still the predominant level of spiritual sophistication in Arras, and although Maximilien, after learning about free religion in Rousseau, stopped going to mass any oftener than he had to at Louis-le-Grand, he fell smoothly back into step when he returned to his home town. The twenty-six cases he has argued in the last two years, before the "Higher Provincial Council of Artois," have been entangled wranglings over property in which he pled the cause of whoever was paying him, plaintiff or defendant. The career of a small-time lawyer, inching his way forward . . .

After May 30, 1783, however, it takes a new turning. That morning he follows his habitual itinerary and alters nothing in his customary routine, but he knows his life is about to change: he's preparing to plead the "lightning-rod case" being fought not only in Artois but by learned societies all over France, as far away as Montpellier.

---

text we have in his own hand, just as the Beugny *Mémoire,* dated May 25, 1782, was his first printed legal text.

35

JUNE 1783

A Head So Beloved, So Sacred

BENJAMIN
FRANKLIN

Gentlemen,

The Arts and Sciences are Heaven's richest gift to mankind; through what fatality, then, have they encountered so many obstacles in establishing themselves on earth? Why must it be that we cannot pay to the great men who have invented or brought them closer to perfection the fair tribute of gratitude and admiration owed them by the whole of humanity, without at the same time being compelled to bemoan the shameful persecutions that have rendered their sublime discoveries as destructive of their repose as they are useful to the welfare of society? Woe unto him who dares to enlighten his fellow citizens! Ignorance, prejudice, and passion have formed a formidable league against all men of genius, to punish them for their services to their fellow men.

Galileo . . .[1]

And he's off. Robespierre's rhetoric is well oiled and ready to run; the opening phrases of the "lightning rod speech" demonstrate the tone of his style, the early defects of which—prolixity and pedantry in particular—long remain with him. But this time his propositions are bolstered by thought. The text quivers with the passion for progress. It is nominally addressed to a president and two assessors appointed by their peers for a two-year term, or in other words to an emanation of that clerical and backward magistrature navigating blind through the inconceivable maze of religious and civil jurisdictions that ultimately go back to Charles V in the Artois—this "allegedly foreign province" still steeped in Hispanism.

And Maximilien calls upon Galileo for support at the start of his second paragraph, bringing in Descartes as a reinforcement soon after. For the first time, he feels the joy of the intellectual when his work is in harmony with his ideas.

It's a weird customer he's defending here, though, you must admit: another lawyer, a retired one named Vissery de Bois-Valé, whose late-blooming flair for do-it-yourself inventions has caused an eruption in the proud little burg of Saint-Omer sixteen leagues away, where the population of ten thousand find it highly vexatious to be governed (for appeals and important cases) by the courts of Arras. Vissery has invented, or so he claims anyway, "a means of preserving the King's troops in battles, sieges etc.;* another for saving people exposed to the perils of water; another that will keep fresh water incorruptible for a year or more; a fourth that enables a diver to breathe a keen and fortifying air while in the depths of the sea; and still others for heating the poor, removing heavy burdens with ease . . ."[2] Perhaps he was a shade ruffled by his neighbors' lack of interest in his genius; to make them sit up and take notice, he built with his own hands a lightning rod corresponding more or less to Franklin's specifications and, early in 1780, erected it on the chimney of his house.

Now, this was the first such contraption not only in Saint-Omer but in the whole of Artois, and when Robespierre delivers his impassioned defense the rooftops of Arras are still uniformly barren.

Vissery was more than half-expecting what happened next. In a small town, disputes are always begun by gossiping women. "Knowing that the conductor of the lightning rod in question was braced against the gable of the Sieur Cafieri, and that his wife was afraid of lightning, it followed that her disputatious neighbor, who is similarly affected, would by her talk increase this fear, which she communicated to other neighbors, by saying that she would leave her house whenever she heard thunder, etc. In short, it was decided by a council of women to present a petition the effect of which would be to have this allegedly terrifying instrument removed."[3] One thing led to another, more petitions began circulating, the noise grew, Saint-Omer saw itself in flames. A complaint was lodged with the aldermen† who, on June 21, 1781, ordered Vissery to take down his lightning rod immediately or have it forcibly taken down by the "lesser bailli" of the town and laborers hired at Vissery's expense.

Darkly gloating, he complied. He had become a martyr to innovation. First, he erected a clandestine lightning rod just to get even with them; then he appealed to the Council of Artois to settle the point of law, and to the scholars of France to uphold the honor of science. There's one man, at least, who's found a way to keep himself occupied in his old age.

> Had they sought to dismantle my entire apparatus by force I should not have borne it patiently; firm in my right, I should have defended it, I and my friends, like Whigs and Tories, Guelphs and Ghibellines, and the Big-endians and Little-endians of Lilliput. That is the form of sedition to which the ruling of a miscon-

*Unfortunately for the science of warfare, this "means" has been lost; all we have is his enumeration of his discoveries.

†The aldermen *(échevins)* were elected by townsmen, usually from the merchant class; they formed an embryonic town council whose decisions, adopted collectively, were locally binding. The "lesser bailli" was a sort of police commissioner but without powers of jurisdiction.

ceived sense of order would have given rise . . . It is with strong repugnance that I removed the sword-blade in order to pacify the seditious ignoramuses, and I consoled myself in some measure by replacing it with another, shorter blade which, with the weathervane supporting it now forms my lightning rod. And that is how one gets the better of the ignorant multitude.[4]

For his appeal to the high-court judges, Vissery, to whom money was no object, consulted one of the best-known of the twenty-two members of the Arras bar: Antoine Buissart, noted for his interest in the natural sciences. As was the custom, Buissart drafted the outline of the argument, or at least set out the facts to be covered in the plaintiff's defense, and handed it to one of his younger colleagues to polish and deliver in public. The "lightning rod" defense, thus, was produced by two lawyers, a veteran and a novice, working from documents sent to them by jurists and academicians in Paris (where Condorcet seems to have opted out of the case, possibly through sheer laziness, as he did when Marat was seeking his support), Dijon (chiefly Guyton de Morveau* and Maret), and also Montpellier, where one Abbé Bertholon, "the Franklin of Languedoc," throws himself heart and soul into Vissery's defense. One sees a sort of jagged line, like that made by a bolt of lightning, zig-zagging across a France that still can't make up its mind between the new sciences and the bristling hackles of tradition, and coming to earth in the hands of Buissart and the voice of Robespierre. What made him choose Maximilien? Well, he was a social acquaintance, and Mme Buissart had taken a liking to the nice, neat young man newly emerging from his cheerless past. He had acquired a reputation as a hard worker, too, a rare thing at his age; and in addition to his ordinary attorney's job, he has just been appointed a judge on the bishop's tribunal, to hear civil [*sic*] cases, which proves that he also has connections in ecclesiastical circles. However, they don't prevent Buissart from hearing an answering echo when the two of them sit talking about Franklin and Descartes and Galileo . . . What a temptation, what fun it would be to give a little jolt to the drowsy world in which he is in danger of being permanently caged, even if it's only a kid-gloved verbal jolt. Robespierre recites his speeches in the first person so there's no way of telling what is his and what is Buissart's in this cascade of language. Except—as is also the custom—the beginning and end, which are more or less improvised at the last minute;[5] and except for a tone, occasionally, that makes you prick up your ears—the man is there.

He reads on his feet, text in hand, facing the three judges and standing profile to a fairly dense crowd—because the case has also stirred up the townspeople of Arras—in the old hall with the giant beams which is called the "cour-le-

*The first, a future Conventionnel; the second, the future Duc de Bassano and Napoleon's right-hand man.

Comte" from the time when the counts of Flanders and Artois used to hold their beds of justice there in the days of their greatness. Endless chambers and corridors covering a large tract of ground "between the Place de la Madeleine and one arm of the Crinchon."[6] Louis XIV's portrait hangs in the vestibule, alongside that of Charles V.

No representation of Robespierre will ever adorn the walls of such an august place (and how could he imagine anybody might want to put one there?); not even the portrait some anonymous artist* has just produced for posterity, showing him still young but already ageless, with warm, wide-open eyes beneath the sweep of a slightly balding, high, thinker's forehead. Flaring nostrils, which must be quick to quiver, above a no more than ordinarily sensual mouth, an average chin. Hard to fix one's attention on this face because everything in it is so restrained, and that's the effect he wants to achieve, by the fineness of the single roll of powdered hair and the sophisticated scaffolding of a thrice-wound cravat over a starched jabot glimpsed between the folds of a striped coat. Voice? A shade high and squeaky at the ends of his phrases, for want of lungs and breath. The merest touch of Artesian accent when he gets hot under the collar, or in other words seldom. The authority he radiates comes not from the orator but from his belief that what he has to say is more important than how he says it. In fact, his delivery is rather monotonous; you have to listen if you want to hear him, but if you do you may be rewarded by the conviction and density of his text. Today is one of those times.

A revolutionary text? Far from it: rational, ironic, lyrical at the end, almost a panorama of the physical sciences of the day and the persecutions to which they had been subjected. Franklin is invoked on the fourth page, along with Harvey who had been condemned for discovering the circulation of the blood† "by the Faculté de Paris, which had commanded the blood to remain motionless."[7] The aldermen of Saint-Omer are scoffed at for their reactionary behavior, "which would better befit one of those remote lands in which the torch of the arts has never burned and the name of science was never yet uttered." Ten pages on the absurdity of this coalition of the respectable, almost an outline for a comedy; a mass of precise information on the discovery of electricity and its applications; a detailed history of the spread of the lightning rod, in general use in the Anglo-Saxon world but much less seen in France; a dozen stories about how houses, and even a munitions works, were preserved from lightning by them; and now, Maximilien de Robespierre's hymn to the princes:

"Notwithstanding our aversion to lightning rods, they tower over pow-

---

*Perhaps it was Boilly; but even the date—1783—is disputed. In any case the portrait, with that date on it, hangs in the Musée Carnavalet in Paris and is certainly the best pre-1789 likeness of Robespierre.

†Announced in his *Exercitatio anatomica . . .* in 1628.

der magazines in Geneva and protect those of Venice as well, along with her public buildings and her ships. In 1778 the Senate itself decreed that they be placed under their safeguard. What a host of illustrious sovereigns has vindicated the conduct of these two republics by imitating it! The Grand Duke of Tuscany, the Empress of Russia, the Empress [Maria Theresa], the Emperor [Joseph], have shown similar proof of their trust in electrical conductors. Every prince seems to have taken it upon himself to accredit them by setting the example, committing his palaces to their care. A lightning rod defends that of the King of Sardinia in Turin. The château of the Elector of Bavaria at Nymphenberg is armed with a like object . . . Need I refer to other authorities? Must I cite Sweden, too, and Saxony, and the Palatinate?"

In France, does it signify nothing that Buffon has erected a lightning rod on his Château de Montbard, that Voltaire put one up at Ferney? They're beginning to blossom in Dijon and Lyons too. Only two have been reported in Paris,* but Louis XVI has just had one stuck "on top of the *cabinet de physique* in the Château de la Muette . . . Had any doubt remained as to the effectiveness of these objects, they would never have been experimented with in the air above a head so beloved, so sacred, as is proclaimed by the sentiments of France for a prince who is her delight and her glory . . ."

Ah, well, if Louis XVI himself . . . The exhausted judges adjourn for twenty-four hours. The reply is given by a clearly outclassed Sieur Foacier de Ruzé, whose only hope is to gain time by asking the court for permission to have further investigations made by a different academy. But Robespierre bounces back with what was supposed to be an improvisation but is actually, he having foreseen or been forewarned of his adversary's last-minute maneuver, the second part of his speech. Brandishing a promise of fresh reports and accounts and case histories of experiments, he easily reduces the judges to gibbering terror. Are we supposed to be engineers or physicists or something? Haven't we had enough of Paris and Dijon and Montpellier and Philadelphia and, oh Lord, there he goes again! Another twenty pages charged with static electricity, Morveau, and Bertholon. When the last night of May falls upon Arras, Robespierre has won, if only by sheer stamina.

And pride. Take note, Gentlemen of Arras, it isn't so often you get the whole world listening to you. You're being observed. A curious sense of universal focus, encyclopédiste rather than Rousseauist in spirit, rises to the surface in the young lawyer's peroration:

> The judgment that is to vindicate us will no sooner have left your lips, Messieurs, than it will resound to the outermost confines of Europe. Those same public papers which reported the decision of Saint-Omer and have promised the entire

*This is a possibly unintentional indication of Vissery's originality and enterprise. In 1783 there were four hundred lightning rods in Philadelphia.

history of this singular trial to every nation are now preparing to present the decision that will end it. Paris, London, Berlin, Stockholm, Turin, Petersburg will all hear, almost as speedily as Arras, of this monument to your wisdom and devotion to the progress of the sciences . . .

But please, not another word about that man Vissery and his accursed hardware! The length of the pleadings is equaled only by the brevity of the preamble to, and especially the substance of, the ruling:

"This Court hereby authorizes the client of Maître de Robespierre to re-erect his lightning rod."[8]

One for me.*

He wants to tell the whole world. One wonders what chain of friendships and connections led to the first mention of his name before a nationwide public, on June 21, 1783, in the *Mercure de France,* a periodical printed in Paris and fairly widely distributed throughout the country. One link, at any rate, was a Benedictine from Arras named Dom Devienne, who had just written a *Histoire de l'Artois* and knew people on two Paris papers well enough to get a paragraph added at the bottom of the column telling the story of the trial:

"Maître Robespierre, a young lawyer of rare ability, showed proof, in this case in which the arts and sciences were at stake, of an eloquence and sagacity that give the highest impression of his knowledge."[9] Dom Devienne also gets him into the *Journal encyclopédique* and *L'Esprit des Journaux.* Six months after the printed speeches from the hearings go on sale in Paris, second compliment from the *Mercure:* "These pleadings do great honor to M. de Robespierre, who is hardly more than a youth."

The learned monk also seems to have acted as agent for the printing and distribution of the brochure containing the two texts—a proper little book, one hundred octavo pages, "on sale in the provinces for twelve sols, including two for the bookseller, and in Paris for fifteen, including three for the bookseller." Dom Devienne offers to furnish three hundred copies—that is, three-fifths of the total run of five hundred, "to a correspondent who would see that they were distributed to the booksellers of the Palais Royal, Luxembourg, Tuileries, Quai des Gesvres, etc."[10] One hundred copies are stocked by Topino, bookseller at Arras, and the last hundred are to be kept by the authors (Buissart must have been a nice guy, because he let Robespierre take all the

*Vissery de Bois-Valé is not overjubilant, however, since he had to pay costs. The population of Saint-Omer continued to show its hostility to him "and to sing Malbrouck under his windows" ["Malbrouck" being the French rendition of Marlborough, the great seventeenth-century English general who fought campaigns in Flanders and was immortalized in a French song, "Malbrouck s'en va-t-en en guerre" (Marlborough Goes Off to War)—*Trans.*]. The neighbors lodge fresh complaints the moment his lightning rod goes up again, but they are unsuited. Vissery dies soon after, in 1784.

credit in the title) for distribution to their friends. Robespierre uses them to set up a little press service for the scholars who helped the lawyers prepare their case and takes the liberty of sending one to his living god, old goodman Franklin, on October 1, 1783*—another almost-forged link between two men of liberty.

"Monsieur, a judgment passed by the alderman of Saint-Omer against electrical conductors has afforded me the opportunity to plead, before the Council of Artois, the cause of a sublime discovery that the human race owes to you. My desire to help uproot the prejudices impeding its progress in our province has prompted me to have the speech I made in this case prepared for publication . . . etc."[11] The letter is signed "De Robespierre, attorney at the Council of Artois" and Buissart's name doesn't appear in it once.

June 12, 1783.

For the first time in his life Robespierre is happy. It's June in his heart too. Summer has hit Artois with a vengeance, bending over the ears of wheat and swelling the hayricks along the country road he took a few days ago, in "the peasants' wagon that makes the return trip once a day" from Arras to the little burg of Carvin l'Epinoy, where one of his innumerable cousins in the region, one who has an excellent pastry shop, has invited him to celebrate his victory. The Robespierre clan is overjoyed: at last, somebody who can even the score for us. He'll go far, our lad Maximilien. Hardly shed his milk teeth, and already a lawyer and famous throughout the region!

The letter he writes to his friends the Buissarts that day is like a glimpse under the collar of this excessively prim overgrown youth, it's a letter in shirt-sleeves, a letter from the other Robespierre. He tries to be interesting. He babbles. He makes an awkward stab at humor and narrative description. The "letter of June 12" is a door pulled ajar to reveal an adolescent fragility lurking within, however hard he tries to hide it from himself in these unexpected caperings. He begins with a solemn MONSIEUR, as though the letter were meant for the older man alone; but his whole tone gives him away, even without the rash insertion of a huge compliment to MADAME at the end of the letter. He's writing to them both, he can imagine her leaning over her husband's shoulder and observing with satisfaction and surprise that he's really not bad at all, their little Robespierre who can make Arras eat out of his hand and then, just ten days later, write us such a long and bubbling letter, showing off almost for the sheer joy of pleasing them . . .

---

*Did Franklin answer? It seems unlikely; one doesn't imagine Robespierre mislaying such a missive or failing to mention it to anybody. Franklin did keep Maximilien's letter, though, among the rest of his papers, where it was found in 1903. It is in the Free Library of Philadelphia.

Monsieur,*

No pleasures can be agreeable if they are not shared with one's friends. I am accordingly about to depict for your eyes those I have experienced in the last few days.

Do not expect an account of my travels: there has been such a prodigious proliferation of that type of book in recent years that the public might well have had its fill of them. I know one author who journeyed five leagues and celebrated the fact in verse and prose. And what is such an undertaking in comparison with the one I have just effected? It was not five puny leagues I covered but six, and lengthy ones at that, so long that in the opinion of the inhabitants of this region they are worth a good seven of your ordinary leagues. But I shall tell you not one word of my trip even so, although I am much chagrined on your account therefor, as it is a great loss for you; the tale would furnish you with infinitely thrilling adventures, alongside which those of Ulysses and Telemachus are as nothing.

It was five in the morning when we set forth; the chariot bearing us emerged from the gates of the town† at the very same instant as that of the Sun lept up from Ocean's breast; it was adorned with a cloth of dazzling white, one portion of which drifted abandoned to the breath of the zephyrs; and it was thus that we proceeded triumphantly past the clerks' little inn . . . I leaned over the side of the vehicle and, doffing a new hat that covered my pate, greeted them with a gracious smile, counting that it would be fairly returned. But, would you credit it? These clerks, motionless as boundary-markers at the entrance to their hut, stared upon me fixedly without returning my salutation. As I have always had a confoundedly high opinion of myself, this mark of superiority cut me to the quick, leaving me in a frightful ill-humor for the remainder of the day.

Meanwhile, our coursers were bearing us forward with a speed beyond human powers to conceive. They seemed to be seeking to vie in lightness with the flying chargers of the Sun overhead; and just as I, with my courtesy, had confounded the scribes at the Méaulens gate, so they, with one bound, crossed the suburb of Sainte-Catherine; a second brought us into the square at Lens, in which town we paused for a moment. I took advantage of our halt to contemplate the beauties that this place offers to the traveler's curiosity. While the rest of the company were refreshing themselves, I escaped and mounted the hill atop which stands the calvary. From these heights I projected my gaze with mingled feelings of affection and admiration out over that vast plain upon which Condé, at the age of twenty, won the celebrated victory over the Spanish that was the salvation of our homeland . . .

We regained our coach, and no sooner had I settled myself upon my bale of straw, than Carvin presented itself to my eyes . . . The inhabitants of this village received us in a manner that liberally compensated us for the indifference of the

---

*The epistle is twelve pages long; I give only brief excerpts here, to show this unfamiliar side of its author.

†Of Arras, of course. The "little inn" he refers to is a sort of guardhouse in which the "commis de la Ferme" (who would be called municipal tax officials nowadays) were installed at the exit of every town. They supervised the peasants' trade.

scribes at the Méaulens gate. Citizens of every class displayed abundant evidence
of their haste to see us arrive: the cobbler, preparing to pierce a boot sole, stayed
the tool in his hand to look his fill upon us; the barber, abandoning a beard half
shaved, ran to meet us razor in hand; the housewife, to sate her curiosity, incurred
the risk of removing her pies burnt from the oven. I saw three gossips break off
a highly animated conversation to fly to their window; at last, during this, alas,
all too brief procession we savored the satisfaction, so flattering to one's self-
regard, of occupying the undivided attention of a numerous populace. How sweet
is travel, said I to myself! How true that one is never a prophet in one's own land.
At the very city gates one is disdained; yet venture but six leagues beyond, and
one becomes a personage worthy of the public interest . . .

Since our arrival, our every moment has been overburdened with pleasures.
Like it or not, I have been consuming pastries without interruption since Saturday
last.* Fate decreed that my bed should be placed in a room that is the storehouse
for the pastry shop, thus exposing me to temptation the whole night long. But I
considered that it was beautiful to master one's passions and so slept soundly,
surrounded by all these alluring objects. It is true, however, that in the daytime
I have made up for so trying an abstinence.

And with that he knocks off twelve alexandrine verses as flat as the pies
they praise. And he still hasn't finished:

But merely eating the pie is not all: it must also be eaten in good company,
and this advantage I have had. Yesterday I received the greatest honor to which
I may ever aspire: I dined with three lieutenants and the son of a bailli; the entire
magistracy of all the neighboring villages was united at our table. In the center
of this senate, M. le lieutenant de Carvin† blazed like Calypso among her nymphs.
Ah, could you but have seen his goodness, conversing with the rest of the company as though he were a mere mortal; his indulgence, when judging the champagne poured out for him to taste; his air of contentment, as he beamed upon his
image reflected back at him in his glass! I, who am speaking to you now, I have
witnessed all . . . But I shall have scant difficulty in consigning my baillis and my
lieutenants to oblivion. However engaging a lieutenant may be, Madame, you
may rest assured that he can never stand in the same world with you. His features,
even when tinted a blushing incarnadine by champagne, fall far short of portray-
ing the charm that nature has bestowed upon yours, and the company of all the
baillis in the universe could not repay me for the loss of your amiable discourse.

I am, with most sincere friendship, Monsieur, your very humble and obedient servant.

Carvin, June 2, 1783.[12]

---

*Fruit pies have remained a specialty in Carvin, where there is an annual celebration in their
honor.

†Military commander of the little garrison, and also the representative of the King.

36

JUNE 1783

The Contrivance . . . Leaped . . . into the Air

The Arras verdict is pronounced on May 31, 1783. It marks, in addition to the first foothills of Robespierre's career, the beginning of a change in mentality reaching even to the provinces; after it, at least some of the judges in Artois have ceased to be scared of science. Five days later, on June 5, in the Vivarais —a province even more remote and neglected by Parisians—science, working in close alliance with technology, wins one of mankind's greatest victories over nature when the Montgolfier brothers cause a balloon to fly "in less than ten minutes, to one thousand fathoms of elevation."[1] The calculated temerity of a couple of paper industrialists puts a kind of final period to the *Encyclopédie.* They don't risk their lives, of course, they let their contraption fly on its own; but they do risk their future and their reputation in a country in which ridicule is reputed to kill. From this day forth, man begins his conquest of air.

People had been talking about it for several months, and not only in France but in every branch of the international club of inventors and savants, where the latter habitually jeered at and poohpooed the former. A year ago the distinguished astronomer Joseph-Jérôme Lefrançois de Lalande, a pontiff if ever there was one in the Paris Academy of Sciences, emitted a definitive ruling on the question in the *Journal de Paris:*[2]

> Messieurs, you have been talking of flying ships and spinning wands for so long now that one might end by thinking that you believe all this nonsense, or that the learned men collaborating on your paper can find no words with which to set aside such absurd pretensions. In their absence, therefore, Messieurs, pray permit me to take up a few lines of your publication in order to assure your readers that if the savants keep silent it is only out of contempt.
>
> It is demonstrably impossible in every sense that a man should rise into or even maintain himself in the air: M. Coulomb, of the Academy of Sciences, read a paper at one of our sittings over a year ago, in which he shows, by experimentally established calculation of human strength, that to do so would require wings measuring 12,000 to 15,000 feet, moved at a speed of three feet per second; only an ignorant person, thus, could postulate such an endeavor . . . The impossibility

of remaining airborne by beating the air is as certain as is the impossibility of rising aloft, owing to the specific gravity of bodies containing no air.

This was aimed at Restif de la Bretonne, the prince of the people's dreamers, who had just published four small volumes entitled *La Découverte australe par un homme volant, ou Le Dédale français: Nouvelle trés philosophique avec de nombreuses vignettes* * [The Austral Discovery (that is, discovery of the other side of the world) by a Flying Man, or The French Daedalus: A Highly Philosophical Story, Profusely Illustrated], whose hero Victorius skims round the world by means of mechanical wings attached to his body, with nothing less than a miniature parachute fixed to his head. Daydream of a utopist? If so, it won't be utopia for long: there are some tinkerers of genius around, neither poets like Cyrano nor novelists like Bretonne nor painters like Leonardo da Vinci but proper researchers fitted out with workshops and material and money (usually supplied by philanthropic private backers), who are determined to transform it into reality, except that they haven't quite decided which to test first, the "lighter-than-air" or the "heavier-than-air" hypothesis.

The "heavier" champions almost carry the day. One who might have edged out the Montgolfiers was Jean-Pierre Blanchard, a "skillful mechanic" from Les Andelys in Normandy, who has just turned thirty and has already thrilled and divided the Parisians by running "a horseless carriage worked by sails" through the Champs Elysées gardens.[3] He has installed his workshop in a big garden on the Rue Taranne (where Diderot spent so many years) put at his disposal by a millionaire courtier-abbé named de Viennoy. Since 1781, Blanchard has been trying to get one of history's first helicopters† off the ground by means of ever higher bounds. The resurrection of Icarus. Blanchard was a real zealot, he believed in his contraption heart and soul and defends his faith with references to the birds Buffon has been studying. "The objection is also made that a man is too heavy to rise from the ground by means of wings alone, much less in a ship, whose very name implies a great weight. To this I reply that my [flying] ship is exceedingly light; and in point of weight I would have people heed what M. de Buffon says in his *Histoire naturelle* on the subject of the condor; this bird, albeit enormously heavy, can easily lift a two-year-old heifer weighing at least a hundred pounds, with wings having a span of thirty to thirty-six feet . . . The ascension of my machine, with its conductor, depends therefore upon the force with which the air is beaten, in proportion to its weight."

*Dated Leipzig 1781 but actually printed by himself in Paris, on the presses of his "book-shop." Apart from the long speeches, one could almost believe one was reading Jules Verne a hundred years before his time.

†The word didn't yet exist, of course.

At the beginning of 1782 he managed to get it eighty feet into the air—with the help, it is true, of a counterweight sliding along a mast. But the counterweight weighed only twenty pounds . . . If Blanchard can just lighten his "ship" by that much, and increase the bearing surface of its four wings, each of which is only ten feet long . . . It was touch and go when that nasty Lalande and his article came along to clip his wings and turn against the inventor all those people in Paris who can find nothing better to do with their time than sneer at somebody else. However, they are no longer *all* of Paris; other people are beginning to react, such as Marat,* who had a grudge against Lalande and later addresses a resounding retort to "that grubby monkey parading three or four budding jades from another century at the end of a leash . . . , that skeletal demi-dwarf of an age more than ripe who is most often seen in a goose-shit green coat with extremely short tails over an olive-hued vest with extremely long ones and wine-colored breeches that do not reach even to his knees."[4]

Blanchard was grimly hanging on, encouraged by such ill-assorted people as Louis-Sébastien Mercier and Philippe de Chartres, who had promised him a thousand louis† if he could get from the Pantin hill to his gardens at Raincy, where the "flying man" had made a date with the prince for the beginning of June 1782[5] . . . But in vain. The ship did not get off the ground—still too much weight and not enough "strokes beating the air." Redoubled gibes, digs, and ditties. Blanchard, although bruised, was doggedly pursuing his experiments in the hope of vindication in the "fine season" in 1783. But news of the Montgolfiers' exploit shifts public opinion in France—followed by that of enlightened Europe and even of Blanchard himself—over to the "lighter-than-air" school. Which means farewell, and for a long time, to the alternative solutions: the century was still too blinkered to grasp the idea of parallel research. It's everything for the Montgolfier brothers now, who also happen to have edged out the competition on their own team by the merest nose. In Paris, a physicist named Charles and a few textile and paper manufacturers were conducting research along the same lines and later swear they were on the verge of success when . . .

When the Montgolfiers beat them to it, and that fact nobody has ever been able to dispute.

Two brothers. Joseph-Michel, five years older than Etienne, forty-three and thirty-eight years respectively in 1783: one, the vaguely poetic dreamer

---

*Yet he's one of the detractors of the first balloons! Despite Lalande's unprepossessing appearance, aggressive pedantry, and obsession with petticoats, he must not be judged on the strength of this one diatribe or of his attitude toward Blanchard. However nearsighted he may be on earth, he was busily engaged in determining the exact positions of thousands of stars in the sky.

†More than 110,000 modern francs ($22,000).

with the vagabond tendencies, aided by an antlike but also artistic and ingenious younger brother, an architect resigned to industry. They worked together like twins on this scheme, maybe because they were both from "the tail of the litter" as they say in the Vivarais, the twelfth and fifteenth scions of pious, robust, and rich parents who produced sixteen in all. Almost a tradition, their paternal grandparents also had sixteen children. A tough family, strongly rooted in a tough country, but originating in Rhenish Germany a long time before.[6] If you go back to the Crusades you will find a Johann Montgolfier, who took advantage of his captivity in Damascus to learn the secrets of paper manufacture. One branch of his descendants, presumably driven out of Germany by the great wounds of the late Middle Ages, had strayed through Auvergne, Beaujolais, and finally the Vivarais, in search of waterfalls beside which they could set up their mills and turn the ancestor's secret to good account. Two of the line finally struck it lucky in the course of their migrations—two brothers, Michel and Raymond Montgolfier—when they married, during the reign of Louis XIV, the two daughters of Antoine Schelles, founder of the paper mill at Vidalon-les-Annonay. A union of money and ideas, from which issued both prosperity and Raymond's sixteen offspring bestriding the seventeenth and eighteenth centuries. Pierre Montgolfier, born in 1700, inherited the running of the mill, which gradually became embedded in one of the most handsome factories of the region, a majestic U-shaped edifice with a proper little palace in the middle to house the owners' clan and two wings at right angles devoted to the works, filled with creaking, sluicing noises and dust. They became "paper-purveyors to the Estates of the Vivarais," that is, suppliers of immaculate sheets, struck with the appropriate arms, to the cream of the prelates, nobles, and upper middle classes between the Rhône and the Massif Central. Many of the men and women of Annonay (397 "hearths" counted under Louis XIV), fed up with trying to cultivate their thankless soil,[7] became the employees not only of Pierre Montgolfier but also of a number of manufacturers of "Languedoc cloths" and, with a population of two thousand-odd, the little town was one of the first in France to become predominantly industrial in the days when Pierre was taking his turn at siring four daughters and twelve sons with his wife Anne née Duret—an Annonay girl, of course. Coincidentally, the "marquisate of Annonay" belongs to the Rohan-Soubises.

Pierre Montgolfier was not a frivolous type. "He was small in stature, stern of face and character, had extraordinary strength of will and was unyielding in his decisions. He was feared and respected by his entire family. None of its members would ever have dared to make a remark to him or raise their voices in his presence.

"Rising at four in the morning, he would go at once, whatever the time of year, to the manufacture canal where he washed his head and hands. In the evening he invariably went to bed at seven and never left his bed thereafter, no matter what occurred inside his house."[8]

. . . It's easy to see why, for Joseph-Michel (born 1740), home was more like a prison. With a father like that, it's all or nothing; either you bow, first to him and then to everybody else your whole life long, or you grit your teeth and clear out as fast as you can the first chance you get, which is what he did before he was a grown man. "Bold in action, as he proved by saving more than one of his fellow-pupils when swimming, he was exceedingly shy about expressing his desires. Did he ask to be taken away from the school at Tournon? In all likelihood, he did not dare consult his parents and deserted instead.

"Fearing pursuit, the schoolboy, who was then twelve or thirteen, took to the fields with the plan of living on shellfish from the shores of the Mediterranean"[9] only to be hauled by the scruff of the neck back from the silk-farm where he had been found tearing the leaves off mulberry trees, trying to breed silkworms. A sound licking awaited him at home, but it didn't cure him. Next time, though, at the school in Annonay, he found a better escape hatch: physical and natural science. For young people trapped in his kind of dead-end, passionate involvement with any fad or hobby is the only salvation. He must have been a real porcupine, because his parents finally let him go to Forez, the adjoining province, to turn into a hermit or the next best thing in some obscure hideaway in Saint-Etienne, where he studied chemistry and conducted his first experiments in rough earthenware vessels.[10] For a time he lived by peddling the salt he refined; but as soon as he invented a high-quality blue dye,* his father pricked up his ears and treated him to a trip to Paris. The rapscallion might bring home some bacon after all. Follow your head, Joseph-Michel, as long as we don't have to pay for you! No doubt he already had that stubborn chin and large mouth clamped tight over his dreams, and those eyes which were not easily lowered. A good-looking fellow, soon mature but long to age. He made the trip to Paris in order to meet, or at least listen to, the savants, his childhood sorcerers. He returned home on foot, determined to invent something, anything—why not a better paper mill? suggested his father, by now almost intimidated by the boy. Okay, why not; but on my own and far from the master: at Rives, at Voiron,† in the company of a first cousin named Thérèse Filhol whom he married at twenty-one. That put him into no-man's-land, half-worker half-boss; was he as tough on the workmen as his dad? Indifferent to them, rather, because of his other side. Inventors are often egotists. For ten years he dreamed of pouring the scattered energies of his youth into some practical, concrete project, and listened intently to all the intersecting debates about "aerial navigation." The heavier-than-air school?

*Later known industrially as "Guimet blue."
†The Rives paper mills (Isère) still manufacture some of the finest paper in France.

He toyed with the idea; but then the series of chemical discoveries relating to "combustible" or "volatile air" made by the English and French scientists Priestley and Lavoisier,* combined with his work as a boy and even more with the materials he used every day in his trade, led him to the flash of all utterly simple great inventions: "While waiting for some learned mechanic to concern himself with that important object [the "heavier-than-air" approach] one of my brothers and I thought of enclosing, in a light container, a fluid whose specific gravity was lower than that of atmospheric air."[11]

"One of my brothers" is Etienne, his accomplice for the past five years. He too began by trying to escape from the paper mills, in his case by being a good student at Sainte-Barbe in Paris and an apprentice architect in the office of Monsieur Soufflot, and by having tremendous luck, which led to a really interesting first job—the plans for the church at Faremoutiers in Ile-de-France.

But paper caught him on the rebound, when he was commissioned to design a new manufacture for M. Réveillon, the biggest paper maker in Paris, in the Faubourg Saint-Antoine. And Réveillon was one of those industrialists (they existed, even in those early days) who was ready to lend an ear, and some money, to the research projects of the physicist Charles. Etienne Montgolfier just missed teaming up with him rather than with his own Joseph-Michel, but the death of another of their brothers caused him to be recalled to the bosom of the family firm by his father, who wasn't getting any younger. When Joseph-Michel and he joined forces, the older brother was almost the director of the Annonay paper mills, "engaged in perfecting the paper industry, especially glues and dryers," and he too came back to the cradle with his head full of his own ideas. What could be better, as an envelope for "volatile air," than a mixture of canvas and paper? "Thereafter the two brothers pooled their ideas; aeronautics was born from their collaboration, which was so intimate that it is impossible to determine what was the work of whom."[12] Like all the other young people in town, François-Antoine Boissy d'Anglas,† son of an Annonay doctor, follows their experiments with bated breath and testifies for History on their behalf:

"It has been claimed"—Boissy d'Anglas writing—"that chance had a great deal to do with the invention of aeronautics. But the discovery of the Montgolfier brothers was the product of a theory supported by facts and observations that had previously escaped the attention of the vulgar [*sic*]." "They realized that it would be possible to lift a mass of great weight to a great

---

*The former discovered hydrogen while the latter was discovering oxygen.

†Boissy d'Anglas (born 1756) is a representative of the Third Estate in the Constituent Assemby, then a member of the Convention, both times elected by the town of Annonay. He sits among the moderates and is president of the Assembly during the riots of Prairial An III; in 1826, he ends his days a Restoration peer . . .

height by filling its interior with a fluid lighter than the air in the atmosphere, so that the mass, being no longer in equilibrium with it, could rise by its relative lightness like an empty bottle floating upon the water."[13]

Arm in arm, their noses pointed skyward, the Montgolfier brothers spent two or three years strolling along the banks of the little streams running down to the Ardèche or Rhône, and observing, mainly in summer, the big fat clouds driven so swiftly along by the violent storms that rage above this green and white country: steep meadows cleft by the gaping wounds of quarries. "It seems that the angle from which they studied this great problem of lifting solid bodies into the air was that of the clouds, those great masses of water that, for reasons we have not yet deciphered, contrive to rise and float in the air and at considerable altitudes."[14] There's "water-gas" in them thar clouds. So? Manufacture hydrogen and fill a sphere with it? But they looked elsewhere too, they snooped into everything. One day Etienne was fascinated by the tails of a drying shirt rising above a current of hot air. He tried several times to fill paper cones with it, but they all fell down again.

Time's a-wasting, though, for them and for Blanchard, and for Charles and the rest; this is the year of the siege of Gibraltar. "What turned them to this research was the desire to devise some means of penetrating the besieged fortress that would be more efficacious than the floating batteries."[15] War has ever been a stimulus to inventors . . . Joseph-Michel's *eureka!* burst forth on November 23, 1782, when the peace treaty was still unsigned. He was sitting by the fireside in the home of some friends in Avignon and staring at the rising curls of smoke while everybody else deplored the disaster of the *prasmes.* Quick! The next day he buys some cloth, builds a light wooden cube, glues the taffeta onto it, and burns a pile of paper beneath it. Under the landlady's incredulous gaze, this cousin to a kite with a capacity of forty cubic feet shoots up to the ceiling. He races to his desk, dashes off a message to Etienne, and sends it by the fastest post: "Prepare immediately supply of taffeta, rope, and you will see one of the most astonishing sights in the world."[16]

There weren't many slack hours between November and June. The peace was finally signed, but it brought no abatement of their fever. In fact, nobody had many slack hours at the best of times in that manufacture. The workers— almost half of them women—put in a twelve-hour day on average, except for Sundays and the high holidays.* First the sorters searched out the finest rags for shredding; then the steepers supervised their perfect deliquescence in the steeping vats; the thrashers and washers further refined the magma, extracting the minutest particles; next, the throwers poured it all into the mills (cylinders were used here instead of pistons, the Montgolfiers having adopted the Dutch

---

*When the church bells imperatively summoned them to mass under pain of committing a mortal sin: the feasts of Christ, the Virgin, the twelve apostles, and the local patron saint.

process); then the drainers carefully inspected the long drying-out of the pulp in the bins, as though they were maturing cheese . . . and then came the pourers and molders to give shape to the sheets, and the couchers who lovingly spread them "on cloths of soft white wool that must be seamless and all of a piece so as to leave no mark upon the paper; they must always be clean, and must not go a week without washing";[17] then there were the posters, who stacked the reams in layers, and the lifters, who detached them from the web sheet by sheet, and the pressers and gluers, who dipped up their pungent porridge from the big vats in the damping room, the *saleranes* or stretchers perched on benches of different heights to supervise the final drying-out in vast corridor-halls a hundred feet or more in length, the smoothers, who assiduously rubbed every sheet with flint as it lay spread on hides of sheep or goats, and then more sorters and counters, sizers and finishers . . . The whole little world of paper making, relatively well-off in comparison with those of weavers, miners, and many others. "The work was no less demanding, but the workers, who were independent and thus all the more indispensable, undertook to 'arrange' their hours of work to suit themselves; as they had a set quota to meet, the 'companions' "*"—but certainly not the women or apprentices —"were free as soon as they had manufactured the prescribed quantity. Thus the length of the working day depended upon the workers' dexterity, and the more skillful took advantage of the time they gained to do some extra work for payment"[18] . . . such as helping the Messieurs to reinforce their huge lengths of taffeta, cunningly assembled in the form of a sphere, with cardboard and paper supports, and anointing them as best they could with nonflammable gums. Classified as "middle-ranking laborers," they earned a daily wage of 20 to 30 sous,† in a very narrow "career" having only three steps (whereas there were twenty-eight at the glassworks of Saint-Gobain and sixty-seven at the Vierzon forges); with this, they could buy two to four four-pound loaves of bread a day, depending on price fluctuations. Urban housing, on the other hand, was expensive: rooms were rented for 30 to 35 francs a year,** and hardly any laborer owned his own home. "But the workers in the Rives and Annonay paper mills, who represented a privileged minority, were placed in a position of strength by their skill and their small numbers, and so they could dictate to their employers, demand"—in addition to their wages—"three or four copious and varied meals a day, real feasts on the holidays when they did not work, and butcher's meat to eat and wine to drink."[19]

It was this relatively comfortable proletariat, light-years away in those

*[*Compagnons* are something like members of a guild; the system dates from the Middle Ages but still survives in some trades.—*Trans.*]

†Representing an average of approximately 30 to 70 modern francs [$6–14] *per month.* In this period, workers' wages showed mind-boggling anarchy in the variations between localities, trades, and corporations: the law of supply and demand at its most savage and primitive.

**180–210 modern francs [$36–42].

days from any thought of comparing its income with the astronomically higher one of its masters, that energetically contributed its arms and ingenuity to the Montgolfier brothers' first experiment: two awkward hiccups, shrouded in darkest secrecy, in a friend's garden. Then came the great day, June 5, and the die was cast. The Assembly of the Estates of the Vivarais was meeting in Annonay, respectfully to ratify the figure demanded for tax by the King's intendant, although not without haggling over a few small items. The Montgolfiers decide to take advantage of the occasion to try their double-or-nothing throw. Either they would fall flat on their faces, like Blanchard, or they would stride into History through the front door, like Prometheus and Christopher Columbus, the men who thumb their noses at the gods. Having just found the ideal mixture for inflating their balloon "with a damp smoke resembling cloud"—a combination of rope, wool, and damp straw—they are feeling quite confident.

Annonay, eleven in the morning, Place des Cordeliers. A small crowd of sightseers has crossed from the other shore of the Rhône on the ferry that was always so badly battered by the current that it made the timorous squeal with fright. More have come from the mountains, scrambling down "a road as long as it is steep but which cannot be avoided, to the valley where the town lies at the junction of three valleys and two streams that might better be called torrents."[20] A limpid spring sky, a sun that has finally eased away the chill that lingers so long in these parts. The "square" is more like a village green, a plot of ground planted with trees and bushes, and a squat old church and a dozen houses playing puss-in-the-corner. The people hang together in knots, according to their kind: the priests here, there the gleaming gentlemen with their white-clad ladies—the new fashion having now made its way down from Versailles—and over there the big bourgeois in black or gray, but wearing beautiful fluffy cravats: the members of the Estates of the Vivarais, the only thing that unites a dismembered region "whose diocese is in Vienne, its parlement in Toulouse, its intendance that of Languedoc, its *Généralité* [or tax collection center] in Montpellier, and whose lieutenant-general of marshalsea lives at Puy-en-Velay!"[21]

But the rest of France is shortly to hear of the existence of the Vivarais, by means of that big blue-and-red loudspeaker (the vertical strips of taffeta were in alternating colors) in the form of a sphere that is about to rise into the sky from the Place des Cordeliers. A local savant, the author of *Recherches sur les volcans éteints du Vivarais et du Velay* [Research Concerning the Extinct Volcanoes of the Vivarais and Velay], is on hand to play the part of Amerigo Vespucci in the rape of the only America still to be deflowered: the sky. True, Faujas de Saint-Fond does not give his name to the balloon, which is immediately baptized *Montgolfière,* but he does form the link between Annonay and Paris and confers nationwide impact upon the experiment by printing and circulating a book about it. His testimony:

What was not the delegates' surprise, and that of the spectators too, when they saw in the public square a species of balloon measuring one hundred and ten feet in circumference, fastened by its lower end to a wooden construction sixteen feet square!* This vast envelope and its base weighed five hundred pounds: it could contain twenty-two thousand cubic feet of vapor.

Then, to the amazement of all, the inventors of the contrivance announced that once it had been filled with a gas that they could produce at will by the simplest of procedures, it would rise into the clouds under its own power! It must be admitted then that, despite the public's confidence in the enlightenment and sagacity of MM. de Montgolfier, this experiment seemed so incredible to those who were about to witness it that the most learned persons, those who were in fact most favorably disposed, were almost unhesitating in their doubt of its success.

At last, MM. de Montgolfier set to work, proceeding to develop the vapors that were to produce the phenomenon; the contrivance, which then looked to be nothing but a cloth envelope lined with paper, a sort of gigantic bag thirty-five feet high, depressed, wrinkled, and void of air, began to swell, grew larger as we watched, assumed consistency, adopted a fine form, stretched taut at every point, and made as if to rise: stout arms held it back;† the signal was given, it sprang away and rapidly leaped into the air, where its accelerated motion carried it, in less than ten minutes, to a thousand fathoms of elevation.

It then described a horizontal line of 7,200 feet and, as it was losing a substantial part of its gas, at that distance it slowly descended but would undoubtedly have remained longer in the air had it been possible to construct it with the required solidity and accuracy; the goal had been achieved, however, and this initial attempt, crowned with such happy success, entitles MM. de Montgolfier to the unending glory of having made one of the most astonishing of all discoveries.[22]

Another stroke of luck for the Montgolfier brothers was the presence of all those VIPs, which makes possible the instant authentification of the event by a memorandum written in the hand of an eyewitness, Henri d'Ormesson himself, the comptroller-general of finance whom the King had just appointed to take over from the invisible Joly de Fleury. A genuine minister, and a major one at that, to spread the news: the Court will hear about it within the week. What a help it would have been if every inventor in those days had been an industrialist too . . .

That's all it takes to bring on the Orléanses, who always have to stick their second-best fingers into every fashionable pie. The Duc de Chartres offers Faujas de Saint-Fond free run of the Palais Royal, not only to get his book published on the double but also, with the help of the prince's inexhaustible

*Within which were the materials to build the fire that would produce the "volatile gas."

†By twenty ropes attached to a large hoop placed around the widest point of its circumference.

wealth, to become the promoter of other and much bolder experiments. It takes the center of interest of this human invention less time than ever before to move from province to capital: not even two months.

BARNAVE

37

AUGUST 1783

The Greatest Happiness of All

Starting in Annonay and drawing a line eastward across Mandrin's country— Saint-Etienne, Saint-Geoires, and Moirans—it would be six stages, more or less, to Grenoble, the pride of the Dauphiné, where the Isère absorbs the Drac at the bottom of the narrow bowl often flooded by the thawing edges of the glaciers that drain into it and cause both streams to writhe in their beds like sleepers in the grip of a perpetual nightmare—until the day, if it ever comes, when they build those great dikes people have been talking about for centuries.

Grenoble is stifling in this month of August, ringed by its mountains, which lost their crowns of snow two or three months ago and in whose parched meadows, an hour away by muleback, one can climb to a cooler air. Here, in the smothering valley heat, another lawyer, Antoine-Pierre-Joseph-Marie Barnave, achieves local celebrity at the age of twenty-two with another epoch-making speech like that of Robespierre three months earlier in the lightning rod case.*

While he was writing it, Barnave may have learned, from the *Affiches du Dauphiné*—the only paper of any consequence around here—that the "Royal Society of Agriculture of Lyons is offering, for 1784, a prize of six hundred livres to whoever succeeds in installing, in Grenoble, a bread oven burning nothing but coal," like those used by many English bakers who have already learned how to do without wood; because wood is a precious commodity around Grenoble, it has to be brought down from the pine forests far away on the heights, whereas coal from the mines at La Mure is arriving in increasingly numerous convoys. "The prize will not be awarded until twelve perfect batches have been baked."

The leaden heat of that year's strange spring has provoked some fierce

*Barnave is a key figure in the Constituent Assembly and later becomes Marie Antoinette's secret counselor; he is guillotined during the Terror.

storms: on July 4 there was hail in the valley of Graisivaudan north of Grenoble; at Saint-Pierre de Chartreuse the crops were destroyed by hail on June 15, and the earth quaked on the 25th of that month. During the second half of July a mantle of fog "thick as in winter" but unhealthily tepid hung over the region "and has also been reported throughout the whole of France." On June 25 at Château-Bert in the Vivarais, the next province southward, a man was struck by lightning. "He is presumed to have been asphyxiated by the vapor of the thunder. The monks of the town are to dissect the body in order to determine the manner in which death was effected." If Château-Bert had put up a few lightning-rods . . . The population statistics for the Dauphiné have also been published: 13,756 male births and 11,098 male deaths; 13,092 female births and 10,869 deaths; 5,436 marriages were celebrated. The population of Grenoble itself is rising and will undoubtedly top 25,000 by the end of the century.* The only shrinkage seems to be among the monks: a mere 34 newly ordained, as against 42 dead. And on July 25 the *Affiches* inform the Dauphinois, over a month after the event despite the proximity of the provinces, that "MM. de Montgolfier have recently produced a truly curious spectacle at Annonay, causing a contrivance made of paper-covered cloth to rise into the sky by means of fire."[1] Versailles and Paris have known about it for weeks.

Barnave must have taken in these items while preparing the speech that is to give him his big break: the address to the closing session of the Grenoble parlement, third in France after Paris and Toulouse. Every respectable eye in Grenoble, a law town if ever there was one, will be fixed upon him; he will affront the intimidating silence of the ten chamber presidents in their majestic pie-shaped mortar-boards, and of the fifty-five councilors, of the chief prosecuting attorney and the one hundred and fifty ordinary attorneys, among whom his own father is not the least awesome, and of the twenty-one "consistorial" attorneys, meaning those with the highest positions at the bar, who rank almost as nobility, and of all the other lawyers who will have to crowd in and stand along the four walls of the great hall in the Palais de Justice. There won't be room for them all—over five hundred.

Why Antoine,† who has only been admitted to the bar for two years and defended a mere twenty cases? It was a custom,** a way for a novice to become known and assessed in legal circles. He was selected by his colleagues, or rather by a committee of twelve or fifteen chosen annually among the most eminent to direct the affairs of the bar. They were always careful to pick a

---

*Making up for the sudden drop after the revocation of the Edict of Nantes, which drove out 3,000 Grenoblois in 1685.

†He chose to use his first given name, because a man (and especially a clandestine Protestant) couldn't be called Marie.

**Lasting until 1789.

young speaker who was not too soporific and who had already been marked out as promising. It was an honor to be chosen, a sort of first reward. It could make a man's career, provided he were capable of deserving it by carrying his audience.

The object here is not to plead for a litigant; there is no adversary, no refutation. One has to choose one's own subject, and the choice is left to the neophyte; one has to treat it in a manner that will show off one's rhetorical talents but also one's inspirational ability. Woe unto the youth who sends his audience to sleep. The coveted honor would turn into a booby prize; he'd be lucky to find many clients to defend the following year.

Barnave has opted for the hard way out, and that alone sets him apart from the rest of the Dauphiné law tribe. Will he give a dissertation on civil law, Roman law, or some point of jurisprudence? Or, to avoid treading on anybody's toes, will he speak of the arts, literature, maybe even science, which is beginning to be fashionable? No; he'll make a sensation: he'll tackle politics, and from their thorniest angle: "The division of powers." Come again? I thought all powers reposed in the hands of the King, the Lord's Anointed, possessor of innate wisdom, incarnation of the law, and sole master of its application? Or at least that's the view into which France, a constitutionless land, has subsided, out of lassitude, since Louis XIV. Every province retains some shreds of tradition that pass for freedoms; for the rising middle class, they are vested in the magistrature and aldermen; for the artisans, in the corporations and guilds; and for the nobility and clergy, in their assemblies; and all are designed to preserve or increase the privileges of each and all are pulling in opposite directions, to the profound satisfaction of the representatives of the King who remains sole arbiter and master of the game.

And here comes a scrawny little sparrow of a lawyer flapping his wings in the heart of the Dauphiné, the land that has given its name to the King's first son, and daring to speak ill of our gracious pleasure. He leads trump in his opening paragraph:

"I was sensible of the uniqueness of this opportunity, and, to employ it as usefully as possible, I sought out the subject on which it was most important to determine my views."[2]

He sought, that is, the common denominator of everything he has studied, one can even say everything he has lived thus far, hacking his way through the jungle of codes. And when he begins to speak the language of the coming generations, it is with the voice of reason no less than that of the heart:

"All these collections of principles, bound together under the denominations of policy, jurisprudence, natural law, law of nations, public and private civil law, and containing so many further divisions almost all of which are lacking in clear demarcation, are most assuredly united by one common principle, by the sole and general aim of all sound legislation: the greatest happiness of all."

Happiness . . . There's the key word he tosses out to his listeners, the oldest of whom broke Mandrin on the wheel; to men who wield the sword more readily than the scales, the men Laclos chose as his cast of characters two years ago. (Not a woman in the house, of course; who could imagine a female councilor, even a lawyer? It would be sacrilege, it would mean that Eve did not do the serpent's bidding; but Laclos has shown them too, the ladies of Grenoble, waiting to take their revenge, in the boudoir, at the harpsichord or embroidery hoop. How many cuckolds are sitting there today among the councilors and consistorial lawyers? The *Affiches* somehow omitted that statistic.)

Barnave opens, thus, with happiness, a calculated challenge, a glove thrown down in the heart of Grenoble's past, which is held as in the palm of a hand by the lovely Place Saint-André. "A cunning stage designer seems to have tried to assemble the entire history of the province here in a shrine of stone: the hoary old houses and stout round tower of the Hôtel de Lesdiguières, evocative of the Middle Ages; the collegiate church of Saint-André, the former chapel of the Dauphins" just across from the carved façade of one of the oldest law courts in France erected on the site of the palace of those same Dauphins, in which the future Louis XI, immured in his strategy of the sulks, opposed his father Charles VII in the last years of his reign. To reward the Dauphinois for backing him, Louis XI promoted the "Conseil delphinal" to the rank of a parlement. The original palace became too small. Under Charles VIII, followed by Louis XII, it was transformed into this vast thick-walled edifice filled with corridors and misshapen rooms. Barnave inaugurates the language of the nineteenth century in the sumptuous mid-fifteenth-century setting of the second chamber, where sculpted wood sings out on all sides from walls covered with panels of linden carved into fruit and leaves and flowers in high relief, flowing in every direction and enclosing a retable almost delirious in its Gothic flamboyance, with eighteen pinnacles and four recesses for statuary. The whole *joie de vivre* of the Renaissance is contained in this room, in which so many have been sentenced to die.[3]

"The happiness of all" . . . At last a phrase more congenial to the invasion of nature that stormed in here with the sculptor's chisel only to freeze like the Great Ice Barrier around the paraphernalia of the law. One wonders if the young man telling them about happiness is happy himself? Not overwhelmingly so, but not positively unhappy either. He's slightly stiff too; after all, he's a Dauphinois, that says everything, those people would sooner die than talk about themselves. And besides, what could Barnave have to say, at his age? What he mainly displays, as his discourse unfolds in shapely periods following all the laws of the genre, is the precocious gravity and extreme application of a young man trying to impress his elders. He's thin, narrow in the shoulders, but a good-looking boy nonetheless, with a fiery expression beneath dark brown brows and a heavy mass of hair, powdered white and pulled into two fat rolls at either side of his ears, after uncovering, as is the fashion, the forehead of an intellectual, but in his case a shade low, a thought stubborn. His long neck, so well-suited to triple-tied cravats, bears a pointed chin, lips neither thick nor thin, and a funny sort of nose—heavy, with wide nostrils that almost turn it into a trumpet.[4] Willpower. He speaks with the lower part of his face jutting forward: "My name is Barnave . . . "

That jutting chin, that affirmation of himself comes from his mother, an aristocrat if you please, and of good family: Marie-Louise de Pré de Seigle de Presle; after a century, her Huguenot relations still hadn't digested either the revocation of the Edict of Nantes or the necessity to disguise their wholly Protestant faith behind a mask of Roman Catholic weddings and funerals. On provocation, *she* might look for and find a scandal, whereas her husband, also a secret Protestant, was better at nodding and smiling. On August 21, 1783, Barnave repays the world for the spectacular humiliation he suffered only a few yards away at the age of ten when he and his mother were expelled from a theater box that had been reserved for one of the governor's favorites, the King's man, the Duc de Clermont-Tonnerre. Does he ever think of it consciously now? No doubt he does, but more as a legend, because he's heard the tale so often and because ever since then the Barnaves have been held up by the bourgeoisie as perfect victims of the latent persecution of heretics . . . though religion had nothing to do with the incident.

It happened in 1770. There was to be a performance of *Baverley, ou Le Joueur anglais* by God alone knows whom, and anglomania had filled the house. Mme Barnave arrived late, holding her little man by the hand, and Antoine all puffed up at the thought of going to the theater like a big person. The boxes were sold out, their doors had been marked with the arms of the provincial dignitaries. Marie-Louise saw one unmarked door and barged in with all the arrogance of her youth and beauty. Either she didn't see, or pretended not to see, a sign indicating that the box was reserved for a Sieur Beauvallon, commissioner of war and friend of the governor. The senior M. Barnave had gone downstairs, as was the custom, to join the rest of the long gownsmen in the pit.

The theater manager was apprised of the intrusion of Barnave mère and fils and hustled up to ask them to vacate the box, but he almost got his wig pulled. Really, oust a Pré de Seigle de Presle for a mere Beauvallon! She slammed the door in his face. He then sent the marshalsea officer on duty at the theater that evening; Mme Barnave dispatched him with a few raps of her fan. The entire house, delighted by this unexpected curtain raiser, was staring. The despairing gendarme retreated downstairs to implore M. Barnave please to extirpate his tigress of a wife if he didn't want her to spend the night in jail. Sorrel, a prosecuting attorney at the parlement, advised his colleague to avoid a scene. Barnave climbed up to the box, and for a moment everybody thought all three were going to barricade themselves inside it, but then he beat a dignified retreat with his family, loudly proclaiming "that they were leaving by order of the military commander of the province." The pit, already much agitated by the sight of a soldier addressing Attorney Barnave and unaware that the box had been reserved in advance, sided with the expellees to a man. There was a fine ruckus. "Their friends were rushing about, leaving the theater; the ladies in the bourgeoisie followed suit, and found Mme Barnave in the lobby where she invited them all to spend the evening in her home. Everyone proceeded there immediately and danced away part of the night. The next day M. Barnave was summoned to the military commander, made his excuses, and there was an end of the matter."[5]

Nevertheless, a dim halo of the martyr, or rather "resistant," has enveloped the Barnaves ever since in Protestant circles, which were still strongly rooted in Grenoble, and the incident left a lasting mark on Antoine and became amplified in his memory. He often speaks of it in later years. In fact, it is almost the only noteworthy feature of an otherwise transparently clear, not to say empty, childhood. His mother was twenty-six and his father forty-nine when he was born, on September 21, 1761, in an old house on the Rue Pérollerie in the center of Grenoble and not far from the parlement, the first child of a hard-won marriage. The de Presles needed a lot of arm twisting before they would bestow their daughter upon a man without a handle to his name—despite the fact that there were several mere cavalry officers in its own ancestry, which may account for Antoine's lifelong love of horses and lonely gallops along the Isère.

By dint of sheer tenacity, Pierre Barnave finally managed to bring off this marriage, composed of a good deal of reason and some love. He worked hard and late at his office and earned a good income, even if piling brief upon brief tended to increase his natural melancholy and bring it into sharper contrast with the petulance of his wife. Owing to a slight speech defect, he had not been able to become the kind of lawyer who pleads cases; as a *procureur* or prosecuting attorney he spent most of his time writing.

Protestant self-discipline and their shared faith* helped the couple stay together without incident, except for the birth of three further children, a boy and two girls, and the painful death of the second son, Jean-Pierre, at the age of twenty, "carried off by the fevers" in Paris, where he was beginning a career as an officer. Antoine went to be with him and stayed to the end: the brothers,

---

*With a dispensation from the Bishop of Lyons, they were married in church in that city, outside the Protestant circle of Grenoble but with strong mental reservations. This was becoming the custom for "tolerated" Protestants in the southeast, so that their children would not be declared illegitimate. Similarly, Barnave was baptized in Saint-Hugues church in Grenoble but brought up in the Reformed faith.

almost the same age, were deeply attached to each other, and this death left its mark on Barnave by increasing his natural craving for solitude. His brother had had a fiancée, but he was unattached. He filled several pages of his diary with his thoughts on the event: "If I were to die, I should like, as you did, to choose the eyes whose tears I should cause to flow."[6]

Their youth had been cooled and refreshed by the lawns and trees of a country home their father had bought at Saint-Egrève, a league away from Grenoble in the Isère valley that opens out of the town at "the gate of France" and runs north to Voreppe. The valley beloved of Laclos. Antoine rode up and down it so many times that he contracted a sort of back-to-nature romanticism, an inner reserve that kept him somehow apart from the urban bustle. He obtained his law degree at Orange without any difficulty: to people of his standing and background the examiners handed out the answers along with the examination questions.

He's a big boy now. His already well-disposed listeners regard him with even greater benevolence because the people of the Dauphiné are anti-authority by instinct, their parlement was one of those that gave Louis XV the most trouble at the end of his reign:

> Thus, the ministry of the altars, the activities of the military forces and those of public education, perverted by human ambition, have served as instruments to enslave men;—thus, the attributes of the judiciary include that of being a public authority employed in the enforcement of sentences; in the ordinary way they also imply some share in legislative power and general administration—because experience of the law teaches legislation—because jurisdiction is a great means of learning about the needs, forces, and resources of the republic*—because, finally, the judiciary authority reconciles the people to those who wield it, creating trust and submissiveness in them, and the habit of belief and obedience that makes them the interpreters of its desires and repositories of its power.

A trifle heavy and stodgy, but pleasing to the ears of these magistrates who are being so tediously relegated to the judiciary when they are so longing to get their fingers into politics. There's a heady tang of subversiveness in Barnave's speech, a little American flavor that has been spicing up debate everywhere in the last few years:

> To my mind the attribution of power is improved the more widely it is divided, so that every part of the state should be invested with a portion of it and enabled to defend its interests more effectively. Such is (at least by law) the constitution of several governments in Europe whereby, concurrently with the prince, the three orders making up the population share in the general administration.

*He uses the word here, of course, in the sense of *res publica,* "public affairs."

His light but supple voice can be heard throughout the room. A sort of fever rises in him—that "added something" of people who believe what they're saying—when, toward the end, he comes to speak of the one thing everybody has forgotten about all these many decades: the people. Perhaps that's the essence of Barnave—a kind of sincerity:

Relegations and deportations will ensue. The laws can neither spare the weak nor strike the strong. Sometimes forms will be invoked only to be broken, but of regular justice there will be none, except between people of equal credit.

The prince may also provide himself with a standing body of men under his orders; the need for a guard, increasing by degrees, and the depredations of troops discharged in time of peace, will gradually have justified its institution. The people, dazed, enfeebled, made frivolous, will applaud and rejoice to see the growth of this army, which enslaves them and which they pay. The people pay, and will have to pay more: the prince has need of gold, because his brilliance increases with his power.

Gold is necessary to those high and mighty persons who, with great credit and many honors, have but little possession.

Gold is necessary to the priesthood, because its empire has been taken away and now its voice must be bought.

The source of all this gold is in the people, but there must also be hands to collect it, and the people, seeing part of their subsistence torn from their grasp; the people, in their joys as in their sorrows seeing only the immediate authors, will vent their indignation upon the tax collectors.

He has quickened the pace; he seems to be trying to make his audience hear something, sounds, giant strides outside the hall, is it Caliban, Cromwell? The speaker is not, ostensibly, trying to portray France under Louis XVI; but what else can account for this surge of emotion, this sense of immediacy in his vision of the Apocalypse?

In the end, bodies and souls languish as a result of depravity; a multiplicity of arbitrary actions annihilates property. Then there is no more hope, no more fear, no more desire, no more movement; the slave yields himself up to apathetic repose, the only positive aspect of his condition; the prince is no longer in command, save through the numbness of his subjects and the force of his army: the state, lying fallow, produces scarce enough income to pay it, and murmurs and threats begin to ferment within its ranks. The day when the building that stands on such ruinous foundations will collapse and turn to rubble is fast drawing nigh. On that fateful day, the soldier wakes and thinks at last to weigh the roles of satellite and master in the same scales: he observes, and he acts. When the signal is given, prince, empire, government, all fall and in their places remain nothing but a pack and its prey.

True, "one glimmer of hope is left, in such crises of states. To affirm that an upset equilibrium can never be restored save by violent revolution would,

I believe, show a poor knowledge of the inconstancy of human vicissitudes,"
but . . . "let princes ever remember that there can be no great king who is not
also the leader of a free people."

The applause is loud and long. From this moment forward, Grenoble and
the Dauphiné have heard of Barnave.

"I made a speech to the parlement of Grenoble," he says later, much later—
ten years, ten centuries later—"on the division of power, a proposition that
in itself constituted, in the eyes of the despotism of the day, a capital crime.
From that day I could be counted among the defenders of the rights of the
French nation."

On January 23 of that same year Henriette Gagnon, wife of another Grenoble
procureur named Chérubin Beyle, gave birth to their first child, Henri, on the
Rue des Vieux-Jésuites in the center of the old town.* "The street is narrow
and twisting; the house very tall, black, quite dilapidated. Within, one's heart
sinks: neither air nor light."[7] Lack of money can't be the reason, because even
the wealthiest people in Grenoble live in these dungeons, escaping to their
country homes as often as they can. Even so, the children who first open their
eyes in them, like Barnave, like Stendhal, are as though stricken by some
sorrowing secret.

38

AUGUST 1783

So Much I Hated . . . Soldiering

Not everybody in France had such a high opinion of prosecuting attorneys,
and Jean Rossignol [the name is the French word for nightingale—*Trans.*], an
infantryman in the Royal Roussillon regiment, is expressing a view widely
held among what the Barnaves would call the "lower orders" when he writes,
in the first part of his *Mémoires,* that he had, in Santo Domingo, "an uncle on
my mother's side who was very rich. He must have been a scoundrel, because
he was a prosecuting attorney. I cannot prove the fact, but the proverb says

---

*Today called Rue Jean-Jacques Rousseau. A plaque above the door of No. 14 commemo-
rates the birth of the child who was to become Stendhal.

'clothes make the man' and I confess that even when I was very young I had already formed a poor opinion of his estate.''[1] He sounds as though he was writing back in the days of Racine's *Plaideurs,* and as far as the law courts are concerned it's true enough: the prosecuting attorney [or *procureur;* the terms are not really equivalent—*Trans.*] was a sort of bastard byproduct of lawyer and *huissier* [who was an enforcement officer without much legal training—*Trans.*], a parasite on civil proceedings. Plaintiffs were presumed not to understand the esoteric jargon of the whereases, nor did they, of course, if they had not studied law—if, in other words, they were any man or woman of the people; and so they had to employ him to present their cases in writing. If he was a greedy man his object, pursued in league with his colleagues or even the judges, was to drag out the case as long as possible and thus get more money from his client.* This is a clear instance of the relations within the three-tier structure of the France of Louis XVI: the men of the long gown, in the middle, may be right to complain of the unliftable lid crammed down on their heads by a decadent aristocracy; but how much more bitterly, then, can the people at the bottom of the edifice complain of unending extortions of the legal racket every time a base commoner has to address himself to it.

But at last, at last! we have the voice of a "man of the people"; for the historian, this means a witness to the period *in* the period, whose testimony comes straight from him to the reader today. Let us attend to Jean Rossignol, former goldsmith's apprentice, who is suspicious of the law and who, in this summer of 1783, escapes from the soldier's life† to which he has been condemned for the last eight years. He's only twenty-three; how many lives has he already lived?

Longwy, in northern Lorraine: the top of the shoulder France shoved into Germany following Louis XV's painless appropriation of the province on the death of Stanislas Leczinski. A stronghold of two thousand inhabitants, its houses squeezed in by ramparts around a big château flanked by towers, looking a little like the Bastille in Paris. A military town *par excellence,* ever since the Romans laid out the camp of *Longus vicus* there two thousand years before. The soldiers of the modern empire are close at hand, too, in their

---

*The lawyer's interest, on the other hand—this shows the difference between Barnave and his father—was to speed up the proceedings so that he could get as many clients as possible and gain popularity among them as a defender, not a quibbler.

†Jean-Antoine Rossignol (1759–1802) is one of the "Conquerors of the Bastille" in 1789 and is included in the official list of their names. He plays an important role in the Paris "sections" and is a leading figure on August 10, 1792. He is Hébertist [i.e., extremist] by inclination but moderated by Robespierre; made a colonel, then a general in 1793, he commands the Convention's army against the Vendéens for a few weeks, following Lauzun-Biron, but is demoted for tactical errors and wanton violence. Arrested by the Thermidorians, he conspires with Babeuf and is deported by Bonaparte in 1801, dying soon after his arrival in the Seychelles.

"Austrian Netherlands" garrisons and sprinkled about among the Rhineland vassals. But what's the point? The military is treading water on both sides, there's nothing but dress parades and maneuvers. Everybody in this part of the world has been resigned to peace for decades; who could imagine the emperor making war on his own sister's armies? So Jean Rossignol can shake off the dust of his garrison life, where he's damned if he's going to rot alive, without a backward glance. If he re-enlists it means another eight years; no thanks. He wants no part of the dismal prospects offered him by the army before 1791. This inveterate brawler can find some better way of using up his excess energy in civilian life. Indifferent to nature, he doesn't linger long over the meadows scorching in the Assumption-Day sun, pricked and smeared by the scarlet glare of poppies. He's on his way back to his old haunts, his native Paris. "I hired a coach that took me half the way from Longwy to Verdun" along narrow roads of white dust whose rising swirls powder the pears and plums bending down their branches within arm's reach. Rossignol won't be around for the *mirabelle* festival [delicious small sweet yellow plums, not much bigger than cherries—*Trans.*]. "I left [on August 14, 1783] after selling everything connected with my military dress; I wanted to own nothing in any way related to soldiering, so much I hated it."

It's been uphill all the way for him. It isn't so much the regiment he's fleeing as the regimental prison, into which he was thrown for the tenth or twelfth time when he rejoined his detachment near Chalons-sur-Marne after casually treating himself to a faked furlough for "a week of amusement in Paris." In punishment for which he was made to march at the head of his regiment with his pretty white coat on backwards, like a dunce-cap on a misbehaving schoolboy. Of Verdun and Longwy, whence the Royal Roussillon was migrating in the long backwash of infantry from Brittany who no longer had anything to do in the West, all he has seen is the guardhouse. His latest stint lasted a month, during which he was made to stand to attention once a day while his comrades marched past at the foot of his pillory at parade time.

Of all the punishments I had to undergo, that was the one that hurt me most.

I also carried guns to the number of ten, five on each shoulder. That was the punishment meted out to me at Saint-Servan; I had gone out to fetch wood for Saint Martin's Day, so we could use the money for a few jugs of cider. We were at fault . . . but mostly for being caught; the sergeant-major denounced us. Although it was the fashion to be given blows with the flat side of a saber,* I didn't get any. Nor did I get any water to drink—because those who were unlucky enough to get tipsy had to drink a gallon bucket of water the next day.

Ever since the Marquis de Vauborel, who was nothing more nor less than a bigot, came to be colonel of that regiment, there were morning prayers and evening prayers in every room, and the corporal in charge of the barracks room

*One of Saint-Germain's reforms.

had to say them every day; the morning at roll call and half an hour after tattoo at night. Every Sunday and holiday we had to go to the regimental mass. The colonel never missed vespers and even less the benediction, and the other troops called us the Capuchins' regiment, which led to quarrels now and then in which several men were killed, not to mention the injured. I remember one day I was the oldest in the barracks room because the corporal was on sentry duty, so the sergeant-major I mentioned before wanted to make me read the prayer, I told him I didn't know how to read, and he put me in the guardhouse for two weeks.

One can understand his being fed up. There is a sort of parallel between the liberation of this uncultivated youth and the escape of the hypersensitive Schiller a year earlier, except that Schiller really was deserting whereas Rossignol's term of enlistment was up, and the poet had always loathed the army from the start.

Jean Rossignol, on the other hand, enlisted with all the illusions of his fifteen years—sorry, fourteen.* You may well rub your eyes but that's the way it was in July 1775, Coronation year; the boy was trapped between an unloving mother and the dead-end of a goldsmith's apprenticeship that was longer than he could bear. He was shooting up and had reached "five feet three inches [more like five feet seven or eight by our reckoning—*Trans.*] in height, was quite well-made, not pretty but passable"—or so the mirror told him at the time of the first great break in his life, the break with childhood. "I decided to go for a soldier" to get a little farther away from his mother. His father had never done him any harm, except maybe by dying too soon; he was God-the-Father. A Burgundian by birth. "He came up to Paris and looked for a wife. He met my mother and they were married. Of the five children they had, three boys and two girls, I was the last. For his good conduct my father had been given a place in the Lyons post office; he was a postman and my mother was a postwoman.† I was only nine when my father died, but I was old enough to know him and I recall that he was very fond of me because I was the most mischievous of my brothers."

That may have been the reason why his mother was so very unfond of him; in any case his family situation was the source of the anger that inhabited Rossignol all his life. "I could lie well enough at home, especially when I had been beaten: either I had fallen or been pushed. I had a mother nobody could ever complain to, she was very hard; she never defended us, on the contrary, 'Fine,' she would say, 'today you've met your master.' That made me so angry that I often left the house in a temper and vented my spleen on the first person I met, after which I felt better. One day I remember we were a party of ten against six on the half-moon at the boulevards,"

*He was born in Paris on November 7, 1759.

†In other words, they delivered both letters and small parcels that had come up on the Lyons stagecoach to addresses in Paris.

that large grassy space growing up to the ramparts in the shadow of the Bastille just near the Place Royale.* Already a scrapper, then, was Jean-Antoine, his fists never quiet in his pockets; already dismissed from "the choirboys of St. Catherine's church" because he quarreled with a cook; already a soldier in the wars between his primary school, taught by Monsieur Roland, "a master celebrated for his penmanship," and the boys of another local school kept by somebody named Bourmera. "Two or three times a week we would fight, using schoolboys' weapons: rulers, compasses, pocket-knives, the lot; I got hurt several times but it didn't discourage me."

"At last my mother determined to have me learn a trade, and I chose that of goldsmith" at the end of his eleventh year. He could just about read, write a bit, count, and fight. But he liked the work, you had to be both strong and delicate at once, and might have saved his youth in it.

> The agreement was that I should stay there four years for four hundred francs in silver.† I was glad to leave the paternal home. The bourgeois I lived with was a decent man, but his wife, an old bigot, was the Good Lord at church and the devil at home. On Sundays and holidays I was forced to go to mass in the parish church with her, and I was pretty bored by it; but since I had a very loud voice I did all I could to prevent her from praying and sang my head off to get her mixed up in her prayers; that made her decide to send me out to the Cours, but I was supposed to come back and collect her as soon as the high mass ended. I took the opportunity to go play with the other apprentices outside church, then I went back in to pick up my bourgeoise.
>
> I stayed three years in that shop and having learned two or three things about the work I imagined that larks would drop ready-roasted into my mouth out in the provinces, so that decided me to travel; it was all in order to be my own master.

At fourteen. One year from qualifying for membership in his guild.

He clears out. Just takes off, alone, on foot, going along the roads with his pack on his back, all the way to Bordeaux, where he meant to embark for Santo Domingo and the *procureur*-uncle, see above . . . The voyage costs three hundred livres. He's only got two hundred,** saved from his wages over the last three years. He gives up the trip and finds a merchant-goldsmith "who gave me work. He did not like the way I worked and showed me the door at the end of the week. I began to feel what it was like in the provinces and was sorry I had ever left Paris"; oh, you little Parisian devil, addict of the half-moon on the boulevard . . .

Next, La Rochelle, long enough to have a fight "with a first hand who made fun of me." Then Niort and the home of another goldsmith, for a breather lasting "all summer long until the end of the grape harvest" at

---

*Now the Place des Vosges.
†2,400 modern francs [$480].
**1,200 modern francs [$240], in other words, of the 1,800 [$360] needed for his passage.

eighteen livres a month,* but he got his bed and board too, until the night he left his clothes, his one and only suit of clothes, in the hands of some drunken Poitevins in a scrap at the entrance to an entertainment hall. Next-door to naked. "The merchant-goldsmith was sympathetic and had one of his old coats made over and gave it to me until my month was up. Then I went straight out and bought a suit of clothes with my eighteen livres; as you can imagine, it was not of the first quality."

Back to Paris, and from goldsmith to goldsmith. Here it's almost riches, sometimes he earns twenty francs a week—four times as much as at Niort, it makes him dizzy. "One day I took it into my head to learn about women" at the same age as Restif—fourteen, the regulation initiation age in those days for boys of almost every social class, "and I caught the little joke," gonorrhoea no doubt. "The men with whom I was working noticed it and I was the laughingstock of the whole shop. It made me desperate, and caused arguments with my comrades. I fought often, and turned all my mates against me." The world of masters and friends was starting to look like the world of his mother, like rejection. Well, if he must be fighting all the time . . . There was talk of a war with England; why not try the army.

Easy as pie for a child of Paris, all he had to do was walk along to the Pont Neuf where the sergeants went scouting every day for their colonels' under-manned regiments. "My recruiter, a trader in human flesh, had also recruited a baker . . . I found an officer who gave me one hundred livres for enlisting and a ten-écu note to get to the regiment.† I sold my tools and went, taking the officer with whom I had enlisted, to bid farewell to my mother. He had his own plan; he thought my mother wouldn't let me go and was apparently counting on a few gold louis of profit. But the moment my mother saw me with a cockade she said, 'Aha! Monsieur, you've made your bed, now you can lie in it!' Then the officer said to her, 'Madame, if you wish, he won't go; for a small consideration I shall return your son to you.' I spoke up and said that in that case I would enlist with somebody else. My mother then chose to say, 'Well, Monsieur, go ahead, and behave yourself.' I left, regretting noth-ing . . ." And comes back the same way. Jean Rossignol is not a sentimental type.

He has been a soldier, in other words, from August 13, 1775, to August 14, 1783, but he never sets foot in America. First garrison: Dunkerque. At that point the army was looking more toward England. "And there I was, in the Royal Roussillon infantry regiment,"** one of those belonging to the King

---

*110 modern francs [$22].

†A bonus of 600 modern francs [$120] in other words, and 180 [$36] more for the road.

**Which becomes, in the Revolution, the 54th Infantry. This regiment was made up of two battalions, each containing 484 noncommissioned officers and ordinary soldiers (only the first nineteen regiments of the army had four battalions, or twice the number of men). Each battalion

himself, who distributes its colonelship as a mark of favor. Most of the men are Catalonian, and it takes Jean-Antoine a while to catch on to their lingo, but he's not the only Parisian around. It was impossible to dump the whole of the weekly Pont Neuf catch into the Ile-de-France, so they were scattered through provincial regiments to plug up the holes. This practice gave a special fillip, a tang to the units from Rouergue, Saintonge, or Brittany—the jeering Paris banter, like a wink exchanged across the banks of the Seine, skittering through the entire army.[2]

The greatest cause of Rossignol's loneliness was his youth. His fellow soldiers were between fifteen and forty or fifty years old, depending on their physical condition and number of re-enlistments. They led the city brat a merry dance, and for eight years he used the technique he had perfected long ago —that is, get in first with both fists—to prove that he was not to be sneered at because of his tender years. Until 1776 he was called *Francoeur;* every ordinary soldier had to take a nickname, like a household pet, and he was lucky they let him choose it himself. But in 1776 his company was enlarged, and he was able to divest himself of this humiliating alter ego. "In the company to which I was then joined there was an old soldier with the same *nom de guerre,* which meant that I had to adopt a different one and I opted for *Rossignol"*— nobody needed to know it was his real name—"that was my family name, which I have borne ever since and will never change. There has never been any shame in my family."

His first bayonet duel took place by moonlight three months after his arrival in Dunkerque, and he almost killed *La Giroflée,* his bedmate,* who was twice his age. "This first attempt made me bolder, and I heard people saying about me, 'There he goes, that's the one who sent La Giroflée to the infir-mary!' "

A month later he sent somebody called Malfilâtre to keep La Giroflée company. "Since that time, we have always been friends and never had any further argument. That made me a name in the company, and the lads began to hang about with me. I was glad to see that I was no longer looked upon as a greenhorn."

Be that as it may, in Havre-de-Grâce, his second garrison, he fought again, with other fusiliers, "against the grenadiers and chasseurs, who wanted to keep us from drilling on their terrain." Such were the pastimes of the King's army while it waited for ships to carry it to the great De-scent on England. There were hundreds of such footling private feuds, as

---

had nine companies of about fifty men each, eight of fusiliers, and one of grenadiers. In all, there were a little over 102,000 men in the royal infantry in the reign of Louis XVI, all supposedly "volunteers" and required to sign on for at least eight years.

*Like sailors and hospital patients, soldiers slept two and often three to a bed.

in the days of Louis XIII and the first musketeers, between these big babies who were bored to death wandering around from Le Havre to Brest to Saint-Malo. "In one day I received three wounds in the arm from a master of grenadiers."

After four years of this, he came within an inch of being hanged one day at Paramé, in northern Brittany. In theory, it was his turn to take the soldier's one furlough, a half year in the middle of his term of service. But a man "from the country of the red stocking merchants, I mean a Catalonian," got his name through ahead of Rossignol's. Every drop of that blood that we now know to be in a state of perpetual overboil rushed straight to his head. And bless me if he doesn't go off to tackle his company commander, "who was with his marquise," and commit a crime of *lèse-majesté* by insulting a superior officer, which was punishable by death, no less than if it had been the King.

"Sir, I have just heard the names of those who have their turn for home leave and I am not on the list; my sergeant-major says that it was you who opposed it, and I've come to find out the truth."

He insolently replied that I could clear out on the double and that he didn't have to give me any explanations. Then I told him I wanted to know what he had against me and said I didn't think I had deserved any reproaches as far as probity and honor were concerned. He lost his temper and said to me, "Monsieur, we can leave your probity out of this, because it is certainly the one virtue you do possess!"

He again told me to leave, I said I wouldn't, I wanted him to give me a reason; in the end he threatened me with his sword. I was so angry then that I told him, "You're said to be the fairest officer in the regiment, but right now those who call you so don't know you as well as I do."

He drew his sword, I told him I didn't give a damn for his sword or for him, that he was not worthy to be my captain, that he had a Cross of Saint-Louis that he never earned, he must have stolen it. He wanted to take me to the guardhouse, but I wouldn't go. He struck me several times, shoving me along, but I gave back as good as I got; one way and another our fight lasted nearly a quarter of an hour. A company sergeant came past, and I surrendered to him.

The sergeant led me to the camp guard. As soon as I got there I was tied to a tentpole with my hands behind my back, and they detailed an extra sentry to guard me and fire if I tried to escape. It was only after several hours of thinking it over that I realized I had been grossly wanting in respect to my captain and that the King's orders were very severe for such cases.

I was inconsolable and kept telling myself, according to the ordinances you'll be hanged. I spent the night in thoughts like that, and I own it was enough to give me a holy terror. It wasn't death I feared, I have never been afraid of that, but the dishonor of being hanged.

He even gives a comrade all the money he had saved up for his furlough —twenty-one livres!*—to buy some poison from an apothecary, "to put in my food as a means of escaping the gallows." But his major (the commander's auxiliary) and the chaplain and some other officers "joined together with the captain's marquise [sic] and got him to say I should only do six months in solitary. My friend, who had overheard their conversation, came to notify me and told me, 'You've been spared! You won't go before the council.' I fell in a faint; they gave me some water to drink and after a few minutes I came back to my senses. I embraced my master-of-arms for joy, for it was he who brought me the news.

"Camp was broken and we were garrisoned at Saint-Servan–Saint-Malo. I was put in prison in the Solidor tower. It didn't take long to find the garrison because it is only one league from Paramé to Saint-Servan. I made the march like all the other military prisoners, at the head of the guard, coat on backwards and gun-butt in the air. I was very happy with this punishment [sic]," but that was the beginning of his disgust with the army. He became allergic to it, as to his mother and the cruel world of apprenticeship. From expulsion to expulsion, when would he ever manage to give birth to himself?

At Saint-Servan, one dark night in a narrow alleyway, he attacks a sergeant with the full fury of his pent-up resentment, giving him "five or six good whacks of a stick," a miracle if his victim survives. The sergeant weakly moans, "I suppose that was Rossignol!" and the captain who had already spared him once, not such a bad devil after all, gives warning:

"Keep this a secret, for if I ever learn it was you I'll put you in solitary until you rot!"

He gets his furlough in the end, a year later. "I came to Paris and arrived in the midst of my family, who were not expecting me, and was pretty well received. I spent several days visiting my relatives and friends, all of whom were workers at my old trade . . . During my term off I had several quarrels with the military, and drew sword seven times." One wonders if he'd have had it out so often in a real campaign. In the course of one of these vicious games he kills a man, a soldier named Patrès, in the Bois de Boulogne. Another miracle, and the protection of the local lord—the Marquis de Livry, an accidental witness to the fray—keeps him from court martial once again.

1781. Somewhere between Brest and Morlaix, waiting to embark with his battalion to give Suffren a hand in the Indies. Oh, but it's so deadly just hanging around. "It was in this interval that I was mortally wounded [sic] and in a most unfortunate way" by a jealous sailor who had his eye on the fair Isabeau, a serving girl in an inn at Morlaix, and who ran him through the stomach from front to back in the course of a drunken brawl, "with the

*130 modern francs [$26].

roasting spit that had the haunch still on it," after taking him for the girl's lover —his friend Bourgeau, alias *Baisemoy* [Kiss—or Fuck—me—*Trans.*]. "I was eighteen days in a transport"—a coma—and eight months on crutches, not to mention the hernia which sometimes bends him double in excruciating pain and which he drags around for the rest of his days. That quells whatever desire he might have had to campaign. "I own that I didn't want to go make war on people in the Indies without knowing what for." But the Marquis de Langeron,* military commander of Brest, is of a different opinion. "I was convalescing when a second convoy was to leave. Langeron passed us in review. I explained to him that injured as I was I would not be able to survive the sea-voyage; his reply, with that brutal air so well known to all soldiers, was that my injury would not prevent me from boarding the ship and that I should get well just as fast at sea as in a hospital." At sea! In those between-decks in which one healthy seaman out of three rotted on every trip. If Our Lady was praying hard for him, Rossignol would have a slim chance of getting himself buried at Cuddalore or Pondicherry . . . but the ship's surgeon wanted no surplus cadavers on board and saved him the very next day, with a certificate that would brook no argument:[3]

> We the undersigned, surgeon in chief of the military hospitals of Brest, hereby certify that Jean Rossignol called Ibid, fusilier in the Royal Roussillon regiment, is affected with a hernia of the stomach resulting from a wound with a roasting-spit received at Morlaix from a corsair volunteer [*sic*]; it is needful for this injury that he be exempted from boarding ship, and we have bound up the wound expressly.
> In earnest whereof the present attestation.
>
> Brest, April 28, 1782,
>
> Giraudeau,
> Surg. in chief.

"I went back to Morlaix to join the depot that had remained there. It consisted of all sorts of infantries [*sic*] that had fallen ill on the road. Many had not wanted to embark and had employed all the ruses of which the soldier is capable."

Morlaix. Mortagne (in the Perche). Verneuil. His costly fling in Paris. His final prisons. Verdun. Longwy. Freedom. He is now awake and aware. It's not just pointless wars he hates now, it's their armies of slaves as well.

He and his pal (we're back in August 1783) don't have enough money to hire a coach beyond Verdun. They continue on foot. "No mishap befell us and we got to Paris after five days of walking." Their military life had inured them to seven-to-ten-league daily marches.

The pal leaves for his native Anjou. Rossignol goes back to his goldsmith's

---

*Whom we shall meet again as a leader of the émigré army, after which he takes service with the tsar and fights against Napoleon's army until and including the fall of Paris in 1814.

trade, and apparently not without pleasure. Oh, miracle! A whole year without a fight, it's too much: in the summer of 1784 he comes to blows with his boss, "a man named Sommier, proud and haughty," who wanted to demote him in favor of a new worker. "I took my accounts to the master telling him that I wouldn't work for him any longer; I didn't want to find myself a miller after being a bishop." Forward march, Rossignol, to the end of your road. "This quarrel earned me so much hatred that nobody would give me work . . . I was forced to leave Paris and spent three years in the provinces. I hadn't been to Provence before, so I went to see the sights in that part."

MARAT

39

MARCH 1783

The Celebrated M. Marat

Another hothead has landed himself in trouble in 1783: Jean-Paul Marat, with a whole hive in his bonnet. If he wanted to make a good living from his sinecure as physician to the Comte d'Artois's life guards,* enlarge his upper-class clientele, and let himself be undramatically loved by his nice Marquise de L'Aubespine, all he would have to do is take it easy . . . He's getting on toward forty. Isn't it about time he settled down? But the devil in his flesh won't take no for an answer.

He's a great savant, in his eyes at least, a French counter-Newton, and nobody's going to tell him any different. His discoveries relating to "the taming of fire" and the improvement of ocular instruments have been hushed up, he swears it to his dying day, by a coalition of Encyclopédistes and Academicians. All right, then; he sets off in another direction. Beginning in 1782 his beautiful official apartment on the Rue de Bourgogne in Paris is transformed into a laboratory full of curious instruments that snort, glitter, crackle, and sputter, not to mention the occasional smells and cries of animals . . . His latest research has to do with the possibility of curing people by "medical electricity," and it is true that this science is very much in its infancy. He electrocutes a pigeon, "which dies instantly in convulsions,"[1] then a frog, then some rats whose chests he opens, after the electrical shock, "to reveal the beating of the heart." He's been engaging in vivisection for some time now

---

*I have backtracked here (from August) in order to introduce Charles by means of this famous anecdote involving him and Marat.

and continues to proclaim his remorse: "Physical knowledge acquired at the expense of pity is paid very dear," and if he has "resolved to torment dumb animals," it is only because he is driven "by the keenest desire to be useful to men." He nevertheless confesses, in his *Mémoire sur l'électricité médicale* [Dissertation on Medical Electricity], that for almost ten years he has been a past master "at slitting the throats of sparrows, chickens, or rats."[2]

He has now determined to reject the method of "electrical treatment" by baths, which he deems ineffective and dangerous; "this practice must therefore be confined to methods of electrification by friction, sparks, and concussions" for paralytics, people subject to convulsions, "those suffering from debility and languor, patients with hypochondria, wet or dry asthma," all of whom should in his opinion by improved by his ministrations. On May 15, 1783, he begins treating them, in groups "separated according to sex," sometimes for three hours at a stretch. He has become more and more convinced of the benefits of his method, going so far as to move a patient into his home for seventeen days to undergo treatment in a special room "the air in which is to be electrified at twenty-minute intervals during five hours of the night." On this occasion he speaks for the first time of something not quite right in his own physical system: "Although the onsets of the spasms [gastritis? palpitations?] from which I was suffering came fairly regularly, I observed no increase in my afflictions during the fifteen out of every twenty-four hours that I spent in an atmosphere saturated with electricity."

Perhaps he will finally go down in History as the father of electrotherapy. The idea was floating around, like so many other scientific novelties that the publication of the *Encyclopédie* had put into the minds of sensible and scatter-brained alike. That very year, for instance, the Académie royale des Sciences, Belles Lettres et Arts* of Rouen sets the following question for competition: "To what extent and in what conditions may one have recourse to electricity, both positive and negative, in the treatment of disease?"† Marat leaps at the chance. It's happened before in his life, primarily in 1780 with the *Plan de législation criminelle* [Plan for Criminal Legislation] proposed by Bern: an academy's question created a sort of vacuum that he filled with torrential inspiration—the only kind he ever experienced—hurling his thoughts onto paper like a cyclone sweeping away everything in its path. After all, it was a question on science and the arts, set by the Academy of Dijon in 1750, that had plunged Rousseau into a state of permanent overexcitement . . .

So Marat eagerly dashed off a hundred-page manuscript and sent it in a sealed envelope to M. d'Ambournay, perpetual secretary of the Rouen Acad-

*In those days "arts," we recall, most commonly meant crafts and trades.

†The method of shock treatment in water had been termed "positive" and was intended to rectify "an overabundance of electricity in the organism," whereas Marat's method, which worked by means of contact with the skin, was called "negative" and was claimed to "recharge" bodies having an inadequate supply of electricity.

emy of Science, anonymously, as required by the rules; the manuscript bore only the initial "M" and "Paris, 1783." One of his Parisian friends, the Baron de Feldenfeld, acted as go-between for him. Jean-Paul puts a year of his life into that envelope and reveals, here as in his other scientific publications, an occasionally brilliant premonition of what electrical treatment could accomplish for some patients; but his knowledge is intuitive rather than deductive, it is an occasional nugget swamped in a gallimaufry of spurious suppositions. He can't concentrate in any one direction, he's forever losing focus in the gush of his excess energy.

And yet this paper may finally bring fame, and with it the firm position in the world of science that he so desperately needs. And oh, miracle: he wins the gold medal! At last, a prize! Will he rush to greet it with open arms? Far from it; he hangs back, he minces and simpers, is he that frightened of success? Has he become addicted to failure? The Academy informs the Baron de Feldenfeld that the award-winning applicant cannot remain anonymous, "the regulations of our constitution and the interest of the author himself requiring that his name be recorded in our books."[3] Marat hesitates, waits almost a month before coming out of hiding—although perhaps for the very simple reason that people in the service of princes of the blood were theoretically forbidden to engage in any other public activity. And the prize-winning *Mémoire* would inevitably uncover the intensive experimentation he had been conducting in his official residence on a very different clientele from the life guards entrusted to his care. This is not the first time that the Comte d'Artois's entourage has been startled by the eccentricities of his peculiar physician. Marat stood out in sharp relief against his background of mediocrity.

But the temptation is too great, he finally consents to identify himself, and the Baron de Feldenfeld can inform d'Ambournay that the author of the prize-winning *Mémoire* is "the celebrated M. Marat, so advantageously renowned among the learned of Europe for his beautiful discoveries in physics." To this letter he appends a copy of each of the winner's works, in homage to the Academy . . . most of whose members are horrified—too late!—by certain passages in the *Plan de législation criminelle.*

It's lucky for him that he didn't send them *Les Chaînes de l'esclavage* [The Chains of Slavery]* as well (at that point the text was still in the original English). The Academy can't take back its decision, however, and sends him —also too late, as we shall see—a copy of his *Mémoire* along with a payment order to the cashier of the Mint (directed by the abhorred Condorcet), instructing him "to issue without cost to the winner the medal struck for the purpose."[4]

Why too late? Because the prizewinners' names are not made public until

---

*The first outcry of the revolutionary Marat, written in 1774.

the autumn of 1783, when Marat's tide has just reached another low ebb. He had a "disease of exhaustion" at the winter's end, possibly brought on by the feverish composition of his *Mémoire,* and a series of written and verbal quarrels, and even one sordid physical row, and all of this friction had abraded the raw flesh of a man who was too thin-skinned to begin with, and increased the animosity of the officials in the Comte d'Artois's household. There was an ill wind blowing his way again. What was the use of a stupid medal if he couldn't earn his daily bread anymore, and above all if he couldn't perform the experiments that were his only true nourishment?

Also, the Rouen Academy slipped a few tight-lipped observations into its "whereases"—just the sort of thing to spoil Marat's pleasure. Giving way to the polemicist in him, he had peppered his text with criticism and jibes aimed at the famed Abbé Bertholon of Montpellier, who was that season's self-appointed arbiter in all matters pertaining to physical science: a Lalande in a cassock. To the increasingly Manichean Marat, whatever Bertholon said was good must be bad, and he therefore expressed strong reservations at the time of the lightning-rod trial in Arras.* Which, in the eyes of the Rouen academicians, was going too far; they accordingly regretted "that the author [Marat] did not show more moderation when refuting the views of an estimable man endorsed by nine scholarly societies, almost all of which have rewarded his efforts."

Moderation? They'll be lucky. Before he even received this thorn-encrusted rose Jean-Paul had gone to war against Abbé Sans, a colleague of Bertholon,† who was leading a new wave of confirmed, patented, constipated savants into battle against the mouthings of our savage. In number 16 of the *Année littéraire* Sans published a *Lettre à M. Marat,* containing what he deemed to be the most devastating reproach possible: that of having set electrotherapy back several decades by rejecting the effectiveness of water treatment and clinging to the methods of the physicians of the early part of the century—Jallabert, Sauvages, Nollet**—all of whom had advocated "sparks and concussions in the tissues and arteries" but would venture no further.

Him, a retrograde? He might have shrugged, but he blows up instead. This kind of criticism affects him like acid poured on his brain. He publishes —instanter, of course—some *Observations de M. l'amateur AVEC à M. l'abbé SANS, sur la nécessité indispensable d'avoir une théorie solide et lumineuse, avant d'ouvrir la boutique d'électricité médicale*⁵ [Observations by Amateur WITH, ad-

---

*At this point in my research I have not been able to learn whether Robespierre ever knew this.

†Originally thought to be an alias of Bertholon himself, Sans actually existed and was conducting his own experiments in Perpignan. [His name is the same as the French word for "without"; see below.—*Trans.*]

**Who introduced first aid by electricity into France around 1740, in the form of the "Leyden jar," which had just been invented in Holland.

dressed to Abbé WITHOUT, on the absolute necessity of having a solid and luminous theory before opening up a medical electricity shop], and this time he really lets his hair down. His disputatious side, never more than half asleep, takes the bit between its teeth and gallops furiously away with the poor abbé, who had been guilty of nothing less than proposing to supplement the diet of certain patients with "electrification." My goodness, what a lion's roar squirting from the quill of Dr. Marat, who lives in his jewelbox of elegant tables and damascened draperies but has not forgotten "the people":

> To maintain health and strength in the body, thus, all you require is an electrical machine and a fountain? First, you will assemble all the exhausted laborers of Versailles, all the poor wretches languishing from hunger; you will give them some beautiful pure water, place them on your insulating stool, and cram them with electrical material. Then, if they feel their energies restored beneath your hand, *then,* monsieur l'abbé, you may count me among your champions . . . Thereafter our fruits, cereals, wines, and livestock, having become useless to the nation, can be taken away to our neighbors; we shall consume all their gold and want nothing ourselves, so long as we may keep our daydreams and machines.[6]

These abbés are a long way away, Bertholon at Montpellier and Sans at Perpignan. Another foe now rises up practically at his feet: Jacques-Alexandre César Charles,* the physicist in fashion and also a "right sort," a man who receives an annuity from the King and who gives public lectures on electricity in a hall in the Louvre, that sovereigns' palace transformed into a sort of gypsy encampment for artists and scholars with friends at Court. Charles has his own suite of rooms there, to accommodate a considerable crowd of people captivated by his glib tongue and talents as a popularizer. He too is said to be cherishing a scheme to master the sky by means of "volatile air" and to be at least as far along toward its realization as those provincial Montgolfiers. What a spring!

　　Every person who comes to hear him, and they're all from the upper reaches of society, means one less listening to Marat, and that in itself is enough to anger Jean-Paul. But then Charles takes it into his head—possibly to get a few easy laughs—to poke holes in Marat's experiments and writings and does so at several successive lectures, calling him an out-and-out charlatan and comparing him to the notorious Ledru, alias Comus, a far more eccentric physicist† who began his career performing experiments in the streets.

　　Too much is enough. This isn't the first Beaumarchais-style skirmish into

　*Born at Beaugency in 1746 and known by his second given name, Alexandre. In 1816, when he is seventy, his much younger wife Julie née Bouchaud des Hérettes, meets the young Lamartine at Aix-en-Savoie (Aix-les-Bains), where she had gone to treat a "chest complaint," and becomes the Elvire of his *Lac.*

　†Although not without merit. He was in favor of free medical care and was constantly asking permission to treat the hospital poor; his request is partially granted at the end of 1783.

which Marat has dived head first. Two or three times before, he has come to physical blows with what he terms the "offenders."* Sardinian blood boils quickly when heated by a sense of persecution and the stifled feeling of people who are convinced they have something to say but nobody will listen to them. Alexandre Charles is asking for it, and he's going to get it.

Saturday, March 15, 1783. The whole Louvre is agog, what a treat for the loiterers—two physicists going at each other hammer and tongs! The scene is worthy of the masters of the *Bourgeois Gentilhomme.* What's got into that M. Charles and that M. Marat? The fewer eyewitnesses there were, of course, the more versions make the rounds. They spin from Paris to Versailles, pop up in the gazettes, reappear during the Revolution, and create a few problems for the historians. Simplified by the centuries, they can be classified into three main categories:

(A) Based solely on hearsay and totally improbable: Marat slips incognito into the audience at one of Charles's lectures and interrupts noisily just as the lecturer is calling him a harlequin and charlatan. Jack pops out of his box, it's Marat waving a sword.† Charles draws too; duel on the platform. Marat is carried out unconscious, wounded in the left thigh. Curtain. It's not true, we may as well forget it. One scholar has managed to prove that Charles was not lecturing that day.[7] Besides, it is hard to imagine either Marat challenging him in front of a high-society audience or that audience allowing them to skewer each other unimpeded.

(B) The anti-Marat version spread around by Charles's friends and infused with the peculiar tone that the bourgeois were soon to adopt when talking about Marat and have preserved through the centuries; at least it has the merit of identifying the precise location and main lines of the quarrel: "M. Charles having cited the charlatanism of Marat in his physics lectures, the ruffian, armed with a long rapier, went to Charles's home and challenged him to single combat, but the other man replied that he could not measure swords except with people who were respected. Thereupon Marat drew, right in Charles's study, and the physicist picked the little man up by the collar, threw him to the floor, disarmed him, broke his sword, and had him turned out of the house."[8] The version given by Charles himself, in a letter to chief of police Lenoir, is substantially the same:

---

*Especially in December 1777, with a Comte de Zabielo, a Spanish gentleman who accused him of not curing his mistress fast enough. Marat tried to strangle him, and there was a general fracas in which the servants became involved and Marat had a fair amount of hair torn out.

†One thing is certain; since entering the service of the Comte d'Artois he has considered himself to be more or less a "gentleman" and has taken to wearing a sword in public.

He appeared at my home in the morning and, refusing to state his name or his grievances, injuriously provoked me, calling me by the most insulting appellatives. I leaped at him, breaking his drawn sword, and I have the stump of it at home; everyone agrees that it is a most dangerous and murderous weapon. Which of the two is the aggressor; he who tries to force the sword into one's hand for a matter of mere opinion, or he who, attacked in his home by an unknown person, seeks to avert his most doubtful intentions? . . . If I have permitted myself, in my lectures, the slightest personal invective against M. Marat, let him prove it and I stand ready to make public reparation. I have attacked his systems and I promise him that I shall do so again; but if one had to fight over that, it would be necessary to arm all Europe against him.[9]

(C) Marat's version; we have it complete, taken down live and in most succulent form by one Antoine Joachim Thiot, commissioner at the Châtelet de Paris:*

The year one thousand seven hundred and eighty-three on Saturday fifteenth March at eight-thirty in the evening, having been sent for we proceeded to the Rue du Sépulcre, Faubourg Saint-Germain, into a house of which Sr Bergeot, bourgeois of Paris, is principal tenant, where, having mounted to the first floor, we entered a back room looking onto a courtyard, and we found there, lying in a bed, Sr Jean-Paul Marat, physician of the life guard of Mgr le Comte d'Artois, dwelling in the house in which we now are.†

The said person lodged with us a complaint against Sr Charles, physics professor dwelling in this city, Place des Victoires, against one of his relations lodging with him, and against another individual whom the plaintiff believes to be the servant of Sr Charles, and told us that this morning around ten o'clock he went to the home of the said Sr Charles to have with him an explanation concerning the asseverations and reports conveyed to the plaintiff as having been uttered against him by the said Sr Charles, namely a parallel drawn between the plaintiff and Sr Comus, which made the plaintiff appear ridiculous and was highly offensive; that, having found the said Sr Charles in his rooms, the plaintiff explained to him the object of his call; that the said Sr Charles replied that he had no explanations to give him; that the plaintiff having resolved to withdraw, the said Sr Charles had taken advantage of the moment at which the plaintiff had turned away to leave, to strike him, before the plaintiff was able to take notice or avert it, a very violent blow of the fist upon his left temple and eye, which were damaged thereby; that the force of the blow did considerably bemuse the plaintiff who, having returned to his senses, found himself invested by two other men and by the said Sr Charles who tore his sword from its scabbard and broke it; that the plaintiff had then strenuously exerted himself to free himself from their grasp and,

---

*The somber château then standing on the site of the present-day Théâtre du Châtelet fulfilled something of the function of the Quai des Orfèvres today: it was the headquarters of the Paris police force.

†Another entrance, and the stables, gave onto the Rue de Bourgogne. "Sr" is an abbreviation for "Sieur."

succeeding in so doing, had retired and returned to his home with the help of a vehicle, with the intention of lodging his complaint, which he had been unable to do beforehand owing to the dazed condition in which he had been until the present moment, and the plaintiff having summoned us to examine the marks of the blow he had received, we observed that his left eye is red and inflamed, both beneath that eye and at the temple, with swelling in those parts.[10]

Charles, hence, emerges unbruised and the possessor of a piece of Marat's sword whereas the latter, poor fellow, has nothing but a big black eye. Much ado about precious little. There might have been more, for Jean-Paul is still fuming between his sheets and, the very next day, sends a friend to issue a regulation challenge to Charles:

> However much cause you may have given me to suspect your principles, Monsieur, I do not believe you coward enough to fail your word of honor, which you have given me so many times. You will find in me a generous enemy, who would blush to take his adversary by surprise and seek advantage from his superiority. To convince you of this, find but a second, and I shall find another. The bearer will tell you the rest.
>
> This day Sunday, at two o'clock.
>
> Marat.[11]

A duel? Now, now, boys! Alerted by his commissioner, and perhaps by Charles as well, Lenoir dispatches one of his staff to warn Marat that he wants to hear no more of such nonsense. This was the way in which private quarrels were being dealt with increasingly often: a veto from the chief of police removed the stain of dishonor from the belligerents. He probably summoned Marat to his office as well, just to calm him down a little. By the following Wednesday, at any event, Jean-Paul was sufficiently recovered to call on Lenoir. But, whether it was a deliberate misunderstanding or he unintentionally mistook the hour of his appointment, Jean-Paul contrives to emerge from even this incident with a renewed taste of bitterness in his mouth. The door is shut in his face. Without pausing for breath, he writes to Lenoir:

> Monsieur,
>
> I arrived at your door at the time stated to M. de Sessart. The Swiss informed me that M. Lenoir was ill and seeing no one. I having observed that I was expected, he looked at the list, did not find my name upon it, and refused to let me in.
>
> You know, Monsieur, what an outrage I suffered in the house of M. Charles. However unworthy it might appear to a man of honor, I was prepared to make you the sacrifice of my resentment. I therefore await your further instructions, and hasten to present to you the homage of the respect and attachment that I share with the public, and with which I have the honor to remain, Monsieur, your very humble and very obedient servant.

Marat, physician to the life guard of
Mgr le Comte d'Artois.
    This day Wednesday, at two o'clock.[12]

He knuckles under—or appears to. Why does Charles get all the breaks and
he all the knocks? It's enough to make him doubt the utility of a job with the
King's brother. He works himself into such a lather of resentment that he falls
ill again, neglects his duties, and earns a scowl from his "employers." Could
this mean the end of the natty Marat in satin and sword? Is he about to hit the
road again?

    Lenoir was well advised, however, to ensure the security of Alexandre
Charles: the physicist is on the eve of his greatest exploit. Momentarily abandoning electricity, he is about to prepare the launching of the first Parisian
balloon, and, supported by the entire town, he is counting on his superior
technique to beat those Montgolfier rubes in Annonay, if only by a few days.
This is no time to let him risk his neck over the temper tantrums of a Marat.

40

AUGUST 1783

The Child That Was Born Today

Marat having been sent, at least briefly, to the showers, the field is now clear
for one of those great matches that thrill the human race and mark its progress.
The stadium: enlightened France; the teams: in Paris, Alexandre Charles and
two industrialist brothers, the Roberts; in the Vivarais, the Montgolfiers—who
also have a powerful Parisian ally in the person of Réveillon. After all those
centuries and centuries of staring at the birds and mulling over the punishment
of Icarus, the rivalry between these two now makes the conquest of the air
seem like an endless back-stretch suddenly headed for dead-heat. There's more
at stake than which brow is going to wear the laurels; it's a question of rival
techniques. In opposition to the perilous tinkering of the Montgolfiers who
mean to send up their balloon with a ball of fire hooked underneath it, Charles
proposes to inflate his with a substance that can now be produced at will, after
ten years of chemical experimentation: hydrogen—fourteen times lighter than
air.

He's been working on it for a year, and he always insists that he had the balloon idea long before the Montgolfiers ever thought of it. Maybe so; but the only thing that matters in disputes like this is the stopwatch and the results. And the news of the flight at Annonay hits Charles in mid-June, just as he is preparing to put his theory into practice.

The first round goes to the Montgolfiers. All he can do now is lay on speed in an attempt to win the second before the Montgolfiers pile up a whole season of successful trials.

He accordingly mobilizes both the financial resources and the spirit of enterprise of the Robert brothers, his neighbors on the Place des Victoires. Paper manufacturers again? Not just. Small builder-industrialists rather, specialists in paper- and cloth-hung walls and ceilings, mainly for all those pretty homes that the aristocrats and *nouveaux riches* are causing to mushroom up out of the Paris soil. They're an inquisitive pair, the Roberts, always looking for new ways to do things. In 1782 they invented a process for dissolving rubber—that still rare and novel substance from the colonies—so as to render fabrics impermeable to gases. This is at the very moment when Charles was cudgeling his brains in search of an envelope less porous than the *Montgolfière,* which could hardly retain heavy smoke—and there was no conceivable collage of cloth and paper that would hold hydrogen. Long live the Robert brothers' "rubber varnish"! Without pausing to curse the successful trial at Annonay, Charles gets them to build "in less than twenty-five days [in July] a spherical globe of rubber-varnished silk measuring twelve feet and two inches in diameter" (much less high than wide, though; a sort of pear pointed at both ends) in the courtyard of their workshop-home that covered a good fifth of the Place des Victoires.[1]

This was the starting point in Paris, a very different setting from the meadow-square of Annonay: almost at the heart of the right bank, not far from the Louvre and Pont Neuf and just next to the gardens of the Palais Royal. Mansart designed the square a century ago* in the form of a truncated circle, to serve as a monumental setting for a statue of Louis XIV in the days when his sun was still making Europe sweat, before the clouds cast a chill over his reign. At the feet of the bronze giant whose beautiful legs are bare almost up to the buttocks, and whose upper parts are enfolded in classical draperies, stand enchained statues symbolizing the four nations he conquered: Germany, the Piedmont, Spain, and Holland.† All this solemnity is lapped and occasion-

---

*It was inaugurated, unfinished, in 1686.

†The statue, by Martin Desjardins, was torn down by the people on August 11, 1792; its first version is preserved in the museum at Versailles. It was replaced during the Restoration by Bosio's mediocre equestrian statue, which still stands today on the Place des Victoires; after many vicissitudes the statues of the "victories" themselves ended up in the Parc de Sceaux, where they have been since 1962.

ally flooded by the ebb and flow of the local ants, the little people crisscrossing the star paved with round stones on their way from the boulevards to Les Halles and the mansions in the Marais, an unending bedlam of cries and smells, "Get your pleasure here, ladies, get your pleasure [that is, gingerbread] here . . . "

The crowd gathers thicker than ever in the July and August heat outside the handsome sculpted façade of the Maison Robert et Robert where workmen strut about explaining what's going on behind the scenes although they don't really understand themselves what the savant and his assistants are up to. Actually, this is one of the most important physics experiments ever undertaken, as far as scale is concerned. Hydrogen has only just emerged from the laboratory, where it was handled cautiously and in tiny quantities; this time over a hundred cubic feet of it will be necessary. The process, like hydrogen itself, could hardly be simpler. You fill a barrel with iron filings, acid, and water. You let the gas produced by this mixture escape through a hole, and a leather tube carries it to the balloon. Through a second hole you pour water and sulphuric acid back into the barrel to replace the material consumed. But simple or not, it will take no less than one thousand pounds of iron and five hundred pints of sulphuric acid to inflate the sphere little by little, while simultaneously spraying the outside of the balloon with cold water to guard against its overheating. Since August 20, the object has been swelling steadily, its top can now be seen over the Roberts' courtyard wall, and the crowd has assumed such proportions that archers have had to be posted permanently in the Place des Victoires to keep it under control.

Forget the Montgolfiers, forget the Vivarais: now you're going to see some real action, and in Paris of course, where else could anything happen? Philippe de Chartres, the "prince of Paris," has unblushingly switched his allegiance from Blanchard to Charles, giving him the full benefit of his prestige. Snobbery? A desire to improve his public image by backing the right horse? Sincere interest in progress? A little of all three. Anyway, that puts him one up on the King, who, although personally interested in science, follows events from Versailles through the gazettes and police reports and therefore seems to have no part in the event. Philippe, meanwhile, has moved Faujas de Saint-Fond, the Vivarais-scholar-turned-Parisian-journalist, right into the Palais Royal, to the Café du Caveau, where he can keep in touch with everything that speaks or stirs in Paris. Faujas, in turn, has taken charge of the box office: every person purchasing a one-écu ticket* gets three seats in the Champ de Mars outside Paris, almost a league from the workshop, where preparations for the takeoff and solemn ascension are in full swing. Street-level Paris is soon in a flutter,

*3 livres, or 18–20 modern francs [$3.50–$4].

thanks to the button-and-trim sellers who start turning out balloons made of treated animal membrane for a few sous apiece. But the excitement has spread to every level of society: at Mousseaux, one late moonlit night after the footmen have been sent away, the Duc de Chartres distributes dozens "of little phalloid balloonlets" to his male and especially his female guests, "which, escaping and flying above the table, moved the whole company to mirth."[2] Everything is going their way; Charles and the Roberts can make their bid. They will have the same faithful eyewitness as the Montgolfiers did almost three months ago, oh, blessed Faujas de Saint-Fond, who will be the first man ever to see two holes made in the sky and tell the tale the next day. A premonition of the magnitude of the event gives his text a sensitivity that is still apparent two centuries later:

On August 24, 1783, at seven in the evening, the globe was straining against the ropes that held it back. The most stringent precautions were taken to ensure that no mishap should occur in the night: the tap was carefully shut, the key removed, and everyone withdrew content.

As may easily be imagined, on the next day, the 25th, people were fighting to see who should be first to visit the device. It was allowed by all to be in the finest condition: a little gas was introduced to repair the inevitable loss of the night, resulting either from imperceptible pores or needle holes that the elastic gum had not completely filled. It was weighed at six in the morning, after being freed from its bonds, and although no more than half full it lifted twenty-one pounds: the public experiment having been set for the 27th, it was not to be filled any further at that point, for fear of fatiguing it. Weighed again at nine in the evening it would lift only eighteen pounds, and had thus lost three pounds of its weight in fifteen hours.

On the 26th, the globe was visited at daybreak and pronounced to be in very good condition: it had lost inflammable air in the same proportion as the previous day. Work was resumed to increase the gas and at eight in the morning the balloon was removed from its harness and attached to thin ropes, and we had the pleasure of seeing it rise over one hundred feet.

The following day [that is, August 27] at two in the morning the transport of the fully inflated balloon began from the Place des Victoires to the Champ de Mars.

It was deposited on a stretcher standing ready to receive it. The same cords that had kept it suspended in the courtyard now held it steady, and the convoy began to move.

Nothing could be more singular than the sight of this balloon borne along in such a fashion, preceded by lighted torches, surrounded by a cortege, and escorted by a detachment of the watch, mounted and on foot! The nocturnal march, the form and capacity of the body being carried with such pomp and precaution, the silence reigning all round, the unwonted hour; all tended to confer upon this operation a uniqueness and mystery that were truly designed to impress anybody unprepared for the spectacle. The coachmen we met along the way were so awed that their first impulse was to pull up their vehicles and prostrate themselves [*sic*] humbly, hat in hand, all the while we passed before them.

At last, after traversing the Rues des Petits-Champs, de Richelieu, de Saint-Nicaise, the Carrousel, the Pont Royal, the Rue de Bourbon and the Invalides, the balloon came to the Ecole Militaire, where it was placed in the middle of the Champ de Mars in a specially prepared enclosure.[3]

Dawn. Make no mistake: this nocturnal procession, like none other, is the first wholly secular ceremony in the history of the world. On this day the people of Paris exchange the ritual of religion for an unintentional and unconscious communion with the private world of the erudite, who have become for the nonce their teachers of object lessons. "At the first light of day, work began to produce more gas; by noon the balloon was full enough to have assumed a beautiful shape; *but the conclusion of the operation was delayed until the people should be present, to give them an idea of how the gas was produced.*"* The heart skips a beat; here indeed is a world overturned, when the proprietors of culture open up their Pandora's box before they know what's in it themselves—"and ye shall see signs in the heavens"—but once that big ball has flown out over the head of Paris, nobody will ever be able to shut it again.

We're standing in the fields in which, less than thirty years ago, vegetables were still being grown by market gardeners. This was the pantry of Paris, and its name, Champ de Mars or field of Mars, the god of war, dates only from the end of the reign of Louis XV, when the architect Gabriel built the King's splendid military academy there, rising brilliant white and naked in newness out of the sand and mud. This is where the cadets are shut up to keep them safe from big-city temptation, for Paris is miles away, you need a carriage or horse to get there. And since space was needed for maneuvers, especially by the artillery, the huge truck garden between school and river was leveled and in its place were planted two quadruple rows of trees, still hardly more than saplings. This expanse, one of the biggest drill grounds in France, is right at the cadets' door, but it also exerts a growing attraction upon Parisians as a site for entertainments and festivities, when they can be bothered to make the trip. The ascension of August 27, 1783, initiates, although again no one was aware of the fact, the demilitarization of the Champ de Mars, "which was guarded on all sides; orders were given to facilitate the progress of vehicles and prevent accidents. At three o'clock, the Champ de Mars was being flooded with people; coaches were rolling up on all sides and soon could move only in single file. The river banks, the Versailles road, the amphitheater [formed by the hill] of Passy, were all garnished with a dense crowd of spectators. The military academy building and the Champ de Mars were thronged with a most brilliant and numerous assembly . . ."

*My italics. This mass demonstration, at long last scientific, is performed on the Champ de Mars less than seven years before the Fête de la Fédération.

One false note: the archers keep ruthlessly thrusting back a tall youngish man dressed in black, as provincials think is proper for great occasions in Paris. He's sputtering with indignation, all he can do is keep repeating:

"But I am Etienne Montgolfier! Etienne Montgolfier . . ."

He's "come up" from Annonay to receive the prize that the Academy of Sciences has just awarded him and his brother, and also to see his friend Réveillon and plan an experiment in the presence of the King at the earliest possible date. He thought he'd take the opportunity to watch his rivals' experiment, but he failed to buy his seat and has come without a ticket.

"Montgolfier? Who's Montgolfier?" inquire the guards in perfect good faith. To them, as to many of those present here, the Annonay ascension is completely unknown. The only people who have heard about it are the readers of a few gazettes. Most Parisians suppose they are about to witness the first balloon flight ever. Charles and the Roberts are the only names recognized here.

Some commentators—including Marat, of course—have tried to blame Montgolfier's eviction on the Robert brothers, which is absurd. Apart from the fact that they were utterly incapable of such shabby behavior, they're far too busy just now, all three of them, out in the center of the field, supervising the final stages of inflation and braving the dual dangers of asphyxiation and explosion. The acid fumes are searing their throats; the globe, inflated to capacity, must fly or burst. It's time to let go.

At five o'clock a cannon fired, announcing that the experiment was about to commence; it also served to alert the savants lodged on the terrace of the Garde-Meuble de la Couronne,* the towers of Notre Dame and the military academy, who were to employ instruments and calculations in their observations. The globe, released from the bonds restraining it, rose up, to the immense amazement of the spectators, so swiftly that in two minutes it had reached 488 fathoms of altitude; there it met a dark cloud, in which it was lost; the cannon was fired a second time to announce its disappearance, but it was soon seen emerging from the cloud. It reappeared for an instant at a very great height, and then vanished into other clouds.

The violent rain that began to fall just as the globe went up did not prevent it from climbing with extreme rapidity, and the experiment was enormously successful; it astonished everyone. The idea that a body leaving the earth could travel in space had something so admirable and sublime about it, it seemed to depart so far from ordinary laws, that the spectators were unable to quell an impression verging upon enthusiasm. Their satisfaction was so great that the elegantly attired ladies, their eyes fixed upon the globe, stood stockstill in the strongest and most abundant downpour, far more concerned to see so wonderful a sight than to protect themselves from the storm.

*[Furniture storehouse of the Crown—*Trans.*] Today, Ministry of the Navy, Place de la Concorde.

There were more than a hundred thousand that day, drinking the rain with mouths agape. For them nothing will ever be the same again. From this moment on the sky is no longer what it used to be.

Round two to Charles and the Roberts.

No sooner won than lost, or seriously compromised anyway. The capital, including its "little people," is, culturally speaking, a sort of island within France, even within Ile-de-France. Everybody has a finger in everything, everybody pretends to know all about everything especially when he knows nothing at all. The moment the balloon is out of sight the Parisians of all classes disperse, with that knowing air of people equal to any event. But the clamor of Paris sinks into the gutters of the boulevards and disappears. A short stagecoach-stop away and we're several centuries in arrears, in places where witches are still to be found, such as Bourg-la-Reine or Montmorency. It's haying time, the second crop, and the peasants are all out tying down their stacks and protecting their livestock from the stormy gusts, praying it won't be hail—their greatest dread in August before the grape harvest.

Now, it just so happens that the Champ de Mars balloon, driven by a fierce south wind, follows the course of the Seine, hardly passing over the city at all, and then heads determinedly northward. Its ascension had been too swift, and it had no valve to regulate the pressure so its surface must have torn almost at once, but it struggles bravely, helped along by rising air currents, and doesn't come down again, deflating as the tear increases, until three-quarters of an hour later. The vileins of Le Bourget (or "little burg"), Aunay, Villepinte, and La Pierre-Fitte are the first men and women ever to observe an unidentified flying object as they peer skyward to see which way the clouds are blowing. Nobody told them to expect it. What sort of devilment is this? The monster speeds past, close to the Senlis road, and finally lands, four leagues from Paris, smack in the middle of the town of Gonesse and its "considerable market"[4]—a few feet from St. Peter's church, in fact, whose belltower, twice rebuilt after being struck by lightning, is firmly glued to the flank of a little twelfth-century nave.

The village, like so many others, has grown up around it any-which-way, in a flatland so fertile that it produces the best wheat in the whole Paris region, thanks to which, in conjunction with the pure water of the Crould that flows across the plain, Gonesse bread has been famous since the fourteenth century and is bought up by the stewards of the rich before its dough is even kneaded. Taller, larger, and older by a century than both belltower and bread are the stolid and perpetually renovated buildings of the Gonesse cloth manufacture (which clothed the Valois kings), still employing the local women. Between the church and the manufacture stand five or six trees, their leaves already yellowing, and some farms with thatched roofs to house the most notable of the fifteen-hundred-odd widely scattered inhabitants.

They're terror stricken.

The huge thing, still half spherical in shape and palpably alive because twitching and making unpredictable leaps and bounds, can only be a danger of the worst possible order: the supernatural. Better hail, a thousand times better! But why has the Lord, or Satan—and how can we tell which—visited it upon us instead of making it fall on the people in Goussainville, our neighbors who make such rotten bread?

Perhaps it is to relieve an unconscious grudge against God, or perhaps it is their fierce desire to drive out the devil: whatever the motive, every man in Gonesse is galvanized into action by the falling balloon. A few, those who were working nearby, have already come running pitchfork in hand. Others —those who have the right to shoot game on their land (far less numerous), hurry home to fetch their guns. But how should we approach the thing? The priest is summoned to exorcise it; who knows if it won't fly away again? The clergyman, every jot as terrified as his parishioners, edges cautiously from tree to tree muttering sacred charms and brandishing his aspergillum. They keep shoving him from behind, but he won't come close enough to the monster to get a single drop of his holy water actually in contact with it; so how will it ever be overcome? One of the armed men finally plucks up his courage and fires a round of buckshot, producing such a hiss from his victim that everyone in the crowd falls flat on his face and starts reciting the act of contrition. The balloon, leaking gas through twenty fissures, falls flattest of all in the end: proof that mumbo-jumbo is not the only means of casting out the devil. The crowd surges forward, the spoils are shredded with blows of spades and pitchforks, and everybody's conviction that he's performing a good deed is bolstered by the sickening smell of gas. People begin firing their guns in all directions, even the dogs join in. A few minutes later, all that is left of the balloon of Charles and the Robert brothers are a few shapeless ribbons tied to a horse's tail and dragged over the countryside. The poor inventors don't hear about it until next day, after scouring the area for traces of their contraption.

It'll take them weeks to build another one, an improved version if possible; you can't make that amount of gas-proof cloth in a day. Etienne Montgolfier, meanwhile, having received an official apology to soothe his injured pride, is hard at work at Réveillon's and, with the extra time in his favor, may well recover his lead.[5]

So in the end, it's a tie.

Paris and Versailles, therefore, have more thrills in store; but it occurs to the authorities that they ought perhaps to give some warning to all those poor dumb brutes who are not among their happy few if they don't want the next lot of balloons shot down like mallards. Bertier de Sauvigny,* intendant of Paris, orders a magnificent poster to be printed in extra-bold-face type on four sheets that could be posted side by side in the designated niches, distributed in brochure form in public places, or (most importantly) read aloud by the priests after the sermon. This is the first "public notice" concerning a scientific event ever written, and it is written in such haste (and backdated) that the incident at Gonesse is added in a footnote at the bottom of one of one page before being officially announced at the end of the text:[6]

From Paris, August 27, 1783.

NOTICE TO THE PEOPLE
Concerning the elevation into the air of Balloons or
Globes; the object in question rose in Paris
on the said August 27, 1783, at five o'clock in the
afternoon, from the Champ de Mars.

A Discovery has been made that the Government has deemed proper to bring to the Public Notice, to forestall the Terrors that it might occasion among the People. By calculating the Difference in Weight between that Air which is called *inflammable* and the Air of our Atmosphere, it has been found that a Balloon filled with this inflammable Air should rise of its own accord toward the Sky, and stop only when the two Airs should be in Equilibrium; which can only be at a very great Height. The first Experiment was made at Annonay in the Vivarais by the brothers MONTGOLFIER, inventors: a Globe of Cloth and Paper five hundred Feet in circumference and filled with inflammable Air rose of its own Accord to a Height that it has not been possible to reckon. The same Experiment has just been repeated in Paris (on August 27 at five o'clock sharp in the Evening) in the presence of an infinite number of persons: a Globe of Taffeta coated with elastic Gum, thirty-six feet around, rose from the Champ de Mars into the Clouds, where it was lost to Sight: it was driven by the Wind in a northeasterly Direction, and it is impossible to predict what Distance it will be borne.† Repetitions of this Experiment are planned, with much larger Globes. Anyone who shall perceive such Globes in the sky, presenting the Appearance of a darkened Moon, must therefore be advised that, far from being a terrifying Phenomenon, this is nothing but a Machine, made in every case of Taffeta or of light Cloth covered with Paper, which can cause no Harm and for which Applications useful to the Needs of Society can be anticipated one day.

*Massacred by the populace on the Place de Grève on July 22, 1789. Readers are reminded that the intendant of a province, acting in the King's name, had a wide assortment of sometimes unlimited powers and was something like what would later be called the "prefect" of a *département* [a sort of governor, but subject to a central authority—*Trans.*].

†"It has since been learned that it fell three-quarters of an hour later at Gonesse, four leagues from Paris" [footnote in the original text].

The *Aerostatic Sphere* or flying Globe, approximately twelve Feet in diameter and weighing twenty-five to thirty Pounds, was abandoned to the Winds at the Champ de Mars on August 27, 1783, at five in the Evening in rainy Weather. It is constructed of gummed Taffeta, closely sealed on the Surface so that the exterior Air shall not penetrate it. It is filled with inflammable Air, a Vapor produced by a Dissolution of iron Filings with vitriolic Oil. In rising, it described a parabolic Curve from South to North, and rose very swiftly in the Air until its Disappearance; and it fell at Gonesse that same day at six o'clock.

Read and approved, September 3, 1783,
DE SAUVIGNY.

One evening that same week, Goodman Franklin is entertaining a few of his friends at Passy. His guests are not in the best of spirits: they are bemoaning the lamentable conclusion of so beautiful an experiment and the brutishness of the people. One of them gives voice to the question at the back of everybody's mind:

"But really, when you come down to it, what is the *use* of these balloons?"

Franklin, who is feeling less and less like cocktail party conversations these days, looks up from his plate.

"What is the *use,* my friend, of the child that was born today?"

MARAT

41

JULY 1783

A Crime to Believe in God

Marat's got his back to the wall and nowhere to turn. His fracas with Charles has rung an alarm bell that nobody else can hear, not even Mme de L'Aubespine who may still be sleeping with him, although less and less often; but if one had to listen to a man's moaning and groaning as well . . . His friends, ill-at-ease in his irritable company, begin sidestepping. His position in the Artois household is hanging by a thread. He had pinned all his hopes—too many, that is—on winning the Rouen Academy's prize for his *Mémoire sur l'électricité.* He won it; and now? Nothing and more nothing. People are talking about him a little more, true, but only to make unfavorable comparisons between him and Charles, and Lavoisier, and all the other savants who "know how to behave." And since the springtime has drawn every eye to the balloon of that abhorred Charles, Marat may now be feeling more restless and dissatisfied with himself than ever before.

His one resource in such cases is to shoulder his pack and move on—Europe's eternal seafarer. They think he's hooked on his Parisian candybox, do they? My eye! He's done Switzerland, Bordeaux, London, Edinburgh, Paris . . . Why not give Spain a whirl? Anything would be better than sitting and rotting here.

One of his new friends—those friends he conquers with love at first sight, like Brissot—another cosmopolitan, named Philippe-Rose [sic] Roume de Saint-Laurent, happens to have just left Paris for Madrid, where, with the approval of the royal, and inquisitorial, authorities, he means to set up an academy of sciences, something totally unheard of in that country. Was it he who seduced Marat with the lure of a share in the scheme, maybe even the leading role? Number-One scientist in Spain, instead of number thirty or lower in Paris? Marat starts dreaming again, he can see himself already. Roume's error may have been well intended, but one ought never to inflict the torture of hope on people one cares for. Jean-Paul is in such a hurry that he starts badgering his friend for news almost before the man has time to reach his destination. He forgets what an ordeal it is, traveling on those roads. But when the fever's on you . . .

From Marat to M. de Saint-Laurent, in Madrid, June 2, 1783:

> The almanach* tells me, Monsieur, that it is but five weeks since you have left us, yet it seems already several years to me. I do not know whether those who have learned to esteem you can ever forget you; but I find that the void you leave behind is not easy to fill. I should feel it yet more keenly had I not the hope of seeing you soon again.
>
> Since your departure, Monsieur, I have made an interesting discovery; the subject of it is the insensitivity to color of certain individuals, a phenomenon that has always seemed somehow prodigious. This article comes into my major work on light, and you will assuredly be one of the first to receive it.
>
> If I were to tell you, Monsieur, that I am not impatient to hear from you, you would not believe me, and you would be quite right; therefore do not keep me waiting too long.[1]

If we forget the Sardinian in Marat, we will never understand his perpetual impatience. It always has to be everything right away and all the way, the instant the comet passes . . . This time, at least, his confidence wasn't too badly misplaced. Philippe Roume (really too much, it would be, to call him Rose) is a likeable Creole who was born in Grenada before the Treaty of Paris, in

*He would have written "calendar" today.

the days when the island still belonged to France. His father, German in origin, was a planter; his mother was related to the La Rochefoucaulds. He's forty now, the age at which boredom in the colonies suddenly becomes unbearable; and he decided, in the last year of the recent war, to use the Franco-Spanish alliance as an argument in his attempt to persuade the King of Spain to adopt a spectacular plan for the "enlightened" colonization of Trinidad, where he had spent some time studying. He came to France first, in search of recommendations to the Spanish authorities. While he was there, the signature of the peace surprised but did not discourage him. During the best part of a year in Paris he sought out everything worth seeing and hearing, including Marat's lectures; listening to them, the utopist in him found a companion soul. Jean-Paul's petulance and fierce convictions subjugated this mild visionary.[2] And what better friend could Marat acquire than one whose presence would revive his chimaeras? Roume, having formed some connections in the Spanish embassy, leaves bearing letters of introduction to Count Galvez, minister for the Indies (West, of course). And it was at the embassy that he first heard talk of this vague scheme for a science academy* . . . More than enough to send Marat into a tailspin of breathless anticipation.

On June 19 his temperature drops a few degrees. He has received a letter from Roume, written almost upon arrival; in it his friend asks his opinion of the experiments in magnetism that Mesmer, now back in Paris,† is resuming with ever greater success among the curiosity seekers. The reply shows that, in comparison with Mesmer, Marat regards himself as a *real* scientist:

> I have received, with much pleasure, my affectionate friend, the letter you sent on May 30. I was relying upon direct news from you and one must know you ill indeed to doubt your word. In the exertions that you have been good enough to make and will in future be good enough to make on my behalf I recognize the tender concern of friendship; and as I am well-acquainted with the negotiator's skill I dare trust to their success. It can never come too soon; in the meantime I am devoting (following your advice) a part of my time to the study of the Spanish language.
>
> I shall look into the matter of M. Mesmer and give you a full account. But it is not to be done in a hurry. You know how I love to examine things, and examine them with care before pronouncing myself . . .

*Roume got nowhere with Trinidad; all the French administration was prepared to do was "lend" him to Spain for a term as commissioner general of Tobago. Returning to France in 1790, he is appointed to a high position in Santo Domingo, where his behavior is on the whole courageous and relatively revolutionary, as regards his support of the Negroes during the time of trouble. He retires under the Consulate and dies in Paris in 1804.

†Since March 1783; his break with the Court of France was not final.

As for me, pray remember, dear friend, that only the keenest friendship can
be the price of that which I have dedicated to you, and do not forget that I love
men only as I esteem them.
     Marat
Paris, this June 19 1783.
There is or will be something about me in the Spanish papers, especially the *Correo
litterario.* [3]

Sure enough, he really does mean to go. His trunks may be half-packed
already. "It was as though Marat felt that his greatest opportunity as scientist
had come and he must grasp it at any cost; even his fierce independence gave
way before it:* he was ready to compromise, to play ball with enlightened
despotism and academism . . . Marat had never before shown, nor would he
ever again, such eagerness to present the most conformist and reassuring
image possible of himself."[4]

The tone he adopts in his very next letter borders on self-caricature, but
that's because he's so desperate. In a century in which everybody, from Voltaire to Diderot to Franklin, has had to crawl in order to achieve even a small
degree of self-fulfillment, are we to imagine Marat not crawling, or half
crawling, toward his Spanish pipe dream? Was it supreme cunning? A moment
of semi-alienation? In later years his unconditional admirers squirm when they
read what follows here. We should remember, however, that at this stage in
his life, Marat was a sincere deist:

To Roume, on July 20, 1783:

Nothing, I make no doubt, could be keener than your zeal for the glory of Spain,
your new homeland. I see with acute pleasure that I might also devote my talents
to the progress of the arts and sciences in a nation that I venerate. But, Monsieur,
my joy is not wholly unmixed, when I think that the ambassador who is instructed
to seek information on my account may well hear the clamors of our *philosophes*
for whom it is a crime to believe in God. You know how fiercely they resent all
who, like myself, have refused to swell the ranks of their criminal sect and
courageously dared to do battle with their pernicious errors. And you also know
how skillfully they can denigrate their adversaries. I flatter myself, it is true, that
the ambassador will see through them now, if he has not judged them already.
But nothing reassures me so much as the profound discernment of M. le Comte
de Florida-Blanca. How fortunate if, in his efforts to ascertain the habits of a man
of letters who has spent his life traveling in his own library and associated solely
with friends distinguished by their piety and virtue, the illustrious minister would
seek his information from such sources. How many respectable ecclesiastics I
could offer as recommendations! . . .

My heart calls me to Spain, as you know, for, apart from the reasons deriving
from my personal inclination, it is sweet to cultivate men whose natural endow-

*Comment by Jean Massin.

ments make them capable of the most beautiful productions of the human spirit.

Farewell, Monsieur, be assured of all the pleasure I shall soon feel, to renew in person the expression of my admiration and devotion.[5]

Florida-Blanca* . . . The minister for foreign affairs in name, but in fact the "principal minister" of the end of Charles III's reign. The man who's running Spain these days, and toward whom the weathervanes of reformist hopes are starting to turn. Enlightened despotism has been dying for ten years now, ever since all the ministers who personified it in Europe were removed from office. People are still vaguely hoping for something from Catherine II or Joseph II or his brother the Grand Duke Leopold of Tuscany, or possibly from the King of the North up there, Gustavus III of Sweden. They say Frederick the Great is dying. In France, it's been all over with Louis XVI since he gave Necker the boot. So this new man on the far side of the Pyrenees, of humble extraction despite his flamboyant title, who lays out canals and roads and promotes agricultural societies as his only means of fertilizing the Spanish soil, who intends to build the country's first observatory and design a botanical garden in Madrid, is beginning to be regarded by "informed" people as the man of the Spanish awakening—when in reality he is the man of the bank of Saint-Charles de Cabarrus,† whose tentacles are creeping north, via Bordeaux, toward the great French and Swiss money manipulators. What better way to make his reputation?[6] And if innocents like Roume or Marat imagine that he's working for the good of the Spanish people when what he's really doing is judiciously encouraging investment among the wealthy (and it was high time!), why, so much the better, his world prestige will shine the brighter for it. He is therefore inclined to lend as benign an ear to Roume's proposals as he would to any other request put to him in homage to his liberalism. But not before making a careful security check concerning the degree of orneriness or servility of potential colleagues, whom he is not at all anxious to see transformed into explosives in his country. Whence the need for Marat to possess himself in patience. The Spanish police don't like to be hurried.

*Don José-Antonio Monino (1729–1808), Count of Florida-Blanca (also written Fiorida-Bianca, and some French called him Floride-Blanche). Despite the long series of plots and conspiracies against him—directed at his authoritarianism rather than any mild "reformist" tendencies, he remains "principal minister" until the death of Charles III in 1788 and is not dismissed by Charles IV until 1792. In his old age, he takes part in the wars against Napoleon.

†Father of Theresa, the future Mme Tallien.

42

SUMMER 1783

The Greatest Enterprise

It just happens to be an image of Florida-Blanca that the artist who may be mankind's greatest photographer is preparing for posterity in the summer of 1783,* the year in which Francisco Goya becomes one of the foremost painters of all time. The minister "is standing in a large room, almost every feature of which proclaims his importance. On the table stands a large clock, showing how precious his time is; the table is piled high with maps, books, documents, scrolls; letters have fallen to the floor. Florida-Blanca is moving forward wearing an absent expression that must be habitual to him, his back to a secretary, who follows with an anxious air . . ."[1] "One spends whole weeks vainly seeking an opportunity to speak to him," moaned the Russian ambassador, "and when at last one thinks one has seized the favorable moment, he suddenly breaks off the conversation on some idle pretext, and again advises you to address him in writing! . . ."

Where an ambassador fails, a painter may succeed in pinning a man down for a few hours. Monino likes the idea of being immortalized "in his resplendent suit, a slender silhouette gleaming with the reflections thrown by the satin cloth, glittering with gold, his chest crossed by a wide band, a star pinned upon his breast. His narrow face, compressed at the temples by the white wig, emaciated and as though consumed from within, is dominated by the tautness in his round, wide-open eyes, as though nothing must be allowed to escape them." A determined impassiveness emanates from the entire painting. A deliberate personification of a sphinx. "The count may be the only person here whose character is difficult to grasp," went on the Russian ambassador, decidedly a psychologist; "no one can know him, so great a master is he of the art of reigning."

He doesn't even pretend to notice the plebeian kneeling before him to present a portrait at which he cannot be troubled to look—his own!

*Impossible to determine exactly when; Goya's biography contains very few and very approximate dates.

Goya repays the snub by repainting the scene at a second level, and giving free rein to his vision in the portrait we see as though in a series of mirrors.

The artist is no peasant, though a disheveled man, already heavy for his thirty-seven years,* "retiring behind his painting, which he holds before him like a shield. His profile is irregular, ugly, with a lumpy brow, a large nose both protruding and thick, his eyes trapped by heavy lids," caricatured by himself in a "piteously menial" posture. But despite his efforts to accentuate his roughhewn side, Francisco Goya is no rube. His father was only a gilder, but his mother, although poor as Job's daughter, came from the lesser nobility of Saragossa. He grew up in proud destitution. "His father died intestate, having nothing to bequeath." Alley-way fistfights, fruit stolen from trees, lessons with the Scolopian brothers (popular appellation of teachers belonging to the *Scolae pie* [religious schools—*Trans.*], which still exist) among "flocks of children led through our streets by a Scolope armed with his stick . . . The little one is humble, they say, when they want to praise one of their charges, meaning that he has already contracted the monastic prostration, fawning or, if you prefer, inveterate hypocrisy." A sentence by Cabarrus,† who, man of wealth though he was, was bringing up his daughter Theresa to assume a very different attitude.

Francisco barely learned to read and write the most common words, but the Scolopian insects** did manage to inject the venom of superstition into him: he always draws a cross at the beginning of his letters and invokes the Lord, the saints, and especially the Virgin del Pilar, patroness of Saragossa, at crucial moments. And in the very marrow of his bones, he retains some sort of respect for authority, whatever its nature, even when it frames him inside his own canvases.

He started painting at twelve, more seriously at fifteen. It was the only thing he could do at all and at first he did it clumsily: bad copies of Velasquez—but they taught him about portraiture; religious paintings on church walls‡—first down-and-out in Saragossa, then down-and-out in Madrid, trying to find a style of his own. Painting in Spain had ceased to exist, it was the void, horse-manure, *nada,* nothing! To Rome on foot, al-

*Goya was born in an extremely poor village, Fuendetodos, on March 30, 1746; he dies in exile in Bordeaux on April 15, 1828.

†[Spanish financier, minister of finance (1752–1810), and father of one of the most spectacular of *merveilleuses* (like *incroyables,* rich youths affecting extraordinary dress and speech and manners in immediate post-Revolutionary France), who married, in turn, the Marquis de Fontenay, Tallien (instigator of 9 Thermidor), and the Comte de Caraman—later Prince de Chimay. —*Trans.*]

**[*Scolopendra:* a kind of carnivorous, poisonous centipede.—*Trans.*]

‡Seeing them again fifty years later he implored, "Don't say it was I who painted that!"

most a beggar, going back to the source. Then Saragossa again, a few academic creations and a long, superficially friendly association with the Aragonese Francisco Bayeu, the fashionable official artist and "King's chamber painter," if you please. Well, if you're going to play that game, you might as well go the whole hog: Bayeu was moaning about his responsibilities—that is, "two sisters, one a virgin, who is attempting to better her condition but to whom he cannot give a dowry." Who cares; Goya marries the colorless Josefa Bayeu, but without renouncing the satyr in him. Before, during, and after Josefa he hurls himself upon every willing female who comes his way, meanwhile producing numerous progeny *via* his wife. He bothered no more about her than about the rest; in the end, he is really married to his work, and tramples underfoot anything that might prevent him from doing it, including, on occasion, his own conscience.

In the spring of 1783 he's still in his prostrate phase, like Marat, but in an even lowlier posture and for longer; his position is similar to that of Mozart in relation to the Prince-Archbishop of Salzburg or Diderot in relation to Catherine II, only worse. But he can see light ahead, he dimly senses that he may be able to stand up straight before too long. "I have some twelve to thirteen thousand *reales* a year; with that I live as content as the most prosperous of men."* His first son was born in 1777. In 1779, thanks to Bayeu, he was presented to the king: at that time his imagination could reach no higher than the marble staircases of the Prado, brand-new, damp, a chillier Versailles. At the end of row upon row of chambers and row upon row of guards, he sees three puppets in black, gold, and silver, like cutouts from a deck of cards: little old King Charles III, wasting away, and his son Don Carlos, Prince of the Asturias, a flabby giant on the arm of his young wife, the former Princess of Parma, with embers in her eyes and a body freely offered at every movement,† notwithstanding an excess of cosmetics and a lantern jaw.

"I kissed their hands; it was the greatest happiness of my life. Never, you may believe me,[2] could I have aspired to more as far as my work was concerned. Shall I tell you how pleased the king was, and even more their highnesses? Thanks be to God! I did not deserve so much honor, nor did my work."

Goya, 1783 . . . The hyperbole of which some great men have been guilty is too harshly judged by people who forget where they started out in life. This one is just completing the long, steep climb from Fuendetodos to Madrid and

*Or 3,000 livres in Louis XVI's day, or 18,000 modern francs [$3,600].

† In 1788 they become King Charles IV and the famous Queen Dona Maria, mistress of the brigadier Godoy and many, many more; Napoleon forces them to abdicate at Bayonne.

cannot be expected to know that kings' palaces are not the end of the line, that the road to infinity, after traversing even them, goes on.

Besides, he gives one the impression, like Marat, that he's beginning to fight for his head before the bit's actually in his mouth. He went back to Saragossa laden with commissions, long enough for a brief triumph; but he's still waiting for the promised advance before starting work on his first truly original creation: a series of frescoes on the life of St. Bernardino for the new Franciscan convent in Madrid. He returns to the capital and lays siege to the financial backers of the project, who include the king and Florida-Blanca:* "The time has come for the greatest enterprise yet offered to Madrid in the field of painting." In the meantime, to soften up the principal minister and keep himself occupied, he paints the portrait in which Goya begins to peep through Goya.

But oh, the patience it takes!

"Goya, we'll see about that later," says the minister, dismissing him without a word of compliment. Maybe the artist's focus was a shade too sharp after all . . . And Goya finds himself back at square one, without another appointment, awaiting not only further instructions regarding the Franciscan convent but also payment for Florida-Blanca's portrait. "Friend, there is no news. At this point my relations with M. Monino are more nonexistent than before I painted his portrait . . . If nothing comes from that side, all is lost; and when one has had such high hopes before, the disappointment is all the more intense . . ."

Goya and Marat. There was one link this year, and only one, between these two men of the same generation: both were waiting for a favorable wind from the most petrified monarchy of their age to waft them to the recognition they deserved. One likes to imagine a meeting between them, to wonder what portraits each would have painted of the other. But Marat never does get to Spain and quickly loses his illusions. Could he have stayed more than a week in this land of Inquisition and indigence? Goya hangs on, finally prises open the palace doors and for a few years becomes the official painter of the Spanish Bourbons. But not for their greater glory.

*The frescoes in the cupola of San Francisco el Grande are still a moving witness to the first flowering of a prodigious genius.

MARAT

43

NOVEMBER 1783

The Revolution That I Have Begun

Meanwhile, physicist Charles has gained his fame, even if it was slightly deflated by the Gonesse pitchforks, and Marat has again been stifled by the silence of the powers-that-be, like the slow-motion closing of a burial-vault door. The nausea of France, or his slice of it anyway, is rising in his gorge.

He keeps trying; Roume can never say he didn't do everything that could be done on his side. He makes appeal after appeal to the "general-judge-at-arms"* to obtain a coat of arms and hence a patent of nobility that he imagines would be useful to him in dealings with the Spanish grandees. But nobody seems to be in much of a hurry there either; of course, getting anything out of civil servants in the summertime . . . Jean-Paul writes to the judge-at-arms:

> Have you received my letter? If you have, I hope you will not refuse me a coat of arms, seeing how certain is the nobility of my family both in Spain and in France. The position I now occupy, which can but improve through the confidence placed in me by Monseigneur,† makes the matter one of some interest to Society. It is honorable for the State that the origins of a servant of its princes should be established by firm written evidence, which I have duly supplied.
>
> J. P. Mara, called Marat[1]

He doesn't seem to have received any reply, or at least any favorable reply . . . He did take the precaution of putting the original spelling of his name first; but looking for the arms of a few odd Maras lost in the dust of centuries in God knows which province of the empire of Charles V was like looking for a needle in a haystack.

On September 17 he tries Aranda, the Spanish ambassador, in response to requests for further particulars from Florida-Blanca. He attempts to make his letter as personal as possible; after all, Aranda could be seen as the very

*A position created by Louis XIII in 1615 to satisfy a desire expressed by the nobility at the previous assembly of the Estates-General; he was responsible for everything relating to quarterings and coats of arms and disputes arising in connection with them. He issued certificates on request.

†He means the confidence of the Comte d'Artois, which he is in fact steadily losing.

essence of a minister in disgrace for liberalism, or at least as a progressive mind, and he can still serve as *deus ex machina* in his country. The French are intrigued by his aplomb, his influential aura, his love affairs, and his gossip; he intimates that when it comes to the crunch in Spain he'll be the one to bail the country out. Marat's letter to him hazards a knowing wink:

Monsieur le Comte,

I have the honor to send you the memorandum you have desired, with a summary of my views.

The plan to devote the fruit of my physics discoveries to Spain did not originate with me but with M. de Saint-Laurent, who is ideally fitted to appreciate the revolution that I have begun in the sciences. I am charmed to have this opportunity to do justice to his zeal for the glory of his new country . . . He asked if I would consent to remove to Spain in the event that the government offered me suitable advantages. I replied that no more pleasant fate could befall me than to be summoned to work for the progress of the sciences in a nation whose natural qualities I knew well . . .

M. de Saint-Laurent, aware of some part of the sacrifices I have made to advance the sciences, and knowing that my research has been interrupted only for want of sufficient means to prosecute them successfully, has indicated to me that the munificence of the King of Spain would supplement my fortune and that I should receive a personal treatment worthy of the grandeur of the monarch and the services that I should render to the nation.

As he desired a definite object, I informed him that the proposals made to me* were for 24,000 livres per annum while active and 12,000 livres upon retirement,† traveling expenses paid. I told him I should be content with the same advantages now; and to prove to him that money was not my principal object I left him free to negotiate with the government and gave him my word to agree with whatever should be decided. I thought M. de Saint-Laurent had made use of the authorization I gave him, but the request that Your Excellency made to me this morning on behalf of your sagacious minister of foreign affairs proves the contrary; I therefore have the honor to assure you that my sentiments in this respect are unaltered.

You have required me, Monsieur le Comte, to explain my position, and I have done so; but I beg of Your Excellency kindly to inform M. le Comte de Florida-Blanca that I have no pretension to set any conditions, that I know the equity of the Spanish government, and that I shall agree to the price it will deem appropriate to set upon my services.

The principal object of my desires would be, under the protection of a great king, to become a benefactor to young people intending to work in the sciences, and I make bold to assure Your Excellency that I am capable of sparing them many years of laborious, tedious, and sterile study. If the government of Spain deigns

*According to Marat, by Gustavus III of Sweden the previous year; to my knowledge no trace of this offer exists.

†144,000 modern francs while working and 72,000 in pension [$28,800 and $14,400].

to approve my views, my happiness will be complete; I shall have the glory of cultivating the fortunate talents of a youth that is destined, in its maturity, to be admired by all of learned Europe.

In addition to a full course of national studies in the exact sciences, I shall offer a method for bringing the lenses used in astronomy and navigation and all optical instruments in general to the highest degree of perfection. It is thus in the power of Spain to appropriate a considerable branch of commerce, which England has been compelled to abandon for want of the proper kind of optical glass, following the death of the only artist who manufactured it. I also have in my portfolio various other objects of equal benefit to commerce and agriculture; not to mention the advantages that would accrue from medical electricity, which has been almost universally abandoned to empiricism, and which cannot be turned to any good account save by a practitioner who is also a physicist, applying it to the treatment of divers afflictions . . .

At the end of the first year I shall be able to bring out half of the national course of study, and in another few years I shall produce it in full, in a form as perfected as pen can make it. And in order that the nation may the sooner reap the fruits of my waking hours I shall give all my time to my work, so honored shall I be to be attached to its service and so determined to devote to its glory the few years of strength that Providence may be pleased to grant me. However considerable this sacrifice may appear, it will not surprise Your Excellency on the part of a man who has forgone fortune, youth, pleasures, and repose for the sake of his reputation and his aspiration to enlarge the domain of human knowledge. These are facts known to all; they shall be the warranty of my zeal and of the purity of my intentions.

You may, Monsieur le Comte, have wished for the power to read the human heart; judge now of mine, with the profound discernment with which nature has endowed you and which is so highly praised by the public voice.

I am, with profound respect, Monsieur le Comte, Your Excellency's very humble and obedient servant,

Marat.[2]

September 26. Hope springs afresh. Did he get some word from the embassy that his letter had been received, or perceive some ambiguous sign from Aranda between two doors? He writes to Roume as though the final decision were just around the corner, almost digging a sword in Roume's side in his haste to remove to Madrid. He asks Charles III for a first payment of twenty thousand livres* for a trip to London to hire copper and glass workers for Spain. Weren't there any in France? He reports two medical cures resulting from his treatment by electricity, one of which restored the sight of a M. de l'Isle who had been blind for thirty-three years. "But it is in Spain that I desire to deploy the resources of this remedy, which is so admirable when administered by a physicist."[3]

*12,000 modern francs [$2,400].

And then another month and more of silence. The shroud falls. Letter to Roume on November 6. Paris is drifting in an All Hallows' fog. Marat feels as though he had been marooned a thousand leagues from the sun of the Estremadura. In this letter bitterness prevails:

> I believed, my friend, that your and my affairs were concluded but I now see that for my part, I still have need of patience. I desire that yours may not have so long a trial to undergo. You tell me that fresh information has been forthcoming. I cannot conceive what it could be. In any event, I flatter myself that I shall be able to sustain the severest scrutiny, although I should have thought myself sufficiently well-reputed among the public to be dispensed with any. You further tell me, on behalf of Monsieur le Comte de Florida-Blanca, that my business will be finished before the 15th of this month, and it is now the 6th, but M. le C. d'Aranda has not said a word to me . . . You urge me to be patient, dear friend, out of consideration for the importance of the matter, for the glory of Spain, and for my own. My own triumph will not fail; but I have set my happiness upon bringing the exact and useful sciences to the highest point they may attain. To succeed, I need the protection of a great king, and all my wishes would be fulfilled could I devote my talents to the welfare of a nation that I love and respect.
>
> Continue what you have begun, therefore, and do not leave the task unfinished.[4]

November 20. It's all over. Roume has notified Marat that about twenty unfavorable reports have reached the Court of Spain, the outcome of the investigation begun in the spring. Denunciations from academicians and scholars, hack writers, and, no doubt, the people in the royal bookshop who know all about his subversive publications. Marat-savant and Marat-inventor are being led to a slaughterhouse at the end of a cul-de-sac; and indeed they will never exist, except for the most diligent of his biographers. But when a man is over forty, isn't it too late for him to become anything except himself? Why has he been pottering around trying to make politico-social pamphleteering mix with scientific research? A man must be One or not at all; no more of the multiple Marat. The forty-one page (!) letter he writes his friend Roume that day, and sends as a cover for a voluminous file containing forty-seven items offered as evidence of his labors during the past ten years, might be taken as a last-ditch attempt; but the tone is so despairing that it sounds more like a bleak summing-up of a lost cause, the Marat nobody knows, or a funeral oration for the only part of himself he had time to bury. It cannot be quoted in full, of course, but here are a few of its louder outcries, the howls of a beast that has been dealt its death blow:

So it is true, my friend, that calumny has flown from Paris to the Escorial to blacken me in the minds of a great king and an illustrious patron.* Twenty letters, you say, have portrayed me in the inkiest of hues.

But what are my detractors? Need one enquire? Jealous cowards, whose multitudinous rabble is forever conniving to lay me low; modernist philosophers, cloaked in anonymity or pseudonyms to defame me. Shall I never come to an end of their doings, the result of my having declined academic honors for the sake of truth, of my having advanced useful knowledge, restored to life a great number of my brothers deemed incurable, defended the cause of virtue? My heart rebels at the thought. And yet I shall not protest against the sacred edicts of Providence; and whatever the lengths to which my adversaries may go, never will they bring me to repent of having been a decent man . . .

From childhood I have cultivated literature, and with some little success, I may say. Hardly had I reached the age of eighteen when our so-called *philosophes* made various attempts to win me over to their cause. The aversion to their principles that had been instilled in me turned me from their company and protected me from their fell teachings. That aversion grew steadily, keeping pace with my maturing reason, and for long it determined the object of my thoughts.

A desire to acquire a background in the sciences and to escape the dangers of dissipation persuaded me to move to England. There I became an author, and the purpose of my first work was to combat materialism by exploring the influence of the soul upon the body, and that of the body upon the soul.—That was the period of my misfortunes . . .†

After seeing how successful my book was in English, I published it in French, with the title *De l'homme* [On Man]. A few of our *philosophes* who cunningly procure new scientific works from abroad before they are offered for sale here received copies of it, and they felt what a blow I was dealing to their principles . . .

Grieved to see that these gentlemen could represent as being dangerous a book that was intended to confute them, and determined to leave them no pretext thereafter, I prefaced it with a dissertation against materialists in the classical form. It is this book, thus retouched and enriched, that I was going to give to the press, with the approval of the Sorbonne, when I made your acquaintance, and you know that I postponed its printing in the design of bringing it out in homage to Spain.

I have fought the principles of modern philosophy: that is the reason for the implacable hatred I have incurred among its apostles. No doubt it is not such as will discredit me in the eyes of the truly wise; but you will soon see how I was to suffer their persecution on more than one account. Leaving no stone unturned in their efforts to expand their maleficent empire, they proliferate on every hand. Our faculties and academies are peopled with them, and I, unable to avoid them, have had to deal with them all in my undertakings.

After spending ten years in London and Edinburgh engaging in research of

*Florida-Blanca.
†He is careful not to mention *Les Chaînes de l'esclavage,* we observe.

every description, I returned to Paris. Several patients of distinguished rank, abandoned by the physicians but restored to health by me, joined forces with my friends and exerted themselves to persuade me to settle in the capital. I yielded to their importunings. They promised me happiness, but all I have found are outrage, griefs, and tribulations.

Word of the striking cures I had effected attracted a prodigious number of patients to me; my door was constantly besieged by the vehicles of persons coming to consult me from every quarter. I practiced my art as a physicist, and thus my knowledge of nature gave me great advantages; swiftness of eye, deftness of touch. My many successes caused me to be called the *doctor of the incurable* . . .

My success gave umbrage to the physicians of the faculty, who reckoned, to their chagrin, the volume of my earnings. They consoled themselves by plotting to dry up those earnings at their source. I could prove, if there were need, that they held frequent meetings to confer as to the most effective means of defaming me. From then on calumny sped in from all quarters, and from all quarters came anonymous letters to my patients to frighten them on my account. A great many persons whose friendship for me is based upon esteem did take up my defense, it is true; but their voices were stifled by the clamors of my adversaires. All these things are public knowledge.

The corruption that is inseparable from the practice of medicine has made me sigh more than once for the confinement of my study, where I could deliver myself up wholly to my beloved research. How could I have anticipated that in doing so I would merely create a new source of envy!

It took me hardly thirteen months in my study to complete my *Découvertes sur le feu* [Discoveries Relating to Fire] . . .

At last, the summary of my experiments with fire saw the day. The sensation it made in Europe was prodigious: all the public papers mentioned it. For six months I had both Court and town at my door. Those who could not see the experiments in my laboratory as often as they wished asked for private lessons, which were given by M. Filassier, a member of several academies. Among his subscribers he counted princes of the blood and the most eminent persons of the state.

While the curious were crowding to my disciple's to see my experiments with fire, I was submitting my discoveries on light for examination by the Academy. Unable to remain incognito, I could no longer rely on the impartiality of my judges, almost all of whom were fierce partisans of Newton . . .

Seven months had been employed in working up my experiments with light, three more were spent in writing the report, and five in soliciting a decision regarding it. The result was a miscarriage of justice. I had expected no less, for it must be said that the task was as delicate as it was unsavory for the gentlemen of the Academy. To admit the truth of my experiments was to acknowledge that for forty years they had been working on false principles, a confession that applied especially to the mathematicians and astronomers, who accordingly formed a redoubtable conspiracy against me . . .

The vexations that I suffered from this conspiracy did not prevent me from conducting further research. My discoveries on light were succeeded by my discoveries on electricity, which were endorsed by several celebrated physicists . . .

But the *Journal des Savants,* published by members of the Paris Academy of Sciences, said not one word of my achievements, although it ought to have been the first to report them.

What flattered me most in my success was the zealousness of a few foreign professors who came expressly from Stockholm and Leipzig to acquaint themselves with my experiments . . .

It follows from all the foregoing that the allegations of ignorance, incompetence, and charlatanism that my adversaries have leveled against me are dictated by the desire to do me harm, and are invalidated by the unanimous testimony of a host of distinguished men of letters, by the suffrage of several learned companies, and by the public voice. But if all these honorable titles did not testify in my favor, I should have still stronger evidence in my work itself: that is the witness whose speech militates with most force against the envious . . .

They accuse me of being a man who promises great things but who is incapable of carrying out what he undertakes. That, beyond doubt, is the description of an ambitious intriguer. But it is a known fact that I have spent almost the whole of my life in my laboratory, that I have never conceived the smallest project with a view to fortune, that I have never become involved in the smallest lucrative scheme. It is also a well-known fact that for the past six years I have given up the wealth accruing from the practice of my art in order to devote myself wholly to the pleasure of increasing useful knowledge. It is a further known fact that all the costly experiments required by my discoveries have been made at my own expense. Nevertheless, I consent not to put these proofs forward against my adversaries; for there are yet more irresistible ones to be advanced . . .

Avert your gaze, please, for one moment, from the black maneuvers of our *philosophes,* and engage with me in a few reflections in which you may find cause for surprise and, even worse, for alarm.

The morality of these messieurs, so well-suited to corrupt hearts, attracts the young in a thousand ways; their proselytes, therefore, are numerous. They multiply daily; spread over the face of the earth, how deeply we would have reason to fear their confederation! A confederation the more to be dreaded because it is invisible; for, having no external marks by which they may be distinguished, they can, without being known, fill every order of society: learned societies, universities, courts, princes' councils.

Even now they have conceived the appalling scheme of destroying all religious orders and annihilating religion itself. To succeed, these madmen are poisoning the very source of all useful knowledge and seeking to put their tools in all the places intended for the edification of the public.

What evils have they not already committed! What greater evils will they not commit hereafter! If one day they come to conceive more ambitious schemes, turning their eyes to political affairs, who will prevent them, acting through their creatures who are soon advised of everything that takes place in government cabinets, from upsetting governments and overturning states?

My friend, I see only one means of averting these misfortunes, and that is to bring every great writer to exert himself to cover the apostles of modern philosophy in ridicule . . .

I weary of contending with chimaeras. But, my friend, judging by the malignity of the allegations made against me by my adversaries, I must expect still greater ignominy to come. It is possible that they have also calumniated my honesty. Let them do so, fine and good, that is their least offensive occupation; but it is for the respectable persons with whom I have been on terms of intimacy to render justice to my religious sentiments, my morals, and my conduct. I shall accordingly transmit to you some testimony that will assuredly not be open to suspicion. . . .

I shall give this testimony to Monsieur le Comte d'Aranda, with the request that he himself seek more ample information from such respectable persons, and pass it on to Monsieur le Comte de Florida-Blanca.

Now at last my task is done. To complete yours, you have only to present my justification to that wise minister, imploring him on my behalf to place it before the king's eyes. Happy, too happy to be judged at the tribunal of his wisdom and his justice,

I embrace you with all my soul.

Marat.[5]

. . . A soul bruised beyond healing. Tomorrow, yes, tomorrow November 21, will be the day of days, the day on which two men are going to fly: d'Arlandes and Pilâtre de Rozier. Another round to the Montgolfiers, but also the first step toward their reconciliation with Charles and the Roberts. Alexandre Charles himself will see the clouds below him before the year is out. But Marat won't even be watching in the crowd. He will not go to Spain. He will be in France, forgotten, his name on nobody's lips. Looked at from Florida-Blanca's point of view, though, who could blame the minister for not wanting to introduce such a virulent virus into Spain?

Where's it gotten you, Jean-Paul, your year of crawling? The King of Spain will give your place to an honorable and obedient creature, a Spaniard into the bargain, the resonance of whose name was made to stifle the sighing fall of yours: Augustin-José Pedro del Carmen-Domingo de Candelaria de Bethencourt y Molina, an "engineer"—which means a man capable of building and inventing things—born on the island of Tenerife in the Canaries, who will never make any trouble for the authorities.[6]

"Marat tried Spain and failed.* And very soon thereafter, by the beginning of 1784, he ceased to be the physician of the Comte d'Artois's life guards. The *Almanach royal* continues to list him as holder of the position until 1786,

*Text by Jean Massin, who has written the last word on this episode.

but the *Mémoire sur l'electricité médicale,* published in 1784, does not mention it. Was he fired—and if so, why? Because the Court of Versailles got wind of his negotiations with Madrid and took offense? Because people had finally divined his true opinions? Or was it rather that Marat himself, feeling the ground less and less sure underfoot for the same reasons, took the initiative and resigned?"[7]

At forty-one years of age Jean-Paul Marat, a total washout, vanishes into the night. Oh, not completely—in 1784 he can be found at number 47 on the Rue du Vieux Colombier hard by Saint-Sulpice. But that's about all he leaves us—an address.

PILÂTRE DU ROZIER

44

OCTOBER 1783

A Sheep and a Couple of Fowls

The ball is briefly back in the court of Etienne Montgolfier and Réveillon, the paper king. He, definitely the top man in the trade in Paris, possesses extensive buildings and several scores of employees in the Faubourg Saint-Antoine beyond the Bastille. His factory runs along part of the Montreuil road. He has the true patron's instincts, and balloon building isn't a bad investment either: what publicity for his linen rag and wallpapers! He turns every hand onto this job, the rest of the work can go hang. Etienne donates to the new balloon the prize of six hundred livres* he has just received from the Academy of Sciences.

In eight days—and nights—an ovoid balloon, pointed at the top, is built at the Réveillon works, "representing a sort of blue tent with awnings and superb gold-colored ornaments."[1] Height seventy feet. Volume 4,500 cubic feet. But September 1783 turns sullen and rainy in Paris, storm follows storm in the wake of the one that half-spoiled the Champ de Mars trial. The segments of the balloon (made of wrapping canvas lined with heavy paper on both sides, an improved version of the Annonay model) can only be assembled outdoors, so several days are lost dragging them out only to rush them back inside again.

On September 11 the contraption nearly kills eight workers by carrying them off into the sky. "A trial was made that same evening; people watched with admiration as the beautiful machine filled in nine minutes, stood upright,

*About 4,000 modern francs [$800].

stretched taut at every point, and assumed the finest shape. Eight men who were holding it down were lifted several feet into the air and would have been carried to a great height had not fresh forces been opposed"—in other words, had not the onlookers rushed up to grab every available inch of rope and haul them back. People are beginning to realize that these monsters aren't just pretty to look at.

But now what? Tomorrow, the Academy commissioners are supposed to be coming to watch a decisive experiment and report back to the King. Don't forget what's at stake, it's the quarrel between hydrogen or smoke as the source of energy. This balloon, in the Montgolfier manner, has a huge hole at its base, beneath which a sort of gargantuan chafing-dish has been suspended to provide fuel. But the technique for manipulating the thing has by no means been perfected. Now it's Réveillon's and Montgolfier's turn to have a setback:

> Thick clouds were moving up to fill the horizon and a storm threatened. However, it was feared that another delay would postpone the experiment too long; the entire machine was ready, it would have taken a long time to dismantle it; so it was decided to fill the balloon.
>
> Fifty pounds of dry straw, set alight in small bundles, over which some ten pounds of chopped wool were sprinkled a little at a time, produced within ten minutes a vapor so expansive and endowed with such force that the machine, notwithstanding its weight and although deflated and folded down upon itself, arose as though in waves to an upright position: its volume and capacity amazed all the onlookers, and when it was fully developed and seeking to rise, their astonishment and admiration redoubled.
>
> The machine left the earth and maintained itself several feet in the air, bearing a weight of 500 pounds. Had the ropes restraining it been cut at that moment, it would have risen to a very great height. Suddenly, rain began to fall; then the wind blew in fierce gusts; the surest means of saving the machine was to release it. But as it was intended for the experiments that were to take place at Versailles, its owners did not want to abandon it, and the efforts they made to force it down, combined with the furious gusts of wind and the rain pouring down upon it, tore it in several places. As the storm worsened and continued for a long time, it was absolutely impossible to handle the balloon in this state. It endured the rain for over twenty-four hours; the paper came unglued and fell in strips, the canvas was laid bare, and this beautiful and splendid machine that had cost so much effort was destroyed in no time at all.

But the King has let himself be persuaded to attend another trial in person, on September 19. And since he leaves home about as often as the Grand Turk, the balloon has to be taken to Versailles. A *new* balloon, and in seven days! Réveillon finishes it in five, which is proof of his authority and his workers' determination, when they put their hearts into a job.

Versailles, September 19. The weather is turning fine, it looks like an Indian summer year [called St. Michael's summer in French, and not a regular occurrence—*Trans.*]. The balloon (deflated and harnessed to a large wagon drawn at a walk) is transported into the château's immense court of honor, in the center of which a high platform—circular scaffolding might be a better description—has been built to conceal the bales of straw for the fire. The gates have to be protected by a double cordon of troops "who had great difficulty containing a huge crowd from Paris and the vicinity." Next to the platform stands a wicker basket, containing a sheep, a rooster, and a duck—not a variation on a fable by La Fontaine, but the King's wish. For days a pack of crazy fools have been volunteering to go up with the balloon, and Louis XVI is stubbornly refusing to authorize any human ascension until he has proof that it will not be fatal. So they're going to use the poor beasties instead.

> At noon the avenues and courtyards of the château, the windows, and even the attics were filled with spectators. All that was greatest, most illustrious, and learned in the nation seemed to have come together of a common accord to do solemn homage to the sciences under the eyes of an august Court, which protects and encourages them.
>
> It was at this moment, and in the midst of this vast concourse of citizens of every estate, that Their Majesties and the royal family deigned to move to the enclosures, and even condescended to penetrate as far as the machine itself, to examine its details and hear an exact account of all the preparations for this beautiful experiment.
>
> At four minutes before one o'clock the sound of a box* announced that the machine was about to be filled; it was seen to inflate almost at once, spreading apart its folds and pleats with great speed; it developed to its fullest extent, its form pleasing to the eye, its imposing capacity astonishing to the mind: it had already reached the height of the tallest mast. Another box gave warning that it was ready to leave, and at the third shot the ropes were cut and the machine rose majestically into the air, carrying with it the contrivance in which a sheep and a couple of fowls had been placed.

There had been some hot moments on the platform, literally and figuratively: just as the sphere reached maximum inflation, a gust of wind struck it full in the flank and two tears almost a fathom long appeared at the summit. Etienne Montgolfier decided to take the chance—anything rather than admit defeat before his sovereign. He called for more fire and produced a little volcano of straw. The race between the inflating smoke and the leaking rips is won by the former, but only just. The balloon remains aloft a mere eight or ten minutes, long enough to convince the public, then glides gently down, as though commanded by remote control, to land at the Vaucresson crossroads a league from Versailles on the Saint-Cloud road, in the middle of the woods where

*Cannon were often called by that name, especially when loaded with blanks.

two gamekeepers phlegmatically (the poster has been widely circulated by now) observe it "come to a stop in the tall branches of the trees, which bowed under its weight. The hamper containing the animals gently touched the ground" just as a large party on horseback came galloping up, having followed the aerostat's trajectory from Versailles—their noses in the air at the risk of their necks. Number-One Witness Faujas de Saint-Fond is among this group, as well as Abbé d'Espagnac and a crowd of others, and, in the foreground, a man of twenty-nine but looking even younger, with big shining eyes above a long hooked nose. Not very tall, a thought underfleshed, but a pretty mouth drawn straight as an arrow, just made for outfacing the whole world. When the Sieur Pilâtre, or Pilastre (nobody knows the origin of his vaguely nobiliary name "de Rozier") has got an idea in his head, you want to think twice before crossing his path. No wonder: A Lorrain . . . [2]

Born in Metz on March 30, 1754, at number 7 Rue de Paris in the new, semi-suburban district of Fort Moselle where his father kept a hostelry.*

For a boy "of base extraction,"[3] he has not wasted his time. At eleven he entered the Saint-Louis collège in preparation for the army, but then, like Schiller, he took a side-turning into military medicine before dropping both at eighteen, out of individualism and a passion for the natural sciences. At twenty he was earning his living as a preparer for an apothecary, which gave him time to study mineralogy, botany, and chemistry in books and "free classes." Like everybody else, the compass of ambition was already pointing him toward Paris. Common sense, however, deposited him for a spell in Rheims on the way, where he became an inspector of pharmacies and professor of chemistry. His tact and poise, an excellent manner at once courteous and unassuming, and his torrential erudition procured for him an ideally soft and secure job—so rare for anyone under thirty—soon after his arrival in Paris: for the past year he has been curator of the natural history and physics cabinets (proto-laboratories) of Monsieur le Comte de Provence.

A better job than Marat's with Artois. But both, without knowing each other,† were suffering from the same itch that kept them constantly on the move. The moment Pilâtre heard about the success of Charles's and the Montgolfiers's experiments, a whole new side of himself suddenly burst into bloom: the spirit of adventure. He's already written a treatise on gases; he decides he will be the first man to fly. He is indisputably the first man to lodge an official application at any rate, with the Academy of Sciences (on August 30), which is in the throes of a rare collective effervescence. From Condorcet to Lavoisier, the question in all of their minds is whether men will be able to

*A plate was put up on the front of his birthplace in 1928 for the district bicentenary, and a café bearing his name has been transformed into a curious little museum.

†Or at least without leaving any trace of an acquaintance.

use these balloons themselves. The Duc de Chartres is longing to try, but he knows full well that his cousin would never let him go first. A few uncredentialed daredevils have also offered their services—the same ones who wanted to rush off to the Islands two or three years back; but for this occasion we need a man who is competent as well as respectable.

Very well, then, you can have Pilâtre, but with strings attached. The Academy, having just awarded its prize to Montgolfier, sends the youth from Metz around to meet him, its conscience easier since the apparently safe return of sheep, rooster, and duck. But it insists upon a series of preliminary trials in a tied, "captive" balloon, to determine in relative security whether a man can acquire some degree of mastery over the craft by jettisoning ballast and adding fresh gas to the envelope—which would require a special cockpit.

Réveillon sets to work. The biggest balloon yet is built, and to it is attached "a wicker gallery two and one-half feet wide with an outer wall three feet high; in addition, in the middle of the space formed by this gallery, there was a sort of wire basket serving as a brazier, in which straw or any other fuel could be burned while the machine was in the air." But that means storing a supply of straw on board. It looks as though the aeronaut, or -nauts, will also have to be something of an acrobat. Another point in favor of the lightweight Pilâtre. And the men who go had better not be the faint-hearted sort, because their little furnace is going to be stoking away under a huge envelope made of highly combustible canvas and paper . . .

Even Louis XVI makes an effort. He stands Réveillon the cost of this latest balloon out of his own pocket money. All through October, the loiterers who are beginning to make a habit of foregathering outside the Réveillon paper-works on the Rue de Montreuil can observe the huge sphere appearing above the trees in the garden behind the works (a miniature princely park it was, too, laid out in the French manner with statues and fountains and orange trees in tubs and even a little Roman-style arch of triumph, and it made a lot of the neighbors jealous) and gliding up and down between two stout wooden posts like masts, at the foot of which workmen give out with rhythmic *heave-ho's!* as though they were deckhands at the capstan. Perched in the gallery is a man making signs to them and calling down through a megaphone: Monsieur Pilâtre de Rozier, training for the first step of the stairway to the stars.

On October 15, his two protective posts are removed but not the ropes, which are firmly held and paid out from the ground, and he rises to one hundred feet. The basket tips too far on his side. On October 17 his weight is offset by an iron counterweight suspended opposite him outside the cage, and up he goes over two hundred feet, almost to the end of the ropes. But there's a hitch when he wants to come down: a gust of wind carries the sphere "over the garden trees, in which it became entangled." Pilâtre keeps his cool, stokes the fire, and takes the balloon up a little higher, while the men come running to saw off the branches in which the ropes are entangled. This experiment proves that one man alone in the crib of an unattached balloon cannot do everything—unload ballast, feed the fire, watch the wind, and observe the terrain. A real ascension would require a team.

"There, you see? I'll have to come too!" crows the Marquis François-Laurent d'Arlandes.

Another nut. And for longer than Pilâtre, because he was a neighbor of the Montgolfiers, born in a primitive manor-house in the region of Saleton* near Saint-Vallier;[4] one of its thick, almost blind towers, built out of big round stones from the Rhône, can still be seen, two centuries later, next to a ruined wall and a hideous modern house. It's clear that the Arlandes must have been almost as poor as their peasants, although sufficiently high-spirited to cross the Rhône. Their ancestors (the d'Arlempdes) go back beyond the Crusades. But eight kids to get rid of (including four girls): Lord, what a visitation! No problem for François-Laurent, he's the oldest so he'll go into the army, like two of his brothers (the fourth boy becomes a cleric). He was sent as a boarder to the collège at Tournon, where he was taught by the Jesuits until their expulsion. There he met Joseph Montgolfier, who was three classes ahead of him, and they seem to have kept up the sort of Christmas-card relations maintained by former schoolfellows until the brothers' first aerostatic experiments incited d'Arlandes to greater intimacy. He has just left the army, ostensibly for "reasons of health" but actually, no doubt, out of boredom and dread of an unpromising future. After twenty years of loyal service and good reports he was still only a "major," or chief captain, in the Bourbonnais regiment which, by remaining mulishly stuck in Brittany waiting for ships, had caused him to miss the American war. (His younger brother François-Pierre was made a captain at Yorktown.)† How could François-Laurent have gone any further? No poor provincial nobleman can ever buy himself a regiment or be given one by the King. Determined that his life should not be over at forty, he had "gone up" to Paris, a confirmed bachelor, and was living there shabbily on his little pension while cultivating a passion for "the astronomical and physical sciences." He was cheerful, clever, and imaginative and easily obtained entry to such salons as that of the Duc de Chartres and Mme de Genlis, which

---

*On September 25, 1742, son "of the noble François d'Arlandes, seigneur of Saleton, and of Dame Marguerite du Pilhon de Dié, daughter of a councilor at the parlement of the Dauphiné." Although hostile to the Revolution he does not emigrate but digs himself in at Saleton, where he dies in total obscurity in 1809.

†Before becoming a colonel and then a general of the Republic; he fights courageously under Bustine before going over to the other side, where he gets killed almost immediately in Condé's army, in a battle in 1793.

drained off considerable numbers of "marginal" gentlemen to form a little "counter-Court" of new ideas.

D'Arlandes occasionally returned home to Saleton, where he kept in touch with the Montgolfiers's research and claimed to have let them use his château towers to try out some primitive parachutes. Now in Paris, he comes to Réveillon's almost every day, his enthusiasm getting in everyone's way and irritating Etienne, who has known him for only a few months. "If anyone is to go up, it will be I!" But Etienne would rather it were Pilâtre, because he has more confidence in the other man's skill and presence of mind. Besides, his trials in the captive balloon give him priority. But they don't discourage d'Arlandes completely, if only because he has connections in high places—which do in fact come in handy. On October 19 they give him a crumb, letting him play human counterweight to Pilâtre de Rozier for the final trial, with longer ropes than ever before: the balloon carries its occupants four hundred feet up—"that is, nearly half again as high as the towers of Notre Dame." But they have to wait for a windless day to do it.

The great time of decision has come: let go of the balloon and two men, and heaven help them.

D'ARLANDES

45

NOVEMBER 1783

All We Could See Were Heads!

Louis XVI is still reluctant. The Gonesse incident made a strong and unfavorable impression upon him, and he observed the Versailles ascension at close quarters and with his eyes open: the last-minute rips did not escape his notice. He therefore maintains his order to his chief of police not to allow any free flights with passengers aboard. Lenoir, rightly mistrustful of the outward docility of a Pilâtre or even a Montgolfier, puts the Réveillon paper mill under twenty-four-hour surveillance.

But Louis XVI also has a horror of nagging, and he's getting plenty of it. He has an idea: suppose they try the experiment with a couple of convicts from the death cells; if they come down unhurt he will reprieve them (but send them to the galleys). What an irony that would have been—two men passing from the shadow of death into the very essence of freedom—sky, sun, clouds, forest—only to be clapped in chains for the rest of their days . . . I wonder if anybody would have put up a monument to them?

Pilâtre is beside himself. "What? Common criminals, men whom society has cast from its bosom, should have the glory of being the first to rise into the air? No, no; it shall not be."[1] He rushes around, writes to the Duchesse de Polignac, implores Monsieur to intervene, and suddenly realizes that the importunate d'Arlandes might be a useful ally. Too bad if he has to share his glory with him; at least he'll be better than a convict. A sacred pact is sealed at Réveillon's, and the marquis spurs away to Versailles as if he were storming it at the head of his grenadiers. On the way, however, he makes a decisive detour to visit the exquisite château called "La Meute," which everybody was beginning to twist into "La Muette": one of the King's hunting lodges [*meute:* pack, as of hounds; *muette:* mute (female)—*Trans.*], situated on the edge of the Bois de Boulogne near Passy. It had been substantially enlarged and remodeled toward the end of the reign of Louis XV and is now a mini-Versailles, with orangery, pheasant preserve, "a circular terrace looking out on the countryside," a large kitchen garden, and a little woods in the English style.[2] Marie Antoinette has persuaded Louis XVI to make a present of it to the dauphin, just turned two, although the present is really for Yolande de Polignac, "governess to the Children of France," who can now hold a little court of her own in it, known as the "Court of Monseigneur le Dauphin." A few gazettes will actually print "that this great prince showed a keen interest in the ascension of Messieurs d'Arlandes and de Rozier, and deigned to express his benevolent solicitude"[3]—goo-goo, kootchikoo.

But it's only natural that he should, because they're going to take off from La Muette! That was d'Arlandes's big idea, to flatter La Polignac and get her into the act. The only problem was to make her think she had had the idea herself, a process that Faujas de Saint-Fond adroitly translates into courtierese: "The court of Mgr le Dauphin was at La Muette; it was composed of learned persons on intimate terms with the fine arts. Mme la Duchesse de Polignac, governess to the Children of France, took an interest in this discovery and thought that the spacious gardens of La Muette would be suitable for the important experiment in which the aerostatic machine was first to rise freely into the air bearing men. By thus encouraging the most beautiful experiment ever performed, she was setting a precious example for her august pupil, making him a witness to a decisively epoch-making event."[4] It's true that the ascension couldn't be held at Réveillon's, where there was no room for a crowd; they'd have been picking the dead off the pavement. But Philippe de Chartres was already offering Saint-Cloud . . . The Queen and her favorite are delighted to score against him. They lay siege to the King, who's got a load on his mind these days, what with his treasury empty and his comptroller-generals going down one after another like bowling pins, d'Ormesson after

Joly de Fleury and now Calonne, each with his magic potion for curing the budget of its languishing disease . . . Louis XVI grumpily consents to spare d'Arlandes two minutes of his time. In comes, or rather in marches, as though on parade, a tall fellow in a captain's uniform with a stubborn brow, piercing eyes, a long beak of a nose with well-drawn nostrils—fine figure of a man upon my soul, and not in the least intimidated by the King:

"Do you think it seemly, Monsieur, for an officer to go gadding about in the air?"

"Sire, I have my reasons for doing so . . . the promises [of promotion] which your minister of war has often made to me have proven to be so much pie in the sky; seeing nothing come of them, I thought the simplest thing would be to go claim them there."[5]

Hoho, a wit! You can always get your way if you can make a king laugh, especially when times are bad. Louis XVI doesn't say yes, but he doesn't say no either. One restriction: neither he nor the Queen will be in any way connected with the matter officially. They will not attend the experiment, where they might risk seeing dead bodies come tumbling out of the sky. A big sacrifice for Marie Antoinette; but since it will make her darling Yolande happy . . .

Anyway, taking off from the dauphin's gardens isn't bad!

D'Arlandes returns from Versailles puffed up like a turkeycock. In his hot-from-the-event narrative on the first human ascension, so precious to us later, he explains that the reason why he is writing it instead of Pilâtre, despite the fact that the other man was a physics professor, is because it was to him, d'Arlandes, that Etienne Montgolfier turned first, and Pilâtre was not chosen to accompany him until the day before the takeoff! "I was accordingly selected by M. Montgolfier to conduct this experiment. One may excusably feel pride in the choice, and it would be unnatural in me to yield to another the acquired right of making public his success."[6] Here's another guy you can't say is positively wallowing in modesty. But for once it's so much the better: his pen is as bright and agile as that of a first-rate journalist.

The sky eater, Réveillon's masterpiece, has now been moved into position. Oh, but she's beautiful,* blue and gold like an exotic fruit sprung from the damp rusty trees of La Meute, a fruit of that late eighteenth century in which everything wrought by man was superb, from Bagatelle to the thatched cottage, from the Queen's white frocks to the peasant's wrap, from the prince's porcelain to the Restifs' soup bowls on the farm of "la Bretonne." For the savants not to have beauty with their perils would have been inconceivable. "The upper part was ringed with fleurs de lys; below them, the twelve signs

---

*20 meters high, 16 in diameter, capacity 2,000 m³.

of the zodiac. In the center, the King's initial, interspersed with suns. The bottom was garnished with masks and garlands; several eagles with outspread wings seemed to be holding up the powerful machine. All the ornamentation was in gold on a blue ground, so that the globe seemed made of gold and azure. The round gallery was painted in scarlet draperies with golden fringes."[7]

The gallery has been enlarged to allow the aeronauts more freedom of movement, and now measures almost a fathom across, with a balustrade protecting what is about to become the highest balcony in the world. In the middle is a large opening, from which hangs the iron cauldron that will feed the combustion. Stacked on the gallery floor, bales of straw and wads of wool. Up we go, into the wild blue yonder . . .

November 21, 1783, is the day. It has taken almost a month to get everything ready. Scheduled time: eleven a.m. "But heavy white clouds appeared, floating in different parts of the horizon." And another scare: Etienne Montgolfier, who feels responsible for the lives of two men, wants to make one last preliminary captive experiment and nearly ruins everything with his obstinacy. The wind drives the sphere against the poles and ropes (a little pink brick scaffolding twenty steps high, built in the middle of the lawn, conceals the red-hot fire that has inflated the balloon in a few short minutes; upstage, the white château —three stories, nine windows each; a few hundred spectators, Polignac's guests, all the last word in elegance, stand neatly parked beneath the trees planted in stiff rows *à la française*) and the same thing happens as at Versailles, a big rip. Reverse gears, down we go again.

A few onlookers, Charles's friends, the supporters of hydrogen *carlines* as opposed to steady-fire *montgolfières,* leap into their saddles and spur back to Paris to announce that the experiment is a failure. All Paris has been fighting their battle for the last six months. But Réveillon is there, with his best workers and a cartload of rubberized taffeta, strong glue, sail-sheets, needles, and thread. A few fluttering fine ladies offer "to lend a hand," and in two or three hours the balloon is patched. A good thing Louis XVI isn't around.

The first two "daring young men" of the air fly away in their weird machine on the stipulated date, at one fifty-four in the afternoon. "This little voyage will live forever in the history of human enterprise.* Openings had been cut all around the cylinder enclosing the flame. Pilâtre and d'Arlandes, compelled to act as counterweights, were deprived of the solace of seeing each other. They had removed their coats and were bare-armed to the shoulder, as they were continually occupied in stoking the fire that kept them aloft . . . One heard them shouting questions and answers back and forth to each other, and

---

*According to an eyewitness, the lawyer Jérôme de Thirolier.

the distance, muffling their calls, made them all the more alarming. And while the contrivance was swaying and clouds of smoke were issuing from it, both men, armed with heavy pokers, were lifting up the straw to stimulate combustion; they stoked the fire and sent down a shower of half-burnt embers, which burst into flame again as they fell. Never did a deeper silence reign upon the earth. Admiration, terror, and pity were engraved on every face."[8]

D'Arlandes gets it all down. He is one of those very rare people who are capable of narrating History at the same time as they make it:*

The position of the machine was such that M. Pilâtre de Rozier was to the west and I to the east: the wind was blowing roughly from the northwest quarter. The machine rose majestically, people say; but few of them noticed, I believe, that just as it came above the treetops it turned half round upon itself, and by this change M. Pilâtre found himself to the front in our direction and I, consequently, at the rear.

I believe it should be observed that from this moment until we arrived, we remained in the same positions with respect to the line we were following. I was surprised by the silence and lack of movement our departure had occasioned among the spectators; I thought them amazed, perhaps frightened by this fresh spectacle, and in need of reassurance. I waved my arm but to little effect; then, having taken out my handkerchief, I waved that, and saw a great stir in the garden of La Muette. It seemed to me that the spectators who had been somewhat scattered about the grounds were moving together into a single mass, and that by some involuntary movement it was being borne along, following us toward the wall, which it appeared to regard as the only obstacle separating us. It was just then that M. Pilâtre said to me, "You're doing nothing and we are hardly climbing at all."

"Sorry," I replied.

I put on a bale of straw, stirred the fire a little, and turned quickly back but could no longer see La Muette. Amazed, I glanced at the course of the Seine, following it with my eye; at last I perceived the confluence with the Oise. So that must be Conflans; and naming the other major bends in the river by the names of the nearest places, I said Poissy, Saint-Germain, Saint-Denis, Sèvres; thus I am still at Passy or Chaillot; and indeed I looked through the inside of the machine and perceived the Visitation of Chaillot beneath me. Just then M. Pilâtre said to me: "There's the river and we're going down."

"Why, then, my good friend, we must have some fire!"

And we set to work. But instead of crossing the river as seemed indicated by our direction, which was bearing us toward the Invalides, we ran alongside the Isle of Swans, returned to the main bed of the river and went up it as far as the barrier of La Conférence. I said to my brave companion,

"This river seems remarkably hard to cross."

"I should think so," replied he, "you're doing nothing."

*Here, in a letter to Faujas de Saint-Fond, November 28, 1783.

"Because I'm not so strong as you are, and we're all right as we are."

I stirred the fire and stuck my fork into a bale of straw, which, too tightly packed no doubt, refused to burn, so I lifted it and shook it in the flames. The next moment I felt myself uplifted as by the armpits and said to my good companion, "We're going up now, at any rate."

"Yes, we're going up," he replied, having looked out, presumably to take some bearings.

That very moment I heard, toward the top of the machine, a sound that made me fear it had burst. I looked and saw nothing. While my eyes were fixed to the top of the machine I felt a lurch, the only one I had felt thus far.

The direction of the movement was down to up.

Then I said, "What are you doing? Are you dancing?"

"I'm not budging."

"So much the better," said I; "here is a new current at last, which will, I hope, take us out of the river."

I turned to see where we were, and found myself between the military academy and the Invalides, which we had already left about four hundred fathoms behind. At the same time M. Pilâtre said to me, "We're over the plain."

"Yes," I said, "we're making good headway."

"To work," he told me, "to work."

I heard another noise in the machine, which I thought must be produced by a rope breaking. This second warning caused me to scrutinize closely the interior of our habitation. I saw that the part facing southward was covered with round holes, several of them quite large. I then said, "We must go down."

"Why?"

"Look!"

At the same time I took up my sponge; I could easily extinguish the few flames that were burning under some of the holes within reach; but when I pressed against the surface of the bottom of the cloth to see if it was still tightly fixed to the circle ringing it, it came away very easily, and, observing this, I repeated to my companion, "We have to go down."

He looked beneath him and said, "We're over Paris."

"No matter," I told him. "But look out, is there no danger on your side? Are you securely fastened?"

"Yes."

I examined my side and saw that there was nothing serious to fear. I did more, I struck my sponge against the main ropes within reach; all held good, only two strands parted. Then I said, "We can cross Paris."

During this operation we had drawn considerably closer to the rooftops; we laid on fire and rose up with the greatest ease. I looked below me and could make out the Foreign Missions with perfect clarity.* It seemed to me that we were moving toward the towers of Saint-Sulpice, which I could perceive through our

*The Foreign Missions seminary and its extensive grounds ran along the Rue du Bac. As for the towers of Saint-Sulpice, new and white, the architect Servandoni had just completed them, thus crowning the hundred years of labor required to build the "left bank cathedral."

opening. As we rose, an air current caused us to depart from our former direction and bore us to the south. I saw on my left a kind of wood that I thought to be the Luxembourg.

We crossed the boulevard and I cried out, "Now then, dismount."

We left off the fire; the intrepid Pilâtre, who kept a cool head, and who was to the fore in that direction, judged that we were heading for the mills between little Gentilly and the boulevard,* and warned me. I threw on a bale of straw and shook it to make it burn more fiercely; we rose up again and another current carried us a little to the left. Good de Rozier cried out again, "Mind the mills!"

But my view through the opening gave me a surer judgment of our direction, I saw that we could not come against them, and I told him, "Let's get down."

The next instant I saw that I was passing over water. I thought it was the river again, but when we were on the ground I recognized it as the pond that works the machines of the clothworks of MM. Brenier et Cie.

We had alighted on the Butte aux Cailles† between the Mill of Marvels and the Old Mill, about fifty fathoms from either. As we were drawing close to the ground I raised myself up on the gallery with both hands. I felt the top of the machine press gently against my head, I pushed it away and leaped down from the gallery. Turning back to the machine I imagined I would find it full. But much to my amazement, it was perfectly empty and completely flattened! I could see nothing of M. Pilâtre; I ran to his side to help free him from the heap of cloth covering him, but before getting around the machine I saw him emerging from beneath it in his shirt, since he had removed his coat before coming down and put it in his basket.

We were alone, and not strong enough to overturn the gallery and remove the straw, which had caught fire. We had to keep it from igniting the rest of the machine. It seemed to us that the only way to avoid that misfortune was to tear the cloth loose. M. Pilâtre took one side, I the other, and by pulling violently we uncovered the fire. The instant it was freed from the cloth that had prevented it from communicating with the air, the straw burst into fierce flames. In shaking one of the baskets we threw the fire onto the one that had carried my companion, and the remaining straw there also caught fire; people came running, laid hold of M. Pilâtre's coat, and shared the pieces among themselves. The guard arrived, and with their help our machine was secured in ten minutes, and an hour later it was at M. Réveillon's, where M. Montgolfier had had it built.

The first noteworthy person I saw upon landing was M. le Comte de Laval. Soon after, the couriers of M. le Duc and Mme la Duchesse de Polignac came for the news. I suffered to see M. de Rozier in his shirt sleeves and, fearing some

---

*Today, the Boulevard de Port Royal.

†So called because of the game [*caille*: quail—*Trans.*] (reserved for the King) then abounding there. Mills had been put up because, like the Butte Montmartre, the place was open to the wind. It had a pretty view of Paris, opposite Montmartre. Today the Butte aux Cailles is part of the XIIIth *arrondissement*.

ill effect upon his health, for we had grown extremely heated while folding up the machine, I insisted that he must go into the first house; the sergeant of the guard escorted him so that he might make his way through the crowd. On his way he met Mgr le Duc de Chartres, who had followed us, as may be seen, very close behind; for I had had the honor to speak with him but a moment before our departure. Finally, some carriages came up.

It was growing late. M. Pilâtre had nothing but a poor excuse for a coat that someone had lent him. He refused to return to La Muette.

I set off alone, although keenly sorry to leave my brave companion.[9]

Does this mean victory for the Montgolfiers? Yes, but for a scant ten days; because Charles and the youngest Robert brother immediately obtain permission to try out the first *carline,* which flies, with them on board, from the garden of the Tuileries on December 1, and is viewed by more than one hundred thousand people. And that is the end of the war of the balloons, for Etienne Montgolfier comes to watch the experiment and receives as great an ovation as they do. He was the father of the first flight, they are the craftsmen of the real aerostats—their success is a clear demonstration of the superiority of hydrogen inflation. Their craft was "the first true spheroid balloon, with rubberized envelope, net, crib,* valve, bags of ballast, and a barometer."[10] The Queen is there, "seated on the palace balcony"; two English observers, Mr. and Mrs. Cradock,[11] are struck by her "serious air," which may perhaps be attributed to the fact that the Duc de Chartres, whom she is beginning to hate with her whole heart (but only for political reasons—his popularity is soaring as hers and the King's declines), is so loudly acclaimed as he goes caracoling about and playing master of ceremonies in the sky game.

Just before takeoff, Charles comes up to Montgolfier and hands him the string attached to a little pilot balloon:

"It is for you, Monsieur, to open our path to the air."

Let's everybody embrace, it's joy all round. The two men rise without mishap to more than a thousand fathoms and drift away over the Park of Mousseaux. Which of the two—Charles or the balloon—is more fit to burst at that moment? "Never can anything equal the surge of exhilaration that filled me as I felt myself escaping from the earth; it was more than pleasure, it was happiness . . . This sentiment was quickly followed by a yet keener sensation: admiration of the majestic sight opening before us. Wherever we looked beneath us, all we could see were heads; above us, a cloudless sky; in the far distance, the most exquisite prospect. 'Oh, my friend,' I said to M. Robert, 'how happy we are here! See what the sky has become for us! what serenity! what enchantment!' "[12]

*Filled with provisions for a long voyage: champagne, cold meat, blankets, furs, etc.

This time they make a proper trip, from the valley of the Seine to the valley of the Oise in the direction of Creil and Pontoise, flying over the great forest of l'Isle-Adam and setting down nine leagues from their point of departure near the pretty little church of Nesles, almost a twin town to Gonesse. But what a difference in the peasants here! Scientific knowledge in the Paris region has shot centuries ahead, thanks to Sauvigny's poster and the priests' elaborations upon it during Sunday mass. As the balloon floats gently earthward it comes within hailing range of the populations of Lannois, Franconville, Eau-Bonne, Taverny, l'Isle-Adam . . .

> We were constantly conversing with their inhabitants, whom we saw running toward us from every direction; we heard their joyful shouts, their good wishes, their solicitude, in a word the thrill of admiration. We called out, *"Vive le Roi!"* and all the countryside returned our shouts. We heard most distinctly, "Friends, aren't you afraid? Are you quite all right? Lord, it's beautiful! God keep you safe. Goodbye, friends!" I was moved to tears by this affectionate and sincere interest inspired by so novel a sight.
>
> At last we came to earth. We were surrounded. Nothing can equal the rustic and loving innocence, the effusion of admiration and enthusiasm of these village folk.
>
> I immediately called for the priests and syndics, who came hurrying forward; a celebration was held on the spot. I quickly wrote out a short report, which they signed. Then a group of horsemen rode up at a gallop; they were Mgr le Duc de Chartres, M. le Duc de Fitz-James, and M. Farrer, an English gentleman, who had followed us from Paris. By a most curious coincidence we had landed near the latter's hunting lodge. He leaped from his horse, came running to our vehicle and said, as he flung his arms round me, "Monsieur Charles, me first!"

The Maréchale de Villeroi, a decrepit lady of eighty-odd and a living relic of the century of Louis XV, had been brought to the Tuileries in her carriage to watch the takeoff, grumbling and railing against this outing imposed upon her by her entourage. But when she saw the balloon rise into the sky, her reaction was that of St. Thomas: doubt gave way to tears. She fell back onto her cushions and sobbed, "Oh yes, now it's certain! One day they'll learn how to keep people alive forever, but I shall already be dead."[13]

BEAUMARCHAIS

46

A P R I L 1 7 8 4

There Is No Salvation Outside Le Mariage

Beaumarchais wasn't one to miss the conquest of the sky; indeed, he didn't miss much that was going on in his day, when he wasn't involved in it as actor. From the daughters of Louis XV to the Chevalier d'Eon and from Franklin to Maria Theresa, he could have built a living museum of his personal encounters. "He was very much struck" by the aerostats (or rather, as he amusingly calls them, "aerambules" or "aerotambules"), according to his faithful companion Gudin de la Brenellerie, "especially as he was then engaged, with a very celebrated mechanician [Blanchard?] in conducting certain experiments relating to the means by which humans might raise themselves into the air. I witnessed a few of these, and I believe they might have been quite successful, with a more judicious attribution of human forces and with long exercise of the muscles employed to propel wings of such large dimension, those of the arms being too weak to obtain the necessary motion.

"The beautiful discovery of M. de Montgolfier and the aerostatic balloon of MM. Charles and Robert seemed entirely satisfactory to us. We attended the splendid trials in the Faubourg Saint-Antoine, Champ de Mars, Versailles, La Muette, and the Tuileries, and they may have inspired greater pleasure and admiration in us than in any other spectators."[1] Pierre-Augustin hasn't minded too much being out of the top ten in 1783, especially as he has every intention of heading the list in 1784. The ice floe around him was finally beginning to break up, as it had ten years before during his great entanglement with the Maupeou parlement. This time, though, it's a king who has to give way, and for that patience is what you need most, especially when the king is Louis XVI.

The news is that they're going to produce *La Folle Journée, ou le Mariage de Figaro* this spring. Who're *they?* The French Acting Company. For whom? Tout-Versailles and Tout-Paris, minus the King and Queen. As the years go by, it begins to look increasingly as though the absence of the royal couple is proof of the importance of the event. They weren't there for the coronation of Voltaire, or for Pilâtre and d'Arlandes. And they won't be there for the explosive launching of the boldest and most prophetic play in contemporary history.

The curtain's rippling again. There go the three warning knocks . . . But what's the scene? This is only 1784.

On March 31 Beaumarchais utters a shout of triumph, in a letter to Préville, an aging but very famous actor who had grown so painfully weary of the heartrendingly mediocre works which the French company had been playing for years to empty houses—sham classics, shepherds and shepherdesses, lachrymose bathos—that he wanted to retire at Easter. Beaumarchais himself was seriously thinking of going into exile in Prussia or Russia so that he could see the play of his life on the stage at last. But.

> We were both wrong, old friend: I was trembling for fear that you would quit the theater at Easter, and you were convinced that *The Marriage of Figaro* could never be performed.
>
> But one must never despair of preserving an actor whom the public adores, or of seeing the triumph of a brave author who is sure he is right and who cannot be disgusted by disgust. My dear old friend, I have the King's *fiat,* the minister's *fiat,* and the *fiat* of the lieutenant of police; all we need now is yours, and we shall see a fine to-do when the season opens. Come on, old man! My play is nothing great, but it has taken four years of battle to get it performed, and that is why I care so much about it.[2]

The end of the fight comes on April 27, less than a month later, part way up the long hill that slopes away from the left bank of the Seine, almost on the outskirts of the city. What's happening? Is this sedition? A carnival? Whatever it is, Paris is up in arms about it. Keep calm, everybody, it's only a play. Although *La Folle Journée* [The Wild (or Mad) Day] has certainly been the occasion for a crazy day. A huge crowd has been standing in the mud since daybreak, fighting to get a seat in the new Théâtre Français, even though the curtain won't go up until half-past five in the afternoon after the Argand lamps have been lit. There are blue-ribboned gentlemen out there, rubbing elbows with chimney sweeps. By eleven in the morning it looks like a riot; the line stretches all the way to the Luxembourg gates and blocks the road leading down to the Seine. The doors are smashed, the guard scattered, and the wrought-iron grills bent by the weight of the assailants. Most of the fine ladies have installed themselves in the actresses' dressing rooms and are lunching there before the show, to be sure of getting a seat. After the final wrestling match, which leaves four out of five contenders outside the doors, three people are picked up dead of asphyxiation. This all takes place in and around a little white palace, the paint hardly dry on its walls, which the Comte de Provence has just put up for the French Acting Company so that he too, like the

Orléanses with their Opéra, can have a theater within walking distance of his home in the Luxembourg. For the moment, the Odéon-to-be still looks a little lost: this part of town, between the Luxembourg and the Palais Mazarin, is in mid-overhaul and has not yet assumed its final aspect. A stone's throw away on the Sainte-Geneviève hill the finishing touches are being put to a gigantic church dedicated to the patron saint of Paris, in the neoclassical style that is about to blossom all over town. One can hardly recognize the place.

A new type of speculation has recently been born: real estate development, for the exclusive profit of the rich. "Masonry"* has rearranged a third of the capital in the last twenty-five years. There has been land speculation; regiments of *limousins*† have been called up, and mountains of cut stone have been rising into the air, all attesting to the rage to build.

> If this fashion served the public welfare one might praise it; but it is masonry, not architecture, that has gained. The parvenu wants spacious rooms and the shopkeeper has ambitions to be housed like the prince.
>
> Places of entertainment have been going up on all sides and the Opéra, the Théâtre Français, and the "Italian" Theater have all been rebuilt, but the Hôtel Dieu still stands penned behind its unsavory enclosure; boudoirs and bathrooms have been put in, everybody has built for himself, abandoned himself to these voluptuous pursuits; but hospital beds are the same as they used to be.
>
> The speculators have called in the builders who, with a plan in one hand and an estimate in the other, have heated the minds of the capitalists. Gardens have petrified and tall dwellings risen to cut off one's gaze over land where the eye had imagined it saw vegetables growing.
>
> The town center has been subjected to the metamorphoses of the stone cutter's tireless mallet; the Quinze-Vingts** have disappeared, and their site now sports a row of new and identical edifices; the Invalides, which seemed to be standing in open countryside, are ringed round with new houses; the Vieille-Monnaie has been replaced by two streets; the Chaussée d'Antin is a new and substantial district.
>
> No more porte St. Antoine. The Bastille alone seems to stand fast, endlessly seeking to shock our gaze with its hideous countenance. Buildings rise on those ditches that bore witness to the murderous games of the Fronde; soon no one will believe any ramparts battered by gunfire could ever have been in their place.
>
> Cranes to hoist aloft enormous blocks of stone cluster around Sainte-Geneviève and the parish of the Madeleine. In the plains of Montrouge, wheels twenty-five to thirty feet across can be seen turning, gutting the quarries.

Sic; the text is by Mercier, who would later have written "the developers."

†Reminder: the "limousins" [from the Limoges region—*Trans.*]—the word was becoming a common noun—came up to Paris, where they worked as journeyman masons, in search of the bare subsistence they could no longer earn from their land; they were an early symptom of the growing destitution of certain provinces.

**Hospital for the blind built by St. Louis.

But despite this great quantity of new buildings, rents are as high as ever; the population has not grown; a crowd of foreigners, sightseers, idle provincials, and lackeys have come. People live in Paris only in the winter. In summer Paris is deserted, yet even so everybody must have vast suites of rooms standing empty half the year.[3]

For the French Acting Company, the move has been all to the good. The jaded public of the banks of the Seine that used to come to their theater on the Rue des Prêtres-Saint-Germain* across from the Café Procope, and to their uncomfortable temporary quarters in the Tuileries, has now been augmented by a new wave of students. "The area of the rue Saint-Jacques, the Montagne Sainte-Geneviève, and the Rue de la Harpe is called the 'Latin Country';† the University colleges are there, and one can see swarms of Sorbonnists in their cassocks, tutors in bands, law scholars, surgery and medical students, their vocation dictated by their degree of poverty.

"When the French Acting Company is playing in the Latin Country, the orchestra stalls are much better composed; this is a public that knows how to form actors."[4]

In front of the theater-temple with its eight Doric columns, connected to the Corneille and Molière pavilions by two passages worthy of the covered bridges of Venice, lies a vacant lot—one can hardly call it a square at this point; and it's a good thing it can hold a lot of carriages, because there are more than seven hundred in it tonight. Over this indescribable chaos presides the voice of the *aboyeur* [barker], one of the most stentorian in Paris, bellowing uninterruptedly: "The carriage of M. le Marquis! The carriage of Mme la Comtesse! The carriage of M. le Président!" His awesome roar resounds to the back walls of the taverns where the footmen are tippling, to the bowels of the billiard rooms where the coachmen stand and wrangle—a voice that can fill a whole district, cover everything, absorb everything, all the mingled cacophony of men and horses. At its imperious signal, footmen and coachmen abandon their pints and billiard cues, return to their horses' bridles, open the door, and bow.

"To give his chest a superhuman force this barker never touches wine and drinks only strong spirits. He is always hoarse, but his very hoarseness gives a harsh and ghastly timbre to his voice, which is like a tocsin. He does not live long at this trade. Another takes his place; bellows like him, drinks like him, and dies, like his predecessor, from imbibing cheap spirits."[5]

"By eleven," relates the actor Fleury, "Mme la Duchesse de Bourbon had sent her footmen to the ticket window to await the ticket distribution, although it

---

*Which became when they left it, and has remained, the Rue de l'Ancienne Comédie.
†*Pays latin.* Now, of course, the *quartier latin,* or Latin Quarter. In those days, masters and students often spoke Latin in the streets to show off their erudition.

was not to begin until four o'clock. To force her way through the throng, Mme d'Ossun did such violence to her nature that she became positively polite. Mme de Talleyrand* gave the lie to her reputation by paying triple for her box . . . People poured in, pushed and shoved, it was stifling.

"Inside the house, another spectacle: the chink of plates and clatter of forks, a deafening pop of corks. Our sanctuary had become a cabaret! Three hundred people were dining in our boxes, to be closer to the office when it opened; there was the fat Marquise de Montmorin who could scarcely squeeze into Mlle Oliver's pretty little niche, and the graceful Mme de Senectère, who mislaid her dinner in the melee; Desessaits† had to be pressed into service so that she could have something to eat. And what an audience, in the main house! Shall I name the illustrious lords who were there, the noble dames, the gifted artists, the renowned authors, the world's wealthy? What a glittering diadem of first boxes! The superb Princesse de Lamballe, the Princesse de Chimay, the indolent Mme de Lascuse, the witty Marquise d'Andlau, the supreme Mme de Châlons, the beautiful Mme de Balbi,** Mme de Simiane more beautiful still, Mmes de la Châtre, Matignon, and Dudrenenc in the same box. It was all sparkle and greetings. Rounded arms, white shoulders, swans' throats, diamond necklaces, cloth from Lyons, blue, pink, white, moving rainbows shimmering, weaving back and forth, fluttering, all eager to applaud, eager to condemn, all for Beaumarchais and all because of Beaumarchais,"[6] who has been hiding for hours in a screened box, unsuspected by the mass— a sign that he wasn't too sure which way the audience would blow and didn't want to find himself facing a torrent of public abuse. As an added precaution, he has chosen a pair of priests for box-mates: Abbé de Calonne, the brother of the new comptroller-general, and Abbé Sabatier de Castres, neither of whom, it is true, is overweeningly pious. But their presence is a sort of official stamp of approval for Beaumarchais. All three are rubicund and armed for an ordeal, having just dined like true gourmets. "From this discreet observatory the joyful author could savor his triumph and measure his stature in the public eye. Once or twice there comes an hour for which one would give the rest of one's life,"‡ and Beaumarchais is living through one of them now.[7]

At the end of four years of one of the bitterest wars ever waged by a creator struggling to get his work before the public. Almost as long as the war in America.

And, like the Rebels, he nearly ran out of ammunition toward the end—that is, of the money he so scorns but can't live without to keep up his handsome

---

*The abbé's mother, who was said to be a skinflint.
†An actor.
**Mistress of the Comte de Provence. Mme de Simiane was being courted by La Fayette.
‡According to the Duc de Castres.

home on the Rue Vieille-du-Temple, to pay for his fine food, his short-lived girlfriends, his carriage, his gorgeous clothes—but also and even more, to support his little tribe of dependents: three sisters, two of whom are in "religious boarding houses" and the third, Julie—his friend and good angel—at home with him; and Marie-Thérèse de Willermawlaz, the mistress of the house; and Eugénie, the little daughter she gave him in 1777; and the servants and clerks; and the episodic and in some instances regular handouts to friends, but also to spongers . . .* Too little tribute has been paid to Beaumarchais's generosity. He was almost incapable of saying no, and on the rare occasions when he did his refusal rankled like a wound.

But in 1783 his coffers were empty. Far from enriching him, his enormous traffic as ship outfitter and arms merchant to the United States had depleted his fortune almost as badly as the Goëzman trial. The King and the Congress in Philadelphia have been volleying America's debts to him back and forth as though they were playing the tournament finals. And then there were the ships that went down and the lost cargoes nobody wanted to pay for . . .[8] Was he about to catch the plague of poverty, which he feared worse than death? On January 19, 1784, one swallow came (but would it make a spring?) in a letter from Calonne, who had taken over the treasury two months before:

> It is my sincere pleasure to inform you, Monsieur, that the King, upon hearing the account of your application, which I submitted to him regarding all the circumstances of your situation and your need of a fresh advance upon the compensation you claim, has deigned to make over to you the sum of 570,-627 livres, which, together with the 905,400† you have already received, will make up the total of what the commissioners instructed to evaluate your compensation have calculated was owing to you. His Majesty has also agreed that the consideration of your further iterations should be entrusted to five dealers proficient in maritime matters, and has approved their appointment as proposed by me.[9]

Hallelujah! That gets him off the hook for a while anyway. Why this gesture from Calonne, just after taking office? Firstly, because the new minister is a man of wit, a cultivated man who has been following Beaumarchais's career for years from the provinces, where he was serving as intendant. Secondly, because, unlike the two shapeless placekeepers before him, Fleury and d'Ormesson, Calonne pretends to have ideas, and even a scheme for getting France off the slippery slope to bankruptcy. He will therefore need the support

---

*Among whom, it's true, there were such great lords as the princes of Luxembourg and Nassau-Spiegen.

†Approximately 3.4 million modern francs [$680,000] as a subsidy, added to 4.5 million [$900,000] already received. This shows the volume of his activity.

of "enlightened" opinion and will also need hacks—talented if possible—to formulate that support. Both Turgot and Necker had them in their teams, and Calonne is on the lookout. His indemnification of Beaumarchais is a down payment on the future.

It left him free to devote his energies to the final phase of his campaign for the production of the *Marriage* . . . or rather *La Folle Journée* as he was careful to call the play then, stressing the first part of the title in order to emphasize its frivolous side. Since reading it to the Comte and Comtesse du Nord—a success with no sequel—Beaumarchais had been using an argument, when whispering to certain "in" courtiers, that was beginning to gain credibility among the people for whom Louis XVI was no longer a total mystery: "The King has forbidden the performance of *La Folle Journée;* that means it will be performed."[10]

In 1783 he quit slithering up from trench to trench and initiated his siege of Yorktown. With his manuscript flapping in the wind like a banner, Beaumarchais chose a new angle of attack and moved closer to the target by deciding to dispense with the Orléanses. There had always been a gulf between him and the Palais Royal—maybe because, however awkwardly and opportunistically, he defended Marie Antoinette at the beginning of her reign; but whatever the reason, the Duc de Chartres, who has just been so ostentatiously present among the aeronauts, takes absolutely no part in the battle of the *Marriage.* The time is fast approaching when relations between the Court and the Orléans coterie will become so strained, and friction so incessant, that people will be forced to choose sides for years to come; even the most agile contortionists can no longer back both the Queen and Philippe de Chartres. It's every man to his territory, like in the jungle.

Beaumarchais plumps for the Queen, Monsieur, and the Comte d'Artois, which means also the Polignacs, the Vaudreuils, Mme de Lamballe, and even the Baron de Breteuil, who is a pretentious pachyderm but who, as minister of the King's Household, has full authority over it in the name of both Queen and King, and hence over the city of Paris as well. Beaumarchais sets out to conquer Louis XVI not by direct assault, but by subverting his entourage; there's still a little of the harp master in him.

At the beginning of February 1783, a final private reading takes place in the home of the Baron de Breteuil, before an audience of a dozen arbiters of fashion and the arts. Beaumarchais's artful introduction:

"Ladies, Monseigneur, dear friends, the play you are about to hear deserves neither the praise nor the blame it has incurred. Excessive opposition to its performance has deformed its content. What is it, in fact? An innocent piece, a pure divertissement in which I have given free rein to my inconsequential temperament. We only jest at what we love. To be sure, it contains many defects, and I shall submit unreservedly to all the deletions and corrections you may deem proper to make."[11]

Oh, the meek little lamb! Toward the end, Breteuil interrupts the reading and proposes one word in place of another. Beaumarchais pounces:

"Monseigneur, that word will save my fourth act!"

Thereby making the minister of the King's Household co-author of *La Folle Journée.* Breteuil gives the signal for applause:

"I do believe, Monsieur, that your comedy could be acted as it is . . . "

Is that the go-ahead? Beaumarchais, who never will stop believing in Santa Claus, tries to rush things and thereby gives Louis XVI the opportunity to administer one last, cruelly refined paw swipe. There was, in Paris, a long gloomy hall with a white glass roof that was never used for much of anything: the Salle des Menus-Plaisirs du Roi. It belonged to the Court. Sometime in February the French Acting Company was ordered (by whom? Breteuil? Papillon de la Ferté, the minister in charge of Menus-Plaisirs, to whom they were directly attached?) "to learn, for the service at Versailles, *Le Mariage de Figaro ou la suite du Barbier de Seville"*[12] and to present it, in the Salle des Menus-Plaisirs, to the Court. According to Grimm it was Beaumarchais who had overstepped the line by telling them that the order had actually come from on high. "Thus it was in a theater belonging to His Majesty that the Sieur Caron [*sic*] undertook to have performed a play that His Majesty had forbidden, and undertook to do so with no more justification than a vague promise said to have been given by Monsieur, or by M. le Comte d'Artois, that there would be no counterorder."

Artois, at least, confirmed this, but which of the two is least frivolous, he or Beaumarchais? The actors, at any rate, were delighted. Notwithstanding their lengthy hassles with Beaumarchais over the rights to the *Barber of Seville* and their irritation at his founding the Société des Auteurs—which would obviously offend them, because until then they had been able to fleece their authors to their hearts' content—the company, almost entirely new, had been awaiting this authorization like manna from heaven. True professionals, they were well aware of the scarcity of playwrights in those days—apart from Diderot, of course, but nobody was allowed to perform him—and they knew that even revivals of Racine and Corneille couldn't fill their new house, the biggest they had ever had: nineteen hundred seats! What they needed was a really first-rate play by a contemporary author. And when they read, enthusiastically applauded, and began rehearsing *Le Mariage,* they showed themselves to be true professionals once again, by willingly relinquishing parts to more suitable players instead of bickering fiercely over them as was their usual practice. Those who were used to leading roles were begging, as a favor, to be given a walk-on as soubrette or peasant, just so they could *be there.* For two years Beaumarchais and his interpreters worked hand in glove: this production of the *Marriage* was one of the first instances of teamwork in the theater since Molière.

Yes, but . . . "as we had formerly heard that the King, after reading the piece, had himself declared it to be *unperformable,* everyone was much surprised to learn that a work which had not been thought decent enough for the city should be commanded for the Court; the author was presumed to have made substantial alterations, and everyone assumed that, on the strength of its success at Versailles, the play would soon be produced in Paris; there was great mystery, however, as to both the time and even the place in which this comedy was to be first performed. The rumor was that it would be in the little *suites,* then at Trianon, Choisy, Bagatelle, or Brunoy. The early rehearsals took place in great secrecy in Paris, on the stage of the Menus-Plaisirs; at last it was decided that the play would be performed at that same theater; but for what audience, and by whose order, and at whose expense? Rather than diminishing, the secrecy seemed to generate layers of cloud that grew denser every day; although a goodly number of people had been let in to watch the final rehearsals. On the eve of the day set for the opening performance [June 13, 1783] the whole Court was talking openly about it; it was even mentioned in the King's carriages. Tickets had been issued, the prettiest tickets imaginable too, striped *à la Marlborough* [?]. The only people who behaved as though they were not in on the secret were M. Lenoir, the lieutenant of police, and M. le Maréchal de Duras, first gentleman of the chamber.

" 'I have no idea,' M. Lenoir said that same morning, 'on whose authority M. Beaumarchais's play is being given at the Menus-Plaisirs this evening; but of one thing I am quite certain, and that is that the King does not wish it performed . . .'

"Not until one in the afternoon did the officials at the Menus-Plaisirs and the police receive an express order from the King to cancel the performance. The following day, the actors of the Comédie Française were summoned to appear before M. le Lieutenant de Police and most particularly forbidden on His Majesty's part to perform the play in any theater or other place whatsoever."

Better luck next time.

But the cup was full. The right-minded Mme Campan herself allows that "this prohibition by the King was perceived as an invasion of public freedom. All the disappointed anticipation aroused such dissatisfaction that the words *opression* and *tyranny* were never uttered with greater passion and vehemence, not even in the days preceding the fall of the throne."[13] The good woman exaggerates, and she was far from Paris in those later fateful times, but her cavatina does bear witness to the dismay spreading through even the most conformist ranks over the battle of the *Marriage.* And Mme Campan would have been utterly incapable of inventing the comment of Beaumarchais, who almost lost his temper for once, as the Salle des Menus-Plaisirs was being emptied in a great mutter of indignation:

"Well, Messieurs, he does not wish it performed here, yet I trust that it will be performed, and perhaps in the choir of Notre Dame."

Not so fast. There will have to be a transitional stage, a real performance, somewhere, with a full cast—but in private, or semi-public might be a better term, for the people whose ears can hear anything because their tongues have already said worse without bringing the world to an end. The Queen's friends now take over. "There is no salvation outside *Le Mariage!*"[14] proclaimed Vaudreuil. On September 4, 1783, the Duc de Fronsac (son of the senescent Richelieu, who remarried in 1780 at the age of eighty-four) writes to Beaumarchais:

> I do hope, Monsieur, that you will not think it ill of me to have undertaken to secure your consent to a performance of the *Marriage of Figaro* at Gennevilliers; but it is true that when I agreed to carry out this task I thought you were still in Paris.* This is the situation: you know that I have ceded my land and house at Gennevilliers to M. de Vaudreuil. M. le Comte d'Artois is coming to hunt there on the 18th, and Mme la Duchesse de Polignac, with her society, will come for supper. Vaudreuil has consulted me about giving them an entertainment, for there is rather a pretty stage, and I told him that none could be more charming than the *Marriage of Figaro,* but that it would be necessary to obtain the King's consent. We did so, and I hurried to tell you this, but was much taken aback and grieved to learn you were so far away. The play is well known, as you are aware: would you give us your approval for its performance?[15]

Would I! Oh, er, hum hum; Pierre-Augustin, purring, lets them twist his arm, insists that the play must be resubmitted to a new bunch of censors; but he can hardly wait and he knows it. Gennevilliers: a bosky fishing preserve in the big loop northwest of the Seine between Asnières and Argenteuil, way out in the country. Fronsac had perpetrated a famous folly there, a multi-tiered cake of stone frosted with gold and rosewood, complete with toy theater. There'll be nobody there but us chickens, how cosy. Will the Queen come? She wouldn't mind, but her imbecile of a husband who lets her have her way in so much else is still putting his foot down about this. Artois, on the other hand, gladly takes a front-row seat and claps his hands with a will. Isn't it comical, all these characters trying to get off with each other. That's all he sees in the play, and all the rest of them see too. Beaumarchais has done a good

---

*Beaumarchais had gone to London for a few days.

job of camouflage. Pierre-Augustin is so ecstatically acclaimed by these fifty super-blasé men and women that he falls into a sort of epilepsy of joy. "He went running about in all directions like a person who has had too much to drink. People were complaining of the heat; he did not even stop to open the windows, but simply broke the panes with his stick." Cavorting about like a *grand seigneur* in the home of his host Vaudreuil: he certainly has learned to ape their manners. "Which caused people to say, after the play, that there had been two smash hits that night."[16] "Ah," sighs Suzanne in Act IV, "I love your joy because it is unreasonable! It shows that you are happy."

Upon his return from Gennevilliers, the Comte d'Artois finally finds the right words to amuse and above all reassure his brother:

"Sire, must I tell you in two words? The exposition [of the play] plot, dénouement, dialogue, the whole and every part of it from the first scene to the last, is nothing but *foutre* and more *foutre.*"*

Whereupon, Louis XVI gives the go-ahead.

Back to April 27. It's silly of Beaumarchais to be cowering behind a screen. This time the battle is won before it starts—but it was worth it. Inside the theater, which "resembles an arena of white sugar," a brand-new chandelier illuminates the signs of the zodiac sculpted in bas-relief around the ceiling and beams down upon the best-filled and most enthusiastic house in the history of French drama, crowded together on benches for the first time. It used to be that the only place where one could sit down was in a box, but the new benches in the orchestra provide not only comfort but also an excuse to double the price of tickets.

His triumph lasts five solid hours, because the actors milk every effect for all they're worth, the intermissions are interminable, and almost every scene is interrupted by rounds of applause.

How different from the teething-troubles of the *Barber!* This time everything goes like a charm from start to finish. Dazincourt plays a Figaro overflowing with wit, Molé an elegant Almaviva, the venerable Préville raises howls of laughter as Brid'Oison—but as usual, the loudest cheers go to the three female leads: the celebrated Contat, who makes a bewitching Suzanne, the tragedienne Sainval, who is delighted to play Rosine with no fear of losing status, and above all Mlle Olivier, an exquisite little actress of seventeen who has only a year to live and who plays the part of Chérubin with wonderful freshness, her transvestism adding to the ambiguousness of the role.

In their rustling, vaguely Hispanified modern costumes, the characters

---

*According to Métra. It may be worth pointing out that the word *foutre* [commonly translated "fuck" or one of its variants—*Trans.*] was the people's and in this instance the aristocrats' everyday word for sperm, a life-oath (recurring again and again in *Le Père Duchesne*), as distinct from the scatological *merde* [shit], which does not come into widespread use until a century later.

sweep the audience along into the five-act farandole of *La Folle Journée,* never giving it time to notice that although they are the same people as in the *Barber* they are also much, much older, stonier in their bitterness, even cruelty. Count Almaviva is a vile and ignominious aristocrat obsessed with his *jus primae noctis,* but his darker side is not belabored by the author. He wants to be unfaithful to his countess with Suzanne, Suzanne wants to marry Figaro, and both women (Suzanne and the countess) are very much aware of the ambivalent charms of thirteen-year-old Chérubin. The characters pursue, intersect, elude each other's grasp, dealing and receiving some nasty bruises as they go, observed by a ponderous trio of caricature-witnesses—Basile, Bartholo, and Brid'Oison-Goëzman—in whom Beaumarchais gets back at the lawyers and churchmen for everything he has suffered at their hands. In the background, a peasant celebration transported from his youth, way back in 1767 when he was supervising the timber felling in the forest of Chinon for the big financier Paris-Duverney.

"The activity involved in this forced labor is quite to my liking:* since my arrival in this retreat, inaccessible to vanity, I have seen only simple and unaffected people such as I often desire to be . . . The furniture in my room, which has four white-washed walls, consists of one bad bed on which I sleep like a log, four straw-seated chairs, one oaken table, a large bare hearth without a mantelpiece . . . Good hard bread, more than modest fare, and execrable wine comprise my meals . . . All the waste land and meadows in the valley are filled with stalwart dark-skinned men cutting and carrying forage by ox-cart; a host of women and girls, their rakes in their hands or slung over their shoulders, sing high, piping songs as they work; I can hear them from my table."[17]

They represent "the people" in *Le Mariage,* and their courage and gaiety make a striking contrast: as the main characters grow more biting (Almaviva cynical, Rosine bitterly disappointed, Figaro vengeful), the rhythm accelerates into a dance, and Chérubin, the foil for adult disillusionment, looks increasingly like innocence personified, which makes him all the more disturbing to the women.

For this opening night, Beaumarchais has magnanimously but regretfully complied with the censors' final request and deleted a few passages† (stunning lines, though), chief among them a sort of feminist manifesto that seems a little incongruous coming from this notorious skirt-chaser. It is spoken by Marcelline at the most throbbing moment of the melodrama, when she is revealed as Figaro's mother. What an outburst, though; what a defense of womanhood!

*Letter to his father, summer of 1767.

†Except for the end of the famous Act V soliloquy, they have largely been restored in modern acting versions.

I was born to be good, and I became good as soon as I was permitted to make use of my reason. But when we are in the years of illusion, inexperience, and need, when seducers beguile us while poverty twists the knife in our sides, what force has a child to oppose so many united foes? And then we are harshly judged by some man who may in his life have been the undoing of ten such wretches!

You worse than ungrateful men, your victims are the playthings of your passions, and you degrade them with your sneers; it is you who should be punished for the errors of our youth: you and your magistrates, so vain of your right to judge us; by your culpable negligence you let any honest means of survival be torn from our grasp! Is there *any* estate for young women of no fortune? All the adornment of womanhood was theirs by natural right; but their places are taken by a thousand workers of the other sex.*

Even in the highest ranks women are treated by you with unspeakable condescension. They are fooled by superficial marks of respect, but they live in actual servitude; where our property is concerned we are regarded as children, but for our faults we are punished as adults; every aspect of your behavior toward us strikes horror or pity.[18]

In the first act Beaumarchais also had to retract a line of Figaro's that Diderot would not have disowned:

"Good day, oh doctor of my heart, soul and other viscera."[19]

But no power on earth could have made him cut Figaro's fifth act monologue:† "What have you done to deserve so much? You gave yourself the trouble to be born, and that was all! . . . Whereas I, by gad! . . . "[20] What pours from the throat of Figaro-Beaumarchais in this speech, more than the revenge he has been waiting for his whole life long, is the rapture that sweeps over every great author when the flame begins to burn brighter and fiercer than his own small candle, giving voice to words unspoken by millions of the mute. "The night is devilish dark . . ." Almost fifteen unrelieved minutes of it. In the house too, even in that Parisian aviary, there must have been—a pregnant pause. *Mene, mene, tekel, upharsin . . .* Did anyone at Belshazzar's feast understand that prophecy of death on the wall? But Beaumarchais didn't want to depress his audience too much, so he also cut, this time on his own initiative, the end of a soliloquy that raises him to the level of Shakespeare:**

Shall I be a man at last? A man! A man grows down as he grew up . . . limping where he ran before . . . then revulsion and disease . . . an old, enfeebled doll . . . an icy mummy . . . a skeleton . . . vile dust, and then, nothing . . . ! [*He lets his head fall upon his breast. Recovering himself.*] Brrr! into what pit have I sunk

---

*Almost a trade unionist's complaint: in those days men were increasingly being trained as weavers and embroiderers. Figaro's reply: "They're even setting the soldiers to embroider . . . "

†The whole soliloquy is worth pondering; it is a monument of the French language and thought. Napoleon said, on St. Helena, that this text was the beginning of the Revolution.

**And looks forward to Musset.

daydreaming here, like a bottomless well? It's turned me to ice . . . I'm cold.
[*Gets up.*] Devil take the beast! Suzon, Suzon, you've brought me to a pretty pass!
On my soul, there's a good square foot of black inside my chest . . .[21]

"This must surely be* the wellspring of romanticism, if the romantic is a man
who feels alien to society and the world, who discovers the emptiness of his
life."

Come on, Figaro, pull yourself together! The countess is coming in Suzon's
clothes and Suzon in those of the countess, and soon Chérubin turns up dressed
as an officer, "merrily singing the refrain to the ballad, 'Once had I a god-
mother, I ever did adore her.' " The house stirs, there is coughing and blowing
of noses, people stretch, the laughs start welling up again, and "everything
ends in song."

A real hit. Twelve curtain calls. A record box office take in the theater's
history: 6,511 livres the first night. 68 performances in eight months. By
January 10, a gross take of 350,000 livres, 41,500 of which are for Beaumarchais. For the first time, a play has actually made money for its author, or at
least it would have if he had not carefully calculated that he had spent 37,500
livres on "public relations" for it: presents, suppers, travel, and the rest. His
net profit comes to 5,000 livres.†

Si ce gai, ce fol ouvrage	[If in this gay and foolish play
Renfermait quelque leçon	Some lesson lurked, for
En faveur du badinage	seasoning,
Faites grâce à la raison . . .‡	Sweet trifling's sake behoves
	you, pray,
	To spare the pain of reason-
	ing . . .]

*According to René Pomeau.

†Approximate equivalents in new francs: 39,000 [$7,800] the first night; gross take on
January 10, 2.1 million [$450,000], of which 249,000 [$49,800] goes to Beaumarchais. But after
deduction of his expenses, he's left with a net profit of only 30,000 [$6,000]—according to him.

**Ninth stanza (sung by Suzanne) of the song that ends the play.

47

APRIL 1784

My Childhood Was Almost Forlorn

Buzot gets married the next day.

What next day? Why, the day after *Le Mariage,* of course, as people were beginning to say and would say forever after, abbreviating the title of Beaumarchais's play.

The triumphant opening night took place in Paris on April 27, 1784; François-Nicolas-Léonard Buzot celebrates *his* marriage at Evreux on April 28; and the word and the date are all the two events have in common. The *Marriage of Figaro* is a festival of joy, or pretends to be, whereas Buzot's nuptials* are no laughing matter. Of course, nobody in Evreux knows about the performance that has taken Paris by storm; people's main activities here are producing not plays but wool and linen and selling wheat and livestock.

We're in the heart of the old town of Evreux in smiling Normandy, ten leagues from Rouen and twenty-five from Paris, by the west road through Saint-Germain and Mantes. The little procession of bride and groom, relatives and guests, didn't need a carriage to wend its way to Saint-Nicolas from the Rue de la Petite-Cité, where Buzot has already taken possession of the family house, although his mother has life use of it. It's only a stone's throw from the church, and hardly more than that from the château at the top of the town that belongs to the ducs de Bouillon, who have been comtes d'Evreux ever since they traded their principality of Sedan to Louis XIV for this expanse of lush green land. You go along the Rue Chiche-Face for a few yards, turn into the Rue Trou-Bailly, another ten or twelve yards along the Rue de la Porte-Notre-Dame and you're at the parish church, one of the three finest in town if you except the enormous ship of a cathedral, full of spires and lanterns, patched and repaired times beyond number after its successive burnings at

*After making a name for himself in the Constituent Assembly, François Buzot (he uses his first given name), born in 1760, becomes one of the most influential "Girondins" or "Brissotins" of the Convention. He is Mme Roland's best friend. After escaping with Pétion and Barbaroux following the indictment of the Girondins in June 1793, he shares their tragic peregrinations and commits suicide with them near Saint-Emilion.

the hands of the Normans, followed by the English, followed by lightning.

It's not so easy to find your way around in this tangle of streets—alleys would be a better name for them—that wind like damp stone corridors through such an agglomeration of religious edifices that the town is virtually obstructed by them.[1] Eight parish churches and six abbeys, two for women, in addition to the cathedral, all squeezed into a pocket handkerchief measuring 300 square fathoms.* The most beautiful convent, however, the monastery of Saint-Taurin, whose depth and mass can vie with those of the cathedral, stands on a hill outside the town walls, looking over the Iton before it splits into three branches, one crossing the lower town, the second lapping its walls, and the third watering the countryside around. This is the abbey of the monks of Saint-Maur, who guard the remains of the martyr Saint Taurin,† patron saint of Evreux, and have guarded them since a pillar of fire in the sky informed the blessed Bishop Landulphe, in the days before the Normans came, where the sacred relics lay. He's done his best to protect the town all these years, but even he was unable to prevent its inhabitants from turning it into a sunless, somber maze with its fifteen houses of God—and the remaining scraps of ground that had to be given to the Hôtel de Ville, the new marketplace, the theater, and the prison. And they had to find room for the bishop's palace, too.

The organ swells. François Buzot, elegant and refined in a pearl gray outfit, moves toward the altar with his mother on his arm, dressed in black and white. He's twenty-four. His father died when he was a child, and this morning a goodly number of the ritual tears shed by a family at any wedding will be in memory of him. Awaiting them, frail and almost buried alive in the multicolored embroidered gown designed to disguise her hunchback, his fiancée Marie-Anne-Victoire Baudry stands clutching the arm of her father, the industrialist—called an ironmaster in those days—of Cosne-sur-Loire in the Nivernais. She's thirty-seven—thirteen years older than Buzot. And as if her deformity weren't enough, there are also her pallid skin, sunken eyes, and expressionless face to make her look even older. Has she ever smiled? Not today, at any rate. She's fond enough of her young fiancé, though; what an unheard-of stroke of luck! One of the most distinguished looking men in Evreux, "a noble face and poised figure, well-combed, powdered hair framing a high forehead below which shine two bright eyes."[2] A slightly aquiline nose, arched brows, and rather disdainful lips mark his pointed face with the signs of swift intuition and considerable vivacity; and Buzot has learned how to set it off with an impeccably fluted muslin jabot. "He conferred upon his attire** that attention, cleanliness, and respectability which denote an orderly mind, taste, and a sense of

*Approximately 55 acres.
†Legendary: there is no historical source for him.
**According to Mme Roland.

the proprieties, the consideration given by a true man of parts to both his public and himself."³ A middle-class assessment of an upper-middle-class man, a lordling, who will often be noticed and indeed envied for a degree of elegance bordering on affectation.

Beneath this very prepossessing exterior lies a gravity precocious in a man of his years, and even some traces of melancholy. "My childhood* was almost forlorn."⁴ Oh come now, François! Want he certainly never knew, or insecurity, or ignorance, or scorn. But the loneliness of the heart—that perhaps, when he was very young, and a lack of love even before his father's death. He has left no record of either his father or his mother, who was presumably a retiring creature. This solemn childhood and a concern for his appearance are points he shares with Robespierre, another young provincial lawyer.

He was baptized on March 1, 1760, also in the church of Saint-Nicolas and at the end of another procession from the same paternal home on the Rue de la Petite-Cité.† He was born the same day, "son of M. François Buzot, *procureur* at the bailliage and presidial seat of Evreux, and of Demoiselle Marie-Madeleine Legrand, his spouse in legitimate wedlock [*sic*]." His godfather, also his maternal grandfather, was "Maître Nicolas Legrand, attorney at the bailliage and presidial seat of Evreux."⁵ Two families of the most "honorable" sort, thus, in legal society, that third estate which was on its way up in Normandy as everywhere else and which counts for a lot, quantitatively and qualitatively, in a town where justice both high and low is meted out to the entire county in the palace hard by the Buzot house and almost next door to the Legrands'. A dual trunk of the old bourgeoisie, a cemetery full of registrars, *procureurs,* and court lawyers in the last two or three centuries, and all of them in Evreux, although the Buzots had a slight lead over the Legrands because their names crop up earlier, as men of the "long gown" but as merchants too, in the local chronicles. On June 6, 1703, a councilor of the king (Louis XIV) named Guillaume Flambart came before the aldermen to complain that "the sieur Jean Buzot,** lawyer of the town, had insulted him and called him a knave and a falsifier, the young man having carried his effrontery to the point of seizing him by the cravat and throwing him to the ground."⁶ If the blood of these impassive Normans has been simmering ever since, what can we expect from the class of 1784?

*Written ten years later when Buzot has suffered great disappointment and is walking in the shadow of death.

†Razed by order of the Convention at the end of July 1793 and replaced by a sort of toy stone pyramid bearing an inscription condemning "the crimes of the scoundrel Buzot." This object was destroyed, in turn, by order of the Thermidorians, in February 1795. Another house was built on the site, and inhabited for many years by a locksmith.

**Presumably a great-uncle of our man.

Honorable and therefore honored, but not all rich. There have been rather too many Buzots in these families, six to thirteen children apiece.* François's father and mother haven't done too badly, their house on the Rue de la Petite-Cité is large and comfortably furnished although by no means a palace. But in other parts of town (were those cousins invited to the wedding?) one can find an Achille Buzot who is a pastry-cook/caterer in the parish of Saint-Denis, and even a Marie-Anne Buzot, "servant-girl of M. Duvivier de Bosc-Roger."[7] In other words Evreux ("6,200 persons of all ages, sexes, and conditions"[8] at the end of the reign of Louis XV) is a town in which the name of Buzot is known on every street.

The François Buzot getting married today has also been lucky in another respect: only one brother and one sister were born after him, in 1762 and 1766, and he himself, the firstborn, came late, after five years of marriage, when his parents were beginning to fear they were sterile. "However, I became acquainted with pain early in life" and also, perhaps, with a propensity for indulging in it. His maternal grandparents died in '67 and '69, his father when only fifty-five, in 1771. But even more, his gloom may have come from the color of his childhood, all dingy gray stone, three children in the shadows of a sad town that turned its back on the games the little peasant boys and girls were playing so close outside its walls. The only affection the three children could always count on, the only ear that was always ready to listen, was that of Marie, a servant who was their one source of knowledge until they were old enough for school. The memory of her flutters across the final page of Buzot's *Mémoires:* "For you, dear Marie, who brought me up for a happier fate."[9]

The Evreux collège was not likely to bring much sun into his life; in a kingdom in which all education was controlled by the clergy, Evreux stood out as a paragon of clericalism. "The school was highly regarded, but it could not have been so in consequence of the educational guidance given to the young people attending it. The establishment must have been subject to ecclesiastical influence, as its principal was also the canon of the cathedral. In addition, the five instructors of belles lettres, even in the philosophy classes [that is, the last year or two of upper secondary education, when philosophy was studied— *Trans.*], were also churchmen chosen by the principal who was himself chosen by the bishop."[10]

François survived by conceiving a passion for Roman history and withdrawing into himself with almost schizoid determination, but also by going for long lonely rambles, book in hand, through the countryside he was finally beginning to discover. He later says that his childhood made him a republican

*Between 1733 and 1752 thirteen children were born to the marriage of Jean-Baptiste Buzot, "sergeant-royal and treasurer of Saint-Pierre" and Marie-Magdeleine Danneboeuf.

before he ever heard the word republic. Even in adolescence the idea of a hereditary and absolute monarchy seemed monstrous to him.

"Born with an independent and proud nature that never yielded to command from anyone, how could I endure the idea of a hereditary master and an invincible man? My head and heart were filled with Greek and Roman history and the great figures who most highly honored the human race in those ancient republics, and I professed their maxims even in youth; I nourished myself on the study of their virtues . . . My passions, concentrated in my fervent and sensitive heart, were violent, extreme, but confined to a single object"— freedom—"they were all directed toward that. Never did libertinage taint my soul with its impure breath; I have always had a horror of debauchery and, even in much later years, no licentious utterance ever sullied my lips . . .

"With what delight I still recall that happy time when my days were spent moving in silence through the mountains [*sic*] and woods of the town where I was born, reading, enthralled, some work by Plutarch or Rousseau, or rehearsing in my mind the most precious traits of their morality and philosophy. Sometimes, seated in the flowering meadows in the shade of a few leafy trees, I would abandon myself with fond melancholy to the memory of the trials and joys that had alternately agitated the first days of my life."[11]

A life that seemed totally preprogrammed, like those of so many other people his age, and made desperate by the total absence of any possibility of adventure on any horizon. He's the oldest, he'll be a lawyer; if he were a gentleman's son, he'd have been a lieutenant. And he'll make a marriage of convenience, of money that is, like all the Buzots in his branch of the family. In the name of what should he try to be different? Buzot certainly has nothing, but nothing at all, in common with Beaumarchais . . . he could almost be an anti-Figaro.

A trip to Paris to study law. About which we know nothing. He must have been a free (i.e., not financed by a religious school or organization) student at the Sorbonne, kept at his family's expense or in the home of some correspondent. Paris brought him not one glimmer of illumination. Which also makes him an anti-Brissot—but Brissot was the son of the proprietor of a cookshop and had revolted against his childhood, whereas Buzot accepts his, dismal though it is. After defending his thesis, he was duly awarded his degree in Paris, on April 24, 1782, and stayed on another year or more in the bustle of the chambers of parlement. Pleading? Not yet. Learning his trade, training.

At the beginning of 1784 he goes back to Evreux and is registered as an attorney of the bailliage.[12] There's plenty of work, even if his eloquence is impaired in those early days by the local twang—Evreux is heaven for office lawyers and hell for those in the courtroom. "The jurisdiction of this bailliage, far more extensive than the diocese, extended to the gates of Caen. Evreux also possessed a presidial court, covering the same territory as the bailliage; it was composed of two presidents and several councilors, who were the same for both courts, a legal monstrosity which meant that both the original trial and the appeal were judged by the same men."[13] Twice the work meant twice the fee for the lawmen; and drifting above them all was that old perfume compounded of incense and burning human flesh, the odor that makes the people of Evreux bow so low under their bishop's crook. In this part of the country, the Inquisition lingered on until the sixteenth century. "Under François I, Evreux had the dubious distinction of being the seat of a sort of inquisition whose pernicious effects were felt by the whole of Normandy. This fanatical and bloodthirsty tribunal sat in the Dominican monastery. In 1722 one could still see its prisons and the seal with which the inquisitor-fathers endorsed their decrees. It was a piece of oval copper with a handle, and on it were engraved the images of St. Dominic and St. Peter."[14] There was a pinch of religion in everything around here, even the payment of the *taille* [a tax] throughout the "election of Evreux,[15] amounting to 120,000 livres."*

But about this marriage . . . It's a matter of course, at least for the parents who arranged it; and neither Buzot nor his wife ever make any audible complaint. They unearthed this cousin, Marie-Anne Baudry, born at Charité-sur-Loire, daughter of "Messire Jean-Pierre Baudry, ironmaster, director-in-chief and controller, on the King's behalf, of the royal forges and manufactures of Cosne-sur-Loire, where anchors, irons, and other utilities for the service of His Majesty's navy and colonies were manufactured, and of demoiselle Marie-Anne Buzot."[16] He's not getting a gold-mine with her, at least not yet: 14,000 livres in cash, and furniture, "wearing apparel," linens and jewelry amounting to 2,800 livres;† but it could be worse, it's better than bare comfort, and they have "expectations"—the word for death when there's money in it—from a few aunts and uncles.

In exchange, Buzot and his mother were offering Marie-Anne a house "in very good condition, having three stories not including the attics, composed of eight chimneyed apartments with their accessories, two vaulted cellars, a stable,[17] an inner courtyard, and a small piece of land with a terrace giving onto the water."**

A good marriage, no? So why this look of disenchantment on the newly-weds' cheerless faces? Because this is the "normal" culmination of a youth spent in their environment?

---

*No connection with any sort of ballot. In the Ancien Régime an election was a jurisdiction established by the baronial or royal authority to determine the basis for calculating taxes.

†85,000 and 17,000 modern francs [$17,000 and $3,400].

**For which they were offered 22,000 livres in 1789 (135,000 modern francs [$27,000]).

48

JULY 1784

We Have Served Mankind

In that time—the time of the first balloons and the *Marriage*—the giants were dying off one after another, as in Genesis. They had done their work and were leaving its fruits to mankind.

D'Alembert died only nine months before Diderot. They hardly saw each other anymore and had stopped corresponding. Both had come to the end of their roads and were devoting what time and energy they had left, more sincerely than many believers, to their preparations for departure. But despite their feud, their names remained linked together by the *Encyclopédie* as closely as those of Castor and Pollux.

For the "'Tout-Paris'" it was as if they were already dead; people talked as though they had long since gone to their graves. Even Grimm can spare them only a few lines in passing.

Late September 1783: "We are about to lose MM. d'Alembert and Diderot: the former of a marasmus [wasting] coupled with a bladder ailment; the latter of dropsy. It is most singular that the two men who together set the tone for the century, who together raised the edifice of a work which will ensure their immortality, seem to have come together yet again to descend into their tombs. M. le Marquis de Condorcet, who is performing for M. d'Alembert the duties that a father might expect of a son, is perpetual secretary to the Academy of Sciences and at this moment director of the Académie Française; in entrusting his final dispositions to him (he has made him his universal legatee), M. d'Alembert said, smiling in spite of his pain:

"My friend, you shall pronounce my eulogy to both Academies at once; you must not waste your time in a repetition of the chore.' "[1]

One month later it's all over: "M. d'Alembert died on October 29, at nearly sixty-six years of age, of a marasmus resulting from the pain occasioned by the stone found in his bladder; it was quite substantial but not adhesive. He would never allow himself to be probed, for he was determined not to endure an operation, which alone could have prolonged his life; he was afraid to know the cause of his sufferings . . . One has some difficulty forgiving the coryphaeus of the *philosophes* for showing so little fortitude in this matter . . . But that quality is determined less by the nature of our ideas, no doubt, than by that of our sentiments; perhaps the mind of a mathematician is too exact to allow of his possessing courage as well. Pain so acute as that which he must have suffered, and for so long, is a source of ill-humor that might readily be pardoned; and it was this pain, far more than the approach of death, about which he entertained not the slightest illusion, that had embittered his nature so excessively. Nevertheless, he never went a single day without seeing his friends. The parish priest having called on the eve of his death, he sent his servant to say that his condition was such that he could not see him just then and would be happy to do so on the morrow; but both his life and his sufferings ended with the night. It has been supposed, with some reason, that the mathematical *philosophe* had calculated, from his degree of weakness, that this lapse of time would be sufficient to spare him the conventional exhortations that the priest owed to his ministry and that the sick man's nature could not render otherwise than odious and, even more certainly, futile. M. d'Alembert was carried to his parish cemetery without a procession and without ado . . .

"M. d'Alembert has left, and could only have left, but a small inheritance; he received an income of 14,000 livres in pensions.* To have more he had but to desire it, but his needs were ever on a par with his ambition. He has named M. le Marquis de Condorcet his universal legatee; he bequeathed 6,000 livres to one of his servants and 4,000 to the other; and instructed his legatee to give them more if the estate should produce enough to do so. It is much feared that the Marquis de Condorcet will reach into his own pocket to comply with this part of the will, as the testator's furnishings, books, and papers will not raise the equivalent of his two bequests."[2]

Condorcet, d'Alembert . . . the two last companions of Julie de Lespinasse, those who didn't hide their tears when they accompanied her frail remains to Saint-Sulpice eight years before. Since then, a loyal mourning affection has persisted between the two big lost children, both without wives or large numbers of friends: at most, they could be said to have small and scattered clienteles, the harvest of their own sowing. D'Alembert, prematurely aged, wrinkled, and crippled, found a source of joyless entertainment in the academic jousts in which he did his best to unhorse the bigots' candidates. But his heart was no longer in it, having broken after Julie's death when he learned, reading through her papers, that she had loved Guibert and Guibert alone—at least then—and hadn't confided in him. It was one thing that she

---

*84,000 modern francs [$16,800] a year—tidy enough. Equivalents for the presents to his servants: 36,000 and 24,000 modern francs [$7,200 and $4,800].

should care for somebody else; but not to have told him about it, him, her nightly caller! D'Alembert had already died twice that week in 1776, and found it hard to survive himself. Condorcet, the only person close to him who felt real grief at his death, wrote to Frederick II—another candle about to flicker out in Berlin:

> From the Marquis de Condorcet to the King of Prussia
>
> Paris, December 22, 1783
>
> Sire,
>
> The friend of M. d'Alembert dares flatter himself that Your Majesty will deign not to reprove the liberty he takes to speak to you of a grief in which you share. Honored with the intimate confidences of that illustrious man, I know, Sire, how great was your esteem and, I make bold to say, friendship for him . . .
>
> M. d'Alembert, who had seemed to fear the sufferings and infirmities of old age, observed the approach of death with tranquil and unostentatious courage. In his last days he amused himself by having read to him, and guessing, the riddles in the *Mercure*. Two days before his death he corrected a page of the new edition of his translation of Tacitus, on which he had been working. With no less equanimity than goodness of heart, he busied himself considering how to ensure that his servants would find relief. It was to this end that he chose me to be his heir and thus gave me this final mark of his friendship and trust.
>
> He would pay no tribute, not even outward, to the prejudices of his country, nor would he do homage on his deathbed to that which he had made it the study of his life to hold in contempt.[3]

From the depths of his lumpy armchair big Frederick replied with a funeral oration consisting of a few brief grunts:

> Pity he did not translate the whole of Tacitus. But a man who had originality himself and who produced an infinity of works on scientific questions has better things to do than spend his life translating the work of other people. Of all the Ancients, Tacitus is perhaps the one most suitable for translation by a mathematician, because he is compact, energetic, and full of force. To my knowledge, moreover, none of our great mathematicians has translated any works of Antiquity. Newton made a commentary on the Apocalypse; but the late d'Alembert is far superior to him by his choice, for there can be no comparison between the wise reflections of Tacitus and the futilities of St. John.

Denis Diderot, meanwhile, was letting himself be carried gently along the awaited stream. Two years before, fatigue, more than illness, finally got the upper hand of the big carcass. For thirty solid years he had "encyclopedized" [*sic*] "like a galley-slave."[4] "In time this work will assuredly produce a revolution in men's minds, and I hope that all tyrants, oppressors, fanatics, and intolerants will be the losers thereby. We have served mankind. But we shall long since have been reduced to cold and insensible clay before anyone feels any gratitude to us for the deed. Why should not good people be praised in their lifetimes, since they shall hear nothing beneath their tombstones?''⁵ The careful craftsman's joy in the future was occasionally marred by bitterness. There was so much more he could have written of his own, instead of accumulating facts for the rich, who would do nothing with them! Almost twenty years earlier (on July 27, 1765), he had shaken the dust from his treadmill-bound feet:

> I write you* from Le Breton's,† where I came to have another look at the copy I am leaving with him.
>
>   I mean never to enter this accursed workshop again, in which I have worn out my eyesight for scoundrels who will not give me so much as a stick to tap my way along with. There are only fourteen quires left to print, the work of eight to ten days. In eight or ten days, thus, I shall see the end of this undertaking, which has occupied me for twenty years; has not made my fortune, and that by a long chalk; has several times exposed me to the choice of leaving my country or losing my liberty; and has consumed a life that I could have made more useful and glorious. Talent would be less often sacrificed to need if it were a matter of oneself alone; one would rather drink water, live on crusts, and follow one's genius in a loft; but for a wife, for children, is there anything to which we cannot resign ourselves? Had I any need to raise myself in their eyes I should say to them not, 'I have labored thirty years for you,' but 'For thirty years I have given up my natural vocation for your sakes, I have chosen, against my inclinations, to do that which was useful for you rather than agreeable to me: that is your real obligation to me, and of that you never think.'⁶

"For a wife, for children . . . " The dig was certainly aimed at a wife, at any rate, who never understood the first thing about the paper he was forever scratching at. His growing sourness had eaten daily a little further into her nerves, and the trench of his atheism had formed an uncrossable barrier between them. Every day she prayed for his conversion. Who says it's so great to be Diderot's wife? He loved other women better than her, and then he loved them against her, and the last of his loves was their only child, his dear and beloved Caroiline de Vandeuil, his final fountain of youth.

Nanette Diderot, the little Parisienne from the Rue Poupée married forty years before at Saint-Pierre-aux-Boeufs;** she had such lovely eyes. She kept a good house for him—when he was there; she gave him excellent food, good wine, and clean sheets. But her lovely eyes had become two large perpetual reproaches "in a wide, full face, reduced to narrow compass."‡⁷ She let him entertain and hold forth to his heart's content upon matters totally beyond her; but she also committed the two deadly sins no man can forgive: she loved

---

*To Sophie Volland.
†The printer of the *Encyclopédie.*
**On November 6, 1743.
‡Diderot's own curious expression.

neither his work nor their daughter. And he had spent half his life longing to live with another woman. There was a streak of fury in Diderot's atheism, his reaction against the idea of the indissoluble union:

> To my mind a nation which believes that people are made decent by belief in God and not by good laws is in a sorry state of backwardness. I regard the existence of God, in relation to a people, as I regard marriage. One is a state, the other a notion; each may be excellent for three or four heads properly put together, but calamitous for the generality. The vow of indissoluble marriage makes, and must make, almost as many miserable human beings as it makes husbands and wives. The belief in God makes, and must make, almost as many fanatics as faithful. Wherever a God is accepted, there is a cult; wherever there is a cult, the natural order of moral duties is overturned and morality corrupted. Sooner or later the moment comes when the concept that prevented the theft of one écu causes the cutting of the throats of a hundred thousand men.[8]

But now all that is over. The great tide is rising. "I shall have no more domestic scenes. The time is past when irrationality drove me into a fury and when, raging at the impossibility of raising my hand against another, I turned it against myself and struck myself; when I went to pound my head against the wall. I have grown used to it . . . This jealousy, of friend for friend, sister for sister, mother for daughter, daughter for mother, is beyond me. I cannot understand it."[9] On one of his last trips to Langres, to the home of his cutler father, he failed to find most of his old schoolmates: "They are almost all gone. Two things point to the fate ahead and give us to think: ancient ruins are one, and the other is the brief duration of those who began to live at the same time as ourselves. We look for them and, finding them no more, withdraw."[10] But "the important thing is to have at the bottom of one's heart a feeling that sets one apart even in a company."[11]

He didn't try to cheat the mirror: "With age I am acquiring the infirmities of my father, and I believe that those traits of resemblance which I did not have before are coming too. My face is growing wrinkled in the same places. There are hollows, lumps, and quite particular signs just where he had them when he died."[12] His "Langrois head" can't snap round in every direction as swiftly as it did, "like the rooster on the weathervane atop a church spire," to grasp and taste everything there was to hear, see, and smell in every instant. His legs are swollen. He coughs and spits at every flight of steps, and soon won't be able to climb them at all. His long solemn sybarite's face has fleshed out a little, there's a growth of handsome gray hair digging into his high forehead, the big arched nose is still scenting the wind, but his long march toward universal tolerance has woven round his large eyes a network, scores and scores, of tiny wrinkles; they may be like his father's but they are also the scars of his goodness. This old and now housebound man, has loved his fellow humans more deeply, more truly than most.

> I am unchanging in my tastes. What I liked once I like forever, because my choice is always motivated. I may hate or I may love, but I always know why. It is true that I am naturally inclined to take little notice of defects and to wax enthusiastic over qualities. I am more deeply touched by the charms of virtue than by the deformities of vice. I turn quietly away from the wicked, but I fly to embrace the good. If in some work, personality, painting, statue, there be one beautiful place, it is there that my eyes stop and dwell; it is the only thing I see; it is the only thing I remember; the rest is almost forgotten.

Almost. Now and then there would be a terrible awakening, a subterranean rumble. In 1782 one flow of lava reached the surface and poured over: his incendiary participation in the new edition of the *Histoire des deux Indes,* followed by the *Essai sur les règnes de Claude et de Néron.* One or two salons had flinched when the mask dropped from their brilliant conversationalist, as if a pirate were suddenly standing by the fireside, gun in hand, like John Paul Jones. "Drive nature out the door, she comes back through the window." We have been too kind to this commoner; now he's talking about tearing up the paving stones, hanging kings and priests! Must we send him into exile like Abbé Raynal, persuade him to leave like Mercier, or embastillade him again as in the days of his juvenilia?* The storm threatened for the last time then, another sign of the growing rigidity of Louis XVI, now freed of Maurepas; with every passing year the King would become increasingly protective toward the "things of religion," increasingly fanatical about the nobiliary hierarchy, and increasingly subject to flashes of irrepressible wrath. Two years ago the gracious pleasure of the gracious King almost sent the greatest French writer to a prison cell. But Diderot was fond of his beef steak and too old to play martyrs. He knew his hour was drawing near, and he wanted to die in peace.

Besides, he had them all in his power. In his files, carefully consigned to friends, was a massive charge of explosive that he would not be taking with him "beneath his tombstone." The still unpublished *Religieuse, Jacques-le-fataliste,* and *Est-il bon, est-il méchant?*—and then there were those hundreds of letters, like Voltaire's, the best of his mind, fire struck in ice, a challenge to more than a society: to the entire Judaeo-Christian civilization. Diderot believed in his own resurrection more than many Christians do, and he had some grounds for his belief.

So he was willing to playact for them one last time, just to be left alone. Also, the Court did not want a scandal on its hands for persecuting the protégé

---

*Diderot had spent a few months in Vincennes in 1749 for his *Lettre sur les aveugles à l'usage de ceux qui voient* and *Les Bijoux indiscrets.*

of Catherine II. Various people, therefore, interposed between the King and him, chief among them Lenoir, the lieutenant-chief of police and sole survivor of the Turgot team, who was not such a bad guy after all and had done what he could for Mirabeau and a few others. He was a Freemason, which meant he could feel some sympathy for the *philosophes,* and he had personally helped to smuggle six hundred copies of the *Essai sur les règnes de Claude et de Néron* into France, in a bundle sent from Holland to his own address![13] To pacify Louis XVI, who at least had the virtue of being easy to dupe, a three-character farce had been enacted in the office of Huon de Miromesnil, the Keeper of the Seals, a man equally disinclined to apply strong-arm tactics. Lenoir himself tells the story,[14] not without an underlying glint of humor:

"M. le garde des sceaux had duly requested the King's orders, and H.M., without further explanation, had said that it was necessary to punish this *philosophe* and enemy of religion.* M. de Miromesnil, out of consideration for his years, wished to hear him first, and sent for him in my presence; he spoke to him with firm dignity, by which Diderot seemed utterly stricken. He instantly made me a sort of *amende honorable,* on bended knee [*sic*]; he reminded M. le garde des sceaux that he had been imprisoned in Vincennes, and spoke as follows:

" 'I deserve yet more fully to be chastised for the faults of my old age than for my former excesses: please deign to accept this avowal and act of repentance.' "

That must have been some time around May 20, 1782. Two days later Diderot sent Lenoir a note of thanks, which was also a sly wink from one old confederate to another:

"The more I consider your government, the more I see that there is an excuse for the error in it,† and that it enables us to feel secure in our persons and property. When I was young I lived on the fifth floor, I wrote nonsense, I was locked in the prison at Vincennes for my *Bijoux indiscrets.* Having acquired fortune and fame I descended to the second floor, where I now live, and where I confess to having propounded even more dangerous works. I have been taught a good and gentle lesson; I stand corrected for the rest of my life,"[15] meaning another two years, to drag through in semidarkness.

Oh, that "bended knee"! Diderot's hard, pure detractors over the centuries must be long on intransigence and short on humor not to see that this was just another of those palinodes which writers everywhere and always are being compelled to sing to the authorities, in order to be allowed to go on writing

---

*Just before this Lenoir has said that Diderot was "regarded as one of the most culpable promoters of irreligion": note by Roth and Varloot, *Correspondance de Diderot,* volume XV.

†He means that religion is a guarantee of morality and property—the Voltairean doctrine; note by Roth and Varloot, *Correspondance de Diderot,* volume XV.

a fourth or a tenth of what they have on their minds. Even today this ritual act is presented by some professorial podiums as an abasement, a quintessence of cowardice. We should only have a few more cowards like Diderot, then, at the age of seventy!* He would turn cartwheels on command, but he never wrote one word against his own thought, never the slightest official retraction; on that score, he has a better record than Helvétius and Voltaire both.

However, performances like this were not likely to improve his health. No one will ever know how many chest-searing coughs that genuflexion cost him. He's only half-alive. He obediently swallows his medicine, at Sèvres or in his daughter's home in Paris. His legs are bloated with edema, so the doctors decide he must have dropsy, and weaken him a little more by bleeding him. He catches a cold in the winter of 1782–83 and barely survives it to wait out another year of undeluded borrowed time. He has left no comment on the death of d'Alembert. The ultimate chill had invaded his large frame, even in the summer.

"And the winter of 1783–84 was a harsh one.[16] There were seventy consecutive days of frost and snow between December 10 and February 20."† Diderot took to his bed again, for good. Bronchia and heart were affected. "On February 19 [1784] he experienced a violent expectoration of blood.**

" 'That's the end of that,' he said to me. 'We must part. I am strong, though. It may not be in two days but in two weeks, two months, a year . . . ' "[17]

One small haven of grace lay tucked away in a corner of his heart. At least he was sure of dying before Sophie, his real wife, whom he had still been going to visit the year before when he was up to it, for she had moved to Paris after her mother's death and the sale of their pretty château at Isle-sur-Marne in Champagne.

She had been half his life, maybe more—the inspiration, the person for whom you stand up straight. The person you write to between two paragraphs of some article for the *Encyclopédie*. "I wanted you to be following me step by step; I wanted to live within sight of your eyes. Nor shall I kill one flea without reporting it to you. How should I dare to call trivial whatever relates to your repose, your peace of mind, your happiness, your health?‡ . . . For whom have

*He was born at Langres in October 1713.

†This marked the beginning of a remarkable series of hard winters followed by torrid summers, culminating in 1788–89 but continuing until Bonaparte, and affecting both the national economy and the psychology of the crowds during the Revolution.

**According to the sympathetic and sensitive *Mémoires* of his daughter Caroiline (or Caroline) de Vandeuil, who hardly leaves his bedside.

‡[This letter begins using *vous* and shifts to *tu* in the last sentence above.—*Trans.*] The transition from *vous* to *tu* occurs fairly frequently in Diderot's letters to Sophie Volland. One

I, who lead the most fragmented and inadvertent [*sic*] life, and that most forgetful of myself, for whom have I spied out all my moments? For one who is far from me and whom I love."[19]

But Sophie Volland dies first—three days after that spout of blood of his, on Sunday, February 22 of that same winter of 1784.

Of what disease; in what circumstances? Nobody knows. To her dying day Sophie Volland, one of the most- and best-loved women ever, remains a mute for History. Her age? No certificate of baptism. It has been conjectured, by cross-checking, that she was born in 1722 and was about ten years younger than Denis. It was he, no doubt, who christened her Sophie, symbol of wisdom. Her real name was probably Louise-Henriette. Social class? The bourgeoisie, comfortable and even cultivated; a father "in charge of purveying salt" about whom nothing else is known and who died early, after building the château at Isle-sur-Marne. There, as in purdah, lived Mme Volland, Sophie, and her two sisters, who (the latter) had traversed brief and unsuccessful marriages to a clod and a swindler as they would have traversed the valley of the shadow of death. The four women lived together for many years, a fragile but self-sufficient society. Sophie, the only one to have any experience of love, never marries, though not because she didn't want to. But when Denis first met her, he was already wearing his ball and chain. "One marries, one gets a wife and children before one has an ounce of common sense. Oh, if I had it to do over again!"[20]

When, how, in what setting did that meeting take place? Another mystery. Rue des Vieux-Augustins, maybe, in Paris, in the home of the ephemeral brother-in-law married to one of her sisters. Sometime around 1755 or 1756. It was love-at-first-sight for both. "We were alone that day, both leaning over the little green table. I remember what I was saying to you and what you said in return. Oh, those happy days of the little green table! . . . When shall I ever

---

cannot imagine why some prudish historians have made such determined efforts to prove that there was no sex in their relationship, which they have tried to fob off as a "sublimated friendship" on the ground that the two had few opportunities to spend a night together and that Sophie was undoubtedly no beauty. But apart from the fact that the idea is an insult to the moral and physical health of both of them, as well as to the simplicity of their love, any ten passages from Diderot's letters are quite enough to establish the opposite. To give just one example, here is the end of a letter written on October 12, 1759: "Farewell, my Sophie, I embrace you with all my heart; your lover and your friend, Diderot"—and here is the delightful *polissonnerie* [a kind of teasing mischief, usually risqué—*Trans.*] of November 21, 1762: "When you are here and I shall have seen you here, when I shall have kissed you a thousand times, when I shall have assured myself of your presence by all the means that the most incredulous and violent love shall suggest to me, then I shall believe you are here. Remember what Thomas said to the apostles when they tried to reassure him on the subject of the resurrection of Christ . . . If I do not have the same proof of your return as that demanded by the doubting apostle, *nisi immittam digitum . . .*"[18] Except I shall put my finger . . .

be free of all other occupation save that of making you happy? Never, never. I shall die without being able to teach you how well I know how to love."[21]

He tried his damnedest, though. Like children, they had a long springtime of furtive encounters in an attic until the day Mme Volland caught them. She said not a word but removed all three daughters—all three of age—to Isle-sur-Marne the following day. Then what? Years of hide-and-seek. They met when they could in Paris. By exerting all his diplomacy Denis even managed to soften the highly principled Mme Volland and made a few brief visits to the château, but it was not an ideal love nest. The two sisters were in on the secret, of course, and mildly infatuated with this unlikely Prince Charming who was giving some spice to their lives. They were jealous of Sophie, but they covered for and helped her from start to finish. Denis and she loved each other through year after year of frustration, never sure they were alone, condemned to the complicity of chambermaids or postmasters. One of the greatest of the men of liberty never knew the liberty to love.

Hence their correspondence—or rather Diderot's, for we do not possess a single letter from Sophie and have no idea what she looked like. She wore glasses. She was on the thin side; she had "a little dry paw." Her portrait, all sweetness, laughter, sensuality, benignity, and curiosity, emerges solely from Denis's gaze, and from that rare trust that enabled him to tell her everything, from childish babblings to quips so risqué that they verge on the scatological . . . Whatever else she may have been, Mlle Volland was no prude. When the years and her ill health had decanted passion into tenderness, his flame never flickered—or so little. Sometimes, to show how even in this he bore no grudges, Diderot's later letters began "Mesdames and dear friends." We can almost see the four women by the fireside, swathed in their shawls against the Champagne winter, deciphering the signs from another world. But there were other sheets tucked into the same envelope and in them, line by line, improvised at the turning of a paragraph or the end of some little disquisition, unfolded the uninterrupted stanzas of one of the finest hymns to a life spent in love that was ever composed—fifteen years of it.* Denis Diderot, a pioneer of the "arts and techniques," the author who first showed the tools of peasants and laborers to people with white hands, was also a great love poet:

> Well, my friend, so you are counting on me? Your happiness and your life depend on the duration of my affections? Fear nothing, my Sophie. They will endure, and you will live, and you will live happy . . . I am everything for you, you are everything for me; together we shall shoulder the trials that fate may choose to inflict upon us. You shall lighten mine, I shall lighten yours . . . The effect of true qualities is to be more keenly felt with every day that passes. Be assured of my

---

*1759 to 1774. After his return from Russia and Holland, Denis no longer needed to write. Liberated from her mother, living in Paris, Sophie saw him every week.

constancy by trusting to yours, and to my ability to discern them. Never was a passion more justified by reason than mine. Isn't it true, my Sophie, that you are lovable? Look into yourself. See clearly, see how worthy of love you are, and you will know how much I love you. That is the unvarying standard of my sentiments.

Good night, my Sophie, I leave you full of the sweetest and purest joy that man can feel. I am loved, and by the most deserving of women. I lie at her feet; that is my place, and I kiss them . . .

What are two lovers' caresses when they cannot be the expression of their infinite regard for themselves? . . .

I constantly have the impression that something is missing, and when I press upon the place I find that it is you . . .

It seems to me that from all eternity reason was made to be trampled underfoot by love . . .

But the thought of death, that tear in the corner of loving eyes, was never very far. There again, though, he found the right words to hold anguish at bay:

And then life escapes, human wisdom has given time a voice to warn us of its light and stealthy flight. But why does the hour sound, if it is never pleasure's hour? Come, my friend; come that I may embrace you, come and let all your moments and all mine be marked by our tenderness; let your clock and mine ever beat the minute in which I love you, and let the long night awaiting us be preceded by a few fine days . . .

They would tell me: "You'll grow old" and I would answer in myself, "Her years will pass with mine." "Both of you will die," and I would add, "If my friend dies before me, I shall weep for her, and shall be happy to weep so. She makes my happiness today; tomorrow she will make my happiness, and the day after tomorrow and the day after that again, and forever, because she will not change, because the gods have given her a just mind, uprightness, sensitivity, openness, virtue, and truth, and these do not change." And I shut my ears to the austere counsel of the philosophers, and I did well to do so, did I not, my Sophie?[22]

Only in love, and through it, was this inveterate doubter prepared to accept a certain notion of eternity:

Those who have loved each other in their lifetime and are buried side by side may not be as foolish as we suppose. Perhaps their ashes press together, mingle, and unite—how should I know? Perhaps they have not lost all feeling and memory of their previous condition. Perhaps they have some remnant of heat and life to enjoy, in their own way, at the bottom of the cold urn enclosing them . . . O my Sophie, that means I could still hope to touch you, to feel you, love you, seek you, unite, and mingle with you when we shall be no more, if there were some law of affinity in our principles, if it were permitted to us to compose one shared being,

if in the course of centuries I were to form one with you, if the molecules of your
dissolved lover were to stir and feel and search out your particles scattered
throughout nature! Leave me this chimaera, it would assure me of eternity in you
and with you.[23]

But there was small chance that the rest of the world would let even their ashes
teach people how to love, in other words be damned. They will not sleep side
by side. Sophie dies, attended by her second sister (Mme de Sallignac), who
lived with her, and four faithful servants, in her pretty little bedroom hung
with crimson serge and damask (red was her favorite color). Her rooms were
on the second floor (less of a climb for Denis) of a house she had rented on
the Rue Montmartre, "near the sewers, the second new house"; and she is
buried in the vault of Saint-Eustache, her parish church. In a will written in
1772, she bequeathed all her worldly goods to her nephews but left "to my
friend M. Denis Diderot, seven little volumes of the *Essais* of Montaigne
bound in red morocco, plus a ring that I call my pauline."[24]

The time for words was over. Caroiline de Vandeuil, who was fond of Sophie
(having never been maltreated by her; it was her mother who was jealous)
made only one comment in her *Mémoires:* "My father shed tears for her but
took comfort in the certainty that he would not long outlive her."

March: inflammation of the chest. Then a stroke. But the Langrois are hard
to kill. His doctors pull him through, leaving him weaker than before but still
able to administer a mild rebuke:
"You are making me live with some very nasty things!"[25]
The buzzards were circling, as was to be expected, but without much
hope. He is spared the obscenity of the clergy's final assault upon the agonizing
Voltaire. His wife, torn between her holy terror of his tantrums and her
conviction that he would go to hell, did notify the priest of Saint-Sulpice,
Jean-Joseph Faydit de Tersac, famous for having extorted that meaningless
retraction from Voltaire and notorious for having thereafter refused to bury
him in his church. Diderot was armed and ready but didn't even have to lose
his temper, according to Caroiline, who in this instance gives due credit to her
mother, the poor muddled, spurned creature in whom respect for her husband
finally won the day.

The priest of Saint-Sulpice heard of his illness and came to see him. My father
received him wonderfully, praised him for his institutions that gave so much
assistance to the unfortunate, and kept talking about all the good deeds he had
done and would do in future; he recommended the needy persons in the neighborhood to the priest, who came to their aid. He called on my father twice or
three times in the week, but they never had any private conversation, so theologi-

cal matters could only be talked about like any other subject, in the way of people in company. My father did not try to broach the question, but nor did he avoid it. One day, when they were in agreement on several points of morality relating to mankind and good works, the priest ventured to say that if he were to print those statements in a little retraction of his writings, it would have a very fine effect in the world.

"I believe it would, father, but you will agree that I should be telling a most impudent lie."

My mother would have laid down her life to make my father believe; but she would also have preferred to die sooner than encourage him to commit a single act that she could regard as sacrilege. Convinced that my father would never change his views, she wished to spare him from persecution and never left him alone with the priest for one moment; we both kept watch over him . . . and it was best that way.

May: last days at Sèvres on the hill, where the pure air did him good and he could take a few quiet turns around the garden. But everybody could see he was fading fast, he wouldn't last out the summer. He allowed his wife, daughter, and a few friends to concoct a small conspiracy so that he might at least be spared what was still regarded as the ultimate indignity in that particular society: to be buried "like a dog." But he couldn't care less what was done with his remains, so long as *they* didn't torture him with their rituals and sacraments.

Parting gift from Catherine II (which must have been solicited by the unvindictive Grimm): she pays for a superb apartment on the Rue de Richelieu, the classiest street on the right bank, and the handsomest dwelling Diderot has ever inhabited—but it's on the fifth floor. He'll never make it up the stairs. Never mind, they carry him up alive to die and then carry him down again dead to be buried, from church. Because the priest of Saint-Roch, the local parish church, was the most accommodating cleric in Paris, and Grimm made over a handsome sum to him for his charities, "on the part of the Empress."

Last move of Denis Diderot, on July 17, from Sèvres to the Rue de Richelieu, his funerary residence.

He had twelve days in which to enjoy it. He was delighted by it; having always lived in hovels, he now found himself in a palace; he was perfectly convinced of his imminent demise but no longer spoke of it; he did not want to give pain to the people he saw plunged into grief. He showed interest only in what might distract or deceive them; every day he found places for some new objects, he had his prints hung on the walls. The day before he died a more commodious bed was brought; the workers were taking great pains with its exact location.

"My friends," he told them, "you are giving yourselves far too much trouble over a piece of furniture that will not be used four days."

His friends came that evening; the conversation turned upon philosophy and the different means of arriving at that science.

"The first step toward philosophy," he said, "is incredulity."

That was the last thing he uttered in my presence;* it was late, I left him, hoping to see him again.

On Saturday July 31, he spends the entire morning in conversation with his old friend the Baron d'Holbach, sole survivor of the glorious host of the knights of atheism. He feels well enough to get up and move "gaily" to the table, where he had contracted so many indigestions in bygone years that he used to be disgusted with himself for days afterward. Menu: soup, boiled mutton, and braised chicory. He says to his wife, "I haven't enjoyed a meal so much for a long time."

He reaches for an apricot. His wife tries to stop him. He bridles: "What earthly harm can it do me?"

He finishes the fruit and leans across the table to help himself to a few stewed cherries. He coughs slightly. Without looking up, his wife asks if he is in pain. He doesn't answer. He's dead.†

CARNOT

49

AUGUST 1784

An Excellent Subject, Highly Intelligent

At long last the Academy of Dijon has found an acceptable text to which it can award the prize for its essay competition for literary tyros on the topic *Un Eloge du Maréchal de Vauban;* and it does so, to its heartfelt satisfaction, at a plenary sitting on July 17, 1784. Thirty-five years before, it had given a prize to another novice, Jean-Jacques Rousseau, for his controversial diatribe against

---

*Caroiline.

†And is buried two days later in great privacy in Saint-Roch, possibly under one of the slabs of the Virgin's chapel! All the tombs were opened and pillaged by the Directoire soldiers in 1796. No one knows what has become of Diderot's remains. His statue on the Boulevard Saint-Germain in Paris stands on the site of the house, on what used to be the Rue Taranne, in which he designed and constructed the *Encyclopédie.*

Le progrès des sciences et des arts. * The honorable assembly of "bishops, canons, abbés, intendants, bourgeois of the highest type, all great dignitaries of Burgundy"[1] was not overjoyed to learn what had hatched out of their egg on that former occasion. "Their learned works might be subtly impregnated with the corrosive spirit of the century, but the only new order they could conceive was swathed in a moral insularity that coincided with the walls of their comfortable mansions. Nothing was remoter from their minds than thoughts of violence or subversion. They did want the public good, but the Messieurs of the Academy of Dijon were prudent, lukewarm, and bourgeois, and above all they were His Majesty's obedient subjects."

Way back in 1770 they had hit upon a topic for a competition that they thought, pardonably enough, could not possibly get them into trouble: a eulogy to one of the province's most illustrious sons, the Maréchal de Vauban, whose talent for building fortifications had transformed France into a sort of hedgehog with stone quills. But what quills! The Academy would naturally have wished to overlook his famous remonstrations with Louis XIV on the fate of the kingdom's poor, and his ensuing disgrace. But perhaps many of its distinguished members were unaware of the kingdom's poor.

Academies are patient creatures: the competition was announced in 1770 and again in 1778, but produced only "five entries, which were found unworthy of the Maréchal's grandeur." As a last resort, they doubled the prize (in other words, offered two gold medals instead of one) when they tried again in 1784. This time they received three acceptable entries, all submitted with due anonymity. Their choice alights, in the words of the official report, upon the author "whose erudition did not appear to have been exhausted by the subject, and who added notes to substantiate his arguments at the end of his *Eloge.* Its qualities do honor to his learning no less than to his patriotism."[2]

They then unseal the envelope attached to his paper, in order to learn the identity of the lucky winner: "Monsieur Carnot, of Nolay near Dijon, captain in the Royal Engineering Corps, garrisoned at Arras."[3]

A letter is dispatched forthwith, summoning him to the official ceremony at which he is to receive his two medals from the hand of the Prince de Condé, most illustrious protector and benefactor of the Academy. Captain Carnot,†

---

*Readers are reminded that the academies played a crucial part in provincial life at the end of the Ancien Régime. Apart from the masonic lodges, they were the only places in which meetings of minds could occur, and they stoutly resisted the self-proclaimed superiority of Paris.

†Lazare Carnot becomes a member of the Legislative Assembly and then of the Convention, where he rapidly gains respect for his military abilities. The victory of Wattignies (October 1793) is won thanks to him. He becomes a member of the "Great Committee of Public Safety" in An II and is baptized "organizer of the victory." He later joins the Thermidorians against Robespierre and is a member of the Directoire but is expelled from it on 18 Fructidor. Napoleon, although

in his first reply dated July 20, expresses profound gratitude and apologizes profusely; his service will prevent him from coming to Dijon in person. He suggests that the award be presented to his brother Joseph, who could receive it in his place. But some of the members of the Academy must have had long arms, or perhaps Condé himself intervened, for Captain Carnot was instantly granted a leave of absence, and here he is under his first floodlights on August 2, 1784, in his trim blue-and-red uniform with the black velvet lapels and gilt buttons and epaulets.

Somebody new for the Dijonnais. Their curiosity is aroused by this military figure who also knows how to wield the pen and shows such a wealth of learning on matters of strategy and tactics. Nobody pays much attention to the rather impertinent epigraph he had borrowed from Fontenelle and used as a preface to his *Eloge:* "He [Vauban] was a Roman, whom our century had seemingly appropriated from the palmiest days of the Republic." Would Captain Carnot be a republican? Certainly doesn't look it; why, he's all bows and humility as he stands on the platform next to the most conservative prince in France. Perhaps Diderot wasn't the only one to do some knee bending that year.

Who is Lazare Carnot?

Thirty years old.* The eighth child of Claude Carnot, notary at Nolay, and Marguerite Pothier, daughter of a big "wine commissioner" and first alderman of the same town. His parents produce eighteen offspring in all, according to the rabbit-like practices of so many families of that day; nine survive. One of Carnot senior's notebooks contains a few lines scribbled on the day of Lazare's birth and (immediately subsequent) baptism (his name was chosen in honor of the relics of St. Lazarus worshipped at nearby Autun): "This child is born in a time of calamity, owing to the sudden and frequent deaths devastating this region and every other part of the province.† May God continue thus to manifest his wrath throughout the course of his life, that he may conduct himself with fear and deserve mercy."⁴ No further research is needed to compose the psychological and cultural portrait of Lazare's father, Claude Carnot. His mother, according to Joseph (another son), was "helpful, humane, devout, and very loving" but also "of a jealous disposition that occasionally troubled the couple's peace."⁵

---

more or less strongly opposed to his government, makes him a Comte d'Empire. Carnot does not side with Bonaparte until it is too late, during the Hundred Days, when he is minister of the interior. The Second Restoration drives him from power, and he dies in exile at Magdeburg in 1823.

*Born at Nolay on May 13, 1753.

†I have been unable to identify the famine or epidemic to which this may refer. Perhaps it was only a fantasy of a man obsessed by a series of deaths.

Childhood? Nolay, the Burgundy of the great wines, not far from Beaune but already beginning to look like the Morvan, which makes Autun the southern limit of the region as well as the seat of the bishopric. Nolay itself is a biggish village of vineyards and crops; over a thousand inhabitants and a few comfortably off notables, all buried in a sort of narrow combe where the houses are piled on top of one another. The handsome Carnot home was just next door to the even handsomer and larger Pothier home, "with an imposing façade and ample terraces giving on to the main square of the village in front of the château."[6] Who needs any better reason for marrying? These dwellings are big enough to hold eighteen children.

First lessons, in reading and writing, administered by his father in person. Brrrr . . . Then the "little collège of Nolay" until the age of fourteen: Latin and rhetoric. Then Lazare (with his favorite brother and almost-twin Joseph, born a bare year before him, who becomes his biographer) migrates to Autun. Joseph enters the little seminary because his father wants him to become a priest (he doesn't), and Lazare goes to the collège of the Oratorian fathers* in preparation for the army. Here his mind is opened up by those excellent successors to the Jesuits; he learns history, geography, mathematics, even the philosophy of Descartes. Lazare begins to write poems and little pieces on the Ancients. He remains a firm believer but turns anticlerical.

So after adolescence comes the army; where else can you put a boy who has no gift for the law? But the trouble with the army is that it's closed to commoners. And the Carnots, although typical representatives of the prosperous third estate, would have a hard time finding so much as the first letter of a particle in the lineage of their wine-making and merchant ancestors. However, the Marquis de Nolay—who is also, and more to the point, Duc d'Aumont—takes an interest in the children of his local notary, just as Mgr de Marbeuf, the Bishop of Autun, will later look out for the Buonapartes on his brother's recommendation. On the other hand, the 1760s were when the nobiliary backlash that reaches its zenith in the reign of Louis XVI began to affect the army: the upper nobility, increasingly remote from the land, tightened and multiplied, for its own benefit, all the locks blocking access to the higher ranks. There was one loophole: the engineer corps, a new and still rather ill-defined body, held in contempt because you had to be not only a trainer of men but an "engineer" as well, and why not a ditch digger while you're at it, before you could qualify. You were actually expected to dirty your hands. November 1769—thanks to the Duc d'Aumont, and to the sponsorship

---

*Ten years before Napoleon Bonaparte. Lazare also attended classes at the little seminary, to complete his background in the humanities.

or godfatherhood (albeit posthumous) of people who might themselves have become officers, Lazare Carnot manages, at the age of sixteen, to slip through the net and swim off in the direction of the engineer corps. First official document concerning him:

"Carnot; his father is an [honorary] attorney at the parlement of Dijon. This young man is the nephew of the Sieur Carnot, Chevalier de Saint-Louis, who, after serving in the naval regiment, entered the Modena regiment of royal grenadiers; cousin of the Sieur Carnot, captain in the Cambrésis regiment; and of the Sieur Carnot de Bessey, who died a captain in the Auvergne regiment."[7]

Even this only makes him a "candidate." To be admitted to Mézières, which was becoming a sort of proving-ground for engineer corps officers, applicants had to pass an examination given by the famous and feared Abbé Bossut of the Academy of Sciences. Twenty-six out of ninety-five get through. Lazare doesn't; even after a solid year of cramming, during which he seems to have conscientiously ingested every subject in the syllabus, he emerges almost at the bottom of the list. Abbé Bossut's evaluation: "Shows much intelligence, has only a superficial knowledge of the course; but he is extremely young."[8] So the door to Mézières remains, just barely, ajar. Before he can knock a second time he is sent, like so many others, to languish in a preparatory school in Paris. At least there do not seem to have been any money problems in this ascetic youth, whose only joys were those of earth, wine, forests, and friendship—you feel it blossoming (the latter) when you first set foot in Burgundy. It wasn't easy for Lazare to leave his native land, and he always feels a bit of an exile outside it.

He duly spends his year in Paris without learning anything about Paris, in the boarding school kept by the Sieur Longpré, one of Abbé Bossut's teachers.* The object is to jockey for position before the next examinations, and it has been announced that only twelve out of ninety applicants will be accepted. Carnot's capacities as a grind are now confirmed. "He set to work with such energy and intemperance [sic] that there was some fear for his health, as he had a delicate chest."[9] Result: in 1770 he comes in third, which automatically gives him the rank of second lieutenant. "An excellent subject, highly intelligent, knows his course very well, and supplements it with other useful knowledge."

Details: his Catholic faith was shed that year like an old coat, without breast beating. He becomes and remains a deist à la Rousseau; he and a friend even embark upon a pilgrimage to the house on the Rue Platrière, where the master receives them in a fractious mood[10] but does not shatter their belief; his works remain in Carnot's library until his death. The main

---

*Cost for one year, board and tuition included: 1,600 livres or 9,600 modern francs ($1,-920).

elements of his personality are now traced out: he is sentimental, he has "a head for figures"; in short, he is a little Condorcet of the military common-alty.

MONGE

50

AUGUST 1784

He Waded Straight Across a . . . Stream

Mézières, 1770–73. A not uncomfortable school for thirty "brains," where even the sons of noblemen had to learn how to draw and take their turn at blackboard demonstrations like anybody else. What could an uprooted young Burgundian do there but work, in this "sort of long square surrounded on all sides by water, situated at the narrowest part of a peninsula formed by the Meuse and wrapped in an old high wall with round towers in the ancient style"?[1] The town, with its thousand inhabitants, grows up a hillside, with only the Meuse between it and Charleville. The Champagne of the Ardennes, "its climate as severe as that of Flanders." The school was housed in government buildings.

> The pupils had their private rooms, one apiece, their construction or wetting room,* their physics laboratory, and their lesson and study rooms. They took their meals outside, at their own expense. We must not forget that they were officers and expected to live as such . . . .
>
> Making ends meet was a daunting problem. Their pay was 720 livres;† it had been 600 at first. With that they had to purchase their clothing, laundry, food, wood and light, and pay the wigmaker and chambermaid, the surgeon-major and chaplain, not forgetting their contributions to the veterans' fund. Their families were required to pay an additional 200 livres a year.
>
> Carnot, wishing to be a burden on his family no longer, resolved to make his emoluments cover all his expenses. A heroic decision, no less heroically implemented. His case remained famous, if not unique, as witness the words of an officer in a later class: "We were told," he observed, "of a pupil who had lived solely upon his emoluments."[2]

Carnot's youth was not a total loss, thus, at least as far as character building was concerned; but even more, because of one of those encounters that shape

---

*The plaster workshop, to which plebians were systematically assigned.
†4,320 modern francs a year [$864].

a whole life. His chief teacher, "tutor in mathematics and physics demonstrator," was a sort of prodigy, barely seven years older than himself: Gaspard Monge, who had just been appointed to fill both positions at the age of twenty-four. He could have made a potato love science.* In 1766, at the age of twenty, like another d'Alembert, he invented, yes actually invented, descriptive geometry—"the art," as Monge himself calls it, "of representing on a sheet of paper, which has only two dimensions, objects that have three, and are susceptible of rigorous definition."[3]

Monge and Carnot, the spark of human contact. Love isn't the only thing that happens at first sight. Monge was in no sense either an orator or a charmer, but he was a real professor, a teacher in every sense of the word, with true pedagogical intuition, a passion for learning, and an affection for his pupils that communicated itself to them.

> Twelve lessons were set aside for physics; another twenty, followed by numerous manipulations, dealt with the principles of chemistry. Geometry, stone cutting, the theories of perspective and shadow, entailed the execution of many drawings in which Monge put his new geometry into practice. He was wholly absorbed in communicating his method, within the limits imposed upon him.
>
> Monge was not a fluent speaker; some have even said he occasionally stuttered. But he made up for this defect, slight as it was, with his remarkable precision. An enemy of high eloquence, which moves but does not teach, Monge thought affected language as bad as positively wrong language. The clarity of his demonstrations was further augmented by a highly expressive use of gesture. Speaking of a plane, line, or intersection, he would associate the gesture to the word; his hands situated the figures being studied in space, flapping over to indicate a rabatment, for example, in an intelligent gymnastics that rendered almost visible what was addressed to the mind alone.
>
> The sympathy that Monge had seen the Oratorian fathers lavish upon their pupils, he gave in turn to his own. It was expressed in his lessons, and even more in the educational walks he took with them around Mézières, in a landscape which lent itself admirably to any kind of lesson after nature and which contained many manufactures and factories.
>
> Goujon, one of his pupils, has written that the young professor transmitted all his enthusiasm to them and that often, to reach his destination more quickly without bothering to seek out the roads and bridges, Monge, in the full spate of his explanation, waded straight across a wide stream, fording it without any

*Gaspard Monge becomes (deservedly) one of the most illustrious scholars of the revolutionary and imperial periods. Minister of the navy after August 10, he is involved in all the Convention's scientific and national defense activities. A member of the Council of the Five Hundred, and then of the Elders during the Directoire, he accompanies Bonaparte to Egypt as a scientist and becomes a convert to him. Made a Comte d'Empire and member of the Senate, he remains loyal to the emperor to the end, including the Hundred Days; he dies in 1818.

interruption in his speech, and with all the young men crowding after him, so great was his power over their minds.[4]

Monge was a living encyclopedia of all the subjects by which Carnot was already fascinated: ballistics, the best materials for military fortifications, the manufacture of gunpowder, the history of weaponry. Traces of Vauban's renovation of the old ramparts of Charleville and Mézières were still clearly outlined on the horizon of those walks. "What more is a great life but a thought conceived in youth and brought to fruition in adulthood?"[*]

There was a strange community of destiny between the two men, too. Monge started out further down the ladder than Carnot and had already climbed higher. Wasn't that proof that it was possible, by dint of merit and determination, to break through the partitions of a society even as arthritic as theirs? And then, the teacher came from Beaune and the pupil from Nolay, almost the same river of vines between them, the same childhood songs, the same colors in their memories. Monge's father, being a mere "casual laborer," was certainly "beneath" a notary. He was a Savoyard who had settled in Beaune[†] at the age of seventeen and come up the hard way: itinerant vendor, journeyman, craftsman, market contractor, and finally "merchant mercer in the Rue Douverte." He married a drayman's daughter. Why on earth should all three of their sons have a passion for mathematics? A pretty puzzle for the geneticists![**] Their father did everything and then some to encourage and push them as far as possible. Gaspard never forgets him. At fourteen, he was already building a model fireman's pump that shot water fifty feet in the air! The Oratorian fathers in Lyons soon perceived what a blessing had come their way. They proclaimed him *puer aureus*, "golden boy," a distinction very rarely conferred; and they were right. At eighteen, during his summer holidays, he was designing a plan for the town of Beaune that was so complete and so clear that it was shown to Colonel du Vigneau, then (1764) second in command of the Mézières school, who was passing through Burgundy. The tongue of fire, gift of fate: "We must have that young man."

He was accordingly admitted to Mézières as a mark of quite exceptional favor, but immediately consigned to the plaster room. He too had tasted all the mortifications meted out to Carnot, and never lost the same sense of hurt at the bottom of his heart, the anger against the nobility, the unwavering

---

*Alfred de Vigny.

†Where a small colony of Savoyards, driven out of their duchy by growing destitution, had established themselves as farmhands, just as those who went to Paris specialized in chimney sweeping [*Savoyard* is another word for chimneysweep in French.—*Trans.*].

**They also have two girls. In addition to Gaspard, there is Louis, the second boy, who is a companion of La Pérouse on board the *Astrolabe* and one of the few survivors of his tragedy; and Jean, the last of the three. All become science professors: mathematics, hydrography, navigation, astronomy.

opposition to class inequality. You must never humiliate a Burgundian: he says nothing, and that means it's serious.

Like everybody else, Monge will go on saying nothing as long as he has to. The authorities at Mézières had no choice but to give him a job as their youngest professor. He made a strong impression on the young Comte de Charlus, son of the Marquis de la Croix de Castries (then governor of Flanders and Hainault, but after 1781 minister of the navy during the American war), when Charlus made his tour of French military schools at the end of his boyhood before entering the army by the front door. Monge found the young nobleman alert and intelligent but was much more strongly attracted to his peculiar tutor, a Swiss "of base extraction" but radiating a jumble of learning and kindliness, Jean-Nicolas Pache.*[5] Like a younger brother of Rousseau. A good idea, a sign of originality in Castries, to have entrusted his son to a man who started out in life as the concierge of his Paris town house. He won't regret it. Monge and Pache, meanwhile, keep in touch. Thanks to the latter, and perhaps also to Charlus, Castries, after becoming minister, protected Monge—who had married by then, on the strength of his reputation, the rich and pretty widow of a Rocroy ironmaster—and "brought him up" to Paris where he is now (in 1784) professor of hydrography and "examiner of the navy guards and cadets." All the officers-to-be of the royal navy pass through his hands. It is ten years since Lazare Carnot stopped needing him and began to fly alone. But he had been one of Monge's best pupils, and these two men never forget each other either.

MARQUIS DE VAUBAN

DIPLOMA GIVING MEMBERSHIP
IN THE ACADEMY OF DIJON
TO CAPTAIN CARNOT

51

AUGUST 1784

The Excessive Inequality of Fortunes

Second official entry in the archives relating to Lazare Carnot:

> Today, the first day of the month of January 1773, the King being at Versailles, on the accounts rendered to him of the Sieur Lazare-Nicolas-Marguerite Carnot,

*Under the Restoration Charlus becomes the first Duc de Castries; he was one of La Fayette's boon companions in Virginia and helped to obtain aid from his father. Pache is a future mayor of Paris and a Montagnard minister of war.

and also on strength of the abilities displayed in the examinations he has sat in the different branches relating to the fortification, attack, and defense of military positions, His Majesty has appointed, ordered, and established him in his service as one of his engineers, whose numbers have been set at four hundred, desiring him to be hereafter known in that capacity by all to whom it may pertain, and to enjoy the ranks, prerogatives, and other advantages attributed thereunto, and the emoluments that shall be ordered to be paid to him by His Majesty.[1]

This made him a sublieutenant and thus a tiny step higher up in the army hierarchy, but the eccentricities of organization of the royal engineer corps also made him an officer-engineer—that is, a sort of half-breed in a bastard corps of troopless officers. "Carnot was first and foremost an engineer,* according to the terms of the appointment; he was an officer or sublieutenant only secondarily, and outside the engineer corps: the orders and commissions specify 'retired lieutenant of infantry,' maintaining a curious administrative fiction that ascribed what one might call honorary rank to the different classes of engineers, implying neither authority nor command and artificially attaching the engineer to the infantry staff only to justify his higher pay and prestige.

"Despite the efforts of Vauban and his successors, the engineer corps had no troops. The sappers and miners, who should rightly have composed them, belonged to the artillery. Carnot, thus, had no men to command, which explains many aspects of his military and political thinking. Like all engineers he dealt only with works contractors, and then only through his superiors."

And yet there was plenty of *esprit de corps* among the engineers, God knows! "The engineers set great store by their time at school, their competitive examinations, and the studies preceding them. This, combined with a particular turn of mind acquired at Mézières, was intensified by their subsequent work. Consciousness of their superiority as a 'talent-corps' was their dominant trait. Only the artillerymen could rival them in this respect, but the academic level was said to be lower in the artillery, and this would appear to be true. The engineers looked down upon the cannonry officers as commonplace instructors. On the other hand, they were jealous of the technician-artillerymen, who were officers or inspectors at army posts. The engineer corps was characterized by self-confidence, an abstract, dogmatic, and trenchant turn of mind, a habit of argument carried to the point of quibbling—it was not for nothing that the engineers were nicknamed the Jesuits of the army—a pretension to be better fitted than anybody else to occupy every position, and the pride of being the sons and successors of Vauban; these traits endowed it with a sort of superiority complex."[2]

Still shabby but proud, thus, Carnot, like the artilleryman Laclos, began dancing the garrison waltz, flicked hither and thither at the whim of their governors or the needs of the service. No protector defended him; the Duc

*Analysis by Marcel Reinhard.

d'Aumont had long since forgotten about him. All he could do was shoulder his pack and march, keeping a weather eye open for a passing chance.

1773. Calais. Rough climate for a Burgundian who didn't like the sea. Six thousand taciturn inhabitants, not counting the ordinary seamen with whom an officer did not associate. But with Dunkerque dismantled, this little town, pinched between its ramparts and its narrow streets, was the "port of France" to the north, facing the English. Fortunately, Carnot liked his work. In December 1775, a qualified pat on the back from his engineer-in-chief:

"M. de Carnot [sic], with M. Blondel, has completely finished the levels of the citadel and plan of the underground galleries, which have been submitted to me. M. de Carnot is very willing, but he would be well-advised to show greater regard for the details of our service, to which he does not give sufficient consideration because he prefers to spend his time applying himself to geometry, which he likes better. His conduct is good."[3]

1777. Cherbourg. War. At last somebody realizes the strategic importance of this port, which has been systematically neglected in favor of Le Havre. Vauban (him again) had called it "the inn of the Channel." He wanted to transform it into a military port so that the Channel would become French and our ships could no longer be "enchanneled" in it. He denounced the "terrible consequences" of an English disembarkation in the Cotentin. "It would be a hundred times better for them to make a landing at Calais or Boulogne than in the peninsula of Cherbourg,"[4] but once he was gone, everybody forgot the scraps of ramparts that had been begun and the port was never built up. This time it was more serious. The British fleets were patrolling the Channel and France was going to jeopardize its famous "Descent" upon England at least partly for want of adequate ports.

Finally, a major works program was launched, in which Carnot might have given the best of himself except that it was launched in total anarchy, with no general plan. There was friction between the intendant, the civil engineers, the navy, the military engineers, and the military commander of the post, a General du Mouriez who had a mysterious past as a secret agent and had even gotten a taste of the Bastille shortly before the death of Louis XV, but was gradually being rehabilitated. He took it into his head to oppose what he called "the ruinous scheme" of the engineer corps, in a series of inflammatory *Mémoires* to the ministers.[5] Not calculated to endear him to Carnot, who was forced to work on drawings instead of buildings. He was then shuffled off to fortify the little port of Granville (which already had nearly ten thousand inhabitants) west of the Cotentin peninsula, "to render it safe from capture."[6]

But it made Lazare furious, although not because of any excess bellicosity, to find himself always on the sidelines. He was primarily a technician, not a lover of bloodshed; he was not afraid of it either, however, and he knew that the only place where one could get a promotion those days was in America or the Islands or Gibraltar. And what did he get instead? A transfer to Béthune, in 1780. It was beginning to look as though this poor Burgundian had been visited by some curse condemning him to the chilly north. And Béthune is purgatory. Forty lawyers or rich merchants with whom one might associate, in a population of five thousand; fortifications—by Vauban, to be sure—but derelict, silted up, strangled. And as Joseph II was most unlikely to invade us from his Low Countries, Carnot could expect no money to spend on arousing this sleeping beauty. Once again, the poor fellow had to console himself with compliments: "M. Carnot, lieutenant. This officer is very diligent in the service of posts, assiduous in his efforts; he works hard at perfecting his own learning at home, and lives very quietly."[7]

And at the end of 1781, just to make sure he stayed chained to the north, they sent him to Arras; well, as the first decent-sized town in his career, it represented a substantial improvement over Béthune at any rate. There, on December 14, 1783, he received his captain's appointment, couched in the picturesquely antiquated style that was the hallmark of all royal writings:

> Louis, by the grace of God King of France and Navarre, to our dear and beloved Sieur Lazare-Nicolas-Marguerite Carnot, one of our first lieutenants in our Royal Engineering Corps, greetings.
>
> Placing under consideration the services that you have rendered Us upon the occasions arising, and desiring to give you proof of our satisfaction, for these causes and others having so prompted Us, We have appointed, ordered, and established you, and do hereby order and establish you by our signature to take and occupy the rank of captain in our Royal Engineer Corps, as from the day and date of this communication and under our authority and for their part under that of our lieutenants-general, and as We or they shall command and order you for our service; to perform which we give power, commission, authority, and special instruction; and instruct whomsoever it may concern to receive and recognize you in that capacity, that in so doing you shall be obeyed; for such is our pleasure.[8]

Captain at thirty; not so bad, eh? He might well thank his lucky stars and start to dream, especially as he has recently fallen in love.

Instead of which, he is utterly dejected. He feels strangled, pushed aside, stymied. Louis XVI's latest nobiliary edicts have blocked all hope of his ever reaching a higher rank. Ursule de Bouillet's parents force him to break off their engagement.

Lazare Carnot—another man buried alive.

The Marquis de Ségur, immediately upon taking up office in the Ministry of War (but wasn't that why he was put there?) got Louis XVI to sign an order, on March 22, 1781, requiring every candidate for an "officer's commission" to produce at least four quarterings of nobility* approved by the King's genealogists. The only exception was for sons of the Knights of Saint-Louis, a decoration awarded for exceptional bravery on the field of battle. But to so few commoners. With every passing year, this absolutely arbitrary straitjacket, which would have been inconceivable even under Louis XV, was sowing revolt and perplexity in the ranks of the upper middle classes—the summit of the third estate that was, on the contrary, feeling increasingly justified, as its wealth grew and it began to take a more active hand in the affairs of the kingdom, in its desire to see its firstborn sons climb ever higher up the military ladder.

But no more. In the middle of the American war, just when an infusion of fresh air might have widened the career prospects of all the Duponts, Buzots, and Carnots, the door to the higher ranks was slammed in their faces.

Lazare Carnot can never become so much as a colonel or lieutenant-colonel, let alone a marshal or brigadier (which then meant general). The wound rankles, and ambition, his strongest driving force and the one that has inspired all his laborious struggles from early youth, rubs salt in it. Oh, to be able to stand up to his father, his brothers, all the people in Nolay, all those teachers and classmates who humiliated him at Mézières and in the garrisons. And to repay Monge for his good will and confidence.

Now his ambition is left with precious little more to feed on than that of Soldier Rossignol. He can vegetate in his captaincy, amass a little nest egg while awaiting early retirement, gain some sort of renown from writing. At least he can write. And also, perhaps, after his monastic youth, he can try to get a little enjoyment out of life. When Carnot is transferred to Arras he sags, true, but he also relaxes. As a Burgundian, asceticism was not his strong point, and his voluntary acceptance of the amputation of a large part of his youth had done violence to his nature. Even so, he had occasionally joined his comrades in a carouse, raised his glass to innumerable toasts, and flirted in moderation from garrison town to garrison town. Neither prude nor Romeo, he now decides to adopt a more comfortable lifestyle.

He frequents the "best" society. He dresses—he might even be said to adorn himself—so as to set off his good figure, "his assured features full of energy and refinement, and his firm and upright bearing."[9] His cravat is made of lace. His hair is elegantly tied. He has a ring engraved with his coat of arms. At what point did he make the acquaintance of a rising young lawyer by whom he was not unduly impressed, Maximilien de Robespierre? Soon, no doubt, in '83 or '84; when he first came to Arras, people were still talking about the lightning-rod case, and the "right" people are soon talking about the newly arrived engineer corps officer with the dead-end career, who surprises his

---

*Meaning a title of nobility held by his direct ascendants for at least three generations.

temporary hometown with a prize from the Dijon Academy. Carnot orders his clothes from the same "merchant of cloth, silks and braid manufacturer" as Robespierre—a good reference in the dress department: Duplessis, whose shop is in the "little square" of Arras. One account Carnot receives from him asks for payment of two hundred and fifty livres* for "blue serge, fustian, alpaca, England flannel, black velvet, and *prunelle en calimade*† of scarlet, gray and white cotton, gold epaulets, and a decoration of fleurs de lys similarly embroidered in gold."

He tries his hand, with no apparent difficulty, at becoming a *bel esprit.* Versifying is a major pastime in this little Aix "of the Artesian Provence," so Carnot starts rhyming too, and, in the company of a few northerners who finally seem to possess a little warmth, proves himself a legitimate heir to the truculence of his native province:

Buvons outre mesure	[Immoderately let us drink,
Aux enfants d'Epicure;	To the possessed our glasses clink,
Buvons à tous les fous;	To the scions of old Epicurus;
Messieurs les raisonnables,	And the reasonable gents be
Allez à tous les diables	damned
Ou trinquez avec nous.	Who with a restraining hand
	From our bottle would try to lure
	us.
Noé, ce joyeux père	Noah, that stalwart sire
Qui montrait son derrière	Who, when wine had set him afire,
Quand il avait bien bu	Would bare his gallant behind,
Valait, sur ma parole,	Outweighs a hundredfold
Cent fois mieux que le drôle	The slavering limp cuckold
Qui rit de l'avoir vu.	Who tittered to see him so blind.
Vous avez lu, peut-être,	In books you may have read
Que la Grèce vit naître	How in ancient Greece was bred
Le docte Anacréon **	Anacreon the wise;
Moquons-nous de l'histoire:	Well, never trust History,
Il vaut beaucoup mieux croire	For that hero could only be
Qu'il était Bourguignon.	A Burgundian in disguise.

* 1,500 modern francs [$300].
†A woolen fabric with a slight satiny sheen.
**Greek poet (born *circa* 570 B.C.), who celebrated love and feasting.

Pour triompher des belles,	To conquer the cruel dame
Pour dompter les cruelles,	And the fair fierce maid to tame,
Avalez du vin vieux:	Old wine must you swallow;
Dans l'amoureux mystère	For without this gift from above,
Nous ferions de l'eau claire	In the mysteries of love,
Sans ce présent des dieux.*10	We'd all be beaten hollow.]

He might have ended as a quiet man of quality busying himself with frontier fortifications, improving the army at the head of a staidly maturing family. In 1782, for example, he began "keeping company" of the most platonic sort with a "local," young Ursule de Bouillet of Dijon, during the seven months that his "semesters" of leave entitled him to spend back in Burgundy every other year. "The Chevalier de Bouillet"—a mere Dijon lawyer who had gently propelled himself into this minor title by successive purchases of land—"had been a friend of our father† for many years. We sometimes saw him at Nolay, sometimes in Dijon," where her parents treated Carnot "as a son of the family."11 Ursule was twenty and Lazare twenty-eight when he first took a closer look. She must have been pretty and fetching, and in any case forward enough to make the first move, by correspondence, between Dijon and Arras; whereupon Lazare, also in writing, promised to marry her.

But the "Chevalier" de Bouillet had something to say in the matter. His daughter was under age. And marriage is a question of "assets." Love and friendship come into the bargain, if at all, as extras. Bouillet went to Nolay to see his old friend the notary Claude Carnot for a little straight talk and some careful counting. How much are you giving Lazare? Because as far as his pay in the engineer corps is concerned . . . "Expectations." When his father and mother are dead, and they're in excellent health for the moment, God be praised, and the property is shared out among his numerous brothers and sisters, why, he'll have around twenty thousand livres, most of it in vineyards.**

We don't know how much M. de Bouillet was promising on his side. Lazare Carnot, in any case, was weighed in the balance and found wanting. At the end of 1783, with no vain beating of breasts, we're all decent people here, Ursule, "on order from her father," informs Lazare that she must break off relations "to her keen regret" and asks him to restore "her imprudent written

*Carnot published a few poetic opuscules during the Revolution; this piece is recorded by an Arrageois as dating from the same period as the *Eloge à Vauban.*

†According to Joseph Carnot.

**A capital, in other words, of 120,000 modern francs [$24,000].

promise," which he does by return mail. Nobody ever knows what he feels at that moment. He keeps quiet about that as well—the deeper the wound, the deeper the silence. Ambition's done with and now love too, at the age of thirty, when a man's patience might begin to wear thin.

It was during that period, jolly good fellow on the outside and bleak despair within, that he wrote the *Eloge à Vauban*. As an escape? For revenge? On fate, perhaps, but not yet on society: he's no Marat. He's still obediently pouring himself into the imposed mold. But as slowly as possible, with his ears wide open and his gaze unclouded.

His text contains muted intimations, that are more perceptible to us than they were to the merry old souls in the Dijon Academy, who were totally oblivious to the byways of military promotion or a young "townee's" heart-strings.

It isn't literature, it's an effortlessly written compilation: Carnot has been living shoulder-to-shoulder with Vauban for over ten years. He has read his major writings, sought out his precursors. He formulates the problems of the engineer corps and its links with the other "talent corps"—that is, the artillery, general staff, and mathematician-surveyor-engineers—in terms of Vauban's day. He hints at wider horizons: economy, demography, finance, even a tinge of politics—but with all the necessary precautions. To demonstrate his erudition, he quotes from thirty authors ranging over the whole history of literature. He also brings a lot of geometry into his paper, no doubt as a result of Monge's influence. Otherwise, his style conforms to contemporary standards: flat and bombastic. Carnot is no writer now and seems unlikely to become one later.[12] In a pinch, prophecy-lovers may try to read the text as a portrait of the man he would have liked to be himself: he depicts Vauban "in the midst of peril but alone and silent; he sees death, but must contemplate it coolly; he must not run at it like the heroes of battles but calmly observe it coming; he goes where lightning strikes, not to act but to watch; not to be dazed but to deliberate."

We can fish out one or two portentous reflections, those of a man who has been hurt and who wants to apply the past to the present and maybe even to the future:

> Vauban ever recommended moderation; he could not endure to see buildings destroyed or the houses in besieged towns fired upon; he spoke with satisfaction of the camps he had designed because, more than any other thing, they helped to save the troops by keeping them out of the enemy's sight; in his own words, he studied to find the least bloody means that might be employed . . .

Vauban never stifled the voice of nature, and always gave way to the first promptings of his soul . . . Woe unto you, Philosopher, who dare contest with your dialectics the foundations of the sacred law you found so clearly graven in your own heart! From the instant in which you sought to subject emotion to analysis, it lost forever the affecting grace nature gave when she bestowed it . . .

Vauban saw the source of social disorder in the excessive inequality of fortunes . . .

Cast your eyes [here he is very close to La Bruyère] upon that ill-favored being whom you scarce deign to count among your fellow creatures; behold him dying of hunger within reach of the nourishment he is incessantly engaged in sowing, reaping, and preparing for you: go, give him pity and comfort; but are you yourself worthy of his pity? . . .

Governments should prevent the appalling misery of some and opulence of others, and that odious multiplicity of prerogatives that condemns the most precious class of men to want and scorn. There can be but one remedy for so many evils, and Vauban saw it: to strike out all exceptions, abolish the finance offices, tax the rich, and relieve the poor . . .

It was Vauban's great quality, as "the friend of men yet unborn," to have been unable "to dissimulate an afflicting but precious truth . . . He knew that the soldier's sole reward is the approval he earns in his own heart . . . O Vauban, die, for you have no more services to render your country . . ."

Nobody rose in protest against this exhortation for the very good reason that most of the men attending the ceremony on August 2 hadn't read the *Eloge* through to the end and had trusted their rapporteur. And if any of them had caught a whiff of subversion and been made a bit queasy by it, Carnot himself is there to dispel their dyspepsia with his brusque military assurance—second nature by now—as he bows before the Prince de Condé to reel off the statutory compliment:

"Monseigneur, it is a priceless honor to be crowned by a hero bearing the name of Condé, and the laurels dispensed by your hand, like those adorning your august brow, are of a kind that never fades."[13]

And yet, on June 25 he had applied to the secretary of state to be sent "to the Windward Islands, if possible, as an ordinary engineer."[14]

52

AUTUMN 1784

I Have Had My Day

The pages turn quickly in Paris, where nothing changes faster than fads. In 1783 the balloon craze spread like wildfire. In 1784 hardly an eye is raised to watch one drift across the sky, as happens at least once a week and sometimes oftener; not to mention those that are floating up from scores of provincial towns and the grounds of the larger schools, manufactured and even manned by the teachers themselves.

This year's big event is Mesmer. What, is he back again? He wasn't long out of Paris, in fact, after the squabble in 1781 that ended in his getting his knuckles rapped for asking too much too soon. Spa bored him, although it also left him free to take his long walks in the forests, singing to himself at the top of his lungs. Not enough clients. Not enough big names to be converted to his doctrine before passing it along to the foot of the throne. And then his associate, his "disciple" d'Eslon, was trying to go it alone in Paris now that the ground had been cleared and, having sensed the potential of psychotherapy, was attempting to steer "animal magnetism" in that direction. Was that such a bad idea? At any rate, They had begun persecuting d'Eslon too—*they* being the physicians, Molière's heirs. Nothing new, please, under the Hippocratic sun. Hearing this, Mesmer decided to come back and do battle in Paris, defend d'Eslon but also recapture first place for himself.

In this second try he was morally and materially aided by two curious characters. One was an Alsatian banker named Kornmann, who swore that Mesmer had cured his son of a fatal illness and told him all about his undoubtedly self-provoked conjugal misfortunes in which his poor wife was the real victim. The other was a lawyer from Lyons, Nicolas Bergasse, a sickly creature but one whose liberality, provided there was sufficient religious exaltation in the cause being touted, was open to every passing illumination. The crossroad: Spa. The seat of their joint investment: Paris.* Both had provided the initial

---

*We meet Kornmann and Bergasse again, facing Beaumarchais in one of his last great "affairs." Bergasse becomes a Third Estate representative to the Constituent and is later actively involved in the counterrevolution.

outlay Mesmer needed to make a strong takeover bid in Paris. Why shouldn't the money that Maurepas–Louis XVI had refused him be supplied by "a company of one hundred shareholders, each contributing one hundred louis"?[1] This form of enterprise was also coming into fashion.*

In March 1784 the *Almanach du Voyageur* published the following announcement: "At the Hôtel de Coigny, Rue du Coq-Héron, the foundation by the illustrious M. Mesmer of a substantial establishment for the treatment of illness by animal magnetism. This establishment is to be known as the Society of Harmony. It comprises halls for treatment and chambers for the patients. The pediment over the door bears, by way of arms, the image of an altar beneath a starry sky with a full moon, and the motto *Omnis in pondere et mensura.*"†

And who should be one of the company's founding members and stockholders, joining on April 5, but Gilbert de La Fayette. The form certifying his accession was printed in advance and would be used for all the other stockholders; he has carefully filled in the blanks in his own hand, however, and it's worth reproducing in full, as a witness to the vast longing for something secret —a challenge to clerical esoterica—from which so many "people of quality" were suffering. Membership in the Freemasons was perfectly compatible; any way to gain possession of higher, incommunicable knowledge that could change the world.

We the undersigned, Antoine Mesmer, doctor of medicine, party of the first part** and *M. le marquis de La Fayette, maréchal de camp residing in Paris, Rue de Bourbon,* party of the second part, have jointly agreed between ourselves as follows, viz:

I, Antoine Mesmer, having ever desired to communicate the doctrine of Animal Magnetism to all honest and virtuous persons, do hereby consent and undertake to instruct in all the principles composing the said doctrine *M. le Marquis de La Fayette* named above, on the following conditions:

1. He may instruct no pupil or transmit, directly or indirectly, to anyone whomsoever, the whole or the least part of the knowledge relating in any respect to the discovery of Animal Magnetism, without prior written consent signed by me.

2. He shall not conclude, with any Prince, Government, or Community whatever, any negotiations or treaty or agreement of any sort concerning Animal Magnetism, that faculty being expressly and privately reserved to myself.

3. He may not, without my express written consent, engage in any public treatment or assemble patients to be treated jointly by my method, but may only see and treat patients privately and singly.

*Basic capital: 1.2 million modern francs [$240,000].
†All things in due weight and measure.
**I have put the words in La Fayette's hand in italics, the rest is a printed form. He signs Lafayette in this instance.

4. By the sacred oath of verbal and written honor he shall give me his undertaking to comply scrupulously and unreservedly with the above conditions, and not to set up, authorize, or encourage, directly or indirectly or in any part of the world in which he may reside, any establishment to which I shall not be formally attached.

And I, *Marquis de La Fayette* undersigned, considering the doctrine of Animal Magnetism to be the property of M. Mesmer its author, and that it is for him alone to determine the conditions in which he may consent to communicate it, accept in every particular the conditions set forth herein and hereby give in writing, as I have previously done orally, my most sacred word of honor to respect the contents hereof in good faith and with the most scrupulous exactitude.

Signed severally between us in free and private contract, with promise to ratify by notary at the first requisition by either party and at the cost of the party so requesting. Paris, the *fifth April one thousand seven hundred eighty-four.*

La Fayette.[2]

Gilbert-the-Butterfly, one might have guessed—when did he ever do anything but flitter? Snobbery remains one of his prime motives. If there had been any societies to promote balloons or deep-sea divers the year before, his name would have headed their lists of patrons as well. But this looks a little more serious; in the ensuing months, we see other names alongside his on the roster of "members of the Society of Universal Harmony," such as the Duc de Chartres; Duval d'Eprémesnil,* the "star" councilor of the Paris parlement; another young member of the same body, active, impulsive, and eloquent, named Adrien Duport;†[3] Jaucourt, the up-and-coming writer in all the smart salons; Cabanis, the rich man's doctor; and the whole little "set" of the Queen's friends (some of whom were La Fayette's too): Lauzun, Noailles, Montesquiou, Ségur (the son). Not too shabby a crew he's patched together this time, has Doctor Mesmer. With his ears forever attuned to his beloved music and his thoughts deep in his medical research, he probably isn't even aware of the molecular process spreading around him, for which he is only a pretext. It is a first, rudimentary gathering of the progressive forces that would like to be the artisans of change, provided it occurs through them and for their benefit and provided they are its sole distributors. A revolution wrapped in mystery, to be passed from one fair hand to another until it reaches the Queen. This seems to be becoming a rather common aspiration, in 1784, in this circle, which, although small, is very powerful, if only by virtue of its connections and fortune.

---

*Who becomes noted very early on for the vehemence of his opposition to the Revolution.

†Toward the end of the Constituent, Duport becomes a leader of the monarchist party, along with Barnave and the Lameth brothers. He emigrates and escapes the guillotine.

La Fayette was invited to make a good-will tour of the United States—his reward, his prize. But he's so badly bitten by his new bug that on May 14, before setting out, he writes to Washington as follows:

"A German doctor named Mesmer, having made the greatest discovery on animal magnetism, has formed pupils, among whom your humble servant is accounted one of the most enthusiastic . . . Before leaving I shall obtain permission to confide Mesmer's secret to you, for you may believe it is a great philosophical discovery."[4]

Since there wasn't any "Mesmer's secret"—only methods, an atmosphere, and a style—Washington's solid Protestant skepticism was in small danger of being overwhelmed by it. But for Louis XVI—possibly alerted by Lenoir and other police reports—it was another matter: he was very upset by anything that might interfere with or "take over" the Catholic Church. When La Fayette comes to bid the King his official farewell, Louis delivers himself, with habitual tact, of one of those little witticisms of which he was such a master and which left pools of resentment in its wake:

"What will Washington think when he learns that you have become Mesmer's first apprentice apothecary?"[5]

Washington, meanwhile, has just sidestepped a nasty snare and soared far above the "victorious generals" class into the tiny pantheon of History's truly great men. The United States had won their war but were divided and, even more, diverse; they didn't know quite what to do with themselves now, politically or economically. The leaders in every state were exhausted at the very thought of the interminable discussions that would have to take place before a constitution could be adopted. And all those underpaid soldiers to be demobilized and sent home again . . . It was *their* half-baked idea: let's have a king. What a relief! And since Washington, now shrouded in clouds of glory, has so often declared himself a champion of central authority as the means of creating a dynamic centrifugal force, why not see what he thinks of the idea? On behalf of his companions-at-arms, one of their habitual spokesmen in dealings with him put out a cautious feeler and drew it back again in a hurry.

From Washington to Lewis Nicola, on May 22, 1782:

It is with mingled surprise and pain that I have attentively perused the thought you submitted to me. Rest assured, Sir, that no event in the course of this war pained me so much as to learn through you that such ideas were circulating in the army. I must regard them with horror and condemn them severely. For the present, they shall remain locked in my breast, unless some further manifestation should render their disclosure a necessity. I look in vain for anything in my behavior that could encourage a proposal that, to me, seems pregnant with the greatest misfortunes that could ever befall my country. Unless I am much mistaken on my account, you could find no one to whom your plans would be more disagreeable.[6]

Few men in history have refused a crown with so much good sense and indignation, understanding absolute hereditary authority to be the kind of gift it is: a turd.

On March 15, 1783, Washington hastily disbanded his staff and bade a brief farewell to his troops, doing his best to master his and their emotion. He urged them, when they became civilians again, to exert themselves to the utmost to increase the power invested in the Federal Congress by the new constitution. A monarchist he definitely was not, but a centralist, yes. And he didn't let them go without one verbal caress, the only one in his power to bestow:

"By the dignity of your conduct you are going to make posterity say, when it speaks of the example you have set for the universe: Had this day not existed, the world would never have contemplated the highest perfection that human nature is capable of achieving."[7]

Soon afterward he turned to La Fayette, whose letters radiated the boredom and misery of his mandarin monarchy. Washington had been truly fond of the boy, despite his giddiness. On February 1, 1784, he wrote:

> At last, my dear marquis, I am now a simple citizen on the banks of the Potomac; and in the shade of my vine and my fig-tree, freed from the tumult of camp and the agitation of public life, I rejoice in these peaceful pleasures of which the soldier, always in pursuit of renown; the statesman who devotes his days and nights to schemes that will make the greatness of his nation or the ruin of other ones; . . . the courtier ever scrutinizing the features of his prince in the hope of a gracious smile, must have very little understanding.
>
> Not only have I withdrawn from all public employment, I have returned to myself and can recover the solitude and resume the paths of private life with a deeper sense of satisfaction. Bearing malice to none, I am resolved to be content with all, and in this disposition of mind, my dear friend, I shall flow gently down the stream of life until I rest with my fathers . . .
>
> I thank you very sincerely for your invitation to live with you if I should come to Paris. I see at present little likelihood that I shall be able to undertake such a voyage. The disruption of my private affairs during these late years not only compels me to postpone but may prevent me from ever satisfying that desire. Since no such motive exists for you, come, with Mme de La Fayette, to see me in my home here.[8]

La Fayette lost no time. But he took only a few friends along and definitely *not* his wife who, according to him anyway, would never have left the children and was needed to supervise their estate in Auvergne, where she was now settled. There was little chance of her making a fuss. "Dear heart" never said no. And God in his wisdom had created her to consent to all her husband's escapades.

La Fayette's trip to the United States lasts from June 18, 1784, to January 20, 1785 (embarking at Brest on an ordinary packet, the *Courrier de New York,* and returning to the same port on board a frigate placed at his disposal by Congress). In fact, he is the official guest of that body rather than of Washington and has also been invited by several city and state assemblies.

Triumph, delirium, hero worship: the incarnation in his person of everything the Americans confusedly felt they owed to France. One might get a swollen head for less, and since he was disposed that way in any event, this trip marks him for the rest of his days. So much has happened—and he's still only twenty-seven. He's the first to go back and receive the full blast of the reverse side of the flame of war: the victors' joy. Neither Rochambeau nor Vergennes, Castries nor Ségur, de Grasse nor Beaumarchais will know it. And as La Fayette is so likeable, so comely, and has got such a gift of gab and gesture, and there are hardly any bones to pick between the Allies, what a party it is!

It intoxicates him. Far more than at Yorktown, where he was elbowed out of the limelight, he now becomes self-aware.

Banquet in New York; entrance into Philadelphia to the sound of ringing bells and twenty-one-gun salutes; ten idyllic days with his adoptive father under the shade trees of Mount Vernon; a dinner for three hundred followed by a ball in the Baltimore Town Hall, where he had tipped his frail weight into the seesaw of war and where all the ladies and misses had so willingly plied the needle for his ragged men; and there is even a wonderful cruise on the Hudson, starting in Albany and traveling north through the September russet of the great forests to play mediators between the Oneidas, an Iroquois tribe, and the Americans[9] and endorse a commercial treaty in the name of France. Everything was settled ahead of time by negotiators sent out for the purpose, but the French stood high in the esteem of the "six Indian nations" that had federated long before the Rebels did and could make serious trouble if they started listening to any English Loreleis. And La Fayette, presented as "father," "great chief," and close kin to the King, makes the interview a ceremonial act and confers the necessary solemnity upon it.

On his return, "the entrance into Boston"—whose inhabitants had such a bad memory of d'Estaing—"was triumphant. La Fayette, accompanied by the Comte de Granchain, commander of the frigate *La Nymphe,* the Chevalier de Caraman and Major General Henry Knox, preceded by fife and drums and other musicians, and escorted by a huge crowd, marched to the Whig tavern and made a speech thanking the citizens from its balcony. Knox made a speech in return, on behalf of the officers of the Massachusetts Line, and the general glorified him as Washington's adoptive son and disciple. On October 19, 1784, the city of Boston celebrated the anniversary of the surrender of Cornwallis at Yorktown. On that occasion the executive council and members of both chambers of the State of Massachusetts gave an official reception for La Fayette. There was a banquet for five hundred at the Town Hall, and at one point a curtain behind the general fell to reveal Washington's portrait crowned with laurel and flowers and framed by the French and American flags."[10]

Then come another five or six lesser metropolises, but the tune is the same everywhere. A pilgrimage to York, on the shores of the Chesapeake, and Williamsburg, where Washington is awaiting him. Together they visit Maryland, of which La Fayette and his descendants are all made citizens. And Annapolis, and Trenton, where the entire congress has assembled.

No Frenchman of that day was ever given such a reception by an entire nation. No military chief, no prince, no king.

La Fayette and Washington make their farewells in Annapolis.* Washington's emotion is all the more forceful for being restrained, in the lines he writes to Gilbert from Mount Vernon on December 8, 1784. During the previous seven years, a real bond had grown between these two men who could hardly be more dissimilar:

> At the moment of our parting, on the road, during the journey, and since then, at every hour I have felt deeply all that the course of years, a close union, and your merit have inspired in me, of affection, respect, and attachment for you. As our carriages drew apart, I often asked myself if I had seen you for the last time. And despite my wish to say no, my fears replied yes. I called to mind the days of my youth, I found that they had long since fled, not to return, that I was now descending the slope I have seen diminishing before me for fifty-two years; for I know we are short-lived in the family, and although I have a strong constitution I must expect soon to lie in the last resting place of my fathers. These thoughts darkened the horizon for me, spread a cloud across the future, and consequently across my hope of seeing you again. But I shall not complain, I have had my day.[11]

La Fayette has just had his, too. Who among the people he sails toward that December can boast of comparable memories? But who was able to feel as deeply as he the tremendous gulf between the two worlds?

He's young, though; memories aren't enough for him. The wind from America catches him up again in 1784, but if anybody imagines that it's going to deposit him placidly in Auvergne or leave him dancing at Trianon . . . Especially when, upon reaching Versailles on February 9, 1785, with his eyes

*A figure of speech, but this time it's true; they never meet again.

and mind still full of a nation in the process of inventing itself, he encounters the same somnolent king, the same frivolous courtiers, the same fossil society, the same resigned masses, the France of Louis XVI. *Nothing,* except science and horse racing.

NAPOLEON AT BRIENNE

53

OCTOBER 1784

More Champenois Than Corsican

Napoleon de Buonaparte's first trip to Paris is made in a hearse; or a basket, at least, which was what the Parisians had nicknamed the "water coach" that plied the Seine between Nogent and Corbeil and went so slowly that its name almost inevitably became attached to the vehicle transporting the dead, called a *corbillard** to this day.[1]

Five youths finally "sprung" from Brienne, and not seventy years among the five of them. Crazy puppies, mere infants unleashed from the semi-prison that had been their excuse for a youth—and where are they going for their first spree? To Paris! Enough to make them giddy, and so they are: Dampierre, Comminges, Bellecour, Castres, and Buonaparte (each of whose names ought rightly, of course, to be preceded by that particle of which they are so proud, and which entitles them to be known as "gentleman-cadets of the King"; Castres de Vaux is not to be confused with anyone of the name of Castries) have been singing and generally horsing around all the way, although within very moderate limits because they are escorted, as was the rule, by a Minim father—the school superior, if you please, no less a person than Father Berton himself.

Their exhilaration was also slightly dampened by a coolness, not really a quarrel, between Buonaparte and the sweetly pretty Laugier de Bellecour, one of the favorite "nymphs" of the big boys at Brienne, where pederasty reigned almost officially "in the dormitories and 'conveniences,' and where means were found of practicing it, despite the supervision of the Minim fathers—not very close supervision, it must be said—under the reading and gaming tables."[2] At first Napoleon had been drawn to the gentle, charming boy, who,

*[*Corbeil:* the town; *corbeille:* basket. The vessel serving the town would naturally be called a *corbeillard,* and the name then slipped into *corbillard:* hearse.—*Trans.*]

unlike so many of the others, did not make fun of him. But when he under-stood that Bellecour . . . ! His Corsican blood froze in his veins. His *mamma* and all her tribe had inculcated in him a shudder of primitive horror at the very thought of homosexuality. With the uncompromising authority of his fourteen years (Bellecour was only thirteen) he proclaimed:

"You have attachments that I cannot approve. Your new friends will ruin you. You must choose between them or me."

Laugier de Bellecour chose his "new friends," and apparently for life. They made his time at Brienne a little less dismal. Buonaparte seems not to have had much success with his first attempts at moralizing; and there was plenty more ahead of him at the military academy.

They caught the mail-coach at Bar-sur-Aube—a stout, large-bellied, heavy-jowled vehicle that creaked at every spring and was deformed by hernias of luggage on its roof. That night they slept at Arcis, the town where Georges-Jacques Danton, a young graduate ten years their senior, was finish-ing off his uneventful youth and preparing to go up to Paris and become a lawyer. The next day they dragged along behind their weary nags as far as Nogent-sur-Seine, where they all slept in the same room at the sign of "La Ville de Jérusalem." In the morning, boarding one of those fat barges that were all the joy of water travel, they paid nine livres and seven sols* each to be transported down the Seine for two days, by water-coach, past Montereau and Melun to Corbeil and at last, along the main artery into the very heart of Paris.

There they disembarked, on October 21, 1784, at the port of Saint-Paul not far from that shapeless sandy bank still known in those days as *la grève,* † next to the square where the town hall stood by the scaffold. Five in the afternoon, almost dusk. They cross the Pont Marie, which is beginning to be divested of the houses crowding its flanks, and sup at the "Coq Hardi," the first cheap caterer they come across. Afterwards, they take a little stroll through the noise of carriages, shouting, and crowds, along streets so poorly lit that they have to hold hands to keep from getting separated. The second-hand booksellers already have their stalls along the riverbanks, and Napoleon in his excitement is said to have bought** on that occasion the first novel he ever owned: *Gil Blas* by Lesage—already fifty years old. At this point their chaperon decides to take them in hand again, and shepherds all five of them along to pray inside the Abbey of Saint-Germain-des-Prés in the heart of a

*About 55 modern francs [$11].

†[*Grève:* strand; public executions had been held there for centuries, and also for centuries workers in certain trades had gathered there to look for jobs; *faire la grève* in those days meant to be out of work, and by extension became applied to a voluntary stoppage of work, so that today *faire la grève* means to go on strike.—*Trans.*]

**With money lent by Castres; but it's Lenôtre who says so, and he quotes no source.

conglomeration of chapels and barkers' stalls, a distillate, in a few hundred square yards, of all the shapes and colors of Paris. Then, curtains: still following the Seine but on the left bank, he leads them out of town to the Champ de Mars, where young Buonaparte takes "his place in the company of gentleman-cadets established by the King in his Military Academy."

The first contact is pretty painful, especially after that tantalizingly brief dip into a free world. This time it's not a convent, it's the army. "The place had a very different feeling from Brienne," Napoleon later says. "The classes were commanded by four officers of Saint-Louis and eight sergeants, their orders were high and mighty and their tone military." And he's not yet fifteen. On the outskirts of Paris, in the Grenelle fields still separated from the city by gardens, he will be almost as penned-up as at Brienne, although in one of the most striking settings of the period. The military academy was planned in 1750, partly built, after various vicissitudes, between 1751 and 1773, incomplete in 1784 and incomplete in 1980.

Year by year its budget had dwindled, its plans shrunk, and its attributions altered. One can't really call the Invalides a failure because the building is— if only the façade and state rooms—a fine example of eighteenth-century architecture; but its mind-boggling jumble of beauty, nobility, improvisation, and oversight, with building sites agape in one place and rubble in another, gives a pretty fair idea of the majestic mess that had been the reign of Louis XV. As seen by Napoleon in 1784, it nevertheless offered a sight like no other in the world, and one no foreign visitor ever missed: a completely self-sufficient little town on the edge of the big one, with housing for officers, pupils' dormitories, infirmary, commons, the riding school still a-building, chapel, stables, specially laid sewers running straight to the Seine, and a monumental clock, "the most beautiful ever seen for both design and masterful execution," a masterpiece by Sieur Lepaute, with nine hundred and sixty-two parts showing "all the revolutions of the sun" and 120-pound hammers ringing eight times an hour.

Buonaparte's initially unfavorable impression of military discipline does not last. A few days later he is filled with pride at the thought that this immense institution revolves, at least a little, around his small self—because the profusion of higher officers, instructors, inspectors, bursars, and a countless horde of minor servants are all there for the sole purpose of transforming one hundred and twenty pupils into the elite of the army to come. At last, a background worthy of a Buonaparte! "We were fed, served, and treated with magnificence in all things, as though we were officers possessed of considerable fortunes, far more considerable than those many of us would later have in reality."[3] For the first time in his life Napoleon has servants, the ones who wait on the cadets in the dining room and riding school. He finds the idea quite to his taste. And then he likes this healthy life, punctuated by the kind of physical exercise that really does build strength and character. Classes are taught by sixteen first-rate masters, with emphasis on the sciences in which he is becoming increasingly interested. He begins to learn algebra, analytical geometry, mechanics, hydrostatics. He even makes some progress in belles lettres and his French teacher, M. Domairon, feels himself shaken, whenever he can decipher his pupil's compositions (already almost illegible; his teachers at Brienne, out of negligence or despair, had allowed him to develop truly abominable writing and spelling), by the tremor, the fever in them: "They were granite heated in a volcano."

He hadn't remained long at the collège in Autun, where the little wild creature from Ajaccio had been dumped at the age of nine in December 1778. The Benedictines of Tiron* turned out to have no room for him; but in May 1779 his protector Mgr de Marbeuf, the Bishop of Autun, found him a place at Brienne.

He was already complaining about the climate in Burgundy, and then the poor boy had to go shiver in Champagne. When he said good-bye to his brother Giuseppe—sorry, Joseph—the companion of his first ten years, his confidant, his only true friend in Corsica, and even more in France where everything bruised and offended him, something broke inside. That day he said good-bye to his childhood too and really, it was a little early, before his tenth birthday. Joseph burst out sobbing. Napoleon, however, had learned one thing no less important than the French language at Autun, and that was self-control. In three months and twenty days he had understood that people would tease him if he showed his emotions. The brothers were not alone so he immured himself in silence, but could not prevent one tear, just one, from rolling down his cheek. Abbé Simon, the deputy principal of the collège, was no fool, and turned to Joseph; "Your brother shed only one tear, yet it proves as much as all of yours."[4]

Brienne at that time was a trifling village in Dry Champagne, four hundred inhabitants, you couldn't even call it a burg. The nearest proper town, Bar-sur-Aube, was six leagues away. Stripped flatlands full of fox and brambles, a few scrubby copses where the jackdaws nested, dusty or muddy paths leading over them, and at the end, in contrast to the fair town of Autun, plump and clean as a canoness, this mound of thatched half-hovels. The school was the only building with a tile roof—except of course for the "big house" up there, its imposing mass flattening the handful of cottages huddled around it, on the

*At Rosny-sur-Seine not far from Paris; the school was said to be "situated in a desert of brambles and bracken from which the pupils never emerged." The Benedictines would undoubtedly have given Napoleon a more extensive literary baggage, but at the expense of mathematics.

summit of the hill where the very high and puissant lords of Brienne, vassals of the counts of Champagne for nigh onto a thousand years, used to keep their garrison and were now living in splendor in the huge château they had just had built. One of them was Bishop of Toulouse.

Napoleon caught the merest glimpse of all this on his way into the school, which had been installed in the buildings of a former convent only two years before. It was long and straight, a perfect symbol of those years and years of gloom, each exactly like the last, which any boy entering a boarding school imagines stretching out before him to the crack of doom. The boys too were all alike. They wore blue woolen uniforms with red facings on collar and cuffs, black breeches, and white stockings. One hundred and ten budding officers under the easy-going command of twelve Minims* assisted by a few lay teachers, all garbed in black.

That night the young immigrant from the island of liberty suffered a fearsome sensation when he was locked, like every one of his comrades, into a space six-foot-square adorned with a trestle bed, a washbasin, and a chamber-pot: a former monk's cell. No outings, no holidays, no vacation, except in September and October, when there were no afternoon lessons, and then only long walks in conducted groups known as spaciments, like the Carthusians' weekly breaks. It was forbidden to receive books, clothing, or money from the outside world. The collège met all the pupils' needs out of the King's treasury and even gave them a little pocket money: one franc a month until they were twelve, two francs thereafter. Their parents were relieved of financial responsibility, provided they sent a trousseau with their son consisting of a uniform, three pairs of sheets, twelve towels, twelve handkerchiefs, twelve white collars, twelve shirts, six cotton bonnets, a powder-bag and ribbon for the hair (which they wore in a cadogan), a knife and fork and silver mug marked with their arms.

Mass came first, then ten hours of study every day. The Minims, also known as Bonshommes [Goodfellows] taught the humanities: no Greek, not too much Latin, a bit of German (Napoleon never really took to it), French, sacred and profane history, literature—of course no mention was ever made of the great authors of the century, but the pupils traded secret copies of Voltaire, Diderot, and Rousseau. The lay masters, some of whom were former officers or noncommissioned officers, were responsible for the sciences, which were beginning to occupy a much larger place in the curriculum, under pressure from the *Encyclopédie.* They gave lessons in mathematics,† geography, astronomy, physics, and draftsmanship, but all were slanted toward the school's

*Related but not directly attached to the Franciscans.

†It has been alleged that the future General Pichegru, who did teach mathematics at Brienne, was one of Napoleon's professors. This is untrue; the dates do not coincide.

objective, which was the practice of the art of war. What Brienne had to produce were dozens of little gentlemen capable of leading untutored boors who didn't even know the alphabet through gunfire and on to their deaths, and making them maneuver as though they were possessed of intelligence. Because the "new spirit" was beginning to blow even through the King's schools, they also had lessons in deportment, fencing, dancing, and the art of fortification. In theory, equality was supposed to reign among the pupils, and they were all treated alike, rich or poor, since their equally noble births were taken for granted.

The teachers were not saints, though, and some of them felt an instant dislike for the scrap of a boy with the sallow complexion and abrupt manners, who answered in monosyllables less out of shyness than fear of making a mistake in French, and who stiffened at the drop of a hat into a sort of superior scorn that initiated eyes would have identified as a massive inferiority complex. However, to anyone who would take the trouble, he showed the better side of his Corsican origins—a serenity, mildness, and application to work that earned him the affection of his fellows. When rubbed the wrong way, on the other hand, he was horrid. A brute of a quartermaster, "without regard for the specific physical and moral qualities of the child" as Napoleon himself was to say later when telling the episode, punished him for insolence by ordering him to clothe himself in a brown homespun frock (worn by the lay-brother servants) and kneel throughout an entire meal at the door of the big dining room where teachers and pupils ate together. At first he said nothing, donned his penitent's gown, went to his place of punishment, and got down on his knees—but when the school filed past on the way to dinner, his will broke. He began vomiting uncontrollably and had an attack of nerves almost like an epileptic fit.*

It was even worse where his schoolfellows were concerned. His first year at Brienne—his sixth-grade year—was a time of emotional solitude so intense that many youngsters less highly strung than he might well have been destroyed by it. The desert of the thousand faces. It wasn't so much because he was poor—plenty of the King's scholars had not a farthing more than he—as because he was Corsican and because, as at Autun, he was looked upon as a foreigner, an alien from a country that France had defeated and conquered only a short time before, still peopled with "bandits." His sensitivity on this point made him all the more vain and aggressive. Who did the little Wop take himself for? Well, of course, he really had been a big fish in Ajaccio, but here at Brienne he was a very minor minnow swimming in a shoal of the glittering great names of France, borne by the scions of families filled with their own importance, who burst out laughing when he said his name was *Napolioné di*

*These attacks continue, although infrequently, throughout his life.[5]

Buonaparté. He had a nasal twang, too, and didn't know how to place his voice, so they soon nicknamed him "Straw-in-the-nose," and the name stuck for many a day.

The turning point in his adolescence came during the winter of 1782, when it was so cold that the water in his basin was frozen one morning, and he ran to alert his neighbors, thinking some terrible cataclysm had occurred. But people were already teasing him less. He was beginning to make himself respected in the only way possible for a boy in his position: by work. He developed a taste for reading. His French became extremely polished, all the more so as it was an acquired language—although he spoke with a strong Mediterranean accent that never completely disappeared. That winter, he and a few friends decided to engage in some extracurricular preparation for their future vocations, with the help of the snow that lay deep on their recreation ground. Armed with picks and shovels, they set the boys to work digging trenches and built a whole system of horn-work, parapets, and fortalices.

And now let's split into two camps, besiegers and besieged.

A fortnight of warplay ensued, with snowballs for weapons, during recreation periods; but it ended before the thaw because a few boys had the bright idea of packing their snowballs with gravel and stones. The casualties were transported to the infirmary covered in glory.

At barely fourteen years of age, thus, Napoleon learned that in spite of his cultural handicap, he had and could exert a natural authority over others; that he possessed a certain magnetism of voice and gesture. By dint of hard work and his struggle with solitude, he contrived to establish a sort of equilibrium. He was no longer shut up in himself, he was becoming a good scholar in arithmetic and geometry and beginning to develop a passion for history and geography.

At bottom, however, he remained what he had always been—Corsican to the marrow, isolated by his resentment of the French, a rather unforthcoming boy, not on the whole a top student, and often rebellious.

He found solace in the company of some new soulmates, the heroes of ancient history. Plutarch, Tacitus, Sophocles, and Aeschylus were almost the only books in the Minims' library, apart from the lives of the saints and theological works. In the evening by candlelight he spent hours and hours in Sparta, Athens, and Rome, with Pericles and Alcibiades, Caesar and Brutus and the Gracchi. He was especially fascinated by the Spartans, he identified with them. He discovered that he had unconsciously been a Spartan fellow-traveler all along, and the fact that he was losing his religion made it easier for him to become one in reality. He had never been particularly devout, but he respected the Catholicism of his compatriots and his mother—a religion of externals, motivated less by the evangelical spirit than by superstition. But at

Brienne, beneath the weight of the prayers parroted in unison morning and night, low mass every day and high mass chanted on Sundays, and the vespers and the lectures, his childhood faith collapsed. An underground draught of skepticism, blown in by the century, was seeping through the pupils' cell doors, becoming almost a form of snobbery. And the Minims, who were religious civil servants rather than priests, were poorly equipped to fight it. The straw that broke the back of his faith came from a tactless reference to his beloved Romans:

"I heard a sermon in which the priest was saying that Cato and Julius Caesar were damned. I was eleven years old. I was shocked to learn that the most virtuous men of Antiquity should burn eternally because they had not followed a religion of which they had never heard . . . From that time on, I had no more religion."[6]

His parents came to see him in the summer of 1782 at the end of three years, three centuries that had wrought lasting changes in him. His mother had a badly knitted fracture of the leg and was being conducted by Charles to "take the waters" at Bourbonne-les-Bains in Champagne; she was alarmed by her son's scarecrow thinness and the transformation in his features, for a moment she didn't even recognize him. He reassured her by explaining how he sat up late at night working, how he sacrificed his recreation periods, how he could not bear not to be at the head of his class. In fact, he never was, but he certainly knew how to talk to parents! They did not disappoint him, either: "What gave him the keenest pleasure, although he would not show it, was to see how everyone in the school admired his mother. He later said to Montholon, 'My mother at twenty-nine was as beautiful as Venus. Teachers and pupils alike were all talking about the beauty of Mme de Buonaparte.' "[7] Napoleon loved many women later in his life, but one wonders if he ever admired one more than his own mother. Carlo-Maria, his father, whom he was learning to call Charles-Marie just as he now called himself Napoleon, dropping the final *e,* was euphoric as always, decked out in yellow like a big canary, bursting with optimism, schemes, and plans. He had just received an inheritance from an uncle and sent to Italy for a whole boatload of furniture, mirrors, and statuary for the *casa* in Ajaccio. And there were two more babies on the Rue Malerba, Pauline and Maria-Nunziata, and the undreamed-of luxuries of a chambermaid and a cook.

Joseph, on the other hand, was not living up to expectations. They had continued to write each other regularly, but in the stiff-jawed style that schoolteachers imposed upon their pupils in those days, pedantically compelling the brothers to inform each other that "they were greatly affected to receive news" of each other, that they remained each other's "obedient and faithful servant," and that "the inviolable attachment which they owed to Holy Religion and to the Sovereign was being expressed in the felicitous pursuit of their studies." Underneath all this gibberish one thing became clear to Napoleon and that was that Joseph was feeling less and less enthusiasm for the priesthood. As in many noble families, the careers of older sons were mapped out in advance on purely material grounds. Joseph might hope to become a bishop and Napoleon a general. And here was the eldest taking it into his head to have a military career too, and in the only branch in which poor gentlemen could see a dim possibility of promotion, the artillery. Now if Joseph turned stubborn he could easily bar the way to his beloved Nabulione, for the rules of the monarchy strictly forbade the award of scholarships in the same branch of the army to two brothers. Well, so much for friendship. Napoleon's first authentic letter, written in Brienne on June 25, 1784, to his uncle Paravicini, is a counterattack upon the brother who had been his most cherished companion a few years before:

> Joseph is mistaken for several reasons . . . He is not bold enough to affront the perils of combat. His poor health will not allow him to sustain the fatigues of a compaign, and my brother is looking only at the garrison aspect of the military condition; yes, my dear brother will make a very good camp officer, well formed, quick spirited, and consequently well suited to frivolous compliments, and with his talents he will always come off well in society, but what about a battle? . . . He was educated for the ecclesiastical condition. It is late in the day to change directions now. Mgr. the Bishop of Autun would have given him a fat living . . . What advantages for the family . . .

A family in which family love was beginning to turn a peculiar shade of green. When Napoleon writes these lines he hasn't seen Joseph for five years, he no longer knows the person he is talking about. What he is really doing is echoing the disenchanted comments of his father who has just come to see him for the second time and for whom, now, everything is going wrong. In two years, the Italian uncle's inheritance has been spent, the family increased by one last baby, Jerome, and he has even more worries than before. In the parlor at Brienne Napoleon and Charles sound like conspirators as they plan the family's future. Joseph will have to wait at Autun while they find out whether an exception can be made in his case so he can go to another military school, the one in Metz. He may be the oldest but priority goes to the one who's done best for the last five years. When the gates of Brienne collège finally clang shut behind the spare, slight youth, another brother, Lucien, remains behind them, unregretted by his elder. Charles-Marie brought him up at the beginning of a summer during which the two boys quarreled nonstop. "The chevalier Lucien," aged nine and no less gifted than Napoleon, finds the tone in which his older brother was trying to order him around highly offensive, and never forgives him.

Brienne made Napoleon into a man, capable of courage, intelligence, toughness, and spite. On St. Helena, Gourgaud later hears him say, "I am more Champenois than Corsican, for from the age of nine I was a pupil at Brienne."[8]

In the morning of March 23, 1785, in the military academy in Paris, Napoleon sees one of the fathers coming toward him with solemn mien; he leads the boy into a parlor with an unusual show of solicitude, and it doesn't take Napoleon long to guess what's up: this is the standard procedure for announcing a death. When he has understood that the dear departed is his own father, the priest suggests that he might like to go to the infirmary—also standard procedure—"so that he might be alone in the first moments of grief." Napoleon curtly rejects the idea. Not for nothing has he spent all those years hanging around with the Romans.

"Do you believe I lack strength of character?"

THE BIRTH OF
THE DUC DE NORMANDIE

54

MARCH 1785

The Queen of France Was Delivered

February 24, 1785. Montpellier. A man is dying. Abandoned, or almost, by heaven and earth. And only thirty-nine, so young, and so handsome—the pity of it! It is an atrocious spectacle for the three or four witnesses to his agony.[1]

Charles-Marie de Buonaparte writhes, jaundiced and gaunt, on his bed of pain; his bones jut through the skin of his perspiring face, a tangle of brown locks lies plastered to his high forehead. The rain has been pelting down for two days in the stately capital of Languedoc; the poor man hardly caught sight of it when he dragged into town exhausted a month ago and crawled to the "Auberge du Parc" in the suburban Sonnerie district.

He was already too sick to stay at the inn, its proprietor wanted no part of any boarder who had death written so plainly on his face. He took refuge in this rich winegrower's house, eight haphazard rooms built of stout yellow stone, standing between the city walls and the barracks. He rented one floor of it for a few écus from a woman named Delon, meaning to stay just long enough to be doped up with asses' milk and gum powder, as prescribed by the gentlemen of the medical faculty of Montpellier, the most renowned physicians in the world for stomach ailments. But he never went out again. For three weeks he's been unable to keep anything down, asses' milk, biscuits soaked in the strong local wine, even sabayon, that cream made of egg yolks, sugar, wine, and herbs that the women whip so fine and thick—you could want to be sick just to have the right to eat it. When Mme Delon saw that Charles-Marie couldn't digest her sabayon, and when she saw the large spots of blood on her linen napkins and sheets, she shook her head, took council with Mme Permon—his only friend here*—and decided it was time to send for the priests.

He'd been asking for them for the past week anyway, and was in no danger of going without, for the Franciscan fathers, or *cordeliers* as they were called around here, lived almost next door at the Font Putanelle,† and were now taking turns at his bedside, with their long beards and the heavy, clicking wooden rosaries they wore instead of belts around their long gray robes. He mixed them up in his delirium, Father Ange-Bastien, Father François-Marie, Father Seraphin. But even though he had sent for them, he treated them as though they weren't there once they had come. Their presence did not displease him. A gentleman ought not to die without the ministrations of the church; but they were not to trouble him with talk. Their job was to pray, his to die; let each man tend to his business.

But why isn't he dying ceremoniously in Ajaccio, in the corner room on the third floor of the Via Malerba—Weed Street—surrounded by his weeping clan, in the big bed in which Letizia gave birth to their twelve children? (Except, it's true, for Napoleon; he was born on the living room sofa on the ground floor one August 15th. She barely had time to leave the Assumption Day high mass, where her pains had come, and hurry home across the square, oh it was so hot that morning, everything white and burning.) Why does he have to die here in this deluge of lukewarm rain falling in huge, limp drops? You can hear them streaming down the round tiles; the whitewashed walls are sweating with damp.

Another moan; he wants more opium. The doctors let him have all he asks for, and even procure him a supply of it once they see that there is nothing more to do. Bigouroux, Sabatier, even the great Barthès himself, whose long, dry octogenarian fingers, lightly exploring his esophagus, instantly found the sensitive spot, the pylorus, from which a black sun of pain radiates fiercely through every part of his body. The Sieur de Bonaparte is mortally afflicted with what was then, for want of a better term, known as a scirrhus of the

*Corsican-born but of Greek parentage, Laura Permon was the mother of Laure Junot, Duchesse d'Abrantès, who wrote some highly fanciful *Mémoires* of the Empire.

†"The Wise Women's Fountain."

stomach. Cancer? Ulcers? Whatever science may call it, its real name is worry.

There's Giuseppe, trying to wriggle out of being a priest. And Maria-Anna's wardrobe at Saint-Cyr to be renewed every year. And to which school should they send Luciano, now on the waiting list at Brienne? And then there's that batch of nestlings in Ajaccio, still playing in the new town's back streets that reek of dirty water, weeds, and bitter oranges. No trace of a sewer in town, every little rivulet is a gutter, what a stench from April on—ah, if he could only have that stench in his nostrils for one short hour! Maria-Paoletta, Luigi, Maria-Nunziata, Girolamo, what will become of them?

He is dying of obsessive anxiety . . . and of this last trip, a walking nightmare. He had to see Giuseppe at Autun, reason with him, try to persuade him to enter the seminary, get him to understand that that was his duty as the eldest son, because Napoleon was making out pretty well at the military academy at Paris and would become an artillery officer. And he also had to see whether Maria-Anna was beginning to turn into a properly trained socialite doll at Saint-Cyr. If only they could marry her off soon to some rich, elderly seigneur!

Charles-Marie set out in midwinter. In those days people traveled in every wind and weather; they went up into the mountains or north to St. Petersburg come storm, come blizzard, come hurricane. Seven years before, at the age of eighty-four, Voltaire had screwed himself into a coach at snowbound Ferney in the dead of winter, to triumph and die in Paris. He had been more than twice the age of Charles-Marie. Who expects the end to come at thirty-nine . . . ?

His ship had been forced back twice from the coast by those treacherous January storms in the Mediterranean; and suddenly, battered alike by waves and worries, something inside him gave way. He stubbornly insisted on continuing the trip; no, never, he would not go back to the Via Malerba and take to his bed, admit defeat, give up this whole latest program of favor begging and visiting. He would, however, make a detour to consult the doctors in Montpellier, the men who cured princes and dignitaries all over Europe by correspondence; but to do that he would have to make a third crossing. He landed in Marseilles at the end of his rope, having eaten nothing for two weeks, looking twenty years older, unrecognizable. The Aix road, with those wicked hairpin bends in the piercing cold, finished him off. At Aix, Abbé Fesch was speechless when he met him in the seminary parlor. Fesch was Letizia's half-brother, a mixture of Swiss and Corsican; he was only twenty-two but already oozing priest from every pore: ageless. Clerical ambition incarnate.* The only person Charles-Marie could turn to in that hideous January. Fesch

*By the grace of Napoleon, he becomes Archbishop of Lyons and primate of the Gauls, then serves as Archbishop of Paris before being driven out by the Restoration and ending his days in Rome, cushioned by the immense fortune he had amassed over twenty years.

had thrust his brother-in-law into a coach and headed for Montpellier, summoning Joseph by letter.

Montpellier the white, so beautiful, its outline so sharp beyond the gardens of the Peyrou; you can see the sea in the distance, dozens of mansions handsome as any in Aix or Nancy, a constant whirl of coaches and carriages, students in square caps, professors in togas, life, the city, and all just to lie down and never get up again . . .

He sinks deeper into his pillows. The hiccup weakens. The pulse too. His eyes begin to turn. Mme Permon, motherly, affectionate, wipes his lips, takes his hand, tries to make him swallow a few mouthfuls of orange-flower water. She's about the same age as he, she may have loved him a little, who knows, when her idiot husband was tax collector for the King in Ajaccio. She's so much more lively and chatty than that great statue of a Letizia, and she knows so much more.

"A little calomel?"

The last doctor shakes his head—no point. Fesch and one of the Franciscans take turns reciting the prayer for the dying. Only one person here is really upset, overwhelmed in fact—that tall dark shapeless adolescent kneeling in a corner, afraid of death: Joseph, the one who was causing his father such anguish a month ago. But the dying man hasn't even tried to make him promise to become a priest. Everything is different now. Now the oldest son will have to go back to Corsica and take his father's place, or try to; he'll have to supervise the sharecroppers and clerks because Letizia can hardly write her own name. Napoleon and Lucien will stay on in the King's schools. Joseph's beautiful dark eyes search his father's, looking for a spark of life; but it's all over. Charles-Marie twitches a little, then grows still, except for the sound at the back of his throat, as though somebody else were moaning. Even his mind has ceased to fret.

Between two shores, did his heart turn once to the four little ones, the "angels" as Letizia called them—how odd—whom he had lost in their infancy, before the mingled blood of Buonapartes and Ramolinos grew thick enough to keep their babies alive? Letizia and he baptized and buried two Maria-Annas before the third one survived.

He has joined them. What a stillness in the room, at four o'clock in the morning. Charles-Marie de Buonaparte is dead, killed by his family and the storm in his heart.

His body can't be sent to Corsica because there isn't a farthing left for the burial. Mme Permon herself has to pay the costs; he is interred in a cellar in the Franciscan convent.*

*Of this convent, rebuilt once in 1622 after the Spanish had razed it to the ground, all that remains today is one building whose external appearance is still reminiscent of a church. It stands

His straitened circumstances also give four eager Montpellier physicians an excuse to take a firsthand look at a body that has died so surprisingly young of a disease that has run so swift a course:[2]

> The opening of the corpse of M. Buonaparte confirmed the views of the doctors of Ajaccio as to the cause of the wilful, obstinate, and hereditary [*sic*] vomiting that carried him off. When he came to this city and placed himself in our care, we could but acquiesce in the views of his own physicians, and we agreed with their opinion, that the large tumor he had located in the lower abdomen was seated in the lining of the stomach toward its inferior orifice, and that there were grounds for supposing the pylorus implicated in it. Following this approach we concluded, in accord with the physicians of Corsica, that the vomiting was incurable, that it would end the patient's days, and that the most our skill could do was to prolong his life by alleviating the symptoms accompanying the vomiting. The body was opened by M. Bousquet, surgeon-major of the Vermondois regiment, and M. Fabre, student surgeon of this town, co-signed with us in the presence of several officers of that regiment.
>
> The viscera of the lower abdomen were found to be in fairly good condition, with the exception of the stomach, which was distended by the liquid taken by the patient. The lower orifice of this organ formed a tumor of the length and volume of a large potato or elongated winter pear. This tumor was very resistant and of an extremely firm, semi-cartileginous consistency. The lining of the stomach, toward the middle of the great bend, was very thick and firm in consistency, becoming more cartileginous as it approached the pylorus, and this lower orifice of the stomach was contained within the center of the tumor and so foreshortened that it was necessary to make an incision with a scalpel before it was possible to introduce a fingertip. The tumor did not extend beyond the pylorus; the duodenal intestine was in its natural state.*

The military academy, Paris. Napoleon, as everybody calls him now except in Corsica, takes plenty of time to suffer in silence—until March 29—before accepting a professor's help in composing a letter to his mother in which, for once, there are relatively few spelling mistakes and not one hint of natural emotion. The conventional language of "the best people," the

---

near the Montpellier railway station and is now a cinema. The site of the house in which Charles-Marie died, long since demolished, is occupied by a five-story building, 3 Rue Castilhon, on which a plaque has recently been placed commemorating him. Napoleon took no interest in his remains, which were exhumed by Louis in 1803 and finally taken to Ajaccio in April 1951, after remaining a century and a half in Saint-Leu.

Napoleon subsequently becomes Emperor of the French; Joseph, King of Naples and then of Spain; Maria-Anna (the third), alias Elisa, Grand Duchess of Tuscany and Princess of Lucca and Piombino; Louis, King of Holland; Pauline, Princess of Guastalla; Maria-Nunziata, alias Caroline, the wife of Murat and Queen of Naples; Jerome, King of Westphalia. Lucien, having quarreled with Napoleon, was never more than Prince of Canino, and that thanks to the pope.

*Napoleon himself dies in almost exactly the same way at St. Helena on May 5, 1821, as confirmed by the report on his autopsy.

language imposed by the priest who was guiding his pen, stifles his letter like a gag:

> My dear mother.
>
> It is only today that time has somewhat allayed the first transports of my grief, and I hasten to send you some sign of the gratitude that the goodness you have ever shown us has inspired in me. Be comforted, my dear mother; circumstances require it of you. We shall double our concern and gratitude, and shall be happy if, by our obedience, we can in some part make up for the inestimable loss of a beloved husband. I now close, my dear mother, my grief bids me do so, with the prayer that you will calm your own. My health is perfect, and I pray Heaven every day to send you an equal blessing.[3]

Did Napoleon ever really love his father? He saw so little of him, Charles-Marie was so far away, so high up, someone on whom one was always dependent, a little god to whom one said *vous*. He seldom mentions him in later years. Even now he is aware of something more than his loss: he's listening to the happy murmur of Paris rejoicing—bells, gun salutes, fountains of wine and fireworks—from which the premature death of an obscure Corsican in Languedoc was so remote. Napoleon snatches up his pen before sealing the letter and adds a few words of his own, the only ones that come from him. He can no longer confine his attention to the fate of the Buonapartes, even in a family crisis:

> P.S. The Queen of France was delivered of a prince, named the Duc de Norman-die, at 7 in the evening of March 27.
>
> Your very humble and affectionate son,
>
> Napoleone de Buonaparte.*

Louis-Charles de Bourbon was baptized two hours after his birth (on Sunday March 25, in fact; Napoleon was wrong by two days); his godfather was Monsieur,† a godfather who, after the poor health of the first boy-child had sent his hopes soaring again, now sees the throne snatched definitively from his grasp. M. de Calonne, Grand Treasurer of the Orders of the King, who is, as everybody knows, about to save the kingdom from bankruptcy, brings the baby the cordon and cross of the Holy Spirit. "Louis XVI seemed highly pleased. He attended the Te Deum that was sung in the chapel of the château, sent word to the Corps of the City of Paris, and instructed Vergennes to convey the news to all foreign courts."[4]

The King has two reasons to be jubilant: not only has he another son, he

---

*Marie-Antoinette's second son becomes dauphin in June 1789 after his brother's death, of cachexy. It is he who is "the poor little prisoner" of the Temple, known to History as Louis XVII, and who dies or disappears in 1795. Napoleon will mount the imperial throne on May 18, 1804, less than twenty years from this time.

†The future Louis XVIII.

has also evened up a private score. For more than a year his ears have been aching from the howling success of that awful *Marriage of Figaro*. He bides his time; then, on March 10, on some trumped-up police charge that leaves the Parisians gasping, he orders Beaumarchais thrown into prison. Which one? The Bastille? Too good for him. No, Saint-Lazare, "where they put young scamps who have been sowing wild oats that good families want to hush up,"[5] and where a Lazarist brother, the "flogger-father," is detailed to spank the inmates soundly every morning.

Two direct heirs to the throne, a seductive prestidigitator in charge of the treasury, Beaumarchais in jail and humiliated, and the people mute if not euphoric. All's right with the world, there is no tiger at the gates. With Turgot expelled and Necker out of the way, the reign of Louis XVI can get down to business at last; the King himself is devoting all his spare time to the preparations for the great voyage of exploration that the Comte de La Pérouse is to make around the world in search of new lands to conquer for him.

On February 1, 1785, Böhmer and Bassenge, the top Paris jewelers, hand the most expensive necklace in the world* to Cardinal Louis de Rohan, Archbishop of Strasbourg and Grand Almoner to the King. He ordered it from them in the greatest secrecy, on the Queen's behalf;[6] and she, according to the cardinal, has undertaken to pay for it "in four quarters" or six-monthly installments, the first payment falling due at the beginning of August 1785.

*One million six hundred thousand livres, or 9.6 million modern francs [$1,920,000].

Notes

Titles appearing in Volumes I and II, where fuller descriptions will be found in some cases, are marked with an asterisk (*) upon first mention here.

I

1. *Histoire des environs de Paris* (no author's name) (Paris, 1837), II, 199.
2. *Dictionnaire historique des moeurs, usages et coutumes des François* (Paris, published by Vincent, Rue Saint-Séverin, 1787), I, 536. Hereafter abbreviated as *Dictionnaire des François.*
3. Victor Fournel, "Collot d'Herbois comédien," article in *Le Correspondant,* July–September 1893. Unnumbered quotations in this section are from the same source. In his article Mr. Fournel says that the "dialogue in *Les Français à la Grenade* is lively and well-paced on the whole," but that the reason is because it is copied word for word from a play by Dancourt, *L'Impromptu de garnison.*
4. Guy Lemarchand, "Les Troubles de subsistance dans la généralité de Rouen," in *Annales historiques de la révolution française,* XXXV (1964), 422.
5. *Dictionnaire géographique, historique et politique des Gaules et de la France* by M. l'abbé Expilly (Amsterdam, 1770), VI: "Rouen." In future I give this as Expilly's *Dictionnaire.* Recent research in historical demography, especially that of Marcel Reinhard, has established Expilly's tendency to inflate French population figures, and I have made allowance for this.
6. Albert Soboul, *La Civilisation et la révolution française,* I, *La Crise de l'ancien régime* (Paris, Arthaud, 1970), p. 312.
7. Anecdote mentioned in a letter dated December 25, 1781, written by Ludovico Pio, the chargé d'affaires of the King of Naples in Paris. H. Flammermont, *Nouvelles archives des missions diplomatiques* (Paris, 1887), VIII, 434. The complete lyrics of the song are given there.
8. Letter from Collot d'Herbois to his friend Armand Desroziers, actor and theater director, published by Mr. A. Preux, *Mémoires de la société centrale de Douai,* 2d series, vol. IX. This one was written in Bordeaux on July 28, 1772; those from Rouen, ten years later, show the same longing for Paris and (with greater intensity) the same contempt for the provinces.
9. Etienne Destranges, *Collot d'Herbois à Nantes* (Nantes, 1888).

*10. Grimm, *Corréspondance littéraire,* Tourneux edition, VIII, 319.

11. In the foreword to *Le bon Angevin,* published in Angers in 1775. Same reference for the next two quotes.

12. *Corréspondance littéraire,* V, 349.

13. A. Preux, footnote 8 to the article mentioned in note 8, letter from Rouen, undated.

English translation by H. E. Bolton (Berkeley, 1913). [Retranslated—*Trans.*]

9. Engelbert, *Junipero Serra,* p. 255.

10. Francisco Palou, *Evangelista del mar pacifico, Fray Junipero Serra* (Madrid, 1944) (reprint of the *Vida* by the same author published in 1784), chap. 14.

11. *Ibid.,* chap. 6.

2

1. Omer Engelbert, *Le Dernier des conquistadores, Junipero Serra* (Paris, Plon, 1956), p. 253.

2. Dr. Lewis Hanke, "Pope Paul III and the American Indians," in *Harvard Theological Review,* XXX (1937), 20–1. [Not verified—*Trans.*]

3. Letter from J. Serra to the Viceroy de Croix, dated October 29, 1779, Archivo General de la Naçion de Mexico, "Californias," II, folio 20–1.

4. Engelbert, *Junipero Serra,* p. 66.

5. *Encyclopaedia universalis,* published by Encyclopaedia Universalis France, 1968, X, 121: "Los Angeles." The entry gives a first-rate description of the city and its setting.

6. Engelbert, *Junipero Serra,* p. 254. Other unnumbered quotations in this passage are from the letters of Junipero Serra to his superiors or to the viceroy; they are quoted from the same source and most are stored in the Mexican Archives under the heading "Californias."

7. Memorandum No. 4 by Junipero Serra to the viceroy, Mexican Archives, "Misiones," XII, 350.

8. Fray Pedro Font, *Journal,* XXIV,

3

1. George Kay, *La Traite des noirs* (Paris, Laffont, 1968), p. 117. Unnumbered quotations in this chapter are from the same source. [Quotes from the logbook and those relating to the subsequent legal proceedings have been retranslated.—*Trans.*]

2. Gaston Martin, *L'Ere des négriers,* from unpublished documents (Paris, 1931), p. 75.

3. *Ibid.,* p. 112.

4. *Ibid.,* note on p. 111: Extract from the diary of Jacques Savary, a slave trader from Nantes.

5. *Ibid.,* p. 29.

6. Kay, *La Traite des noirs,* p. 121.

7. F.O. Shyllon, *Black Slaves in Britain* (Oxford University Press, 1974), p. 191.

8. Kay, *La Traite des noirs,* p. 144.

4

1. Duc de Croÿ, *Journal inédit, 1718–1784* (Paris, 1894), spring 1782, p. 242.

2. *Ibid.,* p. 239.

* 3. Louis-Sébastien Mercier, *Tableau de Paris* (Amsterdam, 1783), VI, 137.

4. *Journal du libraire Hardy,* January 8, 1782, quoted by Jean

Harmand in *Mme de Genlis, sa vie intime et politique, 1746–1830* (Paris, Perrin, 1912), p. 147.

5. Frédéric Masson, *Le Cardinal de Bernis depuis son ministère* (Paris, Emile Paul, 1884), p. 377.

6. *Mémoires* of Louis-Philippe, 1773–1793 (Paris, Plon, 1973), I, 19.

7. *Mémoires* of Mme de Genlis, quoted by Gaston Maugras, *L'Idylle d'un "gouverneur," la comtesse de Genlis et le duc de Chartres* (Paris, Plon, 1894), p. 62. The whole of the decisive scene is related by Mme de Genlis in this text.

8. *Ibid.,* p. 63. Also for the following reply by Louis XVI.

9. *Mémoires* of Louis-Philippe, p. 11.

10. Letter from Mme de Genlis, quoted by Marguerite Castillon du Perron, in *Louis-Philippe et la Révolution française* (Paris, Perrin, 1963) I, 49.

11. *Mémoires* of Mme de Genlis quoted by Jean Harmand, *Mme de Genlis,* p. 48.

12. *Ibid.,* p. 54.

13. Mme de Genlis to the Duc de Chartres, Forges-les-Eaux, on July 24, 1772, in Gaston Maugras, *L'Idylle d'un "gouverneur,"* p. 23.

5

1. Castillon du Perron, *Louis-Philippe,* I, 50.

* 2. Amédée Britsch, *La Jeunesse de Philippe Egalité, 1787–1785, d'après des documents inédits,* p. 356.

3. Amédée Britsch, "Mme Lafarge et Louis Philippe," in *Le*

Correspondant, April 10, 1913. Mme Lafarge is the daughter of another English child, Hermine, whom the Orléanses import in 1785 on the same terms, as a double for Pamela, and for whom they eventually find a "good marriage."

4. *Mémoires* of Louis-Philippe, p. 13.

5. *Ibid.,* p. 20; also for the following quotation.

6. Castillon du Perron, *Louis-Philippe,* I, 61.

* 7. Bachaumont, *Correspondance secrète,* April 14, 1782, quoted by Harmand in *Mme de Genlis,* p. 163. *Ibid.* for the following quote.

8. *Mémoires* of Louis-Philippe, pp. 25 and 26.

6

1. Alfred Ritter von Arneth, *Joseph II und Leopold von Toscana, ihr Briefwechsel von 1781 bis 1790* (Vienna, 1872). Both correspondents wrote or dictated their letters in French. Subsequent extracts from the brothers' letters are from the same source; here, pp. 78, 79, and 81.

2. François Bluche, *Le Despotisme éclairé* (Paris, Fayard, 1968), p. 127.

* 3. Fernand Hayward, *Le Dernier siècle de la Rome pontificale,* I, 83.

4. Pierre Chaunu, *La Civilisation de l'Europe des lumières* (Paris, 1971), p. 209.

5. A. Leopold, quoted by Bluche, *Le Despotisme éclairé,* p. 121.

6. *Ibid.,* p. 135.

7. *Ibid.,* p. 137.

8. Victor Tapié, *Monarchie et peuples du Danube* (Paris, Fayard, 1969), p. 240.
9. Bluche, *Le Despotisme éclairé*, p. 143.
10. See the article by W. von Hippel, "La désagrégation du régime féodal en Allemagne," in *Annales historiques de la Révolution française*, special issue for April–June 1969 on "L'abolition du régime féodal dans le monde occidental," p. 245.
11. To Leopold again, in their correspondence, p. 110. *Ibid.* for the whole of the "Pope's journey" that follows.
12. Grimm, *Correspondance littéraire*, XIII, 120. D'Alembert hastened to show this letter to all his friends, especially Meister.

7

1. Letter from de Grasse to Rochambeau, November 1, 1781.
* 2. Jean-Jacques Antier, *L'Amiral de Grasse, héros de l'indépendance américaine*, p. 299. This book has helped me a great deal already in the reconstruction of naval movements in the Chesapeake, and is my guide to the battle of Les Saintes.
3. Campaign notes of the Comte de Vaudreuil, published by the Association des Amis des Musées de la Marine, in Antier, *L'Amiral de Grasse*, p. 311.
4. *Revue historique*, LII (1893), 411.
5. *Journal du comte de Grasse depuis le 6 avril 1782*, Paris, Archives de la Marine [Navy], in Antier, *L'Amiral de Grasse*, p. 315.
6. Archives de la Marine [Navy], C I, 5.
* 7. G. Lacour-Gayet, *La marine militaire de la France sous Louis XVI*, (cited hereafter as *Marine française sous Louis XVI*), p. 430.
8. Memorandum presented by de Grasse to the council of war, which tries him at Lorient, quoted by Antier, *L'Amiral de Grasse*, p. 310.

8

* 1. La Varende, *Suffren et ses ennemis*, p. 206; this was my main guide to the battle of Provédien (or Providien), but I also consulted Lacour-Gayet, **Marine française sous Louis XVI*, and J.-J. Roux, *Le Bailli de Suffren dans L'Inde* (n.d).
2. Letter to his mistress, Mme de Seillans, from Brest, on March 18, 1781 (in Lacour-Gayet, *Marine française sous Louis XVI*, p. 474).
3. In Roux, *Le Bailli de Suffren*, p. 98.
4. Lacour-Gayet, *Marine française sous Louis XVI*, p. 510.
5. La Varende, *Suffren et ses ennemis*, p. 190.
6. Quoted by Lacour-Gayet, *Marine française sous Louis XVI*, p. 514.
7. *Ibid.*, p. 513.

9

* 1. The lemon incident is related by Charles Lewis, in *Admiral de Grasse and American Independence* (Annapolis, U.S. Navy Institute, 1945), p. 308.
2. From a letter by an English officer written on board the *Formidable* on April 20, 1782, after a long conversation with de Grasse. Archives de la Marine [Navy], B I, 97, folio 22.
3. Notes by the Marquis de

Saint-Simon on the battle of Les Saintes, published in the *Revue d'histoire diplomatique,* I (1930), 31.

4. This text and the following ones by de Grasse are from his Memorandum to the council of war, quoted by Antier, *L'Amiral de Grasse.*

5. Quoted by Antier, *L'Amiral de Grasse,* p. 330. [Retranslated— Trans.]

10

* 1. Louis-Sébastien Mercier, *Tableau de Paris,* V, 301.

2. *Ibid.,* IV, 230.

3. *Mémoires de la baronne d'Oberkirch sur la Cour de Louis XVI et la société française avant 1789* (Paris, Mercure de France, 1970), p. 201. Other unnumbered quotations describing the festivities at Chantilly are taken from the same passage.

4. Arthur Young, *Travels in France,* Constantia Maxwell, ed. (Cambridge University Press, 1950), p. 10.

5. *Histoire des environs de Paris* (Paris, 1837), III, 180.

6. *Ibid.,* p. 181.

7. J. Crétineau-Joly, *Histoire des trois derniers princes de la maison de Condé* (Paris, 1872), p. 29. The entire book is steeped in the fury of a reactionary historian newly traumatized by the Commune. He screams out for the people's blood on every page.

8. *Ibid.,* p. 31.

9. *Ibid.,* p. 40.

10. Edmond Soreau, *Ouvriers et paysans de 1789 à 1792* (Paris, "Les Belles Lettres," 1936), p. 64.

11. *Mémoires de la baronne d'Oberkirch,*

p. 275. The Grand Duke makes this remark, a few months after his visit to Chantilly, to the Duke of Württemberg, who was showing Paul the stables he had built at Stuttgart in his youth, almost as beautiful as those of the Condés, and saying, "I repent of them now . . ."

11

1. Report from Bérenger, French chargé d'affaires in Russia, to Choiseul, December 10, 1764; Archives des Affaires Etrangères (Foreign Affairs), Russia, LXXVI.

2. *Ibid.* Reported firsthand by Bérenger, who heard the words spoken by the little tsarevich.

3. Report from Breteuil to Choiseul, October 9, 1762, Archives des Affaires Etrangères [Foreign Affairs], Russia, LXXXI, folio 32.

* 4. For the description of Paul see Zoé Oldenbourg, *Catherine de Russie* (1966), p. 177.

5. Said by Chichakov, in K. Waliszewski, *Le Fils de la grande Catherine, Paul Ier* (Paris, Plon, 1912), p. 50.

6. Letter from Catherine II to Grimm, June 29, 1776, in *Recueil de la société impériale d'Histoire russe,* XXIII, 49.

7. Von Arneth, *Joseph II und Leopold von Toscana,* p. 116. Letter dated June 5, 1782.

8. *Ibid.,* p. 128.

9. *Revue des antiquités russes,* XI (1874), 165; and LXX (1885), 71

10. Prince de Ligne, *Mélanges militaires* (Brussels, 1882), XXVII, 14.

11. Comte Golovkin, *La Cour et le règne de Paul Ier* (Paris, Librairie Académique Perrin, 1910), p. 111.

12. *Mémoires* of Mme Campan, 1829 ed., I, 241. Marie Antoinette was struck by the remark and immediately mentioned it in a letter to Joseph II.

13. I should like to express my very sincere thanks to Mme Dominique Maroger, the author of several books on Russia and Tolstoy in particular, for letting me see the unpublished text of her translation of Catherine II's letter to her son Paul in 1781 and 1782. The originals have been published in Russian. The following quotations have been taken from this text, which is in the Bibliothèque nationale (B.N.), "Nouvelles acquisitions" [recent acquisitions], 12 412.

14. S. Schilder, *L'Empereur Paul Ier*, I, appendix, p. 555, a text also procured through Mme Maroger.

15. *Receuil de la société impériale d'histoire russe* (1872), May 22, 1782.

16. *Mémoires de la baronne d'Oberkirch*, p. 242.

17. *Ibid.*, p. 254.

18. *Ibid.*, p. 230; also for the following quotation.

12

* 1. Letter to his wife, October 22, 1781, in *Mémoires, correspondance et manuscrits* of General La Fayette, I, 472.

* 2. Quoted by A. Bardoux in *La Jeunesse de La Fayette*, p. 152.

* 3. *Mémoires secrets* by Bachaumont, February 11, 1782.

4. The descriptions of this famous full dress ball of June 8, 1782, are taken partly from the *Mémoires de la baronne d'Oberkirch* and partly from those of the Duc de Croÿ; see reference 8 below.

5. *Mémoires de la baronne d'Oberkirch*, p. 145.

6. Henri Leclerc, *Mme Bertin, ministre des modes de la reine Marie-Antoinette* (Paris, n.d.), p. 88.

7. *Ibid.*, p. 198.

8. Duc de Croÿ, *Journal inédit, 1718–1784*, B.N. 8°, Ln 27, 52 216, p. 264.

9. *Notice sur Mme de La Fayette* by her daughter Mme de Lasteyrie (Paris, 1852), p. 203.

10. Vicomtesse de Noailles, *Vie de la princesse de Poix, née Beauvau*, p. 46, quoted by *André Maurois, *Adrienne, ou la vie de Mme de La Fayette*, p. 133.

11. *Mémoires de la baronne d'Oberkirch*, p. 194.

12. *Ibid.*, p. 199.

13. Benjamin Franklin, *Journal des négociations de paix entre la Grande-Bretagne et les Etats Unis d'Amérique*, in his *Correspondance*, II, 242. [Retranslated—*Trans.*]

14. *Ibid.*, p. 257.

15. *Ibid.*, p. 265. [Retranslated—*Trans.*]

16. *Journal* of the Duc de Croÿ, p. 240.

17. *Ibid.*, p. 239.

18. This unique item was found by André Lebey, *La Fayette ou le militant francmaçon* (Paris, Librairie Mercure, 1937), p. 48. It is in the Lionel Hauser collection.

13

1. *Mémoires de la baronne d'Oberkirch,* p. 168.
2. In her *Mémoires,* original edition (Paris, 1817), I, 129. Mme Campan's recital must, of course, be taken with a grain of salt; she is known to have embroidered considerably. But this scene, when compared with the correspondence between the Duc de Breteuil (minister of the King's Household) and Lenoir, the chief of police, has an authentic ring, and on this occasion she had no cause to exaggerate.
3. Jacques Scherer, *Le Mariage de Figaro de Beaumarchais,* edition with dramaturgical analysis (Paris, S.E.D.E.S., 1966), pp. 354 and 356. Jacques Scherer adds these penetrating lines: "In Greek comedy the term *parabasis* was given to the moment when the author stepped out of his character and addressed the audience directly, like the modern-day Brechtian actor, and, appearing to shed the rules of the theater, began talking about himself with total freedom. Figaro's monologue is the only parabasis in the eighteenth century" (p. 357).
* 4. Letter (undated, but written in 1782) from Beaumarchais to the Duc de Breteuil, minister of the King's Household, quoted by Louis de Loménie, *Beaumarchais et son temps,* II, 294.
5. *Ibid.,* II, 301.
6. Grimm, *Correspondance littéraire,* XIII, 128 (May 1782).
7. *Ibid.,* p. 178.

8. *Mémoires de la baronne d'Oberkirch,* p. 168.
9. According to Julie, Beaumarchais's favorite sister. Text taken from Anne and Claude Manceron, *Beaumarchais, Figaro vivant* (Brussels, Arts et voyages, 1968), p. 141.
10. *Ibid.,* p. 140.
11. Louis de Loménie, *Beaumarchais et son temps,* II, 296.
12. End of Figaro's soliloquy in Act V of *Le Mariage,* p. 360 of the Jacques Scherer edition.
13. Beaumarchais's preface to *Le Mariage de Figaro,* Scherer ed., p. 18.
14. L. de Loménie, *Beaumarchais et son temps,* II, 302, note.
15. Letter from Beaumarchais to the chief of police, quoted in *ibid.,* p. 304.

14

1. From the edition of *Les Liaisons dangereuses* which I have used throughout this chapter, in the Pléiade collection (Gallimard, 1951); *Oeuvres complètes de Choderlos de Laclos,* presented by Maurice Allem.
2. Letter CLII in the "Correspondance littéraire adressée à Son A. I. Mgr le Grand-Duc, aujourd'hui Empereur de Russie et à M. le comte Schovalov, chambellan de l'Impératrice Catherine II, depuis 1774 jusqu'en 1789," in the *Oeuvres* of La Harpe (Paris, 1820), XI, 473.
3. According to the contract between Laclos and Durand, which is preserved in the Bibliothèque nationale, Ms fonds français, 12 845, folio 36.

* 4. *Mémoires* of the Comte de Ségur, I, 188.

5. *Mémoires du comte Alexandre de Tilly, pour servir à l'histoire des moeurs à la fin du XVIIIe siècle* (Paris, Jonquières, 1929), I, 221.

6. Moufle d'Angerville was one of the obscure pen-pushers who had taken over Bachaumont's *Mémoires secrets* after his death in 1773. This is an extract from vol. XX (London, 1782).

7. *Correspondance littéraire,* Grimm, XIII, 108.

8. *Ibid.,* p. 110.

9. *Oeuvres posthumes* of Charles Baudelaire (Paris) I, 598.

10. *Mémoires* of Besenval, quoted by Frederic Dard in *Le général de Laclos, un acteur caché du drame révolutionnaire* (Paris, Librairie Académique Perrin, 1905), p. 41.

15

1. Dard, *Le Général Choderlos de Laclos,* p. 26.

2. In this instance the Marquise de Coigny, with whom Lauzun was so infatuated. She knew Laclos but forbade him her door after the *Liaisons* came out, presumably fearing he might use her as a model one day. (Dard, *Le général Choderlos de Laclos,* p. 45).

3. *Ibid.,* p. 17.

4. Said by Mme Riccoboni, *ibid.,* p. 4.

5. Dard, *Le Général Choderlos de Laclos,* p. 5.

6. His own words. *Ibid.,* p. 5.

7. Mémoires of Louis-Auguste Lepelletier, *Une famille d'artilleurs* (Paris, Hachette, 1896), p. 37.

8. *Mémoires* of the Comte de Tilly, I, 222.

9. Extracts from the *Oeuvres complètes* of Laclos, pp. 461–95.

10. My very sincere thanks to Président René Fonvieille, whom I shall have occasion to thank even more warmly in connection with Barnave, and to my friend Marie-Henriette Foix de Montalais, for guiding my steps through the Grenoble keys to *Les liaisons dangereuses.* They spared me the long and arduous task of clearing away the brush. See in particular, in *Le vieux Grenoble,* published by Arthaud, II, 259, the article by M. H. Foix de Montalais on "Choderlos de Laclos et Grenoble," which she supplemented for me with many precious manuscript notes.

11. Dard, *Le Général Choderlos de Laclos,* p. 28.

12. *Mémoires* of the Comte de Tilly, I, 223. After relating this rare confidence by Laclos, Tilly adds, to confirm the accuracy of the statement, that "these somewhat oratorical expressions, which I recall as if it were yesterday, seemed all the more striking to me as his unemotional and methodical conversation never took on such hues under ordinary circumstances."

*13. This and the preceding description of La Rochelle are taken from Reichard's *Guide des Voyageurs en Europe,* II, 149.

14. Dard, *Le Général Choderlos de Laclos,* p. 29.

15. Archives de la Guerre [War], Laclos file, AR. X, b. 730.

16. Correspondence between Laclos and Mme Riccoboni, published

after the 13th edition of the *Liaisons dangereuses,* in 1787. *Ibid.,* for Laclos's reply. (Cf. *Oeuvres complètes* of Laclos, p. 697.)

16

1. The full text of the speech is given on p. 416 and ff. of volume I of the *Oeuvres* of Condorcet (Paris, 1847), which is the source of the above and following excerpts (on pp. 416–25).
* 2. Marcel Marion, *Dictionnaire des institutions de la France aux XVIIe and XVIIIe siècles,* p. 385.
3. Grimm, *Correspondance littéraire,* February 1782, XIII, 83. *Ibid.* for the next two quotes.
4. *Ibid.,* p. 84.
5. *Oeuvres* of Condorcet, I, 390.
6. Same reference as for note 1.

17

1. Letter published by Charles Vellay in the *Revue historique de la Révolution française,* January-March 1911.
* 2. *Mémoires* of Brissot, I, 271.
3. These particulars are given in the excellent foreword, by M. Claude Perroud, to the *Correspondance et papiers de Brissot* published at his expense by Perrin in Paris, in 1912. For Brissot in Geneva, see p. XXII.
4. Court de Gébelin papers in the BN: L 27/n 36 988, no. 2.
5. Same reference as for note 2.
6. Edouard Chapuisat, *La Prise d'armes de 1782 à Genève* (Geneva, 1932), p. 49.

7. Emile Rivoire, *Bibliographie historique de Genève au XVIIIe siècle* (Geneva and Paris, 1897), II, no. 2281.
8. Jules Anspach, *Un citoyen de Genève* (Geneva, 1902), p. 31.
9. Chapuisat, *La Prise d'armes,* p. 49.
10. Page 80 (verso) of the manuscript narrating the events written by Rochemont, secretary of state of Geneva; quoted by *Edouard Chapuisat, *Figures et choses d'autrefois:* "Etienne Clavière."
11. According to a lawyer–stool-pigeon named Sinner, who supplied information to the Court of France: Archives des Affaires Etrangères [Foreign Affairs], political correspondence (Geneva, 1782).
12. Chapuisat, *La Prise d'armes,* p. 82.
13. *Mémoires* of Brissot, I, 273.
14. Chapuisat, *La Prise d'armes,* p. 86.

18

1. *Mémoires* of Brissot, I, 272.
2. Otto Karmin, *Sir Francis d'Ivernois 1757–1842, sa vie, son oeuvre et son temps* (Geneva, 1920), p. 6.
* 3. Said by Voltaire; see Paul Chaponnière, *Voltaire et les calvinistes,* p. 138.
4. Karmin, *Sir Francis d'Ivernois,* p. 63.
5. These *Mémoires* of d'Ivernois are now in the Geneva archives.
6. Archives des Affaires Etrangères [Foreign Affairs], political correspondence, Geneva, LXXXVI, folio 115.

7. *Ibid.,* LC, folio 131.
8. *Mémoires* of Brissot, I, 220.
9. Cornuaud, *Mémoires politiques,* (cited in note 1, ch. 7, above), p. 142.
10. *Mémoires* of Brissot, I, 274.
11. *Ibid.,* p. 275.
12. According to the *Notice abrégée de la vie d'Etienne Clavière,* manuscript signed by his brother Jean-Jacques but actually written by his daughter, Mme Vieusseux Clavière. This manuscript has been kept by the Rivier family at Prilly and was used by Chapuisat in *Figures et choses d'autrefois,* especially p. 11.
13. As remembered by du Roveray, quoted by F. de Crue in *Necker, Mirabeau et les Genevois de la Révolution* (Bibliothèque universelle et revue suisse, July 1923), CXI, 5.
14. Etienne Dumont, *Souvenirs sur Mirabeau* (Paris: Presses Universitaires de France [PUF], 1937), p. 299.
15. Letter from Clavière to his friend Stadnitsky, on January 13, 1782, in J. Bouchary, *Les Manieurs d'argent à Paris au XVIIIe siècle* (Paris, Plon, 1897), p. 75.
16. Dumont, *Souvenirs sur Mirabeau,* p. 200.

19

1. His portrait as a younger man, by Van Loo, can be seen in the Château de Crans (Vaud).
2. Journal of Saladin de Crans, p. 20, quoted by Chapuisat, *La Prise d'armes,* p. 58.
3. Henry Tronchin, *Le Conseiller François Tronchin et ses amis* (Paris, Plon, 1907), p. 228.
4. Cornuaud, *Mémoires politiques et historiques,* p. 367. This enormous 800-page work was photocopied for me by the iconographic department of Editions Laffont; it is kept in the Bibliothèque nationale, where it is registered as 8° M 16 318.
5. *Ibid.,* p. 365. The following unreferenced quotations are from the same work.
6. Victor Cherbuliez, who wrote a lengthy introduction to Cornuaud's *Mémoires.*
7. Michel Launay, "Qu'entend-on par peuple à Genève au XVIIIe siècle?" in *Images du peuple au XVIIIe siècle,* published by the Centre Aixois d'études et de recherches sur le XVIIIe siècle (Paris, Armand Colin, 1973), p. 59.
8. From a pamphlet by Cornuaud, *Les Aveugles devenus occulistes* [*sic*], Geneva, December 27, 1779.

20

1. Chapuisat, *Figures et choses d'autrefois:* "Etienne Clavière," p. 44.
2. Letter from HE M. le Comte de Vergennes to HE the ambassador of France at Soleure (Solothurn), Versailles, May 12, 1782, in Rivoire, *Bibliographie historique,* No. 2 364, p. 376.
3. Quoted by Karmin, *Sir Francis d'Ivernois,* p. 51.
4. Letter from Vergennes to Gabard de Vaux, the previous French ambassador to Geneva, Versailles, July 23, 1782, Archives des Affaires Etrangères [Foreign Affairs], political

correspondence, Geneva, LXXXVI, folio 13.

5. *Mémoires* of Brissot, I, 281.

6. *Ibid.,* p. 282.

7. According to the manuscript recollections of Reverend Pierre Picot, quoted by Chapuisat, *La Prise d'armes,* p. 94.

8. Letter from d'Ivernois to his English friend Mount Stuart, dated June 26, 1782, quoted by Karmin, p. 95. In order not to burden the story of Geneva's fall with too many references, readers are informed that unless otherwise specified my sources are this book by Otto Karmin and other previously cited works, by Chapuisat *(La Prise d'armes),* Cornuaud *(Mémoires),* and Chapuisat again ("Etienne Clavière," in *Figures et choses d'autrefois*).

9. Article by Alex Guillot in the library of the Société de l'Histoire du protestantisme français, cat. no. D2 7 546 (Au Foyer Chrétien, 1894, pp. 231 to 278): "Du rôle politique de la Compagnie des pasteurs de Genève dans les évènements de 1781 à 1782." Other unnumbered quotations on the pastors' part in the surrender of Geneva are from the same article, for the use of which I am most grateful to Mlle Guillot, Reverend Guillot's niece.

10. Henri de Ziegler, *Itinéraire genevois* (Neuchâtel, Editions du Griffon, 1945), p. 32.

11. Reported by Saladin de Crans in the first series of his *Correspondance,* published in Geneva, V–VI; letter dated July 8, 1782.

12. The expression is by François Descotes, Mallet du Pan's biographer.

13. Quoted by Guillot; see reference 9 above.

14. On July 29, 1768. Text quoted by Karmin, *Sir Francis d'Ivernois,* p. 30.

15. Chapuisat, "Etienne Clavière" in *Figures et choses d'autrefois,* p. 47.

21

1. The Paris Academy of Sciences had organized a competition on the subject, which was of direct concern to Roland as inspector of manufactures. Occupational diseases were also of interest to Gosse, who writes another monograph in 1785, also for a competition, on the *Nature et causes des maladies des ouvriers employés dans la fabrique des chapeaux, et moyens de les prévenir de ces maladies.* (Note by Claude Perroud in the complete edition of the *Lettres de Madame Roland* (Paris, Imprimerie nationale, 1900), I, 199. Her letter to Bosc, quoted later in the text, is on the same page.)

2. Georges Huisman, *La Vie privée de Madame Roland* (Paris, Hachette, 1955), p. 168. Further particulars of her determined nursing of Eudora are from the same source (pp. 169–71). The author rightly concludes, "One cannot know the real Madame Roland unless one remembers what she did for her daughter during the autumn of 1781 and winter of 1782."

3. Letter from Mirabeau to Jean-François Vitry, quoted by

Antonia Vallentin, *Mirabeau avant la Révolution* (Paris, Grasset, 1946), p. 235. Other unnumbered quotations in this passage are from the same source, pp. 228–42.

4. Alfred Stern, *La Vie de Mirabeau* (translated from the German) (Paris, Emile Bouillon, 1896), I, 178.

5. After Mirabeau's death, Legrain writes a few halting pages of manuscript recollections, still unpublished; excerpts appeared in the *Nouvelle Revue rétrospective* for 1901 and 1902. The following passages on his role during their trip and stay in Pontarlier are taken from or based on these recollections.

6. Dauphin-Meunier, *Autour de Mirabeau* (Paris, Payot, 1926), p. 231.

7. Letter to Vitry dated July 17, 1782, missing from the 1806 collection of his letters. It was found by Alfred Stern in the Geneva Municipal Library (Stern, *Vie de Mirabeau*, I, 184).

22

1. Collection of unpublished letters by L. S. Mercier, Neuchâtel Municipal Library; II, 388.

2. *Ibid.* II, plate 386.

3. I have been unable to identify him, as was Léon Beclard, author of the monumental *Louis-Sébastien Mercier, sa vie, son oeuvre, son temps,* volume I of which I have used for this passage. In this instance, see the note on p. 459 (Paris, Champion, 1903).

4. Letter by Mercier published in the *Journal de Paris* for May 20, 1784.

5. Neuchâtel Municipal Library, IV, folios 274–8; there are a dozen more pages in the same vein.

6. The only—but excellent— portrait of L. S. Mercier of which I have any knowledge, dated 1787 and engraved by Dujardin, serves as a frontispiece to Beclard's book.

7. *Le Tableau de Paris,* "new original edition" of 1788, VIII, 304 (published anonymously and falsely declared printed in Amsterdam). All other unnumbered quotations from the book in this section are from the same edition; I shall, however, give specific references for a few of the most significant.

8. From a text by Mercier entitled *Le Parnasse Saint-Jacques,* quoted by Beclard, p. 9.

9. *Ibid.,* p. 10.

10. *Mémoires secrets* of Bachaumont, V, 297.

11. *L'An deux mille quatre cent quarante,* no author's name, London, no publisher, 1772. This must be the second or third edition, and is the one I shall use. This quotation is on page 5; I shall not weigh down the chapter with detailed references for those that follow, all of which are from the same volume.

23

1. *Mémoires* of Brissot, I, 286. The full title of Raynal's enormous work, we recall, is *Histoire philosophique et politique des établissements et du commerce des*

Européens dans les Deux Indes. The remainder of the Brissot quotation follows on directly, on the same page.

2. *Ibid.,* p. 284.

3. See Béclard, *L. S. Mercier,* p. 465.

4. *Le Philadelphien à Genève, ou lettres d'un Américain sur la dernière révolution de Genève, la constitution nouvelle, l'émigration en Irlande, etc.,* no author's name (Dublin, 1783), p. 60.

5. *Ibid.,* p. 66.

6. *Ibid.,* p. 205.

7. *Tableau de Paris,* III, 300.

8. *Ibid.,* p. 239.

9. Jaucourt to Vergennes, July 17, 1782, Archives des Affaires Etrangères [Foreign Affairs], LCII, folio 145.

10. *Note* (from Jaucourt to Vergennes, July 13, 1782) *sur la manière dont il conviendra de punir ceux qui ont eu part à la dernière sédition de Genève,* Archives des Affaires Etrangères, volume LCII, folio 89.

11. From Vergennes to Jaucourt, October 16, 1782, Archives des Affaires Etrangères, volume LCIII, folio 147.

12. *Mémoires* of Cornuaud, p. 413.

13. Letter from F. d'Ivernois to his English friend Mount Stuart, written in Neuchâtel, July 3, 1782, Bibliothèque universitaire de Genève, Ms. Spl. 32, folio 370.

14. Francis Dobbs, *A History of Irish Affairs from the 12th of October 1779 to the 15th of September 1782, etc.,* (Dublin, printed by M. Mills, 1782), p. 150.

15. Neuchâtel Municipal Archives, municipal council handbook, volume XXVI, p. 298.

16. J. Bouchary, *Les Manieurs d'argent à Paris au XVIIIe siècle, Etienne Clavière d'après sa correspondance,* p. 24.

17. *Mémoires* of Brissot, I, 293.

18. Brissot's marriage registration, or its facsimile, is in the Roux collection of the Chartres Municipal Library, Ms No. 1501.

19. *Mémoires* of Brissot, I, 300.

20. Letter from Mirabeau to Rilliet, in the Saussure papers (Why? Saussure was an aristocrat; was Rilliet a double agent?) Quoted by F. de Crue, *Necker, Mirabeau et les Genevois de la Révolution,* Bibliothèque universelle et Revue suisse, vol. CXI, No. 331, July 1923, p. 7.

*21. Reichard, *Guide des voyageurs en Europe,* II, "Suisse", p. 115.

22. Noted by Miranda in his account of his travels through the principality of Neuchâtel in 1788, in *Le musée neuchâtelois,* 1934, No. 1, p. 27.

23. *Mémoires* of Brissot, I, 297.

24. *Ibid.,* II, 124.

25. Foreign Archives, Geneva, vol. LCIII, memorandum from Mirabeau to Vergennes written by a copyist (presumably a copy for Jaucourt) noted "Neuchâtel, 8 October 1782" in Mirabeau's hand.

26. Protocol of the Neuchâtel Conseil d'Etat, 10 October 1782 (Neuchâtel Archives).

24

1. [This English translation is from *The Robbers* in *The Works of Frederick Schiller: Early Dramas and Romances,* "translated from the German,

chiefly by Henry G. Bohn,"
Bohn's Standard Library,
London, 1849. The first German
edition was published at the end
of 1781, and the quoted lines
(from Act IV, scene 5) were, of
course, expurgated for
performance. A 1793 English
translation by Lord
Woodhouselee does not contain
them—*Trans.*]

2. A few years later Streicher writes
a detailed and apparently entirely
accurate account of Schiller's
escape. Long unpublished, it was
incorporated *in toto* into Richard
Weltrich's book, *La jeunesse de
Schiller* (Stuttgart, 1899). The
quoted passages and other details
of their escapade were taken
from Weltrich by Robert
d'Harcourt, *La jeunesse de Schiller*
(Paris, Plon, 1928), and by
Albert Kontz, *Les drames de la
jeunesse de Schiller* (Paris, Ernest
Leroux, 1899).

3. Baronne d'Oberkirch, quoted by
Adrien Fauchier-Magnan, *Les
Petites cours d'Allemagne au XVIIIe
siècle* (Paris, Flammarion, 1947).
Other details relating to the
reception at "La Solitude" are
from the same source, p. 240.

4. In her reminiscences, taken
down shortly after her brother's
death. D'Harcourt, *Jeunesse de
Schiller,* p. 8. The following
quotation, by Schiller, is from
Act II, Scene 5 of *The Robbers.*

5. An expression employed by
Schiller himself in his third play,
Kabale und Liebe (Intrigue and
Love).

6. Told by Charles Eugene to
Kerner, quoted by d'Harcourt,
Jeunesse de Schiller, p. 21.

25

1. A. Berdot, *Voyage de Montbéliard
à Berlin* (Paris, *chez* Richard,
1775), p. 128.

2. Jotted in a memorandum book in
1783 by Charlotte von
Lengefeld, who later becomes
Schiller's wife (Fauchier-Magnan,
p. 219).

3. *Ibid.,* p. 218.

4. Written by Schiller in 1784 in
the *Annonce de la Thalie rhénane*
(Thalia, the muse of comedy,
being the title of Schiller's
review). Quoted by d'Harcourt,
Jeunesse de Schiller, p. 38.

5. Schiller, *Essay on the Theater,*
quoted by d'Harcourt, p. 163.

6. Schiller, *L'Annonce de la Thalie
rhénane,* quoted by d'Harcourt,
p. 125.

7. Reminiscences recorded by
Richard Weltrich; see reference
2 to Chapter 25 above.

8. D'Harcourt, *Jeunesse de Schiller,*
p. 78.

9. *The Robbers,* Act II, scene 1.

10. D'Harcourt, *Jeunesse de Schiller,*
p. 124.

11. *Ibid.,* p. 127.

12. *Ibid.,* p. 131, according to a
contemporary.

13. *The Robbers, a Tragedy, translated
from the German of Frederick
Schiller* (by Alexander Fraser
Tytler, Lord Woodhouselee)
(Dublin, John Archer, 1793),
Act I, scene 3.

14. *Ibid.,* Act I, scene 7.

15. Schiller, *Anthologie auf das Jahr
1782,* published with no author's
name, in Stuttgart, 1782, and
allegedly printed in Tobolsk!
(p. 42).

16. *Ibid.,* p. 123.

26

* 1. Lescure, *Correspondance secrète,* I, p. 514 (at October 24, 1782).
2. *Ibid.,* p. 521 (at November 19, 1782).
3. Vicomte de Reiset, *Louise d'Esparbes, comtesse de Polastron* (Paris, Emile-Paul, 1907), p. 76.
4. M. N. Bouillet, *Dictionnaire universel d'histoire et de géographie* (Paris, Hachette, 31st edition), entry on "Lavater."
5. Lavater, quoted by Grimm, *Correspondance littéraire,* October 1782, XIII, 207. The next two quotations come from the same article by Grimm.
6. *Ibid.,* January 1783, XIII, 258.

27

1. According to Robin, the chaplain attached to the French expeditionary corps. Quoted by Maurice-Charles Renard, *Rochambeau* (Paris, Fasquelle, 1951), p. 158. The following quotation is from the same page.
* 2. *Lettres d'Axel de Fersen à son père* (Paris, Firmin-Didot, 1937), p. 135.
3. Renard, *Rochambeau,* p. 162.
4. Lescure, *Correspondance secrète,* I, 493.
5. J. Crétineau-Joly, *Histoires des trois derniers princes de la maison de Condé* (Paris, Berche et Tralin, 1872), I, 33.
6. *Ibid.,* p. 43.
7. Lescure, *Correspondance secrète,* I, 500.
8. *Mémoires du chevalier de Cotignon, gentilhomme nivernais, officier de marine de Sa Majesté Louis le seizième,* presented by A. Carré,

physician-general of the Naval Academy (Grenoble, Editions des 4 Seigneurs, 1974), p. 112. All the quotations by Cotignan are from this work.
9. Lescure, *Correspondance secrète,* I, 507.

28

1. *Mémoires du chevalier de Mautort, capitaine au regiment d'Austrasie* (Paris, Plon, 1895), p. 255.
2. *Ibid.,* p. 238.
3. *Ibid.,* p. 242.
4. Roux, *Le Bailli de Suffren dans l'Inde,* p. 130.

29

1. Archives des Affaires Etrangères [Foreign Affairs], Paris, *United States,* vol. XX.
* 2. Bernard Faÿ, *Louis XVI ou la fin d'un monde,* p. 232.
* 3. Bernard Faÿ, *Benjamin Franklin, citoyen du monde,* II, p. 238.
4. H. Forneron, *Histoire des débats politiques du Parlement anglais* (Paris, Plon, 1871), p. 42. [It has been impossible to retrace the original English of this anecdote, which has accordingly been retranslated—*Trans.*]
5. Lord Mahon, *History of England,* Tauchnitz edition (Leipzig, 1854), VII, 132. *Ibid.* for the following quotations by Lord North and Burke.
6. H. Forneron, *Histoire des débats politiques,* p. 112. [Apart from George III's statement upon accession *(Bartlett's Book of Quotations),* retranslated.— *Trans.*]
7. *The Correspondence of William Pitt,*

Earl of Chatham, edited by William Stanhope Taylor (London, John Murray, 1838), vol. II.

8. According to the Duchess of Hamilton, quoted by Françoise de Bernardy, *George IV d'Angleterre, un Falstaff royal* (Paris, Perrin, 1970), p. 17. *Ibid.* for the following quotations by Cavendish and Fox, p. 16. [All retranslated—*Trans.*]

30

1. De Bernardy, *George IV d'Angleterre,* p. 23. [Retranslated —*Trans.*]
2. Roger Fulford, *George the Fourth,* (London, Gerald Duckworth, 1935), p. 17.
3. De Bernardy, *George IV d'Angleterre,* p. 27, told in confidence by Lord Melbourne to the young Queen Victoria, many years later. The Prince of Wales's comeback to George III is from the same page. [Retranslated—*Trans.*]
4. Charles de Rémusat, *L'Angleterre au XVIIIe siècle* (Paris, Didier, 1865), II, 331. [Retranslated—*Trans.*]
5. *Ibid.,* p. 482. [Retranslated—*Trans.*]
6. Edward Lascelles, *The Life of Charles James Fox* (Oxford University Press, 1936), p. 160.
7. According to A. S. Turberville, *English Men and Manners in the 18th Century* (Oxford, 1932); quoted by Françoise Châtel de Brancion, in *R. B. Sheridan, personnalité, carrière, politique* (Paris, Didier, 1974), p. 57.

8. *Ibid.,* p. 93.
9. Forneron, *Histoire des débats politiques,* p. 17. [Retranslated—*Trans.*]
10. Jacques Chastenet, *William Pitt* (Paris, Fayard), pp. 15 and 20.
11. *Ibid.,* p. 17. [Retranslated—*Trans.*]
12. Lord Mahon, *History of England,* VII, 135.
13. Said by George III to Lord Temple in February 1783, in Forneron, *Histoire des débats politiques,* p. 181. [Retranslated—*Trans.*]
14. *Considérations sur la paix de 1782, envoyées par l'abbé Raynal au prince Frédéric-Henri de Prusse, qui lui avait demandé ce qu'il pensait de cette paix* (Berlin, 1783), pamphlet, 18 pages.

31

1. I had the good luck to get hold of the original edition of *La Vie de Benoît-Joseph Labre, mort à Rome en odeur de sainteté,* translated from the Italian text of Mr. Marconi, reader at the College of Rome, Confessor of the Servant of God (Paris, "chez Guillot, libraire de Monsieur, frère du Roi, Rue Saint-Jacques, vis-à-vis celle des Mathurins," 1783). This quotation is from p. 161; all other unnumbered quotes, as well as biographical details, are from the same source.
2. Letter written when he left the Trappists of Sept-Fons, on October 2, 1769.
3. On August 31, 1770, before

crossing the Alps to begin his wanderings in Italy.

4. From Abbé Marconi's account, p. 50.

5. In a letter to Benoît-Joseph Labre's father, placed at the end of his book, p. 198.

32

1. *Plaidoyer prononcé par le comte de Mirabeau à l'audience de M. le lieutenant-général de la sénéchaussée d'Aix* on May 23, 1783, in *Mémoires sur Mirabeau et son époque,* published anonymously by "Peuchet" (Paris, Bossange frères, 1824), II, 176. The intentions of these four volumes of memoirs *about (sur)* Mirabeau are strictly dishonorable (they were published during the Restoration), and they are not to be confused with the eight volumes of memoirs *by (de)* Mirabeau published ten years later, under Louis-Philippe, by his recognized illegitimate son Lucas de Montigny; these, on the contrary, are pure hagiography. The chief value of both sets lies in the large amount of primary source material they contain.

2. *Ibid.,* II, 192.

3. *Ibid.,* II, 193.

4. Expilly's *Dictionnaire* (cited note 5, chapter 1, above), I, 53–80. The description of the courtroom is from the same source.

* 5. *Voyages en France de François de La Rochefoucauld, 1781–1783,* I, 205.

* 6. According to the *Journal autographe du parlement* (p. 61) by M. Fauris de Saint-Vincent, quoted by Georges Guibal, *Mirabeau et la Provence,* I, 213.

7. Letters from the Marquis de Mirabeau to his daughter Caroline du Saillant, July 15, 1783, in *Mémoires de Mirabeau* (Lucas de Montigny edition) (Paris, Adolphe Guyot, 1834), III, 408.

8. Fauris de Saint-Vincent, op. cit., p. 62.

9. *Mémoires* of Vitrolles (Paris, Gallimard, 1950), I, 44.

*10. Etienne Dumont, quoted by A. Lebois in "Comment parlait Mirabeau" in *Les Mirabeau et leur temps,* acts of the symposium of Aix-en-Provence, p. 126.

11. *Ibid.,* p. 127. This time it is Chateaubriand reporting, who heard him speak at the Constituent on one or two occasions.

12. Quoted by Guibal, *Mirabeau et la Provence,* I, 215.

*13. Letter from the marquis to the bailli, quoted by A. and C. Manceron in *Mirabeau,* p. 32.

14. *Ibid.,* p. 42.

15. Letter from Mirabeau to his sister Caroline du Saillant, October 22, 1782, in *Mémoires de Mirabeau,* III, 312. Extracts from the bailli's letters to the marquis are from the same source.

16. From the bailli to Caroline du Saillant, then to the marquis, on October 22 and 28, 1782, in Guibal, *Mirabeau et la Provence,* I, 171. The following excerpts were addressed to the same and are on p. 172 (dated September 3 and August 28, 1782).

17. From the bailli to the marquis on November 8, 1782, in *Mémoires de Mirabeau,* III, 314.

18. A. and C. Manceron, *Mirabeau,* p. 90.

33

1. According to the bailli of course, in a letter to his brother, February 4, 1783, in Guibal, *Mirabeau et la Provence*, I, 195. For the preceding quote by the marquis, *ibid.*, p. 197.
* 2. The facsimile may be found on p. 264 of Dauphin-Meunier's *La Comtesse de Mirabeau*.
* 3. Text quoted, this time in its entirety, by Ch. de Loménie, *Les Mirabeau*, III, 729.
4. Seligman, *Mirabeau devant le parlement d'Aix*, p. 31, quoted by Guibal, *Mirabeau et la Provence*, I, 217.
5. See Lydie Adolphe, *Portalis et son temps* (Paris, Sirey, 1936).
6. And by Anne and Claude Manceron, alas, in *Mirabeau*. Anybody who gets involved with the life of this devil is condemned to perpetual revisionism. The best refutation of Portalis's alleged collapse is in Guibal, *Mirabeau et la Provence*, I, 217.
7. *Mémoires sur Mirabeau*, II, 245.
8. Expilly's *Dictionnaire*, p. 53: "Aix."
9. *Mémoires de Mirabeau*, III, 412.
10. Adolphe, *Portalis et son temps*, p. 21.
11. Letter from Mirabeau to Hugh Elliott, undated but presumably written in late June 1783, in the *Memoirs of the Countess of Minto*, quoted by Guibal, *Mirabeau et la Provence*, I, note to p. 228.

34

1. *Oeuvres complètes de Maximilien Robespierre*, published by Victor Barbier and Charles Vellay, Paris, Revue historique de la Révolution française, I, xix of introduction.
2. Collection of the *Délibérations importantes prises depuis 1763 par le bureau d'administration du collège Louis-le-Grand et des collèges réunis* (Paris, 1781), p. 218.
3. A. J. Paris, *La Jeunesse de Robespierre et la convocation des Etats Généraux en Artois*. The work is out of print, and the Laffont publishing company's documentation service photocopied it for me in the Bibliothèque nationale, 8⁰, LN 27, 52499. Hereafter given as "Paris, *Jeunesse de Robespierre*"; this quote is on page 18.
4. Expilly's *Dictionnaire*, I: "Arras," p. 278.
5. This description of Robespierre's routine in Arras is based on Charlotte's *Mémoires* as decanted by Paris, *Jeunesse de Robespierre*, here, p. 72. Everything in quotes comes from Charlotte's *Mémoires*.
6. *Oeuvres complètes* of Robespierre, I, 2–13.
7. Expilly's *Dictionnaire*, I: "Arras," 277. *Ibid.* for the next quotation.

35

1. Original text, printed in Arras in 1783 by the printer Guy Delasablonnière, 100 pages in octavo. Reproduced verbatim in the *Oeuvres complètes de M. Robespierre*, I; the text begins on

p. 24. The title of the 1783 publication is *Plaidoyers pour le sieur de Vissery de Bois-Valé, appelant d'un jugement des Echevins de Saint-Omer, qui avait ordonné la destruction d'un Par-à-tonnerre élevé sur sa maison.*

2. See the articles by Charles Vellay on "Robespierre et le procès du paratonnerre" in *Annales révolutionnaires,* II (1901), of which I have made considerable use in this passage; this quotation is on page 26.

3. *Ibid.,* p. 27, again according to Vissery.

4. Letter from Vissery to Attorney Buissart, Arras, October 25, 1782, quoted by C. Vellay in the article mentioned above.

5. In his monumental *Robespierre,* I, 36 and ff, Gérard Walter sets out to demolish Robespierre's share in the writing of this text. This is the first manifestation of the great historian's repressed hatred of the man who was his chief subject of study and to whose moral assassination by the Thermidorians he has made a signal contribution with his posthumous *Neuf Thermidor,* published by Gallimard in 1974. One might speculate at length on the strange fate that befell Robespierre at Walter's hands. In connection with this particular instance of it, a note by A. Birembaut (in the *Annales historiques de la Révolution française,* 1958, XXX, fascicule 3, pp. 85–90) makes a judicious criticism of Walter's hasty judgment and reinstates Robespierre as having had a substantial share not only in the utterance but also in the substance and, above all, the effectiveness of the "lightning rod speech."

6. Bernard Nabonne, *La Vie privée de Robespierre,* p. 66.

7. From this point on, I refer to the complete text; see reference 1 above.

8. *Oeuvres complètes* de M. Robespierre, I, 99.

9. Paris, *Jeunesse de Robespierre,* p. 57. *Ibid.* (but see footnote) for the following quotation from the *Mercure.*

10. Article by C. Vellay in the *Annales révolutionnaires* (1909), p. 214. It was previously unpublished and comes from the dispersal of a collection of autographs.

11. Albert Cousin, *Franklin et Robespierre,* from the "Mélanges Baldensperger" (Paris, Champion, 1930), p. 8.

12. Full text published by Aulard in the *Revue de la Révolution française* for January 1901. The letter was previously unpublished and comes from the dispersal of a collection of autographs.

36

1. Faujas de Saint-Fond, *Description des expériences de la machine aérostatique de MM. de Montgolfier* (Paris, Panckoucke, 1783), II, 168.

2. *Journal de Paris,* May 23, 1782.

3. J. Lecornu, *La Navigation aérienne, histoire documentaire et anecdotique* (Paris, Nony & Cie, 1903), p. 36. The rest of the

material on Blanchard's machine is from the same source.

* 4. Quoted, unfortunately without any exact reference (from the *Ami du Peuple,* however), by Dr. Cabanes, in *Marat inconnu,* p. 328.

* 5. *Correspondance* of Métra, May 8, 1782.

6. According to Abbé Filhol, a relative of the Montgolfiers who has written a *Histoire religieuse et civile d'Annonay,* which can be consulted in the municipal library of that town, the cradle of the family is the village of Frankendals near Mainz.

7. Expilly's *Dictionnaire,* I, 220: "Annonay."

8. Portrait by one of his grand-nephews, Marc Seguin, in Lecornu, *La Navigation aérienne,* p. 42.

9. Quoted in the same book, same page; excerpt from an (unidentified) work by J. de la Landelle called *Dans les airs.*

10. Geneviève Touzain-Lioud, *Le Marquis d'Arlandes, premier navigateur aérien* (Le Puy, Editions Jeanne d'Art, 1971).

11. From the *Mémoire* by Joseph-Michel de Montgolfier presenting his invention to the Academy of Lyons in July 1783, quoted by Faujas de Saint-Fond, *Description des expériences* II, 98.

12. Lecornu, *La Navigation aérienne,* p. 44.

13. Comte Boissy d'Anglas, *Essai sur les fêtes nationales* (Paris, 1809) p. 23.

14. *Rapport à l'Académie des Sciences de Paris,* December 23, 1783, signed by Lavoisier and Condorcet, quoted by Lecornu, *La navigation aérienne,* p. 45.

15. *Correspondance littéraire,* Grimm, XIII, 347 (August 1783).

16. M. de Gerondo, *Biographie de Joseph de Montgolfier* (Paris, Mestre, 1841), p. 54.

17. *Dictionnaire portatif des Arts et Métiers* (Paris, Chez Lacombe, bookseller, Quai de Conti, 1766), II: "Papetier," p. 330. Other particulars of the stages of the process are from the same source.

18. Pierre Léon, "Morcellement et émergence du monde ouvrier: la condition ouvrière," in *Histoire économique et sociale de la France* (Paris, PUF), II (1660–1789), p. 664.

19. *Ibid.,* p. 673.

20. *Voyages en France de François de La Rochefoucauld,* II, 186.

21. Expilly's *Dictionnaire,* same reference as note 7.

22. Faujas de Saint-Fond, *Description des expériences* II, 166.

37

1. I am extremely grateful to my friends Grosjean and Sansot, who spent hours poring over the Grenoble municipal archives for me and who have supplied all these details. To Roger Grosjean I also owe a photocopy of the reproduction, by Jules de Beylié, of one of the two rough drafts of Barnave's speech that are kept in the Grenoble archives.

2. From the complete text of the speech, published in Jules de Beylié, *Barnave avocat* (Grenoble, Allier frères), p. 34. All other excerpts from the speech are from the same source.

3. See the note by *Président* [chief

justice of a court, more or less—
Trans.] René Fonvieille on "Le palais de justice," in the handsome two-volume work on *Le vieux Grenoble, ses pierres et son âme* (Grenoble, Roissard, 1968), II, 63. René Fonvieille, chief justice in the Grenoble court of appeals, made me a present of these superb volumes and was also of enormous assistance (as was my other friend in Grenoble, Henriette Foix de Montalais), for example by providing me with a copy of the first part of the manuscript of his *Barnave,* a major work to be published soon. I owe the whole passage on Barnave's youth to René Fonvieille; the lines by Paul Dreyfus on the Place Saint-André, quoted earlier, are from *Le vieux Grenoble,* II, 69.

4. The best portrait of Barnave is undoubtedly the admirable bust made by Houdon during the Revolution, in the Grenoble museum; it is reproduced among the plates at the end of volume II of *Le vieux Grenoble,* There is another portrait of him, a little younger, by Victor Cassien.

5. Champollion-Figeac, "La Légende de Barnave au théâtre de Grenoble," from *Chroniques dauphinoises et documents relatifs au Dauphiné pendant la Révolution* (Vienna, Savigné, 1884), pp. 209–12. This article rectifies the Peter-to-Paul, or rather Bérenger de la Drôme–to–Sainte-Beuve (*Les Lundis,* II, 24) tale that built this very trivial incident into a prime example of the persecution of the Protestant bourgeoisie by the creatures of the King.

6. *Oeuvres* of Barnave, published by Bérenger de la Drôme, IV, p. 330.

7. V. del Litto, *Album Stendhal,* in the Bibliothèque de la Pléiade (Paris, Gallimard, 1966), p. 5.

38

1. *La Vie véritable du citoyen Jean Rossignol, vainqueur de la Bastille et général en chef des armées de la République dans la guerre de Vendée (1759–1802),* based on original writings and published by Victor Barrucand (Paris, Plon, 1896), p. 6. These writings were the notebooks filled by Rossignol during his imprisonment by the Thermidorians in the fortress of Ham, in 1795. The notebooks— whose spelling and syntax have unfortunately been "restored" at some points by V. Barrucand— are kept in the Archives historiques de la Guerre in Paris. The following details of Rossignol's youth and service and all other unnumbered quotations in the passage are from the same source, pp. 1–64 (forming eight chapters, artificially separated by V. Barrucand, from the first notebooks).

* 2. See Paul Boiteau, *Etat de la France en 1789,* pp. 239–43, on the infantry.

3. Found by Victor Barrucand (p. 52) in the Archives administratives de la Guerre.

39

* 1. Walter, *Marat,* p. 68. Also for the other unnumbered quotations in this passage, pp. 68 and 69.

2. On page 75 of the single edition, published anonymously in Paris in 1784 by N. T. Méquignon, Rue des Cordeliers near Saint-Côme; the manuscript was awarded the prize by the Rouen Academy on August 6, 1783. The next quote is on p. 89, and that concerning Marat's health on p. 91.

* 3. Cabanès, *Marat inconnu,* p. 277.

4. *Ibid.,* p. 278.

5. Published in pamphlet form, in 1783, by Méquignon the elder, who was then his official bookseller and remained so until 1787.

6. *Observations;* see preceding reference, p. 14.

7. M. Guillemot, in two articles published in the newspaper *Le Rappel,* September 10 and 11, 1874.

8. B. G. Sade, *Supplément aux Institutions de physique* (Paris, 1812), p. 29, note 1. Note the date: the high point of a period of imperial and antirevolutionary reaction.

9. Letter published by the *Amateur d'autographes,* 1864–65, no. 51, item 42.

10. Archives Nationales, Y 13 806, Ancien Régime: le Châtelet de Paris.

11. *Correspondance de Marat,* collected and edited by Charles Vellay (Paris, Fasquelle, 1908), p. 15.

12. *Ibid.,* p. 16.

40

1. Lecornu, *La Navigation aérienne,* p. 53.

2. Britsch, *La Jeunesse de Philippe-Egalité,* p. 424.

3. Faujas de Saint-Fond, *Description des expériences,* III, 51–5. Other unnumbered quotations relating to the 1783 ascensions are from subsequent pages of the same volume.

4. My information on Gonesse, then spelled Gonnesse, comes from Expilly's *Dictionnaire,* III, 620, and from the *Histoire* [anonymous] *des environs de Paris* published by Philippe in 1837, I, 319.

5. The entire tale of the disaster of the balloon is reconstructed by Lecornu, *La Navigation aérienne,* p. 56.

6. Tousain-Lioud, *Le Marquis d'Arlandes,* reproduces a facsimile of the copy of the poster in the Cabinet d'estampes of the Bibliothèque nationale, Paris (pp. 35–38).

41

1. *Correspondance de Marat,* p. 17.

2. See the article by F. P. Renaut, "L'odyssée d'un colonial sous l'Ancien Régime: Philippe-Rose Roume de Saint-Laurent" in the *Revue de l'histoire des colonies françaises,* 1920, pp. 327–48. There is also a bulky file on the colonial official in the Archives nationales, "Colonies," EE 1878.

3. This letter, which Charles Vellay was unable to find, was published in the *Annales historiques de la Révolution*

française, III (1967), 398, by M. A. Birembaut, following the dispersal of an autograph collection.

4. Massin, *Marat,* p. 63.
5. *Correspondance de Marat,* p. 19.
6. See the first two chapters of *La Véritable Madame Tallien* by F. Maricourt, Paris.

42

1. Antonina Vallentin, *Goya* (Paris, Albin Michel, 1951), p. 77. *Ibid.* for all other unnumbered quotations in this passage.
2. Letter from Goya to his boyhood friend Zapater, in *ibid.,* p. 59.

43

1. *Correspondance de Marat,* p. 88. The top of the sheet has been torn and bears neither date nor superscription. But Charles Vellay has worked out an approximate date (August or September 1783) by cross-reference.
2. An unpublished letter, not in the *Correspondance.* It was found in the Spanish Archives by Dr. Claudius Roux, who gave the reference in his *Documents bio-biblio-iconographiques sur Marat* (Lyons, Albums du Crocodile, 1954). Following his indications, Marat's letter of September 17 to Aranda was published in the *Annales historiques de la Revolution française* for 1970, IV, 661.
3. Summary and quote jotted down by Charles Vellay from a catalogue of autographs; in *Correspondance de Marat,* p. 21.
4. *Correspondance de Marat,* p. 22.

5. This enormous letter, followed by all the evidence reproduced in extenso, begins on p. 24 of the *Correspondance.*
6. *Annales historiques de la Revolution française,* 1967, III, footnote on p. 397.
7. Massin, *Marat,* p. 65.

44

1. Faujas de Saint-Fond, *Description des expériences,* III, 61. Other unnumbered quotations in this passage are from the same volume.
2. One of the best portraits of Pilâtre de Rozier is in the Cabinet d'estampes of the Bibliothèque nationale. It is reproduced in the book by Geneviève Touzain-Lioud, *Le Marquis d'Arlandes,* p. 13, across from an excellent portrait of the marquis himself, from the same source.
3. Details from an (unsigned) article in the *Républicain Lorrain* of June 15, 1975.
4. A copy of his certificate of baptism is reproduced in Touzain-Lioud's book on him, p. 141. Also worth noticing, on page 143, is a reproduction of another fine portrait of the Marquis d'Arlandes in his captain's uniform, dated 1772, printed in Montpellier; it is now in the Musée de l'Air in Paris.

45

1. Letter quoted by Dupuis-Delcourt in his *Manuel d'aérostation* (Paris, n.d.), p. 39.
2. *Voyage pittoresque des environs de*

Paris, ou description des maisons royales, châteaux et autres lieux de plaisance situés à quinze lieues aux environs de cette ville, by M. D . . . (Paris, *chez* Debure *l'aîné,* bookseller, Quai des Augustins near the Pont Saint-Michel, 1775), p. 13.

3. *Mercure de France,* December 1783.

4. Faujas de Saint-Fond, *Description des expériences,* III, 129.

5. Note communicated to G. Touzain-Lioud by the Marquis de Digoine, heir to the Arlandes family papers.

6. Touzain-Lioud, *Le Marquis d'Arlandes,* p. 62.

7. Caption from a contemporary print in *ibid.,* p. 45.

8. Commentary quoted in *Histoire de l'aéronautique* by Charles Dollfus and Henri Bouche (Paris, Hachette, 1932), p. 58.

9. This letter by the Marquis d'Arlandes, quoted in extenso here (less three opening courtesy paragraphs), was published by Lecornu, *La Navigation aérienne,* p. 63.

10. Pierre Gaxotte, *Paris au XVIIIe siècle* (Arthaud, 1968), p. 161.

11. *La Vie française à la veille de la Révolution,* journal of Madame Cradock, 1783–6 (Paris, Perrin, 1911), p. 1.

12. From his narrative of the trip published in Lecornu, *La Navigation aérienne,* p. 73. *Ibid,* for the following quotation.

13. *Ibid.,* p. 76.

46

* 1. *Histoire de Beaumarchais* by Gudin de la Brenellerie, p. 323.

* 2. Letter published by Louis de Loménie in *Beaumarchais et son temps,* II, 324.

3. Louis-Sébastien Mercier, *Le Tableau de Paris,* VIII, 193.

4. *Ibid.,* I, 220.

5. *Ibid.,* III, 20.

6. From Fleury's *Mémoires,* quoted by the Duc de Castries in *Figaro, ou la vie de Beaumarchais* (Paris, Hachette, 1972), p. 373.

7. Duc de Castries, *Figaro, ou la vie de Beaumarchais,* p. 374.

* 8. See in this connection Roger Lafon's *Beaumarchais, le brillant armateur.*

9. Quoted by Louis de Loménie in *Beaumarchais et son temps,* II, 251.

10. Georges Lemaître, *Beaumarchais* (New York, 1949), p. 275.

11. Jacques Boncompain, *Auteurs et Comédiens au XVIIIe siècle* (Paris, Librairie Académique Perrin, 1976), p. 306.

12. Grimm, *Correspondance littéraire,* XIII, 322. The rest of the story of the Menus-Plaisirs incident is taken from the same source (quoted parts).

13. Quoted by L. de Loménie, *Beaumarchais et son temps,* p. 306. *Ibid.* for Beaumarchais's retort.

14. In a letter to Fronsac, undated but written the same month, quoted by Loménie, II, 311.

15. *Ibid.,* II, 308.

*16. *Souvenirs* of Madame Vigée-Lebrun, published by Pierre de Noilhac, p. 79.

17. Letter from Beaumarchais to his father, May 6, 1767, quoted by Loménie, *Beaumarchais et son temps,* I, 82.

18. Complete text of *Le Mariage de Figaro,* Act III, scene v.

19. Quoted by Loménie, *Beaumarchais et son temps*, II, note to p. 322.
20. *Le Mariage*, Act V, scene iii.
21. Quoted by René Pomeau, *Beaumarchais* (Paris, Hatier, 1967). The following commentary by René Pomeau is on the same page.

47

1. *Histoire des environs de Paris*, II, 8.
2. Jacques Herissay, *Un girondin, François Buzot, député de l'Eure, 1760–1794* (Paris, Perrin, 1907), p. iii of preface. Part of this description has been borrowed from Mme Roland, but as she had every reason to be partial the author has compared her portrayal with those of other contemporaries. The frontispiece of the book shows a very good portrait of Buzot, the original of which is in the Evreux museum.
3. J. Manon Philipon-Roland, *Notices historiques sur la Révolution* (Paris, édition de l'An VIII), I, 231.
4. *Mémoires inédits de Buzot* (published, together with those of Pétion and Barbaroux, by Charles Dauban) (Paris, Plon, 1866), p. 39. Other quotations by Buzot relating to his youth are on the same page.
5. Extract from the entry recording Buzot's baptism in the archives of Saint-Nicolas parish church for the year 1760 (Evreux municipal archives).
6. Evreux municipal archives, quoted by Hérissay, *François Buzot*, p. 16.

7. Hérissay, *François Buzot*, p. 19.
8. Expilly's *Dictionnaire*, II: "Evreux," 807.
9. *Mémoires* by Buzot, p. 101.
10. *Histoire des environs de Paris*, II, 9.
11. *Mémoires* by Buzot, p. 40.
12. These details are all given by Hérissay, *François Buzot*, p. 21.
13. *Histoire des environs de Paris*, II, 9.
14. *Ibid.*, p. 13.
15. Expilly's *Dictionnaire*, II: "Evreux," 823.
16. Registry office acts of La Charité-sur-Loire, quoted by Hérissay, *François Buzot*, note on p. 22.
17. See Albert Soboul's note on "La Fortune de Buzot" in the *Annales historiques de la Révolution française*, 1951, XXIII, 181, based on the Buzot file in the Archives nationales, F 7, 4627/5.

48

1. Grimm, *Correspondance littéraire*, XIII, 364 (October 1783).
2. *Ibid.*, p. 371.
3. Condorcet, *Oeuvres complètes*, I, 299. For Frederick's reply, *ibid.*, p. 303.
4. A remark he made to Grimm, reported by Paul Ledieu in *Diderot et Sophie Volland* (Paris, Publications du Centre, 1925), p. 171.
5. *Lettres de Diderot à Sophie Volland*, published in two volumes by Gallimard (André Babelon, ed.), II, 8. I shall be taking a number of quotations in this passage from this important collection, and their source is abbreviated hereafter as *Lettres à S.V.*
6. *Lettres à S.V.*, II, 52.

* 7. He said this in 1770; quoted by André Billy, *Diderot*, p. 279.

8. *Lettres à S.V.*, II, 77.

9. *Ibid.*, I, 130.

10. *Ibid.*, I, 42.

11. *Ibid.*, II, 281, in undated fragments. This must be one of Diderot's last letters to Sophie.

12. *Ibid.*, I, 45.

*13. Letter from Pierre Rousseau, editor of the *Journal encyclopédique,* to his father, on January 2, 1782, published by Georges Roth and Jean Varloot in XV (final volume), 286, of their monumental *Correspondance de Denis Diderot,* previously cited; it was published in Paris by Editions de Minuit and sets an example for any critical edition of an author's correspondence. I follow their absolutely comprehensive volume XV point by point in re-creating Diderot's last days.

14. Orléans municipal library, Mss. I 423, f⁰ 327 (mentioned by Roth and Varloot).

15. Roth and Varloot, *Correspondance de Diderot,* XV, 302.

16. *Ibid.*, p. 317.

17. Quoted by *ibid.,* p. 322.

18. *Lettres à S.V.*, I, 67 and II, 35.

19. *Ibid.*, II, 44.

20. *Ibid.*, II, 42 and 43.

21. I have taken a liberty in this chapter, indulging my fancy by assembling these montages on death and love in order to reveal, to the best of my ability, a great and hitherto unknown Romantic poet, one of the first: Denis Diderot. The four excerpts (here and below, ending "trampled underfoot by love") are from *ibid.,* I, 34 and 35, and II, 141.

22. *Ibid.*, I, 147 and 88.

23. *Ibid.*, I, 70.

24. Details supplied by Roth and Varloot in the *Correspondance de Diderot,* pp. 322 and 323. *Ibid.* for the following remark by Caroiline de Vandeuil.

25. From this point on, and for all the circumstances of Diderot's death, I follow Roth and Varloot, vol. XV of the *Correspondance de Diderot,* pp. 325 to 339.

49

1. R. Tisserand, *Au temps de l'Encyclopédie: l'Académie de Dijon de 1740–1793* (Dijon, n.d.), p. 159. *Ibid.* for the next quote.

2. Gaston Duthuron, "Un éloge de Vauban par Carnot" in the *Annales historiques de la Révolution française,* XVII (1940), 152.

3. *Mémoires de l'Académie de Dijon,* Dijon municipal library, IX, 13.

4. Quoted by Marcel Reinhard, *Le Grand Carnot* (Paris, Hachette, 1950), I, 11. For the details of Carnot's childhood and youth I have closely followed this full and documented work; and I take this opportunity to express my deep gratitude to the memory of Marcel Reinhard, historian and professor of the French Revolution at the Sorbonne, who died, too soon, in 1973. He took an interest in my first historical novels twenty years before that and was ever ready to help with advice and good will as my work advanced, even though we did not always see eye to eye. He was a great person, and I owe much to him.

5. Reinhard, p. 15. This will be the reference for the rest of this passage, all of which relates to the material in volume I.

6. Joseph Carnot, *Précis historique de la famille des Carnot en Bourgogne, avec quelques notes critiques sur divers personnages de la Révolution,* Paris, "composed between 18 Fructidor An V and 18 Fructidor An IX" and found by Marcel Reinhard, p. 330.

7. Applicants' records, in the Archives administratives de la Guerre [War], quoted by Reinhard, p. 20.

8. *Ibid.,* p. 25.

9. *Ibid.,* p. 28. *Ibid.* for the next quote.

10. Hippolyte Carnot, *Mémoires sur Carnot,* I, 87, quoted by Reinhard, p. 20.

50

1. Expilly's *Dictionnaire,* IV, 502: "Maizières."

2. Reinhard, *Anecdotes du comte de Bony avec quelques souvenirs sur l'Ecole du Génie,* p. 33.

3. Maximilien Marie, *Histoire des sciences mathématiques et physiques* (Paris, 1887), X, 12.

4. R. Pautet, "Eloge de Gaspard Monge" (Beaune, 1849); previously published in the *Revue de la Côte d'Or* on February 15, 1836.

5. See in this connection, and on Monge's youth in general, the excellent book by Paul-V. Aubry, *Monge, le savant ami de Napoléon Bonaparte, 1746–1818* (Paris, Gauthier-Villars, 1954); here, p. 41.

51

1. Reinhard, *Carnot,* p. 43. The following observations on the curious status of the engineer corps under Louis XVI are taken directly from Marcel Reinhard.

2. *Ibid.,* p. 46.

3. Archives historiques de la Guerre [War], Engineer Corps, X°, 135; Engineer Corps Inspectorate, section III, article I, box I.

4. Reinhard, *Carnot,* I, 55.

5. Calvados Archives, memorandum by Dumoriez, May 20, 1778, C 1770.

6. Archives historiques de la Guerre [War], Memoranda on Granville, boxes 1085 and 1093.

7. Archives historiques de la Guerre [War], Engineer Corps, X°, 136.

8. Reinhard, *Carnot,* I, 64.

9. After a portrait sketched at that time by his younger brother Feulint Carnot. See Reinhard, *Carnot,* I, 91. *Ibid.,* for the details of dress that follow.

10. Published in the *Annales historiques de la Révolution française,* 1947, XIX, 170; identified by Le Gay, *Mes souvenirs et autres opuscules* (1788), quoted in the same issue of the *Annales.*

11. Reinhard, *Carnot,* I, 67.

12. Excerpts from the *Eloge à Vauban,* of which we unfortunately possess no original —it having been published by the Academy of Dijon in 1785 but in a "tightened and corrected [*sic*] form"—are taken either from Reinhard, *Carnot,* chap. VI: "L'Eloge à Vauban"

or, more often, from the previously mentioned article by G. Duthuron on the same subject, in *Annales historiques de la Révolution française,* 1940.

13. *Mercure dijonnais,* Dumay edition (Dijon, n.d.), p. 318.

14. Archives des Colonies (Colonial), E 64, letter from Captain Lazare Carnot.

52

* 1. F. A. Mesmer, *Le Magnétisme animal* (works published by Robert Amadou), p. 22. *Ibid.* for the following quote, p. 23, the excerpt from the *Almanach du voyageur.*

* 2. Etienne Charavay, *Le Général de La Fayette,* p. 102. Facsimile.

3. Georges Michon, *Essai sur l'histoire du parti Feuillant: Adrien Duport* (Paris, Payot, 1924), p. 4.

4. Charavay, *La Fayette,* p. 103. [Retranslated—*Trans.*]

5. *Correspondance littéraire,* XIV, footnote p. 25.

* 6. Sparks, *The Writings of George Washington etc.* (Boston, 1838), VIII, 300. [Retranslated—*Trans.*]

* 7. B. Faÿ, *Washington,* p. 244. [Retranslated—*Trans.*]

8. Sparks, *The Writings of George Washington,* IX, 17. [Retranslated—*Trans.*]

9. In this connection see Vicomte de Montbas, *Avec La Fayette chez les Iroquois* (Paris, Firmin-Didot, 1929).

10. Saint-John de Crèvecoeur, *Lettres d'un cultivateur américain,* translated from the English (Paris, Cuchet, 1878), III, 346. [Retranslated—*Trans.*]

11. Sparks, *Washington's Writings,* IX, 73. [Retranslated—*Trans.*]

53

1. Most of this chapter has been taken from chapter IV of my book on *Le Citoyen Bonaparte,* published in 1969 by Laffont in the "Plein Vent" series, pp. 63–73. The necessary corrections and emendations have been made, of course, and the page notes are new.

2. *Souvenirs d'un cadet de Brienne* quoted by Paul Bartel, *La Jeunesse inedite de Napoléon* (Paris, Amiot-Dumont, 1954), note on p. 80. Same page (body of the text) for the following quotation by Napoleon.

3. *Mémorial de Sainte-Hélène,* Las Cases's original edition, II, 108.

4. J. B. Marcaggi, *La Genèse de Napoléon, sa formation intellectuelle et morale jusqu'au siège de Toulon* (Paris, Librairie Académique Perrin, 1902), p. 69.

5. Doctor P. Hillemand, *Pathologie de Napoléon* (Paris, La Palatine, no date), p. 30.

6. *Mémorial de Sainte-Hélène,* II, 121.

7. Bartel, *Jeunesse inédite de Napoléon,* p. 88.

8. Gourgaud's reminiscences on St. Helena, quoted by *ibid.,* p. 63.

54

1. For this passage I have borrowed a few pages from the book by Anne and Claude Manceron, *La Comédie des Bonaparte* (Brussels, Editions Arts et Voyages, 1969), pp. 13–23. The page notes are new.

2. Archives of Prince Napoleon, box 110, copy of the original kept by Abbé (later Cardinal) Fesch. Published by Doctor Hillemand, *Pathologie de Napoléon,* p. 197.

3. Published by Bartel, *Jeunesse inédite de Napoléon,* p. 131, from Napoleon's correspondence, published under Napoleon III.

* 4. B. Faÿ, *Louis XVI ou la fin d'un monde,* p. 266.

5. Nicolas Ruault, *Gazette d'un Parisien sous la Révolution,* letters to his brother, 1783–1796 (Paris, Perrin, 1976) (a completely new and very exciting text, of which I shall say more hereafter); here, p. 53.

6. Frantz Funck-Brentano, *L'Affaire du collier* (Paris, Hachette, 1901), p. 178.

Index

A

Abrantès, Duchesse d' (Laure Junot), 394 n.
Académie Française, 155 n.
  Condorcet, 80, 111, 112, 113–14, 347
academies, 110, 36 n.
Academy of Sciences, 92 n., 110
  ballooning, 250, 291, 310, 312, 315, 316
  Condorcet, 110–11, 113 n., 114–15, 347
Achem, King of, 201
Adams, John, 186, 203, 215
Adelaïde, Mme (daughter of Louis XV), 188 n., 188–9
Agoult, Comtesse d' (Marguerite-Françoise de Blacons), 105
Aix, 224, 234–5
  military garrison, 101, 102, 108, 109
Alembert, Jean d', 46, 110, 112, 113, 347–8, 348–9, 354
Alexander I, Tsar of Russia, 74, 75, 76 and n., 77
Alexis, Tsarevich, 71
Ambournay, d', 279–80
American Indians, 10–18 passim, 382
American Revolution, 31, 37, 47, 54, 67, 80, 81, 93, 97, 168, 185–6, 191–2, 203 n., 204–6, 207, 327, 332, 372, 380, 382
  peace negotiations and treaties, 81, 86, 167, 186, 192, 202–3, 213, 214–16, 327
  Yorktown, 4 n., 35, 46, 81, 185, 211, 382, 383
Amiens, peace of, 207 n.
Andlau, Baronne d', 29–30

Andlau, Marquise d', 331
Angoulême, Duc d' (Louis de Bourbon; later Louis XIX), 29
Anne, Empress of Russia, 71 and n.
Anspach, Isaac Salomon, 119
Antoine, Jacques-Denis, 112 n.
Aranda, Conde Pedro de, 203, 304–6, 307, 311
Arcon, d', 195 n., 197 n.
Arlandes, Marquis François-Laurent d', 311, 317–25 passim, 327
Arlandes, François-Pierre d', 317 and n.
army (French): artillery, 101–2, 369, 392
  engineers, 363, 366, 367, 369
  floating batteries, 194, 195 and n., 196–7
  fortifications, 119, 360, 367, 369, 370, 371, 375
  Geneva's "revolution," 116–21 passim, 127, 134–43 passim
  Gibraltar, 191, 193–8 passim, 202, 203, 215, 256
  India, 202
  infantry, 273–4 and n.
  mercenaries, 133 n., 134, 178, 217 n.
  military schools and education, 290, 363, 365, 366–7, 369, 384–92
  officers' ranks restricted, 273–4, 363, 371–2
  Order of Saint-Louis, 57, 275, 372, 386
  punishments, 270, 275–6
  recruitment, 273, 274
  regiments sold, 82 n.
  sleeping arrangements, 274 n.
  soldiers' nicknames, 274
Artois, Comte Charles d' (later Charles X), 3, 7 n., 63, 84, 189 and n., 193, 194

C

A NOTE ABOUT THE AUTHOR

Claude Manceron was born in 1923, the son of a French naval officer and a Greek princess. His formal schooling ended after he was crippled by polio at age eleven, but he continued to read and became a teacher and a writer—at first of historical novels. His research, undertaken to make the characters' backgrounds authentic, led him to give up fiction and become a historian. He has been working on the Age of the French Revolution series since 1967. M. Manceron has given up teaching to devote himself full time to this work. He and his wife, Anne, live in a small village in the south of France, where they do research and write.

A NOTE ABOUT THE TRANSLATOR

Nancy Lipe Amphoux was born in Rockford, Illinois, and was educated by the cornfields there, at Vassar and Carnegie-Mellon, and in Europe, where she has lived since 1959. Her interests and activities include teaching and social work, horses and tropical fish, and Zen. Some of the books she has translated are Henri Troyat's biographies of Tolstoy, Pushkin, and Gogol; Edmonde Charles-Roux's biography of Chanel; François Ponchaud's *Cambodia Year Zero;* and an earlier volume in the Age of the French Revolution series, *The Wind from America.* She now lives in Strasbourg, France.

A NOTE ON THE TYPE

The text of this book was set, via computer-driven cathode-ray tube, in Garamond, a modern rendering of the type first cut by Claude Garamond (1510–1561). Garamond was a pupil of Geoffroy Tory and is believed to have based his letters on the Venetian models; it is to him we owe the letter we know as old-style.

Typography and binding based on designs by Earl Tidwell.